EIGHT AMERICAN AUTHORS
A REVIEW OF RESEARCH AND CRITICISM

EIGHT AMERICAN AUTHORS

A Review of Research and Criticism

By JAY B. HUBBELL, FLOYD STOVALL, WALTER BLAIR, LEWIS LEARY, STANLEY T. WILLIAMS, WILLARD THORP, HARRY HAYDEN CLARK, *and* ROBERT E. SPILLER. *Edited by* FLOYD STOVALL

Bibliographical Supplement by J. Chesley Mathews

The Norton Library
W · W · NORTON & COMPANY · INC ·
NEW YORK

First published in the Norton Library in 1963 by arrangement with The Modern Language Association

Published simultaneously in Canada by
George J. McLeod Limited, Toronto

PRINTED IN THE UNITED STATES OF AMERICA

5 6 7 8 9 0

PREFACE

THE plan for this volume was suggested by *The English Romantic Poets: A Review of Research,* edited by Thomas M. Raysor, and published by the Modern Language Association in 1950. In the summer of 1951, Randall Stewart, then Chairman of the American Literature Group, after consulting with the late Stanley T. Williams, presented the plan to the Advisory Council, which approved it as an undertaking of the Group. After many vicissitudes and delays the project has been brought to a conclusion in approximately the form in which it was first conceived: not a detailed bibliography, but a series of bibliographical essays.

The book is addressed primarily to students of graduate and advanced undergraduate courses in American literature, but it should prove useful to others, including more advanced scholars. The essays are not designed to take the place of more formal bibliographies; hence only selected titles are mentioned, and only essential bibliographical facts are given. To conserve space, titles that occur frequently are abbreviated, and masculine Christian names, except those of persons who have only one, are reduced to initials.

The first question which the eight contributors had to answer was, What authors are to be included? That did not prove difficult. Professor Stewart and his advisers had originally proposed the eight authors on whom the essays of the volume are written, having, no doubt, carefully weighed the relative merits of such other important American writers as Edwards and Franklin in the eighteenth century, Longfellow, Lowell, Howells, and Emily Dickinson in the nineteenth, and perhaps some of the older twentieth-century writers. After I became editor, only the names of Howells and Dickinson were presented as candidates for inclusion, and only the latter was seriously considered. No one proposed that we could omit any of the eight originally selected. Doubtless most readers will agree that at this time and for the purposes of this volume they are the most important American writers. They were chosen both for their intrinsic worth and for the significance of the biographical and critical writing that has been done on them and their work.

The essays are consistent in bibliographical details. Where they differ in organization it is for reasons which the author and the editor believe to be sound. Each contributor was free to develop his materials in the way that seemed to him most effective and is of course solely responsible for his own essay.

The project was slow to develop because the contributors were all scholars with many interests and obligations. The deadline for completion of the manuscripts had to be set forward more than once. As a consequence, two or three of them were completed by the end of the summer of 1954, whereas two or three remained unwritten until the spring and summer of 1955. Two of the essays were completed on the supposition that the terminal date for the inclusion of publications would be 31 December 1953. When all were done, it was found that some included publications of the early part of 1955 and others omitted those of 1954. It was finally agreed that 31 December 1954 should be the approved terminal date except for special reasons. Some essays exclude everything published after the agreed terminal date. Others mention, but usually do not discuss, important items appearing in the early months of 1955. Only the Whitman essay discusses in any detail all important publications up to the summer of 1955. All contributors agreed that an exception in this case was justified by the unusual number of significant books and articles on Whitman called forth by the centennial anniversary of the first publication of *Leaves of Grass*. In several essays mention is made of important studies known to be in preparation even though the date of prospective publication is not definitely known.

Some essays mention unpublished dissertations whereas others do not. This inconsistency stems, it must be admitted, partly from a difference of opinion among the contributors. It results also, in part, from the fact that unpublished dissertations constitute a more significant part of the criticism of some authors than of others. It seemed to the editor that the only practical course was to allow each contributor to use his own judgment on this point. No one of them has attempted to discuss all the dissertations that have been written on the subject of his essay. The user of this book is therefore advised to consult other available sources for such works, and in particular to check the following compilations: "Doctoral Dissertations in American Literature," by E. E. Leisy and J. B. Hubbell (*AL,* 1933), "Doctoral Dissertations in American Literature, 1933-1948," by Lewis Leary (*AL,* 1948), and the "Research in Progress" sections of *AL* and *PMLA*. Such a minor inconsistency, though perhaps regrettable, is less serious in its consequences than the loss of freedom in the treatment of individual essays which might have been the price of enforced uniformity.

The question was raised whether this book, like the one on the English Romantic Poets, should devote a separate essay to the discussion of works of a general nature that are not sufficiently accounted for in the essays on individual authors. Since there is in American scholarship nothing quite corresponding to the vast literature dealing with the Romantic Movement in English poetry, the decision was against the preparation of such an essay. There are some works of general reference indispensable to the student of American literature, however, which there was no reason to mention in any of the essays on individual authors. While it is impossible to include in a preface a complete list of such works, their importance should at least be indicated. I have set down here the titles of a few representative and essential works, and for the rest refer the reader to fuller bibliographies, one of the best and most recent of which is Vol. III of the *LHUS*. The first section of that volume, entitled "Guide to Resources," will be found particularly useful in this connection.

In the field of bibliography the most important new undertaking is the monumental *Bibliography of American Literature,* compiled by Jacob Blanck and in process of publication by the Yale University Press, which when complete will run to eight or nine volumes. Only the first volume is in print at this writing. When complete this work will include all writers of literary importance (as determined by a committee of the Bibliographical Society of America) from the time of the Revolution through the early part of the twentieth century. The purpose of the compiler, as stated in his Preface, is to limit his work to belles-lettres and thus to complement the earlier compilations of Charles Evans and Joseph Sabin. The work of Evans does not extend beyond 1800 and that of Sabin and his successors is not limited to strictly literary works. Blanck's list includes all first editions of the authors covered together with a selected number of biographical and critical works.

Other bibliographical sources which the student will be constantly in need of consulting are the Library of Congress Printed Catalog, the British Museum Catalogue of Printed Books, the United States Catalog of Books in Print (Cumulative Book Index), *Poole's Index to Periodical Literature* (1891, extended by supplements to 1907), the Reader's Guide and the International Index, Lewis Leary's *Articles on American Literature, 1900-1950* (1954), and the bibliographical lists in *AL, NEQ,* and *PMLA*. Among works of a more specialized nature the following may be mentioned: P. K. Foley, *American Authors 1795-1895: A Bibliography of First and Notable Editions* (1897), Merle Johnson, *American First Editions* (rev. by Jacob Blanck, 1942), B. M. Fullerton, *Selective Bibliography of American Literature, 1775-1900* (1932), and Lyle Wright, *American Fiction, 1774-1850* (1939). A new and valuable tool is the microfilm library. The Philadelphia Bibliographical Center published in 1942 a *Union List of Microfilms* for the United States and Canada. Among biographical digests, besides the *DAB,* Duyckinck's *Cyclopaedia of American Literature* (1855; *Supplement,* 1866), Appleton's *Cyclopedia of Biography* (1887-

1900), and *The National Cyclopaedia of American Biography* (1892-1954) will be found useful. A handy reference is J. D. Hart's *Oxford Companion to American Literature* (rev. ed., 1948).

Every effort has been made to secure accuracy in the bibliographical descriptions of these essays. The collection was approved for book publication by the Book Publication Committee of the Modern Language Association, the American literature member of which is William Charvat. In addition, each essay has been read critically by the editor and at least one disinterested scholar who has special competence to judge research and criticism on the author concerned. The comments and criticisms of these specialists have proved of great value to the respective authors of the essays, and both they and the editor of the volume take pleasure in expressing here their debt and their thanks for the services so generously rendered. The specialist readers, of course, are in no way responsible for the opinions expressed in the essays. The names of these readers are as follows, arranged in alphabetical order: Raymond Adams of the University of North Carolina, Oscar Cargill of New York University, Charles T. Davis of Princeton University, Leon Edel of New York University, Walter Harding of the University of Virginia, Harrison Hayford of Northwestern University, Thomas O. Mabbott of Hunter College, Sherman Paul of the University of Illinois, Henry A. Pochmann of the University of Wisconsin, Lyon N. Richardson of Western Reserve University, Randall Stewart of Vanderbilt University, Arlin Turner of Duke University, and Stephen E. Whicher of Swarthmore College. Also, for suggestions on European criticism, thanks are extended to Marcel Le Breton of The Sorbonne and Hellmut Bock of the University of Kiel.

FLOYD STOVALL, *Editor*

CONTENTS

Abbreviations

AL	*American Literature*
AM	*American Mercury*
AN&Q	*American Notes and Queries*
AS	*American Scholar*
Atlantic	*Atlantic Monthly*
AWS	American Writers Series
BB	*Bulletin of Bibliography*
BNYPL	*Bulletin of the New York Public Library*
BPLQ	*Boston Public Library Quarterly*
CE	*College English*
CHAL	*Cambridge History of American Literature*
CL	*Comparative Literature*
DAB	*Dictionary of American Biography*
EIHC	*Essex Institute Historical Collections*
Ethics	*International Journal of Ethics*
Harper's	*Harper's Magazine, Harper's Monthly Magazine*
H&H	*Hound and Horn*
HLB	*Harvard Library Bulletin*
HLQ	*Huntington Library Quarterly*
JEGP	*Journal of English and Germanic Philology*
JHI	*Journal of the History of Ideas*
KR	*Kenyon Review*
LAP	*Literature of the American People*
LHUS	*Literary History of the United States*
MLJ	*Modern Language Journal*
MLN	*Modern Language Notes*
MLQ	*Modern Language Quarterly*
MP	*Modern Philology*
NAR	*North American Review*
NCF	*Nineteenth-Century Fiction*
NEQ	*New England Quarterly*

Abbreviations

N&Q	*Notes and Queries*
PBSA	*Papers of the Bibliographical Society of America*
PMLA	*Publications of the Modern Language Association of America*
PQ	*Philological Quarterly*
PR	*Partisan Review*
PULC	*Princeton University Library Chronicle*
QJS	*Quarterly Journal of Speech*
QQ	*Queen's Quarterly*
RAA	*Revue Anglo-Américaine*
RR	*Romanic Review*
SAQ	*South Atlantic Quarterly*
SE	*Studies in English*
SP	*Studies in Philology*
SR	*Sewanee Review*
SRL	*Saturday Review of Literature*
TLS	*London Times Literary Supplement*
TSB	*Thoreau Society Bulletin*
UKCR	*University of Kansas City Review*
UTQ	*University of Toronto Quarterly*
VQR	*Virginia Quarterly Review*
WHR	*Western Humanities Review*
WR	*Western Review*
YR	*Yale Review*

I

POE

I. Biography

FOR NEARLY every major British and American author of the nineteenth century there is an official biography prepared by some relative or friend who felt it his duty to present his subject in a favorable light. Christopher Wordsworth suppressed the story of his uncle's love affair with Annette Vallon, and Samuel Longfellow presented his brother Henry in such a fashion that the poet strikes the modern reader as a prig. But when Poe died in Baltimore on 7 October 1849, there was at hand no friendly biographer to gloss over his failings and emphasize his better traits. There was no compact circle of disciples comparable to those who jealously guarded Whitman's reputation after his death. There was, it is true, what appeared as an official Memoir; but it was written by R. W. Griswold, who at that time was certainly no friend of Poe. Apparently it was not Poe but his wife's mother who asked Griswold to bring out a collected edition of Poe's writings. If Mrs. Clemm had read the obituary article which, under the pseudonym "Ludwig," Griswold had published in the New York *Tribune* only two days after Poe's death, she would have better understood the editor whom she appointed. In that article Griswold had stated that the poet "had few or no friends"; that he was cynical, arrogant, and envious; and that he had "no moral susceptibility" and "little or nothing of the true point of honor." In the Memoir, which first appeared in September 1850, in the third volume of Poe's *Works,* Griswold replied to those friends of

Poe who had protested against the "Ludwig" article and amplified the picture of Poe which he had drawn in it; and to justify himself he printed what purported to be his correspondence with Poe. Although Griswold was long suspected of making changes in these letters, the extent of his malicious forgeries was not fully revealed until 1941, when A. H. Quinn published his life of Poe. There was a vindictive streak in Griswold's character, and he never forgave Poe for harsh criticism of *The Poets and Poetry of America* and perhaps also for Mrs. Osgood's partiality for the poet. Poe as Griswold painted him was the one black sheep in the American literary flock, and very black indeed he seemed when placed beside the great New Englanders.

The conception of Poe as a man of unprincipled character was formed and perpetuated largely by Poe's literary enemies, the men who never forgave him for his criticism of them in his book reviews and "The Literati of New York City." As long as they lived, L. G. Clark, T. D. English, and C. F. Briggs continued to defend Griswold's Memoir as an accurate portrait; and they repeatedly suggested that Griswold had mercifully refrained from publishing the most damning facts in his possession. English published his "Reminiscences" in the *Independent* as late as 1896, and the Griswold tradition colored the *Recollections* of R. H. Stoddard, published in 1903, well over half a century after Poe's death. The conception of Poe which comes from Poe's enemies colored not only many later biographical sketches but also a large number of the literary estimates published in both England and the United States.

It should be noted, however, that some of the factual errors in Griswold's Memoir came directly from Poe's own memoranda. Poe himself was in part responsible for the legend which still colors much that is written about him. It should also be remembered that J. R. Thompson, J. M. Daniel, and J. E. Cooke, who knew Poe only in the last two years of his life, regarded the Memoir as a fairly accurate account. There were undoubtedly two sides to Poe's character. He was not an easy person to get on with. His fondness for rebuking literary pretenders or charging better writers with plagiarism did not endear him to those whose books he reviewed. And it was apparently impossible for those whom he had abused while intoxicated ever to think of him as the courteous and considerate gentleman portrayed for us in the reminiscences of his friends.

These friends, N. P. Willis, C. C. Burr, G. R. Graham, L. A. Wilmer, Mrs. Frances S. Osgood, and others, protested against the injustice which Griswold had done to Poe. None of them, however, produced a biography which might have superseded Griswold's Memoir; and for a quarter of a century it had no rival. After Griswold's death, Mrs. Sarah Helen Whitman, the Providence poet who had been at one time engaged to Poe, published her able defense, *Edgar Poe and His Critics* (dated 1860 but copyrighted in 1859). It was reissued in 1949 with an excellent introduction and notes by O. S. Coad.

The first real biographer of Poe was an Englishman, J. H. Ingram, who in 1874-75 published a four-volume edition of Poe's writings which included a ninety-page biographical sketch. In 1880 Ingram brought out a two-volume biography, *Edgar Allan Poe: His Life, Letters, and Opinions*. Ingram detested Griswold, and throughout his life he made it his business to reply to hostile English criticism wherever it appeared. Although he did not come to America for biographical materials, he obtained valuable information by correspondence with the poet's American friends, especially Mrs. Whitman and Mrs. Annie Richmond. Ingram in fact unearthed many of the basic documents on which later biographers have had to rely. Ingram, however, was reluctant to admit any shortcomings in his hero. He was egotistic and unwilling to give proper credit to G. E. Woodberry and others who brought to light important new materials. Woodberry, on 8 March 1885, wrote to E. C. Stedman: "Ingram did an extraordinary amount of lying about Poe, and I still wonder at it." Ingram certainly altered some of Poe's letters to Mrs. Richmond. (See J. C. Miller's unpublished Univ. of Va. dissertation, "Poe's English Biographer: John Henry Ingram," 1954.) Most of Poe's nineteenth-century critics and biographers were partisans of either Griswold or Poe. In 1877 W. F. Gill, who hated Griswold, published a very partisan and quite inadequate biography, which is indebted to Ingram as well as to Mrs. Whitman and other friends of the poet.

Both as scholar and as critic Woodberry was better equipped than either Ingram or Gill; and his *Edgar Allan Poe,* which in 1885 the Houghton Mifflin Company added to its American Men of Letters series, is a better biography than any of its predecessors. Woodberry was not, however, aware of the full extent to which Griswold had tampered with Poe's letters, and the Memoir seemed to him a truer account than we now know it to be. Woodberry strove hard to be just to Poe, but he was lacking in sympathy for him both as a man and as a writer. As a New Englander and a friend of Lowell, he shared to some extent the unfavorable view of Poe held by other New England writers. In 1909, the year of the Poe Centenary, he brought out a revised and enlarged edition in two volumes under the title *The Life of Edgar Allan Poe, Personal and Literary, with His Chief Correspondence with Men of Letters.* Poe's expanding fame and the new materials which had become available since 1885 led Woodberry to take a somewhat more favorable attitude toward both Poe's character and his writings. The book, now out of print, is still one of the two or three most useful biographies of Poe.

A more sympathetic biographer than Woodberry was J. A. Harrison of the University of Virginia, who in 1902 published a two-volume *Life and Letters* as a part of his seventeen-volume Virginia Edition of Poe's *Works.* Harrison's best service to Poe scholarship was as editor rather than as biographer. While his *Life* contains what was at that time the fullest account of Poe's year at the University of Virginia, it is poorly organized and written in too rhetorical a style. Harrison was so partisan in his attitude that he rarely admitted Poe's personal shortcomings. He did, however, print or summarize many important letters written by Poe and a considerable number of letters addressed to Poe by J. R. Lowell, P. P. Cooke, and other writers.

Two new lives of Poe were published in 1926. The better of the two is Hervey Allen's *Israfel: The Life and Times of Edgar Allan Poe* (reviewed by J. S. Wilson in *VQR,* 1927). A slightly revised edition (reviewed by Killis Campbell in *AL,* 1935) appeared in 1934. Allen was a less scholarly but more sympathetic biographer than Woodberry. He had the twofold advantage of being himself a poet and writer of prose fiction and of having lived in the South. He was among the first to make use of the correspondence (preserved in the Valentine Museum in Richmond) between Poe and John Allan, first published in 1925. He also made some use of the Ellis & Allan papers in the Library of Congress. *Israfel,* which its author first projected as a novel, is brilliantly written in some passages, carelessly written in others. Allen occasionally overworks his evidence and writes scenes which savor more of romantic fiction than of sober biography. His documentation is unsystematic, and his footnotes in one way or another irritate the reader. Allen also wrote the sketch of Poe in *DAB;* and he and T. O. Mabbott edited *Poe's Brother: The Poems of William Henry Leonard Poe* (1926), which throws light upon the Baltimore period.

Miss Mary E. Phillips' huge two-volume *Edgar Allan Poe—The Man* (1926) is profusely illustrated, and it contains some materials that the scholar cannot afford to overlook; but it is badly written, poorly arranged, and inadequately indexed. It is also, unfortunately, in the words of Hardin Craig, "not conspicuous for literary knowledge and insight . . ."

The most recent and on the whole the best life of Poe is A. H. Quinn's *Edgar Allan Poe: A Critical Biography* (1941), which fortunately is still in print. (For reviews, see Hardin Craig in *VQR,* S. T. Williams in *YR,* and J. S. Wilson in *AL*—all in 1942.) The author of *American Fiction* (1936) understood Poe's literary background better than any of his predecessors. Quinn also had the advantage of the new materials which had come to light since 1926. He himself unearthed some new biographical materials—the marriage record of Poe's parents, for instance—and he suggested new sources for some of the poems and tales.

He revealed for the first time the full extent of Griswold's forgeries, which served temporarily to alienate so friendly a critic of Poe as E. A. Duyckinck. Like Woodberry, he gave much space to a careful critical discussion of Poe's writings. He took issue with J. W. Krutch and Hervey Allen, who had thought that Poe was sexually impotent, at least in his later life. A few readers have felt that Quinn was too ready to defend Poe against all comers, and some younger scholars have regretted that he did not employ the newer critical approaches to Poe's poems and tales. And yet in Quinn's *Poe* the student has available a better biography than is to be found for any of Poe's major American literary contemporaries except Irving, Emerson, and one or two others.

J. W. Ostrom's carefully edited *The Letters of Edgar Allan Poe* (2 vols., 1948) appeared too late to be used by any of Poe's abler biographers. In *AL,* November 1952, Ostrom published a "Supplement to *The Letters of Poe.*" Scholars have regretted that Ostrom did not include at least some of the more important letters addressed to Poe by Beverley Tucker, P. P. Cooke, T. H. Chivers, and J. R. Lowell. Occasionally Poe's letters throw light upon his literary aims and methods; but the strongest impression they leave upon the reader is that of a hardworking journalist, not without friends. Presumably there are few unpublished Poe letters. Great caution must now be taken with any manuscript materials that have turned up in recent years. Forgeries abound and some of them are extremely dangerous, especially the work of one man who is known to be a notable student of Poe, Lincoln, and methods of keeping "within the law."

Apart from Ingram's *Poe,* which is now only of historical interest, the only good biography writen in England is Dame Una Pope-Hennessy's *Edgar Allan Poe* (1934), which is a sensible book. Edward Shanks's long-awaited biography, which finally appeared in the new English Men of Letters series in 1937, has no value as biography and very little as criticism. *The Haunted Man: A Portrait of Edgar Allan Poe* (1954), by the British novelist Philip Lindsay, is so highly romanticized that one wishes the author had projected it as a novel.

Poe's critics, like those of Whitman, have always been too ready to read into his poems and tales their own facile interpretations of his character and personality, and the man they have seen is generally, in the words of J. S .Wilson, "a creature fashioned out of hearsay and cheap journalism and fabricated likenesses by painters and penmen" (*AL,* 1942). In "The Early Psychologists and Poe" (*AL,* 1951) Philip Young discussed the earlier speculations as to what was the matter with Poe, and he promised a much-needed sequel dealing with the theories of later writers. Among later speculations are those to be found in Lorine Pruette's "A Psycho-Analytical Study of Edgar Allan Poe" (*Am. Jour. of Psychol.,* 1929); *Edgar Allan Poe: A Psychopathic Study* (1922), by J. W. Robertson, M.D.; and J. W. Krutch's *Edgar Allan Poe: A Study in Genius* (1926), which owes something to Robertson. (See also Krutch's "The Strange Case of Poe," *AM,* 1925.) Krutch's book is a brilliant interpretation based upon the belief—shared in some degree by Hervey Allen but repudiated by Quinn—that Poe was sexually impotent. Krutch has since expressed doubts as to the validity of his thesis.

Among the better French biographies are Camille Mauclair's *Le Génie d'Edgar Poe* (Paris, 1932) and Emile Lauvrière's *L'Etrange vie et les étranges amours d'Edgar Poe* (Paris, 1934, reviewed by Albert Schinz in *AL,* 1934), published in an English translation by E. G. Rich as *The Strange Life and Loves of Edgar Allan Poe* (1935). See also Lauvrière's "Edgar Poe et le Freudisme" *(La Grande Revue,* 1933). Dr. Lauvrière devoted many years to the study of Poe, and the first of his three biographical studies appeared as early as 1904. The chief defects of his latest biography are that it is highly imaginative and very partisan. He expects his reader to admire the man Poe as highly as he does the poet and writer of tales.

Lauvrière's book is, however, a more dependable biography than the Princess Marie Bonaparte's *Edgar Poe: étude psycho-*

analytique (Paris, 1933). A German version was published in Vienna in 1934. It was again published in 1949 in an English translation by John Rodker as *The Life and Works of Edgar Allan Poe*. Sex and psychoanalysis play so large a part in her interpretation of Poe that Lauvrière condemns it as untrustworthy. The Princess Bonaparte's thesis is that Poe's writings are deeply colored by "intense emotional fixations and painful infantile experiences." If only she did not see sex as the explanation of nearly everything that Poe did or wrote, one would have more confidence in her interpretation of his poems and tales. The Index reveals a truly astonishing array of references to the sex organs, sex acts, impotence, castration, dreams, etc. She laid great stress upon the color of Poe's cat, not knowing that he had *two* different cats. Marie Bonaparte would have done well to bear in mind the caution which her master Sigmund Freud expressed in his Foreword to her book: "Investigations such as this do not claim to explain creative genius, but they do reveal the factors which awaken it and the sort of subject matter it is destined to choose." The actual Poe, however, has always seemed too pedestrian a figure for many of his critics and biographers, particularly on the European continent.

If Poe were alive, he would undoubtedly be a prime case for the physician and the psychiatrist. But since he is dead and we do not have even such a record of a post mortem examination as exists for Whitman, we can do little more than speculate as to what was the matter with him. Dr. Robertson thought Poe was a dipsomaniac; Mrs. Shew, who nursed him, thought he had a lesion of the brain; a Texan physician, Dr. E. G. Reuter, whom Haldeen Braddy consulted, diagnosed the disease as tuberculosis; Mabbott has suggested athlete's heart. Until the physicians can produce from the meager evidence available an accurate diagnosis of the poet who died in 1849, we shall have to rely upon the traditional scholarly methods used by Woodberry, Campbell, and Quinn. These methods were used to good advantage in Campbell's "Self-Revelation in Poe's Poems and Tales" in *The Mind of Poe* (1933). Much of what in Poe's writings has seemed significant to the psychological critics of Poe can be explained by the literary fashions of his time. Some psychologist who is attracted to Poe might do well to study the psychological concepts which were current in America in the early nineteenth century for their possible influence upon Poe's treatment of character.

In spite of the work of able biographers, the Poe legend has flourished ever since Griswold compared the poet to Francis Vivian, the villain of Bulwer-Lytton's *The Caxtons*. More accurately, there are several confused and often intermingling conceptions of Poe which still survive. Poe has been portrayed as an unprincipled man of genius, a drunkard, an American Byron, a Bohemian, *le poète maudit* of Baudelaire, an Ishmael whose hand was against every man and every man's hand against him, the sexually impotent husband of a child wife, an erotic pervert who might have been given a chapter in Mario Praz's *The Romantic Agony*. Or Poe is seen as the lonely artist, the lover of the Beautiful, dwelling in an Ivory Tower somewhere "Out of SPACE—out of TIME." For his partisans Poe is too often the sinless hero persecuted by a horde of Philistines. In none of the legends do we find the literary journalist or the fastidious author slowly composing and endlessly revising his poems and tales to make them as perfect as possible.

In *The Histrionic Mr. Poe* (1949) N. B. Fagin rides very hard the thesis suggested by his title; namely, that the poet was an actor *manqué* who carried his histrionic talents into the writing of poems and short stories. (See also Fagin's "Edgar Allan Poe," *SAQ,* 1952.) Often he throws out an illuminating suggestion such as that Poe did not live his tales but acted them instead; hence their air of unreality. Poe's characters, according to Fagin, are not people but masks. Poe was undoubtedly something of a poseur; like many another writer, artist, politician, journalist, and businessman, he felt that it was desirable to present to the world a somewhat romanticized portrait of himself. It may be doubted, however, whether he carried his pose as far as did Byron or Whitman or Ezra Pound. Fagin presses his thesis so hard that the reader finally protests: "If Poe's talent was essentially histrionic, why did he not become an actor like his father and mother or attempt to make a living by writing plays for the stage?" Leo Spitzer has pointed out a semantic error involved in Fagin's terminology: "the main fallacy in such reasoning is that, through the use of the metaphorical *word* 'histrionic,' the fundamental difference between the art of writing a dramatic story and the art of the stage is blurred. With the same reasoning the author of the *Commedia* could be represented as a frustrated producer" ("A Reinterpretation of 'The Fall of the House of Usher'," *CL,* IV, 361-362, n. 13, Fall 1952).

Among special studies of some biographical interest are D. K. Jackson's *Poe and The Southern Literary Messenger* (Richmond, 1934) and Agnes Bondurant's *Poe's Richmond* (Richmond, 1942), which occasioned the essay "Mr. Ritchie's Richmond" in J. B. Cabell's *Let Me Lie* (1947). For the Baltimore period we have May G. Evans' "Poe in Amity Street" (*Md. Hist. Mag.,* 1941); L. C. Wroth's "Poe's Baltimore" (*Johns Hopkins Alumni Mag.,* 1929); and two articles by J. C. French: "Poe and the *Baltimore Saturday Visiter*" (*MLN,* 1918) and "Poe's Literary Baltimore" (*Md. Hist. Mag.,* 1937). For Poe's Philadelphia and New York backgrounds, little has been published outside of the biographies by Quinn, Allen, and Woodberry.

Some work but not enough has been done on Poe's relations with his literary contemporaries. Among the more helpful studies are Joy Bayless' *Rufus Wilmot Griswold* (1943), which, however, Mabbott finds not altogether just to Poe (see his review in *SAQ,* 1944); H. E. Spivey's "Poe and Lewis Gaylord Clark" (*PMLA,* 1939); S. P. Moss's article in *AL,* 1956, "Poe and His Nemesis—Lewis Gaylord Clark," which presents a much less favorable view of the editor of the *Knickerbocker;* J. B. Reece's unpublished Duke University dissertation, "Poe and the New York Literati" (1954), which, like Perry Miller's *The Raven and the Whale* (1956), gives some account of New York social and cultural life as Poe saw it; R. B. Davis' "Poe and William Wirt" (*AL,* 1944); Joseph Jackson's "George Lippard: Misunderstood Man of Letters" (*Pa. Mag. of Hist. and*

Biog., 1935); Gerald Grubb's "The Personal and Literary Relationships of Dickens and Poe" *(NCF*, 1950) and Ada B. Nisbet's "New Light on the Dickens-Poe Relationship" (*NCF*, 1951); T. O. Mabbott's "Poe's Obscure Contemporaries" (*AN&Q*, 1942) and Elizabeth Binns's "Daniel Bryan: Poe's Poet of 'the Good Old Goldsmith School' " (*William and Mary Quart.*, 1943). See also my "Charles Chauncey Burr: Friend of Poe" (*PMLA*, 1954) and *The South in American Literature* (1954), which deals principally with Poe's Southern background and his relations with other Southern writers, especially Simms, the Cooke brothers, and J. R. Thompson. The better biographies discuss Poe's relations with Lowell, Longfellow, Hawthorne, and Willis, but they have by no means exhausted the subject.

For the complex relationship between Poe and Chivers, see S. F. Damon's *Thomas Holley Chivers: Friend of Poe* (1930) and L. C. Bell's *Poe and Chivers* (1931), which takes issue with Damon on the question of influence. There is an unpublished biography of Chivers by Mrs. Lewis Chase. R. B. Davis' *Chivers' Life of Poe* (1952) is based upon manuscripts in the Huntington Library which were first published in part and somewhat inaccurately by Woodberry. For the tangled relations between Poe and T. D. English, see L. B. Hurley, "A New Note in the War of the Literati" (*AL*, 1936); Reece, op. cit.; C. F. Schreiber, "The Donkey and the Elephant" (*Yale Univ. Library Gazette*, 1944) and "A Close-up of Poe" (*SRL.*, 9 Oct. 1926); F. B. Dedmond, "The War of the Literati: Documents of the Legal Phase" (*N&Q*, 1953) and "Poe's Libel Suit against T. D. English" (*BPLQ*, 1953); and three articles in *PULC* (1944) by Willard Thorp, T. O. Mabbott, and W. H. Gravely, Jr., discussing English's novel *Walter Woolfe*. See also Gravely's "The Early Political and Literary Career of Thomas Dunn English" (Univ. of Va. dissertation, 1953).

II. Editions

By the standards of his time Griswold was a competent editor; but when he published *The Works of the Late Edgar Allan Poe* (4 vols., 1850-56), he missed "The Elk," omitted many reviews, and allowed many typographical errors to escape him. He omitted the first "To Helen," perhaps because it was included in Lowell's essay, which Griswold included in the *Works*. He did, however, print from manuscripts in his possession revised versions of some of the "Literati" sketches. Ingram's *The Works of Edgar Allan Poe* (4 vols., Edinburgh, 1874-75) is better than Griswold's edition and includes some new materials. Later American editions which too often reprinted their texts from Griswold and are of little value today are those of R. H. Stoddard (6 vols., 1884), C. F. Richardson (10 vols., 1902), and Edwin Markham (10 vols., 1904). A better edition, though far from complete, was *The Works of Edgar Allan Poe* (10 vols., 1894-95; reissued in 1914), edited by E. C. Stedman and G. E. Woodberry. The most useful of all editions—though like all I have mentioned it has been long out of print—is the Virginia Edition of J. A. Harrison, *The Complete Works of Edgar Allan Poe* (17 vols., 1902), which included Harrison's two-volume *Life and Letters*. The largest collection of Poe's writings now in print is the Borzoi Poe, *The Complete Poems and Stories of Edgar Allan Poe with Selections from His Critical Writings* (2 vols., 1946), edited by A. H. Quinn, who wrote the biographical introduction and the explanatory notes, and E. H. O'Neill, who established the text and supplied the brief bibliographical notes. The selections from Poe's non-fiction prose, which in the Virginia Edition fill nine volumes, occupy only about 200 pages in a total of less than 1,100. A really complete edition with full editorial apparatus is now the chief desideratum of students of Poe; and it is to be hoped that Professor Mabbott's projected edition may not be long delayed.

The latest important edition of Poe's poems is Mabbott's *Selected Poems of Edgar Allan Poe* (1928), which does not include *Politian*, of which he had published a fine scholarly edition in 1923. Editions of much historical importance are those of C. W. Kent (Vol. VII in the Virginia Edition, 1902) and J. H. Whitty (1911; rev. ed., 1917). The most useful of all editions, now out of print, is Killis Campbell's *The Poems of Edgar*

Allan Poe (1917), which contains an admirable Introduction, copious and illuminating notes, and textual variants carefully collated.

Since 1917 much new material has accumulated that has found no place in any edition of the poems. Since 1917 also a few new texts of certain poems have become available. See in particular D. R. Hutcherson's "The *Philadelphia Saturday Museum* Text of Poe's Poems" (*AL,* 1933). Of the four facsimile editions of *Tamerlane* the latest and best was edited by Mabbott in 1941. The Facsimile Text Society, which printed that volume, also brought out *Al Aaraaf* (1935) and *The Raven and Other Poems* (1942), both with introductions by Mabbott, and the 1831 *Poems* (1936), with a bibliographical note by Campbell.

Aside from the Borzoi Poe, the best editions of the tales are J. S. Wilson's *Tales of Edgar Allan Poe* (1927), which has an excellent Introduction, and Campbell's *Poe's Short Stories* (1927), which lists the various known texts of the tales. For a later checklist, see J. C. Wyllie, "A List of the Texts of Poe's Tales" (*Humanistic Studies in Honor of John Calvin Metcalf,* 1941). Poe's five earliest stories, to which Campbell had called attention in the *Dial* (1916), were reprinted in facsimile by the University of Virginia in *Edgar Allan Poe and the Philadelphia Saturday Courier* (1933), with an Introduction by J. G. Varner.

Not many of the numerous published volumes of selections from Poe's writings have been carefully edited. A conspicuous exception is *Edgar Allan Poe: Representative Selections, with Introduction, Bibliography, and Notes* (AWS, 1935), edited by Margaret Alterton and Hardin Craig. Miss Alterton, who died before the book was published, wrote the first two sections of the Introduction; Professor Craig wrote the third and final section and supplied the bibliography and notes. The Introduction emphasizes the unity of Poe's thought. The student should be warned that the recipient of the letter of William Wirt to a law student (pp. xxv-xxvii) which Miss Alterton thought was addressed to Poe was H. W. Miller, a student at the University of

North Carolina. See R. B. Davis, "Poe and William Wirt" (*AL,* 1944).

A useful volume of selections is the Modern Library College Edition of Poe's *Selected Poetry and Prose* (1951), edited by Mabbott with excellent brief textual and explanatory notes drawn mainly from his projected edition of the complete works. W. H. Auden's *Selected Prose and Poetry* (1950) in the Rinehart Editions contains a thoughtful Introduction but no notes. Auden's selections are far from conventional. He reprinted only eleven poems and omitted "The Sleeper," "For Annie," and the first but not the second "To Helen." He reprinted the whole of *Eureka* and the *Narrative of A. Gordon Pym,* the conclusion of which Malcolm Cowley once pronounced the finest passage in Poe's prose writings ("Aidgarpo," *New Republic,* 5 Nov. 1945). In "Poe, 'The Raven,' and the Anonymous Young Man" (*WHR,* 1955), H. M. Jones expressed dissatisfaction with Auden's selections and critical estimate of Poe.

Few poems or tales have been added to the Poe canon since Killis Campbell published "The Poe Canon" in *The Mind of Poe* (1933). Two poems which had been first printed by E. L. Didier under what seemed to Campbell suspicious circumstances may now be safely assigned to Poe. "Alone," of which W. H. Auden and Allen Tate speak highly, first appeared in *Scribner's Monthly* for September 1875 in what appeared to be a facsimile. Didier, who claimed to have found the verses in the album of a Mrs. Balderston in Baltimore, later admitted that he had written on the manuscript the title and the place and date of composition, both of which were demonstrably wrong. The manuscript has come to light, and I. B. Cauthen, Jr., has found evidence which indicates that "Alone" is a genuine Poe poem. See his "Poe's *Alone:* Its Background, Source, and Manuscript" (Univ. of Va. *Studies in Bibliography,* 1950). "O, Tempora! O, Mores!" perhaps the earliest of Poe's extant poems, was published in the first number (Oct. 1889) of Didier's Baltimore *No Name Magazine* without any indication of its source. An earlier and somewhat different text of the poem which appeared in the Richmond weekly *Southern Opinion* for 7 March 1868, came from J. R. Thompson. See my "'O, Tempora! O, Mores!' A Juvenile Poem by Edgar Allan Poe" (Univ. of Colo. *Studies,* 1945). Poe's unfinished story, "The Light-House," to which Woodberry first called attention, is printed in full in Mabbott's *Selected Poetry and Prose* (1951). See also Mabbott's "Poe's Tale, 'The Lighthouse'" (*N&Q,* 1942). In "The Spectacles: The Lost Story by Edgar Allan Poe" (*Liberty,* 24 Sept. 1938) Edward Doherty reprinted a very inferior story ascribed to Poe by a Poe collector, Richard Gimbel, who refused to tell where it was first printed. No scholar that I know of believes that Poe wrote it.

Since 1902 scholars have discovered some important prose items which were not included in the Virginia Edition. Among these are *Doings of Gotham,* which Poe in 1844 wrote for the Columbia, Pa., *Spy* and which in 1929 was published in book form by Jacob Spannuth in Pottsville, Pa., with introduction and comment by Mabbott. The Virginia Edition does not include two installments of the "Marginalia" which E. H. O'Neill has reprinted in "The Poe-Griswold-Harrison Texts of the 'Marginalia'" (*AL,* 1943). Other uncollected items were reprinted in C. S. Brigham's "Edgar Allan Poe's Contributions to *Alexander's Weekly Messenger*" (*Proceedings of the Am. Antiquarian Society,* 1942). Some of Poe's uncollected reviews have been identified through references to them on magazine covers, which too often librarians are accustomed to remove before binding. See, for example, Mabbott's "Newly Identified Reviews by Edgar Poe" (*N&Q,* 1932). Of some interest also is Vincent Starrett's "A Poe Mystery Uncovered: *The Lost Minerva Review* [by J. H. Hewitt] *of Al Aaraaf*" (*SRL,* 1 May 1943).

In the Bibliography of the Virginia Edition (XVI, 355-379), Harrison included what was intended to be a complete list of Poe's writings—though he did not reprint all of the reviews. It has long been suspected that the review of Bryant's poems (VIII, 1-2), which first appeared in the *Southern Literary Messenger* in January 1835, was not by Poe, whose connection with the magazine had not then begun. Some of Harrison's mistakes in attribution are corrected in D. K. Jackson, *The Contributors and Contributions to The Southern Literary Messenger* (1936) and in an unpublished University of Virginia dissertation by William Doyle Hull II, "A Canon of the Critical Works of Edgar Allan Poe with a Study of Poe as Editor and Reviewer" (1941). It is now known that the reviews of Manzoni's *I Promessi Sposi* and Paulding's *Slavery in the United States* were written not by Poe but by Beverley Tucker and the review of the *Crayon Miscellany No. 2* by E. V. Sparhawk. There are uncollected Poe items in the *New York Evening Mirror* which Mabbott plans to publish, and J. B. Reece expects to republish some uncollected items from the *Broadway Journal*. More of Poe's writings may well be discovered when complete files of periodicals to which he is known to have contributed become available—especially the *Baltimore Saturday Visiter* and the *Philadelphia Saturday Museum*. There are some still uncollected reviews in *Graham's Magazine* and Burton's *Gentleman's Magazine*.

III. Bibliography

No one has as yet published a Poe bibliography comparable to that which the late T. F. Currier compiled for Whittier; but there are—besides Harrison's in the Virginia Edition—a number of useful bibliographies of various kinds. Two bibliographies which are of especial interest to collectors must be used with caution by the scholar. J. W. Robertson's *A Bibliography of the Writings of Edgar A. Poe* (2 vols., 1934) is a chronological list of Poe's publications which includes facsimiles of important rare documents. Some of Robertson's errors were pointed out by David Randall in "Robertson's Poe Bibliography" (*Publishers' Weekly*, 21 April 1934). Somewhat more useful to the student is C. F. Heartman and J. R. Canny's *A Bibliography of First Printings of the Writings of Edgar Allan Poe* (1940; rev. ed., 1943). This book represents a thorough revision of Heartman and Kenneth Rede's *A Census of First Editions and Source Materials by Edgar Allan Poe in American Collections* (2 vols., 1932). Mabbott contributed information and advice to Heartman and Canny's *Bibliography,* but their listings from Burton's *Gentleman's Magazine* and *Graham's* are from another source.

There are good but not complete bibliographies in *CHAL* (1918), and *LHUS* (1948), which includes no materials published after 1946. The student will profit from consulting the selective and annotated bibliographies in the AWS volume of selections from Poe (1935), compiled by Hardin Craig, and *Major American Writers* (1936), edited by H. H. Clark. These, however, list almost nothing published in the last two decades. A few of the later materials are listed in the brief bibliography in *LAP* (1951), and in the Borzoi Poe, edited by Quinn and O'Neil. There is a useful selective bibliography in Haldeen Braddy's *Glorious Incense: The Fulfillment of Edgar Allan Poe* (1953).

By far the most nearly complete list of articles about Poe's life and writings, for the period it covers, is Lewis Leary's *Articles on American Literature 1900-1950* (1954), which supersedes Leary's 1947 checklist, which covered only the years 1920-45. The best available list of articles published before 1900 is in *CHAL.* For articles published since 1950, see the checklists in each number of *American Literature* compiled by a committee of the American Literature Group of the Modern Language Association. The *Index* to the first twenty volumes of *American Literature,* compiled by T. F. Marshall and published by the Duke University Press in 1955, lists both articles concerning Poe and reviews of books about him. Later articles and reviews can be located by consulting the annual indexes. For dissertations on Poe, see "Doctoral Dissertations in American Literature" (*AL,* 1933), compiled by E. E. Leisy and J. B. Hubbell, and "Doctoral Dissertations in American Literature, 1933-1948" (*AL,* xx, 169-230, May 1948), compiled by Lewis Leary. For the years since 1948, see "Research in Progress" in each number of *AL.* The student should also consult the "American Bibliography" and "Research in Progress," which appear annually in *PMLA*.

IV. Criticism

1. *General Estimates*

More than any other American writer except perhaps Whitman, Poe has been a controversial figure in literary criticism. Until 1880, when John Ingram published his life of Poe, there was no good source of biographical information to counterbalance the ugly portrait and the factual errors in Griswold's Memoir. The estimates of many of the earlier critics were deeply colored by what they thought they knew about Poe's character and personality. Legend, indeed, has distorted much of what has been written about him ever since his death in 1849. See, for example, Alice L. Cooke, "The Popular Conception of Edgar Allan Poe from 1850 to 1890" (Univ. of Texas *SE,* 1942) and D. R. Hutcherson, "Poe's Reputation in England and America, 1850-1909" (*AL,* 1942). Those critics who accepted Griswold's Memoir as trustworthy conceded Poe's technical skill, but they belittled his critical writings and concluded that his poems and tales were largely vitiated by a lack of moral purpose. In the 1850's Southern magazinists began praising Poe as a neglected Southern genius, but they showed no very clear understanding of his aims and methods. In the twentieth century, however, much of what is best in Poe scholarship has come from the South, principally from Killis Campbell and his students at the University of Texas, and from the University of Virginia, where J. A. Harrison, C. W. Kent, C. A. Smith, J. S. Wilson, and Floyd Stovall have inspired students with their own enthusiasm for Poe.

Throughout the nineteenth century Poe's standing was much lower in New England than it was anywhere else in his own country. For this situation Poe himself was of course partly responsible. In his praiseworthy desire to promote a national as opposed to a sectional literature, he had attacked the New

England writers for their provincialism and condemned their fondness for moralizing. He had ridiculed Boston as the "Frog-pond" and charged Longfellow, Lowell, and Hawthorne (though he often praised them highly) with plagiarism. At the close of the nineteenth century William Dean Howells, who knew them all, thus summed up the New England attitude:

> The great New Englanders would none of him. Emerson called him "the jingle-man"; Lowell thought him "three-fourths [two-fifths] sheer fudge"; Longfellow's generous voice was silenced by Poe's atrocious misbehavior to him, and we can only infer his slight esteem for his work; in a later generation Mr. [Henry] James speaks of Poe's "very valueless verses." Yet it is perversely possible that his name will lead all the rest when our immortals are duly marshalled for the long descent of time ("A Hundred Years of American Verse," *NAR,* 1901).

While Poe was scandalizing the New England literati in the "Longfellow War," he failed to foresee that the Boston-Cambridge-Concord view of the function of literature would dominate American literary criticism throughout the later nineteenth century. On 27 May 1893 the New York *Critic* announced the results of a poll which it had taken of its readers to select "The Best Ten American Books." Emerson's *Essays* and Hawthorne's *The Scarlet Letter* were at the top of the list with around 500 votes apiece; and the poems of Longfellow, Lowell, Holmes, and Whittier were all among the first ten; but nothing by Poe got as much as twenty votes. Edmund Gosse wrote from England to protest against the exclusion of Poe, "the most perfect, the most original, the most exquisite of the American poets." The exclusion of Poe seemed to him "extraordinary and sinister." For a modern New England poet, Amy Lowell, Poe and Whitman were the first and greatest American poets; but, she said in 1916, "the dominance of New England culture over the whole country . . . kept them from being understood for many years" (S. F. Damon, *Amy Lowell,* 1935, p. 331).[1]

The high praise heaped upon Poe in New England and elsewhere during the Centenary year made it evident that at last his own country had accepted him as one of its major writers. Presumably Poe's great vogue in Europe, to which Gosse had called attention, had something to do with the growth of his American reputation. Yet even today there is wide disagreement among critics as to Poe's merits and his place in our literature. Those who accept Poe's views of the nature and function of poetry and fiction almost invariably give him a high rank, but critics for whom content is more important than form are generally reluctant to concede that he is more than a minor writer. Killis Campbell in 1917 rightly attributed much of the critical disagreement as to the merits of Poe's poems to "the world-old difference among critics as to the province and aims of poetry, the traditional clash between those who insist on the inculcation of moral ideas as the chief business of poetry and those who adhere to the doctrine of art for art's sake." Yet it may be said that today only a small minority of competent critics would deny Poe a place in our literary pantheon. Among academic students of American literature there are few indeed who would not concede him a place beside the greatest of his American contemporaries. The poll of twenty-seven specialists, undertaken in 1949 for UNESCO by the American Literature Group of the Modern Language Association, gave Poe a total of 163 points, only one less than they gave to Hawthorne, whose name headed the list.

From all that I have said it follows that hardly more than half a dozen of the critical essays on Poe written in the last century are intrinsically worth reading today. Two of the best of these, however, appeared during his lifetime. These are

[1] Soon after Bryant's death in 1878 J. G. Holland wrote in *Scribner's Monthly,* XVI (Oct. 1878), 896: "Of one thing we may be reasonably sure, viz., that when the genuine geniuses of this period shall be appreciated at their full value . . . , their countrymen will have ceased discussing Poe and Thoreau and Walt Whitman."

Lowell's "Edgar Allan Poe" (which emphasized the poems), published in *Graham's Magazine* in February 1845, and P. P. Cooke's "Edgar A. Poe" (which is concerned mainly with the tales), published in the *Southern Literary Messenger* in January 1848. Lowell's essay was written before a coolness developed between himself and Poe. It was reprinted by Griswold in 1850 in a revised version which distinctly qualified the high praise that Lowell had bestowed in 1845. The earlier version was reprinted, along with Cooke's essay, in Harrison's biography in 1902 and again by Edmund Wilson in *The Shock of Recognition* in 1943.

Of the later nineteenth-century essays written by Americans much the best is that of E. C. Stedman, which after first appearing in *Scribner's Monthly* for May 1880 was reprinted in book form in 1881 and included in his *Poets of America* (1885). For Stedman's continuing interest in Poe, see Laura Stedman and G. M. Gould, *The Life and Letters of Edmund Clarence Stedman* (1910), II, 209-239, and Stedman's introductions to Vols. I, VI, and X of the Stedman-Woodberry edition of Poe's *Works* (1894-95).

In November 1875, when a monument was placed over Poe's grave in Baltimore, Walt Whitman was the only major American writer to attend the ceremonies. In spite of a distaste for Poe's poems, he had come to recognize the power in them. And yet the brief essay on "Edgar Poe's Significance," which he wrote in 1880, reveals a fundamental lack of sympathy with Poe's aims: "Almost without the first sign of moral principle, or of the concrete or its heroisms, or the simpler affections of the heart, Poe's verses illustrate an intense faculty for technical and abstract beauty, with the rhyming art to excess, an incorrigible propensity toward nocturnal themes, a demoniac undertone behind every page—and, by final judgment, probably belong among the electric lights of imaginative literature, brilliant and dazzling, but with no heat."

Of British essays on Poe perhaps the best—though it suffers from inadequate biographical information—is that of the

Scotch critic, J. M. Robertson, in his *New Essays towards a Critical Method* (1889). James Hannay's introduction to Poe's *Poetical Works* (1853) contains an excellent discussion of Poe's poetry as well as incidental high praise for Melville's recent novel, *Moby Dick*. George Saintsbury, who early and late praised Poe, in his old age published an excellent essay in the *Dial* (1927), which was reprinted in his *Prefaces and Essays* (1933).

In France Charles Baudelaire, who translated the best of the tales, was Poe's chief champion. Although he knew little about Poe's life or background, he was nevertheless one of the most discerning and sympathetic of Poe's critics. His three widely influential essays, published in 1852, 1856, and 1857, together with other relevant comments, are available in English in *Baudelaire on Poe* (1952), translated and edited by Lois and Francis E. Hyslop, Jr.

Of the critical estimates occasioned by the Poe Centenary the ablest and least sympathetic was that of W. C. Brownell, which first appeared in *Scribner's Magazine* in January 1909 and was in the same year republished in his *American Prose Masters*. Brownell's conclusion (not unlike Whitman's) was that "whatever his merits as a literary artist," Poe's writings lack "substance" and hence as literature are "essentially valueless." From *William Crary Brownell: An Anthology of His Writings* (1939), compiled by Mrs. Brownell, we learn that in his later years the critic was troubled by a feeling that he had not done full justice to Poe's poetry. In 1923 he slightly modified some of his severest passages when he published a revised version of the essay in the Modern Student's Library edition of *American Prose Masters*.

Few of our earlier literary historians, most of whom were New England professors of English, revealed any thorough understanding of Poe; and most of them had great difficulty in fitting his writings into the national literary tradition as they conceived it. The chapter on Poe in Barrett Wendell's *A Literary History of America* (1900), which is chiefly concerned with the writers of the New England Renaissance, is unsympathetic and suffers from various misconceptions of Poe's life, character, and background. The Centenary address which Wendell delivered at the University of Virginia on 19 January 1909 reveals for the first time in Wendell's writings a comprehension of the real importance of Poe. There is a brief account of Wendell's changing opinions and the nineteenth-century New England attitude toward Poe in my *The South in American Literature* (1954), pp. 542-549. Poe was treated with some sympathy and understanding in *American Literature, 1607-1885* (1889), by C. F. Richardson, a Dartmouth College professor who in 1902 brought out the Knickerbocker Edition of Poe's *Works,* and in W. P. Trent's *A History of American Literature, 1607-1865* (1903). See also Trent's "The Centenary of Poe" in his *Longfellow and Other Essays* (1910).

Poe has fared somewhat better at the hands of most later literary historians. In 1913 John Macy included an impressionistic and appreciative essay on Poe in *The Spirit of American Literature,* sometimes referred to as the first "modern" history of our literature. Still of value are Killis Campbell's chapter in Vol. II (1918) of *CHAL* and the admirable Introduction to his edition of Poe's *Poems* (1917). Before Professor Quinn wrote his biography, in which he discussed Poe's chief writings, he had treated the tales in *American Fiction* (1936). The best summary of what Quinn has to say about Poe appears in *LAP* in a chapter entitled "Beauty and the Supernatural." That chapter and the chapter on Poe in *LHUS* (which first appeared in *SR,* 1946) by the late F. O. Matthiessen are the two best summary accounts of Poe's literary career. Matthiessen's approach to Poe is similar to that which in his *American Renaissance* (1941) he had applied with notable results to Poe's chief literary contemporaries. He was, however, in the space allotted him, unable to treat Poe's writings as fully as he had discussed those of Emerson, Hawthorne, Thoreau, Melville, and Whitman; and he did not bring to Poe the full knowledge and sympathetic understanding that he had brought to them. He should have devoted more attention to Poe's early development and to his Southern background; and he might to advantage, one feels, have studied more carefully Poe's reviews of books.

In two chapters in *The World of Washington Irving* (1944) Van Wyck Brooks discussed Poe more sympathetically and much more fully than he had done in *America's Coming of Age* (1915). He carefully placed Poe in his Southern and Northern backgrounds, and he managed to make him come alive, so to speak, in the various cities in which he lived and wrote. One wishes, however, that so gifted a critic as Brooks had devoted more space to an appraisal of Poe's best poems and tales. Brooks, like Wendell, Parrington, and other literary historians, found it difficult to fit Poe into the American literary tradition. To H. S. Canby, Poe seemed closer to that tradition as we see it in the twentieth century than most of his New England contemporaries. He wrote in *Classic Americans* (1931): "Poe the writer is nearest to our norm; the New Englanders belonged to a culture so differene from our megalopolitan civilization that they might well have come from that star which Poe was always seeking. Professionals in the life of the soul, they often seem amateurs—sometimes of genius—in the craft of writing. . . . Poe . . . as a man of letters, was the true professional" (pp. 263-264). Parrington in Vol. II (1927) of his *Main Currents in American Thought* devoted two thoughtful paragraphs to Poe and then proceeded to dispose of him as follows: "The problem of Poe, fascinating as it is, lies quite outside the main current of American thought, and it may be left with the psychologist and the belletrist with whom it belongs." Poe's claim to a place in our literary tradition is nowhere better summarized than in H. M. Jones's *Ideas in America* (1944):

> Now Poe was not, as Parrington seemed to think, merely an "aesthete and a craftsman" who "made a stir in the world." He was not merely a disappointed artist or merely a disgruntled and deracinated Southerner. He was, so to speak, a complete product of the publishing world of his

> time and of American taste and sensibility in the same epoch. The seventy-odd stories he wrote had been anticipated in almost all their aspects by British and American magazine fiction; and what Poe was principally trying to do was, like O. Henry and Ring Lardner, to master a market. His originality consisted in doing better than anybody else what everybody else was trying to do. His famous critical theories are to a surprising degree the rationale of successful magazine writing in his day. He had, to be sure, a difficult personality, but to think of Poe in terms of a damaged and therefore ineffectual angel, a misunderstood genius, a Satanic being, a problem for the psychologist and the belletrist only, is to give up literary history as an instrument for cultural analysis. (p. 41)

When we turn from the more academic scholars and critics to the English and American poets and novelists who have put on record their estimates of Poe, we find a great diversity of opinion.[2] For this there are a number of reasons. The creative writer, though often gifted with an insight denied to the mere scholar, is likely to think chiefly in terms of the kind of literature which most attracts him; and this too frequently is just the kind of writing he himself does best. Hervey Allen remarked shrewdly of "The Poetic Principle": "Like all poetic criticism by poets, it was, in its final analysis, a special and ingenious plea for the kind of poetry he himself wrote." When Poe maintained that there is properly speaking no such thing as a long poem, one cannot help suspecting him of rationalizing, for both "Tamerlane" and "Al Aaraaf" had been comparative failures. Just as Poe judged the work of other poets by his own high but rather narrow standards, so creative writers have frequently judged him without taking into consideration

[2] My distinction between academic and non-academic critics of Poe may seem an artificial one. And yet although T. S. Eliot, Allen Tate, and Yvor Winters have taught or lectured in universities and colleges, their point of view is that of the widely-read man of letters rather than that of the scholar.

his aims and methods or the attitudes and limitations of the age in which he lived and wrote.

The two decades which followed the First World War were a period of violent revolt and unrestrained experimentation. To some of the creative writers—Sinclair Lewis, for example—the standards of the academic critics, especially those of the New Humanists, were wrong-headed or obsolete. New literary fashions had come in, and Poe's reputation suffered somewhat from the general reaction against the Victorians. A new canon of the Great American Writers was in the making. To a few of the younger writers, who had read nothing of his since leaving high school, Poe seemed simply a writer for adolescents. His Gothic machinery was outmoded, and they turned eagerly to the newer and more exciting poetry and fiction coming from the European continent. Some of the creative writers—notably Aldous Huxley, T. S. Eliot, and Yvor Winters—complained that there was much bad writing in even Poe's best poems and tales. His style seemed artificial and much too rhetorical. Their critical attitude was that of Paul Verlaine: "Take eloquence and wring its neck." To be sure Byron, Milton, and Shakespeare —not to mention Homer, Aeschylus, and Pindar—had also striven after eloquence; but the twentieth-century rebels wanted to write in "the language of common speech," the new American literary language being so effectively employed in verse by Robert Frost and in fiction by Ernest Hemingway.

Nevertheless, Poe's work has stood the severe test of time's sifting better than that of his more popular English and American contemporaries. (See, for example, Harriet Monroe's "Poe and Longfellow," *Poetry*, 1927.) He was obviously a professional writer of high standards and a critic who had no patience with mediocrity. He was an artist who never stooped to sermonizing or to the writing of "namby-pamby love tales." His pessimism, like that of Melville and Henry Adams, proved more congenial than the somewhat complacent optimism of Emerson and Whitman. For some of the younger writers of the 1920's, Poe was useful as a symbol since he seemed to them a rebel against the tyranny of mob opinion who had as little faith in democracy as H. L. Mencken.

The literary expatriates who fled to Paris could not help being impressed by Poe's great vogue in France and by his obvious influence upon the French writers whom they admired. They discovered, when they reread his poems and tales, that he was not only an early symbolist, but a pioneer explorer into the workings of the minds of men obsessed by irrational fears and impulses. Since there is unfortunately no study of Poe criticism for the years after 1909 (except for G. W. Allen's unpublished "American Criticism of Poe since the Poe Centenary," 1931), a glance at some of the estimates which have come from men of letters may help us better to understand the variety of meanings that Poe's works have had for twentieth-century readers. The man of letters when he writes criticism may go wrong through a lack of scholarship, but he often understands better than the scholar what it is in Poe that means most to contemporary lovers of literature.

Among the most extreme British admirers of Poe's poems was the Irish novelist George Moore, who had lived long in France and was deeply influenced by the French advocates of *la poésie pure*. In his *Anthology of Pure Poetry* (1924) Moore included only poems which seemed to him free from ideas, moralizing, and subjectivity. He found it difficult, as he explained in his Introduction, not to overburden his pages with selections from Poe, whose poetry seemed to him "almost free from thought." He reprinted six of Poe's poems, more than he chose from any other poet except Shakespeare.

In *Studies in Classic American Literature* (1923) D. H. Lawrence included an essay on Poe (published earlier in *English Rev.*, 1919) which W. H. Auden has described as "conspicuous for its insights" but which has seemed less sound to more conservative critics. Lawrence was among the first to see in Freudian psychology a key to the understanding of Poe, who, he thought, was "absolutely concerned with the disintegration-processes of his own psyche." "He was an adventurer into vaults and cellars and horrible underground passages of the human soul. He sounded the horror and warning of his own doom." The essay consists in large part of quotations from, and comments upon, "Ligeia" and "The Fall of the House of Usher." Lawrence's comments on Poe's poems betray the naïve notion that Poe composed them with great facility.

In 1930 Aldous Huxley published an essay, *Vulgarity in Literature* (also in *SRL,* 1930), in which he noted that the French translators of Poe had eliminated much of his bad writing; and, employing his own very special definition, he pointed to Poe as an eminent example of literary vulgarity. In England fashions in literature and language would seem to have suffered a radical change since 1909 when Norman Douglas wrote: "What is Poe's life-work? His influence upon literature was a civilising and purifying agency. Poe is a great anti-vulgarian" ("Edgar Allan Poe from an English Point of View," *Putnam's,* 1909; the essay was reprinted in Douglas' *Experiments* in 1925).

American novelists and poets are no more in agreement about Poe than their British contemporaries. J. B. Cabell, whose grandfather witnessed Poe's famous boyhood swimming exploit in the James, expressed the opinion in *Ladies and Gentlemen* (1934) that of our nineteenth-century American literature about all that is of any importance is "A sufficing amount of Poe; and a tiny fraction of Mark Twain." Very different is the estimate suggested a year later in *Green Hills of Africa* by Ernest Hemingway, who apparently cares little for any of our older writers except Mark Twain: "Poe is a skillful writer. It is skillful, marvellously constructed, and it is dead." And yet perhaps Malcolm Cowley was right when, speaking of "The Snows of Kilimanjaro," he wrote in *The Viking Portable Hemingway* (1944): "For all his accurate transcriptions of reality, he [Hemingway] is a haunted and nocturnal writer in the tradition of Poe, Hawthorne, and Melville."

In their youth many American poets have been fascinated by the music of Poe's poems; but most of them, I suspect, like

Sidney Lanier and Robert Frost, have been more deeply influenced by other poets. Not so, however, with Vachel Lindsay, whose "The Wizard in the Street" is one of the best poetic tributes to Poe. In the Autobiographical Foreword to his *Collected Poems* (1923) Lindsay wrote that in the histories of American literature which he read in the Springfield, Illinois, High School: "There was nothing to be found but the full-page portraits of a famous mutual-admiration society. I knew exactly Poe's opinion of these whiskered worthies. . . . I was a kind of literary outcast because I championed Poe and his view."

For W. C. Williams, who in his *In the American Grain* (1925) included a highly eulogistic essay, Poe was "in no sense the bizarre, isolate writer, the curious literary figure. On the contrary, in him American literature is anchored, in him alone, on solid ground." Poe seemed to Williams much more essentially American than Longfellow or even Hawthorne. Poe's criticism was "a movement, first and last to clear the GROUND." "On him," wrote Williams, "is FOUNDED A LITERATURE—typical; an anger to sweep out the unoriginal . . . to annihilate the copied, the slavish, the FALSE literature about him. . . ." In Poe's five best poems "the place itself [America] comes through. This is the New World." Hart Crane, after reading Williams' essay wrote: "I was so interested to note that he puts Poe and his 'character' in the same position as I had *symbolized* for him in 'The Tunnel' section [of *The Bridge*]" (*Letters,* 1952, p. 278).

T. S. Eliot, reviewing Allen's *Israfel* for the *Nation and Athenaeum* (XLI, 219, 21 May 1927), pronounced Poe "a critic of the first rank," but he added: "In the end, Poe remains inscrutable." In later years Eliot has inclined to a more favorable view, but he still has difficulty in making up his mind about Poe's merits. In *From Poe to Valéry* (1948), also published in the *Hudson Review* (1949), he wrote: "Poe indeed is a stumbling block for the judicial critic. If we examine his work in detail, we seem to find in it nothing but slipshod writing, puerile thinking unsupported by wide reading or profound scholarship, haphazard experiments in various types of writing, chiefly under pressure of financial need, without perfection in any detail." Poe's intellect seemed to Eliot that of "a highly gifted young person before puberty." "What is lacking," he said, "is not brain power, but that maturity of intellect which comes only with the maturing of the man as a whole, the development and coordination of his various emotions." Eliot was much impressed by Poe's influence upon three French poets whom he greatly admires, Baudelaire, Mallarmé, and Valéry; and he noted that the French found in Poe's writing both an essential unity and literary theories of great value. In his *Notes towards a Definition of Culture* (1949, p. 115), Eliot, in speaking of the French poetic tradition "which starts with Baudelaire, and culminates in Valéry," wrote: "I venture to say that without this French tradition the work of three poets in other languages—and three very different from each other—I refer to W. B. Yeats, to Rainer Maria Rilke, and, if I may, to myself—would hardly be conceivable. And, so complicated are these literary influences, we must remember that this French movement itself owed a good deal to an American of Irish extraction: Edgar Allan Poe." In his earlier years Eliot seemed to value Hawthorne and Henry James above all other American writers; but in *American Literature and the American Language* (1953)—an address delivered at Washington University in St. Louis on 9 June 1953—he expressed the opinion that the most important of our writers are Poe, Whitman, and Mark Twain.

Allen Tate included in *The Forlorn Demon* (1953) two related essays: "The Angelic Imagination: Poe as God" and "Our Cousin, Mr. Poe." See also his "Three Commentaries: Poe, James, and Joyce" (*SR,* 1950). Tate agreed with Eliot that most of Poe's ideas "seem to be entertained rather than believed"; but he noted one important exception. This he illustrated by a discussion of *Eureka* and those neglected shorter pieces, "The Conversation of Eiros and Charmion," "The

Colloquy of Monos and Una," and "The Power of Words," in which the pessimistic poet expressed his distrust of democracy, industrialism, and the doctrines of nature and progress. In these Poe sets forth "a cataclysmic end of the world, modelled on the Christian eschatology" and "adumbrates a philosophy of impressive extent and depth." Taking his cue from D. H. Lawrence, Tate suggested that "Poe is the transitional figure in modern literature because he discovered our great subject, the disintegration of the modern personality ['a disorder that has since become typical'], but kept it in a language that had developed in a tradition of unity and order." Poe's critical style seemed to Tate excellent, but his fictional style uneven, descending sometimes to "the bathos of 'Ligeia'." Poe, he concluded, "will remain a man of letters—I had almost said a poet—whose interest for us is in the best sense historical."

The severest judgment passed upon Poe in recent years by a reputable critic is found in Yvor Winters' "Edgar Allan Poe: A Crisis in the History of American Obscurantism" (*AL,* 1937; reprinted in *Maule's Curse,* 1938). Winters, poet, critic, and professor of English at Stanford, practically charged that there was a conspiracy among scholars to maintain Poe's traditional standing as a great American writer. His own opinion was that Poe is "a bad writer accidentally and temporarily popular," "an explicit obscurantist," and a critic of poetry who did not understand the fundamental principles of versification and whose poems are "an art to delight the soul of a servant girl." Obviously Poe would not have agreed with Winters that poetry is "a refined and enriched technique of moral comprehension." Could he have lived to read the essay, Poe might with some reason have challenged this recrudescence of the old "heresy of the didactic" and quoted Archibald MacLeish's lines in "Ars Poetica":

> A poem should not mean
> But be.

After Winters' thorough damnation of Poe we may turn to a passage in Paul Valéry's essay, "Situation de Baudelaire," published in his *Variété* (1930), II, 141-147. I quote from *Variety: Second Series* (1938, p. 87), as translated by W. A. Bradley:

> Thus it is not astonishing that Poe, possessing so effective and sure a method, should be the inventor of several different varieties, should have offered the first and most striking example of the scientific tale, of the modern cosmogonic poem, of the novel of criminal investigation, of the introduction into literature of morbid psychological states, and that all his work should manifest on every page an intelligence which is to be observed to the same degree in no other literary career. This great man would today be completely forgotten had not Baudelaire introduced him into European literature. Let us not fail to observe here that Poe's universal glory is weak or contested only in his native country and England. This Anglo-Saxon poet is strangely neglected by his own race.

Poe of course has been less neglected by Englishmen and Americans than Valéry thought; but the centenary of Poe's death in 1949 occasioned the publication of few important articles. Perhaps the best of these is Darrel Abel's "Edgar Poe: A Centennial Estimate" (*UKCR*, 1949). Unlike many other critics, Abel was more deeply impressed by Poe's critical writings than by his poems. He selected the short stories as "that part of his work most likely to endure."

2. *Special Studies*

The two best studies of Poe's literary theories are Margaret Alterton's *Origins of Poe's Critical Theory* (1925) and Norman Foerster's *American Criticism: Studies in Literary Theory from Poe to the Present* (1928), pp. 1-51. But see also George Kelly's "The Aesthetic Theories of Edgar Allan Poe" (Iowa State Univ. dissertation, 1953); Marvin Laser's "The Growth and

Structure of Poe's Concept of Beauty" (*ELH,* xv, 69-84, March 1948); Summerfield Baldwin's "The Aesthetic Theory of Edgar Poe" (*SR,* 1918); A. J. Lubell, "Poe and A. W. Schlegel" (*JEGP,* 1953); and Miss Alterton's briefer and more mature discussion in sections i and ii of the AWS *Edgar Allan Poe.* Foerster's attitude is somewhat less sympathetic than that found in G. E. De Mille's *Literary Criticism in America* (1931; an earlier version of the chapter on Poe was printed in *AM* in 1925); but Foerster is one of the few critics of whom one can be certain that he studied systematically and thoroughly the critical materials in the Virginia Edition of Poe's *Works.*

Like T. S. Eliot, Edmund Wilson has pronounced Poe a critic of the first order ("Poe as a Literary Critic," *Nation,* 31 Oct. 1942). Griswold, it will be remembered, had considered him as "little better than a carping grammarian." George Snell in "First of the New Critics" (*Quart. Rev. of Lit.,* 1945), advanced the view that " 'Textual' criticism, as we know it today, was born" with Poe; and, without noting significant differences, he pointed out similarities in critical method between the New Critics and Poe. The classical background of Poe's criticism is ably treated in J. P. Pritchard's *Return to the Fountains* (1942), which is chiefly concerned with the debt of American writers to Aristotle's *Poetics* and Horace's *Ars Poetica.*

A. G. Halline's "Moral and Religious Concepts in Poe" (Bucknell Univ. *Studies,* 1951), not included in Leary's checklist, is a more thorough and more sympathetic study than those found in A. H. Strong's *American Poets and Their Theology* (1916) and E. J. Bailey's *Religious Thought in the Great American Poets* (1922). Poe's religious ideas are discussed in *Biblical Allusions in Poe* (1928), by W. M. Forrest. See also Killis Campbell's "Poe's Knowledge of the Bible" (*SP,* 1930) and his review of Forrest (*AL,* 1929).

The best general study of Poe's versification is in G. W. Allen's *American Prosody* (1935); but see also C. A. Smith's *Repetition and Parallelism in English Verse* (1894), and three articles in *AL:* W. L. Werner's "Poe's Theories and Practice in

Poetic Technique" (1930), R. C. Pettigrew's "Poe's Rime" (1932), and Anthony Caputi's "The Refrain in Poe's Poetry" (1953).

Some miscellaneous items follow which seem significant because they embody new materials or approaches or explore neglected topics. The influence of the pseudo-sciences has been treated in Edward Hungerford's "Poe and Phrenology" (*AL,* 1930); S. E. Lind's "Poe and Mesmerism" (*PMLA,* 1947); and C. D. Laverty's unpublished Duke University dissertation, "Science and Pseudo-Science in the Writings of Edgar Allan Poe" (1951), which also discusses the scientific background of *Eureka.* J. S. Wilson's "The Devil Was in It" (*AM,* 1931) and W. F. Taylor's "Israfel in Motley" (*SR,* 1934) are almost the only studies of Poe's humorous stories. The best recent study of another neglected topic is N. F. Adkins' " 'Chapter on American Cribbage': Poe and Plagiarism" (*PBSA,* 1948). One of the few good studies of Poe's influence upon American writers is A. C. Miller's "The Influence of Edgar A. Poe on Ambrose Bierce" (*AL,* 1932). Ernest Marchand's "Poe as Social Critic" (*AL,* 1934) supplements Campbell's treatment of the subject in *The Mind of Poe* (1933). The best of the various articles dealing with "The Mystery of Marie Roget" are S. C. Worthen, "Poe and the Beautiful Cigar Girl" (*AL,* 1948) and W. K. Wimsatt, Jr., "Mary Rogers, John Anderson, and Others" (*AL,* 1950).

In a paper on "Scholarship and Literary Criticism" (*YR,* 1925), which he read at a meeting of the Modern Language Association in December 1924, a French scholar, the late Albert Feuillerat, noted regretfully that the practicing literary critics were seldom scholars and that the scholars rarely wrote criticism. He wished that the divorce between scholarship and criticism might be done away with. The situation in 1955 is somewhat better, and more of our literary critics would now agree with Feuillerat that scholarship must be the foundation, the springboard, if criticism is to lead to "that intimate apprehension of the inner meaning of literary works in all their aspects, historical, psychological, philosophical, and aesthetic . . . which is the goal of all criticism."

In the space allotted to me I can discuss only a few significant examples of the various reinterpretations of the poems and tales. I begin with "Ligeia," to which Poe more than once referred as his best story. Clayton Hamilton, lamenting that Poe wrote no analysis of any one of his tales comparable to his dissection of "The Raven," included in his *A Manual of the Art of Fiction* (1918; first published in 1908 under the title *Materials and Methods of Fiction*) a useful classroom analysis modeled upon "The Philosophy of Composition." In "Poe and Phrenology" (*AL,* 1930) Edward Hungerford showed how Poe used the terminology of a popular pseudo-science to point up Ligeia's will to live and her gift for languages.

Not much attention has been paid to the revisions which Poe made in his short stories. A notable exception is Ruth Hudson's "Poe Recognizes 'Ligeia' as His Masterpiece" (*English Studies in Honor of James Southall Wilson,* 1951). "In writing *Ligeia,*" she says, "Poe gathered up the threads of his dreams—the figures of speech, the phrases, the ideals of characters and interiors, the poetic overtones—which had been taking shape in earlier stories and wove them unconsciously into its fabric." In revising the tale, which he knew to be his masterpiece, he transferred from "The Assignation," "Bon-Bon," "Berenice," and other stories "favorite details and images" to enrich the story which he had written at "the peak of his creative vigor as a tale-writer."

In "The Interpretation of 'Ligeia' " (*CE,* 1944; reprinted in his *Sex, Symbolism and Psychology,* 1948) R. P. Basler made skillful use of the methods of the nonrational psychologists to show that "Ligeia" is not to be interpreted as a story of the supernatural, as Quinn and others see it, but as a study of "the *idée fixe* or obsession in an extreme form of monomania." For Basler "Ligeia" illustrates "the power of the psychical over the physical and the power of frustrate love to create an erotic symbolism and mythology in compensation for sensual disappointment." The story, he suggests, is to be interpreted on two planes, like the first-person stories of Henry James; and Poe's hero reveals to the discerning reader much that he has no intention of disclosing. Basler, after considering other interpretations, comes to the conclusion that Poe's ending is "artistically perfect and unassailable if the story is understood to be that of a megalomaniac, a revelation of obsessional psychology and mania." After Ligeia dies the narrator's obsession becomes "an intense megalomania motivated by his will to restore her to life" in the body of the second wife (whom he has murdered) "through a process of metempsychosis." By way of postcript I note that in *The Selected Poetry and Prose of Edgar Allan Poe* (1951) Mabbott suggests a partial source in Dickens' "A Madman's MSS" and, without developing it in detail, expresses his belief that Ligeia is a witch and that the pentagonal chamber in which she returns to life was intended to suggest "real magic."

Edward Hungerford and H. R. Warfel ("Poe's Dr. Percival . . .," *MLN,* 1939) have contributed useful notes on "The Fall of the House of Usher," and D. H. Lawrence and Allen Tate have briefly discussed it. In *Supernatural Horror in Literature* (1945) H. P. Lovecraft noted that the story "hints shudderingly of obscure life in inorganic things, and displays an abnormally linked trinity of entities at the end of a long and isolated family history—a brother, his twin sister, and their incredibly ancient house all sharing a single soul and meeting one common dissolution at the same moment" (p. 58). Darrel Abel's "A Key to the House of Usher" (*UTQ,* 1949) is a study of the symbolism in the story.

The earlier of two notable reinterpretations appeared in that influential text, *Understanding Fiction* (1943) by Cleanth Brooks and R. P. Warren. In their "Interpretation" the editors maintained that "The horror is relatively meaningless—it is generated for its own sake; and one is inclined to feel that Poe's own interest in the story was a morbid interest." The story, in the editors' view, lacked both "tragic quality" and "pathos" since the leading character does not engage our interest like Lear or Macbeth.

In "A Reinterpretation of 'The Fall of the House of Usher' " (*CL,* 1952), Leo Spitzer, the author of *Essays in Historical Semantics* (1948), discussed the story "from a comparatist viewpoint" and vigorously attacked the Brooks-Warren interpretation. The subject of the story, he pointed out, is not Roderick Usher but the fall (in a double sense) of the house of Usher; and the story itself is a study of the psychological consequences of fear. Spitzer concluded with an illuminating analysis of the term "atmosphere"—"a poetic expression of sociological-deterministic ideas which were in the air in 1839"—by pointing out its literary and scientific background.

Since 1917, when Killis Campbell brought out his edition of Poe's *Poems,* investigators have added many small bits of information or interpretation; but few of these have yet found a place in any edition of the poems. Except for Floyd Stovall's "Poe's Debt to Coleridge" (Univ. of Texas *SE,* 1930) and T. P. Haviland's "How Well Did Poe Know Milton?" (*PMLA,* 1954), no one has added much to Campbell's discussion of Poe's indebtedness to other poets. Scholarship and critical insight, however, have combined to bring about excellent reinterpretations of certain poems. See, for example, H. M. Jones's "Poe, 'The Raven,' and the Anonymous Young Man" (*WHR,* 1955), O. S. Coad's "The Meaning of Poe's 'Eldorado' " (*MLN,* 1944), and Mabbott's "The Sources of Poe's 'Eldorado' " (*MLN,* 1945), and many brief articles in the *Explicator.* In "On Poe's 'The City in the Sea' " and "Poe's 'The City in the Sea' Again" (*AL,* 1934; 1936) Louise Pound pointed out the background of the poem in the Bible and in the many tales of cities engulfed by water. She justified the scholar's approach to the poem when she wrote: "There will always be interest in a poet's play of mind over his materials, the operation of his 'shaping spirit of imagination.' Yet, to follow these, there must be a survey of what the materials are, and herein lies the justification of the source-hunter—a type of scholar often disparaged." Among the various interpretations of that difficult poem, "Al Aaraaf," the most thoroughgoing is Floyd Stovall's "An Interpretation of Poe's 'Al Aaraaf' " (Univ. of Texas *SE,* 1929); but see also W. B. Cairns's earlier article, "Some Notes on Poe's 'Al Aaraaf' " (*MP,* 1915) and R. C. and Marie M. Pettigrew's "A Reply to Floyd Stovall's Interpretation of 'Al Aaraaf' " (*AL,* 1937). The discussion of the poem in Quinn's *Poe* is the only one to take into consideration Poe's letter to Isaac Lea, printed for the first time in Quinn's biography.

There has been continued speculation about the meaning of "Ulalume," but apart from the light thrown upon certain details interpretation has not gone very far beyond the theories which Campbell summarized in 1917. But see "The Astrological Symbolism of Poe's 'Ulalume' " (*N&Q,* 1931), in which Mabbott suggested that the poet's relations with Mrs. Osgood are hinted at in the poem, and "Poe's 'Ulalume' " (*N&Q,* 1933), in which he noted Poe's indebtedness to Elizabeth Oakes-Smith's poem, "The Summons Answered." If a certain schoolgirl who in 1847 heard Poe himself explain "the ideas intended to be embodied" in the poem had only taken the trouble to record them in her "Recollections of Edgar A. Poe," published in the *Home Journal* for 21 July 1860, she would have saved Poe's commentators much futile speculation and no doubt have forestalled various interpretations of the poem. (See C. D. Laverty, "Poe in 1847," *AL,* 1948.) The critics still disagree as to whether "Ulalume" is one of Poe's best and most original poems, as Woodberry thought, or is one of his least successful experiments. W. H. Auden regards it as "an interesting experiment in diction but only an experiment, for the poem is about something which never quite gets said because the sense is sacrificed to the vowel sounds." Hardin Craig, who regards it as one of Poe's finest poems, wrote in 1935: "The age in which 'Ulalume' appeared was incompetent to cope with it, and it is possibly doubtful if Poe himself realized fully the thing he had done." "Ulalume" has seemed to some critics to anticipate the practice of the French symbolists. Mallarmé referred to the poem as "perhaps the most original and the most strangely suggestive of all Poe's poems." Aldous Huxley and T. S. Eliot have accused Poe of misusing the word "immemorial"; but Saintsbury thought Poe's use of it singularly effective and the editors of the *Explicator* (1942) defended it against Huxley's charge of "vulgarity."

Among critics of the twentieth century as well as the nineteenth there has been great disagreement as to which are Poe's best poems. Killis Campbell in 1917 rated "Israfel" (Stedman's favorite), "The City in the Sea," and "The Sleeper" as "certainly as richly poetic as anything that Poe wrote." Auden did not include "The Sleeper" (which Poe thought superior to "The Raven") among the eleven poems he reprinted in Poe's *Selected Prose and Poetry*. He did, however, include "To One in Paradise," which W. C. Williams in 1925 thought the best of the poems. Auden omitted that general favorite, the first "To Helen," which he thought could have been written by Landor, and commented that "Poe's best poems are not his most typical or original."

There is disagreement also about Poe's most famous poem, "The Raven," which Brownell referred to as Poe's "star performance" but to which not many critics have been willing to concede a place among the best of his poems. Various suggestions for sources of the poem, some of them very plausible, have been put forward. No one, however, has made a thorough study of these materials or of "The Philosophy of Composition," utilizing what is known or can be inferred from Poe's sources and revisions about the genesis of "The Raven" (or any other poem) and his methods of composition. Since the publication of "The Philosophy of Composition" over a century ago scholars have made available a mass of materials on how certain important poems by other poets were written. There is also available a great deal of information and plausible speculation about the psychology of poetic composition. Not much of this material, however, has been brought to bear upon the genesis of any of Poe's poems or tales.

3. *Cosmopolitan Fame*

The best general study of Poe's reputation outside his own country is Haldeen Braddy's *Glorious Incense: The Fulfillment of Edgar Allan Poe* (1953), which includes a useful selective bibliography classified by countries. An earlier and briefer study is Brander Matthews' "Poe's Cosmopolitan Fame" (*Century,* 1910), reprinted in his *Gateways to Literature* (1912).

Poe's earlier critics in England, influenced by Griswold's Memoir, were disturbed because they thought his character was bad and they could find no useful lessons in his works. Ingram's various writings contributed to the more favorable view of Poe taken by later English critics. For further details, see D. R. Hutcherson's "Poe's Reputation in England and America 1850-1909" (*AL,* 1942), condensed from a University of Virginia dissertation, and Clarence Gohdes, *American Literature in Nineteenth-Century England* (1944). The most detailed study of Poe's influence in England is H. H. Kühnelt's *Die Bedeutung von Edgar Allan Poe für die englische Literatur* (Innsbruck, 1949), the work of an able Austrian scholar who was at that time unable to consult many of the best articles and books by American scholars. He gave most of his space to the discussion of Poe's influence on Rossetti, Morris, Wilde, Swinburne, and Stevenson.

It was in France that Poe found his most enthusiastic admirers. There, too, he has had a continuous influence upon important writers ever since Charles Baudelaire discovered him in 1846 or 1847 while Poe was still alive. The French took seriously Poe's theory of the nature and function of poetry and fiction. Indeed, one may say that he is the only American writer of the nineteenth century who made any substantial contribution to European literary theory. Poe was exceptionally fortunate in his French translators: Baudelaire, who translated many of the tales, and Mallarmé, who rendered the poems into rhythmical prose. Indeed, Baudelaire's prose may well be, as T. S. Eliot and others have suggested, superior to the original. The French enthusiasm for Poe spread to other countries, notably to Spain and Spanish America. Poe's great fame in France has had repercussions upon his standing in England and America. See, for example, René Taupin's *L'Influence du Symbolisme français sur la poésie américaine* [from 1910 to 1920] (Paris, 1931). In *From Poe to Valéry* (1948) Eliot has traced one line of development which runs from Baudelaire through Mallarmé to Valéry and to Eliot himself; but Poe would seem to have influenced in some degree many other writers, including Théophile Gautier, Rimbaud, Villiers de L'Isle-Adam, Maupassant, Jules Verne, Sardou, Sue, the Goncourt brothers, Alain-Fournier, Maeterlinck, and probably Sartre and Gide. Poe's poems and tales have inspired musical compositions by Debussy and other French composers. See May G. Evans, *Music and Edgar Allan Poe* (1939).

A good early appraisal is C. H. Page's Centenary article, "Poe in France" (*Nation,* 14 Jan. 1909). In 1912 G. D. Morris published *Fenimore Cooper et Edgar Poe d'après la critique française du dix-neuvième siècle* and in October 1915 his "French Criticism of Poe" (*SAQ*). All of these, however, were largely superseded by C. P. Cambiaire's *The Influence of Edgar Allan Poe in France* (1927). Better than Cambiaire's study in some respects are three volumes by Léon Lemonnier: *Edgar Poe et la critique française de 1845 à 1875* (Paris, 1928), *Les Traducteurs d'Edgar Poe en France* (Paris, 1928), and *Edgar Poe et les poètes français* (Paris, 1932). See also Lemonnier's articles in Leary's checklist; Paul Valéry's "Situation de Baudelaire" in his *Variété* II (1930); Louis Seylaz's *Edgar Poe et les premiers Symbolistes français* (Lausanne, 1923); Régis Michaud's "Baudelaire et Edgar A. Poe" (*Revue de Littérature*

Comparée, 1938); Marcel Francon's "Poe and Baudelaire" (*PMLA,* 1945); W. L. Schwartz's "The Influence of E. A. Poe on Judith Gautier" (*MLN,* 1927); and Claire-Eliane Engel's "L'Etat des travaux sur Poe en France" (*MP,* 1932).

Poe's vogue in Spain and Spanish America had its beginning in writers who discovered him in Baudelaire's translation of the tales. There is an informative section on Poe in J. D. Ferguson's *American Literature in Spain* (1916). Both Spain and Spanish America are covered in J. E. Englekirk's *Edgar Allan Poe in Hispanic Literature* (1934). See also his " 'The Raven' in Spanish America" (*Spanish Rev.,* 1934) and "Bibliography of Mexican Versions and Criticism of Poe" (*PMLA,* 1937) and Muna Lee's "Brother of Poe" (*Southwest Rev.,* 1926), which treats the influence of Poe on the Colombian poet José Asunción Silva.

Italian studies of Poe have not been numerous or particularly significant. It will suffice here to mention one book, *Edgar Poe,* by Federico Olivero (Torino, 2nd ed., 1939; translated from the Italian by Dante Milani). American students will find the criticism of Poe's work of some interest.

Poe has perhaps interested more German scholars than creative writers of importance except Rilke, whom Eliot thinks indebted to Poe. Studies of some merit are P. Wächtler, *Edgar Allan Poe und die deutsche Romantik* (Leipzig, 1911), and Fritz Hippe, *Edgar Allan Poes Lyrik in Deutschland* (Münster, 1913). Dr. H. H. Kühnelt has published two informative articles: "Deutsche Erzähler im Gefolge von E. A. Poe" (*Rivista di Letteratura Moderna,* 1951) and "Edgar Allan Poe und die phantastische Erzählung im österreichischen Schrifttum von 1900-1920" (*Ensinger-Festschrift,* Innsbruck, 1952.

For Poe's reputation in Russia, see Avrahm Yarmolinsky, "The Russian View of American Literature" (*Bookman,* 1916), and Vladimir Astrov, "Dostoievsky on Edgar Allan Poe" (*AL,* 1942). Yarmolinsky was mistaken in thinking that Poe's writings were known in Russia in the 1830's (Braddy, *Glorious Incense,* pp. 124-126).

4. *Conclusion*

Few scholars who have read any considerable portion of the books and articles written about Poe will, I think, wholly agree with the compiler of the bibliography on Poe who wrote in *LHUS:* "No American writer has been more competently studied and edited than Poe . . ." We do have, it is true, some admirable biographical and critical studies; but as yet we have nothing approaching a definitive edition of his writings, and there are many aspects of his life and work about which our knowledge is far from complete. Until a quarter of a century ago, most of the substantial work on Poe was done by Ingram, Woodberry, Harrison, Campbell, and two or three other scholars. Much of what was written about Poe came from writers without sound critical standards and untrained in scholarly procedures. They were often misled by one or another legendary conception of Poe, and they passed judgment on his work too confidently, often indeed without having read any of it apart from the best-known poems and tales and perhaps an essay or two. Like Shakespeare, Poe has attracted amateur critics with fixed ideas and dubious theories which lead them to disregard known facts and to ignore the complexity of the mind of a creative writer. Scholarship would be as well off if much that has been published about Poe had never been written.

Since the early 1920's there has been a remarkable development of American studies in our graduate schools; and as a result we now have some important monographs and many articles about Poe, published chiefly in the learned journals. And yet as the student examines these articles, he is disappointed to find that, in spite of their technical excellence, many of them are mere notes and many of the longer articles present only isolated bits of information or speculation or else incomplete studies of important topics and thus have little significance when considered by themselves. Eventually of course we hope they will find a place among the notes in a definitive edition; and we should be grateful for them. Many of these articles and notes, it would appear, were written by graduate students or young instructors (perhaps under pressure from their superiors to publish something) who after printing an article or a note either gave up research or turned to other subjects which interested them more deeply. Poe is a less fashionable subject for research than he was in the 1930's, and the younger scholars now seem more interested in Melville, Mark Twain, Henry James, and T. S. Eliot. The number of competent scholars and critics who have year after year pursued their researches into the life and writings of Poe has always been small. I can think of few names to place beside those of Ingram, Stedman, Woodberry, Harrison, Killis Campbell, A. H. Quinn, J. S. Wilson, and T. O. Mabbott.

The best of the later critical discussions of Poe's work have a more solid basis in scholarship than those which were written before 1926. And yet it is evident that we have accumulated a considerable amount of material which has not yet been brought fully to bear upon the interpretation and critical appraisal of his writings. Some even among university scholars who have discussed his work seem not to have gone systematically through his critical writings, and few indeed have bothered to read his uncollected reviews. Some of the scholars, like the more popular writers, have looked for critical shortcuts to an easy understanding of Poe. These they have sought in the study of myths and symbols or in the methods of the nonrational psychologists, especially as regards sex. These approaches are to be sure legitimate and they have led to some valuable insights, but they are likely to betray the unskillful critic who fails to use as a springboard all the pertinent and ascertainable facts. In the end it will be found that Poe is still a highly complex figure for whose life and writings there is no simple and easy explanation.

We have far from exhausted the potentialities of the traditional scholarly methods of research. We do not have as yet, for instance, any thorough published study of Poe's development as a poet, as a writer of tales, as a critic, or as a magazine editor. Many sources have been suggested for some of the poems and tales—notably "The Raven" and "The Cask of Amontillado"—but we do not have a complete study of any poem or story which brings together its multiple sources and studies the genesis, the actual writing, and the various revisions of the poem or story and uses the materials for a fresh critical appraisal. Such a study should be done by a scholar with a keen sense of literary values and some knowledge of the psychological processes involved in composition. No one seems to have systematically examined in detail all of the books which Poe reviewed (C. F. Schreiber has a notable collection of them) for their influence upon his own writings. Killis Campbell carefully studied the numerous revisions which Poe made in his poems, but no one as yet has paid much attention to the changes he made in the successive published versions of his short stories. Except for Walter Blair's "Poe's Conception of Incident and Tone in the Tale" (*MP*, 1944), no one has paid much attention to his critical vocabulary; and we do not know exactly what he meant by such words as "keeping," "identification," "ideality," "arabesque," "grotesque," "taste," "grace," "truth," "beauty," "analogy," "moral," or "undercurrent of meaning." Poe's reviews and his own practice, for example, show that in his mind the relations of truth and morality to beauty and art were much more complex than is generally inferred from his too brief treatment of "the heresy of the didactic" in his popular lecture, "The Poetic Principle."

We need to know more about Poe's background in the various cities in which he lived and wrote; and there is still work to be done on his relations with other writers, the obscure as well as those whose names are in every history of American literature. We need to study more closely his policies as editor of four different magazines in three different cities. There is room for further research into Poe's reputation and influence both in the United States and in the many other countries where his name is well known. In particular, we have not assessed his influence upon American writers from the time of Fitz-James O'Brien to that of Vachel Lindsay. There is need for a study of Poe criticism at home and abroad since 1909. We need also a thorough examination of the various Poe legends and of their impact upon biography and criticism. And some Poe scholar should investigate the role which Poe has played—second perhaps among famous Americans only to those of Washington and Lincoln—in the numerous poems, plays, novels, in which he has figured conspicuously. More work needs to be done on Poe's knowledge, and the use he made, of the other arts, music, painting, architecture, interior decoration, and landscape gardening. And, finally—as is unfortunately the case with many another author—there are obsolescent studies which need or will soon need to be done over in the light of new materials and changed critical points of view. Perhaps few of the topics I have mentioned constitute suitable subjects for doctor's dissertations—upon which our scholarship depends too heavily for the advancement of knowledge—but they will eventually, I hope, attract competent scholars, young or old, with a keen sense of critical values. For the life and writings of Poe offer to the investigator the abiding satisfaction which comes from the study of a fascinating personality and a major American writer.

2

EMERSON

I. Bibliography

BIBLIOGRAPHIES of Emerson, though not all that one might wish, are adequate and generally accessible. G. W. Cooke's *Bibliography of Ralph Waldo Emerson* (1908) is an indispensable guide to editions and to biographical and critical works, including a number of contemporary reviews of Emerson's books, up to the date of its publication. H. R. Steeves compiled the bibliography in *CHAL* (1917), which is selective but is intended to include all publications of importance that appeared during the years intervening since Cooke. The American Art Association catalogue of the *Stephen H. Wakeman Collection of Books of Nineteenth Century American Writers* (1924) contains much useful and interesting bibliographical information, though the book titles listed can doubtless be more conveniently seen elsewhere. The Emerson section (Part 4) of the *Index to Early American Periodical Literature, 1728-1870* is useful but not intended to be complete. It does not, of course, include British periodicals, and it omits some items listed by Cooke, though it contains a few that Cooke did not include. A supplemental bibliography prepared by R. A. Booth and Roland Stromberg (*BB,* 1948) is intended specifically to fill the gap between Cooke and 1920, the first year covered by Lewis Leary's volume, *Articles Appearing in Current Periodicals, 1920-1945* (1947). A new edition of Leary's book, corrected and greatly expanded, was published in 1954 as *Articles in American Literature, 1900-1950*. The annual bibliographies of *American Literature* and *PMLA* are easily accessible. Good selective bibliographies may be found in the following books: T. H. Johnson in the *LHUS* (1948); F. I. Carpenter in *Emerson* (AWS, 1934), with annotations; H. H. Clark in *Major American Poets* (1936), with annotations; and Harry Hartwick in W. F. Taylor's *History of American Letters* (1936). The most recent extensive bibliographical information is to be found in the classified lists of F. I. Carpenter's *Emerson Handbook* (1953), where many books, including some foreign publications and some unpublished dissertations, are summarized and discussed. For doctoral dissertations on Emerson, consult the lists compiled by E. E. Leisy and J. B. Hubbell (*AL,* Jan. 1933) and Lewis Leary (*AL,* May 1948), and the lists of "Research in Progress" in *AL* since May 1948.

An extensive manuscript collection owned by the Ralph Waldo Emerson Memorial Association, including the unpublished journals, a large number of letters to Emerson, lectures, sermons, and a typed volume of notations found in the books of Emerson's library, is deposited in the Houghton Library of Harvard University. Some of these materials are now being edited for publication. Persons wishing to examine these manuscripts should write in advance for permission to Mr. William A. Jackson, Houghton Library, Harvard University.

II. Editions

Emerson has been fortunate in his editors, and his works have now for more than half a century been available in the excellent Centenary Edition in twelve volumes (1903-04), edited by his son Edward Waldo Emerson. It has extensive notes and a useful index. It is based upon the twelve-volume Riverside Edition, edited by J. E. Cabot (1884), which in turn was based on collected editions of 1869, 1876, and 1881 which had the benefit of Emerson's personal supervision. Both Cabot, Emerson's literary executor, and Edward Waldo Emerson, though not literary scholars in the present limited sense of the term, were well fitted for the work they accomplished. However, these "complete" editions have since been supplemented by several volumes, and others are to come. In 1912 C. C. Biglow edited *The Uncollected Writings: Essays, Addresses, Poems, Reviews and Letters by Ralph Waldo Emerson,* which contains fifty-four items altogether, mostly short. In 1938 A. C. McGiffert in *Young Emerson Speaks* edited twenty-five of Emerson's sermons, chosen from approximately one hundred and seventy manuscript sermons available. His introduction and notes throw much light on the intellectual development of Emerson during the critical years from 1826 to 1836. A list of all sermons is appended.

Three of Emerson's college compositions not in his collected works have been made available. In 1896 E. E. Hale edited two essays, "The Character of Socrates" and "The Present State of Ethical Philosophy," written respectively in 1820 and 1821 in competition for the Bowdoin Prize. In 1954 K. W. Cameron edited Emerson's college poem "Indian Superstition," with an introductory essay and notes on "Emerson's Orientalism at Harvard."

Some of Emerson's lectures are printed in the Centenary Edition, and many others are summarized in an appendix of Cabot's *Memoir.* Still others are listed by Cabot for which no manuscript copies were available. Some of these were reported, with summaries, in contemporary newspapers, and have been found and reprinted. Jeanne Kronman edited "Three Unpublished Lectures of Ralph Waldo Emerson" (*NEQ,* 1946), and Clarence Gohdes edited a volume made up of newspaper reports of *Uncollected Lectures* by Emerson in 1933. Of these lectures, Gohdes states that the newspaper accounts are full in two of the seven reported lectures and contain material not available elsewhere.

Emerson's complete writings have been printed several times in cheap editions, and there have been numerous volumes of selections. K. W. Cameron's facsimile edition of *Nature* (1940) has interesting notes on the text. F. I. Carpenter's *Emerson*

(AWS) is of interest to scholars. *The Portable Emerson,* edited by Mark Van Doren (1946), should also be mentioned here as of use to students, and also the Modern Library and Rinehart paper-bound editions. The *Essays* have been frequently reprinted, and since 1892 the poems have been available at modest prices in the one-volume Household Edition.

G. S. Hubbell's convenient and dependable concordance of the poems (1932) is based on the text of Vol. IX of the Centenary Edition.

Ten volumes of selected material from the manuscript journals, edited by E. W. Emerson and W. E. Forbes, were published in 1909-14 in a format uniform with the Centenary Edition of the *Works.* The editors state that they have omitted much that had been incorporated by Emerson in his essays and other materials of little significance, but that they have included "the greater part of the contents" of the journals. Yet a doubt has been raised (by H. A. Pochmann in "The Emerson Canon," *UTQ,* 1943) whether the journals have been published in sufficient fullness and accuracy. For those who do not require the full text of the published journals, Bliss Perry's *The Heart of Emerson's Journals* (1926) may be consulted.

Emerson's correspondence has received a good deal of attention and is now available in great quantity, though not yet in completeness. R. L. Rusk's edition of the *Letters of Ralph Waldo Emerson* in six large volumes (1939) contains all the letters known to him at the time which were available for publication, with the exception of about 200 previously published, and has a calendar of other letters both published and unpublished. The text is a literal printing from the original manuscripts or reproductions of them, without corrections. The editor's introduction is a biographical and critical essay based on information available in the letters. His notes are a mine of useful information and his index is a model. The letters not here published are listed among the printed letters in their chronological order, where they are described, and, if they have been published elsewhere, bibliographical reference is made to that fact.

Among the collections of Emerson letters needed to supplement Rusk's edition, *The Correspondence of Thomas Carlyle and Ralph Waldo Emerson, 1834-1872* is the most important. It was edited by C. E. Norton and published in two volumes in 1883. In 1888 a revised edition was issued containing thirteen additional letters, and another edition is now in preparation by Joseph Slater. Less important but very useful is *A Correspondence between John Sterling and Ralph Waldo Emerson,* edited by E. W. Emerson (1897) with a brief account of the circumstances leading up to the correspondence. Of special interest as illustrations of the character of Emerson's friendship with younger men are *Letters from Ralph Waldo Emerson to a Friend, 1838-1853,* edited (1899) by C. E. Norton. The friend was Samuel Gray Ward. In this connection should be mentioned also *Correspondence between Ralph Waldo Emerson and Herman Grimm,* edited by F. W. Holls, originally published in 1903 in the *Atlantic* and reprinted in book form the same year; and the *Emerson-Clough Letters* (1934), edited by H. F. Lowry and R. L. Rusk. *Records of a Lifelong Friendship, 1807-1882,* edited by H. H. Furness (1910), contains the correspondence of Emerson and W. H. Furness. "The Emerson-Thoreau Correspondence," edited by F. B. Sanborn and published in 1892 in the *Atlantic*, includes interesting letters written while Emerson was editor of the *Dial* and others written while he was in Europe in 1847-48. Other Emerson letters of less importance have been published, some before and others since Rusk's edition, and Rusk is preparing a seventh volume of letters for publication in the near future.

Among new editions announced as in preparation are the following: an edition of lectures and sermons, by R. E. Spiller and Stephen Whicher, work on which is now well advanced; a new edition of the poems, by C. F. Strauch; and an edition of Emerson's translation of Dante's *Vita Nuova,* by Chesley

Mathews. It should be noted also in this connection that Louise Hastings is editing for publication the Journals of Mary Moody Emerson, which should be important source material.

III. Biography

There was little biographical writing on Emerson until after his death in 1882. It is true that G. W. Cooke's *Ralph Waldo Emerson: His Life, Writings, and Philosophy* (1881) has about 200 pages of biography, but it is based exclusively on published materials and is intended, as the author states, merely as a background of biographical facts for the discussion of Emerson's ideas. The first book-length biography was that of Holmes (1885) in the American Men of Letters Series. This work, though quickly superseded, still makes lively reading and is valuable to the modern reader of Emerson chiefly as it reflects the friendly but somewhat skeptical Bostonian attitude towards the Concord transcendentalist at the time of his death. The introduction is widely known for Holmes's comment on Emerson's ministerial ancestors and his opinion that one from so superior a stock ought to have superior qualities. The book is also valuable for the information it gives of Emerson's immediate family, most of whom were known to the author. The narrative includes a good many statements especially prepared for this volume by persons intimately acquainted with Emerson.

The best early biography, and still an indispensable primary source, is *A Memoir of Ralph Waldo Emerson* (2 vols. 1887), by Emerson's literary executor and authorized biographer, J. E. Cabot. Though a personal friend of Emerson, Cabot wrote an unbiased and thoroughly dependable biography, consisting largely of extracts from the journals and letters then in manuscript, together with many personal reminiscences of Cabot and other contemporaries. The appendixes contain a list of Emerson's contributions to the *Dial,* valuable letters, and a chronological list of Emerson's lectures and addresses, with summaries of many not available in substance in Emerson's published works.

Others who knew Emerson personally contributed during the 1880's and later many reminiscences and impressions which have supplemented Cabot's *Memoir*. M. D. Conway's *Emerson at Home and Abroad* (1882) is a treasury of delightful anecdotes, some from books, some from letters, and some from conversations with Emerson and others, including, no doubt, a deal of gossip and rumor. Alexander Ireland's *In Memoriam: Ralph Waldo Emerson* (1882) records his recollections of Emerson's visits to England in 1833, 1847-48, and 1872-73, with extracts from unpublished letters. The same year this book was largely augmented with an extended biographical introduction and republished as *Ralph Waldo Emerson: His Life, Genius, and Writings*. J. B. Thayer's *A Western Journey with Emerson* (1884) describes a trip by rail which Emerson made, in a party of twelve persons, to California in 1871. D. G. Haskins' *Ralph Waldo Emerson: His Maternal Ancestors* (1886) is worth mentioning for its firsthand reminiscences of Emerson's mother and father during their first married years and the childhood of Ralph Waldo. More important is E. W. Emerson's *Emerson in Concord* (1889), an intimate, firsthand account of Emerson's private life by his son, who supplements his recollections with extracts from the journals. Much of this material is incorporated in later biographies. Three books afford valuable insight into Emerson's remarkable influence on younger men. John Albee's *Remembrances of Emerson* (1901) relates to the 1850's; C. J. Woodbury's *Talks with Emerson* (1890) covers the 1860's; and F. B. Sanborn's *The Personality of Emerson* (1903), the most important of the three, gives the author's impressions on visiting Emerson when he was a college student, and again later when he was the teacher of Emerson's children, and reports many of Emerson's conversations with him and other persons through many years.

There was no further full-length biographical study of Emerson based on original sources for half a century, though there were some good biographical studies based on these earlier sources. Richard Garnett's *Life* (1888) was based chiefly on

Cabot but contains some appreciative criticism; and G. E. Woodberry's *Life* (1907) was based on Cabot's *Memoir* and such additional records as those named above. Yet Woodberry's is, for the general reader, a very satisfactory biography. It is scholarly and yet very readable; it is not wholly sympathetic, yet it is fair, and his last chapter is a fine characterization. Of later biographies, D. J. Snider's (1921) attempts to coordinate Emerson's life with his intellectual development according to a logical scheme; Phillips Russell's gives a readable account of the facts of Emerson's life but hardly justifies its subtitle, "The Wisest American," since it does not enter deeply into a discussion of his ideas; and Van Wyck Brooks's has the charm of Emerson's own style, in addition to the considerable gifts of the biographer, for it is largely presented in the language of the journals. Its impressionistic manner holds the reader's interest and gives him the sense of reality, with many side glances at personalities, places, and moods of the time. One misses specific dates and the orderly progression of events. André Bruel's *Emerson et Thoreau* (Paris, 1929) deals justly with the growing coolness between Emerson and Thoreau during the 1850's, following their earlier intimacy, and Townsend Scudder's *Lonely Wayfaring Man* (1936) is an entertaining account of Emerson's visits to England and his relations with Carlyle based on a fresh examination of the original sources. H. H. Hoeltje tells the story of the friendship of Emerson and Alcott in *Sheltering Tree* (1943), often in the language of the diaries and other original sources. *Ralph Waldo Emerson* (1915), by O. W. Firkins, and *Emerson Today* (1931), by Bliss Perry, have some biographical materials, but they are primarily works of criticism and will be discussed in that category. Biographies written by foreigners are not likely to provide the American student with values which he cannot more readily come at in English, but he may find different points of view. One of the best books on Emerson by a foreigner, though it is not primarily biographical, is Marie Dugard's *Ralph Waldo Emerson: sa vie et son œuvre*

(Paris, 1907; rev. ed., 1913), a thorough and scholarly book. The author understands Emerson, but her lack of sympathy with transcendentalism inhibits her in doing what she often insists the critic must, viz., see Emerson whole. Régis Michaud's *La vie inspirée d'Emerson* (Paris, 1930; translated and published in America the same year as *Emerson, the Enraptured Yankee*) is very readable but popular rather than scholarly in treatment.

The definitive biography is *The Life of Ralph Waldo Emerson* (1949), by R. L. Rusk, the only detailed and thorough factual biography since Cabot's, and as such it will remain for many years an indispensable tool for all students of Emerson. Rusk has made use of all published materials, including Cabot's biography, but he has also made a minute examination and analysis of the original manuscripts, particularly the manuscript journals, much of which is unpublished. Although the book is mainly a factual account, as a good biography must be, there is enough of interpretative criticism to reveal Emerson as a developing mind as well as an actual person in the midst of events. Considering the great condensation of materials, the biography is remarkably clear and readable. The work is thoroughly documented, and yet the reader who does not care for bibliographical details may read ahead without impediment of reference numbers or footnotes. It must be admitted that one who attempts to follow the author through his source materials will find the notes and bibliographical apparatus at first puzzling, but it can be done without vast trouble. Critics have found objections to the book: that Emerson's personality is obscured by the multitude of facts; that it does not add as much as one might expect to an understanding of the structure of Emerson's thought; that it is not brilliant or profound. Yet they have agreed that it is a complete and living portrait, that it is readable, and that it introduces us for the first time to the real and great Emerson. It is an authoritative work, designed for the student, and more likely to be consulted for information than read for pleasure, though it is by no means barren of promise for the casual reader who comes to it conditioned by an interest in the subject.

IV. Criticism

It was through his character and personality that Emerson made the strongest impression upon his own generation, but he survives into our own time primarily as a thinker and an artist, although his rank in both categories has been disputed. Much criticism is therefore to be found in the biographies, particularly in Cooke, Firkins, Woodberry, Dugard, and Rusk. Of works exclusively of criticism, there are, in general, three types: (1) the book-length study of varied aspects of Emerson's works, (2) the general critical essay, and (3) specialized studies, whether books or essays. It seems most convenient to organize the criticism under the following heads: (1) General Estimates, (2) Sources, (3) Philosophy, (4) Science, (5) Practical Affairs, (6) Aesthetics, and (7) Reputation and Influence. Since many of the books and essays discuss several aspects of Emerson's work, it will be necessary sometimes to mention a critical work and discuss it in part under two or more of these heads.

1. *General Estimates*

Margaret Fuller wrote an appreciative review of Emerson's essays for the *Tribune*, 7 December 1844 (reprinted by Mason Wade in *The Writings of Margaret Fuller*, 1941), but the most important early essay on Emerson was written by Theodore Parker (*Mass. Quart. Rev.*, 1850; reprinted in Parker's *Works*, Centenary Edition, 1907), who calls him the most American of American writers, though he is also the most cosmopolitan. Thus the clear-eyed Unitarian minister sees at once what generations of critics, in America as well as in Europe, have not clearly seen; namely, that an American writer need be none the less American for belonging in the European tradition. Emerson, he thinks, exaggerates the value of intuition and is defective in the power to organize his thought; yet he would rank him higher than any other writer since Milton. Less perceptive, Lowell ("Emerson the Lecturer," in *My Study Windows,* 1871) remembers his personal charm and inspirational power over youthful minds, but is somewhat condescending in reference to Emerson's lack of substance. A. B. Alcott (in an essay on the genius and character of Emerson, written in 1865, published in *Ralph Waldo Emerson: Philosopher and Seer,* 1882) sees that Emerson is a realist as well as an idealist (as Lowell had seen too in *A Fable for Critics,* 1848), and that he is also at once a poet and a moralist in the same class with Plutarch, Epictetus, Montaigne, Bacon. His only "subtraction" is that Emerson is too impersonal. Another contemporary and friend of Emerson, Henry James, Sr. (see *Literary Remains,* 1885, and *Atlantic,* 1904; see also W. T. Stafford, "Emerson and the James Family," *AL*, 1953), attributes Emerson's authority to his character more than to his ideas; he brought his hearer, or reader, face to face with the infinite in humanity. Like many later critics, James could account for Emerson's concept of evil only by supposing that he had no personal experience of it and therefore no conscience. Henry James, Jr., who reviewed the Carlyle-Emerson *Correspondence* for the *Century* in 1883 and Cabot's *Memoir* for *Macmillan's Magazine* in 1887 (reprinted in *Partial Portraits,* 1888), agreed in part with his father's opinion: he said that so far as evil was concerned Emerson's eyes were "thickly bandaged," but that he had a faculty, never surpassed, for speaking to the soul in a voice of authority. Yet it seems obvious that Henry James, Jr., could find little in Emerson to interest him and that he never attempted seriously to understand him. Holmes and Woodberry, though unsympathetic, did make an effort to understand Emerson, yet both placed the value of his character above that of his ideas. Holmes thought he was very near an embodiment of his own ideal of humanity. Woodberry agreed and added that he embodied also the American spirit in his works and was himself "a shining example of it." This personal force Bliss Perry defined as the "emanation of spiritual energy." Yet he recognized the dynamic quality in Emerson by calling him "the herald and attendant of change, the son and father of Revolution," and he rated him as "the only great mind that America has produced in literature." E. C. Stedman (*Poets of America,* 1885) has a balanced criticism of Emerson, but he was among those who viewed Emerson's writing in verse and prose as a means to an end, and that end not art but the "enfranchisement and stimulation of his people and his time."

British opinion of Emerson in the nineteenth century was appreciative but always sharply critical. Carlyle's attachment was to Emerson the man more than to Emerson the transcendental philosopher. Richard Garnett, his biographer and most appreciative British critic, thought that the "diffused beauty" in which his works lie "bathed" is ample recompense for his defects as an artist, and he saw that he is at one with the moral consciousness of the American nation. More objective appraisals were made by Matthew Arnold, Leslie Stephen, and John Morley, all eminently qualified to judge the worth of a man of letters. Arnold's essay (in *Discourses in America,* 1885) has been widely quoted, agreed with, and disagreed with. Arnold declared Emerson does not rank with the great men of letters (Plato, Bacon, Pascal, Swift, Voltaire) because his style does not have the "requisite wholeness of good tissue." He is not a great philosophical writer (like Aristotle, Spinoza, Kant) because he cannot build a philosophical system; his ideas have no evolution. He gives Emerson high praise nevertheless. He is "the friend and aider of those who would live in the spirit," and his essays are the most important work done in prose in the nineteenth century. Leslie Stephen (*Studies of a Biographer,* 1902, Vol. IV), while he condemns Emerson's thought as too vague to have meaning or else meaning something which is "palpably absurd," yet assures us that Emerson is worth reading because he is inspirational and because his optimism teaches us how to maintain a cheerful temper and make the best of things. John Morley ("Emerson," in *Critical Miscellanies,* 1904, Vol. I) finds fault with Emerson's inconsecutive thought, his faulty diction and grammar, and his inability to appreciate the darker side of life; yet he declares that he is among the most persuasive and inspiring of those who awaken us from the "deadening slumbers of convention and conformity" and lift us up from "low thoughts and sullen moods of helplessness and impiety." Morley believes, and J. M. Robertson agrees ("Emerson," in *Modern Humanists*, 1895), that Emerson's reaction against what is superficial in Locke and Hume blinded him to much besides that is sound and valuable. Robertson points out that Emerson denied inspiration to analytic processes of thought and thus made the way easy for the bigot and the crank as well as for the seer. Yet he inclines to agree with Arnold that Emerson wrote the most important prose of the nineteenth century, and he rates the poetry higher than Arnold.

But Emerson has had strong defenders both as an artist and as a philosopher. J. J. Chapman ("Emerson Sixty Years After," in *Emerson and Other Essays,* 1898; reprinted 1909), after describing Emerson's literary effects, says: "If the man who can do these things be not an artist, then must we have a new vocabulary and rename the professions." Yet he says the poetry is too intellectual and the prose is more effective because it is more emotional. Santayana (*Interpretations of Poetry and Religion,* 1900) begins by saying that Emerson is "not primarily a philosopher, but a Puritan mystic with a poetic fancy," yet in the end he concludes: "If not a star of the first magnitude, he is certainly a fixed star in the firmament of philosophy." No other American, he thinks, has earned a place there. Though he denies originality to Emerson's thoughts, he praises the originality and beauty of their expression. William James, in an address at Concord on the centenary of Emerson's birth (published the same year in a volume containing fifteen centenary addresses), declared that the matter and manner of Emerson's expression are inseparable, and that if he must be defined in a word we must call him Artist. "He was an artist whose medium was verbal and who wrought in spiritual material." James says that the "headspring" of all his writing is that "the commonest person's act, if genuinely actuated, can lay hold of eternity"; and that for this truth, posterity will call him a prophet. Hugo Münsterberg, on the same occasion, declared that it was Emerson's influence that brought him from his native Germany to America. The highest tribute by a philosopher to the philosophy of Emerson was paid by John Dewey at an Emerson memorial meeting in Chicago in 1903. (The address is printed in *Characters and Events,* 1929.) Dewey charges that the critic who complains of Emerson's lack of method simply "writes down his own incapacity to follow a logic that is finely wrought," and he affirms that he knows no writer "whose movement of thought is more compact and unified." In fact, Dewey calls Emerson more than a philosopher, saying that he is "a maker rather than a reflector," a perceiver more than a reasoner. Yet he agrees in effect with William James that Emerson is essentially an artist, though none the less a genuine philosopher; in fact, he calls him the Philosopher of Democracy. Emerson, says Dewey, is "the one citizen of the New World fit to have his name uttered in the same breath with that of Plato." His final word is that the heart of Emerson's philosophy is "the identity of Being, unqualified and immutable, with Character." A few years later another philosopher of a very different school, Josiah Royce, said (in *William James and Other Essays on the Philosophy of Life,* 1911) that there were then only three representative American philosophers, and they were Jonathan Edwards, Emerson, and William James.

The critic W. C. Brownell, in his judicial appraisal of Emerson in *American Prose Masters* (1909), says that he "has limitations but no infirmities." He proceeds to place him in the company of Plato and Pascal, of Shakespeare and Goethe. More specifically, he said that Emerson's nature was "flooded with light, but it lacked heat"; and that his philosophy had elevation but not depth. Such antitheses sometimes led Brownell to inconsistency and distortion, as when he said that Emerson is not essentially religious because he is concerned with the mind yet calls him less the descendant of Erasmus than of Luther. He concludes with many others that Emerson serves best as a stimulus, not a literal guide, for which he is too extreme a nonconformist. Yet in saying that Emerson is the enemy of "culture" he is surely going too far. He adopts the view that the poems lack art and sentiment and are inferior to the essays. In general it may be said that his total estimate, which is very high, contradicts his detailed criticism, which finds many faults. John Macy says in *The Spirit of American Literature* (1913) that Emerson "gathers the wisdom of twenty sages into one discourse," but fails in his attempt to be a poet. P. E. More writes in *CHAL* (1917) that "Emersonianism may be defined as romanticism rooted in Puritan divinity." He repeats the complaint, originating with Lowell, that whereas Emerson is the inspirer of youth, older men turn from him. In *Main Currents in American Thought* (1927) Parrington agrees that he was largely the product of the romantic movement, yet he too recognizes the Puritan influence—"Roger Williams and Jonathan Edwards come to more perfect fruition." He classifies Emerson as a Jeffersonian in politics. S. P. Sherman (*Americans,* 1922) sees Emerson as a humanist bent upon liberating all the "properly human powers," and he extenuates Emerson's apparent defects (lack of design, incoherence, etc.) as due to the excess of his virtues. The idea that Emerson is one of the romantics is pursued by Charles Cestre (*RAA,* 1929). It is a mistake, he thinks, to call Emerson a pure intellectual; he was rather a mystic. Although H. W. Garrod (*Poetry and the Criticism of Life,* 1931) finds fault with Arnold for not exploring the hiding places of Emerson's power, he agrees with him that Emerson is a poet only in epigrams and that only his ardor saves him from triviality. But he agrees with William James that in his prose Emerson is a verbal artist. Where Arnold found a disconnectedness in his sentences, Garrod finds a "diffused eloquence." In contrast with Parrington, H. S. Canby says in *Classic Americans* (1931) that when we think now of democracy it is in terms of Emerson, not Jefferson, of potentiality, not right. Though Emerson valued the great inventors (like Goethe, Shakespeare, Sophocles), he himself, Canby thinks, lacked invention, and this was his great weakness. In English belles-lettres, he concludes, Emerson must take his place with Pope, not with Milton or Shakespeare.

But the twentieth century has witnessed another type of criticism, a wholesale condemnation and repudiation, which is unlike anything said of Emerson since the first alarmed protests of the 1830's and 1840's. There have been chiefly two grounds for such repudiation. The first is his alleged shallow optimism, and the second is his alleged heretical and anarchic doctrine of self-reliance. J. T. Adams, in an essay called "Emerson Re-Read" in the *Atlantic* (1930), revived the old complaint that Emerson is not to be taken as a serious thinker. He has tried to reread Emerson at fifty but finds it almost impossible, although he was stirred by him at sixteen. He is "amazed" at the "shallowness" of the essays. He cites Emerson's estimates of Swedenborg and Alcott for the purpose of ridiculing his critical judgment. Emerson's fatal weakness, according to Adams, is that he "makes life too easy by his insistence on intuition and spontaneity." The judgment of F. O. Matthiessen (*American Renaissance,* 1941), though less severe, has probably influenced some young people against Emerson. He says that Emerson, like his poet Saadi, is limited by the very virtues imputed to him—his cheerfulness and his resources against pain and failure—as if pessimism and skepticism might be proofs of spiritual strength. Yet Matthiessen also had a seminal influence on many young scholars.

In two essays ("Emerson" and "The Puritan Heresy") in *H&H* in 1932, H. B. Parkes rejects Emerson on the basis of a formal analysis of his thought. He returns to the argument of Orestes Brownson almost a century before, that Transcendentalism is the logical end of all Protestantism and is the supreme heresy; it is "Edwardian Calvinism modified by European romanticism, French and German." It is marked by a refusal to accept authority, a tendency to obey impulse as the voice of

God, a worship of enthusiasm, a belief in perfectibility in this world. Emerson accepted the New England values, says Parkes, which rested on supernatural and traditional buttresses, but imagined naïvely that he could destroy those buttresses and yet retain the structure of values. He finds the source of Emerson's error not in his mind so much as in his character; he was himself without a sense of evil (as Henry James had said) and was hence led into the delusion that the soul is of the substance of God and untouched by original sin. He is therefore not a true Christian mystic but a heretical pseudo-mystic, in the tradition of Eckhart and Jacob Boehme. After Emerson, whose ideas he thinks no educated man could believe, there was no way to go but back; hence he finds the heirs of Emerson to be Henry Adams, who turned to St. Thomas, and after Adams, T. S. Eliot, who made an attempt to recapture the "lost traditions of Catholicism." Parkes reverted to the subject of Emerson in *The Pragmatic Test* (1941) and *The American Experience* (1947) with somewhat milder judgments but, so far as I can see, retracted nothing. Yvor Winters attacked Emerson on the same logical and theological grounds. In *Maule's Curse* (1938), Winters states that Emerson's central doctrine is the submission to emotion, which destroys all values and renders man an automaton. He concludes that Emerson is "a fraud and a sentimentalist," and devalues him by comparing him unfavorably with Jones Very. Later, in an essay ostensibly concerned with Hart Crane (*In Defense of Reason,* 1947), Winters returns to the attack on Emerson, asserting that Emerson's whole philosophy is based on the theory of natural goodness and reliance on irresponsible impulse. He then argues, from the example of Hart Crane, that any one who believes sincerely in Emerson's philosophy should logically become insane and commit suicide. Such an extreme position does not provide the clear perspective needed for a fair estimate of Emerson.

F. I. Carpenter *(Emerson Handbook)* shows on what grounds Parkes and Winters may be answered. With regard to the often-remarked dichotomies of Emerson's philosophy (nature and the soul, law and impulse, etc.) Robert Spiller believes (*LHUS*, 1948, Vol. I) that Emerson sets up a provisional dualism in order to explore the ultimate unity; the dualism is of method only. In this view, Emerson's philosophy can be called anarchic only by ignoring his ideal of unity, his faith in the power of the Over-Soul to make itself felt in the individual. The extent of Emerson's later compromise and withdrawal from an extreme optimism and self confidence is explored and stated by S. E. Whicher in "Emerson's Tragic Sense" (*AS*, 1953). His conclusion that Emerson was an extremist, that "he had to have entire assurance or he had none at all," is itself perhaps an extreme view, but the essay is valuable as a correction of the common misconception of Emerson as a man of easy faith. The evidence of Emerson's awareness of actuality and the means by which he reconciled the real with the ideal are shown by Sherman Paul in *Emerson's Angle of Vision* (1952). F. I. Carpenter, among others, has pointed out Emerson's tendency towards pragmatism in the reconciliation of his apparent dualism in experience (Introduction to *Emerson,* AWS, 1934). The prevailing pessimism of the last three decades in America has made Emerson appear to many to be a naïve idealist merely. Others have attempted to show that Emerson was aware of evil (see C. E. Jorgenson's "Emerson's Paradise under the Shadow of Swords," *PQ*, 1932), and that his philosophy of power is not a denial of evil but an affirmation of the ability of man to cope with it by building up his potential spiritual resources. It is recognized that the inspirational value of Emerson cannot be saved in an age of skepticism without first restoring confidence in his common sense.

2. *Sources*

The main sources of Emerson's thought are not difficult to discover and have often been pointed out, though there has been much disagreement on their relative importance. In broad terms they may be stated as follows: (1) New England Puritanism and related English thought of the seventeenth century; (2) Platonism, especially in the form of Neoplatonism, and related ideas from Swedenborgianism; (3) European romanticism as derived through the English romantic poets and German romantic philosophers, especially as the latter were interpreted by Coleridge; and (4) Orientalism, particularly the Hinduism of the sacred writings of ancient India. All of these were mentioned by Cooke in his critical biography of 1881. Stedman pointed out (*Poets of America,* 1885) that Emerson "refined and digested what was good in all philosophies," but that his earliest and chiefest models were Plato and Plotinus. Stedman also cited Emerson's debt to the English poetry of the seventeenth century and to the Persian Saadi and Hafiz. P. E. More *(CHAL)* expressed the view of many others in saying that he owed much to his New England background, to German thought through Coleridge and Carlyle, and to Greek philosophers and the poets and preachers of the English seventeenth century as they were interpreted in the light of the romantic movement. Parrington associated Emerson with the French romantic school and with Jefferson. Spiller *(LHUS)* expresses a view now widely held in saying that Emerson was essentially romantic by disposition, akin to Goethe and Coleridge, and that he was strongly influenced by Neoplatonism, German idealism, and Oriental mysticism, but that he never departed from the Christian tradition.

Comparatively little has been written specifically on the survival of early New England thought in Emerson's mind because it was derived not so much from discoverable sources in his reading as from early religious teaching and his theological studies at Harvard. The most detailed study of this aspect of Emerson's thought is to be found in Perry Miller's article "Edwards to Emerson" (*NEQ*, 1940), in which he traces the pantheism and mysticism of Emerson back through Edwards to an inherent tendency in orthodox Calvinism. One should consult in this connection also "Emerson and Quakerism," by F. B. Tolles (*AL*, 1938). His Puritanism and his Quaker tendencies had their roots in the English seventeenth century. For light on this relationship, see J. R. Roberts, "Emerson's Debt to the Seventeenth Century" (*AL*, 1949). Roberts believes that the vitality and spirit of the English seventeenth century armed him against rationalism and expanded his idealism to the point where it broke through the limits of Unitarian dogma. This reading antedated Emerson's reading of Coleridge and Carlyle. Another step towards these nineteenth-century contemporaries was by way of the Scottish philosophers, whom he read as college assignments and independently, and from whom he learned the distinction between the "moral sense" and the "affections." This is discussed by M. R. Davis in "Emerson's 'Reason' and the Scottish Philosophers" (*NEQ*, 1944). The influence of the seventeenth century on Emerson's poetry is discussed incidentally in several general criticisms, and more particularly by N. A. Brittin in "Emerson and the Metaphysical Poets" (*AL*, 1936). Brittin shows that Emerson was fond of all the metaphysical poets, but especially of George Herbert, to whom he says Emerson shows a strong kinship. The next strongest influence he finds was that of Marvell. The American seventeenth century had no significant poetry, and Emerson found the eighteenth-century literary fashions, whether in England or America, unattractive.

Strong as was the hold upon Emerson of New England Puritanism, Platonism was the dominant influence upon his philosophy. The first book-length study of Emerson's sources was J. S. Harrison's *The Teachers of Emerson* (1910), which attempts "to show the essentially Platonic quality of Emerson's thought," though it also deals less extensively with other sources. Harrison says Emerson derived his Platonism chiefly from Thomas Taylor's translations of Plato and the Neoplatonists, from Ralph Cudworth's *True Intellectual System of the Universe* (1820 ed., 4 vols.), from De Gerando's *Histoire comparée des systèmes de philosophie* (2nd ed., 4 vols., Paris, 1822-23), and from Coleridge, whose *Aids to Reflection* and *Friend* he read as early as 1829. Taylor's identification of Platonism with Neoplatonism was, Harrison thinks, at first accepted by Emerson, and not greatly questioned later when he had read Plato in the more accurate Bohn translation (1848). He says Emerson's theory of opposites reconciled in the One, originally derived from the Neoplatonic interpretation of Pythagoreanism, was later confirmed by his reading of Victor Cousin. He derived most of the ideas in *Nature,* Harrison thinks, from Plato and the Neoplatonists, and also the later idea that intellect has power to amend fate. His theory that art is the universal mind working through plastic nature was suggested by Cudworth, who quotes Plotinus. (In this connection see Vivian Hopkins, "Emerson and Cudworth: Plastic Nature and Transcendental Art," *AL,* 1951, who develops this thesis in some detail.) Harrison wrote his book without the benefit of Emerson's published journals, and while it is the basic work on Emerson's Platonism, it must be supplemented by later studies. F. I. Carpenter thinks (*Emerson and Asia,* 1930) that Harrison ascribed too great an importance to the influence of Platonism, pointing out that Emerson had not read Taylor's translations when he wrote *Nature,* though he had read many excerpts from Platonists in Cudworth's volumes. It is Carpenter's opinion that Neoplatonic books formed an important but small fraction of his reading. S. G. Brown, however, agrees with Harrison that the essence of Emerson's thinking is Platonic, though the taste of the time required him to disguise it in the cloak of German idealism and Oriental mysticism ("Emerson's Platonism," *NEQ,* 1945). Many of the Neoplatonic ideas to be found in Emerson may also be found in the writings of the Swedenborgians. Clarence Hotson has made an intensive study of Emerson in relation to Swedenborg and the Swedenborgians (see "Emerson and the Swedenborgians," *SP,* 1930; "Sampson Reed, a Teacher of Emerson," *NEQ,* 1929; also numerous articles published in the *New Church Magazine* and elsewhere between 1928 and 1934). Hotson thinks Emerson became interested in Swedenborgian ideas through reading Sampson Reed's *Observations on the Growth of the Mind* (1826) and his later articles (1828 ff.) in the *New Jerusalem Magazine,* citing many passages from the *Journals* as evidence. He emphasizes especially the importance of Swedenborg's doctrine of correspondence in determining the thinking of Emerson. Sherman Paul (*Emerson's Angle of Vision,* 1952) thinks Emerson had been working towards this idea before he knew Swedenborg's doctrine, and that Channing had given him help in that direction. For evidence that Emerson was influenced appreciably by other Greek writers, particularly by Aristotle's *Poetics,* see J. P. Pritchard, *Return to the Fountains* (1942).

Though Emerson, as noted by Stedman, drew from all philosophies, and though his own thinking was in the Platonic tradition, he was in fact, as P. E. More declared, a product of the Romantic Movement as it manifested itself in New England in the early nineteenth century. Perry Miller's *The Transcendentalists* (1950) will prove useful in this connection, especially as background material for the early essays of Emerson. H. C. Goddard (*Studies in New England Transcendentalism,* 1908) and H. D. Gray (*Emerson,* 1917) agree that Schelling was a more stimulating if less continuous influence than the Platonists. Coleridge was Emerson's most important helper in the formulation of his idealistic philosophy, and through him chiefly he knew the German idealists, particularly Schelling. Carlyle was his next best source of German thought. F. B. Wahr says in *Emerson and Goethe* (1915) that Emerson was comparatively ignorant of German ideas until he read Coleridge in 1829 and Carlyle's essays in 1829-30. Later he read all Goethe's works in German, which he learned for the purpose, but Wahr believes he read merely for corroboration, maintaining his independence of thought. In a later study, "Emerson and the Germans" (*Monatshefte für deutschen Unterricht,* 1941), Wahr says that Emerson was more or less familiar with the works, in translation chiefly, of Schiller, Herder, Lessing, Schlegel, and others, and with German idealistic philosophy from Kant to Hegel, but that the foundation of his thought was already laid in Plato and the Neoplatonists. René Wellek's "Emerson and German Philosophy" (*NEQ,* 1943) is a careful study of the subject. Wellek says that aside from his secondhand knowledge through Coleridge, Carlyle, Cousin, and De Staël, Emerson knew the Germans at first hand, including Böhme (though "Emerson was no mystic") and Kant in the early years and Hegel later. He was chiefly interested in Kant's moral philosophy, Wellek thinks, and could not have penetrated very deeply into Kant's *Critique of Pure Reason* (though he owned a copy of the translation of 1838), since he misunderstands Kant after the fashion of Coleridge and Carlyle. He knew Leibniz, Fichte, and Schleiermacher but slightly; Schelling he knew much better, but chiefly through Coleridge. In this connection see also F. T. Thompson's two essays in *SP*, "Emerson's Indebtedness to Coleridge" (1926) and "Emerson and Carlyle" (1927). Thompson says Emerson spent the autumn and winter following his European tour in "mastering Coleridge's interpretation of Kant's philosophy." He states that Coleridge was the means by which he bridged the gap between Platonism and romanticism, and that this was done by 1834.

A recent article of some interest is J. O. McCormick's "Emerson's Theory of Human Greatness" (*NEQ,* 1953), where it is asserted that Coleridge gave sharpness and clarity to Emerson's idealism, provided him with a method, and clarified for him the organic theory of art and the doctrine of correspondence between mind and nature. McCormick emphasizes the importance of Cousin in introducing Emerson to the Hegelian philosophy and particularly to the idea of the great man as representative. The most exhaustive study of Emerson's sources before 1837 is K. W. Cameron's *Emerson the Essayist* (2 vols., 1945), which contains numerous excerpts from books read by Emerson with parallel passages from Emerson's *Nature* and the *Journals*. While not minimizing the importance of Emerson's Platonism from other sources, Cameron affirms that "Coleridge is pre-eminent among the teachers of Emerson." He read Marsh's edition of *Aids to Reflection* (1829) as soon as it appeared, and by 1831, according to Cameron, "the larger outlines of Emerson's philosophy were complete." Cameron devotes much space to Swedenborg and the Boston Swedenborgians (whom he associates in large part with the Neoplatonic tradition), and next to Coleridge he rates them as the most important influence on Emerson at the time he was developing the ideas presented in 1836 in *Nature.* (See also Cameron's earlier study, *Ralph Waldo Emerson's Reading,* 1941.) The question of Wordsworth's influence on Emerson is studied by J. B. Moore ("Emerson on Wordsworth," *PMLA,* 1926), who concludes that though Emerson was deeply interested in Wordsworth, he was not profoundly influenced by the latter's view of nature. F. T. Thompson points out in "Emerson's Theory and Practice of Poetry" (*PMLA,* 1928) the importance to Emerson of Wordsworth's odes and other later poetry and also of the influence on him of Coleridge's criticism of Wordsworth's poetry in the *Biographia Literaria,* especially the distinction between the Fancy and the Imagination. J. W. Beach (*Concept of Nature in Nineteenth-Century English Poetry,* 1936) thinks that Emerson's philosophy is mostly a "loose and popular rendering of Schelling," who is "no better than a Kant run wild." He thinks Emerson's Schelling came through Coleridge, and that he missed some of the metaphysical implications of Coleridge's statement. This is much the position that H. D. Gray (*Emerson,* 1917) had taken in his study.

Emerson's Orientalism was well known to his contemporaries even as early as 1845, as evidenced by an anonymous article on "Mr. Emerson and Transcendentalism" in the *American Whig Review* in March of that year. It was the subject of a lecture at the Concord School of Philosophy by the Hegelian, W. T. Harris, which F. B. Sanborn published in *The Genius and Character of Emerson* (1885), and it was recognized by G. W. Cooke and other early critics. Yet no thorough study was made until the end of the third decade of this century, when F. I. Carpenter published (1930) his *Emerson and Asia.* Two years later (1932) A. E. Christy's *The Orient in American Transcendentalism* appeared. In 1928 George Williamson in "Emerson the Oriental" *(Univ. Calif. Chron.)* had said there are four Emersons: the Yankee, the Romantic, the Platonist, and the Oriental; and by an analysis of "Brahma" and comment on the essays, particularly "Experience," "Fate," and "Illusions," had decided that Emerson was more Oriental than Platonic. Carpenter shows how Emerson was introduced to Orientalism through his reading among the Neoplatonists between 1830 and 1837. He had also been introduced to Kalidasa and some of the Persian poets through Goethe. By 1845 he had become "an Orientalist in earnest." The essence of Orientalism for Emerson, Carpenter says, was Hindu philosophy, which is most fully represented in Emerson's writings in the poems "Brahma" and "Hamatreya," and in the essay "Illusions," which Carpenter analyzes in detail. The influence of Persian, Arabian, and Chinese literature is also discussed. Carpenter concludes that he was drawn to Hafiz and Saadi for their "joyful humanity and love of nature," and that he was repelled by the formalism of Chinese literature. Christy begins by reminding the reader that Emerson, like Thoreau, was interested, not in metaphysics, but only in the literature of the Hindus. Though Neoplatonism and Western mysticism generally prepared the way for Oriental mysticism, Emerson, Christy points out, never accepted the fatalism of the latter. He says Emerson's Over-Soul is the Hindu Brahma, his doctrine of Illusion is like the Hindu concept of Maya, and his theory of Compensation is comparable to the Hindu Karma, except that Emerson did not subscribe to the doctrine of Transmigration. Christy attributes Emerson's optimism, in part at least, and his belief in evil as negative, to the influence of Hinduism. Christy says it was the urbane Emerson that was attracted to Confucius, but he was held by the corroboration he received of his belief in the goodness of man. The Persian contribution is only in the realm of poetry, and Emerson profited in his own verse by the example of the pithy, epigrammatic wisdom of the Persian poets. For a discussion of Emerson's poetry in relation to Persian models, see two articles by J. D. Yohannan (*AL,* 1943), "Emerson's Translations of

Persian Poetry from German Sources" and "The Influence of Persian Poetry upon Emerson's Work." For Emerson's early attitude towards Orientalism, see K. W. Cameron's introductory essay and notes to his edition (1954) of Emerson's college poem, "Indian Superstition," in which he appears unsympathetic and not well informed.

There were, of course, numerous other sources not to be included in any of the groups discussed above. Obviously, the Bible was such a source, as indicated in Harriet R. Zink's *Emerson's Use of the Bible* (Univ. of Nebraska Studies in Lang., Lit. and Crit., 1935). Paul Sakmann, in *Emerson's Geisteswelt* (Stuttgart, 1927), has linked Rousseau with Goethe and Swedenborg as one of the antecedents of his nature-philosophy. For Emerson's interest in Dante see J. C. Mathews, "Emerson's Knowledge of Dante" in Univ. of Texas *SE,* 1942, and for Milton, R. C. Pettigrew, "Emerson and Milton" (*AL,* 1931). Many have commented on Emerson and Montaigne, including D. L. Maulsby, *The Contribution of Emerson in Literature* (1911), W. L. Ustick, "Emerson's Debt to Montaigne" (Washington Univ. *Studies,* 1922), and, most completely, C. L. Young, *Emerson's Montaigne* (1941). Young says Emerson read Montaigne chiefly as a tonic, and cared more for him as a moralist than as a skeptic.

3. *Philosophy*

Something has been said already, under the heading "General Estimates," on the question whether Emerson may or may not be called a philosopher, and we have seen that the most distinguished American philosophers have been willing to acknowledge him as one of themselves. The historians of American philosophy have usually treated his philosophical ideas with respect. Woodbridge Riley (*American Thought from Puritanism to Pragmatism and Beyond,* 1915, rev., 1941) discusses the sources of Transcendentalism and analyzes Emerson's *Nature* in detail but does not deal effectively with the later essays. (On Transcendentalism the student will find O. B. Frothingham's *Transcendentalism in New England,* 1876, still useful.) H. G. Townsend (*Philosophical Ideas in the United States,* 1936) finds fault with Emerson because his thought is not stated in a logical and systematic fashion, but in the main his discussion is just and useful, especially in his sound view of Emerson's treatment of evil and in his statement that there was in Emerson a latent pragmatism. P. R. Anderson and M. H. Fisch (*Philosophy in America,* 1939) find a causal relationship between Transcendentalism and the maturing of democratic thought. They designate the essay "Experience" as Emerson's masterpiece and take note, as most significant in his work, of the "gradual shift from the neoplatonic doctrine of emanation and return, to the scientific theory of evolution," culminating about 1849. H. W. Schneider (*History of American Philosophy,* 1946) deals inadequately and somewhat condescendingly with Emerson as philosopher. *Men and Movements in American Philosophy* (1952), a recent textbook by J. L. Blau, has a useful discussion of Emerson.

Of books that attempt a full statement of Emerson's philosophical ideas, the first was G. W. Cooke's biography, and it is remarkably sound considering the fact that it was based solely on the works published before 1881. He says Emerson's "intuition" is the same as Schelling's "intellectual intuition" and Coleridge's "reason." His "moral sentiment" is much the same as the "inner light" of the Quakers, the "ecstasy" of Plotinus, and the "divine illumination" of Swedenborg. Like Kant, he does not distinguish between morality and religion. "Fate" is the term, says Cooke, which Emerson uses to indicate the limits of intuition, spontaneity, and freedom; yet freedom is itself, for man, a necessity.

Marie Dugard's long book on the life and work of Emerson (1907, 1913), already mentioned as biography, should not be ignored by any student who would make a serious study of him. The author summarizes Emerson's thought and provides ample extracts. She concludes that Emerson was a monist, that he rejected the past as a dead letter, and that he believed truth cannot be reached through the rational faculties but only by intuition. Human problems have no solution but in idealism, since the individual is but a momentary fixation in which certain powers and functions of the Spirit become active and are then released. Evil exists, but only conditionally; and in all its variety of forms, nature only repeats two laws: the law of compensation and the law of universal amelioration. The continuation of life after death is certain but the survival of the individual consciousness is not assured except in the externalization of the present moment. Ethics comprises and is not distinguished from religion; and each man may find for himself, in union with the Divine, the spiritual life he needs. Mme. Dugard has some acute criticism of Emerson's ideas. She says that he fails to reconcile the many antinomies he recognizes, that his complacent optimism is useless and unintelligible to those who are discouraged and defeated in life, that if truth comes only in a series of moods it is lost in the flux and is not dependable, that his Universal Spirit is "confounded with its attributes" and provides the individual no support, that if the individual soul is dissolved in death the terrestrial phase of existence "loses all significance, and human life appears less as a mystery than as nonsense," that in seeing nothing in evil but non-being he exaggerates the power of the individual, and that his thought lacks vital authority because he did not feel great pity and great love. In spite of these defects, she concludes, Emerson "was very great and he did a good work."

Firkins' biography (1915) has a long chapter on Emerson's philosophy which has stimulating insights. Firkins says that Emerson was "perfectly capable of using the syllogism" if he chose. He was impatient, not incapable, of logic. The center of his philosophy is the value he put on the unit experience. The moment of experience contains all, annihilates time and space, cancels the authority of custom, and solves the problem of immortality. The perceived object expands to the dimensions of the cosmos and the perceiver to the stature of God when the perceiver has that self-reliance which is reliance on God. Emerson was not an idealist in the sense of a disbeliever in the actuality of matter, but he was in the sense of one who "maintains the absolute dependence of sense impressions on character and intelligence." Firkins thinks Emerson's theory of evil is a logical outcome of his faith in benevolence and in the perfection of the cosmos as a moral mechanism analogous to its perfection as a physical mechanism. Firkins does not believe that the moral world has the precision of physical laws. Some of Emerson's statements are mere rhetoric, Firkins says, such as "If a man is at heart just, then in so far is he God," which is identifying the part with the whole. Firkins sacrifices directness and sometimes clearness for liveliness that often verges on flippancy, but his interpretation of Emerson's philosophy was based on a sympathetic, though critical, study of his work.

The earliest and one of the best books devoted exclusively to a study of Emerson's philosophy is H. D. Gray's *Emerson: A Statement of New England Transcendentalism as Expressed in the Philosophy of Its Chief Exponent* (1917). Gray says that Emerson was primarily a poet and that he approached philosophy with a religious attitude, but he denies the popular notion that his want of logic and system was congenital, saying it was rather the result of a perpetual openness of mind to receive new truth, and a distrust of formalism. Emerson believed, according to Gray, that the laws of nature are the laws of the mind and that the evolution of nature back to spirit produces in progress the individual human minds. To state the laws of nature is to summarize Emerson's philosophy, and he names these as the law of permanence, the law of correspondence (of nature with spirit), universality, progress, and the moral law, which underlies the rest. Intellect is primary, nature secondary; intellect takes body in nature, for nature "will not remain orbed in thought, but rushes into persons." When persons break the laws they lose their hold on reality. Gray raises the question: How does that which is "never a cause but a perpetual effect" produce those persons "who have this fatal ability to lose hold on the central reality"? He answers by saying that the confusion in Emerson's mind arose from "his endeavor to equate an inherited idealism, to which his adherence was largely emotional, with a theory of evolution which more and more forced itself upon him in his attempt to take account of an individual whose impulses proceed from within himself." In 1836, Emerson conceived of God as pure spirit and the world as an illusion which God uses for the education of individuals. Then he came under the influence of Lamarck. Gray objects to Emerson's statement that man seeks to abstract himself from effects and dwell with causes—to ascend into the region of law, where all men belong. He says man cannot "belong" in one kind of existence and "be" in another. To Emerson's statement that man is related by his form to the world about him and by his soul to the universal, Gray objects that this "leaves an impossible dualism in the nature of man." What Emerson wanted, Gray continues, was "thoughts which are more than thoughts,—which in being 'plastic forces' are not thoughts at all." Hence he was driven from the theory of emanation to the theory of evolution, but continued to cling to idealism out of a fear, half realized, that his thinking will end in materialism. It becomes his task, then, to find a common ground for spirit and nature, and for this he turns to Schelling's theory of the identity of subject and object in a substance older than either mind or matter. This Reality is difficult to name, and when Emerson calls it Spirit or Nature he is speaking symbolically. In his effort to define this ineffable One he "rises out of the realm of Philosophy altogether and dwells in the pure region of Religion." Gray thinks Emerson came finally to believe that this underlying Reality rises in the lower animals to the point of instinct and arrives at consciousness in man. Whether there is a self-consciousness in the Totality, as well as in man, Emerson seems to question, though he is not clear on such matters. Gray thinks Emerson remained a pantheist to the end, that his philosophy had no room for a theistic conception of God. He says Emerson's concept of immortality in the moment, by abolishing time, has no meaning, and he doubts whether he ever gave up completely the idea of individual survival. He says Emerson's ethics is a consistent part of his idealism. The "fall" of man is his coming to the plane of consciousness, the attainment of a moral will at the expense of innocence. The moral law is the groundwork of our being; hence the virtue of obedience. To attain intermediate goods the will must struggle, but to attain the highest good the will negates itself and attains supravolitional freedom. Emerson is aware of evil, but only as a part of the process of evolution. His optimism is "the ethical reading of the great fact of evolution."

It was ten years before another important study of Emerson's philosophy was published, and this was the German Paul Sakmann's *Ralph Waldo Emersons Geisteswelt nach den Werken und Tagebüchern* (Stuttgart, 1927). Sakmann's is one of the few important studies by foreign critics. He says Emerson's thought on the sovereignty of virtue is in harmony with the virtuous idealists of all times from the Sermon on the Mount and from Plato to Kant. He finds the parallelism with Kant particularly close. Emerson agreed with Hegel's saying that all things move towards the right, and it disturbed him as little as it did Hegel that so much time is required to achieve justice. With the sovereign romantic "I" and with the godless superman of Nietzsche, the Emersonian soul had hardly anything in common other than the denial of happiness in slavery. Nature was throughout affirmative, and had nothing of the negation of one weary of society, of world-sickness, wherewith Rousseau, Schopenhauer, and Nietzsche confined it. As to immortality, Sakmann says Emerson felt as did many enlightened spirits from Spinoza to Schleiermacher, that we can know nothing of it except that it is to be, in the midst of the finite, one with the Infinite, to exist eternally in each moment. In his mystical philosophy of nature he was in line with Rousseau, Goethe, and Swedenborg as against the theories of Newton, Voltaire, and the materialists. Sakmann concludes that Emerson appeals, as America does, especially to youth and to those who have faith.

F. O. Matthiessen says (*American Renaissance,* 1941) that

Emerson wanted, like Plato, to bridge the gap between reason and the understanding, the one and the many, but never could, and now, paradoxically, "The Over-Soul" proves unreadable, whereas on the level of the understanding he "has left us the best intellectual history that we have of his age." Matthiessen also asserts that although Emerson claimed to be a "seeker," all his mature work "proceeded from *a priori* deductive assertion."

Two important books on Emerson's philosophy have recently appeared, demonstrating the fact that Emerson's ideas are still dynamic and susceptible of new and broader interpretations than those to which we have been long accustomed. In date of publication (1952) the first of these books was Sherman Paul's, entitled *Emerson's Angle of Vision: Man and Nature in American Experience*. Paul says Emerson begins with the dualism of mind and matter, and seeks by means of the theory of correspondence to bridge the gap and pass from the eighteenth-century concept of the universe as mechanism to the concept of the universe as an organism. The act of intuitive perception is the means by which the gap is bridged, unifying the finite (outer) and the infinite (inner) worlds in the experience of the self. Kant, though retaining the dichotomy of noumena and phenomena, indicated the way to unity by asserting that the moral self in its acts of will transcends the limits of the knowing self and takes its inspiration from noumenal sources. With the help of Fichte and Schelling and Coleridge, Emerson came to see how the two worlds are united in perception as the expressive unfolding of the self. For though knowledge begins with reception, the mystical union of finite and infinite, it ends in action. The mind is the lens converging the days of the spirit on the daily affairs of men. The faculties of the mind are seeds planted in man in anticipation of the nutrition they find ready for them in a universe designed to call them forth, and self-culture begins with the calling out (the education) of these faculties. Modern science is a manifestation of the polarity of the mind as it represents the human concern with commodity and limit. But it is balanced by the "organic vitality" of the mind's other pole of intuitive perception by means of which man overcomes this limitation in moments of insight. From his position at the center of the universe, man looks through nature in such moments and perceives an arc of the spheric unity of the soul. This is his "angle of vision," by means of which the expansive, creative faculty of the Reason is able to complete the circle. The condition of this experience is the correspondence of nature and spirit and the mind's mediative relationship to both. Since the expressive aspect of perception is inseparable from the receptive aspect, self-culture becomes a duty and results in the development of character. In this process, limitations become benefits, the self becomes knowable by being objectified, and man attains sphericity by taking the world into himself. Paul says that Emerson's theory of correspondence owed much to the "sympathetic" character given to it by Cudworth and even more to his reading of the Swedenborgian books and articles of his early years, particularly those of Sampson Reed and J. J. Garth Wilkinson (the friend of Henry James, Sr.).

The second of these books is S. E. Whicher's *Freedom and Fate: An Inner Life of Ralph Waldo Emerson* (1953). Part I discusses Emerson's loss of faith in historical Christianity, and his discovery of a new ground of faith about 1831-32 in the recognition of man's potential greatness by the power of God working through him. Part II shows how Emerson's faith in the greatness of man was later impaired and "driven underground" by a clearer understanding of the facts of experience. A new skepticism seized him, such as he expresses through the mouth of Montaigne in the essay on him in *Representative Men.* The skeptic's position (recognizing fate and illusion) is based on life not as it ought to be but as it is. Yet though in the essay "Experience" he openly and honestly deals with the facts of experience, he does not consciously yield to skepticism, but he saves his faith only by transferring it from the "impotent self" to the "All-disposing fate," from "the God within" to "the

God of the universe." From teaching men their power to rise above fate, he turns to teaching them "how to make the best of it," chiefly through the means of Vocation and Intellect; that is, "obedience to his genius" and "the habit of the observer." (See also H. N. Smith's "Emerson's Problem of Vocation: A Note on *The American Scholar," NEQ,* 1939.) Whereas before he had believed that "every man was equal in his potentiality," now he recognized the idiosyncrasy of individuals, each of whom must obey his peculiar bias. Hence the wise man, instead of being a rebel withdrawing from society, must be one who participates in society by following his vocation—doing his own work. His best method of overcoming the limitations of freedom through doing his own work and freedom through observing is to resolve both Doer and Knower in the Sayer, which is accomplished in the essay "The Poet." Eventually the acceptance of the theory of evolution completed the process by which his concept of man as the God-possessed creator of nature became the concept of man as the latest product of nature. *The Conduct of Life,* according to Whicher, states Emerson's latest attitude: that we are subject to necessity, yet must act as if we were free. Fate and freedom are still reconciled in his thought, but freedom is not, as in its transcendental phase, the release of greatness, but the natural and relative power of choice. This, Whicher says, is the position of the humanist.

In contrast with Whicher's well-documented statements on Emerson's persistent tendency towards skepticism, F. O. Matthiessen remarks in *American Renaissance* that in spite of his fondness for Montaigne, Emerson "had not a trace of skepticism in his being." Essays which are worth consulting on Emerson's philosophical ideas include C. E. Jorgenson's "Emerson's Paradise under the Shadow of Swords" (*PQ,* 1932), which is devoted to the exposition of Emerson's view of evil as privative only and of fate as immutable limitation only when unpenetrated by thought; A. R. Caponigri's "Brownson and Emerson: Nature and History" (*NEQ,* 1945), which affirms that Emerson's doctrine of intuition as a principle of nature and related doctrines are intended by him to prove that man's life is independent of history (apparently ignoring Emerson's acceptance of the theory of evolution); and P. F. Quinn's "Emerson and Mysticism" (*AL,* 1951), which, by narrowly defining mysticism as an experience beginning with "conversion," proves that Emerson was not a mystic; but in the "sporadic" and "pantheistic" sense defined by William James in *Varieties of Religious Experience* Emerson undoubtedly does qualify as a mystic.

But Emerson was also something of a realist and even a pragmatist, as many critics have recognized ever since in *A Fable for Critics* Lowell referred to him as having a "Greek head on right Yankee shoulders." Among those who have made a special study of the pragmatic aspects of Emerson's philosophy, F. I. Carpenter is preeminent. His essay "Points of Comparison between Emerson and William James" (*NEQ,* 1929) was the earliest and his later "William James and Emerson" (*AL,* 1939) is the fullest treatment available on the subject. He also discusses Emerson's pragmatism in the introduction to his *Emerson* (AWS, 1934), and in his *Emerson Handbook* (1953) he summarizes his own ideas on the subject as well as other works, including the German scholar Eduard Baumgarten's *Der Pragmatismus: Die geistigen Grundlagen des amerikanischen Gemeinwesens* (Frankfurt, 1938). E. C. Lindeman in "Emerson's Pragmatic Mood" (*AS,* XVI, 1946-47) says Emerson's "allegiance to the experimental approach to life . . . guarantees his permanent place in American life and thought."

4. *Science*

Emerson's identification in the popular mind with idealism and romanticism has made it difficult for critics to estimate properly his lifelong interest in science. Yet this interest has not gone unnoticed. John Burroughs wrote in 1889 ("Science and the Poets," *Works,* 1924, Vol. V): "In chemistry, in botany, in physiology, in geology, in mechanics, he found keys to unlock his enigmas. . . . There is hardly a fundamental principle of science that he has not turned to ideal uses." It is precisely because he turned science to ideal uses, because as Burroughs says again he "fertilized it with his own spirit," that critics have often thought he rejected it or ignored it. Richard Garnett said in 1888 that "science has found no such literary interpreter as Emerson," and he quoted Tyndall as saying, "By Emerson scientific conceptions are continually transmuted into the finer forms and warmer hues of an ideal world." Norman Foerster expressed the view of most critics in "Emerson as a Poet of Nature" (*PMLA,* 1922) when he said that Emerson is essentially an idealist though he was deeply interested in the science of nature. Paul shows in the last chapter of *Emerson's Angle of Vision* how he used science in his "astronomy of ideas."

The first and only detailed study of Emerson's reading in the scientific literature of this time is H. H. Clark's "Emerson and Science" (*PQ,* 1931). Clark says Emerson became acquainted with Newton's *Principia* at the age of twenty, and that it was the reading of works on astronomy by Mary Somerville, F. W. Herschel, Laplace, and others in the summer of 1832 that precipitated his resignation from the pulpit of the Second Church. Helping him to an acceptance of the theory of evolution were the evolutionary philosophers Leibniz, Kant, Goethe, and Coleridge, and the evolutionary scientists Linnaeus, Buffon, Cuvier, John Hunter, Erasmus Darwin, Saint-Hilaire, Lamarck, Lyell, Robert Chambers, and later, Asa Gray and Charles Darwin. German transcendentalism and science, Clark believes, "were not mutually exclusive in their influence." He finds evidence of scientific reading in *Nature,* "The American Scholar," and "The Divinity School Address." His study does not go beyond 1838. The most thorough study of Emerson's reception of the theory of evolution, first from the philosophers and later from the scientists, is J. W. Beach's "Emerson and Evolution" (*UTQ,* 1934). Beach repeated and expanded the materials of this essay to give them a setting in philosophy in his book *The Concept of Nature in Nineteenth-Century English Poetry* (1936). Beach says that Emerson's scientific opinions "were not shaped primarily by the great scientific writers, Buffon, Lamarck, Saint-Hilaire, and Darwin, but by a succession of second-rate, popular, and more or less dubious authorities, and the first of these was Coleridge." He says Emerson's early concept of evolution was really not evolution at all but the "graduated scale of being" theory, which was held by many philosophers in the eighteenth century, and which Emerson took from Coleridge, who took it from Schelling. This was a "mere logical, or conceptual, unfolding, or disinvolvement, of the lower category of being from the higher, or *vice versa,*" and not a chronological evolutionary sequence of events. Emerson's transition from belief in this scale-of-being theory to a belief in scientific evolution was very gradual, and he was not himself wholly aware of the process. The change, Beach says, began after the writing of *Nature,* had made considerable progress by 1841, and had so far advanced by 1844 that the reading of Robert Chambers' *Vestiges of Creation* gave him no shock. Beach thinks Emerson had fully accepted the scientific theory of evolution by 1854, that his transcendentalism enabled him to accept it "without a qualm," and that the more he learned of natural history the more certain he was that "it is all a projection of the mind, an expression of the inherent moral purpose of the universe which is found in the human spirit." He thinks it never occurred to Emerson that ethical concepts may also be a product of evolution, for his remained arbitrary, traditional, and vague, whereas those of naturalism are relative and precise. It is evident that Beach is unsympathetic with idealism and transcendentalism, and that he is thoroughly in sympathy with scientific naturalism.

A much more sympathetic study of the subject is that of F. W. Connor in his book *Cosmic Optimism* (1949), though his conclusions are not materially at variance with those of Beach. Connor agrees that Emerson's evolution was not that of the scientist, that he never mentioned natural selection, and that he was not interested in the immediate cause of the transformations of organic nature. He saw no gulf between the ultimate cause of things and the things themselves; hence for him there was no question whether living forms were attributable to a natural or a transcendental purposive cause, there being for him no such distinction. Whether species developed through the survival of chance variations or the inheritance of acquired characteristics, Emerson saw "only the phenomenal manifestation of a Creative Mind." Such a view of the cosmos made possible an optimistic view of life.

5. *Public Affairs*

Many have recognized that Emerson had a good deal of "Yankee" common sense to balance his idealism, and we have seen to what extent he is thought to have been a precursor of the pragmatic philosophers and how he kept abreast of the scientific thought of his day. Indeed, Emerson is a notable example of the obvious fact that a thinker may be an idealist and a realist without inconsistency. John Morley said half a century ago (*Crit. Misc.,* 1904), "It is only the great idealists, like Emerson, who take care not to miss the real." It was also Morley who said that Emerson "values mundane circumspection as highly as Franklin." It is well known that he took an active interest in the civic affairs of the town of Concord (see H. H. Hoeltje, "Emerson, Citizen of Concord," *AL,* 1940), and his very opposition to some of the prevalent attitudes of his time is proof that he was keenly aware of their existence. (See P. H. Boynton, "Emerson in His Period," *Ethics,* 1929, and Mildred Silver, "Emerson and the Idea of Progress," *AL,* 1940.) He belonged to the "Party of the Future," as H. N. Smith has said ("Emerson's Problem of Vocation," *AL,* 1939), and he chose the part of student rather than active reformer; yet he had no objection to reform except as it hardened into institutional patterns or organized movements.

One of the earliest and fullest studies of this phase of Emerson is Raymer McQuiston's *The Relation of Ralph Waldo Emerson to Public Affairs* (1923), which deals with Emerson's political, economic, and social ideas and his attitude towards slavery and the Civil War. McQuiston says Emerson preferred democracy, though he recognized its weaknesses, particularly the crudeness of its leaders of the Jacksonian period. At first he was a Whig, but he eventually lost confidence in their leadership (Webster, especially about 1850), and allied himself with the Republican Party in the late 1850's. Emerson opposed the tariff, but had no other strong economic views. In his individualism he tended to undervalue society and theoretically refused to recognize social classes though he was aware of their existence and the practical need of them. He spoke in favor of equal political and educational rights for women. He disliked the early anti-slavery agitators, but was driven into their camp by his dislike of the Fugitive Slave Law. He thought Lincoln too conservative in the Civil War, and after the war he favored the radical reconstructionist policies of Sumner and Stevens. This proves that Emerson's reasoned theories could be broken down by the passions evoked by public events.

Of specialized studies, the student should read A. I. Ladu's "Emerson: Whig or Democrat" (*NEQ,* 1940). Ladu says Emerson thought the Democrats had the more laudable objectives but the Whigs had the better men. His chief objection to the Democratic Party was that it failed to base political action on morality or to promote individual culture. He objected to the Whigs because they seemed to treat property as an end in itself and not a means to cultural ends. Ladu appears to feel that Emerson's natural sympathies were more with the Whigs than with the Democrats, in spite of a continuing theoretical democracy. Perry Miller, in "Emersonian Genius and the American Democracy" (*NEQ,* 1953), shows how Emerson struggled to reconcile his democratic philosophy with his Boston distaste for crudeness in men like Jackson and Lincoln, and he is able to do so by his theory of genius. "The genius is great not because he surpasses but because he represents his constituency." J. J. Chapman had remarked in 1898 that Emerson, though an individualist, was not an equalitarian democrat. Brownell had said that he hated the mob and shrank from the vulgar. Perhaps, as Parrington pointed out, he was a democrat only in the Jeffersonian sense. Marie Dugard said Emerson's attitude was not anti-democratic, but he believed democracy could succeed only if the people were wise enough to choose their best instead of their worst men as representatives in government. (See also W. M. Salter, "Emerson's Views of Society and Reform," *Ethics,* 1903, who says Emerson's sympathies were with democracy; C. G. Shaw, "Emerson the Nihilist," *Ethics,* 1914; and the chapter on Emerson in R. H. Gabriel's *The Course of American Democratic Thought,* 1940.)

As to economics, Emerson had no theory, says A. C. Kern in "Emerson and Economics" (*NEQ,* 1940), but he was in effect a laissez-faire expansionist who was saved from materialism by his demand that wealth and material growth shall be not ends in themselves but means to the enlargement of man's spiritual and moral world. J. C. Gerber, in "Emerson and the Politcal Economists" (*NEQ,* 1949), is more specific, agreeing that Emerson was for laissez-faire and free trade, much after the school of Adam Smith, though he favored an agricultural economy rather than Smith's balance of agriculture and industry. (Cf. D. C. Stenerson, "Emerson and the Agrarian Tradition," *JHI,* 1953.) Of the developments out of Adam Smith—utilitarianism, pessimism, and optimism—he approved only the third. He disliked utilitarianism, though he seems not to have known Bentham or Mill (Cf. R. T. Harris, "Nature: Emerson and Mill," *WHR,* 1951-52.) He agreed with the American school of Raymond, Everett, and Carey only in part, they being too close to the Hamiltonian view for Emerson's taste. Gerber says Emerson's ideal economic system probably would "combine socialistic ends with capitalistic means." With this latter estimate J. T. Flanagan ("Emerson and Communism," *NEQ,* 1937) seems to agree, saying that Emerson was sympathetic with the aims of the Brook Farm and Fruitlands experiments, but against their methods. His individualism predisposed him to distrust any reform that does not begin with the inner life of the individual. While recognizing that Emerson's admiration for men of power unwittingly gave comfort to ruthless manipulators of wealth in the Gilded Age, Daniel Aaron sees him chiefly as a "transcendental democrat" who encouraged men rather to "cultivate their inward greatness," and as a founder of the progressive tradition in America (*Men of Good Hope,* 1951).

On Emerson and the abolitionist movement, Marjory M. Moody's "The Evolution of Emerson as an Abolitionist" (*AL,* 1945) should be consulted. She indicates the progressive steps from 1837 to 1862 by which Emerson moved from an attitude of "detached criticism" to "unqualified demand for emancipation." (See also Rudolf Schottlaender, "Emerson as Abolitionist," *NEQ,* 1933.) Emerson, according to W. A. Huggard, saw in the Civil War not only the liberation of the Negro but "a hope for the liberation of American culture." (See his "Emerson and the Problem of War and Peace," Univ. of Iowa Humanistic Studies, No. 5, 1938; also, by the same author, "Emerson's Philosophy of War and Peace," *PQ,* 1943.)

Doubtless Emerson's lecture tours over the country, particularly in the West, affected his attitude towards democracy and public affairs in general. Ernest Marchand, in "Emerson and the Frontier" (*AL,* 1931), takes the view that native culture exercised a more powerful influence over Emerson's thinking than foreign philosophy, and tends to minimize the influence of Puritan New England in order to emphasize that of the Western frontier. (See also Lucy Hazard, *The Frontier in American Literature,* 1927, and for a view at variance with Marchand's, Ladu's article above mentioned.) It may be that Emerson taught more than he learned in the West; for as Willard Thorp has pointed out in "Emerson on Tour" (*QJS,* 1930), he made his strenuous lecture tours less for the fees he earned than to fulfill a need to teach and improve the American mind where he could. Several articles, giving details of Emerson's lecture tours, have been published by H. H. Hoeltje (three), Louise Hastings, R. B. Nye, Eleanor B. Scott, C. E. Shorer, and others.

Emerson's interest in educational theory probably grew out of this need to teach. His turn from the ministry to the public lyceum was the first proof of this need. H. D. Gray said that the one reform to which he could devote himself with consistency was in the field of education, where he might hope to provide a better means for the development of the powers of the individual. R. M. Gay says in *Emerson: A Study of the Poet as Seer* (1928) that Emerson's pedagogy rested on the belief that "education consists in invigorating the imagination," and that his own purpose was not to inculcate ideas but to "increase sensibility." H. C. Carpenter's "Emerson, Eliot, and the Elective System" (*NEQ,* 1951) reviews and marshals the evidence, including Eliot's own statements, that Emerson was an important influence in shaping the educational theory of Charles W. Eliot. The subject is discussed briefly in Carpenter's *Emerson Handbook.*

6. *Aesthetics*

Emerson made no attempt to develop a theory of art, and most of what he has said on the subject is casual and fragmentary. Several attempts, however, have been made to formulate what appear to have been his aesthetic principles. H. D. Gray's book has a chapter on the subject. Gray thought it surprising that "Emerson should have so little of value to offer us by way of an esthetic theory"; yet he accounts for the fact perhaps in suggesting that the doctrine of intuition and Emerson's Puritan ancestry "predetermined all he had to say regarding the meaning of beauty and the utility of art." Emerson believed, according to Gray, that beauty is that which inheres in the object to be imitated, and art is the expression which genius is able to give it. While beauty is perceived by the Reason, art must be wrought under the guidance of the Understanding. The office of art is "to educate the perception of beauty," and the principles of art are to be deduced from the nature of beauty. Whatever is adequate to its purpose must be beautiful, Emerson thought, and he saw no antagonism between sensuous charm and moral beauty. It is this, Gray says, that prevents Emerson's aesthetics from being more than "a mere offshoot from his ethics."

The next book on this subject is E. G. Sutcliffe's *Emerson's Theories of Literary Expression* (1923), the aim of which is by means of related quotations from Emerson to show the connection between his philosophy of style and his philosophy in general. Sutcliffe says the reason for Emerson's lack of unity is in his theory, which is dualistic, as Gray had said. Emerson was not willing to deal with "the high inspirations of the Reason" according to the methods of the Understanding. He found some comfort in the belief that the whole is mirrored in each part, so that a faithful adherence to his inspired moments will give him the image of eternity. An art so produced must depend largely upon symbols adequate to express the correspondence between mind and nature. Hence the best style must be both simple and symbolic.

Norman Foerster, in "Emerson on the Organic Principle in Art," (*PMLA,* 1926), speaks of "qualitative and quantitative" beauty, the one derived through intuition and the other through the externalization of this intuition. This is much the same as the distinction made by Gray and Sutcliffe in terms of the Reason and the Understanding. A work of art is supreme when it is a synthesis of these two, and such a synthesis Emerson found in the work of Michael Angelo. (For the influence of Michael Angelo on Emerson, especially in "The Problem," see F. B. Newman's "Emerson and Buonarroti," *NEQ,* 1952.) Emerson's distinction between genius and talent, Foerster says, is the same. Genius alone, Emerson conceived, is organic. Foerster has a more thorough analysis of Emerson's theory of art in the essay on "Emerson" in *American Criticism* (1928). Here he says Emerson's greatest debt is to Plato and the Platonists, though he probably came to his organic theory immediately through Coleridge and Schlegel. He emphasizes the classical quality of Emerson's taste, perhaps too much, and says Emerson belittled all the romantics except Wordsworth.

He agrees more or less with Gray that for Emerson the highest type of imagination is ethical (or humanistic), and virtue, in the end, becomes superior to beauty. Emerson's ideal is the poet-priest, and he proposes a union of art and religion. In this connection see N. F. Adkins, "Emerson and the Bardic Tradition" (*PMLA,* 1948).

Among others who have written on the subject, Régis Michaud has collected in *L'Esthétique d'Emerson* (Paris, 1927) a large number of statements from Emerson's works illustrating his aesthetic ideas. Art for Emerson, he says, consists in the individualization of the universal, the reduction of the many to the one; it is not an end in itself but is instrumental to the individual's appropriation of the universe. In *American Renaissance* Matthiessen shows from the *Journals* that Emerson does not always belittle talent, and that he realized that genius is ineffectual without the talent by which it is channeled into understandable form. With this compare the interpretation of Jean Gorely in "Emerson's Theory of Poetry" (*Poetry Rev.,* 1931), that in the order of genius thought precedes form, comes from within, and is not subject to the will, though it is conditioned by the artist's physical and mental health and the conventions of his time.

The most extensive study of Emerson's aesthetics is Vivian C. Hopkins' book, *Spires of Form: a Study of Emerson's Aesthetic Theory* (1951). Emerson's theory, as explained by Miss Hopkins, has three phases: first, the creative process, which itself has the three phases of inspiration, imagination, and expression; second, the completed work of art, which in its organic form is derived from nature, but in its spiritual form (objectified in the art form) is derived from the Divine Spirit; and third, the reception of the work of art by an observer, whose imagination is awakened by sense impression, memory, and the subconscious, and who finally, in the climax of recreative escape, shares with the creator the sense of freedom from time and space. See Miss Hopkins' earlier article, "The Influence of Goethe on Emerson's Aesthetic Theory" (*PQ,* 1948), in which she points out various aspects of Emerson's aesthetic theory in which he was indebted to Goethe without minimizing their numerous differences.

Very acute and provocative, though less comprehensive, is Charles Feidelson's chapter "Toward Melville: Some Versions of Emerson" in his volume *Symbolism and American Literature* (1953). Though he prefers Melville's tragic view of the world to Emerson's brighter outlook, he thinks their methods are reciprocal, and that "if we feel Melville as one of ours, we must take Emerson into the bargain, whether we like it or not." For Emerson, say Feidelson, "poetic vision 'is the perception of the symbolic character of things,' and poetic structure, the form of this vision," and yet it did not occur to him, as it did to Melville, "to exploit the most exciting quality of modern symbolism—the tension between opposite meanings in paradox and the tension between logical paradox and its literary resolution—even though this quality was implicit in his own approach." Emerson's great failing, he thinks, "was too simple a confidence in the power of poetic harmony." It seems to me that in emphasizing Emerson's predisposition to find "poetic harmony" Feidelson underestimates his consciousness of the reality of the terms of the paradox.

More recently two books have appeared that deal with Emerson's aesthetics. C. R. Metzger's *Emerson and Greenough: Transcendental Pioneers of an American Esthetic* (1954) is a comparative study of the organic theory of art as expressed by Emerson and Horatio Greenough, the sculptor. It contains some interesting suggestions on the relation of Emerson's "protestant esthetic" with his "protestant theology," both reaching through nature towards God. Metzger's work enlarges and develops the study of Emerson's and Greenough's statements of the organic principle in art made by Matthiessen in *American Renaissance*. In *Emerson as Mythmaker* (1954), which is interesting but less important, J. R. Reaver discusses Emerson's use of the imagination for the purpose of drawing his deepest meanings from the soul through the subconscious mind into the intellectual world of conscious mind. He thinks Emerson is less a mystic than a psychological interpreter and that his method has much in common with the method of present-day psychologists. One of Emerson's achievements, according to Reaver, is the resolution of ethics in aesthetics.

On Emerson's aesthetic practice, a good deal of criticism has been published. From the beginning critics have disagreed, more or less, on the question of the structure of his poems and prose works, and on the merits of his style. W. T. Harris said in 1882 ("Ralph Waldo Emerson," *Atlantic*) that Emerson's poems often lack logical unity but have organic unity. Some of his essays, and Harris names particularly the essay "Experience," have "a true genetic development," whereas others do not, and he specifies "The Over-Soul." Charles Malloy, in a series of articles in *The Coming Age* (1899-1900) and also in *The Arena* (1904), found a clue to Emerson's structure in the *Bhagavat Gita,* and this clue was the Platonic concept of Identity. Firkins has a good deal to say on this subject, and in general he agrees with Harris. He finds the essays structurally sound. "An essay is a structure, a contrivance," says Firkins, "not an efflux; but in its highest evolution, it mimics the efflux . . ." Some of the poems are also structurally sound (he cites "Days"), but most of the philosophical poems, though they contain fine lines, lack organization. Matthiessen attributes Emerson's alleged incoherence to lack of "tension between form and liberation" due to his having escaped completely from the practical restrictions of his age. In his poetry, except where he achieved the condensation of "Days," he was, says Matthiessen, likely to exemplify the "Heraclitean doctrine of the Flowing." Emerson's formlessness was, he thinks, a consequence of his practice of the organic theory of art.

Walter Blair and Clarence Faust, in "Emerson's Literary Method" (*MP,* 1944), describe a method, suggested to them by Emerson's discussion in *Representative Men* of Plato's "twice bisected line" as the key to the two worlds of the mind and the senses, by which Emerson treated a given subject in such a way as to relate it both to that which was above it and to that which was below it in the scale of being, and so achieved a balanced judgment. They successfully apply the method, by way of illustration, to several essays and poems. Sherman Paul says in *Emerson's Angle of Vision* that Emerson also employed this method in the organization of some of his books. In the *Essays, First Series,* for example, "History" is balanced by "Self-Reliance," and in *The Conduct of Life* the first three essays are preparatory to and balanced by the last three. R. P. Adams continues the theme in "Emerson and the Organic Metaphor" (*PMLA,* 1954), but he thinks the "twice bisected line" is too rigid an analogy and that Emerson explains his own method, if not Plato's, better when he says in "Plato: New Readings" that Plato "represents the privilege of the intellect, the power, namely, of carrying up every fact to successive platforms and so disclosing in every fact a germ of expansion." Such expansion, Adams says, is organic; and he thinks it is closer to the romantic than to the Platonic conception of organicism.

Other studies of Emerson's style that may be of interest are R. M. Gay's book, already mentioned; G. W. Allen's chapter on Emerson in *American Prosody* (1935), which shows that Emerson places greater importance on "images, cadenced phrases, and rhetoric than on rimes and meters"; André Célières' *The Prose Style of Emerson* (Paris, 1936, in English), which argues that the three strongest influences on Emerson were Carlyle, Swedenborg, and Montaigne; and Kathryn A. McEuen's "Emerson's Rhymes" (*AL,* 1948), which develops some of the ideas already mentioned by Allen. Brief studies have been made on special aspects of Emerson's poems by many writers, including G. W. Arms, C. P. Hotson, G. R. Elliott, and C. F. Strauch. Studies of Emerson as a practical critic may be found in G. E. DeMille, *Literary Criticism in America* (1931), who agrees with Foerster that there is a "strong vein of classicism" in Emerson's literary taste; J. T. Flanagan, "Emerson as a Critic of Fiction" (*PQ,* 1936); R. P. Falk, "Emerson and Shakespeare" (*PMLA,* 1941), who says that Emerson's one derogatory comment on Shakespeare as "master of the revels" has been ridiculously overstressed. Studies have also been made by T. A. Perry and Leah E. Jordan.

7. *Reputation and Influence*

The extensive critical literature discussed in this essay is proof enough that Emerson's reputation has been great both in this country and abroad. Of his younger contemporaries, Theodore Parker and Thoreau felt his influence before 1850 (see E. D. Mead, *The Influence of Emerson,* 1903, and André Bruel, *Emerson et Thoreau,* 1929). With regard to Thoreau, and the coolness that came between him and Emerson after 1850, see also Charles Cestre, "Thoreau et Emerson" (*RAA,* 1930) and J. B. Moore, "Thoreau Rejects Emerson" (*AL,* 1932). The relationship of Emerson and Whitman is more complex. It seems certain that he was Whitman's most important teacher and that Whitman read him thoroughly and heard him lecture during the late 1840's and early 1850's, though objective evidence is slight. After 1860 Whitman, like Thoreau after 1850, stood more firmly on his own feet and was inclined to minimize his debt to Emerson. Whitman's criticism of Emerson in *Specimen Days* (1882) points up the wide differences between them as well as their agreement on basic issues. Helpful studies of this relationship are J. B. Moore, "The Master of Whitman" (*SP,* 1926), Clarence Gohdes, "Whitman and Emerson" (*SR,* 1929), and Carlos Baker, "The Road to Concord: Another Milestone in the Whitman-Emerson Friendship" (*Princeton Univ. Library Chronicle,* 1946). The progress of the Emerson-Whitman relationship is fully documented in *The Shock of Recognition* (1943), edited by Edmund Wilson.

Others of more or less importance whom Emerson influenced were the mystic Jones Very (see Carlos Baker, "Emerson and Jones Very," *NEQ,* 1934), Margaret Fuller (see H. R. Warfel, "Margaret Fuller and Ralph Waldo Emerson," *PMLA,* 1935), and Herman Melville, though it must be said that on Melville opinion is divided. William Braswell studied Melville's annotations in his Emerson books and discussed his findings in "Melville as a Critic of Emerson" (*AL,* 1937). See also E. S. Oliver, "Melville's Picture of Emerson and Thoreau in The Confidence Man" (*CE,* 1946). For Emerson's relationship to Hawthorne, see B. B. Cohen's "Emerson's 'The Young American' and Hawthorne's 'The Intelligence Office' " (*AL,* 1954).

G. W. Cooke, writing in 1881, says: "The period from 1860 to 1870 is that in which Emerson secures the widest hearing, has the strongest personal influence in molding the thought of his time, and when his character shines out in the most emphatic manner." Emily Dickinson, about this time, was much under Emerson's influence (see G. F. Whicher, *This Was a Poet,* 1938), and in one way or another William James certainly drew largely upon Emerson, as F. I. Carpenter has shown. In an anniversary speech (*New Republic,* 15 Feb. 1943), Irwin Edman placed James in the tradition of Emerson, Thoreau, and Whitman. An interesting analysis of the opinions of the three Jameses on Emerson may be found in W. T. Stafford's "Emerson and the James Family" (*AL,* 1953; Cf. also p. 57 above). As for Chapman, S. G. Brown has said ("John Jay Chapman and the Emersonian Gospel," *NEQ,* 1952) that he understood and believed in Emerson's teachings better than any other man. "He points to Emerson," says Brown, "and Emerson points to the inherent strength and benign power of the human spirit," which America now so badly needs to believe in. Emerson has doubtless influenced many poets and other American writers of the twentieth century, including Robinson, Frost, and Hart Crane certainly (see, for references, Carpenter's *Emerson Handbook),* but detailed studies are lacking.

Emerson was well received on his lecture tours in Great Britain in 1847-48 and 1872-73, an account of which is given by Alexander Ireland in his biography of Emerson (1882). The tour of 1847-48 is outlined and discussed in detail by Townsend Scudder in "Emerson's British Lecture Tour, 1847-48" (*AL,* two parts, 1935), in "Emerson in London and the

London Lectures" (*AL,* 1936), and in "Emerson in Dundee" (*AS,* 1935). For Scudder's story of Emerson's friendship with Carlyle, Clough, and other Englishmen, see his book, *The Lonely Wayfaring Man* (1936). The attitude of Carlyle may be studied in the correspondence of Carlyle and Emerson and in the various biographies, particularly Rusk's. Interesting sidelights may be gained from numerous comparisons of the writers, among which may be mentioned that of Lowell in *A Fable for Critics* (1848), that of Henry James, Jr., in his review of the *Correspondence* in the *Century* (1883), that of E. P. Whipple in *American Literature and Other Papers* (1887), and that of E. D. Mead in *The Influence of Emerson* (1903). See also Clarence Gohdes, *American Literature in Nineteenth-Century England* (1944).

The best survey of the reception of Emerson in France is Hans Keller, *Emerson in Frankreich; Wirkungen und Parallelen* (Giessen, 1932). Among the first in France to write of Emerson were Philarète Chasles, in the *Revue des deux mondes,* 1844, and Edgar Quinet, who hailed Emerson in 1845 as the most idealistic writer of the time. These were followed by Marie de Flavigny, Comtesse d'Agoult (pseudonym, Daniel Stern) in 1846, and Emile Montégut in 1847. Emerson continued to be heard of occasionally during the next twenty years, and in 1871 he was welcomed on his European tour as a master by Renan and Taine. By 1898 he was beginning to be studied seriously by moralists and philosophers. The most important critical result of this growing interest was Marie Dugard's biography in 1907, which was crowned by the Academy. Later studies of importance were Régis Michaud's critical study *Autour d'Emerson* (Paris, 1924), which has an essay on Emerson and Nietzsche, another on Emerson and Achille Murat (see also Mrs. H. L. Richmond's "R. W. Emerson in Florida," *Florida Hist. Quart.,* 1939, on Emerson's relations with Achille Murat), and another on Emerson's reading of the work of G. G. L. Oegger; and also Michaud's *L'Esthétique d'Emerson* and his *La vie inspirée d'Emerson* (Paris, 1930), translated the same year as *Emerson, the Enraptured Yankee,* which were discussed earlier. Evidence of a continuing interest in Emerson may be found in Charles Cestre's "La pédagogie d'Emerson" (*Annales de l'Université de Paris,* 1929), Maurice Chazin's "Emerson's Disciple in Belgium: Marie Mali" (*RR,* 1933), and a series of articles by the same author on Edgar Quinet in *PMLA* (1933) and in the *Revue de littérature comparée* (two essays, in 1935). Besse D. Howard's "The First French Estimate of Emerson" (*NEQ,* 1937) is a study of "Daniel Stern." Margaret Gilman says in "Baudelaire and Emerson" (*RR,* 1943) that Emerson was the only American writer except Poe who "won more than a passing mention" from Baudelaire, and she says his *Journaux intimes* have "an unmistakeable Emersonian tang."

A very good survey of Emerson's reception in Germany is Julius Simon's *Ralph Waldo Emerson in Deutschland* (Berlin, 1937). It appears that interest in Emerson began about 1855 and that Herman Grimm was the earliest important reader of Emerson in Germany. Grimm tried to interest others in Emerson with little success. Simon says the period during which Germans interested themselves most in Emerson was between 1894 and 1907. After the First World War there was another upsurge of interest in Emerson, culminating in the excellent studies by Paul Sakmann and Eduard Baumgarten (1927 and 1938) already discussed. Baumgarten, it appears, emphasized the American characteristics of Emerson's thought, whereas others, including H. S. Chamberlain (1935) and Simon himself attempted to relate it to the current of thought then prevailing among the followers of Hitler. Hedi Hildebrand's *Die amerikanische Stellung zur Geschichte und zu Europa in Emerson's Gedankensystem* (Bonn, 1936) is oriented somewhat as Baumgarten's work. All inevitably discuss Emerson's ideas in comparison with those of Nietzsche. Two younger scholars, Rudolf Schottlaender in "Two Dionysians: Emerson and Nietzsche" (*SAQ,* 1940) and Hermann Hummel in "Emerson and Nietzsche" (*NEQ,* 1946), have carried forward these studies.

Schottlaender seems to believe that Emerson's conception of "Fate" and "Power" indicates a sympathy with Carlyle's "Force" and Nietzsche's "Will to Power," and that both Emerson and Nietzsche derived from antiquity the "identity of value-quantum with power-quantum." Hummel conveniently reviews previous writings on Emerson and Nietzsche, and though like Baumgarten he finds considerable influence on Nietzsche, he condemns those who have tried to derive from Emerson's works a justification of the racial theories of Germany under Hitler. The difference between Emerson's and Nietzsche's interpretation of the operation of the Will is emphasized by Grace R. Foster in "The Natural History of the Will" (*AS,* 1946).

It hardly seems worth while to indicate specifically the evidences of Emerson's influence in other countries. The Soviet Russian point of view is presented in S. L. Jackson's translation, "A Soviet View of Emerson" (*NEQ,* 1946), drawn from a Russian statement of American philosophy. A brief survey of Emerson's reception in a few other countries, such as Japan, India, and Sweden, is given by F. I. Carpenter in his *Emerson Handbook,* which need not be repeated here. There is a good review of Emerson criticism in English and in French up to 1931 in Bliss Perry's *Emerson Today.*

The attempt to saddle Emerson with the responsibility for the "rugged individualism" and materialism of the American Gilded Age and for the philosophy of force in Nazi Germany of the present century has been no less misleading than the opposite effort to identify him with the sentimental optimism that was widespread in his own time. As Rusk and others have seen, Emerson has been a harmonizer of discordant values, and has yet something to teach mankind. (See especially R. L. Rusk, "Emerson and the Stream of Experience," *CE,* 1953.) Firkins said in 1930 ("Has Emerson a Future?" *MLN*): "Emerson means for us pre-eminently an enlargement of the possibilities of man's experience; the inextinguishable thirst of the race for what is larger and deeper in the psychic life cannot finally ignore him." Recent opinion, after all deductions have been made, supports this view. Stephen Whicher concludes his study by saying that "to reject Emerson utterly is to reject mankind." Carl Strauch (*Personalist,* 1952) says that Emerson's moral idealism, resulting from his struggle to maintain his poise in the midst of the conflicting elements of life, puts him in the stream of the most enduring intellectual and imaginative tradition of the Western World. S. A. Brown says (*Ethics,* 1954) his value today is perhaps as great as it was to his contemporaries. Recently H. M. Jones, speaking at the sesquicentennial of Emerson's birth, said that Emerson is badly needed today for the very thing which causes him to be neglected: his faith in the individual man and his courage to face the principal evil of our time, cowardice and conformity. There is, then, evidence of the beginning of a renewed, if more critical, appreciation of Emerson in America.

3

HAWTHORNE

I. Bibliographical Materials

At the time this is written, the available bibliographies of Hawthorne leave much to be desired. Three bibliographies—Nina E. Browne's *A Bibliography of Nathaniel Hawthorne,* W. H. Cathcart's *Bibliography of the Works of Nathaniel Hawthorne,* and J. C. Chamberlain's *First Editions of Nathaniel Hawthorne*—are of use; but all appeared in 1905, before a large share of the best work on Hawthorne had been done. These may be supplemented by the bibliography in *CHAL,* II (1918); Harry Hartwick's bibliography in W. F. Taylor, *A History of American Letters* (1936); and T. H. Johnson's bibliography in *LHUS,* III (1948).

A compilation promised for publication but not available in time for review, possibly would supersede all these, Nouvart Tashjian and Dwight Eckerman, *Nathaniel Hawthorne: An Annotated Bibliography.* This is to be a 416-page volume listing all of the author's works chronologically, then books and articles about Hawthorne and his work (reviews and studies of single works, general literary criticisms, books and articles about Hawthorne, bibliographies—all annotated), then an exhaustive variety of miscellaneous items. The preface and the outline of this book (which are all I have seen) as well as the experience and the intelligent aims of its compilers, augur well for its success.

Eva M. O'Connor, *An Analytical Index to the Works of Nathaniel Hawthorne* (1882), which includes both topics and proper names, is a useful tool.

Bertha Faust's *Hawthorne's Contemporaneous Reputation, a Study of Literary Opinion in America and England, 1828-1864* (1939) is a thorough and competent study of reviews and discussions appearing from 1828 through the months immediately following Hawthorne's death. The author's reputation after 1864 down to the present has been discussed only in three unpublished studies: William Reid, "A History of Hawthorne Criticism, 1879-1932" (1932), written as a master's thesis at the University of Colorado; Helen-Jean Moore, "The American Criticism of Hawthorne, 1938-1948" (1952), a University of Pittsburgh doctoral dissertation; and R. M. Aderman, "Nathaniel Hawthorne's English Reputation to 1904" (1952), a University of Wisconsin doctoral dissertation. The first offers a fairly full bibliography for the period it covers, but deals only with what the author considers important studies. Miss Moore's is a much more exhaustive study which considers in appropriate detail not only the works of the decade being studied but a fair number of the biographical and critical studies preceding 1938. Though brief, Miss Moore's outline of the trends in Hawthorne studies from 1828 down into the 1930's (pp. 217-222) is the best discussion of shifting approaches and interests. Aderman's compilation, exhaustive for English writings about his author, is briefly outlined in *Summaries of Doctoral Dissertations, University of Wisconsin,* XII (1952). Such annotated bibliographies as Austin Warren, *Hawthorne, Representative Selections* (1934), pp. lxxvi-lxxix; T. H. Johnson, "Hawthorne" in *LHUS* (1948), III, 547-552, and the forthcoming Tashjian-Eckerman bibliography will serve to tell the full story.

II. Editions

The standard edition is *The Complete Works of Nathaniel Hawthorne, with Introductory Notes,* edited by G. P. Lathrop, 12 volumes (1883)—the Riverside edition. To this, *Doctor Grimshawe's Secret,* edited by Julian Hawthorne, has been added as a somewhat anomalous thirteenth volume. There are also the so-called Autograph Edition, *Complete Writings* (Boston, 1900), and the Old Manse Edition (Boston, 1900), each in 22 volumes. Better texts of the notebooks, collated and with Mrs. Hawthorne's bowdlerizations and various personal allusions restored from manuscript sources, are available in *The American Notebooks of Nathaniel Hawthorne* (1932) and *The English Notebooks of Nathaniel Hawthorne* (1941), both edited by Randall Stewart. The Italian notebooks, similarly restored, are in preparation by N. H. Pearson. The first complete and faithful printing of the different versions of *Dr. Grimshawe's Secret,* edited by E. H. Davidson, was published in 1954.

Uncollected works include S. T. Pickard, ed. *Hawthorne's First Diary, with an Account of Its First Discovery* (1897); Elizabeth L. Chandler, ed. "Hawthorne's 'Spectator' " (*NEQ,* 1931); N. H. Pearson, ed. "A Sketch by Hawthorne" (*NEQ,* 1933); D. C. Gallup, ed. "On Hawthorne's Authorship of 'The Battle-Omen' " (*NEQ,* 1936); Arlin Turner, ed. *Hawthorne as Editor: Selections from His Writings for the American Magazine of Useful and Entertaining Knowledge* (1941); Randall Stewart, ed. "Hawthorne's Contributions to *The Salem Advertiser*" (*AL,* 1934) and "Two Uncollected Reviews by Hawthorne" (*NEQ,* 1936). The admission of the *First Diary* and "The Battle Omen" to the canon is not established. On the former, Pickard wrote an article, "Is 'Hawthorne's First Diary' a Forgery?" *Dial* (1902), indicating that he had become dubious about its attribution.

Collections of tales and romances are too numerous to list in detail, but these are outstanding: *Nathaniel Hawthorne: Representative Selections,* ed. Austin Warren (1934); *The Complete Novels and Selected Tales of Nathaniel Hawthorne,* ed. N. H. Pearson (1937); *Hawthorne's Short Stories,* ed. Newton Arvin (1946); *The Portable Hawthorne,* ed. Malcolm Cowley (1948); *The Best of Hawthorne,* ed. Mark Van Doren (1951).

A complete collection of Hawthorne's letters, badly needed, is being prepared by N. H. Pearson and Randall Stewart. The chief manuscript collections are those in the Boston Public Library, Essex Institute (Salem) Manning Collection, Henry E. Huntington Library, Houghton Library at Harvard, National Archives in Washington, D.C., the Duyckinck and Berg Collections of the New York Public Library, and the Pierpont Morgan Library. Those in the Huntington Collection are described in Randall Stewart, "Letters to Sophia" (*HLQ,* 1944).

Numerous letters are quoted in the earlier biographies of Hawthorne by G. P. Lathrop, Julian Hawthorne, and Horatio Bridge (listed later) and in Samuel Longfellow, *Final Memorials of Henry Wadsworth Longfellow* (1887). Collections include: Manning Hawthorne, "Hawthorne's Early Years" (*Essex Inst. Hist. Coll.,* 1938); idem, "Nathaniel Hawthorne Prepares for College" (*NEQ,* 1938); idem, "Nathaniel and Elizabeth Hawthorne, Editors" (*Colophon,* 1939); E. B. Hungerford, "Hawthorne Gossips about Salem" [letters of 1830-31] (*NEQ,* 1933); Randall Stewart, "Hawthorne and Politics: Unpublished Letters to William B. Pike" (*NEQ,* 1932); *Love Letters of Nathaniel Hawthorne, 1839-41 and 1841-63,* with a preface by Roswell Field (1907); Manning Hawthorne, "Hawthorne and Utopian Socialism" (*NEQ,* 1939); *Letters of Hawthorne to William D. Ticknor, 1851-1864,* 2 vols. (1910); Caroline Ticknor, *Hawthorne and His Publisher* (1913); Harold Blodgett, "Hawthorne as Poetry Critic: Six Unpublished Letters to Lewis Mansfield" (*AL,* 1940); Rose H. Lathrop, "The Hawthornes in Lenox. Told in Letters by Nathaniel and Mrs. Hawthorne" (*Century,* 1894); R. M. Aderman, "Newly Located Hawthorne Letters [1855]" (*EIHC,* 1952); J. C. Austin, *Fields of the Atlantic Monthly* (1953); Randall Stewart, "The Hawthornes at the Wayside, 1860-1864" and "Hawthorne's Last Illness and Death" (*More Books,* 1944).

III. Biography

Supplementing Hawthorne's letters and journals, books and articles by the author's relatives, friends, and acquaintances provide indispensable primary sources: G. W. Curtis, a Brook

Farmer and a neighbor of the author when he lived in the Old Manse, wrote "Hawthorne" in *Homes of American Authors* (1853) and "Hawthorne and Brook Farm," *From the Easy Chair,* 3rd Series (1894). S. G. Goodrich, publisher, told of Hawthorne's early literary career in *Recollections of a Lifetime* (1856). Elizabeth P. Peabody, sister-in-law, wrote "The Genius of Hawthorne" (*Atlantic,* 1868) and "The Two Hawthornes" (Nathaniel and Julian) in *Western* (1875) and quite probably was the chief source of a long-accepted account of Hawthorne's early years. In addition to editing the notebooks, Hawthorne's wife, Sophia P. Hawthorne, published *Notes in England and Italy* (1869). His publisher, J. T. Fields, who knew him from about 1839, wrote "Hawthorne" (*Atlantic,* 1871), later incorporated in *Yesterdays With Authors* (1872) and published as a small book, *Hawthorne* (1876). His son, Julian, wrote, among other articles, two useful ones on the settings of the tales and novels—"The Salem of Hawthorne" and "Scenes of Hawthorne's Romances" in *Century Magazine* (1884)—and two longer works which, despite their adulatory tone, are extremely valuable: *Nathaniel Hawthorne and His Wife: A Biography,* 2 vols. (1884), and *Hawthorne and His Circle* (1903). M. D. Conway, a disciple of Emerson who was acquainted with Hawthorne, interestingly interpreted him in *Life of Nathaniel Hawthorne* (1890). Horatio Bridge, a friend from college days on, recalled his encounters and reproduced many letters in *Personal Recollections of Nathaniel Hawthorne* (1893). Rose Hawthorne Lathrop, a daughter, wrote "My Father's Literary Methods" (*Ladies Home Jour.,* 1894) and a book, *Memories of Hawthorne* (1897), which offered personal insights. G. B. Loring, Democratic postmaster in Salem, 1853-57, and an acquaintance of thc author, wrote an essay on "Hawthorne" in *Papyrus Leaves,* ed. W. F. Gill (1898). Annie (Mrs. James T.) Fields wrote *Hawthorne* (1889). W. D. Howells showed his usual skill in evoking a personality in the few pages on Hawthorne in *Literary Friends and Acquaintance* (1900). R. H. Stoddard published "My Acquaintance with

Hawthorne" in *Recollections, Personal and Literary* (1903) and F. B. Sanborn, Transcendentalist schoolmaster of Concord, wrote *Hawthorne and His Friends* (1908).

Secondary biographical writings on Hawthorne from the start have tended to be interpretative. Reading any such writings, students therefore need to consider the facts which they include, the weighting of these facts, and also the emphases in the discussions of the sketches, tales, and romances in relation to the theses being developed. Two over-all views of the man—an earlier view which may be called the traditional one and a newer interpretation—are distinguishable.

Details drawn from the letters, from contemporaneous or partially contemporaneous accounts, as well as from statements about Hawthorne's personality in them, furnished the basis for what came to be a traditional view of the author. Biographers with this view saw Hawthorne as a solitary figure, withdrawn from society and from the world, aloof from its problems but driven to brooding over them and treating them fancifully. The keynote was struck in Henry James, *Hawthorne,* English Men of Letters Series (1879). The author's career, said James, "had few perceptible points of contact with what is called the world, with public events, with the manners of the time, even with the life of his neighbors." James believed that Hawthorne's "mind proper—his mind in so far as it was a repository of opinions and articles of faith—had no development." James saw his subject as essentially an unworldly artist with a New England Puritan background, and he treated him as such in a book which avowedly was "a critical essay" rather than "a biographical essay." (See also the section on "Evaluations and Analyses.") The interpretation was developed more briefly, and with some variations, in P. E. More, "The Solitude of Nathaniel Hawthorne" (*Atlantic,* 1901), later published in *Shelburne Essays,* 1st Series (1904).

A detailed biographical study which followed shortly was G. E. Woodberry, *Nathaniel Hawthorne,* American Men of Letters Series (1902). This gave an admirable statement of the characteristic early attitude and offered persuasive arguments for it. Wrote Woodberry: "That recurring idea of isolation, the sense of secrecy in men's bosoms, the perception of life as always lying in the shadow that falls on it, proceeded from predilections of his own, differentiating him from other men; there may have been no perilous stuff in his breast, nothing to confess or record peculiar to himself in act or experience, no intensity of self-life, but there was this temperament of the solitary brooder upon life." His chief relationship to the world—a rather tenuous one—was a "race quality"—an "inheritance from Puritanism": "He took practically no interest in life except as seen under its moral aspects as a life of the soul; and this absorption in the moral sphere was due to his being a child of New England. It was his inheritance from Puritanism. . . . The moral world, the supremacy of the soul's interests, how life fared in the soul, was his region; he thought about nothing else."

Woodberry, however, like others who had written about Hawthorne earlier, saw his subject as in some ways well adjusted. In politics, for instance, he was a sensible and consistent Democrat. And his family life was a solid Victorian achievement, as the concluding words in Woodberry's biography attested: "perhaps even more than his genius the sweetness of his home life . . . as it is so abundantly shown in his children's memories, lingers in the mind that has dwelt long on the story of his life."

With some differences in emphasis and interpretation, this picture was reproduced in general outline in histories of literature and biographical studies both brief and extended down through the 1920's, and in some instances, even beyond. Though students differed somewhat about the precise nature or degree of the man's withdrawal, Hawthorne's solitariness was recurrently emphasized. One of the longer studies reiterated the concept in its subtitle, Herbert Gorman, *Hawthorne: A Study in Solitude* (1927), and frequently stressed, though it did not very systematically develop, its indicated theme. Lloyd Morris, *The Rebellious Puritan: Portrait of Mr. Hawthorne* (1927), was a more thoroughly documented work which also frequently underlined the author's tendency toward withdrawal. It may be of some significance that both Gorman and Morris believed Hawthorne to be somewhat more closely related to his intellectual milieu than Woodberry had; but the emphasis still was upon his dissociation.

Newton Arvin, in *Hawthorne* (1929), showed other deviations as he brought to biographical and critical interpretation some of the techniques of modern psychology to relate his author's abnormal preoccupation with guilt to his unconquerable reclusiveness: "Mark the form that guiltiness habitually takes in his representation of it, and you will be in no doubt of its origin. The essential sin, he would seem to say, lies in whatever shuts up the spirit in a dungeon where it is alone, beyond the reach of common sympathies and the general sunlight. All that isolates, damns; all that associates, saves . . . thus fearfully, we may be sure, did he represent to himself the pitfalls he had peculiarly to avoid." The theme, Arvin held, came not from Hawthorne's Puritan inheritance but from his own tragic struggle, and he was deeply involved in its expression. Thus, though he accepted the general belief in Hawthorne's isolation, Arvin differed from earlier students in his conception of the way this quality shaped the fiction.

The newer interpretation of Hawthorne is based in part, as it must be, upon the primary sources which students used through 1929. But later students question some hitherto accepted "facts," for instance the tradition that the love of solitude of Hawthorne's mother lasted for decades, and infecting her son, quite probably passed along to Julian Hawthorne by imaginative Elizabeth Peabody. These later students use some of the documents previously relied upon—the notebooks, to cite an important example—in more authentic versions. And they utilize materials previously only partly studied or, in some instances, previously unknown. The resultant new picture of Hawthorne shows him as less of an unworldly, isolated, brooding and abnormal man and conversely as better adjusted and more in tune with fellow human beings and the life of his period.

A number of special studies filled in this general outline. To cite a few instances: J. B. Osborne, in "Nathaniel Hawthorne as American Consul" (*Bookman,* 1903), reported that a study of the two volumes of the author's official letters in the Department of State reveals Hawthorne to have been a hard-working and efficient consul with a far from unworldly interest in American shipping and seamen. G. E. Jepson, "Hawthorne in the Boston Custom House" (*Bookman,* 1904), corrected earlier accounts of the author's service in another office. W. S. Nevins, "Nathaniel Hawthorne's Removal from the Salem Custom House" (*EIHC,* 1917), continued the study of the author's political career. N. F. Doubleday, "Hawthorne's Satirical Allegory" (*CE,* 1942), related several satires to current events, and Arlin Turner, "Hawthorne and Reform" (*NEQ,* 1942), studied political and social attitudes. A significant book-length study was L. S. Hall, *Hawthorne: Critic of Society* (1944). This thorough survey of official records, personal correspondence, and writings asserts that Hawthorne, rather than being aloof, was interested in and highly knowledgeable about political, economic, and social issues.

Manning Hawthorne, great-grandson of the author, published a number of articles, drawing a good share of his material from previously unexplored family manuscripts, which argued for reinterpretation of the writer's life, for the most part in his earlier years. The most valuable of these were: "Hawthorne and 'The Man of God' " (*Colophon,* 1937); "Hawthorne's Early Years" (*EIHC,* 1938); "Nathaniel Hawthorne Prepares for College" (*NEQ,* 1938); "Maria Louisa Hawthorne" (*EIHC,* 1939); "Nathaniel and Elizabeth Hawthorne, Editors" (*Colophon,* 1939); "Parental and Family Influences on Hawthorne" (*EIHC,* 1940); "Nathaniel Hawthorne at Bowdoin" (*NEQ,* 1940); "The Friendship between Hawthorne and Longfellow" (*English Leaflet,* 1940); "Aunt Ebe: Some Letters of Elizabeth M. Hawthorne" (*NEQ,* 1947); "A Glimpse of Hawthorne's Boyhood" (*EIHC,* 1947).

Similarly concerned with the author in his youth were N. F. Adkins, "The Early Projected Works of Nathaniel Hawthorne" (*PBSA,* 1945), and N. H. Pearson's "The College Years of Nathaniel Hawthorne," an unpublished monograph which was awarded the Henry H. Strong Prize in American Literature at Yale in 1932. Pearson's unpublished doctoral dissertation, a study of *The Italian Notebooks* in their unedited state (Yale, 1942), has been useful for the new light it cast on Hawthorne's European experiences.

Randall Stewart has been more responsible than any other scholar for expounding and documenting the new concept of Hawthorne. He, like Pearson, restored the texts of some of the notebooks; and in 1932 and 1941, respectively, he published his admirably edited *American Notebooks* and *English Notebooks.* His work on the notebooks persuaded him that the overnice wifely tinkering with their text had contributed much to an erroneous traditional image of Hawthorne. Stewart also wrote a series of articles on various aspects of Hawthorne's biography, most of them in one way or another urging changes in traditional concepts. These included: "Hawthorne and Politics: Unpublished Letters to William B. Pike" (*NEQ,* 1932); "Hawthorne in England: The Patriotic Motive in the Note-Books" (*NEQ,* 1935); "Hawthorne's Speeches at Civic Banquets" (*AL,* 1936); "Hawthorne and the Civil War" (*SP,* 1937); "The Hawthornes at the Wayside, 1860-1864," and "Hawthorne's Last Illness and Death" (*More Books,* 1944); " 'Pestiferous Gail Hamilton,' James T. Fields and the Hawthornes" (*NEQ,* 1944); "Recollections of Hawthorne by His Sister Elizabeth" (*AL,* 1945); "Mrs. Hawthorne's Financial Difficulties: Selections from Her Letters to James T. Fields, 1865-1868" and

"Mrs. Hawthorne's Quarrel with James T. Fields" (*More Books,* 1946).

Stewart's years of work were summarized and climaxed in *Nathaniel Hawthorne: A Biography* (1948) based upon a complete study of the author's papers and manuscripts and of the restored notebooks, upon a rereading and re-evaluating of reminiscent accounts by family, friends, and contemporaries, and upon the use of all relevant recent scholarship. The book was not crowded with factual information nor heavily documented: the biographer took for granted, evidently, that his introductions and notes to the *Notebooks* and his articles, as well as those of other modern scholars, had provided much of the documentation. Stewart at all points in his account portrayed a more worldly, more sociable, more "normal" figure than the older biographers portrayed. More than others, he also showed a philosophically sophisticated author who "touched his times at point after point with admonitory finger"—a thinker with a great positive message. The message, says Stewart in his final chapter, "is essentially the recognition of man's fallibility, the restoration of sympathy, the sharing of the common lot. Hawthorne's 'moral' comprehends the Christian doctrine of charity, the psychological doctrine of participation, the social doctrine of the democratic way."

In contrast with Stewart's graceful but brief biography, two other book-length biographical studies of the 1940's are crowded with rather too much detail. Edward Mather [Jackson], *Nathaniel Hawthorne, A Modest Man* (1940), the first of these, had the extraordinary aim of treating "the biography of Hawthorne as that of a man rather than that of an author" —extraordinary in that such an approach would seem to remove the chief element of the subject's interest. Jackson, however, did not complctely neglect Hawthorne's work: he was interested in it, but as an expression of a strange personality rather than as literature. He accepted the older concept of Hawthorne as a diffident recluse and considered at length the relationship between the man's solitary ways, on the one hand, and the nature of his work and his life, on the other. But Jackson notes that, recluse though he was, Hawthorne had an impact upon many of his contemporaries and he was, furthermore, very perceptive of their characteristics. Jackson therefore was much concerned with Hawthorne's contemporaries, and the details he presented—and the parallels and contrasts between the lives of associates and that of the author—often proved illuminating. Also, "As an Englishman," Jackson writes, "I have been particularly interested in his years of residence in England and in his violent opinions concerning the English." His chief new findings were in this aspect of study.

Another very detailed study was Robert Cantwell's *Nathaniel Hawthorne: The American Years* (1948)—the first volume of what was planned as a two-volume biography. Like Stewart, Cantwell was eager to correct, as he put it, the older "narrow and lop-sided portrait" distorted by false emphasis upon the "brooding seclusion" of his subject. He hoped to restore the real Hawthorne by two means: by giving a "fuller treatment of people whose lives were linked with his," and by dealing at length with "the depth and nature of his political work." Cantwell's discussion of Hawthorne's family and of folk even casually associated with him, though overfull and too often irrelevant, has something of an encyclopedic value for students. The discussion of the author and politics develops a startling thesis. It is that Hawthorne was detached from Salem life during the twelve years after Bowdoin, not because of his temperament or even because of his artistic concentration but because he was engaged in secret work for the United States Treasury Department. There is not much evidence for this hypothesis.

Two other books which appeared after Cantwell's are also particularly useful for the light they throw upon Hawthorne's family. One is Louise H. Tharp, *The Peabody Sisters of Salem* (1950). The other is Vernon Loggins, *The Hawthornes: The Story of Seven Generations of an American Family* (1951), a thorough study which gives an account of the author's family from the fifteenth century down to modern times, ending with the death of Julian's widow in 1949.

IV. Studies of Ideas

When G. W. Curtis published his article, "The Works of Nathaniel Hawthorne," in the *NAR* in 1864, he emphasized the man's isolation from the intellectual movements of his day. In discussions of the author's ideas, especially during the last three decades, the general trend has been toward a conception of the man so at odds with this that, in recent studies, Hawthorne's close relationship to the currents of thought in his time has been emphasized. Nor has the degree of isolation been the only point about which there was disagreement: students of almost every facet of the author's thought have differed. As Austin Warren pointed out in his American Writers Series volume in 1934, "Critics of ability and acumen urge contradictory interpretations of the author's mind: he was, we are told, the defender of Puritanism; its opponent and satirist; a Transcendentalist; the adversary of the movement; a believer; a sceptic; a democrat; a moralist of New England rigor and even prudery; a prophet (albeit perhaps unaware) of the Freudian gospel; a romantic, imbued with belief in the essential rightness of human instincts and faith in the masses; a Christian and realist with suspicion of reform and no credence of 'progress'."

Since such disagreements still exist among competent scholars, it is impossible to cite a definitive treatment of almost any of the areas of Hawthorne's thought. All the leading biographers necessarily have concerned themselves to some extent with Hawthorne's ideas, and all contribute in some way to an understanding of them. Three scholars, however, have done particularly impressive surveys of Hawthorne's thinking in various fields—Austin Warren, F. O. Matthiessen, and Randall Stewart. Others have written useful studies of particular facets of Hawthorne's mind.

Warren's Introduction to his volume, *Nathaniel Hawthorne: Representative Selections* (1934), has as its chief concern "to trace the development of Hawthorne's religious, ethical, political, social and literary ideas—to study his mind." Under the headings, "Theology," "The Problem of Sin," "Anti-Transcendentalism," "Politics," "European Influences," and "Hawthorne as Artist," Warren sets forth intelligently and persuasively a summary of his own and other scholars' explorations in the author's thought. The book therefore affords an excellent introduction to Hawthorne's attitudes. Later scholars, however, have tended to modify Warren's statement that his author "was nearly impervious to the intellectual movements of his day," finding Hawthorne more in tune with the thought of the time than had Warren and his predecessors.

F. O. Matthiessen's *American Renaissance: Art and Expression in the Age of Emerson and Whitman* (1941) deals in a most revealing way with the work of five authors, Hawthorne among them. Since he is concerned with the authors' relationships to one another and to the movement of American literature, he considers Hawthorne in relation to his milieu rather more thoroughly than most predecessors have, and finds revealing parallels between his thought and that of his contemporaries. He is interested, furthermore, as he says, in describing the writings of these authors as works of art. To do this, he feels it necessary to discover "the conceptions held by five of our major writers concerning the functions and nature of literature, and the degree to which their practice bore out their theories." This leads to a study of literary theories. He also feels it necessary to evaluate "their fusions of form and content." His consideration of form leads to his study of other ideas and attitudes, for, like Croce, he thinks of form as "nothing else than the entire resolution of the intellectual, sentimental, and emotional material into the concrete reality of the poetic image and word." So in dealing with Hawthorne in various parts of his complex study, he includes excellent discussions of Hawthorne's ideas about religion, philosophy, politics, society, and art. These are related to excellent analyses of the individual tales and the romances.

Stewart's concern with Hawthorne's ideas is evident in many of his articles, but the most useful extended treatises occur in two books. Two introductory chapters to his edition of *The American Notebooks* (1932), "The Development of Character Types in Hawthorne's Fiction" and "Recurrent Themes in Hawthorne's Fiction," offer valuable generalizations about the author's chief ideas as they are embodied in his writings. The final chapter of *Nathaniel Hawthorne: A Biography* (1948)—"The Collected Works"—is a concise but brilliant essay, based upon a thorough knowledge of Hawthorne's life and all his writings. It considers the works, taken together, as "in the highest sense a criticism of life" and precisely defines the nature of this criticism.

Other studies have been more specialized in their approach or have contributed mainly to the study of one phase of Hawthorne's thought. These may be studied under three headings—Religious and Philosophical Concepts, Social and Political Ideas, and Literary Theories.

1. *Religious and Philosophical Concepts*

The two family biographers, Lathrop and Julian Hawthorne, note that though Hawthorne was reared in the Unitarian Church, he did not belong to a church or attend church as an adult. The implication, which scholars generally have accepted, is that he was not a practicing Unitarian; and few have held that he showed Unitarian bias or used Unitarian terminology in his writings. Discussions of Hawthorne's religious beliefs are largely concerned with his attitudes towards Puritanism, towards Catholicism, and towards nonsectarian attitudes of his time.

Those who have held that Hawthorne was basically a Puritan have differed in defining the nature of his Puritanism. Emile Montégut, "Un Romancier pessimiste en Amérique," *Revue des Deux Mondes* (1860), holds that Hawthorne showed the depravity of man but, unlike other authors, did not do so as "a prelude to recommending the grace of God," thus emphasizing one Puritan doctrine but scanting another. W. C. Brownell, "Hawthorne," *American Prose Masters* (1909), thinks the author so much a Puritan that he almost always succeeded when developing Puritan themes and usually failed when not doing so. In other ways, too, for instance in noting Hawthorne's didactic tendency, he feels that the man's innate Puritanism shaped his works: *The Scarlet Letter* was, he holds, "the Puritan *Faust*." As has been indicated, Woodberry, in his biography—and in an article, "The Literary Age of Boston" (*Harper's*, 1903)—expresses the cpinion of a large share of the earlier writers on Hawthorne's religion. He sees the writer as less a conscious doctrinal Puritan than one who, as it were, absorbed the moral emphasis and atmosphere of Puritanism as his inheritance and as part of his temperament. One result was his deep concern with the moral aspects of life; another was a relentless attitude towards his characters and an emphasis upon the darker aspects of life; still another was a democratic attitude which led him to "see all men as in the light of the judgment day."

Similarly, various writers have held that Hawthorne's Puritanism expressed itself not in his adopting specific dogmas but rather in his arriving at derivative or related attitudes. Thus Arvin sees the author's tendency toward excessive fatalism as a related attitude; Morris and some others, Hawthorne's scepticism as a modification of his Puritanism. H. W. Schneider, in a section on Hawthorne in his brilliant historical study, *The Puritan Mind* (1930), characterizes him as one who "did not need to believe in Puritanism, for he understood it." "He," continues Schneider, "saw the empirical truth behind the Calvinistic symbols. He recovered what Puritanism professed but seldom practiced—the spirit of piety, humility, and tragedy in the face of the inscrutable ways of God." Matthiessen repeats and enlarges upon this conception of the nature of Hawthorne's Puritanism. C. E. Eisinger, "Hawthorne and the Middle Way"

(*NEQ,* 1954), holds that the author "was a champion of a norm" in his sympathetic portrayal of balanced characters and his less sympathetic portrayal of characters abnormally isolated or extremely ambitious. Eisinger's readings of certain stories —though not his general thesis—are questioned in S. R. Price, "The Head, the Heart, and 'Rappaccini's Daughter' " (*NEQ,* 1954).

F. I. Carpenter, in "Puritans Preferred Blondes: The Heroines of Melville and Hawthorne" (*NEQ,* 1936), sees Hawthorne as an uneasy inheritor of some Puritan attitudes. His vestigial belief purportedly forced him, like others of his time, to choose between the ideal of personal freedom (the progressive aspect of Puritanism) and the religious sense of sin (the conservative aspect). Hawthorne wavered, says Carpenter, but in his later novels "denied the progressive ideal of self-reliant experience and returned to the old morality of purity." The thesis is expanded and somewhat modified by Philip Rahv, in "The Dark Lady of Salem" (*PR,* 1941). Carlos Kling, "Hawthorne's View of Sin" (*The Personalist,* 1932-33), holds that the author's concept of sin was less justifiable in Puritan terms than in terms of aesthetics.

Two recent studies of Hawthorne's Puritanism are noteworthy for their careful study of the author's pronouncements on specific doctrines. Barriss Mills, "Hawthorne and Puritanism" (*NEQ,* 1948), is concerned with Hawthorne's approval of certain Puritan attitudes not only towards such matters as seriousness, justice, democracy, courage, "toughmindedness," but also towards various beliefs. He believed, Mills holds, in innate depravity, in the futility of external reforms, and (with some important reservations) in determinism. He differed from the Puritans in his tolerance, his anti-intellectualism, in his sympathy for sinners, in his belief in the educative values of guilt, and in his modifications of such doctrines as that of predestination and that of absolute sovereignty. Mills's interpretation of Hawthorne's attitude toward the role of intellect is a questionable part of an otherwise useful article. A brief but thoughtful and suggestive study is C. E. Eisinger, "Pearl and the Puritan Heritage" (*CE,* 1951). This considers Pearl in relationship to an important Puritan distinction, that between natural and civil law. "She," the author concludes, "is the hypostatization, in miniature, of the Puritan conception of nature and the nature of the state."

Two authors have made useful studies of Hawthorne's relationships to Catholicism. The first, "Hawthorne's Attitude Toward Catholicism," by A. F. Hewitt, appeared in the *Catholic World* (1885). The author cites and examines references to Catholicism dotted through Hawthorne's writings. He concludes that Hawthorne remained throughout life "a Liberal Christian," though evidently not a Unitarian. His contacts with Catholicism in Europe, however, enabled him—in Hewitt's opinion—to find and to formulate what was attractive and what was unattractive. His Christian belief was brightened and his religious views were made "more vivid and elevated by the influence of Catholic art, and the pervading atmosphere of faith, in Italy and Rome." Despite his sympathies, Hawthorne, so Hewitt says, showed "no sign of . . . having attained a perception of the historical and theological evidence that the Catholic Church is the only church of Christ and way of salvation." Gilbert Voight, in a briefer yet equally thorough article, "Hawthorne and the Roman Catholic Church" (*NEQ,* 1946), summarizes available materials from biographies, notebooks and fictional works. He concludes that Hawthorne moved from an initial attitude of hostility to a more judicious view—part way between Kenyon's disapproval and his daughter Rose's later acceptance.

Since Hawthorne was a neighbor of several New England Transcendentalists and otherwise was associated with Transcendentalists and their thoughts, various students have considered the extent to which he was affected by the Transcendental beliefs. Bliss Perry discusses the problem in "The Centenary of Hawthorne," first published in the *Atlantic* (1904) and later reprinted in *Park Street Papers* (1908). He sees the writer as one whose thinking was nurtured by Puritanism but who (as his reading, his friends and associations, and his intellectual environment all suggested) was in fact a Transcendentalist. F. P. Stearns, *The Life and Genius of Nathaniel Hawthorne* (1906), holds that Hawthorne's concern with "the indestructibility of the spirit" and his emphasis upon the spiritual above the physical allied him with Transcendentalism. John Erskine, in his chapter, "Hawthorne," in *CHAL* (1918) discusses (and probably overstates) the direct influence of Emerson and Alcott on Hawthorne's thinking. He holds that the author adopted certain beliefs, modified some "to conform to stubborn and perplexing facts," and rejected others. Similarly, Matthiessen and Floyd Stovall—the latter in a passage on Hawthorne in *American Idealism* (1943)—see Hawthorne as accepting some Transcendental tenets. Matthiessen stresses his beliefs that all things had spiritual as well as literal meanings and that the imagination served as a mediator between spirit and matter. Stovall cites his concern with the human soul, his consideration of the doctrine of compensation, and his distrust of the intellect not controlled by human affection. B. B. Cohen, "Emerson's 'The Young American' and Hawthorne's 'The Intelligence Office' " (*AL,* 1954), argues that Hawthorne and Emerson were mutually more influential, notably between 1842 and 1844, than has been noticed. Cohen details their meetings, and is particularly impressed—quite possibly overly impressed—by the duplication of certain ideas in the works mentioned. His suggestion that Emerson was "the seeker" in "The Intelligence Office" is based upon only slightly better evidence than his belief that the two men influenced one another.

Several other recent studies of a particularly fruitful sort similarly concentrate on Hawthorne's attitudes concerning specific nineteenth-century psychological and philosophical concepts. D. A. Ringe, "Hawthorne's Psychology of the Head and Heart" (*PMLA,* 1950), takes a phrase from Matthiessen as his title and his starting point. Ringe attempts to discover Hawthorne's attitude towards the problem of sin and the Fall of Man by examining the characters in a number of stories and romances in terms of a prevalent psychology. His suggestion, very persuasively documented, is that while one solution was shown to lie in a balance between head and heart (as in the case of Holgrave), another was suggested as superior (as in the case of Hester): "If man is to develop the noblest qualities of mind and heart and so achieve true and profound insight into the problem of human existence, he must sin, incur the perilous state of isolation and sacrifice whatever happiness can be achieved in a troubled world." Both of these solutions, Ringe holds, were presented in *The Marble Faun,* the former in the story of Kenyon and Hilda and the latter in that of Donatello and Miriam. H. S. Kariel, in "Man Limited: Nathaniel Hawthorne's Classicism" (*SAQ,* 1953), asserts that the author consistently spoke out in opposition to the widespread faith of the day in man's ability to achieve perfection in knowledge, behavior, or art: "He worked . . . with the drama of man's contentions and conflicts, with man divided, man torn between his vision of evil and his knowledge of perfection." R. R. Male, Jr., has published two revealing articles which, as he puts it, "examine part of the climate of opinion in Hawthorne's time in connection with a detailed study of his work." "Hawthorne and the Concept of Sympathy" (*PMLA,* 1953) suggests that the writer's preoccupation with the concept was not simply the result of his isolation: it was also "amplified and crystallized by the ideas which had also affected, in varying degrees, the German and English Romanticists." Male's analysis of a number of Hawthorne's symbols and characters offers convincing proof that the writer fully accepted a number of the widespread ideas concerning a concept which was "admirably suited to the sensibilities of an age," and explicitly rejected others. The same author's " 'From the Innermost Germ': The Organic Principle in Hawthorne's Fiction" (*ELH,* 1953) offers evidence to prove that "the organic principle, justly held to be the very root of Romanticism in America, is an essential aspect in Hawthorne's fiction and one which complements his tragic sense; that in viewing the New England past in terms of the organic-mechanical antithesis he was illuminating a crucial social problem of his own time; and finally that in two of his less successful works he was dealing specifically, albeit in his own way, with moral problems related to nineteenth-century evolutionary theory."

2. *Social and Political Ideas*

G. P. Lathrop and Julian Hawthorne saw Hawthorne as a sort of split personality: as a man of affairs, he was said to have proved himself practical and efficient, but as an artist he held himself aloof from contemporary problems. For some time, students following the lead of these biographers tended to believe that the aloofness was not confined to Hawthorne's art, and several defended his detachment—for instance, James and Woodberry. But beginning with Brownell in 1909, a number of writers held that he was uninformed about the society and the politics of his day and that his work was weakened as a result. Herbert Gorman, Lloyd Morris, and V. L. Parrington in 1927—the last in his chapter on Hawthorne in *Main Currents in American Thought*—all so condemned him. Parrington, sympathetic as he was to authors who fought the battles of their day, was particularly sharp in his summary: "He was the extreme and finest expression of the refined alienation from reality that in the end palsied the creative mind of New England." When, a little later, historians writing from the Marxist standpoint discussed Hawthorne, they were at least equally stern. V. F. Calverton, in *The Liberation of American Literature* (1932), saw him as "almost an alien" in his own country, interested in the past and indifferent to the future. Granville Hicks, in *The Great Tradition* (1933), felt that he was a great artist who had lost his importance because he ignored the life around him.

Long before, however, as has been indicated in a previous section (p. 108), authors such as J. B. Osborne, G. E. Jepson, and W. S. Nevins had begun to furnish details for a new portrait —one which showed Hawthorne as much more aware of society and politics than had been thought. In 1932, Randall Stewart published "Hawthorne and Politics: Unpublished Letters to William B. Pike" (*NEQ*), offering proof that the author had not been passive in politics. It was the first of several articles and grist for the biography in which Stewart was to give many specific instances of Hawthorne's political and social awareness. (See p. 110.) Manning Hawthorne's "Hawthone and Utopian Socialism: Two Letters Written to David Mack" (*NEQ,* 1939) unearthed comments which were relevant to the Brook Farm experiment and his preference for another way of living.

N. F. Doubleday shortly afterward published three articles which were relevant. His "Hawthorne's Hester and Feminism" (*PMLA,* 1939) re-examined *The Scarlet Letter* to make the sound point that here—as in the later characterization of Zenobia—Hawthorne was attacking the mid-century feminist movement for failure to recognize the true nature of women. His article, "Hawthorne's Criticism of New England Life" (*CE*, 1941), holds that *The House of the Seven Gables* and *The Blithedale Romance* both offer disproof of "the conventional notion that Hawthorne was isolated from contemporary life." These novels, like others and like several tales, showed that although he was not a spokesman for the spirit of the time, he was an objective and shrewd critic of some aspects of the American scene. The third article, "Hawthorne's Satirical Allegory" (*CE,* 1942), concentrated upon the eight tales and sketches of the years in the Old Manse. Doubleday found that these pieces showed a real interest in contemporary social issues and that some of them at least, in their own terms, had great merit as satires.

A year later, in 1942, Arlin Turner's "Hawthorne and Reform" (*NEQ),* specifically refuted the scholars who had claimed that Hawthorne was indifferent to contemporary affairs. In 1944, L. S. Hall's book-length study, *Hawthorne: Critic of Society,* offered even more decisive refutation of the earlier view. Examining a great deal of evidence, much of it for the first time, Hall found that Hawthorne was keenly aware of the problems of the day and that he studied them and took his stand. He was an admirer of Jackson, a friend of equalitarian society and *laissez-faire* government, and he aligned himself with the Young Americans. He was, moreover, an active and practical politician. Hall's final chapter of the book, "The Social Ethic," considered the themes of the major romances as well as many shorter works in relationship to the author's views. Hall claimed that Hawthorne's works "represent . . . about the most satisfactory expression in art of the basic morality of the democratic life." In 1946, H. W. Schneider, in *A History of American Philosophy,* drew upon Arvin, Morris, and Hall to arrive at a synthesis of the views of all three. Like Arvin and Morris, he saw in the author a fierce conflict arising from his admiration for British aristocratic ways of living; but concluded that he should be denoted not a "conservative" Democrat or a "radical" Democrat, but a "pure" Democrat, "a man of the people." And in 1948, Stewart, in his biography, authoritatively traced the author's growing interest in politics—an interest stimulated particularly by his dismissal from his Salem appointment—to a time when Pierce's election caused him to become a very practical politician indeed. Stewart avoided specific labels, but argued for the belief that, despite the fact that he clearly saw weaknesses in political practices, Hawthorne held to principles which were clearly democratic.

Cantwell's conception of the author, as set forth in his biography of the same year, led him to go rather too far in his representation of the author's political activity as "active" and "vigorous" and even, when he became a secret agent, characterized by "considerable excitement and hazard." Three more recent studies which deal with the author's alleged conservatism remain to be mentioned: Russell Kirk, "The Moral Conservatism of Hawthorne" (*Contemporary Rev.,* 1952), Darrel Abel, "Hawthorne's Skepticism about Social Reform: With Special Reference to *The Blithedale Romance*" (*UKCR,* 1953), and

Morton Cronin, "Hawthorne and Romantic Love and the Status of Women" (*PMLA,* 1954).

Herbert H. Hoeltje, "The Writing of *The Scarlet Letter*" (*NEQ,* 1954), which traces Hawthorne's political relationships from 1844 to the Custom House débacle and the literary work which followed, relates both the writing of Hawthorne's masterpiece and its initial success to Hawthorne's activities in politics.

3. *Literary Theories*

Most writers on Hawthorne have had something to say about his literary theories as they affected his work, but detailed and systematic studies were not made until recently. Warren in 1934 surveyed some of Hawthorne's comments on his artistry. In 1938 Arlin Turner, in "Hawthorne as Self-Critic" (*SAQ*), considering statements the author made on many occasions, held that he was able to make "as accurate a judgment of his own writings as could be passed by any unbiassed critic now." For Hawthorne scolded himself for having qualities which critics often lamented—a love of allegory, a meagerness of detail, and a darkness of outlook too infrequently relieved. But Turner notes that despite his awareness of such tendencies, Hawthorne did not change his ways, probably because he realized that his manner of seeing life, his experience, and his beliefs forced him to write as he did.

Turner mentions that "much of Hawthorne's self-abasement . . . was intended as obvious understatement." In the years that followed, as students became increasingly sympathetic towards Hawthorne's aims, methods and achievements, they paid more and more attention to the ironic tone of the author's talk about his "faults" and noticed that much self-criticism actually constituted a justification. Matthiessen's *American Renaissance* (1941), which conscientiously surveyed statements concerning the author's intentions and procedures, is often favorable at points where previous critics were critical. And not only does Matthiessen notice how the author's peculiar sensibility directed the working of a fine imagination, he also relates his ideas about literature to those of his great Transcendental neighbors. In 1941, also, N. F. Doubleday published an article, "Hawthorne and Literary Nationalism," in *AL,* which discusses Hawthorne's relationship to a group larger than the Transcendentalists. This was the group of authors who, in the early nineteenth century, urged authors to try to achieve in America what Scott had achieved in Scotland. Doubleday cites both Hawthorne's comments and his early historical fiction to show his awareness of the movement.

Probably the meatiest and most useful general survey of Hawthorne's literary belief to date is Charles Foster, "Hawthorne's Literary Theory" (*PMLA,* 1942). Foster notes that the chief purpose of literature, in Hawthorne's view, is the conveying of spiritual truth. This involves an idealization of life which nature initiates but which the author has to complete by "carrying out the tendencies of nature in an imaginative realm." It does not, so Hawthorne held, mean that art escapes from reality: it means that the idealization is so shaped as to convey unusual truth—a value deeper than reality itself provides. The shaping takes the form of modifications of the external world, events and human experience in the service of allegory and symbolism. Foster discusses, finally, the author's concept of the artist and his task. The artist, Hawthorne held, needs intellect and emotion as attributes; he needs also to be able to respond to inspiration. And the task of the artist, in Hawthorne's view, is to live within his age, to comprehend it, and to so work and discipline himself as to realize his capabilities. Foster perhaps oversystematizes Hawthorne's beliefs, and may well overestimate their uniqueness; but his excellent summary of them is intelligently set forth and well documented.

Two useful studies deal with Hawthorne's theories about writing at specific times. N. F. Adkins, "The Early Projected Works of Nathaniel Hawthorne" (*PBSA,* 1945), calls attention to Hawthorne's plans from the start of his career onward to write works which had more coherence than those which he published before 1850—*Seven Tales of My Native Land, Provincial Tales, The Story Teller, Allegories of the Heart* and, later, *Old Time Legends, Together with Sketches, Experimental and Ideal.* The author's comments upon these abandoned collections, each more unified than a miscellaneous collection of tales, throw much light upon Hawthorne's intentions as an author, his way of thinking about his work, and his movement toward longer works. The second of these studies, R. H. Pearce's "Hawthorne and the Twilight of Romance" (*YR,* 1948), discusses the effect of a change which Pearce believes took place in Hawthorne's critical theory when he wrote *The Marble Faun.* The earlier belief, so Pearce claims, is that the aim of romance is conveying moral truth, while the later concept places more emphasis upon a suitable atmosphere—on matter rather than means. This—and the unfortunate shift away from the New England scene which he knew so well to a foreign scene which he did not know well—accounted for the falling off evident in *The Marble Faun.* Pearce makes some valid and illuminating points about the importance of Hawthorne's experience to his success, though a careful reading of the author's earlier passages, particularly of the "moonlit room" passage in "The Custom House" and the Preface to *The House of the Seven Gables,* would seem to indicate that Hawthorne's belief was that both means and matter ("fashion and material" to use his terms) are equally important in his concept of romance before *The Marble Faun,* and it may be argued that the Preface to his final completed novel differs less in its theory than Pearce holds it does.

V. Criticism

1. *Studies of Sources*

Critics of Hawthorne's sketches, tales, and romances have chiefly written about two topics, their sources and their artistry. Discussions of the first of these topics have not always excluded concern with the second. Students of Hawthorne's sources, fortunately, have at times contributed to an appreciation of the man's skill as an author.

Randall Stewart, in the "Introductory Essays" to his edition of *The American Notebooks* (1932), notices that the author's writings derived from three main sources—the notebooks, reading, and Hawthorne's own fiction. Each of these three sorts of sources has been studied by a number of scholars, with varying results. Stewart's discussion is admirable in that often, as in his remarks on *The Scarlet Letter,* he thoroughly explores the diverse sources of the writings and considers how a comparison of sources with the works illuminates Hawthorne's artistry. Another survey of varied types of sources, Arlin Turner's "Hawthorne's Methods of Using His Source Material," in *Studies for W. A. Read* (1940), compares notes in the journals with finished works. Turner fully documents his claim that the author began with a "central theme or basic idea" suggested by personal experiences, reading, or (most often) independent speculations. The author's next task was to find illustrations for the concepts. Turner notes how in many instances meaning and materials are developed as "catalogues" or "processions" presented in a deliberately represented atmosphere which removes happenings from actuality and underlines meanings. These two scholarly considerations illustrate—as too few similar ones do—source studies at their best and most complete. Too many other studies fail to prove that alleged sources are indeed sources, and more fail to show by comparisons how and why the artist molded his materials to his purposes.

An early investigation of biographical sources is Anton Schönbach's "Beiträge zur Charakteristik Nathaniel Hawthornes" (*Englische Studien,* 1884). In a sixty-four-page study, the author makes use of Hawthorne's posthumously published romances to generalize about his methods of writing, and relates the completed romances and the tales to relevant passages in the notebooks.

A briefer but useful and highly suggestive survey is Amy Louise Reed's "Self-Portraiture in the Work of Nathaniel Hawthorne" *(SP,* 1926), which notes how the author pictured himself both as he was and as he feared he might be in both his heroes and his villains, and which gives particular attention to Coverdale, Holgrave, and Kenyon. A similar line of inquiry is carried further—possibly somewhat too far—in perhaps the most valuable part of the Editor's Introduction to *The Portable Hawthorne,* by Malcolm Cowley (1948). The essay also offers perceptive comments on Hawthorne's training for writing and his literary procedures. A recent study holding that characters represent different facets of Hawthorne's character and expiate his feelings of guilt is the highly conjectural *"The Scarlet Letter:* One Hundred Years After," by J. E. Hart in *NEQ* (1950).

P. E. Burnham, in "Hawthorne's *Fanshawe* and Bowdoin College" (*EIHC,* 1944), relates the author's first book to his college and his experiences there. The three works most obviously based on Hawthorne's experiences—a tale and two romances—have naturally been much discussed in biographies and biographical studies. The notebook passages dealing with Hawthorne's stay in North Adams, germinal to "Ethan Brand," are related to the story by Bliss Perry, "Hawthorne at North Adams," published in both the *Atlantic* (1893) and in *The Amateur Spirit* (1904). Like Miss Reed and Cowley, Perry sees the narrative shaped not only by men and events from actuality but also by Hawthorne's concept of his own personality. The suggestion made by Lewis Mumford in *Herman Melville* (1929)—that Ethan's character derived from Melville—is ably refuted by Randall Stewart in a note, "Ethan Brand" (*SRL,* 1929). From the start, there has been much discussion of the precise extent to which actuality entered into *The Blithedale Romance.* To what degree was Coverdale a self-portrait? More important, to what extent was Zenobia a copy of Margaret Fuller? From first reviewers to today's scholars, practically all readers have agreed that the New England bluestocking provided details in the characterization. (An interesting exception was Emerson, in his lecture, "Historic Notes of Life and Letters in New England," delivered in 1880.) A minority holds that Zenobia was a satirical representation of Miss Fuller. This is argued by Margaret's nephew, Frederick Fuller, in "Hawthorne and

Margaret Fuller Ossoli" (*Literary World,* 1885), and by Oscar Cargill, in "Nemesis and Nathaniel Hawthorne" (*PMLA,* 1937). Most students hold that Zenobia was a characterization based upon certain details in Miss Fuller's character greatly modified by Hawthorne's imagination. Arlin Turner so argues in "Autobiographical Elements in Hawthorne's *The Blithedale Romance,*" University of Texas *SE* (1935), as do two replies to Cargill's article, one by Austin Warren (*PMLA,* 1939), and one by W. P. Randal (*AL,* 1939). Lina Bohmer, *Brookfarm und Hawthornes Blithedale Romance,* published in Jena in 1936, in addition to studying Zenobia and Miss Fuller, elaborately analyzes correspondences between book and journal and argues, not very persuasively, that the book should be read more as an autobiographical record than as fiction. N. H. Pearson, in his as yet unpublished edition of *The Italian Notebooks,* offers the best discussion of the author's European experiences in relation to *The Marble Faun.* This, as well as passages by Stewart, Davidson, and Matthiessen on Hawthorne abroad, is used by Christof Wegelin in his study, "Europe in Hawthorne's Fiction" (*ELH,* 1947). Wegelin documents the interesting point that Europe became literary capital for Hawthorne only after he himself had been abroad.

Discussions of literary sources fall into three groups, one group dealing with Hawthorne's reading, one with those sources which influenced procedures or materials in a number of works, and one centering attention on specific works and their sources. The best studies of the author's reading, in the order of their appearance, have been Austin Warren, "Hawthorne's Reading" (*NEQ,* 1935) and M. L. Kesselring, "Hawthorne's Reading, 1828-1850" (*BNYPL,* 1949). The latter, which revises a study published in *EIHC* in 1932, is the more inclusive.

An early discussion of an author held to be influential is T. W. Higginson, "A Precursor of Hawthorne" (*Independent,* 1888). Higginson argues convincingly that William Austin's famous short story "Peter Rugg" (1824) originally suggested Hawthorne's oft-used device of providing alternative explanations of happenings between which readers might choose. P. E. More, "The Origins of Hawthorne and Poe," *Independent* (1902) and *Shelburne Essays,* 1st Series (1904), lists as influences historical witchcraft and the writings of Cotton Mather, Wigglesworth, Edwards, Freneau ("The House of Night"), and C. B. Brown. The group had in common a concern with "the weirder phenomena of life," which, says More, fascinated both Hawthorne and Poe. A number of influences are considered by Elizabeth L. Chandler in Smith College Studies in Modern Language, VII—*A Study of the Sources of the Tales and Romances Written by Nathaniel Hawthorne before 1853* (1926). Miss Chandler's scholarship is sound, and the contribution to knowledge she has made is important. G. H. Orians, "New England Witchcraft in Fiction" (*AL,* 1930), necessarily deals with Hawthorne's sources among the older chroniclers. Tremaine McDowell's "Nathaniel Hawthorne and the Witches of Colonial Salem" appeared in *NEQ* in 1934. Randall Stewart, "Hawthorne and *The Faerie Queene*" (*PQ,* 1933), finds some very significant relationships which probably merit even more detailed discussion than he gives them. Arlin Turner, "Hawthorne's Literary Borrowings" (*PMLA,* 1936), is inclusive and persuasive. Hazel T. Emry, "Two Houses of Pride: Spenser's and Hawthorne's" (*PQ,* 1954), makes a rather unconvincing case for the influence of a passage in *The Faerie Queene* upon *The House of the Seven Gables.* Alice L. Cooke, "Some Evidences of Hawthorne's Indebtedness to Swift," University of Texas *SE* (1938) defines the New England author's attitudes towards the eighteenth-century writer and holds that Swift was influential on "ideas and literary patterns" in six of his shorter works—"Dr. Heidegger," "The New Adam and Eve," "Earth's Holocaust," "A Select Party," "The Hall of Fantasy" and "The Pygmies." Quaker lore is investigated by M. J. Griswold, in "American Quaker History in the Works of Whittier, Hawthorne and Longfellow," *Americana* (1940). J. C. Mathews, "Hawthorne's Knowledge of Dante" appeared in University of Texas *SE* in 1940. N. F. Doubleday, "Hawthorne's Inferno"

(*CE,* 1940), also deals with the author's acquaintance with Dante and reveals telling resemblances between the treatments by the two authors of the sin of pride. A ten-page chapter in J. P. Pritchard's *Return to the Fountains: Some Classical Sources of American Criticism* (1942) discusses the relatively few influences of classical literary critics upon Hawthorne's theories about literature. Frank Davidson, "Hawthorne's Hive of Honey; a Few Specific Influences of Shakespeare and Milton" (*MLN,* 1946), briefly discusses, in addition to the authors mentioned in the title, Sir Thomas Browne and the Bible, and notices specific influences on "Earth's Holocaust," "The New Adam and Eve," and "Rappaccini's Daughter."

Jane Lundblad in 1946 published *Nathaniel Hawthorne and the Tradition of Gothic Romance,* No. 4 of a series issued by the American Institute of the University of Uppsala—Essays and Studies on American Language and Literature. This matter is incorporated, with a few changes, in a broader study, *Nathaniel Hawthorne and European Literary Traditions,* issued as No. 6 in the same series in 1947. Here, the opening chapters stress continental influences on Hawthorne's reading, his life, and his work. Miss Lundblad then considers, in turn, three literary traditions—the Gothic romance, Mme de Staël, and Balzac. In discussing the first of these, the author deals with twelve common Gothic devices and considers their occurrence in fifteen tales, four romances, and four fragments. Turning to de Staël Miss Lundblad argues that this French writer shaped Hawthorne's depiction of the passionate and exotic type of woman whom he portrayed frequently. Balzac is held to be influential on Hawthorne's ideas on art and architecture and perhaps his depiction of the cold-hearted villain. N. F. Doubleday's "Hawthorne's Use of Three Gothic Patterns" (*CE,* 1946) is an outstanding study of certain aspects of the Gothic tradition. It emphasizes at the outset the fact that Hawhorne's following of the tradition, instead of proving the author morbid or lacking in invention, showed his awareness of a contemporary literary vogue and his remarkable ability—at his best—to adapt conventions to his own requirements as a romance writer. Doubleday then considers, with many insights, his author's adaptation—with varying success—of mysterious portraits (in "The Prophetic Pictures," "Edward Randolph's Portrait," and *The House of The Seven Gables*); witchcraft (in "Alice Doane's Appeal," "The Hollow of the Three Hills," "Young Goodman Brown," and *The Scarlet Letter*); the Wandering Jew, elixir of life and allied occult experiments (in "Dr. Heidegger's Experiment," "Rappaccini's Daughter," and "Ethan Brand"). Frank Davidson turns to a very different source in "Hawthorne's Use of a Pattern from the *Rambler*" (*MLN,* 1948), which discusses the use of the eighteenth-century catalogue form in "A Select Party," "The Hall of Fantasy," and "The Christmas Banquet." He finds, in addition, that other essays by Johnson are echoed in "The Intelligence Office" and "A Virtuoso's Collection." Other useful source studies include: B. B. Cohen, "Hawthorne and Legends," (*Hoosier Folklore,* 1948); Millicent Bell, "Melville and Hawthorne at the Grave of St. John (A Debt to Pierre Bayle)" (*MLN,* 1952); W. S. Johnson, "Hawthorne and *The Pilgrim's Progress*" (*JEGP,* 1951); and G. H. Orians, "Hawthorne and Puritan Punishments" (*CE,* 1952).

The most ambitious discussion of a single body of source material as it was operative in Hawthorne's writings appeared in 1953—W. B. Stein, *Hawthorne's Faust: A Study of the Devil Archetype.* "A simple mythic formula based on the devil-archetype," so the thesis of this study goes, "provides Hawthorne with the medium of inquiry into the riddle of good and evil." The formula is that of the Faustian story—"the devil image," "the diabolic pact" whereby a soul is bartered for superhuman knowledge, the ordeal of sin, and the role of the principle of evil in the scheme of things. The legend, so Stein claims, may have come from various sources. Of these, the Mathers, the "Faust Chapbook," Marlowe, and what is Stein's favorite candidate, Goethe, are not argued for with conclusive persuasiveness. However, as Stein holds, the Faustian elements might well have been drawn from other works; and Gothic romancers such as Beckford, Godwin, Maturin, and "Monk" Lewis, all cited, were demonstrably influential. The author's subsequent effort to "disclose the unbroken continuity of Hawthorne's art and thought" from *Fanshave* through the unfinished romances makes possible his disclosing several interrelationships and developments in the author's thought. Though some of the philosophical readings are oversystematic or overingenious and all need to be carefully checked, the book says important things about the development of Hawthorne's thought and of the artistry with which he expressed it.

Many studies are concerned with the sources of individual works. Arranged alphabetically according to the title of the work discussed, the most useful of these include: B. B. Cohen, "The Sources of 'The Ambitious Guest' " (*BPLQ,* 1952); Frank Davidson, "Voltaire and Hawthorne's 'The Christmas Banquet' " (*BPLQ,* 1951); Louise Hastings, "An Origin for 'Dr. Heidegger's Experiment' " (*AL,* 1938); N. F. Doubleday, "The Theme of Hawthorne's 'Fancy's Show Box' " (*AL,* 1938); G. T. Little, "Hawthorne's *Fanshawe* and Bowdoin's Past" (*Bowdoin Quill,* 1904); G. H. Orians, "Scott and Hawthorne's *Fanshawe*" (*NEQ,* 1938); J. S. Goldstein, "The Literary Sources of Hawthorne's *Fanshawe*" (*MLN,* 1945); Alfred Kern, "The Sources of Hawthorne's 'Feathertop' " (*PMLA,* 1931); M. Jane Griswold, "American Quaker History in the Works of Whittier, Hawthorne, and Longfellow" ["The Gentle Boy"] (*Americana,* 1940); G. H. Orians, "The Sources and Themes of Hawthorne's 'The Gentle Boy' " (*NEQ,* 1941); idem, "The Angel of Hadley in Fiction: A Study of the Source of Hawthorne's 'The Gray Champion' " (*AL,* 1932); K. G. Pfeiffer, "The Prototype of the Poet in 'The Great Stone Face' " (*Res. Studies of the State Coll. of Wash.,* 1941); T. M. Griffiths, *Maine Sources in "The House of the Seven Gables"* (1945)—an expansion of an article, " 'Montpelier' and 'Seven Gables': Knox's Estate and Hawthorne's Novel" (*NEQ,* 1943); Fannye N. Cherry, "A Note on the Source of Hawthorne's 'Lady Eleanore's Mantle' " (*AL,* 1935); L. A. Haselmeyer, "Hawthorne and the Cenci" (*The*

Marble Faun), Neophilologus (1941); Nathalia Wright, "Hawthorne and the Praslin Murder" (*The Marble Faun*) (*N&Q,* 1942); G. H. Orians, "Hawthorne and 'The Maypole of Merry Mount' " (*MLN,* 1938); Darrel Abel, "Le Sage's Limping Devil and 'Mrs. Bullfrog' " (*NEQ,* 1953); Alice L. Cooke, "The Shadow of Martinus Scriblerus in Hawthorne's 'The Prophetic Pictures' " (*NEQ,* 1944); G. H. Orians, "The Sources of Hawthorne's 'Roger Malvin's Burial' " (*AL,* 1938); D. S. Lovejoy, "Lovewell's Flight and Hawthorne's 'Roger Malvin's Burial' " (*NEQ,* 1954); Herbert Read, "Hawthorne" *(The Scarlet Letter)* (*H&H,* 1930); Fannye N. Cherry, "The Sources of Hawthorne's 'Young Goodman Brown' " (*AL,* 1934).

These studies of individual sources or of sources of particular works vary greatly, of course, in their value. Some make pretty doubtful cases for indebtedness, depending upon tenuous farfetched parallels. An instance is T. M. Griffiths' study of the sources of *The House of the Seven Gables.* Here the author moves from the probability that the Pyncheons' legendary holdings are identifiable with the Waldo patent in Maine to the highly improbable identification of the Knox mansion with the House and the equally dubious identification of characters in the novel in fantastic detail with members of the Waldo, Flucker, and Knox families who successively held the grant. Most source studies, fortunately, have been sounder in their arguments for indebtedness; but too few have much of value to say about the author's adaptation of his sources. Miss Chandler, in one of the early studies, despite the soundness of her demonstrations of indebtedness and the value of her findings, regrettably attempted no specific consideration of her author's manipulation of his source materials. When the needed additional step was taken, as I have indicated above, by Doubleday in his study of Hawthorne's use of certain Gothic patterns, the value of the article was greatly enhanced. Even some sources which have been discussed at length, therefore, may still be so studied as to yield important insights into Hawthorne's literary procedures and artistry.

2. *Evaluations and Analyses*

From his own day down to the present Hawthorne has often been fortunate in his critics. Such contemporaries as Poe, Melville, and Whipple took him seriously enough to write carefully formulated discussions of him; and later a number of perceptive readers, not the least of whom was Henry James, wrote at length about him. The discussions of his writings may be most usefully classified and discussed under two headings: those which dealt with a large number or all of the author's works, and those which dealt with individual works.

Though Poe, who wrote an early criticism of a large number of works, died in 1849, before Hawthorne's first novel appeared, he evidently followed the writer's early career with interest, and he wrote about him on four occasions. His famous review of the second edition of *Twice-Told Tales* appeared in two issues of *Graham's Magazine* in 1842; he wrote a paragraph on Hawthorne in "Marginalia," *Democratic Review* (1844), and another in "Author's Introduction" to *The Literati of New York, Godey's Magazine* (1846); and he reviewed *Twice-Told Tales* and *Mosses from an Old Manse* in an article for *Godey's Lady's Book,* "Tale Writing: Nathaniel Hawthorne," in 1847. All four of these criticisms were laudatory, but the last differed interestingly from the first. The first contains the highest praise: it says that Hawthorne's distinctive trait is "invention, creation, imagination, originality—a trait which in the literature of fiction, is worth all the rest." And Hawthorne shows originality in both "tone" and materials. The last holds that Hawthorne was not "original"—merely "peculiar," and his peculiarity, unfortunately, derived largely from an infinite fondness for allegory which showed itself in far too large a proportion of his tales. Scholars have puzzled over the change in Poe's evaluation. H. M. Belden, in "Poe's Criticism of Hawthorne," *Anglia* (1901), suggests that Poe had come to believe, between 1842 and 1847, that Hawthorne, instead of originating his way of writing, had copied the German writer, Tieck: hence he could not be genuinely original. Miss Faust suggests that the difference is accounted for by the different subject matter of Poe's two articles. Stewart suggests that Poe changed his mind because he felt, with some justice, that Hawthorne—as a writer of tales—had somewhat deteriorated during his years in the Old Manse. Another possibility is that Poe's theories about literature had undergone change—a possibility that is supported when one notes that in the four discussions there is a growing emphasis upon Poe's disapproval of the monotony of tone and the mysticism or allegory in the tales, and the last speaks of a sort of originality not before discussed —of effect. Whatever the cause, Poe, in condemning Hawthorne's use of allegory, strikes a note which is to be echoed by critics for a long time. Allegory, he says, is a product of the fancy (rather than the higher imaginative faculty), and its appeals are made to the fancy—"that is to say, to our sense of adaptation, not of matters proper, but of matters improper for the purpose, of the real with the unreal. . . . The deepest emotion aroused within us by the happiest allegory, as allegory, is a very imperfectly satisfied sense of the writer's ingenuity in overcoming a difficulty we should have preferred his not having attempted to overcome." Allegory, Poe continues, can not be made to enforce a truth and if it ever establishes a fact it does so by overturning a fiction: even the best allegory interferes with the unity of effect for which the artist should strive. Only when the suggested meaning is an undercurrent, so Poe holds—only when it is shadowy and unobtrusive—can it fail to injure vitally "earnestness or verisimilitude" in fiction. Hence Poe advises Hawthorne to break away from the American transcendental influences which, erroneously, he believed had encouraged him to allegorize.

The next of the great American authors to discuss Hawthorne at length was Herman Melville. He wrote a lengthy review, "Hawthorne and His Mosses" in *The Literary World* (1850), and in 1851 he playfully reviewed *The House of the Seven Gables* in a letter to Hawthorne, first printed in *Nathaniel Hawthorne and His Wife*. Both critiques have been frequently reprinted, but perhaps they are most easily accessible in *Herman Melville: Representative Selections . . .*, ed. Willard Thorp (AWS, 1938). Melville was less interested in discussing Hawthorne's art—he says nothing about allegory—than the personality and the philosophy revealed by the writings. He writes metaphorically, praising Hawthorne for "the sunlight" in his writings—his humor and warmth—but praising him even more for "the great power of blackness in him"—his sense of the tragic in life which made possible his setting forth deep truths. Melville, who was himself not unaffected by the plea for a national literature, also expresses patriotic pride in the fact that America has produced such a literary genius. Like Poe's discussions, Melville's throw light upon both their subject and their author.

Another writer contemporaneous with Hawthorne—E. P. Whipple—wrote reviews of the longer romances and of one collection of tales as they appeared, and concluded with an evaluation of Hawthorne's whole career. The review of *The Scarlet Letter* appeared in *Graham's Magazine* (1850), that of *The House of the Seven Gables,* ibid. (1851), that of *The Snow Image,* ibid. (1852), that of *The Blithedale Romance,* ibid. (1852), that of *Tanglewood Tales* in *The Literary World* (1853), and that of *The Marble Faun* and the author's whole career in "Nathaniel Hawthorne," *Atlantic* (1860). The last of these was reprinted in Whipple's *Character and Characteristic Men* (1866). The articles have peculiar value, not only because Whipple was a critic of some stature but also because he was Hawthorne's personal friend and his favorite among American critics. Hawthorne left to him the decision concerning the titles of both *The Blithedale Romance* and *The Marble Faun* and called his final study "really keen and profound." From the start, Whipple emphasizes the author's depth of insight into moral laws—the profound philosophy underlying his fiction. He also writes appreciatively and specifically of his originality, of his powers of observation and of his character portrayal. And, like Hawthorne, Whipple is much interested in the author's representing the various facets of his genius, so that his stern pessimism and scepticism would be tempered by his sunnier insights.

The 1870's produced four important discussions of Hawthorne. The first was H. A. Page (pseudonym for Alexander Japp), *Memoir of Nathaniel Hawthorne* (1872). The biographical portion of this is not particularly valuable: Japp as an Englishman writing primarily for his countrymen has nothing to add to previous accounts. But the lengthy essay which follows the memoir admirably interprets and evaluates Hawthorne's writings. The second was G. P. Lathrop, *A Study of Hawthorne* (1876). Though Lathrop, as the author's son-in-law, is at least a shade too laudatory, he is an intelligent and sensitive reader and an articulate critic. He shows some of the prejudices of the time against the allegorical mode of writing, but having drawn upon Coleridge for a distinction between symbolism and allegory, he is able to initiate the discussion of aspects of Hawthorne's artistry which have been of particular interest to recent critics. Furthermore, his analyses of themes in relation to characters and happenings in tales and novels are consistently intelligent and often enlightening. The third was Anthony Trollope, "The Genius of Nathaniel Hawthorne" (*NAR,* 1879). Trollope had heard of Hawthorne's admiration for him as a writer of solid and substantial novels, "written on the strength of beef and through the inspiration of ale." He confesses that he, in turn, likes Hawthorne, though they were as different as any two authors could be. He considers several books by Hawthorne, finding them to be a strange mixture of romance and austerity. The remoteness from reality accounts for Hawthorne's "weird, mysterious, thrilling charm"; the austerity, for a pervasive melancholy endurable only because it, too, was illusory. As Trollope discusses specific works, he shows himself to be one who tends to read them, nevertheless, as if they are realistic creations: the virtues and the faults he sees derive largely from their lifelikeness or lack of it. As a result, some of his summaries sound very strange. One thing he remarks with interest is the vein of drollery, of humor, of satire, which ran through even the darkest of narratives; another is the lack of plot in most tales and novels; still another is the admirable adaptation of the author's tone when he turns from New England to Italy. Trollope shows in its most extreme form the difficulty which lovers of realism then had appreciating romances.

The fourth study, which more subtly showed the same difficulty, was particularly important—Henry James, *Hawthorne,* English Men of Letters Series (1879). This consideration of one author by another is like earlier studies in that it perhaps casts more light upon its writer than upon Hawthorne. Despite this, given its point of view, such a conscientious study by such a great literary theorist is full of insights and is bound to be influential. James, in his role as an expatriate American and a man of the world, underlines Hawthorne's provincialism and makes much of the faults and virtues arising from it. Extraordinary provinciality, he claims, was inevitable for anyone living in New England in the early nineteenth century. The trait drove a man inward and led him, too often, to the excessive use of symbols, conceits and overelaborated allegory. James is in agreement with much that Poe has said about allegory; it is, he asserts, "quite one of the lighter exercises of the imagination" which too often spoils both the form and the development of a theme or moral in a fictional work. On the other hand, James rather wistfully concedes that Hawthorne benefits from his close tie with a section and a country, for his sense of the past and his temperament so definitely derive from his background that both consciously and unconsciously he perforce saturates his writings with local and national flavorings. Indirectly as a rule, since—James repeatedly emphasizes—Hawthornc is not at all a realist, he writes fictional works in which at least half the interest or virtue resides in their impregnation with New England air. Moreover, Hawthorne's past and upbringing made the Puritan conscience his natural heritage. And though (so James thinks—pretty surely erroneously) Hawthorne himself took little stock in Puritan dogma, this old moral sense, this old awareness of sin and hell, lodged in this man of imagination and fancy, stimulate his fancy to manipulate them, to see and utilize their artistic possibilities for entertainment and irony. A very fortunate result, so James feels, is that Hawthorne, at his best, plumbs below surfaces to write—with great artistry—stories and novels which are moral, whose purpose is moral, and which (though James does not say this) therefore resemble those of James in their fundamental aims. Basing his discussion on these partly sound, partly unsound premises, James has brilliant things to say about many of the tales and the novels.

N. Dhaleine, *N. Hawthorne, sa vie et son œuvre,* which appeared in 1905, is interesting as a meaty, generally sound discussion of Hawthorne from the French point of view. It contains acute analyses of the tales and novels, worked into a biography. And it concludes with a series of six chapters on different aspects of the works—the author's style, his intentions as a fiction writer, his methods, his backgrounds, his characters, and his handling of the problem of evil. It is a workmanlike and solid, though hardly inspired, doctoral dissertation written for the University of Paris.

More challenging is W. C. Brownell's chapter, "Hawthorne," in *American Prose Masters* (1909), which caustically attacks the author and, despite its urbanity, shows many signs of exasperation. Hawthorne, according to this critic, wrote one great book, *The Scarlet Letter,* a truly imaginative creation. Otherwise he frittered away his talents, employing his fancy instead of his imagination to mingle bad allegory with worse symbolism. Allegory, according to Brownell's standards, rises to the level of art only when "its representation is as imaginatively real as its meaning." Hawthorne's typical allegory is not, for this critic, imaginatively real: a product of the author's uncontrolled fancy, it lacks the substance of reality. And since Hawthorne is a fatalist in art (as in morality) instead of struggling against his vicious habits, he cultivates them. Brownell thus repeats and enlarges on criticisms which are typical of his period, distinguishing between Hawthorne as imaginative writer and as fanciful writer, and disqualifying most of his fiction because of its lack of reality. Many modern readers will not be so sure of Hawthorne's lack of seriousness, or so prejudiced against his failure to write realistically.

Yvor Winters, in "Maule's Curse, or Hawthorne and the Problem of Allegory," published in the *American Review* (1937) and in the volumes, *Maule's Curse* (1938) and *In Defense of Reason* (1948), condemns Hawthorne's shorter writings because they lack meaning, or they lack reality, or having both meaning and reality (e.g., "The Minister's Black Veil") they seem incapable of justifying the intensity of the author's method. Turning to the longer works, Winters finds *The Scarlet Letter* faultless in scheme and detail. It is faultless because it is pure allegory and because, moreover, Hawthorne here utilizes the material for one great allegory which colonial New England provided: "By selecting sexual sin as the type of all sin, he was true alike to the exigencies of drama and of history. In the setting which he chose, allegory was realism, the idea was life itself; and his prose, always remarkable for its polish and flexibility, and stripped, for once, of all superfluity, was reduced to the living idea, it intensified pure exposition to a quality comparable in its way to that of great poetry." But having treated sin in such simplified terms and having done the best that could be done with allegory, Hawthorne perforce thereafter moved towards the novel. Incapable of developing significant themes or of creating characters, he was doomed to write impure novels in which themes and characters were both insignificant and disparate. Winters holds that Hawthorne illustrates the thesis of his book as a whole—that nineteenth-century authors traded their heritage for a mess of European romanticism, and a result was the great deterioration in their artistry and the validity of their beliefs. Winters is a brilliant though rather peremptory critic, and his perceptions here as elsewhere are of great value. But readers who do not share his disdain for certain romantic beliefs (including a loathing for Emersonianism) or his concept of artistry cannot go along with his sternest criticisms.

In its analyses of Hawthorne's novels and tales, as in its discussions of other aspects of his life and work, F. O. Matthiessen's *American Renaissance* (1941) is outstanding. Not only does this critic discuss the works in their biographical and historical context; he also analyzes individual works perceptively. Some of the best interpretations in a study which is important for any student of the author are those of "Young Goodman Brown," *The Scarlet Letter,* and *The House of the Seven Gables.*

Leland Schubert in 1944 published *Hawthorne, the Artist: Fine-Art Devices in Fiction,* which uses an unusual approach. It deals, he firmly proclaims, with form, not content. This means, he says, that he will discuss Hawthorne's work as he would "the work of any other artist, whether a painter, a sculptor, or even a musician." To do this, he picks various artistic devices, such as rhythmic motifs, color, and sound, used by painters and composers, finds devices analogous to these in Hawthorne's works, and studies in detail Hawthorne's use of such devices. He notices, for instance, that a picture is admirable "when there is a kind of balance, symmetrical or asymmetrical, within the outline." and so on. Now, of course, the parts of a picture are spatially arranged, and nothing in a fictional work exactly corresponds to such an arrangement. But vaguely similar are the successive pages or chapters of a tale or novel. Thus considering *The Scarlet Letter,* "in two parts, or in three parts or better yet in seven parts," he finds it to be "a beautifully constructed novel." He discovers the parts in different ways. The three-part division, for instance, is based on the scaffold scenes, the seven-part division on the characters in the center of the stage and what happened to them in certain chapters. Area on a canvas is thus equated, in a novel, with chapters, and a painting's forms with particular characters and their actions. Again, turning to music, Schubert finds that it may be admirable because of its "recurring use of melodies and chords." Analogous in a novel are "repeated . . . words and phrases, or colors, or masses, or whole images, or even sounds or philosophic concepts." So Schubert studies such repetitions. The present writer has developed two adverse criticisms of Schubert's approach in a review of the book (*MP,* 1944): (1) he believes that most (though not all) of the patterns Schubert discusses lack significance when they occur in literary works; (2) he believes that the divorcing of form from content makes impossible the discovery or demonstration of such significance. And he has coped with similar problems in a way he himself believes (perhaps without justification) to be somewhat more revealing in an article, "Color, Light and Shadow in Hawthorne's Fiction" (*NEQ,* 1942). Here he attempts to demonstrate that in both novels and tales Hawthorne has used color and chiaroscuro as well as other devices for one or more of three purposes—to indicate character, to emphasize narrative changes, and to articulate themes. His prejudice is based upon beliefs that (1) fiction can best be studied in its own terms rather than those of other art forms, and (2) study is most valuable when it relates fictional parts or elements to one another or to wholes.

Mark Van Doren, *Hawthorne,* American Men of Letters (1949), makes an effort to relate the author's life to his works. Van Doren believes that the warring aspects of Hawthorne's nature previously pointed out by biographers are very relevant to the writings. On the one hand, here was a man of the world, with sound sense—watchful, objective, without illusion or ardor, dubious. On the other hand, here was an unworldly poet, imaginative, mystical, capable of being moved deeply by symbolic objects, with a strong instinct to accept. In the works, the former is the man of the fancies and the sketches, the latter the romantic moralist. Both Hawthornes, Van Doren holds, are apparent, in degree, in all the writings, and the two never are made thoroughly acquainted with one another. Both are instrumental in both failures and successes. The man of the world Hawthorne too often forced his imagination to work on the world about him where it was ineffective (e.g., in *The Blithedale Romance).* This Hawthorne crippled the other, and was suspicious of his imagination. But the mystical and moral Hawthorne too often succumbed to gothicism, to melodrama, to contrivances and abstractions, to sentimentality, to vague or oversimple significations (e.g., "Egotism" and "The Great Stone Face"). At his best in allegory—for "without allegory," says Van Doren firmly, "Hawthorne was nothing"—Hawthorne wrote great tales (e.g., "Young Goodman Brown," "Rappaccini's Daughter," "The Birthmark," "Ethan Brand") and great romances (*The Scarlet Letter, The House of the Seven Gables, The Marble Faun*). His greatest allegory keeps its significations both solid and clear: it has reality in characterization and motivation; its characters are good vehicles for its ideas; its thought, brooded over and deeply pondered, is universal and complex. Van Doren, having accepted and modified some of the older biographical interpretations, interestingly adapts these to a discussion of Hawthorne's life which, psychologically, is more up to date. Similarly, he combines what seem to him sound judgments of older critics with evaluations based upon newer critical methods. Van Doren himself indicates that he is dissatisfied with the results of his attempt to span the mysterious gap between Hawthorne's life and works, perhaps because—despite all the safeguards his great common sense provides—he shares the fears of some readers that his interpretation tends to be a bit too neat. Yet his discussions of the writings, in general and in particular, in many instances are excellent.

H. H. Waggoner's Introduction to *Nathaniel Hawthorne: Selected Tales and Romances* (1950), though relatively brief, offers excellent discussions of theme and structure in a number of the tales.

Q. D. Leavis published a lengthy two-part study, "Hawthorne as Poet," in *SR* in 1951 which was intended to correct what Mrs. Leavis considered two misapprehensions of Hawthorne on the part of previous critics—as to matter, the belief that Hawthorne was aloof; as to manner, the idea that he was an allegorist. The essential Hawthorne, so Mrs. Leavis holds, was deeply involved in what he wrote, and furthermore, he was concerned about American society: he was, in fact, a sociological fiction writer. The essential Hawthorne, furthermore, was not an allegorist but a dramatic writer who conveyed his meanings by employing symbolism. To prove both claims, the critic analyzes and interprets a number of tales and book-length romances, finding that they comment upon society and that they employ poetic symbols to communicate meanings. The article is weakened by the author's lack of familiarity with much recent discussion of Hawthorne, by its need to exclude much of his writing to define what is "essential" in him, and by its failure to consider many basic and recurrent symbols. The strength of the study derives from its freshness of approach to important problems and its sensitive (though not always unique) perception and discussion of certain of the writer's symbols.

R. H. Fogle, *Hawthorne's Fiction: The Light and the Dark* (1953), draws together and augments a group of articles which the author previously had published in various learned journals. He argues for his belief that Hawthorne is a great writer in absolute terms by discussing, at length, six tales and four novels and, more briefly, numerous tales and sketches and the uncompleted romances. The "light" of the title stands for clarity of design. In a typical work, "Young Goodman Brown," for instance, "the clarity is embodied in the lucid simplicity of the basic action; in the skillful foreshadowing by which the plot is bound together; in the balance of episode and scene; in the continuous use of contrast; in the firmness and selectivity of Hawthorne's pictorial composition; in the carefully arranged climactic order of incident and tone; in the detachment and irony of Hawthorne's attitude; and finally in the purity, the grave formality, and the rhetorical balance of the style." The "dark" stands for Hawthorne's "tragic complexity" which is achieved by complicated characterization and motivation and also by a deliberate ambiguity in the use of allegory, symbolism, and the author's commentary—all of which allow for, indeed necessitate, "multiple interpretations." Hawthorne's excellence, so Fogle argues, derives from the combination of the light and the dark so defined: "His clarity is intermingled with subtlety, his statement interfused with symbolism, his affirmation enriched with ambiguity." Such an intermingling Fogle sees as an inevitable expression of his author's psychology. Some readers, the present writer among them, will hold that some of the elements of clarity Fogle has described are overneatly formalized, and that some of the ambiguities which he admires are based upon overingenious exegesis or upon actual indecision, on Hawthorne's part, at the time certain works were written. (For detailed discussion of the second of these matters, see Leon Howard's review, *NCF,* 1953.) Nevertheless, many of the careful discussions of imagery, allegory and symbolism reveal neglected but important facets of artistry and meaning.

H. H. Waggoner, *Hawthorne, a Critical Study* (1955), a discussion avowedly similar to that of Fogle, was published too late for the detailed consideration which it deserves in the present essay.

A number of fairly recent surveys of a good share of Hawthorne's writings, although relatively brief portions of books, are valuable in one way or another for the insights which they provide. Listed chronologically, these include: S. P. Sherman, "Hawthorne: A Puritan Critic of Puritanism," *Americans* (1922); D. H. Lawrence, "Hawthorne," *Studies in Classical American Literature* (1923); H. S. Canby, "Hawthorne and Melville," *Classic Americans* (1931); P. H. Boynton, "Nathaniel Hawthorne," *Literature and American Life* (1936); Van Wyck Brooks, *The Flowering of New England 1815-1865* (1936); Carl Van Doren, "Nathaniel Hawthorne, *The American Novel,* rev. ed. (1940); S. T. Williams, "Nathaniel Hawthorne," *LHUS* (1948); George Snell, "Nathaniel Hawthorne, Bystander," *The Shapers of American Fiction, 1798-1947* (1947); Austin Warren, "Nathaniel Hawthorne," *Rage for Order* (1948); Alexander Cowie, "Nathaniel Hawthorne," *The Rise of the American Novel* (1948); Charles Feidelson, Jr., "Hawthorne," *Symbolism in American Literature* (1953).

Especially during recent years, some very useful critical studies have been those concentrating upon single works. In most of these, writers use the techniques of twentieth-century criticism to study and discuss the matter and the manner of tales and novels. The value of the findings varies; but most will be of some value and a few of great value to readers of Hawthorne. The following paragraphs list the best such discussions appearing down to the end of 1954. The order is alphabetical according to the title of the work considered in each.

H. H. Waggoner, "Hawthorne's Beginning: 'Alice Doane's Appeal' " (*UKCR,* 1950), not only analyzes an early narrative of Hawthorne but also discusses the symbols and themes typical of the author which appear in it. "The Birthmark" has been discussed on two occasions—by Cleanth Brooks, Jr., and R. P. Warren in *Understanding Fiction* (1943) and by R. B. Heilman in " 'The Birthmark': Science as Religion" (*SAQ,* 1949). The former discussion deals with the way Hawthorne wrought a sort of parable here to develop a moral, and then considers the relationship between the theme and the fictional work as a whole. Heilman accepts the findings of Brooks and Warren and examines the value of recurrent religious metaphors for enriching the meaning of the tale. Frank Davidson, "Toward a Reevaluation of *The Blithedale Romance*" (*NEQ,* 1952), holds that previous critics have failed to formulate the theme of the book properly and hence to evaluate the work satisfactorily. The book, he claims, "records the tragedy attendant on ambiguities which rise from man's false assumption that his convictions about life . . . are absolute realities." The story and several recurrent symbols, he holds, admirably develop this significant theme. H. H. Waggoner, "Hawthorne's 'Canterbury Pilgrims': Theme and Structure" (*NEQ,* 1949), thoroughly studies the rather complex symbolism in what, at first glance, seems to be a relatively slight tale. C. A. Reilly, "On the Dog's

Chasing His Own Tale in 'Ethan Brand'" (*PMLA,* 1953), makes a detailed comparison between the North Adams entry about the dog in the *Notebooks* and the passage in the story based upon it. He finds a surprising number of alterations, and demonstrates their relevance to the development of the theme of the story. Reilly's article, despite its brevity, is a good example of both enlightening source study and critical analysis. Carl Bode, "Hawthorne's *Fanshawe:* The Promising of Greatness" (*NEQ,* 1950), summarizes and augments the attacks which have been made on this first book. But Bode goes on to consider the aspects of the book which predict the author's future greatness—Hawthorne's superior handling of characters and his devotion to both character and theme at the expense of plot. Louise Dauner, "The 'Case' of Tobias Pearson: Hawthorne and the Ambiguities" (*AL,* 1950), briefly discusses "The Gentle Boy" especially in relationship to Melville's *Pierre.* S. L. Gross, "Hawthorne's Revision of 'The Gentle Boy'" (*AL,* 1954), compares the *Token* version with the final one, and finds in the changes made some valuable clues to the author's method of working and his final meaning.

Harold Orel, "The Double Symbol" (*AL,* 1951), is the first of several recent articles on *The House of the Seven Gables.* B. W. Griffith, Jr., "Hawthorne's *The House of the Seven Gables*" (*Georgia Rev.,* 1954), is an impressionistic study which is suggestive rather than convincing. Clark Griffith, "Substance and Shadow: Language and Meaning in *The House of the Seven Gables*" (*MP,* 1954), examines recurrent symbols in the book connoting substance (the present, human potentiality for good, community) and shadow (the past, sin, isolation) and relates these plausibly to a central meaning which he finds the book has. The author is largely concerned with Chapter xviii of the novel: there he finds Hawthorne using a double symbol involving light and time. The scene, he holds, is a vital one in the book and furthermore typifies the very essence of Hawthorne's literary method. Darrel Abel, "Hawthorne's House of Tradition" (*SAQ,* 1953), suggests that the novel is a poem in five movements—"an allegory of love versus self-love, of human tradition versus personal ambition and family pride, of imagination versus preoccupation with present fact."

Even in Hawthorne's day *The Marble Faun* invited analysis. Shortly after the book appeared, J. R. Lowell wrote a review in the *Atlantic* (1860) discussing the book as a fiction embodying "the most august truths of psychology, . . . the most pregnant facts of modern history, and . . . a profound parable of the development of the Christian Idea." Two other contemporaries published discussions of more than ordinary interest. Martha T. Gale, *"The Marble Faun;* An Allegory, with a Key to its Interpretation," *The New Englander* (1861), found the characters representative of various faculties as mid-century psychology defined them (Soul or Will, Miriam; Conscience or Intuitive Power, Hilda; the Reason or Intellect, Kenyon; the Animal Nature or Body, Donatello) and analyzed the happenings in these terms. The review is also of interest as a statement of objections some Calvinists at least made to Hawthorne's views as too gloomy and morbid for their taste. Elizabeth P. Peabody, the author's sister-in-law, wrote on the book in the *Atlantic* in 1868 and republished her discussion in *Last Evening with Allston and Other Papers* (1886). Miss Peabody, writing from the Transcendental point of view, found the book to contain "an interpretation of Christianity more vital than has yet been symbolized by any ritual, or systematized by any ecclesiasticism." A much more recent study, Dorothy Waples, "Suggestions for Interpreting *The Marble Faun*" (*AL,* 1941), although it disavows any attempt to psychoanalyze Hawthorne, asserts that five Freudian concepts are helpful: timelessness as characteristic of the unconscious; the connection between myth and symbol and the unconsciousness; the idea of repetition-compulsion; the idea of the death instinct; and the contest for the soul between life and death. Miss Waples writes interestingly and persuasively, but the present writer, at least, finds it difficult to use the twentieth-century psychological concepts for purposes of interpretation. Darrel Abel, "A Masque of Love and Death" (*UTQ,* 1953), finds that the various characters represent various degrees of experience and various approaches to living and that Hawthorne tried to make the book his best consideration of the problems with which he long had grappled—the personal ego in relation to the cosmic tragedy and the moral vision of life. Suggestive and valuable though the study is, it does not deal with some aspects of the book which some readers will believe demand explication. John Bricknell, "*The Marble Faun* Reconsidered" (*UKCR,* 1954), holds that this work shows the falling off of Hawthorne's artistry because it indicates he had "lost his hope" that the sinner had the power of redemption. The reading is, the present writer believes, questionable in several particulars.

Mary E. Dichmann, "Hawthorne's 'Prophetic Pictures' " (*AL,* 1951), sees the tale as a revealing of the writer's ambivalent attitude concerning the artist. On the one hand, the ideal artist is godlike in his vision; on the other, the artist is in danger of committing the greatest sin—the violation of the human heart. The critic also finds that the tale is concerned with the responsibility of the artist to society. The most damaging evidence against this plausible interpretation is to be found in Hawthorne's words at the end of the story which seem to summarize a "deep moral" which is much less complex than the meaning set forth in the article. A brief analysis of "Rappaccini's Daughter" is in R. B. West and Robert Stallman, eds. *The Art of Modern Fiction* (1949); another is in F. L. Gwynn, "Hawthorne's 'Rappaccini's Daughter' " (*NCF,* 1952). The former discusses the tale as a symbolic story dealing with innocence and evil; the latter as dealing with Hawthorne's dualism of Head versus Heart. The contrast between the two interpretations, although the terms seem quite different, is not irreconcilable. R. R. Male, Jr., "The Dual Aspects of Evil in 'Rappaccini's Daughter' " (*PMLA,* 1954), elaborately reinterprets the tale to show that it is expressive of Hawthorne's concept of the dual nature of man. Some readers may feel that what Male considers aspects of "rich irony"—if his interpretation is correct—are actually signs of Hawthorne's confusion. And some may be dubious of the part played by psychology in this study. Most, however, will find some insights of value.

Recent articles or essays analyzing *The Scarlet Letter* have been too numerous to discuss here in detail. They include Françoise Dony, "Romanticisme et Puritanisme chez Hawthorne, à propos de la 'Lettre Pourpe,'" *Etudes Anglaises* (1940); F. I. Carpenter, "Scarlet A Minus" (*CE,* 1944); J. C. Gerber, "Form and Content in *The Scarlet Letter* (*NEQ,* 1944)—republished, somewhat revised, as an introduction to the Modern Library College edition (1950); Gordon Roper, Introduction to *The Scarlet Letter and Selected Prose Works by Nathaniel Hawthorne* (1949); J. E. Harte, "*The Scarlet Letter:* One Hundred Years After" (*NEQ,* 1950); Newton Arvin, Introduction to Harper's Modern Classics edition of *The Scarlet Letter* (1950); Rudolph Von Abele, "*The Scarlet Letter:* A Reading" (*Accent,* 1951); Darrel Abel, "Hawthorne's Hester" (*CE,* 1952); idem, "The Devil in Boston" (*PQ,* 1953), on Chillingworth's role. Of these, the discussions of Gerber and Roper (which were worked out, in part, jointly) are perhaps the most comprehensive and illuminating. The second, the more thorough of the two, considers Hawthorne's creative experience preparatory to the writing of his masterpiece—his writing methods and his adaptation of popular fiction and allegory to his purposes. The author then turns to the book itself and considers it in relationship to Hawthorne's theory of Romance, as a work developing a theme, and as a form (the parts and devices in relation to the work as a whole). Finally, C. C. Walcutt, "*The Scarlet Letter* and Its Modern Critics" (*NCF,* 1953), deals with various readings of the book, classifying them as orthodox Puritan, romantic, transcendental and relativist. He then discusses various reasons for these variations—the nature of the symbolism, Hawthorne's sympathetic attitude towards his erring characters, the tendency of readers to identify themselves with the characters, and Hawthorne's contradictory basic attitude towards sin and Providence. The classification in some instances is open to question;

but the over-all distinctions drawn are useful, and the consideration of the reasons for the divergences is in general sound. Quite possibly, however, Walcutt has been too polite to mention a larger reason for disagreement—the shaping of some readings by the readers' preconceptions of what they will find.

Two other brief but suggestive analyses remain to be listed —Andrew Schiller, "The Moment and the Endless Voyage: A Study of Hawthorne's 'Wakefield' " (*Diameter,* 1951), and D. M. McKeithan, "Hawthorne's 'Young Goodman Brown': An Interpretation" (*MLN,* 1952).

3. *Discussions of Hawthorne's Influence*

The question of Hawthorne's influence has not been very carefully explored, although it may well merit exploration. There are some brief dicta on Hawthorne's influence on the short story in F. L. Pattee, *Development of the American Short Story* (1923); Malcolm Cowley, "One Hundred Years Ago: Hawthorne Set a Great New Pattern" (N.Y. *Herald-Tribune Books,* 1950), and Hershell Brickell, "What Happened to the Short Story" (*Atlantic,* 1951). None of these discussions, however, is as precise or as well-documented as one would like it to be.

The influence of Hawthorne on two American authors has been more satisfactorily discussed. Various students of Melville (e.g., Willard Thorp, Howard Vincent, and Newton Arvin) have discussed some of the details of the influence on Melville. In addition, E. G. Lueders writes persuasively about interrelationships between the two authors in "The Melville-Hawthorne Relationship in *Pierre* and *The Blithedale Romance*" (*WHR,* 1950); Randall Stewart discusses personal and literary influences in "Melville and Hawthorne" (*SAQ,* 1952); and Nathalia Wright suggests Hawthorne as the source of the fire imagery in Melville's masterpiece in "*Mosses from an Old Manse* and *Moby Dick:* The Shock of Discovery" (*MLN,* 1952). The best over-all discussion of the relationship, however, is contained in Harrison Hayford, "Melville and Hawthorne, A Biographical and Critical Study," an unpublished Yale doctoral thesis (1945). Some of Hayford's findings have been set forth in two articles by him—"The Significance of Melville's 'Agatha Letters' " (*ELH,* 1946) and "Hawthorne, Melville, and the Sea" (*NEQ,* 1946).

There have been good brief discussions, too, of Hawthorne's influence upon Henry James. F. O. Matthiessen dealt with these at various points in *American Renaissance* (1941) and in *Henry James: The Major Phase* (1946). Marius Bewley, "James's Debt to Hawthorne" (*Scrutiny,* 1949, 1950) reprinted in a book, *The Complex Fate* (1952), considered the chief novels of the earlier writer in relation to the works of James. The discussions of *The Blithedale Romance* and *The Bostonians* and of *The Marble Faun* and *The Wings of the Dove* are quite convincing; those of *What Maisie Knew* and *The Turn of the Screw* are less so.

One other study of influence remains to be mentioned—R. J. Niess, "Hawthorne and Zola—An Influence?" (*Revue de littérature comparée,* 1953), which suggests that *The Scarlet Letter* may have influenced *Thérèse Raquin.*

4

THOREAU

I. Bibliography and Text

THANKS to the careful devotion of students for something more than half a century, Thoreau seems better groomed bibliographically than many of his contemporaries. S. A. Jones's pioneer "Contribution Toward a Bibliography of Thoreau" (*Unitarian,* 1890), reprinted in his *Thoreau: A Glimpse* (1890) and expanded in his *Bibliography of Henry David Thoreau* (1894), was slightly enlarged by J. P. Anderson for the bibliography appended to H. S. Salt's *Henry David Thoreau* (1890). These early listings were superseded, however, by F. H. Allen's *Bibliography of Henry David Thoreau* (1908), supplemented by J. S. Wade's "A Contribution to a Bibliography from 1909 to 1936" (*Jour. N. Y. Entomological Soc.,* 1939), but especially by William White's "A Henry David Thoreau Bibliography, 1908-1937" (*BB,* 1938-39) and by P. E. Burnham and Carvel Collins' "Contribution to a Bibliography of Thoreau, 1938-1945" (ibid., 1946-47).

Since 1941 Walter Harding has contributed "Additions to the Thoreau Bibliography" to each issue of the *Thoreau Society Bulletin.* Helpful selective bibliographies have been prepared by Mark Van Doren in *CHAL* and by B. V. Crawford in *Henry David Thoreau: Representative Selections* (AWS, 1934). Special bibliographies include Raymond Adams' "The Bibliographical History of Thoreau's *A Week* (*PBSA,* 1949), Harding's "A Bibliography of Thoreau in Poetry, Fiction, and

Drama" (*BB,* 1943), his "A Check List of Thoreau's Lectures" (*BNYPL,* 1948), and his *A Centennial Check List of the Editions of Henry David Thoreau's* Walden (1954). Finding lists include Adams' *The Thoreau Library of Raymond Adams* (1936, supplement 1937), Viola C. White's "Check List of Thoreau Items in the Abernethy Library of Middlebury College" in *The Concord Saunterer* (1940), Harding's "The Thoreau Collection of the Pierpont Morgan Library of New York City" (*TSB,* 1947), F. B. Dedmond's "A Check List of Manuscripts Relating to Thoreau in the Huntington Library, the Houghton Library of Harvard University, and the Berg Collection of the New York Public Library" (*TSB,* 1953), and Mrs. H. W. Kent's "A Catalog of the Thoreau Collection in the Concord Antiquarian Society" (*TSB,* 1954).

Textually, Thoreau seems a little more unkempt. The bulk of his writing was issued posthumously. From 1840 through 1860 he contributed some twenty-four items in prose and verse to the *Dial* and something just over a dozen more to other periodicals. Only two volumes were published during his lifetime: *A Week on the Concord and Merrimack Rivers* (1849), in an edition of 1,000 copies printed at the author's expense, and *Walden: or Life in the Woods* (1854), published by Ticknor and Fields in an edition of 2,000 copies. During his last illness, Thoreau worked some of his lectures into essays for the *Atlantic,* where they appeared after his death, in 1862 and 1863. His literary effects, manuscripts, some letters, and thirty volumes of journals were left to his sister Sophia who, aided by Emerson, Ellery Channing, and other friends, saw to the preparation of five posthumous volumes.

Excursions in Field and Forest (1863), prefaced by a memoir by Emerson, was composed of papers collected by Sophia Thoreau from the *Dial*, the *Boston Miscellany*, the *Democratic Review,* the New York *Tribune,* and the *Atlantic. The Maine Woods* (1864), the first two of the three parts of which had appeared in the *Union Magazine* and the *Atlantic* during Thoreau's lifetime, was edited by Sophia Thoreau and Channing.

Cape Cod (1865), also edited by Sophia Thoreau and Channing, was made up in its first four chapters of materials which had appeared in *Putnam's* ten years before. *Letters to Various Persons* (1865) was prepared by Emerson, who selected from and edited the correspondence to present an austere portrait of Thoreau. *A Yankee in Canada, with Anti-Slavery and Reform Papers* (1866) contained in its first three chapters materials which had appeared in *Putnam's* in 1853, but inadvertently contained also an essay on "Prayers" from the *Dial* which Emerson had written. Thoreau's friends did their work devotedly, if not always scrupulously well.

Yet, before he had been dead five years, the best of Thoreau, with the exception of the journals, was available in print. The journals, however, were zealously guarded. "These papers are very sacred to me," wrote Sophia Thoreau in 1866, "and I feel inclined to defer giving them to the public for the present." Channing and F. B. Sanborn each used them in their biographies, but it was not until after Sophia Thoreau's death that Harrison G. O. Blake excerpted from the journals to produce *Early Spring in Massachusetts* (1881), *Summer* (1884), *Winter* (1887), and *Autumn* (1892).

These posthumous volumes, the materials rearranged and obvious errors corrected, but never apparently carefully compared again with Thoreau's manuscripts, form the basis, together with *A Week* and *Walden*, for the ten-volume Riverside edition of *The Writings of Henry David Thoreau, with Bibliographical Introductions and Full Indexes* (1893), edited by H. E. Scudder. A year later Sanborn's *Familiar Letters* was added as an eleventh volume. Then, in 1906, fourteen volumes of the *Journals*, edited by Bradford Torrey and F. H. Allen, supplanted Blake's four volumes of seasonal excerpts to make up the twenty-volume "standard" Walden edition; but, except for a few additional letters and a new distribution of the contents of some of the posthumous volumes, the text for the most part was as casually reproduced as before. R. L. Cook's brief statement of "Thoreau's Annotations and Corrections in the First

Edition of *Walden*" (*TSB,* 1953) points to some textual errors which are uncorrected even after one hundred years.

Thoreau's poems have, finally, fared better. Emerson included nine of them in the *Letters to Various Persons,* G. P. Lathrop printed another in *A Masque of Poets* (1878), and Sanborn published more in the *Commonwealth* (1863), in the *Critic* (1881), in his *Thoreau* (1882), in *Scribner's* (1895), in *The Personality of Thoreau* (1902), and elsewhere. Fifty poems were brought together in *Poems of Nature* (1895), edited by Sanborn and Salt, and the Walden edition contained "A List of the Poems and Bits of Verse Scattered Among Thoreau's Prose Writings," but it was not until 1943 that all available Thoreau verse except the poetic translations was put together by Carl Bode in the *Collected Poems by Henry Thoreau,* which appeared both in a trade and an annotated critical edition, and which Allen (*AL,* 1945) reviewed as "an admirable but not an impeccable piece of work." The letters also, faithfully collected but not always meticulously reproduced by previous editors (see Harding's "Franklin B. Sanborn and Thoreau's Letters," *BPLQ,* 1951), have been recently collected by Bode and Harding into an edition which will, when printed, contain "every available letter written by Thoreau and to Thoreau."

II. Biography

Thoreau's life was not long, he traveled little beyond Concord, and during the years of his maturity he kept a detailed account of what he found important in each day. His biography, then, might be supposed easily written. But Thoreau's journal discloses his mind, his thoughts, his observations; on matters of personal concern, the kind of detail to which biographers are attracted, he was doggedly reticent. He dramatized his ideas through unusual action, so that he became a symbol of quiet rebellion and self-sufficiency, and the center of a local legend which he did little to discourage. He used the first person perpendicular more than most men, yet he was the least inward-looking of writers. He revealed what he saw, seldom what he felt or exactly what he did. As a result, biographers of Thoreau, handicapped by a paucity of particulars, have often been satisfied with presenting him within the limits of the legend or with examining his writings for secret explanations of his actions. Reading between the lines of the record which Thoreau or his friends provided, they have written sympathetic defenses of his way of life or critical examinations of the efficacy or impotence of his ideas.

Because Thoreau has meant *Walden*, and *Walden* seems so dramatically to reveal the essence of Thoreau, much that preceded or followed the two years on Emerson's few acres has until recently been obscured, by Thoreau himself, by his friends, and inevitably by his biographers. Details of his life before or after his adventure in retirement have been remembered and recorded too often only in relation to that premature climax. Reminiscent friends have recalled events of his childhood or youth or of his post-Walden maturity which lead like spokes to a hub in explanation of the Walden experiment. Much early biographical information is untrustworthy, distorted, even contradictory. "All of the sources," Brooks Atkinson has said, "are poisoned by good intentions."

Though recent investigation has revealed important new factual material, Thoreau's life story has not yet been completely told. He has been much at the mercy of goodhearted friends, of his own or later generations, who speak with more enthusiasm than judgment. He has been used too often as a rallier of causes. His prickly character has attracted partisans, so that he has been attacked by people who did not like him, his way of life or his ideas, or who did not like his friends or his friends' enthusiasms. Almost everyone who has written about Thoreau has attempted to prove something—that he was a hermit or not a hermit, a naturalist or a humanist, a scientist or a poet, a warm man disappointed in love or a cold man for whom love in the ordinary sense had no meaning. The best biography of Thoreau is now more than half a century old. There are few present indications that a new and better one will soon be written.

Our first knowledge of Thoreau inevitably derives either directly or indirectly from Emerson's memoir, read as a eulogy at his funeral, then revised for the *Atlantic* (1862), and reprinted often since, notably as the introduction to *Excursions*, Volume X of the Riverside edition, and to Volume I of the Walden edition of the *Writings* of Thoreau. It was "such an address," said Sophia Thoreau, "as no other man could have done." Though some of her friends shared Miss Thoreau's disappointment in Emerson's emphasis on "stoical" elements of Thoreau's character, the essay is remembered today as a "beautifully poised analysis" and even, as Joseph Wood Krutch suggests, the "best thing ever written on Thoreau." It shares with Lowell's review of the *Letters* the distinction of probably having been quoted or paraphrased by succeeding commentators more often than any other single writing on Thoreau.

Bronson Alcott's "The Forester," in the *Atlantic* one month before Thoreau's death, had underlined much the same Spartan and Stoic qualities. Other early essays of biographical interest include Storms Higginson's "Henry D. Thoreau" (*Harvard Mag.,* 1862), the first posthumous article on Thoreau and the first also of recollections by men who had responded enthusiastically to Thoreau as schoolboys; G. W. Curtis' urbane reminiscences in his "Easy Chair" column (*Harper's,* 1862), and Joseph Palmer's brief sketch in the Boston *Advertiser* (1862). More interesting, though to be approached with great care as biographical fact, is Louisa May Alcott's idealized portrait of Thoreau in her first novel, *Moods* (1864), where he appears as Adam Hartwick, a self-reliant wandering scholar who "clings to principles," is "violently virtuous," and devoted to nature.

Thoreau's friends were eager that his life story should be truly told. "I ardently wish," wrote Sophia Thoreau less than a year after her brother's death, "that a faithful record of his life might be written for the profit of all men." She considered with Daniel Ricketson who could do it best. Harrison Blake or Theo Brown, she thought, would "be truer to him than any who knew him"; Bronson Alcott "best understood his religious character"; Emerson possessed the "rare wisdom, discrimination, and taste requisite for the purpose"; and Ellery Channing and Ricketson himself could also be of assistance. "Henry's character," his sister explained, "was so comprehensive that I think it would take many minds to portray it" (*Daniel Ricketson and His Friends,* 1902).

Meanwhile Ellery Channing had himself been at work on a book, the history of which is given in what some students believe is not completely ingenuous detail by F. B. Sanborn in his introduction to the enlarged (1902) edition of *Thoreau: The Poet-Naturalist.* Channing's reminiscences began to appear serially in the Boston *Commonwealth* on 25 December 1863, for the first two installments as "Henry D. Thoreau," and subsequently as "Reminiscences of Henry D. Thoreau." After eight installments, the last on 19 February 1864, the manuscript was withdrawn because the author took offense at the editor's failure to give it precedence over other materials submitted for publication.

Nine years later, in 1873, Channing revised his earlier manuscript, "omitting much," said Sanborn in explanation of his own subsequent corrected edition, and "making portions of the rest obscure and enigmatical, by enriching it with the treasures of his recondite learning." To make the volume large enough to satisfy publishers, Channing filled it out with some sixty-eight pages from another manuscript on which he had worked twenty years before, an account of walks and talks in and around Concord which he had shared with Thoreau, Emerson, and Alcott. Copying, paraphrasing, and sometimes misreading passages from the journals of his companions, he put together a medley, often without indication of who was saying what, so that, explained Sanborn who supplied this lack in his revised edition, "the authors themselves could hardly pick out their share."

Irresponsible and eccentric though it is, Channing's *Thoreau:*

The Poet-Naturalist, in the 1873 edition, but especially in Sanborn's edition of 1902, is a volume filled with indispensable intimate detail. Channing alone among the early admirers seems to have recognized that Thoreau, in addition to being a lover of nature and an austere eccentric, was also, and primarily, a literary artist. As biography the book is poor and sketchy indeed, but as testimony to the ideals and literary inclinations of Thoreau it is, in spite of panegyric and self-glorification, much more useful than some of its critics have admitted.

By the time Channing's volume appeared, Thoreau's reputation needed the kind of fervent defense which his friend provided. The Rev. John Weiss's article on "Thoreau" (*Christian Examiner,* 1865), while not condemnatory, did reinforce current notions of his eccentricity by recalling that the hermit of Walden had been even in college a withdrawn, exceedingly strange figure. Hawthorne's notations on Thoreau in *Passages from the American Note-books* (1868) did little to dispel these opinions. And the Rev. W. R. Alger seemed to Sophia Thoreau "inspired by personal enmity" when in his *Solitudes of Nature and Man* (1867) he found egotism Thoreau's outstanding characteristic. But it was Lowell's review of the *Letters to Various Persons* (*Atlantic,* 1865; reprinted in *My Study Windows,* 1871) which most solidified public attitudes. Though the review pretended to be critical, in some of its most memorable and often quoted passages, Lowell presented a portrait of Thoreau as a strange, perversely eccentric person, lacking grace or any social sense, and through the vigor of his wit established an attitude toward Thoreau the man, and to his writings also, which was pretty much to prevail in the United States through the rest of the nineteenth century.

From England, however, came an ardent defense when, four years after Channing's biography, Dr. A. H. Japp, a Scotchman who read his name backward to come up with the pseudonym "H. A. Page," published in Boston and in London *Thoreau: His Life and Aims* (1877). Page praised Thoreau, not as a person of "morbid sentiment, weak rebellion, and contempt for society," not characterized by "stoical egotism," but as a latter-day St. Francis of Assisi, whose understanding of nature led him surely to an understanding of man. The book, which curiously misdates the last years of Thoreau's life, is of less value as biography than as a forerunner of what we shall discover as an important transatlantic application of Thoreau's ideas.

Meanwhile Thoreau's American friends had not been completely silent. Bronson Alcott remembered him generously in *Concord Days* (1878). The "Thoreau Annex" to the Concord *Freeman* (6 May, 1880) contained Joseph Hosmer's account of a day spent with Thoreau at Walden and some crude drawings from memory of the little house there. "A Graphic Story of Thoreau's Hermit Life" and "Greeley and Thoreau" in the New York *Tribune* (1881, 1882) were from advance sheets of F. B. Sanborn's *Henry D. Thoreau* (1882), which was written as one of the American Men of Letters series. Sanborn, who had known Thoreau from 1855 to the latter's death, had been schoolmaster in Concord and had boarded for a time at the Thoreau home, but he seems never to have been completely accurate in any of the numerous volumes he wrote or edited on Thoreau. He had, says H. S. Canby (*Thoreau,* 1939), the kind of "inconsecutive mind which seemed to be one of the by-products of the Transcendental movement." But his carefully collected reminiscences, his use of Thoreau's journals, his extended quotations from the college essays, and his printing of much of the correspondence with Horace Greeley brought forward for the first time important details of Thoreau's activities.

M. D. Conway's graceful recollections of Thoreau in *Emerson at Home and Abroad* (1882) added still more to the gradually growing fund of stories about the man. His reputation based on an understanding of his life as well as his writings was increasing. He had been briefly noticed in the *British Quarterly Review* (1874), in the London *Spectator* (1883), and in the *Dublin University Magazine* (1877). Theodore Watts-Dunton, reviewing Page's *Thoreau* in the *Athenaeum* (1877), wondered whether Thoreau were not the original of Donatello in *The Marble Faun.* On this side of the Atlantic, George Stewart read a paper on "Thoreau: The Hermit of Walden" before the Literary and Historical Society of Quebec in 1882. John Burroughs wrote a discriminating friendly estimate for the *Century* (1882). W. G. Barton read an essay on "Thoreau, Flagg, and Burroughs" in 1885 before the Essex Institute at Salem. T. W. Higginson in his *Short Studies of American Authors* (1888) presented a measured defense of Thoreau against Lowell's charges of indolence, imitativeness, and pretense, and S. A. Jones, already known for his devoted labors as Thoreau's first bibliographer, spoke fervently in defense against the same charges before the Unity Club of Ann Arbor in 1889.

In 1890 appeared *The Life of Henry David Thoreau* by H. S. Salt, an English critic who had published studies of Shelley and James Thompson, and who had two years before included in his *Literary Studies* an appreciative essay on Thoreau which had first appeared in the *Temple Bar* (1886). Here for the first time a disinterested professional was at work. Salt solicited new information from Thoreau's friends, from Sanborn, Ricketson, Blake, Edward Hoar, Higginson, and E. W. Emerson. He corresponded with Dr. Japp, John Burroughs, W. S. Kennedy, and Dr. Jones, who supplied bibliographical information. "My object," Salt wrote to Ricketson, "is to give (1) a clear and succinct account of Thoreau's life, gathering up and arranging in their due order all the scattered records of him to be found in the periodicals, as well as the information given by Messrs. Channing, Sanborn, and Page. (2) A fuller and more serious estimate of Thoreau's *doctrines* than any hitherto published, and a critique of his literary qualities" (*Daniel Ricketson and His Friends,* 1902).

Salt succeeded well in both objectives. His book remains today the most satisfactory single account of Thoreau's life. Prepared before the journals were made public and before many important small discoveries of modern students, it yet brings together as no other biography does those elements which seem to remain essential to an understanding of Thoreau. The appearance of this book, revised and abridged by the omission of many quotations in 1896 for the Great Writers series, marks the beginning of a new era in Thoreau scholarship. Salt's maturity of judgment and his insights into Thoreau's character have been useful to and used by many students who followed him with better biographical equipment at their disposal.

For more facts were appearing. E. W. Emerson's reminiscent lecture of 1890, expanded to *Henry Thoreau as Remembered by a Young Friend* (1917), was intended to correct contemporary notions of Thoreau as a strange and unsocial fellow. The publication of Sanborn's *Familiar Letters* (1894), A. W. Hosmer's edition of personal impressions in *Three Letters* (1900), S. A. Jones's collection of early articles and reviews in *Pertaining to Thoreau* (1901), F. B. Sanborn's *The Personality of Thoreau* (1901), E. H. Russell's *A Bit of Unpublished Correspondence between Henry Thoreau and Isaac Hecker* (1901), and *Daniel Ricketson and His Friends* (1902) each added something of significant biographical detail. The store of information about Thoreau, his friendships and his person, was increasing.

Annie R. Marble's *Thoreau: His Home, Friends, and Books* (1902) was the first full-length biography by an American not a member of the Concord group. It presents a fair, completely sympathetic portrait, based on materials found in Channing, Sanborn, and Salt. Mrs. Marble used Thoreau's letters and, to a limited extent, his journals, and she interviewed Concord neighbors. She did not, said a reviewer in the *Dial*, try "to paint a striking picture. Thoreau's reputation, she thinks, has already been dragged at the tail of too many epigrams." Her study is not now of great significance, but it performed important service by calling attention to Thoreau's integrity and fundamental consistency.

Meanwhile further bits of biographical evidence continued to appear. M. D. Conway's *Autobiography* (1904) added testimony to that already given in Sanborn's *The Personality of*

Thoreau on Thoreau's anti-slavery activities. Sanborn's printing of a letter dated 1836 from Thoreau to Henry Vose in the *Year Book of the Bibliophile Society* (1906) threw additional light on the early years. New family background was provided by E. H. Russell's note on "Thoreau's Maternal Grandmother" (*Proc. Amer. Antiquarian Soc.,* 1909). F. L. H. Willis added firsthand evidence of Thoreau's attraction for children and his power over birds in the *Alcott Memoirs* (1915). Mark Van Doren's *Henry David Thoreau, A Critical Study* (1916), less important as biography than as criticism, came to the provocative conclusion based on a study of the published *Journals* that Thoreau's life ended in disappointment and defeat—a view shared by Gilbert Seldes in *American Writers on American Literature* (1931) and David Boyd in "Thoreau, the Rebel Idealist" (*Americana,* 1936), and to which H. S. Canby forcefully took exception in "The Man Who Did What He Wanted" (*SRL,* 1936; see also his *Thoreau,* 1939).

The centennial of Thoreau's birth saw the appearance of Sanborn's posthumous *The Life of Henry David Thoreau* (1917), expanded and rewritten from the 1882 American Men of Letters volume, containing "memoirs of his ancestors not before given to the public; and also, in their complete form many essays written in his early youth," mainly college exercises. Every student of Thoreau recognizes large debts to Sanborn. "In matters," says B. V. Crawford (*Thoreau,* 1934), "of family history, neighborhood associations or gossips of Concord, the anti-slavery agitation in which he was also a leader, his testimony is almost final." Sanborn is often irritating because of the freedom with which he treats his material, rearranging paragraphs, deleting at will, and interpolating words and phrases wherever it seems to him proper. He knew the minutiae of Thoreau's life, but lacked understanding of his thought and literary accomplishment, such as had Ellery Channing, at whom Sanborn often looked down his nose. "However much one might be irritated by Sanborn's attitude of ownership of all that pertained to Thoreau," said F. H. Allen, "one had to admit that he occupied a unique position as the only one of Thoreau's biographers who had personal acquaintance with him, and who was at the same time an active and energetic seeker for information about his life and writings, also that he had a keen mind as well as a gift for expression" (*Thoreau's Editors,* 1950).

Léon Bazalgette's *Henry Thoreau, Sauvage* (1924), translated by Van Wyck Brooks as *Henry Thoreau, Bachelor of Nature* (1924), is a dramatized biography in the manner of André Maurois, taking literally Thoreau's admonition (which is used as motto on the title page), "My friend will be bold to conjecture. He will guess bravely at the significance of my words." Bazalgette sometimes seems sentimentally patronizing to his subject, whom he calls Henry throughout; he finds Henry absurdly shy and unable to establish intimacy with anyone, compensating for his failure at friendship with love of natural things; yet he pointed to Thoreau also as one of the most significant intellectual forces of his time.

W. L. Phelps's *Henry David Thoreau* (1924), a reprint of the first essay in his *Howells, James, Bryant, and Other Essays,* contributes nothing new to biography, but suggests that Thoreau "is certain to outlive many of his more showy contemporaries." Mary H. Brown's chapter on Thoreau in *Memories of Concord* (1926) presents affectionate recollections by one who had known him in her childhood. Brooks Atkinson's *Henry Thoreau, the Cosmic Yankee* (1927) is racily written, with infectious enthusiasm and sympathetic understanding and, along with Canby's chapter on Thoreau in his *Classic Americans* (1931), is perhaps the most useful brief biographical introduction to Thoreau.

During the 1930's professional students, already at work in critical evaluation, began to uncover new scraps of biographical evidence. Raymond Adams's "Thoreau's Literary Apprenticeship" (*SP,* 1932), competently exact, established 1841 as the year when Thoreau decided on a literary career, the summer of 1841 as the time when he first became acquainted with

Hindu philosophy; his "Thoreau Buried Twice" (*SRL,* 1933) cleared up a minor point relating to Thoreau's final resting place. J. T. Flanagan revealed something of Thoreau's Western experiences in "Thoreau in Minnesota" (*Minn. Hist.,* 1935). H. H. Hoeltje found important new evidence on "Thoreau in Concord Town and Church Records" (*NEQ,* 1939). Fresh information was made increasingly available about relationships between Thoreau and Emerson (see pp. 171-173 below), Thoreau and Alcott, Channing, and Whitman. Scattered Thoreau manuscripts were being gathered in university or public repositories. Graduate students were at work ferreting out and putting together evidence of almost every variety. The time seemed ripe for a new, detailed and objective biography which would bring these materials together.

Written as if in response to this requirement, H. S. Canby's *Thoreau* (1939) is the most complete of modern biographies, but it has proved to many students a disappointing book. It marked, as T. L. Collins observed in the *SR* (1940), "Thoreau's Coming of Age," but it is marred by an aloofness from its subject which is almost condescending and by what seems even now an inept toying with Freudian psychology. Canby's groundwork was based discriminatingly on Channing and Sanborn, on a study of all available evidence from other printed sources and on manuscript materials not available to or unused by previous biographers. Nine tenths of the story of Thoreau, he tells us, is written, "sometimes plainly, sometimes obscurely, in his Journal."

Thoreau could be described, says Canby, as "a creative artist and thinker in search of a career," as a "Yankee Pan" such as Channing found him, as a poor boy who made good in the traditional American fashion, as a Transcendentalist, as an individualist independent to excess, or as "next to Poe the most truly professional of American writers"—he is all of these, and more: "My feeling is, however, that a life of Thoreau must chiefly emphasize the creative thinker with weighted wings, and the ascetic with a passion for living." To Canby, Thoreau was "typically American," and the story of his life, "contrary to opinion, is not a futility, but a success story, the history not of an ascetic hermit but of a man of letters of deep and troubling emotions." All this was perhaps to the good, and as long as Canby held to this line, his biography succeeded.

Canby's unquestioning acceptance of the accounts of some of Thoreau's contemporaries has been challenged by Raymond Adams in "Thoreau at Harvard" (*NEQ,* 1940) and "Thoreau's Diploma" (*AL,* 1945), and by F. T. McGill in "Thoreau and College Discipline" (*AL,* 1945). Other errors of minor fact have been corrected by Adams, who amplified what he had said seven years before in "Thoreau Buried Twice" about the original and present site of Thoreau's grave in "Thoreau's Burials" (*AL,* 1940); Max Cosman in "Apropos of John Thoreau" (*AL,* 1940) revealed that Thoreau's brother had died of lockjaw, not resulting from tearing his hand on a nail but from cutting himself while shaving. In most essential details, Adams's excellent review of Canby's *Thoreau* (*AL,* 1940) gives a more satisfactory summary of the achievements and shortcomings of the book than there is space for here.

Most evocative, most daring, and perhaps least sound is Canby's treatment of Thoreau's love life, a subject which had briefly intrigued many previous writers. The tradition of an abortive love affair, known in outline since Sanborn's *Thoreau* (1882), had been dismissed by Van Doren as of negligible importance, and by Atkinson as flimsy and a "sop to gossip." Thoreau's reasons for not marrying had been set forth by Channing in 1867, when he wrote in his journal that "Henry made no account of love at all"; it had been hinted at by Stevenson in the introduction to *Familiar Studies of Men and Books* (1891), where, though accusing Thoreau of being "devoid . . . of any quality of flesh and blood," he admits that he "was once fairly and manfully in love"; it had been discussed tentatively in psychological terms by Mrs. Marble in 1902, and mentioned by E. W. Emerson in 1917. The story of Thoreau's refusal by Ellen Sewall, known briefly since Sanborn's *Thoreau,* had been first recounted in detail by T. M. Raysor in "The Love Story of Thoreau" (*SP,* 1926). But the older notion that Thoreau was incapable of love prevailed. Ludwig Lewisohn in *Expression in America* (1932) wrote him off as a "clammy prig . . . hopelessly inhibited, probably to the point of psychological impotence or else physiologically, hopelessly, undersexed."

Canby attacked such "serious misunderstanding, which makes Thoreau a sexless Platonist." He retold the story of Ellen Sewall more completely, drew on the correspondence of the Ward family, selections from an unpublished journal for 1840-41, and deduced meaning hidden in printed passages. This was admirably done. But Canby also suggested that "Thoreau was what the common man would call in love with Emerson's wife," and he commented further without coming to satisfactory conclusion on other women who were or who might have been attracted to Thoreau, one to the point of having committed or attempted suicide when he spurned her, and even speculated that the "idea that Margaret Fuller . . . should have proposed" to Thoreau "is not so ridiculous as it seems," though he concluded that the "probabilities favor Sophia Foord as the tragic heroine, both of the spurned proposal and of the alleged suicide" (see Walter Harding, "Thoreau's Feminine Foe," *PMLA,* 1954, for a confirmation of Canby's guess). Refining Van Doren's and Bazalgette's suggestion, Canby explained that when Thoreau's true love for Ellen Sewall, then for Lidian Emerson, was not returned, he turned then to "new obsessions with nature. . . . He found compensation there."

Canby's position, extreme and not always bolstered by fact, has not been seriously challenged, except mildly by Raymond Adams in his review (*AL,* 1940), by T. L. Collins in "Thoreau's Coming of Age" (*SR,* 1941), and by R. L. Rusk, who in his *Emerson* (1949) dismisses the Lidian Emerson affair as "entirely unconvincing" and suggests, if an actual person must be found to explain the dreamlike figure which Thoreau created in "The Sister," that Mary Russell "who was under Emerson's roof and in the Emerson family circle at the same time with him in 1841 would seem, in the present state of knowledge, to be the most likely choice."

During the past fifteen years additional threads of biographical evidence have been unraveled from the past without serious attempts to reweave them into a complete pattern. During the 1940's, reports Leonard Gray in "The Growth of Thoreau's Reputation" (*TSB,* 1953), research articles on Thoreau increased three hundred per cent over the preceding decade. Max Cosman has written of "Thoreau and Staten Island" (*S. I. Hist.,* 1943), Frank Buckley of "Thoreau and the Irish" (*NEQ,* 1940), and Raymond Adams of "An Irishman on Thoreau" (*NEQ,* 1940), R. L. Straker has found additional information on "Thoreau's Journey to Minnesota" (*NEQ,* 1941) and E. G. Berry on "Thoreau in Canada" (*Dalhousie Rev.,* 1943; see also Max Cosman's "A Yankee in Canada," *Canadian Hist. Rev.,* 1944). F. Henry has put together materials on "Henry David Thoreau and Bronson Alcott" (*Teachers Coll. Jour.,* 1943), Walter Harding on "Thoreau and Horace Greeley" (*TSB,* 1945), and Ruth H. Frost on "Thoreau's Worcester Friends" (*Nature Outlook,* 1945-47). R. F. Stowell has published a useful *Thoreau Gazetteer* (1948) and Leonard Kleinfeld a *Henry David Thoreau Chronology* (1950). Carl Bode has explained "Thoreau, the Actor" (*AQ,* 1953) and presented a brief, definitive account of "Thoreau and His Last Publisher" (*NEQ,* 1953); Christopher McKee has told of "A Week on Mt. Washington and Tuckerman's Ravine" (*Appalachia,* 1954), J. O. Eidson has suggested "Charles Stearns Wheeler, Emerson's Good Grecian" (*NEQ,* 1954) as the man who inspired Thoreau to retire to Walden, and R. J. Harmon has discovered a hitherto unnoticed letter from "Thoreau to His Publishers" (*AL,* 1954).

His abolitionist activities have been briefly explored by N. A. Ford in "Henry David Thoreau, Abolitionist" (*NEQ,* 1946), by Harding in "Thoreau and the Negro" (*Negro Hist. Bull.,* 1946), and by W. P. Glick in "Thoreau and the *Herald of Freedom*" (*NEQ,* 1949). His experiences on the public platform as a lecturer have been set forth by H. H. Hoeltje in "Thoreau as

Lecturer" (*NEQ,* 1949) and by Harding in "Thoreau on the Lecture Platform" (*NEQ,* 1951). R. W. Robbins in *Discovery at Walden* (1947) has told of his search for and excavation of the site of Thoreau's house at Walden Pond.

The most recent extended biographical study is J. W. Krutch's *Thoreau* (1949). Though it provides little new information, it is a mature and sensible appraisal, unmarred by the condescension or the speculation which disfigures Canby's biography. The student will not discover in it the kind of orderly biographical precision that he will find in Salt or even in parts of Canby, but rather a serious and useful attempt at understanding. William Condry's brief *Thoreau* (1954) is an enthusiast's account, but with refreshingly perceptive insights into Thoreau's achievement as a writer.

III. Criticism

"The character and works of Henry David Thoreau, who chose to live alone in the world, have roused stabbing assailants like Lowell and Stevenson, or complete panegyrists like Emerson and the biographers, but few critics." When Mark Van Doren made this charge almost forty years ago, Thoreau was just coming into his own as, if not a major, at least an important American man of letters. As Randall Stewart has reminded us ("The Growth of Thoreau's Reputation," *CE,* 1947), Thoreau at the turn of our century had been singularly neglected: Barrett Wendell had lumped him casually with Bronson Alcott and Ellery Channing as one of "The Lesser Men of Concord" in his *Literary History of America* (1900), and W. C. Brownell had not included him at all in his *American Prose Masters* (1909). P. E. More had seriously reviewed the *Journals* in 1906, but had found Thorcau falling something short of his austere requirements. By 1913, however, John Macy dignified Thoreau with a chapter in *The Spirit of American Literature;* two years later H. S. Canby published in the *Dial* the first of his many evaluations of "The Modern Thoreau"; and soon Norman Foerster was to begin the series of penetrating papers which was to culminate in his essay on Thoreau in *Nature in American Literature* (1923).

Except for these four men, with whom Mark Van Doren takes his place as a fifth, there have been until recently few serious critics of Thoreau as a literary figure. There has been writing about him aplenty. Walter Harding's *Thoreau: A Century of Criticism* (1954) collects much of the best of it. Nevertheless one completes a survey of criticism of Thoreau with a strong sense that much good will, a great deal of pompousness, and an embarrassing amount of repetition which is seldom quite plagiarism have gone into the evolution of the muddied estimate which our generation has inherited. Among us, only F. O. Matthiessen and Raymond Adams have examined him generously as a man of letters. Recent studies by R. L. Cook, Ethel Seybold, and Sherman Paul may indicate that this failure is soon to be remedied, but we still have no available complete analysis of any one of his books, nor even a completely annotated text—though E. E. Leisy's edition of *A Week* is well advanced, and Walter Harding's edition of *Walden* is under way. J. L. Shanley's excellent "A Study of the Making of *Walden*" (*HLQ,* 1951) indicates how much more on the subject remains to be done. Thoreau invites research, such things as the complete editing of his Indian notebooks, the intensive study of his college writings and other incompletely published or unpublished manuscripts; but he invites criticism more, an estimate of his worth, not as a prophet crying alone in the Walden wilderness, but as a writer skilled in his trade.

1. *The Emersonian Eccentric*

Much of the tone of early criticism of Thoreau was set by J. R. Lowell, first in *A Fable for Critics* (1848), a year later in his review of *A Week* in the *Massachusetts Quarterly Review,* but principally in his review of the *Letters to Various Persons* in the *NAR* (1865). Whether in *A Fable* Thoreau was portrayed as the "brother bard" who treads "in Emerson's track with legs painfully short," as Austin Warren has suggested

("Lowell on Thoreau," *SP,* 1930), or whether he is the disciple who "has picked up all [Emerson's] windfalls before," as Sanborn (*The Personality of Thoreau,* 1901), E. J. Nichols ("Identification of Characters in Lowell's *A Fable for Critics," AL,* 1932), and Canby (*Thoreau,* 1939) believe, the indictment is the same: "For all practical purposes the damage was done, and Thoreau went through life ticketed as Emerson's man—a pale, cold luminary reflecting only the radiant glory of Emerson's genius" (Crawford, *Thoreau,* 1934).

After Thoreau's death, his friends were quick to counter this among other charges, but with little effect, and the extent of Emerson's influence on Thoreau has been argued by students ever since. The Britisher Page made first effective public denial: "Thoreau has been too completely . . . treated as a mere disciple of Emerson" (*Thoreau,* 1877). He was soon joined by M. D. Conway who, though he admitted Thoreau "looked not the least like his parents, but closely resembled Emerson," stated with force that "Thoreau was quite as original" (*Emerson at Home and Abroad,* 1882). John Burroughs, acknowledging Thoreau "too directly under [Emerson's] influence," concluded, however, that "Thoreau was just as positive a fact as Emerson. . . . He was no . . . soft-shelled egg to be dented by every straw in the nest" (*Century,* 1882). And a few years later Emerson's son Edward stated unequivocally: "The charge of imitating Emerson, too often made against Thoreau, is idle and untenable" (*Emerson in Concord,* 1889).

Charges of imitation were repeated almost thirty years later by Archibald MacMechan in the *CHAL.* But the tide was turning. Norman Foerster, describing "The Intellectual Heritage of Thoreau" (*Texas Rev.,* 1916), temporized judiciously that "what Thoreau received from Emerson he found in the man rather than his books," and Mark Van Doren (*Thoreau,* 1916) was equally moderate in explaining that even if Thoreau "were insignificant in that he took all his ideas from Emerson, he would be significant in that he reduced them to their practical and visualizable essence." But it was E. W. Emerson again who a year later (*Henry Thoreau As Remembered by a Young Friend,* 1917) expressed the view still held, with one shade of emphasis or another, by many present students: that, rather than imitating Emerson, Thoreau put the older man's ideas into action. By 1921, even the New York *Times* could identify Thoreau as "a literary figure too long overshadowed by St. Ralph, the Optimist."

André Bruel in *Emerson et Thoreau* (1929) has capably brought together evidence of relationships between the two, their shared admiration for natural law, their affirmation of human liberty; Charles Cestre has discussed "Thoreau and Emerson" at considerable length (*RAA,* 1930); but the most convincing study is J. B. Moore's "Thoreau Rejects Emerson" (*AL,* 1932) which, through an analysis of the journals of each man, concludes that Thoreau was early attracted to and influenced by Emerson, but that by the early 1850's he had grown away from him and, in attitudes toward man and nature, beyond him. For an extension and slight revision of Moore's argument, see Leonard Gray's "Emerson and Thoreau" (*Unity,* 1952).

Lowell's review of the *Letters* further saddled Thoreau with charges of morbid self-consciousness, lack of humor, faulty logic, failure to discriminate between the trifling and the significant, cynicism, and misanthropy. Next to the charge of being Emerson's man, that which followed Thoreau most doggedly through all the nineteenth century was the charge of being a strange, cold, misanthropic person, an oddity, a recluse. Emerson himself established something of the pattern in his memoir and in his selection of materials for the *Letters,* in which he omitted, complained Sophia Thoreau, "passages betraying natural affection" in order to present his friend as "a most perfect piece of stoicism" (*Daniel Ricketson and His Friends,* 1902).

Thoreau's friends contributed almost unanimously to the charge, even when they defended him on other grounds, so that it grew out of proportion to its significance in almost all early estimates of his work. Hawthorne's description of him in 1842 as "ugly as sin" seemed more often remembered than the novelist's subsequent qualification that Thoreau's ugliness was honest and agreeable, and became him "much better than beauty" (*American Note-books,* 166). He seemed "stubborn and implacable," Emerson once said (*Journal,* VII, 274), and "rarely sweet." He was argumentative to excess. A college friend remembered him as cold, with a moist hand and slack handshake, loose-lipped, dull and plodding (*Christian Examiner,* 1865). G. W. Curtis in the *Commonwealth* (1853) spoke of the "inflexible Henry Thoreau, a scholastic and pastoral Orson, then living among the blackberry bushes of Walden Pond," and in *Harper's* (1862) described him as a man who "seemed to think that civilization had gone astray; that much fine wisdom had perished with the Indians"; and that the "Stoics were the true heroes, and the Hindoo Vedas and Norse Eddas the most interesting religious legends."

Even among eccentrics, he seemed strange. Bronson Alcott described him in his diary (March 1847) as a "wood nymph," a "sylvan soul," and he wrote publicly of him as a "little overconfident" and "stiffly individual, dropping society clean out of his theories" (*Atlantic,* 1862). Ellery Channing found him a "spartan" who had "gone steadily over the rough places and thorns in order to crucify and kill out the human virtues" (Journal, 1853). To John Burroughs he was "devoid of sympathy, devoid of generosity" (*Indoor Studies,* 1895). O. W. Holmes wittily wrote him off as an oddity who "insisted on nibbling his asparagus at the wrong end" (*Ralph Waldo Emerson,* 1885). The something more than a dozen articles about Thoreau which appeared in the New York *Tribune* before 1902 almost without exception outlined his eccentricities. Nor does the temptation to make a phrase at Thoreau's expense elude writers of our day. Van Wyck Brooks characterizes him (*The Flowering of New England,* 1927) as a "little man" whose "nose and . . . thoughts were the biggest things about him."

But Thoreau was not denied recognition as a man of letters by his contemporaries. Though *Godey's Lady's Book* (1849) thought the anonymous *A Week on the Concord and Merrimack Rivers* was certainly by Whittier because it was so "charming" and "just the book to read in idleness of summer," and though it was slightingly noticed in the *Athenaeum,* Thoreau's first volume did receive some friendly attention. George Ripley in the New York *Tribune* (1849) condemned its "second-hand, imitative, often exaggerated" pantheistic egotism as a "bad specimen of a dubious and dangerous school" and denounced its attitude toward the Christian Bible as "revolting alike to good sense and good taste," but he liked its literary quality. "Nearly every page," he said, "is instinct with genuine Poetry except those wherein verse is haltingly attempted."

Lowell's review in the *Massachusetts Quarterly Review,* patronizing and even flippant, was on the whole good natured and friendly (see Austin Warren, "Lowell on Thoreau," *SP,* 1930). Lowell praised Thoreau's natural history, his spontaneity, even his humor, and—this in contrast to his later estimate—his lack of self-consciousness: "Pepys is not more minute and with no uncomfortable sense of a public looking over his shoulder." Like Ripley, he admired Thoreau's prose for its "antique purity like wine grown colorless with age," but he found the verse bad indeed: "Better things can be got out of Herbert and Donne than the art of making bad verses." Thoreau was at his best, said Lowell, when he remained himself; when he copied Emerson or any other master, then he became obscure and digressive.

Walden, distributed and reviewed more widely (see Walter Harding, "Some Forgotten Reviews of *Walden,*" *TSB,* 1954), seems to have been less favorably received. What was said about it created attitudes toward Thoreau which his countrymen were to maintain for many years. The book was pleasantly noticed in the *NAR* as "more curious than useful," but filled with pithy, piquant suggestions. The New York *Tribune* also found it of "curious interest." C. F. Briggs in *Putnam's* called Thoreau "A Yankee Diogenes" who lived gypsy-like in a shanty rather than a tub, who "lived happily, too, though it don't exactly speak volumes in favor of his system . . . that he only continued his economical mode of life two years. If it was 'the thing,' why did he not continue it?" *Walden* was a pleasant book, but "it strikes us," said Briggs, "that a philosopher like Mr. Thoreau would have done the world a better service by purchasing a piece of land, and showing how much it might be made to produce instead of squatting on another man's premises."

So, the pattern was set. Thoreau was an eccentric, antisocial, a hermit, good perhaps as diarist of wood and stream, but hardly to be taken seriously. Youthful Edwin Morton described *Walden* as charming and its author the "high priest and poet of nature" (*Harvard Mag.,* 1855), but other commentators were less kind. The *Knickerbocker Magazine* (1855) compared Thoreau to P. T. Barnum in a gayly irresponsible article entitled "Town and Country Humbugs": "One sneers at and ridicules the pursuits of his contemporaries with the same cheerfulness and good will that the other cajoles and fleeces them." In England, a contributor to *Chambers's Journal* (1857) followed much the same line, though he did suggest that "if Barnum's autobiography is the bane, Thoreau's woodland experiences may be received as the antidote."

From England, however, came another notice, this by George Eliot in the *Westminster Review* (1856), which found in *Walden* "a bit of true American life (not the go-ahead species, but its opposite pole) animated by that energetic yet calm spirit of innovation . . . which is peculiar to some of the finer American minds." Almost alone among contemporary reviewers of *Walden,* George Eliot took the book and its author seriously. She found in Thoreau a "deep poetic sensibility" and a "refined as well as a hardy mind": "There is plenty of sturdy sense mingled with his unworldliness."

2. *Posthumous American Reputation*

After Thoreau's death, friends published reminiscent accounts which praised him without stint, but which continued the impression that he was, in spite of and even because of their testimony, a very strange man, the archrepresentative of those elements of Transcendentalism which sensible men disdained. As a result, in the United States discussion of Thoreau was for a long time concerned with many things besides his accomplishment as a man of letters. The intimate personal details and rhapsodic praise of Ellery Channing's reminiscences, Sanborn's printing of Thoreau's verse, the activities of Sophia Thoreau, Emerson, and Channing in seeing the posthumous volumes through the press, the fervent discipleship of men like Ricketson and Blake—all these made Thoreau seem, as indeed in fact he was, the property of a cult. With missionary zeal, M. D. Conway presented him to British readers in *Fraser's Magazine* (1866) as a "pious Yogi" who received homage from the little band of literary men which made Concord in truth an "American Weimar."

Reaction to such unqualified admiration inevitably set in. Austin Warren has explained in detail ("Lowell on Thoreau," *SP,* 1930) how Lowell, the humanist, in his review of the *Letters* charged Thoreau, the romanticist, "with substituting egotism and individualism for the social sense, nationalism for the study of man, and eccentricity for centrality." Lowell's brilliant phrase-making about whimsical and superficial aspects of Thoreau have often been better remembered than the critical core from which they radiate, so that his essay seemed to Salt (*Thoreau,* 1890) "a masterpiece of hostile innuendo," to John Macy (*The Spirit of American Literature,* 1913) "the product of a mind from which poetry and youth had evaporated, and of a social outlook grown conventionally decorous," and to John Burroughs (*The Last Harvest,* 1923) a diatribe from a man whose "smug respectability" made him "naturally antagonistic to the Thoreau type of mind." Almost every commentator on Thoreau has pointed his lance briefly toward Lowell, most of them with aim distorted by anger.

But few defenders of Thoreau have penetrated to the essence of Lowell's argument. Some of his charges had already been made in his review of *A Week:* that Thoreau managed form badly, had no sense of architectonics and was unable to select the significant from the trivial, that he needed condensation, that he was self-centered, and that he was not very good at poetry. Now, in reviewing the *Letters,* Lowell extended his indictment by finding Thoreau representative of a whole modern school of unhealthy sentimentalism about nature, "one more symptom of the general liver complaint" which fails to provide for man as part of nature, an argument which in some of its implications was later intensified by P. E. More, and first effectively answered by Norman Foerster. Finally, Lowell attacked the romantic concept of originality as absurd: "A man cannot escape in thought any more than he can in language, from the past and the present." Thoreau's "itch for originality" which "infects his thought and style" leads him only to perversity as he "turns commonplaces end for end."

Two years later, a Unitarian abolitionist, the Rev. W. R. Alger, in *The Solitudes of Nature and Man* (1867) repeated Lowell's indictment of the ultimate social uselessness of a man like Thoreau by attacking again the strain of egotism, of "interior aggrandizement of himself," which isolated Thoreau, which made him a lonely and in every social sense a sterile man. Nature was not enough. Man's responsibilities to other men, his unselfish devotion to the welfare of his fellows—these were to take precedence if society were to advance. Sometimes criticism hostile to Thoreau seems specious, as when J. V. O'Connor suggested in the *Catholic World* (1878) that the "incompleteness of [Thoreau's] life cannot be concealed by all the verbiage and praise of his biographers." He "gave up his life to . . . desultory study and admiration of Nature, and got for his worship a bronchial affliction which struck him down in the full vigor of his manhood."

Raymond Adams has recently called attention ("An Early and Overlooked Defence of Thoreau," *TSB,* 1950) to one critic, not usually remembered among the Thoreau adulators, who spoke out strongly in opposition to Lowell. Eugene Benson, writing of "Literary Frondeurs" (*Galaxy,* 1866), described

Thoreau as "a man of letters without the artistic spirit, but so thoroughly emancipated and so sincere that his writings have the beauty of truth if not the truth of beauty." He was a nonconformist, like Emerson, Poe, and the elder Henry James: "Today, among the rising men we know of none; all are under the rule of conformity, express the average sentiment." It was to the conformity of Boston that "Lowell loaned his wit, his humor, the prestige of his literary reputation, to arraign and pronounce judgment against the most blameless and sincere man of letters who ever in this country resisted the majority."

3. *Reputation Abroad*

As late as 1909 T. W. Higginson, in *Carlyle's Laugh and Other Essays,* supposed that Lowell's criticism, so effective in making Thoreau suspect in this country, had also limited his popularity abroad. Critical commentary in the British press, however, indicates that this certainly was not the fact, for, as J. P. Wood ("English and American Criticism of Thoreau," *NEQ,* 1933) has demonstrated, during the late nineteenth century Thoreau and especially Thoreau's ideas were taken more seriously in England than in the United States. While Thoreau remained in this country essentially the property of a clique concerned with reminiscence and panegyric, he was attended in England as a voice to which industrial and social reformers listened with respect.

The *British Quarterly Review* (1873) responded to Channing's biography by finding "seriousness and severity" in Thoreau and such "fiery hatred of wrong" as to provide the "main ingredients of heroism." He was no American Rousseau who retired to escape men; he went to Walden to discover in himself that which was useful to all men, to prepare himself for a free and vigorous life of action. Three years later, Thoreau was introduced to Irish readers in the *Dublin University Magazine* (1877) as certainly not "only an odd sort of character who lived alone in a wood." The London *Spectator* (1883) described the two years at Walden as "liberty expressed in the clearest language." Walter Lewin in the *Academy* (1884) emphasized the practicalness of Thoreau's ideas and the *Spectator* (1885) suggested that, though "he wrote nothing by which he will be long remembered," yet his fight for freedom will live on. H. S. Salt in the *Temple Bar* (1886) found him a "prophet of warning and remonstrance," more narrow and intense than Walt Whitman, but like him the "incarnation of all that is free, healthy, natural."

To Salt and other liberal Englishmen, Thoreau seemed "in the truest sense an original thinker." The Christian Socialist, Thomas Hughes, then principal of the Workingman's College in London, in the *Academy* (1877) praised Thoreau's contribution of "something simpler and nobler" than the "trappings and baggage of social life." The Fabian Edward Carpenter protested in *England's Ideal* (1887)—a volume which Salt (*Thoreau,* 1890) described as "worthy to rank with *Walden* in the literature of 'plain living and high thinking' "—that the "real truth" about Thoreau was "that he was a thorough economist" who in reducing life to its simplest terms established for all men an understanding of the relationship between labor and the rewards of labor. It is Thoreau as champion of individualism and anarchism, in "vigorous protest . . . against that artificiality in life and literature which constitutes one of the chief dangers of our complex civilization," who finally emerges from Salt's biography. Thoreau to him was an "idealist who looked through the outer husk of life, and saw the true reality" (*Thoreau,* 1890).

Robert Blatchford's popular socialist tract, *Merrie England* (1895), quoted Thoreau along with J. S. Mill, Adam Smith, and Henry George, and recommended *Walden* as a text for English workers. H. M. Tomlinson ("Two Englishmen and a Whale," *Harper's,* 1926) recalls that hundreds of Blatchford's disciples carried Thoreau's book in their pockets, and that literary groups in English industrial areas were often called Walden Societies. "It would scarcely be too much to say," reports Wood, "that the first . . . British Labor government can be traced back to the youthful reformers who were so strongly influenced by Thoreau." His chapter on "Economy" in *Walden* became, as G. F. Whicher has said (*Walden Revisited,* 1945), "a minor gospel of the British Labor Party because of its uncompromising emphasis, not on reform, but on proceeding at once to realize the ultimate values of life and on living only for them."

As the nineteenth century ended, Thoreau reached Holland also, where Frederik Van Eeden established at his home not far from Amsterdam a socialist colony devoted to literature and social reform and called it Walden. It was in 1907 that Mahatma Gandhi first came on the writings of Thoreau (see H. S. Salt, "Gandhi and Thoreau," *Nation and Athenaeum,* 1930, and H. S. L. Pollack, "Gandhi and Thoreau," *TSB,* 1953), and in South Africa translated portions of "Civil Disobedience," the principles of which he was later to work into his doctrine of passive resistance (see Mahatma Gandhi, *Young India,* 1923).

Even writers like Havelock Ellis, who in his remarks on Thoreau in *The New Spirit* (1890) put chief emphasis on his relation to Nature, found timely tonic also in his ethical strictures. When Page in *Thoreau: His Life and Aims* (1877) hailed the American as a modern St. Francis whose "great aim is to recommend Nature to man," he also insisted that Thoreau "went to Nature an individualist, and came back a prophet of society." Theodore Watts-Dunton seconded him strongly in the *Athenaeum* (1877), where he praised Thoreau as a "Child of the Open Air" because he loved the wind, because more than St. Francis or Cowper, Burns, Coleridge, and Bisset he understood that animals were not really dumb, and because he saw through the sophism which lay at the heart of the modern concept of work.

But Englishmen did not unanimously praise Thoreau. R. L. Stevenson, as gracefully witty and patronizing as Lowell, dismissed him in the *Cornhill Magazine* (1880) as an anti-social ascetic, a "melancholy, lean degeneration of human character," a "skulker" who lacked manliness or grace. Page replied heatedly in the *Spectator:* "I think the most charitable assumption is that Mr. R. L. S.'s studies of Thoreau have not been quite so exhaustive as they might have been"; and he presented examples of Thoreau's humanity, his humor, and his friendliness. Some years later, when Stevenson included his essay in *Familiar Studies of Men and Books* (1891), he apologized for the harshness of his first estimate of Thoreau the man, but he never rescinded his strictures on the cold lack of humanity in his ideas. Later critics, like Van Doren (*Thoreau,* 1916), have accused Stevenson, who admitted that he had never written ten words after he had read Thoreau which did not recall him, of something like guilty self-consciousness.

Theodore Watts-Dunton in a second *Athenaeum* article (1882) seems to have agreed with Stevenson. Thoreau was too self-conscious: "what racoon or chickadee in Walden Wood lived in such a perpetual state of sensitiveness as to himself and his fellows as Thoreau?" For all the lessons he had learned from Wordsworth, without whom there would "not have been any Thoreau or Emerson or Walt Whitman," Thoreau could not forget himself long enough to know Nature. It was an American trait: "Nature worship such as Borrow's or even Wordsworth's is scarcely possible in America. . . . Will Nature reveal her secrets to a man who can never look at her with the frank eyes of a child, but looks at her with the eyes of the bookishly, self-improving, transcendental species?" When Watts-Dunton wrote some of these attitudes into his introduction to the Oxford World's Classics edition of *Walden* (1906), he was mildly scolded by Arthur Rickett in his *The Vagabond in Literature* (1906), and more severely by Salt in the *Fortnightly Review* (1908) who defended Thoreau as a thinker with a message which was not easily accepted because it was disturbing to complacent men.

4. *The Student of Nature*

Little of importance appeared in the United States during these years, except by John Burroughs who his contemporaries thought was particularly qualified as a naturalist to interpret—as indeed he effectively did—the writings of Thoreau. Sanborn's *Thoreau* (1882) was in no real sense critical, nor were the brief items about Thoreau which Sanborn and others among his admiring countrymen scattered through the press. W. S. Kennedy's proposal of a "New Estimate of Thoreau" (*Penn Mag.,* 1880) was perhaps typical, in presenting Thoreau as the "saintliest of men . . . whose only crime was to be too pure . . . and to love too well the meadows, woods, and streams." The appearance between 1881 and 1892 of Harrison Blake's extracts from the journals and the publication in 1906 of the *Journals* in fourteen volumes, however, soon brought forth fresh commentary, particularly in respect to the question, never completely neglected before, of whether or to what extent Thoreau was a naturalist or a nature lover or a scientist.

"Thoreau by the charm of his writings," said E. W. Emerson (*Henry Thoreau As Remembered by a Young Friend,* 1917), "led many young people to wood walks and river journeys. . . . A whole literature of this kind has sprung up . . . inspired by him." Even people like Lowell, Holmes, and Stevenson, who found nothing to admire in his radical individualism, responded to his deft descriptions of Nature. A writer in the New York *Commercial Advertiser* (1888) undoubtedly echoed the judgment of many of his contemporaries when he explained that Thoreau's ideas were "of no use to anybody nowadays," but that his pictures of forest, field, and stream have "enduring and great value."

So Thoreau became, as he has to some extent remained, the property of another cult, that of the romantic back-to-nature movement. Thus he was set forth by J. A. Prinzinger as *Henry D. Thoreau, ein amerikanischer Naturschilderer* (Salzburg, 1895). "He was the chief of the poetic naturalists," agreed Brander Matthews in his *Introduction to the Study of American Literature* (1896). He was a maker of "Literature of Field and Hedgerow," said the London *Nature Notes* (1900). Salt wrote of the relationship between "Thoreau and Jeffries" (*Nature Notes,*

1900), between "Thoreau and Gilbert White" (*New Age,* 1900), and of "Henry David Thoreau and the Humane Study of Natural History" (*Humane Rev.,* 1903). His "Gospel of the Open Air" formed the basis for discussion by E. G. Ives in the Boston *Transcript* (1901). Maurice Muret in Paris wrote of him in *La Revue* (1900) as "Une poète-naturaliste Américain." Jeanette Perry in the *Critic* (1903) asked "Was Thoreau a Lover of Nature?" and answered her question emphatically in the affirmative. H. W. Mabie talked of "Thoreau, a Prophet of Nature" in the *Outlook* (1905) and described him as "A Theocritus of Cape Cod" in the *Atlantic* (1912). Will D. Howe in the *Reader* (1905) expressed a popular attitude when he said: "Nature was to Thoreau the solace, the refuge, from the business and worldliness of society. There he found simplicity, variety, harmony, truth, and beauty. . . . He was no seer like Emerson, no artist like Hawthorne, no scholar and man of letters like Lowell, he had no great message like Browning and Stevenson, and yet he lived a life of exceptional purity and has been the inspiration of countless readers."

In vain did Sanborn plead in the *Outlook* (1906) that Thoreau's chief interest "was literature rather than Nature-study, though the world has long otherwise fancied." Even John Macy, who preferred to value Thoreau for more significant things, found (*The Spirit of American Literature,* 1913) the "growing cult of the open air, the increase in number of amateur prodigals returning to nature, have given a fresh vogue to his sketches." F. White brought together "Thoreau's Observations on Fogs, Clouds, and Rain" (*Nature Study,* 1920), and G. A. Parker wrote of "The Moon in Thoreau" (ibid., 1922). Régis Michaud in *Vie des Peuples* (1924) found in Thoreau's writings new revelations of the wonders of Nature. "As Nature's lover," said D. C. Peattie (*NAR,* 1938), "Henry David Thoreau is the greatest in the English language. And it is as a Nature writer that I hope he will be read forever." In this estimate Peattie has recently been joined by J. W. Krutch ("The Wilderness at Our Doorstep," N.Y. *Times Book Rev.,*

1953) who attests that "as a nature writer, Thoreau is still the greatest of them all," and by Alec Lucas in "Thoreau, Field Naturalist" (*UTQ,* 1954).

But many students of Thoreau have found him something more than this. As early as 1877 Page had complained that Thoreau was "rejected all too decisively by the purely scientific men, for whom, nevertheless he has many hints that are equally original and valuable." John Burroughs did not agree. In "Thoreau's Wildness" (*Critic,* 1881) he explained that Thoreau "cared little for science," that what he was "finally after in nature was ulterior to science . . . philosophy . . . [or] poetry; it was something vague which he calls 'the higher law,' and which eludes all direct statement." A year later in the *Century* (1882) Burroughs authoritatively charged Thoreau with "failure to make any new or valuable contribution to natural history." His "ornithology was not sure": Thoreau looked so "intently for the bird behind the bird" that he was even "a long time puzzled to distinguish the fox-colored sparrow from the tree or Canadian sparrow." Burroughs was subsequently to multiply his charges of scientific inaccuracy: Thoreau's "night-warbler" was really the oven-bird; he confused the indigo bunting with the black-throated blue warbler; he failed to differentiate between the song of the hermit and the wood thrush; he misunderstood the habits of the woodpecker (*The Last Harvest,* 1922). But as a nature writer, Thoreau was supreme. Like Peattie, Krutch, and Bradford Torrey ("Thoreau's Demand on Nature," *Friends on the Shelf,* 1906), Burroughs praised his "rare descriptive powers" and proclaimed other nature writers "tame and insipid beside Thoreau."

Havelock Ellis, who thought Burroughs' essay in the *Century* the most discriminating estimate of Thoreau ever made, agreed thoroughly: "It has been claimed for Thoreau by some of his admirers, never by himself, that he was a man of science, a naturalist." He was neither: "his science is that of a fairly intelligent schoolboy—a counting of birds' eggs and a running after squirrels." Thoreau was not a naturalist; he was an artist and a moralist (*The New Spirit,* 1890). Salt agreed also. Though "Nature was the solid groundwork of his faith, and *out-of-doors* was his ritual, Thoreau's methods were not those of the . . . man of science; he held that 'nature must be viewed humanly to be viewed at all'." It was "supernatural rather than natural history which Thoreau studied" (*Thoreau,* 1890). For recent rephrasings of what is essentially Burroughs' view (effectively restated in "A Critical Glance into Thoreau," *Atlantic,* 1919), see Odell Shepard, "The Paradox of Thoreau" (*Scribner's,* 1920) and, especially, Ethel Seybold, *Thoreau: The Quest and the Classics* (1951), who says, "The truth, the quite incredible truth about Thoreau . . . is that he spent a quarter of a century in a quest for transcendent reality, in an attempt to discover the secret of the universe."

P. E. More expressed much the same attitude in "A Hermit's Notes on Walden" (*Atlantic,* 1901; reprinted in *Shelburne Essays,* 1st Ser., 1904). To him Thoreau was the "greatest by far of our writers on Nature, and the creator of a new sentiment in literature." He was not at his best, however, merely in describing Nature: "Much of his writing, perhaps the greater part, is mere record of observation and classification, and has not the slightest claim to remembrance." Thoreau was "far from having the truly scientific spirit; the acquisition of knowledge with him was in the end quite subordinate to his interest in the moral significance of Nature." His writing was successful only when he infused description with "qualities of awe and wonder" inherited from colonial times in New England when men experienced the "strange and often threatening forces of untried wilderness."

More found in Thoreau's attitude toward Nature none of Byron's "fiery spirit of rebellion," Keats's "passion for beauty and voluptuous self-abandonment," or Shelley's "unearthly mysticism"; least of all did Thoreau, like Wordsworth, hear "in the voice of Nature any compassionate plea for the weakness and sorrows of the downtrodden." Nature to him was awful and wonderful; it was a "discipline of the will as much as a stimulant to the imagination." John Macy in *The Spirit of American Literature* (1913) disagreed; "Thoreau misreads Nature as a collection of moral lessons, but he is not blind to her naked loveliness, and he finds her lessons not austere, but consoling." But for Macy, Thoreau was misunderstood as simply a mystic transcendentalist; he was, as people in England had recognized, "an anarchist of great literary power," whose "poetic notes on the seasons are recommended," but whose eloquent social philosophy is ignored.

Lowell had characterized Thoreau's retirement as a search for a physician; Burroughs in the *Century* had suggested that Thoreau's search for wildness was a search for health; and Mark Van Doren suggested (*Thoreau,* 1916) that Thoreau found in Nature a substitute for the kind of friendship he could not find in men. That which will be remembered of Thoreau, said Van Doren, is not what he wrote about Nature, some of which is very prosy indeed, but what he has to say of human relations, "talking of friendship and charity and solitude"—these "will be remembered when Thoreau the visitor of wild flowers will beg for notice."

Norman Foerster explained even more emphatically than Burroughs the relation between "Thoreau and 'The Wild' " (*Dial,* 1917). He pointed to Thoreau's attraction to the Indian, to all wildness, and he underlined both the insistence of Page and Salt that Thoreau had gone to Nature better to know men, and the suggestion of Burroughs that Thoreau looked through Nature for secrets behind those which the observation of the naturalist can disclose. But Nature, excellent for its purposes, was better when its wildness was tamed, humanized as Concord was humanized to become "more expressive, not only of man, but also to man."

Foerster, along with More and Van Doren, with whom in most matters he is substantially in agreement, was one of the first American critics to view Thoreau dispassionately, to consider the man entire, and weigh his weakness and his strength. He builds carefully on what Burroughs had suggested; he accepts but judiciously modifies many of the indictments of Lowell and Stevenson, but explains them in terms of Thoreau's total personality. To him also, Thoreau was at best an "amateur scientist," Rousseauistic rather than truly Platonic. The "leading error in Thoreau's intercourse with nature" seemed to Foerster "the tyranny of observation, and not the abandonment of sentimental mysticism." Full of contradictions, "forever baffling if we insist on resolving into perfect harmony all his ideas, which he never harmonized himself," Thoreau nonetheless gave order and direction to his insights and observations by depending on that "most human of human qualities, the inner voice which places us on the pinnacle of humanity."

Thoreau's conception of "humanized landscape" has been praised by G. P. Morley ("Thoreau and the Land," *Landscape Architecture,* 1934), and Foerster's interpretation of Thoreau as a humanist has been pretty well accepted by such modern commentators as Canby (*Thoreau,* 1939), Whicher (*Walden Revisited,* 1945), and, with some modification, Krutch (*Thoreau,* 1948). The most discriminating recent explanation of Thoreau's mystic humanism is in R. L. Cook's *The Concord Saunterer* (1940), revised and expanded as *Passage to Walden* (1949), which explains how Thoreau found in Nature correspondences which resulted in rare insights into his own nature and the nature of man.

Thoreau's increasing concern after 1845 with the collection of fact was noticed as early as 1865 by T. W. Higginson in his review of *Cape Cod* in the *Atlantic*. Bradford Torrey in *Friends on the Shelf* (1906) and, more recently, Raymond Adams in "Thoreau and Science" (*Sci. Mo.,* 1945) also effectively called attention to Thoreau's turning in his later years toward the accumulation of particulars. The apparently unimaginative piling of detail in the journals of the 1850's led Mark Van Doren (*Thoreau,* 1916) to conclusions concerning Thoreau's final discouragement and defeat, and Canby (*Thoreau,* 1939) blamed the "bog of classificationist detail into which he sank deeper and deeper" on the seductive influence of Agassiz and his disciples.

But Thoreau as a scientist has recently had his champions. C. D. Stewart said "A Word for Thoreau" (*Atlantic,* 1935) in answer to certain of Burroughs' charges, and concluded that Thoreau was capable of the most exact scientific observation. E. S. Deevey in a "Re-examination of Thoreau's Walden" (*Quart. Rev. Biol.,* 1942) challenged Canby's view by contending that, if Thoreau did mistake the means of observation for its end, the fault was not with Agassiz, but with the formal curriculum of Harvard College, together with Thoreau's innate distaste for empiricism. Deevey presented Thoreau as the "first American limnologist" and, as Adams had also suggested (*Sci. Mo.,* 1945), a plant ecologist interested in the relations between organisms and their environments, rather than a botanist. Aldo Leopold and Sara E. Jones in "A Phenological Record for Sauk & Dane Counties, Wisconsin" (*Ecological Records,* 1947) found Thoreau the "father of phenology in this country" because of his detailed notes on the blooming, pollination, and leafing of plants.

P. H. Oesher included Thoreau among "Pioneers in Conservation" (*Nature Mag.,* 1945) because of the conclusion of his essay "Chesuncook" in *The Maine Woods;* and this, said Kathryn Whitford in "Thoreau and the Woodlots of Concord" (*NEQ,* 1950; see also Philip and Kathryn Whitford, "Thoreau, Pioneer Ecologist and Conservationist," *Sci. Mo.,* 1951), "is mild indeed by comparison with the wisdom and bitterness of comments found in the last Journal." Thoreau's science, Mrs. Whitford concluded, cannot be judged "without recognition of the fact that he was working almost alone in this country. To a large extent he had to compile his own textbook in ecology." She claimed for him the true scientist's reverence for factual data, and supposed that, had his career not been cut short, he might have utilized much of the detail with which he filled his notebooks.

Thoreau's interest in the Indian, pointed out but only briefly explained by Channing, Sanborn, and other early commentators, was woven, as we have seen, first by Burroughs and then by Foerster, more closely into the whole fabric of his attitude toward Nature. Since then, the Indian notebooks have been studied by J. A. Russell ("Thoreau, the Interpreter of the Real Indian," *QQ,* 1927) and Albert Keiser ("Thoreau's Manuscripts on the Indians," *JEGP,* 1928, and *The Indian in American Literature,* 1932). Students of the late Arthur Christy have edited transcripts of most of these notebooks for deposit in the Columbia University Library, but the Indian materials have not been studied completely, nor has Thoreau's reading in preparation for the "book concerning the Indian" which Channing insisted he planned to write been satisfactorily explored.

5. *Intellectual Background*

Publication of the *Journals* in 1906 made possible more objective investigations into the workings of Thoreau's mind and of the books which fed it. P. E. More wrote of "Thoreau and German Romanticism" in reviewing the Walden edition (*Nation* and N.Y. *Evening Post,* 1906; reprinted in *Shelburne Essays,* 5th Ser., 1908). To him Thoreau seemed shallow and derivative, with "only a scant handful of ideas"; he was "the shadow of a shadow" who "excelled several of his contemporaries only through greater precision of details." Like other Concord Transcendentalists, Thoreau echoed German romanticism, in his sublime egotism, his reaching out to embrace all nature in ecstatic communion, his attempts to find the basis of man's nature through pure emotionalism; but, unlike his New England fellows, he also rose above what More felt was sickliness in the *romantische Schule* through exercise of "one great offset—character," a will toward self-discipline, a "higher self-restraint."

The sources of this difference between Thoreau, on the one hand, and Novalis, on the other, were five: (1) the inheritance of Puritan religion which made possible a return to the kind of medievalism found among German romantics; (2) the British notion of practical individualism found in the philosophy of Adam Smith; (3) the lesson of austerity in Wordsworth's attitude toward Nature; (4) a "spirit of fine expectancy" drawn from Thoreau's favorite seventeenth-century poets; and (5) the "incalculable force of Emerson's personality." For all its provincialism and tedium, Thoreau's journal presented a record of "romanticism striving to work itself out in character." Thoreau's contemplation of Nature in all its aspects, his "sympathetic knowledge of savage life among the Indians, and the tradition of New England's struggle with the wilderness kept him, in a word, from sentimental softening of reality."

Mark Van Doren in *Thoreau: A Critical Study* (1916) found faults in More's emphasis on German sources of Thoreau's Transcendentalism. Drawing on Thoreau's testimony in the *Journals* and on the testimony of Channing and Sanborn, he explained Thoreau as "most durably nourished by three literary springs": (1) the Oriental scriptures, from which "he took figures and sentences, not ideas"; (2) the Greek classics, which furnished "means for artistic discipline"; and (3) the poets of seventeenth-century England, to whose style and temper he "owes more than any other group."

In "The Intellectual Heritage of Thoreau" (*Texas Rev.*, 1917), Norman Foerster presented an analysis of Thoreau's literary background which agreed substantially with Van Doren's. Foerster pointed to what Channing had called Thoreau's "very uncompleted reading," his avoidance of fiction, his almost complete ignorance of English letters from Dryden to Matthew Arnold, his failure to read the literature in modern languages at his command. In an examination of quotations from *A Week,* Foerster found twelve from Latin and Greek authors, twelve from early English, thirty-four from Elizabethan and seventeenth-century England, fourteen from English and American contemporaries. Among the latter, he suggested that Thoreau owed more to Wordsworth than had yet been recognized, found—as Van Doren had also—more hints of Carlyle in

Thoreau's style than in his matter, and concluded that less had been derived from Emerson the writer than from Emerson the man who drew Thoreau, not only to the Classics and the literature of seventeenth-century England, but also to Goethe and the religious books of the Orient.

Since the mid-1920's there has been a proliferation of brief articles on the literary ancestry of Thoreau, for the most part underlining or changing the emphasis of what Channing, Sanborn, Van Doren, or Foerster had already pointed out. Thus J. H. Birss wrote of "Thoreau and Thomas Carew" (*NEQ,* 1933), Raymond Himelick of "Thoreau and Samuel Daniel" (*AL,* 1952), E. E. Leisy of "Thoreau and Ossian" (*NEQ,* 1945) and "Francis Quarles and Henry Thoreau" (*MLN,* 1945). J. B. Moore found likenesses between "Thoreau and Crèvecœur" (*Papers Mich. Acad. Sci. Arts and Letters,* 1926), A. B. Benson discovered "Scandinavian Influences on the Writings of Thoreau" (*Scandinavian Studies,* 1941), Howard Schultz discovered "A Fragment of Jacobean Song in Thoreau's *Walden*" (*MLN,* 1948), and J. C. Mathews explored "Thoreau's Reading in Dante" (*Italica,* 1950). Fred De Armond compared "Thoreau and Schopenhauer" (*NEQ,* 1950), L. M. Kaiser presented "Remarks on Thoreau's Translation of the *Prometheus*" (*Classical Weekly,* 1953), and Edith Peairs considered the influence of *Zadig* in "The Hound, the Bay Horse, and the Turtle Dove: A Study of Thoreau and Voltaire" (*PMLA,* 1933).

"Sources of Thoreau's Borrowings in *A Week*" (*AL,* 1946) were explored by E. E. Leisy, and "Thoreau's Borrowings in *Walden*" (*N&Q,* 1943) briefly outlined by Joseph Leach. When William Templeton in "Thoreau, Moralist of the Picturesque" (*PMLA,* 1933) claimed Thoreau a disciple of the Rev. William Gilpin and the vogue which he created for the wild and rough in nature, J. G. Southworth answered him (*PMLA,* 1934), not by denying the influence of Gilpin, but by claiming that of Wordsworth more profound. Canby (*Thoreau,* 1939) mediated by acknowledging that Thoreau had learned something of composition and design from Gilpin, but that he had finally found him artificial and unsatisfactory.

Thoreau's political ideas were influenced by William Godwin, said Parrington (*Main Currents in American Thought,* 1927); by Johann Ritter von Zimmermann, said Grant Loomis (*NEQ,* 1937) and Canby. But the sources of Thoreau's ideas are difficult thus to pin down. Almost every modern commentator has recognized him as an eclectic who took what he needed from many sources, using it as he wished. Raymond Adams in "Thoreau's Sources for Resistance to Civil Government" (*SP,* 1945) found that Emerson's "Politics," the writings of the Garrisonian abolitionists, and William Paley's *Moral and Political Philosophy* all contributed to Thoreau's best-known political essay—but, said Adams, "He took from all three and rejected much from all three, and . . . so fashioned the material and individualized it and so intensified it or translated it that it became his own."

"Thoreau's reading, aside from that in natural history, falls into certain clearly marked categories," said Ethel Seybolt in *Thoreau: The Quest and the Classics* (1951): (1) the Greek and Latin classics, (2) the Oriental scriptures, (3) the English poets, (4) New England history and legend, (5) data on the Indian, and (6) early accounts of travel, adventure, and exploration. Of these, she explained, "he valued the classics most," and she appended to her study a list of Greek and Latin books which Thoreau owned or read, and a list of his quotations from the classics. Few have ever disagreed with this estimate. Channing, Sanborn, and Salt had all testified to Thoreau's learning in Greek and Latin; Foerster's statement (*Texas Rev.,* 1917) that "Thoreau without his classical background would simply not have been Thoreau" and Van Wyck Brooks's (*The Flowering of New England,* 1927) that Thoreau was "the best Greek scholar in Concord" were corroborated by Clarence Gohdes in "Henry Thoreau, Bachelor of Arts" (*Classical Jour.,* 1928), Raymond Adams in "Thoreau's Literary Apprenticeship" (*SP,* 1932), and John Paul Pritchard in *Return to the Fountains* (1942). "Alone among American writers," said Pritchard, "he devoted his attention to the [classical] writers on rural life: Hesiod and Theophrastus, and especially Cato, Varro, and Columella." Though "Greek philosophy held no spell over him," as it did over Emerson, and "though he did not care for Plato" and "Aristotle interested him chiefly as a zoologist," he revered Homer and the Greek tragedians, and Virgil and the satirist Persius. Miss Seybolt, however, expanded a study of Thoreau's interest in the classics to an investigation which attempted to locate "in his classical reading the specific foci of his interest and their relationship to the experiences of his life and thought," to his "quest for transcendental reality," his attempt to discover the secret of the universe by following a pattern of Homeric experiment.

Oriental influences on Thoreau, noted by almost every commentator, were studied in detail by Helena A. Snyder in *Thoreau's Philosophy of Life, with Special Consideration of the Influence of Hindoo Philosophy* (1900). His adaptation of Eastern ideas was noted briefly by Frances Fletcher in "Henry Thoreau, Oriental" (*Open Court,* 1930) and touched upon by F. I. Carpenter in *Emerson and Asia* (1930), but was most authoritatively investigated in Arthur Christy's chapter on "Thoreau and Oriental Asceticism" in *The Orient in American Transcendentalism* (1931). Christy took issue with Van Doren's statement that "Thoreau took figures and sentences, not ideas from his Oriental reading," but his own conclusions were not, finally, very different: "He used the Hindus to bolster his own thoughts," and when he read Confucius, it was not to "read mystic divinity into the Chinese; he quoted them in connection with flora and fauna." Christy also seriously considered whether Thoreau really was, as Conway had described him, "like the pious Yogi." He found that Thoreau resembled the Oriental mystic in courting solitude for the purpose of spiritual discipline, but, unlike the Yogi, he had no interest in ascetic self-torture; he consciously sought none of the Yogi disciplines, for he "had no interest in systems"; he did not share the Oriental attitude toward benevolence; he "probably never accepted . . . the Hindu insistence that the man who has reached a stage of true enlightenment is freed from the consequences of his work." What had seemed to Van Doren the ultimate failure of Thoreau's life in his "never succeeding in stepping entirely out of his little private darkness," may however be, Christy suggested, the result of his having accepted the attitude of Oriental mystics that one's individuality is ultimately indistinguishable from Universal being. If by Occidental standards Thoreau was a failure, certainly he was not by standards of the Orient.

The intellectual climate to which Thoreau was exposed during his college years, considered by Sanborn, Canby, and Adams in relation to curriculum and the books he read, was further investigated by J. J. Kwiat in "Thoreau's Philosophical Apprenticeship" (*NEQ,* 1945), who suggested that Thoreau's reaction against the materialism of Locke and the utilitarianism of Paley came by way of the influence of the Scottish common sense philosophy which served him, as it served others of his time also, as transition to the idealism of the Germans and of Coleridge.

More work will undoubtedly be undertaken in tracing the intricacies of Thoreau's intellectual background. Meanwhile G. F. Whicher's *Walden Revisited* (1945) and J. W. Krutch's *Thoreau* (1947) provide excellent summaries of what has been done, and K. W. Cameron's *Emerson the Essayist* (1945), his "Emerson, Thoreau, and the Society of Natural History" (*AL,* 1952), his "Thoreau Discovers Emerson: A College Reading Record" (*BNYPL,* 1953), and his "Thoreau, Sic Vita, and *Harvardiana*" *(TSB,* 1954) supplement the valuable work done by Foerster, Adams, and Seybold (together also with the pioneer suggestions of Ellery Channing) in making available a more complete and accurate record of Thoreau's reading than is found in the appendix to Sanborn's *Life.* The late Arthur Christy's virtually completed index of every literary reference in Thoreau's published or unpublished writings remains in manuscript in the hands of his literary executor, Mrs. Elliott V. K. Dobbie, at Columbia University.

6. *The Social Philosopher*

After John Macy in *The Spirit of American Literature* (1913) took his contemporaries to task for overlooking Thoreau's "eloquent social philosophy" and H. S. Canby called attention to "The Modern Thoreau" (*Dial,* 1915), a gradually increasing number of Americans discovered in Thoreau a reliable guide for the solution of problems of their time. "To our amazement," said Brooks Atkinson in "Thoreau the Radical" (*Freeman,* 1920), "we discover this odd fellow . . . a stupendous radical," worthy of a place beside Samuel Butler, Anatole France, and Bernard Shaw. C. J. Finger wrote admiringly of *Henry David Thoreau: The Man Who Escaped from the Herd* (1922). David Boyd wrote of "Thoreau, the Rebel Idealist" (*Americana,* 1926). John Cournos described him as a "Hater of Shams" (*Century,* 1928). V. L. Parrington (*Main Currents in American Thought,* 1927) rephrased what English commentators had said years before: "The single business of Henry Thoreau . . . was to discover an economy calculated to provide a satisfying life . . . to explore the true meaning of wealth."

During the 1930's commentary of this kind increased. Canby again called attention to the timeliness of Thoreau's social criticism in "Thoreau in the Machine Age" (*YR,* 1931). Gorham Munson pointed to "A Lesson in Thoreau" (*Thinker,* 1931), E. M. Schuster included him in her study of "Native American Anarchism" (*Smith Coll. Stud. in Hist.,* 1932), Sinclair Lewis described him as "a One Man Revolution" (*SRL,* 1931), and Canby's "American Challenge: A Study of 'Walden' " (*SRL,* 1939; reprinted in *Thoreau,* 1939) called attention to the "significant paralleling of dates between *The Communist Manifesto* of 1848 and *Walden,* ready for publication a year later: "The same diseases of the profit system impressed the

American recluse and the German scholars." Max Lerner affirmed "Thoreau, No Hermit" (*Ideas Are Weapons,* 1939) and explained his social thought as "tighter than Emerson's," his economics as anticipating Ruskin's, his pragmatic aesthetics as looking toward William Morris': "It was his tragedy to be forced by the crudities of capitalism into a reclusion . . . that has until recently obscured the real force of his social thought."

In reply to Canby's and Lewis' claim that Thoreau lives on while most of his contemporaries are dated, D. C. Peattie asked "Is Thoreau a Modern?" (*NAR,* 1938), and replied that Thoreau was not; he represented the end, not the beginning of an era, and his time was separated from the present by a gap, "one of the greatest in the history of man. . . . It asks too much of him to bridge it." Science and society had outstripped Thoreau; his way of life could only be practiced by bachelors. In answer to Peattie and also in rebuke to Canby for "virtually ignoring the tremendous weight of Thoreau's social criticism and handling the bombshells of his most explosive thoughts as if they were roses," C. C. Walcutt proposed in "Thoreau in the Twentieth Century" (*SAQ,* 1940) "to consider how [Thoreau's] thought can be applied—and indeed is being applied—to the most pressing modern problems," specifically how Aldous Huxley's *Ends and Means* is an "elaborate application of Thoreau's ideas."

Walter Harding wrote of "The Significance of Thoreau's Walden" (*Humanist,* 1945) and of "Thoreau, Pioneer of Civil Disobedience" (*Fellowship,* 1946), H. F. West pointed to "Modern Values in Thoreau" (*TSB,* 1946), S. E. Hyman emphasized the efficacy of "Henry Thoreau in Our Time" (*Atlantic,* 1946) as an artist, but also as a political writer, "the most ringing and magnificent polemicist America has ever produced." J. M. Dabb described "Thoreau—the Adventurer as Economist" (*YR,* 1947) who prudently developed an economy in order to adventure farther, and F. B. Dedmond called attention to "Economic Protest in Thoreau's *Journal*" (*Studia Neophilologica,* 1953-54). W. S. Thomas presented "Marti and Thoreau

(*Dos Pueblos,* Havana, 1949) as "pioneers of personal freedom," C. R. B. Combellback and R. N. Stromberg followed Canby in comparing Thoreau with Marx, the first in "Two Critics of Society" (*SP,* 1949), the second in "Thoreau and Marx" (*Social Stud.,* 1949), and R. L. Cook in "Thoreau in Perspective" (*UKCR,* 1947) found him "like Thomas Paine . . . one of the watchdogs of human rights," to be remembered "as one of the perceptive moral guides who recall men to their senses when they become confused by the transvaluation of values in revolutionary eras." Townsend Scudder (*LHUS,* 1948) emphasized his effective "reappraisal of life's values in the modern industrial state" and his "ringing challenge to totalitarianism." Heinz Eula described him as a "Wayside Challenger" (*Antioch Rev.,* 1949) who is "as germane today as he ever was in the development of political thought" because of his final "conversion to violence as a legitimate means in social conflict." J. L. Blau wrote of "Henry David Thoreau, Anarchist" (*Men and Movements in American Philosophy,* 1952), and Wendell Glick described "Civil Disobedience" as "Thoreau's Attack on Relativism" (*WHR,* 1952-53).

Nor has his usefulness in other fields gone unnoticed. His influence on education has been discussed by H. E. Hurd ("Henry David Thoreau—A Pioneer in the Field of Education," *Education,* 1929), Raymond Adams ("Thoreau, Pioneer in Adult Education," *Institute Mag.,* 1930), and H. H. Hoeltje ("Thoreau and the Concord Academy," *NEQ,* 1948); on diet by John Davies ("Thoreau and the Ethics of Food," *Vegetarian Messenger,* 1947); on his continuing appeal to youth by Reed Crowell ("Henry Thoreau at Walden Pond," *Methodist Classmate,* 1948) and Robert Ortmayer ("Prescription for Today," *Mennonite Youth,* 1951).

7. *The Literary Artist*

"No writer more demands," said Channing in 1873, "that his reader should look at his writings as a work of art." But like most nineteenth-century commentators, Channing was satisfied to allow description to do much of the work of criticism, pointing to Thoreau's "piquant humor" and his "unstudied felicities." Until recently almost everything which has been said of Thoreau's style has been thus a matter of statement, an acknowledgment of its precision, its raciness, its homely effectiveness. Even Burroughs, most perceptive among the late nineteenth-century critics, did little beyond speak of its "restrained extravagance" and "compressed exaggeration." From Lowell's description of Thoreau's language as of "an antique purity like wine grown colorless with age" in the *NAR* (1849) to E. B. White's description of it in the *New Yorker* (1949) as "100-proof anchovy," phrases have been ingeniously manufactured to picture Thoreau's art. To some, he seemed not an artist at all—on this both Stevenson and the English reformers were agreed—but an edifying proponent of self-improvement, of whom one either approved or disapproved, sometimes because of what he said, sometimes because of the tone in which he said it.

Much of the better recent criticism of Thoreau has been able to see beyond the naturalist or even the mystic supernaturalist to the man of letters. Among the first to analyze Thoreau's achievement as a literary man was Mark Van Doren (*Thoreau,* 1916), who praised his "genius for the specific," his sense of the drama of ordinary things, which allowed him to avoid the fatal lure of generalization which attracted Emerson. To understand Thoreau, one must recognize in him six qualities: (1) his sensibility, by which Van Doren seems also to mean his sensitivity, (2) his concreteness of vision, (3) his thoroughness, (4) his "wild combative self-sufficiency," (5) his humor, which, however, he "priggishly exorcised" from his books, and, finally, (6) his wistfulness. Though mind-intoxicated like Emerson, Thoreau had one natural gift which saved him from obscurity. In his "passion for writing perfectly," his distaste for wooden and lifeless words, his self-consciousness about individuality in style, he was a "nineteenth-century euphuist of the stamp of Flaubert, Stevenson, and Pater; he travailled to catch consciousness itself in the trap of the specific." In this he was a pioneer, but "isolated in America, his wits straying through the endless and utterly formless reaches of a transcendental Journal," he failed to "end his literary career as happily as Flaubert and Stevenson . . . and Pater" because he was "fatally committed to sphericity," to what he described as a sense of "eternity and space gambolling through my depths." In his reach for the transcendental whole, he finally lost disciplined contact with reality.

Norman Foerster in "Thoreau as Artist" (*SR*, 1921) discovered in Thoreau's reading of William Gilpin on landscape and of John Ruskin on painting an interest in aesthetic principles which was reflected in his literary workmanship. Like Van Doren, Foerster recognized Thoreau's unflinching demand for truth in observation and phrase, but he proposed also that Thoreau's perfection of the senses, his physical dexterity, familiarity with natural fact, his knowledge of literary tradition, his moral energy, insight, and imagination were all "given order and direction" by his essential humanism.

Foerster also called attention to Thoreau's humor, as many others had before him (see, e.g., George Beardsley, "Thoreau as Humorist," *Dial,* 1900; H. W. Mabie, "Thoreau," *Outlook,* 1905; and G. T. Coleman, "Thoreau and His Critics," *Dial,* 1906), and concluded that "much of the charm of Thoreau's best pages resides in . . . lurking humor . . . dry wit always ready to kindle." Brooks Atkinson, however, in "Concerning Thoreau's Style" (*Freeman,* 1922), though he admired much besides in *Walden* and especially in *A Week,* described Thoreau's kind of humor, his "strange propensity for puns and plays on words," as disagreeable: "So reserved and austere a writer had no business to deal with elephantine touch in such bastard humor." Thoreau's manner was ungainly, gnarled and knotted: "He could not trip lightly across the slack wire of scintillant jest; but he was not too pompous to try." More recently, J. P. Brawner defended "Thoreau as Wit and Humorist" (*SAQ,* 1945), Tyrus Hillway in "The Personality of Thoreau" (*CE,* 1945) explained that "Thoreau's well-nourished sense of humor saved his egotism from becoming boorish," and E. B. White (*Subtreasury of American Humor,* 1941) offered expert testimony that "there is hardly a paragraph in *Walden* which does not seem humorous to me. . . . Thoreau makes me laugh the inaudible, the enduring laugh." With this Adams, Canby, and Krutch seem sympathetically to agree (see also Constance Rourke, *Native American Humor,* 1931).

On the whole, the critical atmosphere of the late 1920's and the 1930's was not hospitable to Thoreau as a man of letters. Odell Shepard in "The Paradox of Thoreau" (*Scribner's,* 1920) aroused little resentment when he proclaimed that Thoreau never learned to write, only to exclaim. "The world," said a writer in the New York *Times* (12 Sept. 1920), "is altogether too full of people who know how to write." Llewelyn Powys in "Thoreau: A Disparagement" (*Bookman,* 1929) announced him "neither a profound thinker nor a great writer." G. S. Hubbard found him equally inadequate in "Walden Re-Visited" (*SR,* 1929). Ludwig Lewisohn (*Expression in America,* 1932) disliked his literary manner as much as he did his personality. The best product of the period, Raymond Adams's "Henry Thoreau's Literary Theory and Criticism" (Univ. of North Carolina dissertation, 1928), remains unpublished, though much of its detail and many of its conclusions have been utilized by later critics, notably and most effectively by B. V. Crawford (*Henry David Thoreau: Representative Selections,* 1934).

Though Van Wyck Brooks (*The Flowering of New England,* 1937) and H. S. Canby (*Thoreau,* 1939) each have pleasantly judicious things to say of Thoreau's style, it was F. O. Matthiessen's *American Renaissance* (1941) which, just one hundred years after Thoreau decided to become a man of letters, first approached him seriously and sympathetically as an artist. Matthiessen's section on "*Walden:* Craftsmanship *vs* Technique" has already become a classic, setting forth an approach to the literary study of Thoreau which Matthiessen explored briefly in testing to what extent *Walden* meets Coleridge's demand of shaping, "as it develops, itself from within." His emphasis on Thoreau, the artist intent on the exact word and the homely image, owed something to Van Doren and other earlier critics, as did his review of Thoreau's literary and intellectual background and his expert exposition of the organic principle, all of which, however, was extended to consider Thoreau, not in isolation, but as part of the pattern of his time.

Students have found provocative Matthiessen's placing of Thoreau in a literary tradition which extends, not only to the past and to his New England contemporaries, but which stretches forward also, to Hemingway, D. H. Lawrence, Yeats, and Eliot. His suggestions of the relations which Thoreau discovered between symbol and myth, his demonstration of Thoreau's recreation of basic myth as protagonist in the drama of cosmic ritual, led S. E. Hyman in "Henry Thoreau in Our Time" (*Atlantic,* 1946) to claim Thoreau "not only a writer, but a writer in the great stream of American tradition," one with mythic and moralistic writers like Hawthorne, Melville, Mark Twain, Henry James, Hemingway, and Faulkner, and to find *Walden* "a vast rebirth ritual, the purest and most complete in our literature." The relation with Yeats, briefly mentioned by Matthiessen and by R. L. Cook (*Passage to Walden,* 1949), is further discussed by Robert Francis in "Passage to Innisfree" (*Christ. Sci. Monitor,* 1952) and Wendell Glick in "Yeats' Early Reading of *Walden*" (*BPLQ,* 1953).

G. F. Whicher's examination of *A Week* in *Walden Revisited* (1945), J. W. Krutch's chapter on "The Style and the Man" (*Thoreau,* 1947), Townsend Scudder's well-rounded appraisal in the *LHUS* (1948), Cook's chapter on "The Sinews of Style" (*Passage to Walden,* 1949) are all thoughtfully penetrating. Thoreau's use of sound, noted by almost every commentator from Emerson and Channing to Matthiessen and Cook (see Cook's chapter on "Correspondence with Nature"), is carefully explored by Sherman Paul in "The Wise Silence: Sound as the Agency of Correspondence in Thoreau" (*NEQ,* 1949). Something of present-day critical attitudes toward Thoreau is illustrated by Paul's study of his symbolism in "Resolution at Walden" (*Accent,* 1953) and by Charles Feidelson's treatment in *Symbolism in American Literature* (1952). A trend for the future may be discovered in P. W. Brown's "A Metropolite's Notes on Thoreau" (*Re-Appraisals,* Cleveland, 1952), where it is insisted that Thoreau is, first, a transcendental poet, second, a nature-mystic, but supremely an artist. It can even be hoped that the pattern of maturely informed criticism established by Raymond Adams in his address before the Grolier Club in March 1954, recently printed as "Thoreau's Mock Heroics and the American Natural History Writers" (*SP,* 1955), and by Frank Davidson's "Thoreau's Hound, Bay Horse, and Turtle-Dove" (*NEQ,* 1954) will set a standard toward which other contemporary commentators will reach.

Thoreau's poetry has not received intensive critical attention. Early commentators almost without exception pronounced it bad. Ripley found it "for the most part sorry prose" (N.Y. *Tribune,* 1849); Lowell dismissed it as "worsification" (*Mass. Quart. Rev.,* 1849); and Thoreau's classmate John Weiss found it crude and slovenly, seldom "touched with the bloom of beauty" (*Christian Examiner,* 1865). Again, however, Emerson set the critical pattern when he explained (*Atlantic,* 1862) that Thoreau "had the source of poetry in his spiritual perception," but that he "wanted a lyric facility and technical skill," so that his verses were "often crude and defective." In England, Stevenson passed them by and Watts-Dunton (*Athenaeum,* 1882) called them "unmitigated doggerel." There were a few defenders, like H. A. Page who found in Thoreau's verses "rarity and chastity" (*Thoreau,* 1877), and Sanborn (intro. to Channing's *Thoreau,* 1902) who described Thoreau as having "more completely than any man since Keats the traditional poetic temperament, intensive, passionate, capricious."

Most explicit of the early critics was Joel Benton, who discovered in "The Poetry of Thoreau" (*Lippincott's,* 1886) all of Thoreau's salient traits: his sturdy self-assertion, his love of paradox, his defiance of truth which is anti-proverbial and not apparent, his vision of each in all, his emphasis on the present tense, and his almost Swedenborgian belief in the double meaning of things. Thoreau's poetic endowment was unique and not easily grasped: "He would not court the listless or holiday auditor. You must wrestle with his thought, as he did, to entertain it properly." He was not a modern, but an Elizabethan, and his poetry "appeals to the inner spirit, like the lines of Wordsworth and Emerson." But for all of this, "poetry was either Thoreau's diversion or his reliance when prose failed. He believed that, in the main, prose was the better medium."

Most later critics have been less generous to Thoreau the poet, agreeing rather with Emerson, or with Salt, who concluded (*Thoreau,* 1890; see also his "Thoreau's Poetry," *Art Rev.,* 1890) that "strictly speaking he can hardly be called a poet at all," for "although he had a large gift of poetic inspiration, he lacked . . . lyrical fire and melodious utterance" (see also the introduction to Salt and Sanborn's edition of *Poems of Nature,* 1895), or with John Macy (*The Spirit of American Literature,* 1913) who found him in spirit close to the nature poet of all times and very close to Wordsworth, though in execution "his verses were not good."

Norman Foerster, too, in "Thoreau as Artist" (*SR,* 1921) wrote him off as no poet, because "a man can scarcely be a poet without achieving a certain bulk of successful verse, and the total bulk of Thoreau's verse, most of it unsuccessful, would fill less than an ordinary volume." The lines scattered amid his prose "have the odd effect of serving, not to lift the reader aloft on the wings of sudden inspiration, but to make him halt in consternation before a veritable New England glacial boulder, shapeless and inert." Thoreau "tells us repeatedly that he is inspired, but also tells us that the mood is gone before he can versify it; the best poetry, he says broadly, is never expressed." In metrical skill he was even more deficient than Emerson: "Most of his verses are benumbed, and crawl along, with an occasional spurt, like a grasshopper in autumn." Van Wyck Brooks (*The Flowering of New England,* 1937) described the poems as homespun, "well-woven, but indifferently cut . . . not intended to please." Though occasionally "Henry wrote a line or two that shivered its way up the spinal marrow," his verses were more often "sound and scholarly doggerel."

Thoreau's theory of the art of poetry was carefully examined by F. W. Lorch in "Thoreau and the Organic Principle of Poetry" (*PMLA,* 1938), which demonstrated that his conception of the organic principle, whether he got it directly from the German romanticists or from Emerson or Carlyle or Coleridge, "furnishes a key to a better understanding of his basic attitudes toward life" and illuminates his critical point of view. Thoreau never embodied his ideas in a single extended essay, but he was, said Lorch, "deeply interested in the theory of poetry." Like Emerson, he found its basis in beauty, truth, and goodness. No foe to the didactic, he demanded of poetry that it be ethical and useful, as well as beautiful. Form was "inseparably linked with idea, or intuition." Character and style, thought and word, substance and expression were but different aspects of the same thing. By means of poetry, man might establish relationship with the Divine, for poetry, said Thoreau, "is the mysticism of mankind." Because the end of art is the spiritual improvement of man, "its finest expression is not poetry but the character of the poet."

The appearance of the *Collected Poems* in 1943 brought from H. W. Wells "An Evaluation of Thoreau's Poetry" (*AL,* 1944) which G. F. Whicher (*Walden Revisited,* 1945) called the "only competent critical study of the complete poems." Wells noted Thoreau's search for a poetic style in the Greeks, in Horace, Skelton, Ben Jonson, Herbert, Marvel, Blake, and Wordsworth, but found him neither imitative nor derivative: "His scholarship is merely the outward sign of his universality as a poet. . . . Thoreau found all schools of poetry his teachers, none his master." He was in no sense a poet with his face to the past, nor even a "strictly representative figure of either the early or the later phases of romanticism," but was one who, "like Emily Dickinson or Baudelaire, anticipates the bold symbolism, airy impressionism, stringent realism, and restless inconsistencies of modern verse." He has the acute tensions of modern verse, an abruptness and boldness of phrase, a nervous heightening of subjectivity, and his satire "resembles in a broad way the forthright manner of the brilliant satires of Yeats." His "breadth of vision is precisely what our age, tragically seeking a new consolidation of mankind, most of all requires."

The centennial of the publication of *Walden* brought forth in 1954 several pleasantly appreciative commemorative articles, among them those by Raymond Adams in the *TSB,* H. S. Canby in the *SR,* Robert Frost and Reginald Cook in the *Listener,* Joseph Jones in the *University of Texas Library Chronicle,* Lewis Leary in the *Nation,* Samuel Sillen in *Masses and Mainstream,* and E. B. White in the *YR*. None of them added significantly to the sum of our understanding of Thoreau, but in the aggregate they provided evidence that the breadth of his vision is not forgotten.

5

MELVILLE

I. Bibliography and Manuscripts

NO COMPLETE bibliography of Melville can come into being until after the subsidence of the present wave of biographical and critical writing. The detailed eight-page record in the *LHUS* (1948) is already inadequate, and one might conjecture that the 500 articles noted in 1939 by Charles Anderson in *Melville in the South Seas* have tripled in number during the last fifteen years. All existing bibliographies, including that in the *Literary History,* will remain selective until this need is fulfilled. Students may supplement this bibliography with the *Annual Melville Bibliography, 1951* (1952); *1952-53* (1954), sponsored by the Melville Society and compiled by S. C. Sherman, J. H. Birss, and Gordon Roper. (See also *BNYPL,* June-July 1951). There are also checklists of varying extent and wisdom in recent editions and biographies of Melville. Gordon Roper has issued mimeographed sheets, "Bibliography and Works by and on Herman Melville." For up-to-the-minute information one should consult *Doctoral Dissertations on Herman Melville, 1933-1952,* compiled by Tyrus Hillway, and also the current Melville Society *Newsletter* (1945-).

Many biographies, beginning with R. M. Weaver's in 1921, include helpful lists or "bibliographical notes," but the most workable for the scholar is the "Selected Bibliography" in *Herman Melville, Representative Selections* (1938) edited by Willard Thorp. In these classified lists the fourth section is the most valuable, under the heading of "Contemporary Reviews and

Criticism." Additional aid may be had from the still earlier checklists in W. S. Ament's "Bowdler and the Whale" (*AL,* Mar. 1932) or Michael Sadleir's *Excursions in Victorian Bibliography* (1922) or Meade Minnegerode's *Some Personal Letters of Herman Melville,* published in the same year. (See also Roper, pp. 4-7.)

Materials for a detailed bibliography reside in special collections at Harvard and Princeton Universities, in the New York Public Library, and in the libraries of a few private persons. Although some letters survive and a few manuscripts of the later writings, the spine of these collections is books. Out of these, containing Melville's jottings in pencil on Emerson or Cervantes, the scholars are recreating in biography or critical article the intellectual and artistic history of his books and of his mind. Some 350 books (exclusive of his own writings) are known as his. Many of these books are in the three collections mentioned. The Houghton Library at Harvard has letters, manuscripts of poems and prose items, and of the journals of 1849 and 1856, and the Harvard College Library contains most of the books saved by three granddaughters of Melville. Other books were given by a fourth granddaughter to the New York Public Library, which in the Gansevoort-Lansing, the Duyckinck, and the Berg Collections possesses other treasures. More books and other Melville material are available in the Lemuel Shaw Collection of the Massachusetts Historical Society and in the Princeton University Library. An edition of the letters will be published in the near future by W. H. Gilman and M. R. Davis. (See Roper, pp. 4-5.) Although manuscripts are not abundant in comparison with those of more sedentary or more immediately popular authors, the continued analysis of this source material (Jay Leyda, *The Melville Log;* see below) may make possible, say, in twenty-five years, the desired complete bibliography.

II. Editions, Reprints, Selections, Letters, Journals, etc.

It is ironical that for a writer now recognized as, presumably, our foremost novelist, reliable texts are difficult to secure. Apart from such compendiums as the *Romances of Herman Melville,* and the recent, far better *Portable Melville* (see below), we must still rely on *The Works of Herman Melville,* Standard Edition in twelve volumes, published in London in 1922-23, with the additional four volumes of 1924: XIII, *Billy Budd and Other Prose Pieces;* XIV, XV, *Clarel;* XVI, *Poems,* containing *Battle-Pieces, John Marr and Other Sailors, Timoleon,* and *Miscellaneous Poems.* In spite of its cost and unavailability this edition is even now indispensable to the scholar. A new collected edition (*Complete Works,* Hendricks House) under the aegis of young Melville scholars has become a case of hope deferred, but of these projected fourteen volumes (in a trade edition, and also in a numbered set with textual notes) we may now consult editions of the *Collected Poems* (1947), by H. P. Vincent; *Piazza Tales* (1948), by E. S. Oliver; *Pierre* (1949), by H. A. Murray; *Moby-Dick* (1952), by L. S. Mansfield and H. P. Vincent; and *The Confidence Man* (1954), by Elizabeth Foster. In a brief allusion to these five volumes merely as texts, the first, in its inaccuracy, calls for another edition. The second fills effectively a long-felt need for an accessible text of these stories, and the third supplants an edition of 1930, by R. S. Forsythe (see below). The fourth appears to be a "definitive" edition. The fifth contains an excellent introduction. Of these two "collected" editions, the first is doubtful in textual authenticity, if compared with the first American editions of the separate works, and cumbersome in its appendage of four belated volumes. The second is still unfinished, and in the volumes published uneven in both format and editing. We need new definitive editions of all our major writers (save Sidney Lanier), but our suppression of Melville is triumphant. Only a few minor writers have had a more complete Christian burial than our Titan. (For other editions and manuscripts, see Roper, p. 6.)

I am speaking of formal, collected editions. As Melville's stature has revealed itself during the thirty-three years since Weaver's pioneering biography, edition after edition of the separate works has appeared in attempts to fill this blank. A few of these are inferior reprints, profiteering on the tardy fame of an almost forgotten author. *Typee* has had a complicated bibliographical history, including the first American (unexpurgated) edition in 1846. An edition of 1892 is still in print. *Typee* reappeared in 1902, with an introduction by W. P. Trent, in 1907 in Everyman's Library (severely "expurgated") and in 1924 in the World's Classics. Republished in these years as an adventure story or an idyl of the South Seas, *Typee* was eventually to aid in the merciless modern analysis of Melville's mind. Editions of *Omoo* have been numerous both during Melville's lifetime, and later. Curiosity about other books by the author of *Moby-Dic*k is indicated by R. M. Weaver's edition of *Mardi* in 1925 and of *Redburn* in 1924 (See also editions in 1937, 1948, and 1951) or by Carl Van Doren's of *White-Jacket* in 1929, in the World's Classics.

Even the many reprints of *Moby-Dick,* often with corrupt texts, during the first three decades of the century (Everyman's Library, 1907; World's Classics, 1920, with its tribute from Viola Meynell; Modern Library, 1926; or Modern Readers' Series, 1929) seemed to strengthen the conviction first expressed by Archibald MacMechan in 1914. In "The Best Sea Story Ever Written" he pronounced a verdict unacceptable today: "Melville is a man of one book." Other editions of the "one book" have multiplied during the last twenty-five years. Newton Arvin brought out an edition in 1948, and one special edition was Willard Thorp's reproduction in 1947 of the text of the first American printing, with a facsimile title page, a sheaf of pertinent illustrations and diagrams, and a sane introduction.

A reprint of *Pierre,* with an Introduction by J. B. Moore and a Preface by H. M. Tomlinson, appeared in 1929, but the first warning that this novel was a key to the mind of Melville was sounded in R. S. Forsythe's edition (1930, 1941), with its exploratory introduction. There followed a spate of articles (see below) analyzing its relation to the other novels and its disclosure of what Ellery Sedgwick was to call (as the subtitle of his biography) "The Tragedy of Mind." An acknowledgment of

Pierre's importance is the edition of 1949, with its seventy-five pages of "Explanatory Notes," ten of "Textual Notes," and its Introduction of ninety pages, all contributed by H. A. Murray, "a professing psychologist."

Curiosity extended to the writings after *Pierre* (which we now recognize as the third book in a trilogy of which the preceding two were *Mardi* and *Moby-Dick*), and was destined to reach another climax in the posthumous *Billy Budd. Israel Potter,* of minor interest to the serious student of Melville, had been reprinted in 1924, and in 1929 *The Piazza Tales,* a stopgap pending E. S. Oliver's text (mentioned above). In 1927 (reprinted in 1949) Random House issued "Benito Cereno" with illustrations by E. McKnight Kauffer, and in 1940 V. W. Van Hagen brought out *The Encantadas* in a limited edition. Editions of *The Confidence Man* were published in London in 1948 and in New York in 1949. Elizabeth Foster's edition appeared late in 1954 (see above).

Melville's poetry, issued during the last twenty-five years of his life, was to wait almost as long for recognition. In 1922 Henry Chapin offered selections, with an Introduction, but both scholar and general reader remained preoccupied with the prose until about 1944. In this year F. O. Matthiessen gave us *Herman Melville, Selected Poems,* containing twenty-one pages of meticulously selected verse, and a commensurate Introduction of four pages. (In London, in 1943, was published William Plomer's English edition of the poems.) Matthiessen's slender volume, which found room for a few lines from *Clarel,* seemed, as its editor said, "to take advantage of all the various interests attaching to any part of Melville's work." *Clarel* is on the verge of reappearance in the new Collected Works. Although its length prevented its inclusion in H. P. Vincent's *Collected Poems of Herman Melville,* this "first American Edition" aimed at completeness. "The text," says its editor, "of the first 256 pages faithfully follows that of the three volumes of poetry published during his lifetime and under his scrupulous supervision; the text for the rest of the poetry is taken from the manuscripts, of which all but three are in the Houghton Library, Harvard College." The set edition of this volume contains a substantial body of notes, explanatory and textual.

Among all the posthumous pieces of Melville (letters, lectures, contributions to periodicals, reviews, poems, and prose fragments; see Roper, pp. 3-5), many of which are now exhumed and edited, none rivals *Billy Budd* either as a distinguished volume in the Melville canon, or, like *Pierre,* as a part of the "Inside Story" of Melville's mind. Melville died on 28 September 1891. On 19 April he had completed his revision of the manuscript, which then lay among family papers until R. M. Weaver was permitted to examine it in 1919. Its first published appearance was in Volume XIII of the Collected Works in 1924 (see above). Weaver reprinted it in 1928 in *The Shorter Novels of Herman Melville,* and since that date it has commanded, through anthology, play, or opera, an audience almost as devoted as that of *Moby-Dick.* In 1948 appeared *Melville's Billy Budd,* edited by F. B. Freeman. This book was "an attempt to present the first accurate transcription, with all variant readings, of the manuscripts of *Billy Budd;* the first publication of Melville's previously undiscovered short story, 'Baby Budd, Sailor'; the first extended analysis of the novel, together with a biographical account of the neglected last years of his life." Appendixes contain manuscript fragments including the controversial (and perhaps unrelated) "Daniel Orme" item (see below). Here is a new text, unfortunately still inexact, from an almost illegible manuscript, besides an Introduction of 126 pages dealing with the novel (and the short story) in relation to Melville's thought. (*Billy Budd* is also available in *Selected Tales and Poems,* 1950, edited by Richard Chase, and in *Selected Writings,* Modern Library Giant, 1952.)

Among the miscellaneous publications there are now several travel journals. In 1935 (published by *The Colophon*) R. M. Weaver edited (with inaccuracies of transcription) *Journal up the Straits, October 11, 1856-May 5, 1857,* valuable for its relevance to *Clarel.* H. C. Horsford's new edition of this journal, entitled *Journal of a Visit to Europe and the Levant* (1955), corrects Weaver's text and provides a helpful introduction and many valuable notes. Further light is thrown on Melville's outward life in the "Journal of Melville's Voyage in a Clipper Ship" (*NEQ,* 1929), and in Eleanor Melville Metcalf's *Journal of a Visit to London and the Continent by Herman Melville 1849-1850* (1948). (For journals and juvenilia, see Roper, p. 3.) Pending the publication of a complete edition of the correspondence (see above), Melville's letters remain scattered in manuscripts, magazines, biographies of other writers (e.g., Hawthorne), or volumes of selections. In 1922 Meade Minnegerode published *Some Personal Letters of Herman Melville.* Accurate versions of most of these letters and of others in the Duyckinck Collection may now be found in the important section called "Letters" in Thorp's *Herman Melville, Representative Selections.* This volume contains a list of letters in scattered sources and of miscellaneous material, both prose and poetry. (See also Jay Leyda, *The Melville Log.*) We may note here the *Family Correspondence of Herman Melville,* 1830-1904, "Some Melville Letters," in the *Nation and Athenaeum* (13 Aug. 1921), and "Two Letters of Herman Melville," edited by Harrison Hayford (*ELH,* 1944). Melville's letters, which are none too plentiful (e.g., see E. M. Metcalf, *Herman Melville, Cycle and Epicycle,* 1953; *NEQ,* 1932; *AL,* 1943), are usually either dross (mere fact) or pure gold, as in the beautiful revelation of his art and of his association with Hawthorne in "Melville's 'Agatha' Letter to Hawthorne" (*NEQ,* 1929; see also *The Portable Melville* and Roper, pp. 4-5).

Melville has proved to be a problem for the anthologists, but various *Piazza Tales,* especially "Benito Cereno," have been reprinted entire, and *Billy Budd* and even *Typee* have been gathered into volumes of selections. (See *Selected Tales and Poetry of Herman Melville,* 1950.) Thorp's AWS *Representative Selections* now seems the most practical, both for the novice and the devotee, if we remember that no winnowing can take the place of the books themselves. This volume is invaluable for its unpublished material, its wise selections from the prose and poetry, and its workable scholarly apparatus. On the verge of going out of print, it is likely to be supplanted by Jay Leyda's *The Portable Melville* (1952), a stout anthology of 746 pages. Leyda has "strung the work selected along the thread of the life that produced it." This theory is a bit finespun especially since we look in vain for *Moby-Dick*. Leyda acknowledges humorously that "A Melville anthology without *Moby-Dick!*" is startling but argues that the lack is extremely easy to supply. The space saved pays dividends in complete versions of *Typee* and *Billy Budd,* in new letters, journal passages, a lecture, poetry, and marginalia.

III. Biographies

In a bibliographical essay on Herman Melville the age-old problem of the separation of biography from criticism becomes acute. Some of the biographies to be discussed in the present section contain critical judgments of the highest importance, and large sections of the criticism in the next division (both books and articles) are packed with new biographical data. In some instances biography has been austerely divorced from criticism, and in others criticism has voyaged into a dubious infinite, with a lofty disdain of earthbound facts. Usually, however, these books attempt an integration of Melville's life and writings. Such biographies reveal a profound mind, philosophic, humanitarian, artistic, a mind asking questions and postulating answers. Melville used his novels as divining rods in his approaches to the mysteries of God and Man. In this sense the study of Melville is the study of one mind, its genetics, its development, its sensitivity to American life, its explorations in the trackless ways of metaphysical thought.

These varied approaches are apparent in the score of books included in this section, and I shall allude again to their judgments in the subdivision on criticism. For example, articles on *Pierre* supplement or contradict chapters on this novel in the biographies. The distinguishing feature of these books, however, apart from their length, is their awareness, even when they use it for the purposes of criticism, of Melville's daily life. On all students of Melville this exerts an undying fascination partly because the biographer must work for what he gets—facts are still scarce—partly because of the striking analogy between Melville's actual sea and the sea of his imagination. The problems of his novels seem to have precedents in his own life, whether in his adolescence or in the "silent years." Few of the biographers mentioned below would agree with Ronald Mason, an English critic (see below), that "the actual events of Herman Melville's life, except in so far as they are directly recorded or reflected in his books, are not of very great interest or importance, and it is possible to extract a coherent meaning from the body of his writing without having much recourse to biographical narrative."

It is profitable to compare the two earliest "biographical narratives" by friends of Melville with Van Wyck Brooks's version in 1943 in the *DAB*. In comparison with this modern critic's recognition of Melville's genius, the Duyckincks' bleak estimate in their *Cyclopaedia of American Literature* in 1855 seems incredible. By this year *Mardi, Moby-Dick,* and *Pierre,* besides the earlier writings, were available. Yet Amasa Delano in "Benito Cereno" was not more myopic than these intimates who saw Melville almost daily. This is true of his friend, J. E. A. Smith, whose thirty-page biographical sketch, written for the *Evening Journal* of Pittsfield, in 1891, has the maddening gift of silence on questions which we long to ask a contemporary of Melville. The first substantial biography of Melville by R. M. Weaver thirty years later (1921) also fails to satisfy our curiosity, although the biographer had access to Melville's manuscripts, letters, and papers. On the years after 1857 Weaver offers virtually nothing. Yet one is reluctant to note omissions or lacks in this godfather of all Melville criticism, in this discoverer of *Billy Budd. Herman Melville, Mariner and Mystic* remains an important repository of source material, and a beginner may acquire the story of Melville's life from Weaver's pages. The story is, of course, incomplete. Recent scholarship has invalidated, corrected, or added to Weaver's outline. Everything in Weaver is simplified, and if we complain of too many meanings from some recent critics, we may, on the other hand, smile a little at Weaver's vague interpretations of Melville's "mysticism" or at his apologies for the complexity of Melville's genius. *"Moby-Dick,"* he says, "is at once indisputably the greatest whaling novel, and 'a hideous and intolerable allegory'." That we have gone farther we owe in part to this scholar's enthusiasm. His book is still useful.

John Freeman found it so, and in his 200-page *Herman Melville* (1926) added nothing to our knowledge of Melville's life. Instead he condensed Weaver's crowded data into a lucid narrative. To this story, which in the light of modern research appears elementary, Freeman devotes his first four chapters or a little less than half his book. Like Weaver, Freeman was writing for a public for whom Melville was but a name. He employs copious extracts and synopses, and his tone is appreciative, again like Weaver's, rather than critical. After all, it was, as he observes, the first book on Melville to be published in England, and actually, the second biography of this American author. The other six chapters are critical in intent and pleasantly written, but Freeman, though he is sensitive to what he, too, calls the "mysticism" in Melville, and though he submits analogies with Conrad, Hardy, and Blake, fails to explain either the novels or the complexities of Melville's mind. *Moby-Dick,* he declares, must be read "in isolation." In introducing a little-known Melville, perhaps Freeman's greatest service was in Chapter ix, in his early estimates of the poetry, in, for instance, his examination of "After the Pleasure Party," a poem destined to entangle later critics in a thicket of bold interpretations.

The next biographers responded less to fact than to the challenge of Melville's mind. The stage was now set for a long series of magnificent guesses. Lewis Mumford's *Herman Melville* (1929) removed the writer from the uncritical admiration of Weaver and Freeman and created an intimate portrait of the man in relation to his books. Melville's adolescence, his marriage, his "insanity," and his Timonism are all integrated with the thought and passion of his fiction. Mumford's image of Melville has inspired other adventurous interpreters of Melville (Arvin or Chase, see below) while it has distressed critics demanding more demonstrable truth. The portrait is definite in outline, plausible, and admirable in its recreation of a mind, of an "Olympian," a "Titan," and a "Pilgrim." Yet just as Julian Hawthorne once declared that a certain imaginative portrait of Nathaniel Hawthorne, however arresting, was not, after all, his father, so this may be, as Mumford's critics assert, not Melville, but an image born of our ignorance and dreams.

For the biographer relies not as much on the letters and journals as on Melville's own fiction as autobiographical. It is, in certain ways, but recent scholarship has shown conclusively ways in which it is not. We cannot rely on *Redburn* (see Thorp and Gilman below) as a dependable record of young Melville's daily life, and we cannot be as sure as Mumford concerning the relationship of Melville's wife, Elizabeth Shaw Melville, to the characters of Lucy and Isabel in *Pierre*. "Both Melville's father and his mother were monsters." This statement, in the first chapter, "Bitter Morning," is essential to the subsequent full-length portrait which Mumford draws so skillfully. As announced in his Preface, he uses Melville's "own language, wherever possible," and he emphasizes the poetic temper of his book by casting pages 119-131 in the form of a drama.

Yet the importance of this undocumented, semi-fictionized biography is undeniable. We shall not understand Melville merely by knowing when he was in Honolulu or the day on which he deserted ship in the Marquesas. Apparently Mumford was the first to perceive that the cetological passages in *Moby-Dick* were not merely "digressions." He saw the interrelation of the lesser works to this book though he was courageous enough to say that it "stands by itself as complete as the Divine Comedy or the Odyssey stands by itself." He recognized its superb craftsmanship, and, in a brilliant chapter on *Moby-Dick,* he stated a thesis which has withstood considerable shock from later critics. The novel is, he said, "fundamentally, a parable on the mystery of evil and the accidental malice of the universe. The white whale stands for the brute energies of existence, blind, fatal, overpowering, while Ahab is the spirit of man, small and feeble, but purposive." Mumford declared that to understand Melville we must enter into his "deepest consciousness." Later critics took up the theme. The truly great man, Melville had said, is a "diver."

With a vigor unequaled, I think, in the scholarship concerning other major American authors, there now followed an intensive investigation of the tangibles relating to Melville: biographical facts, even of the most minute character (see below), examination of his intellectual habits and tastes, such as his reading, and the exposition and classification of his ideas. In 1937 K. H. Sundermann, acknowledging his debt to the three biographies just discussed, published in Berlin his *Herman Melvilles Gedankengut, eine kritische Untersuchung seiner weltanschaulichen Grundideen.* This final word was apt. After a twelve-page Introduction on Melville's life and his objectives and methods, Sundermann pursues relentlessly these basic ideas (pantheism or patriotism; the theory of innate ideas or capitalism) through novel after novel. He considers three kinds of ideas, religious, philosophic, and historical, with breakdowns in each of these three large sections into special concepts. The elusive Melville does not suffer so fierce a systematization; Sundermann gives the poetic and symbolistic Melville rough handling. Yet, if heavy-footed, this topical method has its uses; the fugue-like recurrence of themes in Melville's thinking is strongly emphasized. Unfortunately a record of the times when Melville analyzes or invokes "Truth" does not tell us much, not much more, perhaps than a list of his visits to New York. The categories, however, will prove helpful.

After a glance at Luther Mansfield's *Herman Melville, Author and New Yorker, 1844-1851* (abstract of dissertation, 1938), with its account of Melville's reading, we turn to another highly detailed biography, to Jean Simon's *Herman Melville, marin, métaphysicien, et poète,* published in Paris in 1939. A professional student of American literature, a visitor from time to time in the United States, Simon created a book of solidity and dimension. In 623 pages it records the whole story of Melville's life and writings as these were known fifteen years ago. In three parts, with exposition, description, and with liberal quotation, Simon discusses the biography, the mind, and, in the most significant section, the "originality" of Melville (The Man, the Thinker, the Artist, the Romancer). In this broad view of Melville the Man and Writer, Simon finds room for particularity, as in the descriptions of the islands in *Mardi.* Like all of Simon's scholarship, this book is valuable for its European frame of reference, especially for its account of translations and European criticisms of Melville.

Meanwhile, in America the untiring search for fact found expression in 1939 in C. R. Anderson's *Melville in the South Seas.* Concerning the travels of 1841 to 1844 Anderson was lynx-eyed. He used the standard collections at Harvard and in New York as well as the Naval Records and Library at Washington, but he drew especially upon "newly discovered manuscripts and documents, widely scattered from Paris to Sidney, Australia, and from the vast, unexplored literature of travel." For his grains of biographical gold he scoured newspapers, logbooks, and registers. The resultant body of evidence is impressive. Melville changes from a romantic Sindbad to an actual sailor in real ships. This book is an excellent check upon impressions of the "Titan" formed from volumes like Mumford's, but Anderson is not content with the names of vessels and ports of call. He shows how Melville used his travels with increasing subtlety, and how he reinforced the verisimilitude of his fiction by passages from travel books. These episodes Melville recast until in comparison the originals seem bare. To create *Typee* he breathed new life into old chronicles. Anderson makes us reconsider the quality of Melville's imagination; it was less wildly spontaneous than transforming.

In their contrasting purposes the foregoing are stimulating studies, but the last decade has witnessed others, swinging in their axis of reality between what most men call fact to psychological conjecture, from Jay Leyda's *Melville Log* to Lawrance Thompson's *Melville's Quarrel With God.* W. E. Sedgwick, who seems to have been only incidentally aware of Lewis Mumford's "integration" of Melville's life and writings, began this important decade with *Herman Melville, The Tragedy of Mind* (1945). This appreciation of Melville, comparable in temper, though not in genius, with Francis Thompson's memorial to Shelley or Henry James's to Hawthorne, scants biography, but establishes and maintains a special point of view. This is a definition of Melville's approach to life, with illustrative chapters on Melville's novels and tales. Gracefully written, even in its presentation of a thesis, this book on Melville has provoked both admiration and disagreement.

Reflecting on Melville's astonishing double intimacy, both with outward life, even in its grossest or most trivial aspects, and with the inwardness of Mind, Sedgwick is, at first, at a loss for a definitive word. In the end he christens this dualism of Melville's his "intensity." Here was an inner quest, reflected in that "indrawn, dim look" of his eyes, recorded by Mrs. Hawthorne. "Importunate," Sedgwick continues, "he was forever precipitating himself against the ultimate truth of creation." This "intensity" was an active as well as passive function, growing in power and delicacy throughout his long life, and finding a progressive expression in the fiction and poetry. The books are "the record, in their innermost recesses, of . . . an unfolding of inward vision." Sedgwick describes the "unfolding panorama" of the mind of Melville, the "slowly lengthening 'landscape in the soul'."

The unfolding, the search for an explanation, begins in *Typee,* in its concept of a society from which the fever of the modern world is beatifically absent. Like Melville, we have all at times longed for the carefree world of the Typees. Sedgwick admits that this unfolding drama of Melville's mind breaks down in *Omoo*. He believes that it is resumed in *Mardi,* in whose second part Melville lives in the heaven of the unfettered intellect. The limbo of *Typee* is exchanged for an intense search for Truth. In *Redburn* the exfoliating mind knows evil and all its disillusionments. In this series of "profiles" of the exploratory mind of Melville, each work, including *Clarel,* has its own particular revelation. In Sedgwick's chapter on *Moby-Dick,* which consumes about one fifth of his 255 pages, the thesis is subdivided into other unprovable dogmatisms. There is "a trinity, a three in one": Ahab, the White Whale, and the sea. Ahab is sentient Man who is set against "the immense mystery of creation," symbolized by Moby-Dick. The sea is "the element of truth." What was at first a provocative idea, if kept fluid and tentative, has become a formula. Critics have found it too precise, as in its application to *Redburn.* (See Gilman, pp. 285-286.)

Richard Chase's *Herman Melville, A Critical Study* (1949) is not, as its author says repeatedly, a biography, but, like Sedgwick's book, it makes use of Melville's life history, and may be included here. Chase is at odds with Sedgwick and other critics who interpret Melville as a searcher after ultimate truth. He is interested in him as an artist and as a critic and analyst of "man and his culture." Although his method is "partly biographical," Chase tries to put the works of Melville before the reader and ask the questions: "What do these works say within themselves and in relation to one another? What do they say to us in our time of troubles?" Like Mumford and Arvin (see below), he gives much attention to the father quest, but for Chase this quest means not God but "a cultural ideal, a great man in a great culture." This study is not always clearcut in carrying out its announced purposes, and it demands sweepingly revisionary judgments of Melville, often based on mere assertion.

If, however, we accept partial or hypothetical truth as the temper of the book we may have some engaging reading. For example, it might be true to say that *one* "theme of Melville's first five books is the education of the young man," but Chase uses the definite article, "the theme." Most critics would agree that in *Mardi,* for instance, other problems also occupy Melville. Perhaps implications of mutilation flit through Melville's mind in connection with Ahab's amputated leg or even in the lameness of the young man in *Typee.* Yet the reader is apt to have reservations on the flat statement that the hero obsessed by the fear of castration is a common one in Melville's novels, or that the "real theme of *Billy Budd* is castration and cannibalism, and eating of the Host." These are not exceptional instances of Chase's method. The first wave in his extreme, unsubstantiated interpretations carries a shock, but once we are used to the water the others break over our heads without much damage. It is lively reading, and does the sophisticated Melvillian no harm.

Although such overtones may be in the novels, precise conclusions are perilous, concerning "the fear of castration (symbolized by cannibalism, decapitation, the injured leg, the horror of women), homoeroticism, narcissism, incest, and parricide." Chase has transformed echoes from Melville's subconscious into doctrines. If, however, we read on, we have a wider view of Melville's protean mind, through which thronged a continual procession of hooded phantoms like those of the White Whale. It is arguable that Melville was interested in two central themes of a myth: the Fall and the Search. The Prometheus myth recurs, and the sixteen sections of the chapter called "Portraits of the Young Man" emphasize not unfairly Melville's sensitive awakening to an awareness of man's insecurity in his civilization and in his relations with the universe.

The virtue of Chase's book is its "suggestiveness," especially in its interpretation of Melville's works in relation to America. We cannot accept unreservedly the notion that Ishmael symbolizes young America or that America is the Prometheus among nations. We may challenge the assertion that Ahab is "the American cultural image," that he is the good, progressive American, and so on. Nevertheless, Chase, in debt to Chapter vi of Constance Rourke's *American Humor* (1931), was the first to make us fully aware of what is now in the public literary domain, the intimate association of the writings of Melville not only with the American scene, but with American attitudes of mind, with American myth, with the American folklore hero. Such "suggestiveness" mitigates the categorical definitions, that "Ahab is the aging American Titan" or that the name "Redburn" means "the Promethean fire."

Almost simultaneously with Chase's book appeared two biographies by European authors, Geoffrey Stone's *Melville,* in 1949, and Pierre Frédérix' *Herman Melville* in 1950. (See also Jean Giono's fictionized *Pour Saluer Melville,* Paris, 1941.) Both these writers seemed to address primarily their fellow-countrymen and offered little that was new for American students of Melville. Stone invokes the "general reader" and renounces "scholarly impedimenta." He treats *Redburn* as sound autobiography and describes Melville's mind as "partly Calvinistic, partly Romantic." Stone's own point of view was Catholic. Frédérix' narrative acknowledges its dependence upon Weaver, Freeman, Mumford, Sedgwick, and Anderson. He recounts plots, dresses up Melville's adventures both in Polynesia and America, and, even if accurate in his reproduction of standard sources, reminds us constantly by contrast of Simon's monumental work.

In his *Herman Melville* (1950) Newton Arvin follows, in some respects, the fashion inaugurated by Mumford, to whom he pays homage in his succinct bibliography. He aims at an integration of Melville's life and works. He is also akin to Chase in pseudo-psychological speculation. He begins by describing Melville as afflicted by "the tormented psychology of the decayed patrician" and he dwells on the staggering consequences of the loss of his father on the edge of adolescence. Although not particularly respectful toward cold fact, Arvin's book, most gracefully written of all the biographies of Melville, contains some sane, perceptive literary criticism. Our attention is called to the influence of space (see articles below) on Melville's imagination, to the obvious need of this imagination for "the coarse stuff of experience," to the weakness of *Mardi,* with its shifting centers of interest and its lack of "a balanced design." Without extravagance Arvin shows Melville's growing consciousness of evil in the period of *Redburn* and *White Jacket,* and he comments on the factitiousness of Melville's feminine characters. In "The Whale"—an effective chapter—he suggests four basic "movements" and two kinds of metaphor, and he is excellent on the language of Melville.

In his survey of the novels after *Moby-Dick,* Arvin is influenced by his conviction concerning the "inescapable effect of anticlimax." *Pierre,* now recognized as an unlocker of Melville's mind, he dislikes for its "badness" and "deadness," and he hardly glances at "Benito Cereno." He calls this story "an artistic miscarriage." It is strange to find this acute critic holding (though for different reasons) to the old illusion of 1914, that "nothing Melville later did [was] comparable to his one very great book." The critical judgments on the writings are suggestive, but again the pitfall seems to be the man Melville, his inner thoughts, his subconscious self. When Arvin moves from the books to the recesses of Melville's mind, we enter a now familiar yet still chartless realm. We tread doubtful ground. Is it true that for Melville "physical sexuality" was "charged through and through . . . with guilt and anxiety"? Is it true that "the masculine and the feminine elements in Melville's own nature were far too precariously balanced, too unreconciled with one another for marriage to be anything but excruciatingly problematic?" These statements are made as facts, but they are not facts. They are surmises.

It was natural that the subconscious or oneiric Melville should be challenged. In some criticism reaction went far, as extreme in its preoccupation with fact as exploratory criticism with its fantasies. I believe, however, that the reader of the present bibliographical essay will discover an over-all balance. Two biographies of the reaction appeared in the same year (1951), and were, indeed, two sides of a common project: Leon Howard's *Herman Melville* and Jay Leyda's *The Melville Log:*

A Documentary Life of Herman Melville, 1819-1891. Out of a devotion to Melville, and out of a common conviction that Melville and his writing had suffered distortion, these two writers embarked on an original approach: two interdependent biographies. In his Preface Howard alludes to the "misinformation . . . in print" about Melville, and Leyda speaks of "the bog of Melville interpretation . . . with its thick growth of wild guesses." He asks: "Is there anyone in American literature who has attracted such a swarm of myths and apocrypha as has Melville?" Nevertheless, we must not think of these biographies as angry rejoinders to more speculative minds. The two books came from the natural temper of these two scholars and probably would have been written had not others declared that the sea stood for "Truth," and (later) that the name *Pequod* meant a "pique at God."

According to the plan, Howard was to write "a formal narrative biography," while Leyda was to create from all dependable materials a day-by-day record of Melville's life. To achieve this end Leyda followed a principle which he derived in part from certain Russian biographies, and which he is now adapting to his forthcoming life of Emily Dickinson. The two authors shared materials, discussed problems, and made the two books separate, but interrelated, not composite but complementary. Although Howard's book is professional, notes are lacking and must be supplied, so to speak, by the reader through a concurrent reading of the *Melville Log*. This technique permits Howard's biography to be a free-running narrative, with suggestions of the sources and authorities in the *Log,* while at the same time the latter has a sequence of its own and a readability never vouchsafed orthodox footnotes. The reader will think of disadvantages, such as the simultaneous use of two different volumes. In one he may miss documentation, and in the other he may find only the bareness of a chronicle. Wings of the imagination are clipped. Yet apart from the interlocking, which some have found valuable, each volume has a kind of authority in its own right.

Howard's closely-packed, factual biography demonstrates the amazing expansion in our knowledge of the actual Melville since the relatively sketchy life histories by Weaver and Freeman. Many of the gaps which hampered Mumford have been closed. Instead of a lonely, meditative philosopher and artist Melville appears as a busy human being, living and writing under the pressures of intense activity. The density of the book, with its garnering of all known facts, we owe to many investigators but also to Howard's determination to present Melville as a living, breathing, nineteenth-century American. But perhaps we should let him define his purpose in his own words. After repudiating a current conception, that of the novel and poem as an independent object of aesthetic experience, he says: "Nor can I share another widespread assumption: that literature draws most of its peculiar nourishment from the substrata of the author's mind, below the level of his conscious motives and desires . . . the sort of critical botanizing that confines itself to speculations about the taproot . . . is not to my taste . . . and in dealing with Melville's books I have concerned myself primarily with the observable evidence of their growth."

There will be agreement about Howard's service to Melville criticism by this synthesis of all our knowledge concerning the everyday Melville. In contrast to some previous biographers, he viewed the autobiographical narratives with suspicion, and used their material only when he could find supporting evidence. He says "there is guesswork aplenty," but the reader feels secure. There will not, however, be agreement that in providing us with the entire external story Howard has recreated the whole Melville. Even a conservative Melvillian has remarked that Howard "has drawn back farther from his subject than he should have." The four pages of the main entry on *Billy Budd,* for example, say nothing which good sense cannot credit, but do not say enough. A few moments ago we considered the opposite situation: too little proved and too much said. It is easy to demand everything in one book. I am trying to estimate critical reactions to these different types of biographies. None cleaves to a single principle more firmly than Howard's *Herman Melville.*

After an Introduction Leyda's book begins with "Biographical Notes on Melville's Associates," a kind of dramatis personae. Volume II concludes with a section called "The Sources." Between these two parts of a simple apparatus is the day-by-day log. In the orthodox sense there is no interpretation. Yet Leyda really gives us the ultimate in that liberty of speculation which other biographers have wooed in their disregard of demonstrable fact. That is, Leyda's purpose is to furnish the data and let the reader weave his own interpretation. "I have tried," he says, "to hold to one main aim: to give each reader the opportunity to be his own biographer of Herman Melville, by providing him with the largest possible quantity of materials to build his own approach to this complex figure . . . to put together everything that could be known about his life." In describing Leyda's method I have, perhaps, suggested an aridity which does not really exist. The *Log* is far more than a place in which to look things up about Melville. Somehow, as in his still incomplete record of Emily Dickinson, Leyda has captured through letters, documents, or press notices something authentic concerning Melville and the time-spirit in which he lived.

The *Melville Log* may be supplemented by *Herman Melville, Cycle and Epicycle* (1953), by Eleanor Melville Metcalf, Melville's oldest grandchild, and for many years the benefactress of all who would study his life or writings. She retells his story, generally in a chronological pattern, with letters (some familiar, some new), and with interconnecting paragraphs. This is a family book, discursive, reverent, and enriched by oral traditions, conversations, and reminiscences known only to the author and her relatives. For contrast we may turn to an English biography, in point of view detached and highly critical. Although in *The Spirit Above the Dust, a Study of Herman Melville* (1951) Ronald Mason denies that his book is "biography proper," it is suitable to our category, in its constant reference to biographical facts and in its scope. After an interesting passage on Melville's reputation in England and its recent, if temporary, decline, the author settles down to the task of "redirecting the interest of English readers and critics back to the swarming complexities and relevances of Melville's unusual art."

At times this need to persuade gives to *The Spirit Above the Dust* a tone of exhortation. Mason's unawareness of some recent American scholarship is noticeable, as in his discussion of what Vincent called the "cetological center" of *Moby-Dick*. Yet these very qualities make this book refreshing. Elements in Mason's over-all pattern—not quite a thesis, but a framework—contradict or diverge from opinions already cited from other biographers. In, for example, the "simple and unsubtle" *Typee* Mason finds a "statement of innocence," an innocence which he thinks, if considered in relation to tragedy, was Melville's central theme. Melville's other books, revealing also his use of the symbol, reflect respectively, the assault upon, the defeat of, and finally, in *Billy Budd*, the victory of innocence, although this last is the innocence of a redemption from evil. The three readable chapters on *Moby-Dick* ("The Prelude," "The Symbol," and "The Myth") also lead Mason into controversial areas. Does Ishmael represent innocence? Is Mason right about the difficult problem of the Parsee? Whiteness, and the concept of a dead universe, also debatable, is eloquently reasoned here, to show Melville's "Vision of Nothing," his nihilism.

IV. Criticism

1. *Books on Special Subjects*

Shortly after Mumford's biography in 1929, and possibly under its stimulus, there began to appear studies of varying length and merit, devoted to special turns in Melville's thought, such as Vega Curl's *Pasteboard Masks, Fact as Spiritual Symbol in the Novels of Hawthorne and Melville* (1931), a Radcliffe honors thesis. Or *Moby-Dick* is used as a sustained illustration of certain kinds of imagery in W. H. Auden's *The Enchafed Flood, or the Romantic Iconography of the Sea* (1950). Or we encounter exegeses (not all published) of particular works or topics, as in the studies by younger Melville scholars (e.g., Gilman, Freeman, Davis, Sealts, Hillway, Bezanson, Pommer, Miss Foster, and Miss Wright). Some of these have written biography more detailed (Gilman or Davis) than Howard's, but their center of interest is usually the genetics, content, and history of a novel (Davis or Freeman), a particular source (Pommer), or a dominant pattern of thought like science (Hillway). I propose to look at these in this, the first of four sections under the general rubric of "Criticism," and in this division, beginning with Curl, to follow an approximate chronology. These books on special subjects, together with the articles, with their restless probing of every recess of Melville's life story and mind, are, considered together, as important as the biographies. Intimacy with them distinguishes the professional Melvillian, analytical, polemical, from the bemused admirer, the dilettantish (so these others would say) reader. Presumably the latter are a happier race than the former, but it is these devotees with whom we are now concerned.

In 1937 at Basel Walter Weber's *Herman Melville, eine stilistische Untersuchung* was an early venture into a region which still offers opportunities for study. Weber's tabulations of similes, tropes, and other techniques are likely to help more imaginative students of Melville's style. In the following year W. S. Gleim discussed Melville's "pyramidal silence" and summarized other criticism in *The Meaning of Moby Dick* (1938), a book inferior to Stanley Geist's *Herman Melville, The Tragic Vision and the Heroic Ideal* (1939). To develop the two themes suggested in the title this Harvard honors thesis narrows its focus and omits Melvillian attitudes as dominant, some would say, as the sense of tragedy or the demand for the heroic in man. In showing the progression from the "outwardness" of *Typee* to the "inwardness" of *Pierre* Geist perceives in Melville an increasing indifference to the external world of events. Moreover, in portraying the intense subjectivity of Melville, Geist speaks of his myths as taking no account of society. These exclusions seem inexact and arbitrary. Yet the firm development of the two complementary ideas of tragedy and heroism makes this essay a distinguished piece of work, even among more comprehensive studies. Out of Melville's soundings in the blackness of his own subconscious emerged his vision of tragedy. Ahab and Pierre struggle with monsters which they created within their own minds. The hero is the man who "dives" (like Shakespeare), and the truly valiant take this heroic plunge into the depths. They face the truth. In comparison other views of life are despicable.

Melville's relations with Christianity, a vexed question in the biographies, receive special consideration in William Braswell's *Melville's Religious Thought, an Essay in Interpretation* (1943). Although only 126 pages in length and expositional in method, this documented and sensible book has carried with it a simple authority throughout the last decade. A more complete, more critical book is needed to synthesize new chapters and articles on this subject. The problem is basic. Melville hesitates between belief and disbelief not merely in preliminary questions in *Typee*, in the introspective *Clarel*, and in the valedictory *Billy Budd*, but in all his writing.

The question recurs boldly and more critically in Charles Olson's *Call Me Ishmael* (1947), in Part IV, with the caption "Loss: Christ." What Melville had learned by his experience in the Pacific, Olson says, "he allowed Christ to undo." Religion, however, is not the primary theme of this short book. It estimates a series of indelible influences: whaling and the real America, space, and Shakespeare. Olson includes the notes which Melville wrote in his own copy of the *Narrative* of the sinking of the *Essex*. With its source material, its originalities, typographical and stylistic (the reader thinks of D. H. Lawrence; see below), with its large claims for Shakespeare (a revision of an essay; see below), and its apocalyptic tone, the book is a little startling. For instance, Olson says of Melville:

"The man made a mess of things. He got all balled up with Christ. He made a white marriage. . . . He rode his own space once—*Moby-Dick*." Yet *Call Me Ishmael* is alive; it has the power to energize our thought about Melville.

More and more during the 1940's students turned to the sources of Melville's novels (see articles below), not always as pedantic exercises, but as approaches to an unfathomable mind. What did he read? Which authors did he underline or annotate? How far did books modify or enrich the stuff of his experience? The awareness of these problems is far more evident in the later biographies than in Weaver, Freeman, and Mumford. Some books concentrated on these intellectual genetics of Melville's masterpieces. Illustrations range from Tyrus Hillway's brochure, *Mellville and the Whale* (1950), to Vincent's *The Trying-Out of Moby-Dick* (1949). This book is a study of the materials out of which Melville created his novel. Vincent examines the five books which provided Melville with most of his whaling data, analyzes his use of them, and illustrates his conclusions by parallel passages. All this evidence is contained in Part IV, in which Vincent destroys forever the illusion that the passages on whaling were merely digressive. He defines "The Cetological Center" of *Moby-Dick*. He shows how Melville vitalized facts in the dull narratives of the books on cetology into the dramatic episodes of the novels, and he offers a valuable running commentary on *Moby-Dick*. He indicates how he raised this material to the level of metaphysical perception and symbolism. Ishmael, who in Sedgwick was negligible and in Mason was merely a symbol of innocence, emerges in Vincent as a major character.

In Melville's manipulation of his reading was a transforming power comparable to Shakespeare's. In *Melville's Use of the Bible* (1949) Nathalia Wright demonstrates his immersion in scriptural imagery, characters, themes, and style, but especially his distillation of the Bible, perhaps his most important single source, in terms of his own time and language, of his own vision. The Bible sank to the deepest level of his consciousness, there constantly transforming and transformed by his thought and imagination. In similar fashion H. F. Pommer in his *Milton and Melville* (1950), lists, like Miss Wright, characters, ideas, and verbal echoes, but finds the vitality of this influence, akin in many ways to that of the Bible or of Shakespeare, in something beyond literalism. Pommer discusses the effect on Melville of Milton's minor writings, of his vocabulary and sentence structure, and of the epic style and poetic temper of *Paradise Lost*. He speaks of the influence of the concept of Satan upon Melville's characters, especially upon Ahab and Claggart. Yet throughout, as in the case of the Bible, he is conscious of "rich connotations," difficult to define, and an "indeterminable total" of parallels which cannot be set down in lists. Whatever Melville touched in travel book, mythology, Holy Writ, or the English classics was reborn into his own world.

In considering Melville's adjectival echoes from Milton or his Biblical phraseology there is danger of forgetting books which guide the unprofessional but civilized reader and increase his pleasure. Such a volume is M. O. Percival's *A Reading of Moby-Dick* (1950). This running commentary takes us on *The Pequod's* voyage, with ideas sometimes familiar, sometimes fresh. It is a pleasant journey, with pauses over mysteries which we have all pondered. In reflecting on the "despair" of Ahab, Percival (in debt to Kierkegaard) reminds us of this theme in other men of genius. He offers observations on Fedallah, though the mysterious Parsee is likely to remain a problem until some Melvillian masters the lore of the Arabians. Does the Parsee represent the "primal mind"? *A Reading of Moby-Dick*, blessedly free from a professional vocabulary, is a helpful monograph for the student still puzzled after his first shock of recognition from the great book.

The temptation to use Melville's fiction as autobiography is well defined in the Introduction of W. H. Gilman's *Melville's Early Life and "Redburn"* (1951). In showing the unwise reliance of biographers from Freeman to Chase upon *Redburn* for the events of Melville's youth, Gilman emphasizes the need of separating fact from fancy in all of Melville's novels. The two parts of this detailed biography of Melville from 1819 to 1841 (Book I), and the three chapters (Book II) about *Redburn* itself, are really one. Through Book I we understand Melville's point of view as an artist toward this story of adventure. Everything in his early career suggests that in writing *Redburn* he would give play to his imagination. A comparison of known facts with the text reveals changes from his own experience and additions from other sources. The character of the boy Redburn was not Melville's, but was "primarily a literary creation." The age, the appearance, the fictional adventures of the hero show Melville as an experimenter with his art, though not yet its master.

In the following year (1952) appeared another intensive study of one book, *Melville's "Mardi," a Chartless Voyage,* by M. R. Davis. Here the author's problem was more complex than Gilman's, from the very nature of *Mardi.* This huge novel has usually been regarded as split in two. Either the realistic voyage of Jarl is an "Introduction" to the world of thought or the entire book is a chaotic, sophomoric fantasy. Davis' first section, "Literary Apprenticeship," beginning only three years after Gilman's biographical terminal, relates the story of Melville's life in meticulous detail from 1844 to 1847. The second part, "The Writing of *Mardi*" is of major significance in our increasing knowledge of Melville's methods of composition. From Melville's own statements, from his reading, from his correspondence (increased here by twelve new letters to the publisher, John Murray), Davis shows the shifts in Melville's purposes and the planned stages in the composition of a book which has often been dismissed as a reckless outpouring of Melville's youthful imagination. In the third part, in his ninety-page analysis, Davis evaluates *Mardi* as a work of art in itself, but omits (for reasons of space and unity) a study of its relationship with Melville's other novels.

Perhaps this is the proper place to mention Gabriele Baldini's *Melville o le ambiguità* (Milano, Napoli, 1952). This book (together with a chapter on Melville in Cesare Pavese's *La litterature americana e altri saggi,* 1953) probably represents the best Italian criticism of Melville. It protests against the systematization of Melville's symbolism, and analyzes its persistent ambiguity.

To define sharply the difference in method of the various books on special subjects we may turn from Davis' *Mardi* to Lawrance Thompson's *Melville's Quarrel with God* (1952). "Throughout *Mardi,*" says this writer, "the reiterated references to the tendency of human and finite minds to hold concepts of God which are distortions of God may suggest that Melville had a related meaning in mind when he chose his pun-like title: the world is inclined to mar deity." *Mardi* represents only one level in the disillusionment which culminated in Melville's hatred of God, in a kind of "inverted mysticism." In another chapter Thompson argues that *Redburn* represents three steps in Melville's spiritual development, of which the third is Melville's secret bitterness expressing itself in satire, not only on his own inherited Calvinism but on all religious belief. Thompson's thesis is that Melville declared war upon God. After outlining this theory clearly in his Preface, he applies it in elaborate detail in a book of some five hundred pages to Melville's major novels.

Rebellion, skepticism, even defiance of God were certainly moods known to Melville. Whether these can be stretched into a single all-motivating purpose some critics of this book have doubted (see below). Thompson, however, goes farther. Since such views of God would be unacceptable to his contemporary readers, Melville concealed his "quarrel" by subtle artistic devices. For example, if we go behind the Christian symbols in *Billy Budd,* we find there the mockery and bitterness that were the mainspring of Melville's being. The last page of Thompson's long exegesis describes the effect upon Melville of the "Divine Depravity." His "vision narrows down to the sharp focus of a misanthropic notion that the world was put together wrong, and that God was to blame. The gist of it is that simple.

He spent his life sneering at the gullibility of human beings who disagreed with him, but also in sneering at God, accusing God, upbraiding God and (as he thought) quarreling with God." Even *The Pequod* really means "to pique God." If this is the explanation of the multipatterned Melville then this author has indeed drawn out "leviathan with an hook." The reader must decide for himself between this and less daring hypotheses.

The social implications stressed by Chase reappear vigorously in C. L. R. James's *Mariners, Renegades and Castaways, the Story of Herman Melville and the World We live in* (1953). Meditating in detention at Ellis Island, James concluded that a century earlier Melville had seen clearly "how masses of men would behave." Leaving James's definition of Ahab as "the embodiment of the totalitarian type," we may end this section by a glance at more conventional, if diverse, estimates in *Moby-Dick, Centennial Essays* (1953). This is a book on a special subject in a technical sense only, but is classifiable here for convenience. Actually it is a sheaf of nine essays, with their unifying thread the centennial ceremonies for *Moby-Dick* in 1951, and, except in two, their centralizing theme the great novel itself.

In another sense these studies belong among the articles in periodicals (see below) where, had it not been for an alert publisher, they would have found their ultimate homes. Since it is the product of four widely separated meetings and more than twice as many points of view, the little book (of not quite 200 pages) has all the merits and defects of a symposium. Ahab is the personification of Satan (Murray) or Ahab is Man in protest against his destiny and limitations (Hillway, also co-editor with Mansfield). *Moby-Dick* is a work of art, with Ishmael its deepest center (Bezanson). It is a masterpiece presenting as a major theme the alienation of the individual from society (H. N. Smith). Or it is a symbolic record of the struggle of its author for answers to the eternal mysteries, especially that of evil. Four other essays deal with the immediate reputation of the book (Hetherington), with Melville's links with Transcendentalism (Miller), with his friendship with Hawthorne (Stewart), and with his knowledge of Nantucket (Heflin).

2. *Introductions to Editions and Selections*

Criticism and scholarship of importance have found their way into the introductions to texts and selections (see above), especially in editions striving to re-evaluate the lesser-known novels, such as *Pierre* (Forsythe and Murray) or *Billy Budd* (F. B. Freeman). Much of the front matter of reprints of *Moby-Dick* for school and college classes is stereotyped, but a few specialists reintroduce the oft-told story with fresh suggestiveness. We may expect more of this concentrated criticism in the forthcoming editions of the new Collected Works (see above). One cannot read of America without Columbus, nor of Melville in the early period of re-estimates without R. M. Weaver, the pioneer, the high priest of the Melville canon, even if most of his writing has now been challenged, amplified, or even discarded. We have known him as a biographer, and we shall encounter him again as editor and as the author of articles.

His pioneer work survives also in his introduction to the *Shorter Novels of Herman Melville* (1928). Weaver was, perhaps, the first to study, though not really the discoverer of the manuscripts. It was natural that after the recognition of the *Billy Budd* papers he should speak too extravagantly of the *Piazza Tales.* A reader of about thirty years ago, unaware that *Moby-Dick* was not just a sea story, would be startled by his declaration that "*Benito Cereno* and *The Encantadas* . . . are slowly coming to be chosen as marking the supreme technical achievement of Melville as an artist." Like his biography, Weaver's Introduction is expositional and obsolescent. We now know, for example, far more of "Bartleby the Scrivener" than Weaver tells us. Yet the book was an early guide to the now classic tragedies of "Benito Cereno" and *Billy Budd.* A similar pioneering spirit animates R. S. Forsythe's interpretation in his early edition of *Pierre* with its first bold foray into Melville's relationship with Shakespeare, especially with *Hamlet.*

In 1938, when Willard Thorp published his Introduction to *Herman Melville, Representative Selections* (AWS), the only important biographies extant were those by Weaver, Freeman, Mumford, and the somewhat inaccessible one by K. H. Sundermann. Thorp speaks of the "extravagancies" of "the new worshippers," but the wildest exaggerations were still to come. Perhaps, then, this long Introduction of about 100 pages is, like some of its scholarly apparatus, dated. Certainly it could not be said today that Melville suffers from neglect, and there have been forceful replies to "the new worshippers." Actually Thorp's own Introduction is such an answer. Indeed, despite our new facts and our stratospheric speculations, it is difficult to think of a better orientation for an intelligent student than this sound introductory essay. It is wonderfully comprehensive, and its six sections leave unexamined no essential areas of Melville's life and writing. We can acquaint ourselves with his trilogy, his social ideas, his fate as a writer in his contemporary world.

Forty pages deal, as a kind of anchor to the criticism, with formative influences, which Thorp summarizes as primarily five. These were the religious orthodoxy surrounding Melville's boyhood; his exposure to the brutality of life, at sea and in primitive societies; his ceaseless reading in philosophy and belles-lettres between 1846 and 1851; his associations with the New York literary group; and his friendship with Hawthorne. The succeeding section on Melville as an artist centers in three chapters in *The Confidence Man,* in 1938 even less known than today. Thorp believes that these chapters tell us much of Melville's aims in fiction even if they lack the revelations of the Prefaces of Henry James or of Hawthorne. Next Thorp passes on to the preliminary novels, and reaches in his third section the problems of *Mardi, Moby-Dick,* and *Pierre.* The unifying concept of pursuit in these three novels is now easy to recognize, and has since been discussed in many a book and article. This early study is rich in suggestion, as in the comparison with André Gide's *Les Faux-monnayeurs,* a parallel which was later to serve well a historian of American symbolism (Charles Feidelson; see below). Of the other sections, the twelve pages on the poetry herald the subsequent study of this province of Melville's work—still, despite scattered articles (see below), an arable field for investigation. As another successor (see above) to *Representative Selections* we may turn to *Complete Stories of Herman Melville* (1949), edited by Jay Leyda, with its faithful texts (excluding *Billy Budd*), its biographical introduction, and its "Notes on Sources."

Thorp's edition, *Moby-Dick or The Whale* (1947), addresses its brief Introduction to readers more sensitive to the "inexhaustibleness" of Melville's meanings. It touches lightly on the various levels of interpretation, leaving the reader to enjoy casually the epic story, the illustrations, and the metaphysical implications. Presumably, we need to renew this point of view. It reappears in another Introduction to *Moby Dick or the Whale* (1946), but here its editor, Montgomery Belgion, is thinking, like Mason, of a British public, less indoctrinated than Thorp's readers by the Melville cultists. Even within his short Introduction Belgion is discursive; he tells us Melville's life story and reports the opinions of the various critics. He urges us "to steer equally clear of the empyreal imaginings of Sedgwick and of the too earth-bound view of Mr. Anderson," and reminds us that *Moby-Dick* is, after all, just a story of pursuit.

There will be other volumes of selections and other editions. The editors now reassess Melville as more than the author of "one indisputable masterpiece," to use Belgion's phrase, so reminiscent of thirty years ago. He is presented as the creator of books which equal *(Pierre)* or excel *(Billy Budd) Moby-Dick*. A common purpose, carried out individually by scholars, inspires fresh transcriptions of texts and gives each the setting of an all-embracing Introduction. Apart from the value of the new text of *Billy Budd* (see above), Freeman insists on a reconsideration of the older Melville. We are acquainted with his appearance, his family life, his moods (no Timonism, despite the earlier biographers), and his reading. We are familiarized with the "outside facts" of this "inside story." Where did Melville secure his solid base of facts for his last grapple with the Ultimate? To understand *Billy Budd* we must know *White Jacket*, the famous Mackenzie case (see below), and other personal experiences.

Most of all, we must study the new text of the novel in its relations to a prior short story and ponder on Melville's creative art during these years when he was almost at the end of his journey. We can learn much from the manuscripts, and also from the printed variants by Freeman, of Melville's ideas on structure, of his ways of portraying character, of his style, and of his symbolism. In *Billy Budd* is evidence of his continued interest in religion, philosophy, and humanitarian thought. Both in comprehensiveness and in detail this Introduction invites comparison with all other estimates of *Billy Budd*, from Mumford to Thompson. Freeman has no thesis. Many questions, especially those touching Melville's creative art, he leaves unanswered, but his labor on this one book has been enormous, and he speaks in the Introduction with authority.

The value of another edition, Henry Murray's *Pierre; or, The Ambiguities,* is more perilous for the layman to judge. Murray (see above) is a professional psychiatrist, but apart from a necessary vocabulary (anima, schizoid, etc.), he has resolutely kept the novel out of the realm of pathology. He has not tried to solve problems requiring "a lengthy or deep or technical analysis," such as Melville's concern with unique and immense sins, with the "Unpardonable Sin," with, perhaps, a secret one of his own, carefully withheld. Slightly embarrassed by his literary audience, Murray limits himself to the clarification of a few critical points in character and plot which, he believes, have been misinterpreted. Nothing could be more reasonable if we concede the desirability for our criticism of a psychiatric approach to the mind of Melville.

Although there are dangers, we do desire this approach. In one book it may be wise to go the whole way and see where such professional analysis leaves the amateurs. Concerning our literary psychologists, however, Murray is tactfully silent. He regards *Pierre* as essentially autobiographical, in the same sense that Shakespeare's tragedies are autobiographical, but not in the sense that specific incidents and characters form the basis for the narrative. Nor do the opinions of characters equate those of the author. Murray believes *Pierre* to be "the hushed story" of Melville's mind, of his deepest impulses. It reflects his "thwarted catharsis of emotions." Indeed, he thinks *Pierre* "a literary monster, a prodigious by-blow of genius," but we study the monster to comprehend the genius. Approximating Sedgwick's point of view that the various books represent profiles, Murray explores Melville's subconscious and its relationships with the vast, unfathomable World of Mind.

Although Murray is merciful toward the incompetence of his readers, in, for example, his explicit definition of the "anima experience," he evaluates *Pierre* as a psychological document rather than as a novel. As such a record the book, despite its confusion, has great interest, in its revelation of the "anima experience" through Lucy and Isabel, in the "mother-son knot of incest" as a primary theme, in the mother fixation, and in other conditions quite comprehensible, Murray says, to any psychiatrist. As if in reply to a question often in our minds as we read the psychiatric interpretations of Hawthorne, Poe, or Melville he says: "It is astonishing that two generations before Jung, Melville, unaided by the findings of depth psychology, should have described with such fidelity, subtlety, and beauty, all the significant features of the first phase of the anima experience."

3. *Chapters in Books*

Thus many biographies, special books, texts, and introductions attest the acceptance, somewhat late, of Melville as an American classic. His contemporary reputation (see articles below) was intermittent and based upon secondary aspects of his genius. Duyckinck's brief biography in his *Cyclopaedia of American Literature* (1855) was friendly but uncomprehending. C. F. Richardson's *American Literature* (1887-89) allotted him one short paragraph, and Barrett Wendell's *A Literary History of America* (1900) one sentence. True recognition in histories of American literature or of American civilization or in volumes of essays began soon after the appearance of Weaver's biography. One early and durable contribution was the brace of chapters devoted to him by D. H. Lawrence in his *Studies in Classic American Literature* (1923). It would be impractical to distinguish between chapters like these, which are integral parts of a literary history, and essays like R. P. Blackmur's, E. M. Forster's, or Carl Van Vechten's. Without a particular frame of reference, the latter study some phase of Melville's writing for its own sake, usually for its artistic or philosophic values. Some of these essays first saw the light in periodicals, but they may be considered here chronologically as separate chapters, along with sections of books whose broader purposes included Melville. We may begin with the brilliant assault on Melville's mind by Lawrence.

Lawrence allots separate chapters to Franklin and Crèvecœur and two each to Cooper, Hawthorne, and Melville. Those on Melville, pre-empting almost a fifth of the entire book, he called "Herman Melville's 'Typee' and 'Omoo' " and "Herman Melville's 'Moby Dick'." Written thirty years ago in language which is explosive, colloquial, and eloquent, the book is both absurd and thought-provoking. There are platitudes: Melville was "at the core a mystic and an idealist." There are odd judgments: Lawrence thinks Melville may be at his best, or at least his happiest in *Omoo*. Facts are unimportant: Melville had *fifty* years of disillusionment; he "writhed for eighty years." There is oversimplification, often delightful: Lawrence says *Pierre* came from Melville's desire "to show that the more you try to be good the more you make a mess of things." Although we tire of Lawrence's apocalyptic tone and even of his humor, both his passion and his perception animate these two chapters. He says that, naturally, the whale is a symbol, but he doesn't think Melville knew himself of what. "That's," he adds, "the best of it." But Lawrence knows: the whale is "the deepest blood-being of the white race. He is our deepest blood-nature. And he is hunted, hunted by the maniacal fanaticism of our white mental consciousness." These ideas and their corollaries anticipated, if they did not inspire, our modern interpretations of the whale and Ahab.

In contrast, other chapters seem, in the light of modern criticism, unacquainted. In "Conrad and Melville," in *Definitions, First Series* (1922), H. S. Canby says, at variance with recent theories of a planned organic structure, that in *Moby-Dick* Melville "lost control of his book." In *Excavations* (1926) Van Vechten outlines the plot of *Pierre* and makes an ardent appeal for a consideration of Melville's later work. In his chapter "Herman Melville" in *More Contemporary Americans* (1927), P. H. Boynton defines the whale as the "symbol of all property and all privilege." This ready seizure upon almost any interpretation is symptomatic of these beginnings in the reappraisal of Melville. Whatever our disagreements with Mumford, criticism of Melville seems to commence with his biography and reach full expression only in the 1940's.

To cite other examples, in a weak and rhetorical chapter in the second volume of *Main Currents in American Thought* (1927), V. L. Parrington dismisses *Mardi* as a prologue to *Moby-Dick* and labels Melville a child of Rousseau. In his "Notes on Herman Melville," in *Emerson and Others* (1927), Van Wyck Brooks hails Melville for his assault on the doctrine of progress. This early paper is in marked contrast to Brooks's article in the *DAB* and his definition of the novelist's place in *The Times of Melville and Whitman* (1947). Similar generalizations, belonging to this early phase of Melville criticism, appear in Canby's "Hawthorne and Melville," in his *Classic Americans* (1931). Here Melville's vision of Nature, beautiful but malignant, is admired as his answer to Emerson and the other Transcendentalists—an interpretation vigorously challenged today (see below).

Before 1940 the historians of our literature and civilization failed to exhibit Melville justly in their long and complicated stories. In contrast to the materials on Emerson or Hawthorne, those relating to Melville were scarce, and critical judgments were still too unformed to permit summaries in a few paragraphs. Apart from the major biographies and the increasing flow of articles (see below), for the slow revelation during the 1930's of Melville's gigantic stature we are in debt to a few critics. These were less interested in fitting him neatly with a generality or two into the American literary family than in an inspection of him as a brilliant apostate, almost a *lusus naturae.* Despite Lawrence's perspective on American literature, this was his point of view, and other examples might be mentioned. One is the memorable section of seven pages in E. M. Forster's *Aspects of the Novel* (1927); another is Yvor Winters' "Herman Melville and the Problems of Moral Navigation," in *Maule's Curse* (1938). Particularly important was the brief but brilliant section in Constance Rourke's *American Humor* (1931, pp. 191-200).

Some of these critics emphasize the poetic spirit of *Moby-Dick*, and Forster, in particular, insists that there is a quality here uncapturable, untranslatable into the phrases by which critics try to hem in its meanings. He concedes that the spiritual theme of the book is a battle against evil, or that the White Whale represents evil, or that the pursuit by Ahab deepens into revenge. But he adds hastily that these are words. Like Lawrence, Forster is sure that Melville himself hardly knew the full import of his symbols. These are words, and we become "false" if we define Moby-Dick too distinctly as a struggle between two unreconciled evils. Beyond the words there is something more; there is some sort of contest. Beneath surface ideas or suggestions runs an undercurrent. It is this undercurrent which we must feel even if we do not understand it. We must not turn it all into symbols for, even if the symbolism is correct, it then silences the book. The undercurrent is a song, a "prophetic song." All that we can say of *Moby-Dick* is that there is a contest. "The rest is song." Novelists are notoriously poor critics of other novelists, but there is something satisfying about these few pages. Nor are they inharmonious with Melville's own doubtful wave of the hand about the presence of allegory in *Moby-Dick.*

Winters is in agreement about the poetic character of *Moby-Dick*; he regards it as a poetic epic rather than a novel. He is, however, convinced that Melville developed his symbolism with unflagging care, and he is not hesitant about definite meanings. The spine of the novel is the antithesis between the sea and the land, and the central problem resides in Ahab the sinner. Fedallah, always troublesome to the critics, represents "the sinning mind as it shows itself distinct from the whole man." Throughout its twenty-six pages the essay has a sustained firmness of exegesis, although Winters believes that many of Melville's own judgments were "desperately confused." This essay is particularly suggestive respecting the union of form and subject in *Moby-Dick*, and Melville's art in creating a magnificent structure.

Yet two years later, in "The Craft of Herman Melville: A Putative Statement," in *The Expense of Greatness* (1940; see also, *VQR,* Spring 1938), R. P. Blackmur declared that he bequeathed nothing to the novel as a form, and commented on the dearth of other novelists writing under his influence. Melville found the available conventions of the novel (and of the drama) inappropriate for his particular species of insight. Therefore he worked not on the representative or dramatic level, but on a nondramatic plane, on that of "putative" statement. Instead of showing characters in action, he created shells of stock characters who take on life only through Melville's own eloquent words. With this theory in mind Blackmur takes us through *Moby-Dick* and *Pierre*, examining their interdependence and discussing them as revelations of Melville's art. He shows the relationship of the "putative" statement to dramatic form and to language. Thus Melville used forms in which he did not really believe, and he relied heavily upon statement, almost on the sermonic. This chapter is not an attack. Blackmur thinks Melville's "the only great imagination in the middle period of the American nineteenth century." Some critics call the essay a tour de force; after all, Melville was a novelist.

Naturally, in the histories of American civilization the figure of Melville the man or Melville the thinker appears more prominently than in these essays bent upon new interpretations of his art. In Jean Simon's *La Polynésie dans l'art et la littérature de L'Occident* (1939) he is shown briefly as a traveler. In a chapter called "Melville, Critic of Mid-Nineteenth Century Beliefs," in *The Course of American Democratic Thought* (1940), his independence of mind is silhouetted by R. H. Gabriel against a smug American democracy. His stay among the Typees showed him that the aim of American society was "security," whereas, look where you would in Christianity, in Transcendentalism, or in science, security remained a mirage. After a consideration of Melville's somber answers to the questions concerning the nature of God and of Man, this historian concludes that Melville was hostile to the democratic concept of progress. For this reason he was a prophet without honor. His "doctrines" were alien to the passionate American democratic faith.

Carl Van Doren's eighteen pages, "Herman Melville," in his revised *The American Novel* (1940), is a reasonable integration of our novelist into the whole pattern of American fiction, but is necessarily out of date. A more recent estimate in a similar frame of reference, with more available material on Melville, occurs in Alexander Cowie's *The Rise of the American Novel* (1948). Both these handbooks allocate Melville in the development of American fiction. (See also E. C. Wagenknecht, *Cavalcade of the American Novel,* 1952.) Melville is associated with four other major figures in F. O. Matthiessen's *American Renaissance* (1941), a massive and profound study, more admired, perhaps, than any other sustained work of literary criticism published in the United States in the twentieth century. The sections on Melville are detailed, taking us deep into his reading, his quasi-philosophical thought, and his craftsmanship.

During many chapters in *American Renaissance* it is impossible to evaluate Melville without sensing common impulses which he shared with Hawthorne and others. We are introduced to Melville's ideas on Hawthorne and on Emerson. We are reminded that the subject of *Pierre* already existed in "The Birthmark," and was "one of Hawthorne's most recurrent themes." In like fashion *Moby-Dick* is spiritually akin to *The Scarlet Letter*. Matthiessen extends this integration of Melville to other literatures, chiefly through his reading. He assesses his debt to Shakespeare and a bondage to Sir Thomas Browne which, if brief, was intense even to the point of "ventriloquism." He discusses penetratingly allegory and symbolism in the light of these interrelations, past and contemporary. We feel the intellectual "wholeness" of this book, very different from the conventional literary history, a "wholeness" which, perhaps, strives too much to include social areas, like democracy. Yet we may read many pages of perceptive criticism of the separate works of Melville. Matthiessen's promise in his Preface to concentrate "on the foreground, on the writing itself" is magnificently fulfilled in the main entries on Melville.

More circumscribed than Matthiessen, more controlled by the purposes, biographical, critical, and bibliographical, of a three-volume work, the *LHUS* (1948), Thorp's "Herman Melville" in this compendium has an air of finality in its grasp upon everything known to date. It is profitable to compare these two capable outlines by Thorp, this in the *LHUS* and that in the Introduction to his *Representative Selections,* written just a decade earlier (see above). In the later study are assumptions of critical sophistication on the part of the reader which would have been unjustified at the writing of the earlier essay. The section on Melville's poetry, necessarily concise in these thirty pages of the *History*, is a valuable definition of the present status of this product of Melville's genius.

The present acceptance of the bellettristic values of our fiction and poetry has led to other critical soundings in these major writers, among them Melville. Twelve years after Matthiessen's book C. N. Feidelson's *Symbolism and American Literature* (1953) sought for a more stable unity. Troubled by the strong "sociological and political bent" in *American Renaissance*, he re-examined the common purpose of these writers. Was it really "their devotion to the possibilities of democracy"? Instead he found solidarity in their "devotion to the possibilities of symbolism." Feidelson thinks them all motivated by the concept of "Man Seeing," of "the mind engaged in a crucial act of knowledge." This point of view shaped both their form and their content. It looked backward to early American symbolism, and forward to the literature of our own time.

Part I, "Four American Symbolists" (Hawthorne, Whitman, Melville, and Poe), outlines this adventurous act of the mind. Ishmael opens *Moby-Dick* by his identification of the voyage with this vision. Part II is a brilliant essay on the symbolistic imagination, and Part III, historical in character, studies the origins of symbolism in the American mind. With Emerson and Melville as "the poles of symbolism," Part IV demonstrates the approach "Toward Melville" in other symbolists (Emerson or Horace Bushnell). These chapters are preparatory to the final chapter. In this section by a study of the novels Feidelson shows the "complex modernity" of Melville, and his part in the underlying unity of the American symbolistic approach.

4. *Articles: General and Special*

Of the multitudinous articles on Melville, apart from those on his separate books (see below), many center on his biography. We must remember his unusual associations with authorship: the years of wandering; the neglect of his genius until thirty years after his death; the subsequent controversy about autobiographical data in his novels. These conditions have given his life story a kind of remoteness, as if he had lived in another age. The difficulties of research have kindled the zest of the investigators. Every provable fact has become precious. Since no one bothered to save the correspondence of a man who had lived among cannibals, who had attacked the missionaries (*NEQ,* 1935), or had written as insane a book as *Pierre*, every letter has become important. Scholars have plundered the logs, the registries of ships, newspapers, hazy personal recollections, the very islands of Polynesia. In this section I shall refer to representative articles which reveal in a fullness of detail impossible in a biography episodes in Melville's career, his contemporary standing, his reading (including his sources and relations with other writers), his use of language, and other aspects of his life or art.

We must omit many pedestrian articles (sometimes under the simple caption of "Herman Melville") which repeat platitudes and shopworn biographical facts. A few contemporary sketches of his personality have value. We learn something from H. S. Salt's article in the *Scottish Art Review* (1889), or from two which appeared in the year of Melville's death: J. E. A. Smith's (see above) and R. H. Stoddard's (New York *Mail and Express,* 8 Oct. 1891). The biographical studies in the magazines seem to have begun with Weaver's (*Bookman,* 1921), and the examination of his associations with particular locales with Stanley Salvidge's "Herman Melville and Liverpool" (*Spectator,* 16 July 1927). After the first three biographies (see above) this search for footprints became assiduous. In 1934 H. A. Larrabee discussed the Gansevoort family *(New York History,* Apr.). The Melville revival came almost too late for reminiscences, but in 1935 Oscar Wegelin recorded his memories in "Herman Melville as I Recall Him" *(Colophon),* with glimpses of the New York background. This factual knowledge was difficult enough to obtain, and it told us very little about the obscure years. In 1935, 1936, and 1937 R. S. Forsythe wrote of Melville as a bookkeeper in Honolulu *(NEQ),* of his life in the Marquesas *(PQ),* and of his stay in Tahiti *(PQ),* with, in 1938, a postscript on this last experience *(PQ).* Almost at the same time in "Gossip About Melville in the South Seas" (*NEQ,* 1937) Clarence Gohdes added details concerning Melville and "Fa-a-wa."

Charles Anderson, the authority on Melville's Polynesian

biography, was now at work ("The Romance of Scholarship: Tracing Melville in the South Seas," *Colophon,* 1938). Meanwhile the surveys of more accessible backgrounds multiplied. L. S. Mansfield's "Glimpses of Herman Melville's Life in Pittsfield, 1850-1851 . . ." (*AL,* 1937) includes an interesting group of letters. Contrasting Melville "the gay excursionist and Melville the recluse," Mansfield suggests that his seclusion in the country changed him. Scholarly inquiry now included Melville's companions in his adventures, especially "Toby" (Richard T. Greene), who is described in Gohdes' article (*MLN,* 1944). In "Melville's Liverpool Trip" (*MLN,* 1946) Gilman established the identity of Melville's first ship as the *St. Lawrence,* and prepared the way for his revisionary study of the "autobiographical fact" in *Redburn* (see above). Gilman also illustrated the holy passion of the devotees for scraps of biography by proving that Melville was once a pinboy in a Honolulu bowling alley (*AL,* 1947). One of the most useful recent studies is W. L. Heflin's "Melville and Nantucket" (*Proc. Nantucket Historical Assn.,* 1951; see above). Further examples are unnecessary. We may readily find in the bibliographies the many brief studies: Melville's income, his office-seeking, his publishing relations with the *Atlantic* or the Ohio Press, his relations with the Shakers, his "silent years"—the list seems endless.

One part of the story aroused curiosity, perhaps because it revealed Melville in an unexpected role. As a lecturer he was not successful, but in the newspaper records of his platform appearances we see him as a personality. Some dozen articles, beginning in 1934, outline his itineraries and his topics, "Statuary in Rome," "The South Seas," or "Traveling." They report on his performances in various cities, in Milwaukee, Yonkers, or New Haven. (See *AL,* 1942; *MLN,* 1945; *AM. Book Col.,* 1934; *N&Q,* 1942, 1943). In "Melville's Midwestern Lecture Tour, 1859" (*PQ,* 1941) M. R. Davis reaches conclusions which probably apply to all these interludes in his career. The fault of the lectures was their bookishness, the result of Melville's dependence upon historical materials concerning the

South Seas and on the "descriptive" parts of his own writing. Awkwardly delivered, the lectures were derivative, generalized, and repetitious. One assumption which comes readily to mind must be dismissed: the failure of the lectures was not due to any burden of philosophic thought (see also Roper, pp. 3-4).

Far less comprehensible than Melville's fiasco as a lecturer was the paradox of his obscurity, in contrast to his posthumous fame. The latter is worldwide, from Hawaii (see *NEQ,* 1935) to Soviet Russia (*CL,* 1953). His exact contemporary status remains controversial. To measure this, critics have exhumed fragments of his writing and his hackwork, such as book reviews (see *NEQ,* 1932; *AL,* 1942). They have dressed him up as a naval historian (*Harvard Graduates' Mag.,* 1930), and as a critic of society. L. S. Mansfield has indicated the breadth of his interests by "Melville's Comic Articles on Zachary Taylor" (*AL,* 1938). The debate began with O. W. Riegel's "The Anatomy of Melville's Fame" (*AL,* 1931). This critic asserted that the attacks on his later works came not from a failure to understand his intentions but from distaste for his point of view. He conceded that British critics did not comprehend his aims, but he denied the "myth" that Melville was forgotten. William Braswell, however, in "A Note on 'The Anatomy of Melville's Fame!' " (*AL,* 1934), attacks all these judgments. For supporting evidence he quotes Weaver, thus becoming, in turn, a target for Anderson in "Melville's English Debut" (*AL,* 1939). Although Anderson's survey is limited to the reception of *Typee* and *Omoo,* he estimates Melville's reception to have been, on the whole, more favorable abroad than at home. For the adjustment of these contradictory opinions, a full-length study of Melville's contemporary fame is needed. (See also *AL,* 1950, and Hetherington, above.)

In turning from the outward Melville (biography and reputation) to his mind, that is, to his reading, his ideology, or his craftsmanship, we find the articles more varied, richer in content, and touched occasionally with the excesses of the Melville cult. Melville's remark about dating his intellectual life from his twenty-fifth year implied that thereafter he plundered all reading. In studies of parallel passages or of his literary preferences he has been bracketed with a score of authors, past and present, in as many articles. It was natural to link him proleptically with Conrad (*Literary Review,* 4 Feb. 1922), and at about the same time he was associated with Hawthorne. Students interested in this relationship should read Randall Stewart's essay invalidating Mumford's statement that "Ethan Brand" was a portrait of Melville (*SRL,* 27 Apr. 1929); Stewart's "Melville and Hawthorne" (*SAQ,* 1952; see above); and Harrison Hayford's "Hawthorne, Melville, and the Sea" (*NEQ,* 1946).

Howard defined Melville's debt to Spenser (*MLN,* 1931), and J. H. Birss, his connections with Whitman (*N&Q,* 22 Apr. 1933), with Blake (idem, 5 May 1934), and with James Thomson (idem, 5 Mar. 1938). His obligation to R. H. Dana, Jr., was political rather than personal or literary, according to J. D. Hart in "Melville and Dana" (*AL,* 1937). Yet in an article supported by two important letters, Hayford shows Melville "fresh from reading *Two Years Before the Mast* when he shipped aboard the *Achusnet* for his second voyage" (*ELH,* 1944). Except for Charles Olson's essay in *Twice a Year* on *Moby-Dick* and *King Lear* (revised for *Call Me Ishmael;* see above), the immense influence of Shakespeare has received its most distinguished treatment in the biographies. Much work remains to be done on Melville's knowledge of the ancients, amazing in the light of his limited formal education, but interesting contributions in this area are Braswell's "Melville's Use of Seneca" (*AL,* 1940) and M. M. Sealts' "Melville's Neoplatonic Originals" (*MLN,* 1952). "Biblical Allusion in Melville's Prose" (*AL,* 1940) by Nathalia Wright is a pemmican-like article packed with examples of Melville's intimacy with both the Old and the New Testaments (see above).

These representative articles suggest the all-embracing character of Melville's reading. He was at home in Cervantes (*Realidad,* 1947; see Ángel Flores, *Cervantes Across the Centuries,* 1947); Dante (*PMLA,* 1949); Emerson (*AL,* 1937); or the

Gothic Novel (*NEQ,* 1949). He was a lifelong student of Christianity (*Friends' Intelligencer,* 24 Feb. 1945), and he commands respect for his knowledge of history, philosophy, foreign literatures, and also of science. The novels reflect his apprenticeship to astronomy, cetology, and geology. Elizabeth Foster's "Melville and Geology" (*AL,* 1945) and her additional note on the same subject (*AL,* 1951) underscore his passion for accuracy in the use of scientific data, as well as his interest in the "vast antiquity of our planet." (See also Hillway's "Melville and the Spirit of Science," *SAQ,* 1949; his "Melville's Geological Knowledge," *AL,* 1949; his "Melville as Critic of Science," *MLN,* 1950; and his "Melville as Amateur Zoologist," *MLQ,* 1951.)

The most systematic analysis of Melville's use of books is contained in M. M. Sealts's articles in six issues of the *Harvard Library Bulletin, 1948-1950,* now offprinted and bound as a single volume, *Melville's Reading, A Check-List of Books Owned and Borrowed.* In a brief Introduction (Part I) Sealts announces his purposes: to assemble all known facts regarding the disposition of Melville's library, and to submit other evidence concerning his reading, "afforded by his correspondence and journals and by booksellers' statements, library ledgers, and similar contemporary documents, including the titles of 93 books which he is recorded as borrowing." To anyone who has struggled with the separate articles and scattered facts Part II is very satisfying indeed, for it records chronologically and with extraordinary condensation the evidence in regard to Melville's reading throughout his life.

These two parts occupy only the first of the six issues in the *Bulletin.* The five subsequent numbers are devoted to the checklist itself (with a brief indication of "Scope," "Arrangement" etc.). For the student of Melville this group of articles (or books) has enormous importance. Even the browser in Melville will find interest in the separate items, in, for example, the copy of Cervantes with its marginalia. The specialist will rely on it as a treasury of "corroborative evidence." The internal evidence of

Melville's reading too often lacks this corroboration, but many gaps will be filled. More items will be located; the book points toward the future. The expert, for instance, in the Oriental background of the mysterious Parsee of *Moby-Dick*, will hope for the discovery (and a recording in a supplement) of the sources used by Melville to create this character.

Future students of Melville's intellectual debts should start from Sealts as a base and range far and wide. Millicent Bell's "Pierre Bayle and *Moby-Dick*" (*PMLA,* 1951; see below), demonstrates what one scholar can do with one influence exerted on one book. W. E. Bezanson shows Melville absorbed in the poetry of Matthew Arnold (*PMLA,* 1954). This essay must be reckoned with in all future studies of Melville's own poetry. For this new light Sealts lit the candle. Between 1862 and 1883 Melville, Bezanson says, "bought, read, and marked six major volumes of Arnold's poetry and prose." He does not guess about the subtle effects of this reading of Arnold's poetry on Melville's mind. But he studies the marginalia; he stresses Melville's preferences; and by other tests he attempts to show the temper of Melville's mind during the years when he was indentured to *Clarel.* The resultant portrait of Melville in these gray middle years may stand (in contrast) with the more familiar image of the young man swept off his feet by Shakespeare and the Elizabethans. Of such explorations we need more, in both English and in Continental literatures.

Articles of a general character on Melville's art are fewer than those on particular books (see below). Apparently critics have found difficult the analysis of an ideological or artistic pattern outside the larger arena of a book. Nevertheless, we encounter in the magazines some comprehensive judgments on Melville's techniques or ideas. In "Melville's Struggle with the Angel" (*MLQ,* 1940), Howard surveys the major technical devices in the early novels, certain artistic interests connected with *Moby-Dick,* and Melville's failure to attain a reliable craftsmanship. We observe the strong continuing excitement about "Melville's 'Agatha' Letter to Hawthorne" (*NEQ,* 1929; see above). This appeared in the year of Mumford's biography, also an inspirer of a subtler study of Melville's art. There now followed a widespread discussion of the artistic implications of this manuscript. In "The Significance of Melville's 'Agatha' Letters" (*ELH,* 1946), Hayford stressed the fact that the document helps to interpret Melville's mind in the months after his completion of *Pierre.* Had he written the story, he would have emphasized "the theme of patient submission."

Before continuing our review of articles on Melville's craftsmanship and thought, we should glance at studies of his fiction on a more matter-of-fact level. The only full-length analysis of his style is in German (see above), but various essays (see below) deal with his manipulation of words, sea lingo, folk materials, or frontier types. One original essay is J. M. Purcell's "Melville's Contribution to English" (*PMLA,* 1941). As a result of an exhaustive study of his language in the fiction Purcell declares that Melville "possessed one of the most individualized vocabularies among American writers of the nineteenth century." He divides his list of 180 words into two classes. First, he groups words not in the *NED* or *DAE,* or used with a meaning not in these dictionaries. Second, he lists words or phrases whose use is earlier or considerably later than the examples quoted in these dictionaries. No major American writer, not even Whitman, was more sensitive to the magic of words than Melville.

Several articles by C. M. Babcock emphasize Melville's interest in etymology and underline the fact that he was an incorrigible neologist. Purcell's list abounds with words of Melville's own coinage. Supplementary material may be found in Babcock's "Melville's Proverbs of the Sea" (*Western Folklore,* 1952). In a salty little paper, "The Language of Melville's Isolatoes" (idem, 1951), he shows that in the works as a whole may be found a lexicon of sea talk (see also *Word Study,* Dec. 1953). This study of the language leads us again (see above) to Melville's consciousness of the frontier (see Nichol, below). Babcock describes his adaptation of folk materials in "Melville's Backwoods Seamen" (*Western Folklore,* 1951). Melville's delight in these homespun materials should be remembered as a balance for his metaphysical vagaries.

A half-dozen essays in the 1930's may be linked with the biographies in their preliminary explorations of Melville's subconscious mind. In 1932 appeared two articles which probably seemed bolder in their own day than in ours: R. M. Wainger's "Herman Melville: A Study in Disillusion" *(Union College Bull.)* and G. C. Homans' "The Dark Angel: The Tragedy of Herman Melville" *(NEQ).* Homans perceived in "the three unautobiographical novels of Herman Melville's first period: *Mardi, Moby-Dick,* and *Pierre* . . . a regularly developed action, complete in the three novels and completed with the catastrophe in the last." Although Homans excluded biography he referred to this action as "the Melville tragedy." He studied the author's identification of himself with his characters, so endlessly discussed in later criticism. Melville was dramatizing his own failure to answer the riddles of the universe, his own refusal to be satisfied with penultimate truth.

A similar subjectivity, although not necessarily autobiographical, is discussed in N. B. Fagin's "Herman Melville and the Interior Monologue" (*AL,* 1935). The flow of meditation in *Moby-Dick* points back to *Hamlet* but also forward to James Joyce. In almost the same year F. I. Carpenter introduced the troublesome question of Melville's women in "Puritans Preferred Blondes: The Heroines of Melville and Hawthorne" (*NEQ,* 1936). Now emerges the theme dear to later biographers, Melville's "worship of the adolescent ideal of purity." This decade of beginnings culminated in Blackmur's original definition of Melville's "putative statement," in "The Craft of Herman Melville" (*VQR,* 1938; see above).

It is impossible to separate Melville's ideas on God and man from his craftsmanship, and some devotees of the latter urge us not to take the former too seriously. After all, they say, Melville was no philosopher. In the articles, however, one detects an inclination toward the study of one or the other of these two aspects of Melville's genius. In the next decade R. E. Watters published several essays, expositional rather than critical, and useful in defining attitudes deeply rooted in all of Melville's writings. For example, in "Melville's Metaphysics of Evil" (*UTQ,* 1940), in speaking of Melville's "ethical cosmos," he summarizes his concept of external nature, with its power, its beauty, and its remorseless evil. To Melville man is inconsequential in an indifferent universe, struggling in body and spirit, and divided within himself.

This definition carries with it the danger of regarding such syntheses as Melville's answers rather than his questions. In contrast, we recall Sedgwick's theory of the exploratory character of each book. An intimacy with Melville's writings, as with Shakespeare's, leaves us with evidence for almost any conclusion regarding good and evil, aristocracy and democracy, solitude and society. For Melville, as for Marcus Aurelius, life is "opinion." In "Melville's 'Sociality' " (*AL,* 1945) Watters finds Melville deeply concerned with "the commonalty of mankind," and in "Melville's 'Isolatoes' " (*PMLA,* 1945), he develops the other side of this theme, that isolation is impossible. The word "isolato" is not in Purcell's list (see above), but Watters says it was invented by Melville to describe the crew of *The Pequod.* The roster of "isolatoes" is formidable: the narrators in *Typee* and *White Jacket,* Father Mapple, Ahab, Pierre, Isabel, Mortmain, Vine, and others. Watters distinguishes between two types of victims: those who are forced into solitude, and those whose solitude is self-imposed. The implication, however, that Melville advocated "shared experience" and a resultant happiness is at variance with evidence that he did not think happiness important. The truly heroic man is a "diver," and so necessarily an "isolato."

Maintaining an approximate chronology, we may go on to studies of techniques, in Tyrus Hillway's "Melville's Art: One Aspect" (*MLN,* 1947) or in Richard Chase's "An Approach to Melville" (*PR,* 1947), with its preview of patterns in his book (see above), with its symbolism of castration, and with its considered judgment that we are justified in discussing Melville as an artist. In "Melville as Symbolist" (*UKCR,* 1949), an essay of only nine pages but richly allusive to various literatures, R. W. Short dwells on Melville's sensitivity to unseen reality, but warns us against trying too hard to interpret his symbols. "Claggart and Billy Budd ray out from themselves, shedding concentric rings of light upon the values of their universe," but the degree of understanding will depend on the experience of the percipient mind. Short discusses Melville's apostasy from strict allegory or from "vaguely felt intimations," and believes that in his nineteenth century he lacked the critical vocabulary to consummate his "artistic strategy," that is, his various kinds of symbolism and of myth. He observes that Melville lets his symbols "accumulate meanings . . . as they knock about in his myth-world." Thus a single meaning attached to one of them has at least "a partial validity . . . he makes his symbols blur through one another and take shape at that vanishing point where the one and the many become indivisible."

Occasionally articles have used the entire body of Melville's works for the purpose of general definitions. In contrast to previous views of this relationship, Perry Miller declares that Melville never escaped from "the incubus of Emerson" (*VQR,* 1953; see above). With barbs for the various schools of Melville criticism, Miller reminds us that Melville wrote romances, and that *Moby-Dick* and *Pierre* derive from transcendental roots. The novels "are, to the end, implacably, defiantly, and unrepentantly Transcendental." In a less polemical vein, in "Melville and the Midwest" (*PMLA,* 1951), J. W. Nichol writes thoughtfully of the sources of the Western imagery in Melville's prose. With few external records of a trip which left an indelible imprint on Melville's imagination, Nichol estimates its influence. Placed beside other discussions of the West (see above), this essay confirms our impression of the strength of Melville's land symbolism as opposed to his sea symbolism. The former was in debt to far more than Melville's experiences in New York State and Nantucket. Nichol demonstrates the extensive use of this Western imagery, and conjectures that from this inland journey Melville sloughed off the "coastal provincialism" which affected some other American men of letters. The conflicting judgments in this section of the present essay the reader must adjust for himself. Melville inspires controversy, and, as we now reach the articles on particular books, we may with reason adapt the old saw: *Quot homines tot sententiae!*

5. *Articles on Particular Works*

All of Melville's novels, and also his poetry, have now received separate attention from the critics. It would be possible to list here, besides "notes," "explications" of passages and of characters, or other brief comment, more than 100 essays. Of the 100 the distribution is about what we might expect. Little has been written concerning *Israel Potter* (see Roper, p. 27), and there are hardly more than half a dozen pieces on *The Confidence Man*. More than one half of the 100 essays are devoted to *Moby-Dick*. My selected list, from which I shall select yet again, contains many trifles. Melville is so inexhaustible that we need not be surprised at any new word from a zealot on the various characters in his fiction, whether on Pip, on Jarl, or on the Old Dansker. My eclectic list, however, includes some of the most distinguished writing on Melville. Such essays should be associated by the reader with items on the previous pages, with biographies, chapters or introductions. When I have been compelled to choose between two items of a special character, I have recorded the one which was supplementary in interest to the longer discussions in books.

Articles on *Typee* and *Omoo* are not comparable in analytical content to the discussions of these early writings in the biographies. We should note their concern with background material (e.g., *SRL,* 24 Nov. 1928; *NEQ,* 1932; *PQ,* 1936; or *AL,* 1938, and, in particular, Ida Leeson, "The Mutiny on the *Lucy Ann,*" *PQ,* 1940), or with the reception of these books

(*AL,* 1937; see also Roper, pp. 17-20). The essays on *Mardi* demand more attention as supplementary to Davis' study of its genetics or to the important sections in Sedgwick or Matthiessen (see above). Scholars now began in earnest the search for sources (*AL,* 1937 or 1952), or for special meanings, for instance, of the star, Arcturus (idem, 1942). In 1941 Davis published a curtain-raiser for his book *(MLQ).* Paralleling the discovery that Melville used travel books (see Anderson, above), he showed his dependence on contemporary "flower books" for the characters of Yillah and Hautia, and for both framework and symbolism. The article contains a "Floral Dictionary" for *Mardi* (from Amaranth to Wormwood).

For interpretation *Mardi* is, like *Moby-Dick,* fertile material (see *American Quart.,* 1950). Hillway opposes the conventional view that, after the end of the book, Taji carries on his search in this world. He argues that he commits suicide and pursues Yillah in the "outer ocean" of eternity. (See "Taji's Abdication in Herman Melville's *Mardi,*" *AL,* 1944, and "Taji's Quest for Certainty," *AL,* 1946.) On the other hand, in a geographical tour through the entire Mardian archipelago, Miss Wright, evidently weary of Taji's infatuation for the somewhat tiresome Yillah and Hautia, refuses to regard them as central. The true object of the quest is "an undiscovered, ideal man," a "whole" man combining both heart and head, a Jack Chase rather than an Ahab or a Pierre ("The Head and the Heart in Melville's *Mardi,*" *PMLA,* 1951).

Whatever the meanings of *Mardi,* it is clearly Melville's first extended experiment in artistic method. *Moby-Dick* was to reflect the lessons learned from *Mardi* and also from *Redburn* and *White Jacket.* Interest in *Redburn* was born with the interest in Melville, simultaneously with Weaver's biography. Possibly Mumford's reckless use of *Redburn* as autobiography begot a caution which reached a climax in Gilman's patient separation of fact from fancy (see above). For Gilman could not agree with Mumford that *Redburn* was "autobiography with only the faintest disguises." A reasonable attitude toward this novel had been stimulated by the work of Anderson, Forsythe, and others, and especially by Thorp's "Redburn's Prosy Old Guide Book" (*PMLA,* 1938). With parallel passages Thorp showed Melville's objectives in the use of this particular source: expansion of material, information (without too much acknowledgment), and satire. But if this episode was transmuted by the imagination, why not the book as a whole? Obviously *Redburn* was not to be taken too seriously. It was a work of fiction.

In the creation of *Redburn* other books were involved, as Keith Huntress indicated (*NEQ,* 1945), and Thorp's article was the forerunner of the new point of view. Melville showed his hero as a naïve and romantic boy, and pictured the fate of a young gentleman condemned to the fo'c's'le. Critics have, however, never given up the dream that *Redburn* contains what J. J. Gross has recently called "spiritually accurate autobiography." In "Rehearsal of Ishmael: Melville's *Redburn*" (*VQR,* 1951) he hails Melville's satisfactory union, for the first time, of "symbolic suggestion with the narrative pattern." Articles on *White Jacket,* on the coat itself, on the fall from the masthead, and on other episodes of the novel reveal Melville the artist in a transitional phase to *Moby-Dick. White Jacket,* however, like *Typee* and *Omoo,* fares better in biography than in article (see *AL,* 1935). A few short studies deal with special aspects of the novel (*AL,* 1935): its sources in character, book, or incident (*SRL,* 4 July 1931; *BPLQ,* July 1951; *AL,* 1945 or 1950). J. W. Nichol has an amusing note on F. O. Matthiessen's mistaken reading of an adjective (see "Melville's 'Soiled' Fish of the Sea," *AL,* 1949). Altogether, bold, original articles on *White Jacket* are still unwritten (see, however, *NEQ,* 1949).

Whether or not Melville can be compared with Shakespeare, as some disciples assert, there now exists a passion for the evaluation and editing of his texts. Except for *Billy Budd,* the original manuscripts are lacking, but the different editions of *Typee,* the altered purposes and revisions of *Mardi,* or the obvious discrepancy in *Moby-Dick* between a straight story of whaling and its present form, demand a full dress study of all Melville's texts. In "Bowdler and the Whale; Some Notes on the First English and American Editions of *Moby-Dick*" (*AL,* 1932), W. S. Ament establishes the distinction between the first American edition, riddled with inconsistencies and textual inaccuracies, but obviously representing what Melville wished to give to the world, and the first English edition, "an uninspired version of the proof of the American." (For a collation of the first English and first American editions, see the textual notes in the set volume of the Mansfield and Vincent edition.)

In a "Melville Number" of *AL,* in January 1954, two of five essays deal with these problems of text. W. M. Hutchinson's "A Definitive Edition of *Moby-Dick*" clarifies the history of its various texts. It faces the lurking doubt about the dependability of the Mansfield and Vincent edition, published in 1952, as a volume in the new edition. Hutchinson's collation of this text with the first American edition demonstrated to his satisfaction that this new imprint may be regarded as a definitive edition, if we condone "compositors' errors and some editorial oversight." The perfect text is always a dream and not a reality, and even the list of "errors" and "oversights" at the end of the article does not qualify too much Hutchinson's faith in the edition.

In "The Two Moby-Dicks" George Stewart has given us equally valuable textual definitions. Like Davis in his *Mardi* and Freeman in his *Billy Budd,* he has taken us into the mind of Melville in the act of creation. This essay shows how Chapters i-xv are presumably the original story, slightly revised, and Chapters xvi-xxii the first narrative with revisions of great significance. Chapters xxiii-Epilogue tell the tale as Melville reconceived it. Yet these chapters, too, may retain parts of the first version, again somewhat revised. After a helpful review of the scholarship on the subject, based chiefly on external evidence, Stewart submits his own beliefs, founded primarily on internal evidence. He mentions shifts in the conception and function of characters, style, Shakespearean influence, and atmosphere. There will be further argument about this mystery, but here is a compendium of what is known or credible in regard to the composition of Melville's greatest novel.

All the topics found in articles about Melville's writing as a whole are repeated in respect to *Moby-Dick.* Special studies of its reputation have been made (e.g., *Jour. Rutgers Univ. Lib.* 1940; *PQ,* 1946). Its sources have been explored, and the task begun of determining the reading which lies behind it—a colossal labor unlikely to be finished for decades. Incidents which may have precipitated or anticipated *Moby-Dick* (*AL,* 1930, or *MLN,* 1934, or *Colophon,* 1936); sources for the grand three-day climax of the chase (*N&Q,* 26 July and 15 Nov. 1941; *AL,* 1948); the curious lore inherent in Ahab's "blood-quench" of the fatal harpoon (*AL,* 1946); these are examples of this endless investigation of our classic.

Many essays concern themselves solely with the sources of *Moby-Dick.* Charles Olson's "Lear and Moby Dick" (*Twice a Year,* 1938, see above) suggested the solid subsoil of English literature in Melville's writing, as Forsythe's paper, however slight, "Emerson and *Moby-Dick*" (*N&Q,* 23 Dec. 1939), hinted at his debts to his peers in America. There can be no doubt of the molding power of Shakespeare upon this novel or upon *Pierre,* but, in the light of other causative factors, Olson's estimate of the "impact" now seems slanted. *Moby-Dick* "was actually precipitated by Shakespeare." Shakespeare's plays became a great metaphor by which Melville objectified his original vision. But there were also Plato, Milton, Browne, Hawthorne, Carlyle, Emerson, and dozens of others; Melville's power of assimilation was boundless. The most exciting study in recent years of his reading is Millicent Bell's learned demonstration of his kinship of mind with Pierre Bayle (see above). Like Bayle, Melville thought the secret of God impenetrable, and like Bayle—perhaps this was the crux of the Melville mystery—he was "a man tossed between the will to believe and the compulsion to doubt."

The periodicals' literary criticism of *Moby-Dick* really began in the 1940's, if we except a few essays at about the time of

Weaver's biography (*Freeman,* 23, 30 Aug. 1922; *Bookman,* 1924; the *Century,* 1925; *RAA,* 1927; *English Jour.,* Nov. 1938). One of the pioneer interpretations of nearly thirty years ago reappears in all the bibliographies of Melville: W. S. Gleim's "A Theory of Moby Dick" (*NEQ,* 1929; see also *The Meaning of Moby Dick,* 1938). Gleim ascribes to each of the sailors an allegorical meaning: "Love," "Common Sense," "Authority," and so on. Forsythe's brief comment six years later on "The Town-Ho's Story" (*N&Q,* 4 May 1935), is a contrast to the detailed studies of this gam by Sherman Paul in 1949 and Don Geiger in 1954. We observe the advance of techniques in these and in J. D. Young's examination of all nine gams (1954) since Lincoln Colcord's elementary "Notes on 'Moby Dick' " (*Freeman,* 23, 30 Aug. 1922).

Beginning in 1940 with S. W. D. Scott's "Some Implications of the Typhoon Scenes in *Moby Dick" (AL),* various critics held Ahab under the microscope. Scott explores the relations of *The Pequod* to the typhoon as a symbol of the conflict between Ahab and Starbuck. In "Captain Ahab's Discovery: The Tragic Meaning of Moby Dick" (*NEQ,* 1942), H. A. Myers explains how Ahab's quest for certainty ends in a revelation: in losing his life he discovers its significance. He realizes that his suffering gives meaning to his unconquerable spirit. But C. C. Walcutt, in "The Fire Symbolism in *Moby Dick*" (*MLN,* 1944), thinks Ahab's spiritual development depends on his comprehension that evil is at the center of reality. He learns the great truth that evil and good are not different entities but are one. Meanwhile, W. H. Auden, contrasting Greek and Christian concepts, finds Ahab close to "The Christian Tragic Hero," the title of his essay (*New York Times Book Review,* 16 Dec. 1945). If none of these Ahabs please us, we may turn to Sophie Hollis' "Moby Dick: A Religious Interpretation" (*Catholic World,* 1946). In the end, we shall probably write our own table of meanings for the mad sea captain. For a balanced diet it is well to read Joseph Jones's "Humor in *Moby Dick*" (Univ. of Texas *SE,* 1945-46).

It is not strange that some critics pleaded for simpler approaches to the old man and his White Whale. In his "Heterodoxy on Moby Dick?" (*SR,* 1947), Montgomery Belgion protests overrefinement in the interpretation of Melville. He deplores the notion that *Moby-Dick* has a cosmic theme, and he joins battle with the exponents of such theories, particularly Sedgwick for his "hypoborean" symbolism (see above). He denies that Ahab stands for "Man" or the sea for "Truth." After discussing *Moby-Dick* as a story of "pursuit," Belgion defines certain American "affinities" of Melville (Emerson, Thoreau, Hawthorne, or Whitman) and also his English "derivations" (the Bible, Thomas Browne, or Shakespeare). Having mentioned one skeptic, we might turn to a complete unbeliever. In "Symbolism in Moby Dick" (*JHI,* 1951), E. E. Stoll assails Melville critics in general and, in particular, Mumford, Sedgwick, Winters, and the "extravagant" Vincent, as confused, eccentric, and with inconspicuous powers of reasoning. His essay rebels against "the present-day criticism in its excesses or vagaries." His cold water, however, is also for the book itself, which he concedes is a good, perhaps even a great story. But it is not, he declares, thinking, presumably, of certain critics, of really "ecumenical or perennial importance." *Moby-Dick* is by no means an immortal masterpiece. Stoll has written a vigorous essay. The faithful should contain themselves and read this blasphemy carefully.

The search for interpretations of the Whale and his pursuers continues in all kinds of periodicals. R. E. Watters has adduced new "meanings" (*UTQ,* 1951), and, in "In Nomine Diaboli," H. A. Murray defines Ahab as the incarnation of the Satanic principle (*NEQ,* 1951; see above). Instead of a cessation of what Belgion and Stoll denounce as "extravagant" criticism, we are likely to have more experimental analysis of *Moby-Dick.* Of this fact there is proof in the papers on the gams to which we now return in our survey of the research on *Moby-Dick.*

In "Melville's 'The *Town-Ho's* Story' " (*AL,* 1949), Paul, besides dealing with the democratic theme of this, the first of the gams, examines it as a miniature version of the book's fundamental idea. "Ahab's tragedy comes to mean the same thing as Radney's." The difference would seem to be one of degree. Don Geiger's challenge of this theory and his disagreement with Thompson's thesis in *Melville's Quarrel with God* (see above) may be read in "Melville's Black God: Contrary Evidence in 'The *Town-Ho's* Story' " (*AL,* 1954). Geiger draws his parallel not between Ahab and Radney, but between Ahab and Steelkilt. J. D. Young's "The Nine Gams of the Pequod" (*AL,* 1954) adopts the familiar metaphor of *The Pequod* as a world in itself, and adds up the significance of all the gams. They illustrate the relation of the microcosm of *The Pequod* to the outside world. As a series they may be divided into groups, and in their integration with the story they form a frame of reference for understanding both the structure and the narrative.

The decoding in the biographies of one of Melville's most difficult books, *Pierre,* has also had its parallel in the periodicals. The early work, with its summaries of the plot, now seems curiously out of date. Foster Damon's "Pierre the Ambiguous" (*H&H,* 1929) and E. L. G. Watson's "Melville's *Pierre*" (*NEQ,* 1930) were among the first in a series of partisan essays. Watson went far. He called *Pierre* "the greatest of Melville's books," and "the height of his achievement," an opinion which in these early days even Forsythe (see above) did not share. The latter alleged that Mumford had "twisted" the plot (*AL,* 1930). In "The Satirical Temper of Melville's 'Pierre' " (*AL,* 1936) Braswell reduced the book to the "laughter of despair," but some years later, Hillway, in "Pierre, the Fool of Virtue" (*AL,* 1949), protested against the acceptance of opinions in the book as Melville's own. He was merely asking questions. Nevertheless, Braswell's theory has had some support, that the author, after the failure of *Moby-Dick,* adopted for himself the "genial, desperado philosophy" described in *Pierre.* Here he is recording "his own sad spiritual history." Fifteen years later Braswell turned again to the book in "Melville's Opinion of *Pierre*"

(*AL,* 1951). One suggestive study in sources is G. Giovannini's "Melville's *Pierre* and Dante's *Inferno*" (*PMLA,* 1949).

If we are ever to be rid of the notion that *Pierre* is only a hodgepodge, a hysterical novel, a bitter satire on the low state of American letters, Charles Moorman's recent article, "Melville's *Pierre* and the Fortunate Fall" (*AL,* 1953), may do much to attain that end. Moorman makes no claims for *Pierre* as literature. In fact, he calls it a bad novel. But he is fascinated by its "dense substratum of theme and imagery so important to the whole of Melville's philosophy." Far from being hysterical, Melville is reworking, systematically through his imagery, the myth of the Fall of Man and the related tradition of the *felix culpa.* Moorman admits that this correspondence is not exact. His tracing of the imagery, the green and gold Arcadian world, the serpent patterns, and the hemlock is well-reasoned, and important as a new evaluation of *Pierre.* The hero returns to the quest; it is a *fortunate* fall.

Israel Potter has received little attention (for its sources see *SAQ,* 1928). Criticism in periodicals of Melville's *Piazza Tales* hardly existed before the 1940's, and a full-length study is needed of their place in the Melville canon. During the past fifteen years the favorites for special study have been "Bartleby the Scrivener" and "Benito Cereno." The lag in exploring these tales is well illustrated by H. H. Scudder's heavy-handed treatment of the last-named story in "Melville's *Benito Cereno* and Captain Delano's Voyages" (*PMLA,* 1928). This is a useful estimate of Melville's expert use of *A Narrative of Voyages and Travels in the Northern and Southern Hemispheres* (1817). The story's wealth of allusion and metaphor, however, is left untouched, except for the dubious conclusion that "Melville himself is Benito Cereno and Babo is the personification of modern criticism." Evaluations of these revealing little sketches really began with E. H. Eby's "Herman Melville's 'Tartarus of Maids' " (*MLQ,* 1940) and with M. M. Sealts's "Herman Melville's 'I and My Chimney' " (*AL,* 1941). In the former appear in symbolic pattern Melville's reflections on woman's destiny. In the latter his somber meditations on the subconscious may allude to fears about his own sanity, after the writing of *Pierre.*

A little later Sealts added "The Publication of Melville's *Piazza Tales*" (*MLN,* 1944), and in "A Second Look at 'Bartleby' " (*CE,* 1945) Oliver continued his work on the various stories and on the book as a whole. (See " 'Cock-A-Doodle-Doo!' and Transcendental Hocus-Pocus," *NEQ,* June 1948, and above. See also *Furioso,* Fall 1947, and *SR,* 1953.) Although Arvin thought "Benito Cereno" negligible, this "sensitively poised" story, as Matthiessen called it, has elicited a considerable body of criticism in the magazines. S. T. Williams discussed its interwoven strands of the Catholic Church, the Spanish empire, and the American civilization (*VQR,* 1947). Mrs. Rosalie Feltenstein stressed its architectural skill, and its characterization (*AL,* 1947). In the most recent study R. H. Fogle says that after *Moby Dick,* "Benito Cereno" is Melville's "most fully achieved piece of writing" (Tulane *SE,* 1952).

Eventually each of the *Piazza Tales* will receive particular attention. Not long after Scudder's exploration of the backgrounds of "Benito Cereno," Russell Thomas gave us "Melville's Use of Some Sources in *The Encantadas*" (*AL,* 1932), and we may now read interpretations of "The Bell-Tower" (*AL,* 1951), of "The Apple Tree Table" (*AL,* 1954; see also 1940), and, with still wider implications, as the title suggests, "Melville's *Bartleby:* Absolutism, Predestination, and Free Will" (Tulane *SE,* 1954; see also Leo Marx's important "Melville's Parable of the Walls," *SR,* 1953). In "The Shorter Fiction of Herman Melville" C. G. Hoffman suggests that Melville, instead of declining in power, "grew as an artist" through these tales and sketches (*SAQ,* 1953).

Criticism now includes *The Confidence-Man,* for the lay reader the most acrid of all Melville's books. We may now add Miss Foster's valuable edition of this novel in the Collected Works (see above) to the discussions in Sedgwick and Miss Wright (see above), and to a few supplementary essays. Oliver finds the portraits of Emerson and Thoreau done "with pointed directness, though almost entirely without bitterness" (*CE,* 1946; see also his "Melville's Goneril and Fanny Kemble," *NEQ,* 1945). Like other readers, H. C. Horsford speculates on Melville's abrupt and cryptic ending for his river saga. In "Evidence of Melville's Plans for a Sequel to *The Confidence-Man*" (*AL,* 1952), he cites passages in the Journal of 1856-57 to indicate that Melville planned continuance. As supplements to the discussions in the biographies, three important articles are Chase's "Melville's *Confidence Man*" (*KR,* 1949), J. W. Shroeder's "Sources and Symbols for Melville's *Confidence-Man*" (*PMLA,* 1951), and R. H. Pearce's "Melville's Indian Hater . . ." (*PMLA,* 1952). Without attacking crucial problems, this latter essay examines, in particular, Melville's Biblical imagery and also his "Indian-imagery."

The *cause celebre* of a century ago, the story of the brig *Somers* and Captain Alexander Slidell Mackenzie, has been revived through the zeal of Melville scholars. They intend to learn everything possible about the origins of Melville's last novel, *Billy Budd.* "Thus out of his reading in 1888," wrote Anderson in "The Genesis of *Billy Budd*" (*AL,* 1940), "and reminiscences of his personal experiences of 1843-1844, heightened through dramatic invention, Melville compounded his last story." In "A Note on the Background of *Billy Budd*" (*AL,* 1948) Arvin shows how a passage in the *Autobiography of Thurlow Weed* betrays the unhappy connection of Guert Gansevoort (Melville's cousin) with this affair. Perhaps Gansevoort was the prototype of Starry Vere. Other details of the historical background will emerge. Already this novel, written on the eve of its author's death, has evoked article after article. These commentaries approach those on *Moby-Dick,* not in number, but in their determination to unravel Melville's complexities of meaning.

Weaver had little to say critically of his great discovery, but all later biographies and introductions focused upon *Billy Budd* for their estimates of the older Melville. The boldest interpretation of his artistic purposes in *Billy Budd* appeared in Thompson's book. I shall not list here the replies to this theory (see above), but Maurice Bewley's "A Truce of God for Melville" (*SR,* 1953) may illustrate the general disagreement. Even if its thesis, evident in its title, seems too strongly stated, we must yield credit to Watson's "Melville's Testament of Acceptance" (*NEQ,* 1933). This was read, reread, and contradicted, as in Chase's direct reply, "Dissent on Billy Budd" (*PR,* 1948). The novel was *not* a testament of acceptance. On the contrary, "the moral situation in *Billy Budd* is deeply equivocal." Watson's verdict was opposed, but it still remains after twenty years a platform for discussion. In his essay Chase repeats his definition of the two kinds of Melvillian hero: the "false Prometheus," and the other, the man great in body, heart, and intellect. "Billy Budd is pre-eminently the beautiful boy of the liberal-progressive myth, the figure who gets 'pushed around'." Apropos of the controversy the student should read Joseph Schiffman's "Melville's Final Stage: Irony . . ." (*AL,* 1950). Besides these full dress essays there are many others (*AL,* 1944, on Daniel Orme; *Explicator,* 1945; *MLN,* 1951; *AL,* 1950; *Accent,* 1951; *UTQ,* 1944).

The most helpful of recent interpretations are Wendell Glick's "Expediency and Absolute Morality in *Billy Budd*" (*PMLA,* 1953), and N. H. Pearson's "Billy Budd: 'The King's Yarn' " (*AQ,* 1951). Both essays are aware of the critical literature on *Billy Budd;* both deal with central problems; and by a coincidence they are complementary to each other. With B. F. Freeman's Introduction (see above) and these two essays, the student has an excellent enchiridion to *Billy Budd.* With these guides we understand why this may be called the best-loved book by Melville. We feel its tranquillity, its tenderness, and its reaching out toward the mysteries which once tormented but now calmed his mind. Glick is interested in the abstract issues, in the ethical conflict of the book. Pearson devotes himself to the characters themselves, particularly to Budd, "a sort of upright barbarian" (as Melville calls him) and to the dreamer-philosopher, Vere. Glick makes much of the episode of Nelson in the story. After a study of the conflict between the expediency of the world, and the code of heaven, he defines Melville's position, perhaps somewhat too precisely. Melville, he says, agrees with Vere "that justice to the individual is not the ultimate loyalty in a complex culture; the stability of the culture has the higher claim." Pearson finds the character of Budd rooted in Melville's conception, profoundly in debt to Milton, of prelapsarian man, and that of Vere in postlapsarian man.

In almost the only critical essay on Melville's verse (*KR*, 1946), R. P. Warren says: "Even behind some of Melville's failures we can catch the shadow of the poem which might have been." Revaluations of Melville's prose have revealed such unexpected depths that one hesitates to dismiss Melville as the poet that might have been. The study of his poetry is just beginning. Sedgwick's sympathetic account and the various introductions may be forerunners, especially in the forthcoming edition of *Clarel* (see above), of a revaluation of Melville's poetry. As so often in prose-writers who are incidentally poets, we find in *Clarel* or in such a poem as "The Berg," condensed restatements of the ideas in the novels. In the main, however, we should expect, despite increasing study of the poems (see *CE,* 1943, on *Clarel*) that Warren's judgments would stand. He notes the unevenness of the craftsmanship and hazards the guess that "the violences, the distortions, the wrenchings . . . [represent an] effort to develop a nervous, dramatic, masculine style." The poems are mixed with "disparate elements" which are seldom assimilated. Reading Warren's expert analysis of the break-up of stanza after stanza, it is difficult to believe that later research will unveil Melville as a poet.

6

WALT WHITMAN

I. Bibliographies

THE FIRST extensive Whitman bibliography was prepared by O. L. Triggs for Volume x of *The Complete Writings of Walt Whitman* (1902). It is still valuable for its listing of the earliest writing about Whitman, under the headings of Essays in Books, Incidental Discussion, Articles in Periodicals, and Poems (i.e., poems with Whitman as a theme). The fullest bibliography is the one assembled by Emory Holloway and H. S. Saunders for the second volume of the *CHAL* (1918). Of particular value, even after forty years, are Sections IV ([Whitman's] "Contributions to Periodicals"); VI ("Biography and Criticism"); and VII ("Translations"). Supplementing the *CHAL* bibliography is G. W. Allen's *Twenty-five Years of Walt Whitman Bibliography,* 1918-1942 (*Bulletin of Bibliography Pamphlets,* No. 38, 1943). The listing of periodical articles about Whitman is carried down to 1950 in Lewis Leary's *Articles on American Literature, 1900-1950* (1954). Some articles written outside America are included, though Leary states in his preface that "no systematic search has been made through foreign language periodicals of the period." There is a useful section on "Reviews of Books and Articles about Walt Whitman" in *Index to Early American Periodical Literature, 1728-1870* [sic]: *Part 3, Walt Whitman* (1941). Collectors and librarians interested in the typographical minutiae of Whitman first editions will find useful information in Frank Shay, *The*

Bibliography of Walt Whitman (1920) and in Carolyn Wells and A. F. Goldsmith, *A Concise Bibliography of the Works of Walt Whitman, with a Supplement of Fifty Books about Whitman* (1922; rev. ed., 1930).

The most extensive critical bibliography is that contained in *LHUS,* ed. R. E. Spiller et al. (1948), III. Briefer selected and annotated bibliographies appear in Floyd Stovall, ed. *Walt Whitman, Representative Selections* (*AWS,* 1934; rev. ed., 1939); H. H. Clark, ed. *Major American Poets* (1936); and W. F. Taylor, *A History of American Letters* (1936). (The bibliography in the Taylor volume was prepared by Harry Hartwick.) In his indispensable *Walt Whitman Handbook* (1946), G. W. Allen discusses in detail all the important biographical studies of book length and supplies briefer comment on other studies under these chapter divisions: The Growth of *Leaves of Grass* and the *Prose Works;* Whitman's Fundamental Ideas; Social Thought; Ideas in Action; Literary Technique in *Leaves of Grass;* and Walt Whitman and World Literature. His "Walt Whitman Bibliography 1944-1954" (*Walt Whitman Foundation Bulletin,* 1955) is especially useful for its listing of foreign works. The seventeen-page bibliography in Roger Asselineau's *L'Evolution de Walt Whitman après le première édition des Feuilles d'Herbe* (Paris, 1954) gives a full listing of works which have appeared since 1942, including a considerable number of reviews. Before this date the listing is selective. Allen intends to publish in time a full-scale bibliography of the writings of Whitman, with a checklist of biographical and critical works about him.

II. Collections

After much selling and buying in the auction rooms the Whitman manuscripts have finally been gathered in ten or so great collections, the majority of which are in public and university libraries. Almost all of this vast accumulation of material derives ultimately from the literary property which Whitman, by his will, gave to his three executors, Harned, Traubel, and Bucke, who were friendly rivals in dividing up their treasure.

The Whitman collection presented to Duke in 1942 by Dr. and Mrs. J. C. Trent is fully described in Ellen F. Frey's *Catalogue of the Whitman Collection in the Duke University Library* (1945). The Whitman materials in the Library of Congress are distributed in twenty-seven individual collections. More than 1,000 items are listed in *Walt Whitman, A Catalog Based Upon the Collections of the Library of Congress* (Reference Department, Library of Congress, 1955). Charles E. Feinberg, himself one of the great Whitman collectors, supplied an illuminating essay for this catalogue: "Notes on Whitman Collections and Collectors." In the Lion Collection and the Henry W. and Albert A. Berg Collection the New York Public Library possesses Whitman materials of great value. One of these collections has been described in detail: Lewis Stark, et al., "Walt Whitman; The Oscar Lion Collection" (*BNYPL,* 1954). There is no printed catalogue of the Berg Collection. Some of the twenty Whitman manuscripts and 400 autograph letters in it may eventually be published in the Berg Monograph Series which will be initiated in 1956. The W. D. Bayley Collection is now in the library of Ohio Wesleyan University. There is a description of it by E. F. Amy (*Ohio Wesleyan Magazine,* 1955). The Van Sinderen Collection of more than 600 items was acquired by Yale in 1940. It has been described by S. T. Williams: "The Adrian Van Sinderen Collection of Walt Whitman" (*Yale Univ. Library Gazette,* 1941). The libraries of Brown University and the University of Pennsylvania possess important collections. The materials at Brown are briefly discussed by J. S. Saunders, "A Gift of Unrivalled Whitmania" (*Brown Alumni Weekly,* 1932). The William Sloane Kennedy Collection is now in the Rollins College Library. A large part of the magnificent collection formerly in the possession of Clifton Waller Barrett has recently been presented to the University of Virginia.

Important private collections are owned by Charles E. Feinberg of Detroit and T. E. Hanley of Bradford, Pa.

Several catalogues of exhibitions of Whitmaniana deserve to be noted. When the collection of Mrs. Frank Sprague (now at the University of Pennsylvania) was exhibited at the Library of Congress in 1939, a catalogue was issued: *The One Hundred and Twentieth Anniversary of the Birth of Walt Whitman* (Government Printing Office, 1939). Drawing on eleven American collections, Charles Feinberg, in 1954, arranged a remarkable exhibition of Whitman material in London. This was shown under the auspices of the United States Information Service which issued a catalogue: *Walt Whitman, Catalogue of an Exhibition held at the American Library, London, March-April 1954.* A portion of Mr. Feinberg's collection was exhibited in Detroit in 1955. There is a valuable catalogue of this exhibition: *Walt Whitman, a Selection of the Manuscripts, Books and Association Items Gathered by Charles E. Feinberg: Catalogue of an Exhibition held at the Detroit Public Library* (1955). For the exhibition at the New York Public Library in 1955 a catalogue was prepared: L. M. Stark and J. D. Gordan, *Walt Whitman's Leaves of Grass* (New York Public Library). This describes many of the Lion and Berg items in such a way that one can get a satisfactory account of the principal treasures of these two collections which relate to *Leaves of Grass.*

One sale catalogue should be mentioned: *Manuscripts, Autograph Letters, First Editions, and Portraits of Walt Whitman,* Formerly the Property of Dr. Richard Maurice Bucke (American Art Association, Anderson Galleries, 1936). This catalogue is of particular interest because the items in the Bucke collection are now dispersed in several libraries. Edward Naumburg, Jr.'s "A Collector Looks at Walt Whitman" (*Princeton Univ. Library Chronicle,* 1941) describes the collection, once his, all or most of which is now in the library of Ohio Wesleyan University.

III. Editions

1. *The Text*

Although the essays in this volume do not discuss in detail the first editions of the works of the authors represented, something must be said of the unique problem which confronts the reader of *Leaves of Grass.* When the ninth separate edition of this work appeared in 1892 (Philadelphia), it was not the usual collective edition prepared by a poet just before his death. Whitman revised his poems extensively over the years. Some he discarded altogether. Some he expanded. Others he broke up, distributing lines and sections in new poems with new titles. Thus it is that the student who wishes to know Whitman's poetry thoroughly must be familiar with the successive editions of *Leaves of Grass,* for each of the first eight editions has its own distinctive form and flavor.

That serious readers would not be content with Whitman's final versions and arrangement of his poems was foreseen by his literary executors when they issued the *Complete Writings* in 1902. O. L. Triggs prepared for the third volume of this edition "Variorum Readings of Leaves of Grass," a compilation which continues to be of use to scholars. A variorum edition of *Leaves of Grass* is called for, though the problems which its editor would have to solve are many. The nature of these problems has been discussed by two scholars: I. C. Story, "The Growth of *Leaves of Grass:* A Proposal for a Variorum Edition" (*Pacific Univ. Bull.*, 1941); and Sculley Bradley, "The Problem of a Variorum Edition of Whitman's *Leaves of Grass,*" *English Institute Annual, 1941* (1942). In the absence of a variorum edition the student will find especially helpful three long discussions of the successive editions of *Leaves of Grass.* These are to be found in G. W. Allen's *Walt Whitman Handbook* (1946), Frederik Schyberg's *Walt Whitman* (1951), and Roger Asselineau's *L'Evolution de Walt Whitman* (Paris, 1954). The fascinating problem of the growth of *Leaves of Grass* from edition to edition has evoked many studies. Though most of these concern themselves in some degree with the texts of the poems, it has seemed appropriate to group them together in the section of this essay devoted to Criticism.

In 1902 Whitman's literary executors, R. M. Bucke, T. B. Harned, and H. L. Traubel, issued *The Complete Writings of Walt Whitman* in ten volumes. This is still the standard edition.

In addition to the works which Whitman published in his lifetime the editors included several items from what has come to be virtually a library of Whitmaniana. Among these are the poet's letters to his young friend Peter Doyle, first edited by Bucke in 1897 under the title of *Calamus,* and *Notes and Fragments,* also issued by Bucke in 1899 (London, Canada).

The best edition of *Leaves of Grass* was prepared by Emory Holloway (1924). The text of this "Inclusive Edition" is that of the 1902 *Complete Writings.* It includes the Variorum Readings (somewhat revised) prepared by Triggs. This edition has been re-issued several times, most recently in 1954.

At the end of his life Whitman tried to make certain just which of his writings should stand as "authorized." The *Complete Poems and Prose of Walt Whitman, 1855-1888* (8th ed. of the poems; 3rd of the *Complete Works*) and the 1892 edition of *Leaves of Grass* have the stamp of finality on them. Nevertheless Whitman was aware that his disciples would not be content with these volumes as his *carte de visite* to posterity. For some time they had been busy gathering in his manuscripts and taking down his table talk. Yet he could not have foreseen what the Whitman "text" would finally become. Seemingly nearly every line of his, published or unpublished in his lifetime, has found its way into print; yet one need not be surprised if next week still another collection of Whitman editorials or sketches, hitherto buried in a newspaper file, is announced for publication.

The flood of such collections began in 1920 when Cleveland Rodgers and John Black edited *The Gathering of the Forces,* 2 vols. This work consists of editorials, essays, literary and dramatic reviews, and other material written by Whitman as editor of the Brooklyn *Daily Eagle* in 1846 and 1847. Wider in scope is Emory Holloway, ed. *The Uncollected Poetry and Prose of Walt Whitman,* 2 vols. (1921; reprinted 1932). This "vast batch left to oblivion," as the editor, quoting Whitman, called his collection, is made up of magazine publications not found in the *Complete Prose* and a selection from Whitman's "countless newspaper stories, book reviews, editorials, criticisms of art, music, drama, etc." Printed for the first time are extracts from the poet's notebooks which are now in the Library of Congress. The value of this work is enhanced by two long introductions, one biographical and one critical, and by a subject-index.

Whitman's early journalistic writing was not confined to editorials, sketches, and reviews. He tried his hand, not very successfully, at fiction. Five of his stories were rescued from a deserved oblivion in T. O. Mabbott, *The Half-Breed and Other Stories* (1927). Four of these stories appeared originally in a rare periodical of the 1840's, *The Aristidean.* Whitman's temperance novel, *Franklin Evans or the Inebriate,* was republished in 1929, with an introduction by Emory Holloway. A piece of hack work, which Whitman once called "rot of the worst sort," written in three days with the help of "a bottle of port or what not," *Franklin Evans* is nevertheless described by Holloway in his Introduction as "a crude foreshadowing . . . of Whitman's remarkable poetic autobiography, to come thirteen years later."

The unpublished manuscripts collected and edited by C. J. Furness in *Walt Whitman's Workshop* (1928) provide an indispensable tool for scholars. The great value of this compilation lies in the intrinsic importance of the manuscripts themselves and in the fact that Furness' aim was to show Whitman at work in notes and introductions, endeavoring to make his intentions as a writer clear and his spiritual message powerful.

When Holloway issued his *Uncollected Poetry and Prose of Walt Whitman* in 1921, he had had only limited access to the files of the Brooklyn *Daily Times* for which Whitman wrote editorials from 1857 to 1859. In 1932 Holloway and Vernolian Schwarz were able to present an ample selection from these editorials in *I Sit and Look Out.* As Holloway says in his Introduction, these writings show us "a Whitman who had at last found himself." He was thirty-eight when he went to the *Daily Times* and the Civil War was only four years in the future. Emory Holloway, with the assistance of Ralph Adimari, provided, in 1936, still another selection of Whitman newspaper articles: *New York Dissected.* These pieces which came from *Life Illustrated* were written in 1855 and 1856. The editors added to the value of their volume by reprinting in it a number of English and American reviews of the first edition of *Leaves of Grass,* several of which were not before known. An addition to the seemingly endless supply of newspaper pieces by Whitman was made in J. J. Rubin and C. H. Brown, eds. *Walt Whitman of the New York Aurora* (1950). The *Aurora* was the first New York daily of which Whitman, then only twenty-two, was the editor. Though he was in charge of the *Aurora* for only two months (March and April 1842), Rubin and Brown were able to uncover more than 180 articles and two poems written for it by Whitman.

As the important collections of Whitman manuscripts find permanent lodging in public libraries, we may expect selections from them to be printed. Much of the material in the Trent collection of the library of Duke University has been edited by Clarence Gohdes and R. G. Silver in *Faint Clews & Indirections* (1949). Aside from fragmentary notes for poems or versions of prose passages, the most valuable section of this volume consists of a selection of letters written by members of the Whitman family. As the editors note: "They afford for the first time a fairly substantial basis for judging the mental abilities of the Whitmans and uncover several skeletons in the family closet."

Several miscellaneous works, issued after the publication of the *Complete Writings* of 1902, should be mentioned at this point. In 1904 W. S. Kennedy published *Walt Whitman's Diary in Canada,* with extracts from other diaries and literary notebooks. In the same year Traubel edited *An American Primer,* a group of interesting notes on the American language apparently intended for a lecture. (The import of this work has been analyzed by Leon Howard: "Walt Whitman and the American Language," *American Speech,* 1930.) Emory Holloway edited, in 1927, *Pictures, An Unpublished Poem of Walt Whitman.* This early poem is of some importance because parts of it were scattered through the editions of *Leaves of Grass* from 1855 to 1881. *A Child's Reminiscence,* edited by T. O. Mabbott and R. G. Silver (1930), reproduces the first version of "Out of the Cradle" as published in the New York *Saturday Press* in 1859. In 1947 Sculley Bradley and J. A. Stevenson published *Walt Whitman's Backward Glances.* The editors reproduce in facsimile the manuscript of Whitman's essay "A Backward Glance on My Own Road" and establish the connection between it and "A Backward Glance O'er Travel'd Roads" as it appears in *November Boughs,* 1888.

As the Whitman manuscripts have become accessible to scholars, additions to the Whitman text have been published in the periodicals. The literary detectives are also constantly reprinting hitherto unknown journalistic writing. Only a few of these discoveries can be mentioned here. An early version of "Hush'd be the Camps To-day" is printed in O. S. Coad's "A Walt Whitman Manuscript" (*Jour. of the Rutgers Univ. Library,* 1938). Manuscripts from the Clifton Waller Barrett Collection of the University of Virginia are published and described in two articles by Fredson Bowers: "Whitman's Manuscripts for the Original 'Calamus' Poems" (*Studies in Bibliography,* Bibliographical Soc. of the Univ. of Virginia, 1953); and "The Manuscript of Walt Whitman's 'A Carol of Harvest, for 1867' " (*MP,* 1954). Bowers also presented in *MP* (1953) a diplomatic reprint of "The Manuscript of Whitman's 'Passage to India' " from the Houghton Library autograph. Holloway has printed two additional notebooks. The first of these appears in his "A Whitman Manuscript" *(AM,* 1924). The second will be found in "Walt Whitman's Visit to the Shakers" (*Colophon,* 1933). Subsequent to the appearance of this article C. I. Glicksberg discovered that this notebook was used by Whitman as the source for a piece in *Harper's* (1857) entitled "The Shakers." See Glicksberg, "A Whitman Discovery" (*Colophon,* new series, 1935). An interesting and unknown travel piece which Whitman wrote for the Philadelphia *Times* in 1879 is reprinted in Herbert Bergman's "Walt Whitman on New Jersey" (*Proc. New Jersey Hist. Soc.,* 1948). Letters which Whitman contributed to the *National Era,* under the pseudonym of Paumanok, were uncovered by R. G. Silver—"Whitman in 1850: Three Uncollected Articles" (*AL,* 1948).

Surprisingly enough few detailed studies of the Whitman text have been made aside from those which fall more properly into the category of criticism. W. L. Finkel, in two important articles, has shown that extensive notes printed in *Complete Writings* as largely Whitman's own work are actually extracts from other writers: "Walt Whitman's Manuscript Notes on Oratory" (*AL,* 1950); and "Sources of Walt Whitman's Manuscript Notes on Physique" (*AL,* 1950). The manner in which Whitman pilfered ideas and phrases from his 1855 Preface for use in his poetry is described by W. T. Weathers, "Whitman's Poetic Translations of his 1855 Preface" (*AL,* 1947). Fredson Bowers' *Whitman's Manuscripts, Leaves of Grass (1860), a Parallel Text,* was published in 1955.

2. *Letters*

There is no complete edition of Whitman's letters. Works which contain a fair number of letters are *Complete Writings,* Vol. VIII; the four volumes of Horace Traubel's *With Walt Whitman in Camden* (1906, 1908, 1914, 1953); C. I. Glicksberg's *Walt Whitman and the Civil War* (1933); and *Faint Clews & Indirections.* There is an excellent selection of letters in Emory Holloway's *Walt Whitman, Complete Poetry and Selected Prose and Letters* (1938). Many of these letters were here printed for the first time.

In 1898 R. M. Bucke published in Boston *The Wound Dresser,* which consists in large part of Whitman's letters to his mother during the Civil War. A convenient reprint of this work was edited by Oscar Cargill in 1949. T. B. Harned, another of Whitman's literary executors, brought together in 1918 *The Letters of Anne Gilchrist and Walt Whitman.* (See also Grace Gilchrist, "Chats with Walt Whitman," *Temple Bar Mag.,* 1898.) In 1936 A. F. Goldsmith issued *Letters Written by Walt Whitman to His Mother, 1866-1872,* with an introductory note by

R. G. Silver. These letters appeared originally in a very limited edition prepared by Harned in 1902. They are also in Volume VIII of *Complete Writings.*

Batches of new Whitman letters turn up frequently in the journals. Only the more important of these will be mentioned here. A half dozen letters to Whitman's brother, Jefferson, written in the 1860's, were printed by Emory Holloway in "Some New Whitman Letters" (*AM,* 1929). R. G. Silver has uncovered several miscellaneous letters scattered in various libraries. These he published in two articles in *AL:* "Seven Letters of Walt Whitman" (1935) and "Thirty-one Letters of Walt Whitman" (1937). In 1937 (*Colophon,* new series) he presented a group of Whitman letters ("For the Bright Particular Star") written to members of the family of Robert Pearsall Smith of Philadelphia. Most of them are addressed to Smith's daughter Mary who, as an emancipated college woman, had insisted on meeting the poet. O. S. Coad printed "Seven Whitman Letters" in the *Jour. of the Rutgers Univ. Library* (1944). The recipient was W. S. Kennedy. In 1948 Horst Frenz collected in *AL* "Walt Whitman's Letters to Karl Knortz," and followed this group of letters with *Whitman and Rolleston, A Correspondence* (Ind. Univ. Publications, 1951). (T. W. Rolleston and Knortz translated *Leaves of Grass* [*Grashalme*] into German in 1889.) "Walt Whitman's Letters to a Danish Friend" (Rudolph Schmidt) were edited by Carl Roos in *Orbis Litterarum* (Copenhagen, 1949). Fourteen letters to various persons were collected by Walter Harding in "A Sheaf of Whitman Letters" (*Studies in Bibliography,* Bibliographical Soc. of the Univ. of Virginia, 1952).

3. *Editions: Selected and Annotated*

It is a truism, often uncritically repeated, that Whitman's poetry has never had a wide audience. Yet from 1886, when *Poems of Walt Whitman* was issued in England in the Canterbury Poets Series, down to 1955 when *The Whitman Reader,* edited by Maxwell Geismar, appeared in Pocket Books, many excellent selections from Whitman's works have been printed for the use of students and the general reader. Only a small number of these volumes can be noted here. Floyd Stovall's *Walt Whitman, Representative Selections* (New York, 1934; rev. ed., 1939), like the other volumes in the AWS, contains an Introduction, Selected Bibliography, and notes. The Introduction stresses Whitman's gospel of freedom. Louise Pound's *Walt Whitman, Specimen Days, Democratic Vistas, and other Prose* (1935) is the best selected edition of the prose writings. The Walt Whitman volume in the Viking Portable Library (1945), edited by Mark Van Doren, offers selections from *Leaves of Grass* and *Specimen Days* and prints the whole of *Democratic Vistas.* Malcolm Cowley's *The Complete Poetry and Prose of Walt Whitman* (1948; reprinted in a cheaper edition, 1954) contains a provocative introduction which first appeared in four issues of the *New Republic* (1946-47). A special feature of The Inner Sanctum Edition of *The Poetry and Prose of Walt Whitman,* edited by Louis Untermeyer (1949), is its long section of critical commentaries about Whitman. In 1949 Sculley Bradley prepared *Walt Whitman, Leaves of Grass and Selected Prose* for the low-priced Rinehart Editions. Another well-edited selection is H. W. Blodgett, *The Best of Whitman* (1953). *Walt Whitman's Poems,* edited by G. W. Allen and C. T. Davis (1955), is strangely enough the first volume of selections which provides ample introductions and critical notes to each of the poems chosen. There is also a long introduction on the nature of Whitman's poetry.

IV. Biography

Whitman is a most difficult subject for the biographer. In spite of the efforts of recent Whitman scholars, notably Emory Holloway, H. S. Canby, Roger Asselineau, and G. W. Allen, to tell the whole story of his life accurately and with the proper proportioning, there are still blank periods for which details will probably never be forthcoming. Not many of the companions of Whitman's early years, from minor newspaper editors to

Broadway omnibus drivers, bothered to set down their recollections of him. On the other hand, the Whitman idolaters of his Camden days took down nearly every word of the poet's table talk, as he sat in the front room of the little Mickle Street house poking among his accumulated memorabilia, on the hunt for the item he needed to support his statements. But much of what they so piously recorded the scholars have had to sift with care. Whitman knew that his interlocutors were eagerly preparing themselves to be his spokesmen to posterity and he intended that his version of his struggles for acceptance as the poet of democracy should be the one the world would believe after his death. Though he seemed to tell all, there was in fact much that he kept back. About his sexual life he was particularly reticent though here, as well, he told the members of the Whitman cult tall tales which some of them were shrewd enough to disbelieve.

At length, after more than a half century of patient searching in the manuscripts, a diligent hunting for unrecorded Whitman articles in the many papers and journals for which he worked, the checking of statement against statement, and—possibly most important—the study of Whitman's complex personality, something like the true story of his life, in outline and, for many periods, in detail, can be arrived at.

First to be described in this section will be two recent and very elaborately documented biographies: Roger Asselineau's *L'Evolution de Walt Whitman après la première édition des Feuilles d'Herbe* (Paris, 1954) and G. W. Allen's *The Solitary Singer, a Critical Biography of Walt Whitman* (1955). Then will follow a chronological account of the earlier Whitman biographies, a story which, because of its surprising turns and shifts in emphasis and the personalities of the biographers, is not without its drama.

Asselineau's work runs to 567 pages. Following the pattern of the French *thèse* in treating first the man and then his work, it is actually two books in one. Though the author asserts that it was not his aim to write a new biography of Whitman, his "Introduction biographique: La création d'une personnalité" (pp. 19-284) cannot be called anything else. True, Asselineau ostensibly begins where Catel (see below, pp. 292) left off, after the birth of the 1855 *Leaves of Grass,* and he is primarily intent on showing how the successive editions of the *Leaves* can be related to the episodes and crises of Whitman's life. Yet this "Biographical Introduction" makes full use of the accumulated knowledge about Whitman.

Asselineau's thesis is, in brief, as follows. Of Whitman's many struggles the most difficult was against his strong homosexual desires. Without doubt it was his art which saved him by permitting him to express (literally) the troubled passions which haunted him. His poetry was for him a means of purification. Yet it is not the song of a demigod but the sorrowful pouring forth of a sick soul which seeks passionately to understand itself and recover its self-possession.

Allen's *The Solitary Singer* is certain to stand for a long time as the most detailed biography. In its 616 pages he essayed to "trace consecutively the physical life of the man, the growth of his mind, and the development of his art out of his physical and mental experience." The extraordinary mass of detail which Allen assembled and organized overbalances his account of the development of Whitman's art, but the amount of new material he uncovered compensates for this deficiency. More disappointing is his hesitancy to commit himself in discussing the important issues in Whitman's life. Allen's labors were lightened by his having received the notebooks, transcriptions of manuscripts, and bibliography assembled over a twenty-year period by C. J. Furness.

The first account of Whitman, a forty-six-page pamphlet by the fiery W. D. O'Connor, *The Good Gray Poet: A Vindication* (1866; reprinted in R. M. Bucke's *Walt Whitman,* 1883) is, as the title shows, a defense rather than a biography. The occasion of its writing was Whitman's dismissal, on 30 June 1865, from his clerkship in the Department of the Interior. O'Connor attacks Secretary Harlan, who had found indecencies in the sex poems in the 1860 edition of *Leaves of Grass,* and announces, in refutation, that there are only eighty of Whitman's lines (out of 9,000) "which the most malignant virtue could shrink from." The pamphlet is interesting biographically because it contains the earliest versions of some of the episodes of the Whitman legend and gives a firsthand description of the poet as he looked at that time. That Whitman wrote a part or parts of O'Connor's pamphlet is asserted by Nathan Resnick, *Walt Whitman and the Authorship of The Good Gray Poet* (Brooklyn, 1948). This view is controverted in an article by W. G. Milne, "William Douglas O'Connor and the Authorship of *The Good Gray Poet*" (*AL,* 1953).

With John Burroughs' *Notes on Walt Whitman as Poet and Person* (1867) begins Whitman's lifelong effort to present his autobiography through the words of others. He wrote parts of young Burroughs' book and used his editorial pencil on the rest. (Convincing evidence of this is presented by F. P. Hier, Jr., "The End of a Literary Mystery," *AM,* 1924.) The enlarged edition of 1871 contains "Supplementary Notes," most interesting of which are extracts from letters and newspaper accounts used by Burroughs to account for the genesis and characteristics of *Leaves of Grass.*

In 1883 Dr. R. M. Bucke, a Canadian alienist who met Whitman in 1877, wrote the first comprehensive biography—*Walt Whitman.* Here again the poet supplied much of the biographical material. (It is known for certain that he wrote the section on his ancestors and his early years.) Much of this material is inaccurate, for instance the account of Whitman's New Orleans sojourn, or is slanted in the direction of the legend of himself which the poet was shrewdly creating. Dr. Bucke's most substantial contribution was the group of reminiscences which he gathered from Whitman's New York and Brooklyn friends. Whitman was so well pleased with Bucke's biography that he hoped no other study of his life would ever supplant it. In 1888 he asked Bucke to "let it stand just as it is."

In the years between the publication of *Leaves of Grass* and the poet's death in 1892 a group of English writers of some stature had built for him a considerable reputation in England. Among them were W. M. Rossetti, unofficial archivist of the Pre-Raphaelites, Edward Dowden, the Shakespeare scholar, Swinburne (who soon deserted Whitman as he deserted most of his demigods), Mrs. Anne Gilchrist, widow of the biographer of Blake, and J. A. Symonds, student of Greek and Renaissance culture. The work which this group did in editing and commenting on Whitman's poetry culminated in Symonds' important *Walt Whitman: A Study* (1893). The biographical portion of this work is derivative but Symonds was the first critic to raise three important questions to which biographers thereafter would have to give attention. In the first place he deprecated the tone of eulogy which prevailed in the Whitman circle in America and called for an objective evaluation of the poet—which he in some measure achieved in his study. Symonds also tackled the important question raised by Whitman's verse: was Whitman the true bard of democracy? And he was the first biographer to look deeply into the import of the poems about sex. To satisfy himself on the question of Whitman's sex life he wrote the poet a frank letter of inquiry to which he received the now famous reply: "Though unmarried I have had six children—two are dead—one living Southern grandchild, fine boy, writes to me occasionally—circumstances (connected with their fortune and benefit) have separated me from intimate relations."

Symonds did not use this letter in his book but his apprehensions were stilled by it. He concludes "that what he calls the 'adhesiveness' of comradeship is meant to have no inblending with the amativeness of sexual love." Symonds did go so far as to note, however, that Whitman appeared to be not wholly unconscious that there were dangers and difficulties involved in the highly pitched emotions he praises in such poems as "Whoever You Are" and "Trickle Drops." From this opinion rose the specter which has haunted all later biographers of Whitman.

The death of Whitman inspired his literary executors, Horace

Traubel, Dr. Bucke, and T. B. Harned to prepare a memorial volume, *In Re Walt Whitman* (1893), which they intended should be regarded "in the light of the 'Annex' foreseen by Walt Whitman" to Dr. Bucke's biography. This collection of twenty-nine items, besides "Poems and Minor Pieces," is a strange potpourri: tributes by such devoted admirers as J. A. Symonds, Dr. Bucke, John Burroughs, W. D. O'Connor, W. S. Kennedy, R. G. Ingersoll, and T. B. Harned; translations from articles about Whitman originally published in Germany, France, and Denmark; a gruesome account of the autopsy as reported by Dr. Daniel Longaker. A hodge-podge though the book is, the student will find in it many useful items. Most important, perhaps, is Traubel's "Notes from Conversations with George W. Whitman." Useful also are the accounts of Whitman's funeral, and of the last Whitman birthday dinner, held in 1891. A stenographer was present and not a word was missed. It was on this occasion that Whitman, replying to the question why he had never married, said: Bucke and Traubel "are the nearest to the explicators" but "the whole thing, my friend, like the Nibelungen, or somebody's cat, has an immensely long, long, long tail to it."

In 1896 two friends of Whitman published intimate accounts of their contacts with him: W. S. Kennedy, *Reminiscences of Walt Whitman*, and Thomas Donaldson, *Walt Whitman, the Man*. Though Kennedy admired Whitman, he wrote more objectively of him than the other members of the Camden circle. Chiefly valuable are records of conversations with Whitman and with friends who had known the poet early and late. Donaldson's book adds much new information, particularly about the means by which Whitman supported himself and was in part supported by his friends in his last years. In this same year John Burroughs, who first met the poet in 1863, published *Whitman, A Study*. As the title indicates, it is more a work of criticism than of biography. (The biographical section occupies less than a third of the book.) The full story of the friendship of these two men was not told until 1931 when Clara Barrus published *Whitman and Burroughs, Comrades*. The author was careful in her documentation and having received assistance from Whitman scholars, notably C. J. Furness, she was able to tell her story accurately.

In 1905 the first scholarly biography was published, H. B. Binns's *Life of Walt Whitman*. Binns was an Englishman, but he came to American in order to acquaint himself thoroughly with the places where Whitman had lived. He cleared up many of the vague and contradictory statements made by early biographers, and tried to date precisely the episodes of Whitman's life. Most important of all, he wrote a connected, well-proportioned account which filled out the poet's early years and brought into focus the Camden days, which the "hot little prophets" (as Bliss Perry called the idolaters) had overstressed. Binns's chief error was his fanciful story of the "lady of the South" who "became the mother of [Whitman's] child, perhaps, in after years, of his children." This invention (for it was sheer invention) was an attempt to reconcile the "evidence" about Whitman's early sex life with the tenor of the poems. Binns also took an unsophisticated view of Whitman's affection for young men. Despite some errors and reticences of this kind Binns's biography is still a reliable work. One of its most useful features is the abundance of illustrations which it contains—thirty-three in all.

Bliss Perry's *Walt Whitman, His Life and Work,* which appeared the next year (1906; rev., 1908), is a less ambitious work than Binns's but it likewise, and more consistently, seeks for the real facts. Where he lacked information Perry frankly says so. The book contains many hitherto unpublished letters and investigates certain episodes which had previously been incompletely discussed, such as the story of Whitman's reading of the Commencement Poem at Dartmouth College in 1872. Some of the value of this biography derives from materials put at Perry's disposal by John Burroughs who had given up his plan of writing a complete life of Whitman. Perry's work was greeted by the reviewers as "calm" and "discriminating."

In the main, Edward Carpenter's *Days with Walt Whitman, with Some Notes on his Life and Work* (1906) belongs with the work of the Whitman idolaters. As a Cambridge undergraduate Carpenter had read the poet in the late sixties. He visited Whitman twice and was so much stirred by his message that he imitated Whitman's style in the poetical sections of *Towards Democracy.* But Carpenter saw more deeply into Whitman's nature than the other idolaters could or wished to do. After reviewing the information available about Whitman's sex life ("Walt Whitman's Children") he concludes—with considerable boldness for the year 1906—"It is clear that throughout his life his intimacies with men were very close and ardent; and it seems possible that these, in the later period, to some extent supplied the deficiency on the other side." Carpenter saw that there were contradictions in Whitman's life and work, contradictions which may have produced "a great tragic element in his nature." Carpenter's Whitman is believable because he is complex.

In 1906 there also appeared the first installment of Horace Traubel's *With Walt Whitman in Camden,* which, as the work now stands in four volumes, constitutes one of the most curious episodes in the history of biographical writing. During the years 1888-89, Traubel, one of the first of Whitman's Camden friends, visited him almost daily. He listened reverently to Whitman's rambling recollections, took notes unobtrusively, and received with gratitude the letters and other items which Whitman dug out of the seemingly inexhaustible pile on the floor. Whitman knew well enough that Traubel was planning to be his Boswell for he charged him to "speak for me when I am dead." Few promises have been so voluminously kept. The first volume of the series is 473 pages long; each of the other three runs to over 500 pages. The second volume appeared in 1908, the third in 1914. At this point publishers seem to have grown weary of Traubel's endless manuscript. The fourth volume was not published until 1953 when Sculley Bradley edited it for the University of Pennsylvania Press. When the rest of Traubel's manuscript is published, his long story will end with the death of Whitman.

This vast and unorganized work has great value for the student of Whitman. In it scores of significant letters were published for the first time—such as Symonds' letter seeking information about Whitman's "adhesiveness" (manly attachment)—and many others which indicate the extent and nature of Whitman's influence on the younger generation of writers who had turned to him for confirmation of their aims. Whitman's garrulous table talk is of much less value, though now and then a pungent judgment on one of his critics or a verifiable fact from his past relieves the tedium.

The first full-length biography of Whitman in French was Léon Bazalgette's *Walt Whitman: L'Homme et son œuvre* (Paris, 1908), a bowdlerized translation of which was published in New York in 1920. This enthusiastic study is a throwback to the worshipful manner of Bucke. Bazalgette is certain that Whitman in New Orleans, "dans le plein épanouissement de sa beauté virile," fell in love with a woman of high birth who was probably French. (It was from her, it seems, that he learned the French words with which he "enamelled" his poems.) Bazalgette concludes his discussion of the Peter Doyle friendship with a surprising analogy which was intended to silence the questioners: "Peut-être celui qui définirait la nature exacte de l'affection qui unissait l'apôtre de Galilée à son disciple Jean pourrait-il éclaircir le mystère d'amour qui se cache dans les tendres camaraderies du Bon Poète aux cheveux gris." The best that can be said for Bazalgette's 513-page work is that it is the most impassioned of the Whitman biographies.

When the Macmillan Company of New York was bringing out its "American Extension" of the English Men of Letters Series it included, in 1909, a biography of Whitman prepared by Professor G. R. Carpenter of Columbia. Walt was at last in respectable company, the other four Americans who were so honored being Emerson, Whittier, Prescott, and Bryant. Carpenter's neatly organized biography adds no new facts but the chapter "Workman and Poet (1850-1860)"—nearly one third of the book—explores, with some success, the impulses which brought the *Leaves of Grass* to birth. Seventeen years later (1926) Whitman's biography appeared in the same series, as issued by the London house of Macmillan. This time the other American representatives were Melville and Poe. John Bailey was the biographer. The title of his last chapter, "The Ultimate Remainder," indicates the tone of the book. The idolaters having departed, Bailey wished to sum up the case for Whitman.

Thirteen years of research went into the production of Emory Holloway's *Whitman, An Interpretation in Narrative* (1926). When it appeared it was by all odds the most scholarly life of Whitman, and though Asselineau's and Allen's biographies have corrected it at various points, it is still a valuable work. Holloway had edited in 1921 (see above, pp. 276) the indispensable two-volume *Uncollected Poetry and Prose of Walt Whitman* on which he drew extensively in his biography. Holloway is something less than candid in discussing Whitman's sex life. Though he had discovered that the poem "Once I Pass'd Through a Populous City" (the city is usually taken to be New Orleans) was, in one draft, addressed not to a woman but a man ("Walt Whitman's Love Affairs," *Dial,* 1920), he clung in his biography to the New Orleans love affair promoted by Binns. Holloway even does some improvising of his own: "Even were there no direct evidence, it is more probable, as it is more charitable to suppose" that the woman in the case was no common prostitute but a "Creole octoroon" who was as faithful to Whitman as "Anne of Oxford Street was faithful to De Quincey and Claire to Stevenson." It was unfortunate that Holloway's biography appeared at a time when footnotes were unfashionable. There are none in his biography. However, Holloway's scholarship is generally sound and his citations can be trusted.

For several years Holloway's biography satisfied the demand for a complete story of the poet's life. The next attempt at a work of this large scope would be Canby's biography, published in 1943. Meanwhile there appeared studies of particular periods of Whitman's life and biographies which were primarily concerned with presenting a thesis to explain the poet's complex nature and its relation to his poetry.

Jean Catel's *Walt Whitman: La naissance du poète* (Paris, 1929) attempted to account for the sudden efflorescence of *Leaves of Grass* in 1855. The problem of the "naissance" of the poem, a work so different from anything the young editor and writer of prose sketches had revealed to the world, had, of course, puzzled earlier commentators. But Catel was determined to pluck out the heart of the mystery with the help of Freud. His boldly stated conclusions have had a very considerable influence. He threw out the legend of the healthy, hearty, virile young man and rejected the various New Orleans romances invented by his predecessors. To Catel there is no doubt that Whitman was autoerotic and continued to be so "jusqu'à un âge avancé." He sees the young Whitman's Bohemianism as an evasion of orderly life. But his early work shows that this attempt to escape did not bring him happiness and security. The tone is not that of a young man who is beginning the conquest of life with assurance. To console himself for his failure to make firm contact with the real world he retreated into his imagination. "Là, ses désirs réprimés lui font un monde sympathique et doux. Là il s'attarde; là sont les images pour le consoler." In sum, the extraordinary 1855 volume was born "tandis que Whitman se séparait des hommes et du réel, d'une extase sensuelle portée au paroxysme. . . . Le miracle vint lorsque de ce qu'il regardait comme un mal s'épanouirent les calices emplis de poésie."

The Danish scholar, Frederik Schyberg, published his *Walt Whitman* in Copenhagen in 1933. This was translated into English by Evie Allison Allen in 1951, with an introduction by G. W. Allen. In almost every respect Schyberg's book is an extraordinary performance. His knowledge of the cultural background of Whitman's earlier years was slight but he made excellent use of the abundant information about Whitman's personal life which was available by 1930. He penetrates deeper into Whitman's psyche than the more doctrinaire Freudian approach of Catel permitted him to do, but he accepts the fundamentals of Catel's thesis of the moody, unsatisfied youth who escaped into his joyful vision of democratic man and society. Schyberg's greatest contribution is his careful analysis of the successive volumes which finally made up the completed *Leaves of Grass*. He defines perceptively the qualities of each of the editions and the moods which formed the poems in each. He follows Whitman's revisions and rearrangements of the poems, suggesting what impulses prompted them. The biography contains a chapter on "Whitman in World Literature" which was revised and expanded for the translation. This excellent essay in comparative literary history, by placing Whitman among the writers of his century, does much to dissipate the image of him as a unique phenomenon.

Among studies which are concerned with a single aspect or period of Whitman's life, Esther Shephard's *Walt Whitman's Pose* (1938) has some slight merit. The book's thesis is that the only true way to explain the change in Whitman which produced *Leaves of Grass* is to find the "pose" he adopted while creating his early poems. "The source of *Leaves of Grass* is, in spite of all of Walt Whitman's protestations to the contrary, in the fragment of a book, the epilogue of a French novel. The novel is *The Countess of Rudolstadt,* by George Sand, which Whitman read in a translation by Francis G. Shaw." Whitman certainly knew this novel and never concealed his interest in George Sand. One critic called Mrs. Shephard's repetitious study a "wrong" book, devoted "not to finding out something *about* Whitman, but to trying to get something *on* him."

In the leftist 1930's it was inevitable that someone should feel impelled to interpret Whitman's life in the light of his social thinking. Such a work appeared in Newton Arvin's *Whitman* (1938). Though Arvin occasionally overstrains his facts in his effort to align Whitman, where he thinks he can do so, with the socialist thought of his day, his conclusions are not far from the truth. "Whitman's political outlook was distorted in at least one way by his emotional organization: it certainly did lead him to hope for too much from the cohesive force of spontaneous affection, and to make much too light—in a carefree, transcendental way—of the 'institutions' which he said he was neither for nor against. It encouraged him, along with his idealism, to feel that he could afford to be ignorant of the practical details of any political program."

More thesis-ridden than Arvin's book is H. I. Fausset's *Walt Whitman: Poet of Democracy* (1942). Fausset's main contention is that the masculine and feminine elements in Whitman were "so ill-adjusted that to reconcile them creatively, whether as prophet or poet, was to prove very difficult." The groundtone of his biography is depreciatory and Fausset frequently contradicts himself because he is seldom content to let any words of praise stand without qualifying them into a shadowy negative.

On its appearance one reviewer called Haniel Long's *Walt Whitman and the Springs of Courage* (Sante Fe, 1938) "an essay in personal biography and public evangelism." Another biographical study with a thesis—that Whitman "dared (and cared) to be Walt Whitman"—Long's book is actually a series of eleven disconnected essays.

After these partial studies of Whitman's life it is a pleasure to come to H. S. Canby's *Walt Whitman, an American* (1943) which still stands as the best biography for the general reader. This is not to suggest that the book is superficial. Canby's training as a biographer, his knowledge of Whitman's America, and his sympathetic understanding of Whitman as man and artist are happily in conjunction here. In his Preface Canby states that "a satisfactory biography of Whitman must be essentially a biography of an inner life and of the mysterious creative processes of poetry." He kept steadily to his purpose of writing such a biography and succeeded. There is enough detail to introduce the reader to Whitman's daily life but the poet is never forgotten for long.

Two popularized biographies of Whitman were widely read at the time of their publication: Edgar Lee Masters, *Whitman* (1937), and Frances Winwar, *American Giant: Walt Whitman and His Times* (1941). The inaccuracies in the second of these were pointed out in a valuable review by C. J. Furness (*AL*, 1942). A recent biography which the author intended should rescue Whitman from the cultists and the wrong-headed critics is A. E. Briggs's *Walt Whitman, Thinker and Artist* (1952). It is too subjective and cantankerous to be of much value. Halfway between biography and fiction, and not succeeding as either or both, is Cameron Rogers' *The Magnificent Idler* (1926). Admiration for Whitman has prompted the writing of three novels based on his life: Grant Overton, *The Answerer* (1921); Elizabeth Corbett, *Walt, The Good Gray Poet Speaks for Himself* (1928); and John Erskine, *The Start of the Road* (1938).

V. Biographical Materials

1. *Books and Pamphlets*

Several visitors to Whitman printed recollections of their talks with him. One of the earliest of these is Sadakichi Hartmann's *Conversations with Walt Whitman* (1895). In 1898 an English physician, Dr. John Johnson, printed his *Diary Notes of a Visit to Walt Whitman and Some of his Friends in 1890*. This work was reissued in 1917, with the added recollections of another English visitor, J. W. Wallace: *Visits to Walt Whitman in 1890-1891 By Two Lancashire Friends.* There is valuable information about Emerson's influence on Whitman, obtained from the poet himself, in J. T. Trowbridge's *My Own Story, With Recollections of Noted Persons* (1903). Further material about Whitman's last years will be found in H. S. Morris, *Walt Whitman, A Brief Biography with Reminiscences* (1929). Beginning in 1882 Whitman was a frequent visitor in the house of Robert Pearsall Smith, a wealthy Philadelphian. A delightful account of the impression the poet made on the college-student son of the house forms a chapter in Logan Pearsall Smith's autobiography, *Unforgotten Years* (1939).

Some of Whitman's friendships have been the subject of special study. Elizabeth P. Gould's *Anne Gilchrist and Walt Whitman* (1900) is too slight and too reticent to be of much use. W. E. Walling's *Whitman and Traubel* (1916) makes a feeble attempt to show the similarities in the thought of the two men; it says almost nothing about their friendship. There is little new information in Edward Carpenter's *Some Friends of Walt Whitman; A Study in Sex-Psychology* (British Soc. for the Study of Sex Psychology, Pub. No. 13, 1924). This pamphlet is of interest, however, because it was written late in Carpenter's life and expresses his final view of Whitman's sexual deviation.

There are a few studies of particular episodes and periods in Whitman's life. In 1921 Elizabeth L. Keller, the professional nurse who tended Whitman in his last illness, published *Walt Whitman in Mickle Street*. The main purpose of her book was to praise the devotion and self-sacrifice of Mrs. Mary Oakes Davis who kept house for Whitman in Camden. Whitman's schooling and his interest as an editor in the problems of education are treated in Florence B. Freedman's *Walt Whitman Looks at the Schools* (1950). The writer prints for the first time editorials on school affairs which Whitman wrote for the Brooklyn *Evening Star* in 1845 and 1846. The part Lincoln played in Whitman's life is inadequately and verbosely discussed in W. E. Barton's *Abraham Lincoln and Walt Whitman* (1928), though the information about Whitman's famous Lincoln lecture is useful. Katherine Molinoff has published three informative monographs on obscure passages in Whitman's life: *An Unpublished Whitman Manuscript: The Record Book of the Smithtown Debating Society, 1837-1838* (1941); *Some Notes on Whitman's Family* (1941); and *Whitman's Teaching at Smithtown, 1837-38* (1942).

2. *Articles*

The substance of most of the significant articles concerned with particular aspects or episodes of Whitman's life has been absorbed into the full-scale biographies of Asselineau and Allen. Therefore only those articles will be mentioned here which are of special importance or are so detailed that these biographers could not make full use of them.

In her "Personal Recollections of Walt Whitman" (*Atlantic,* 1907) Ellen (O'Connor) Calder, wife of Whitman's friend and champion, provided important firsthand information about the poet's Washington days. Among the many accounts of Whitman's last years W. R. Thayer's "Personal Recollections of Walt Whitman" (*Scribner's,* 1919) is of special interest because Thayer, a genteel Bostonian, questioned Whitman closely and argued with him. Brief but shrewd observations about Whitman and his disciples will be found in William White's "Walt Whitman and Sir William Osler" (*AL,* 1939). (Osler was one of the physicians who attended Whitman in the 1880's.)

Whitman wrote for Bryant's *Evening Post* in the fifties and possibly into the Civil War period. What is known of their friendship is told by C. I. Glicksberg in "Whitman and Bryant" (*Fantasy,* 1935). The complicated relationships between Emerson and Whitman—the question of how often they met, the changing attitudes of each toward the other, the extent and nature of Emerson's influence, indirect or direct, on Whitman—are explored in three excellent articles: J. B. Moore, "The Master of Whitman" (*SP,* 1926); Clarence Gohdes, "Whitman and Emerson" (*SR,* 1929); and Carlos Baker, "The Road to Concord: Another Milestone in the Whitman-Emerson Friendship" (*PULC,* 1946). J. T. Trowbridge's efforts to enhance Whitman's artistic reputation in New England and the personal relationships between the two men are fully treated in three articles by R. A. Coleman: "Trowbridge and Whitman" (*PMLA,* 1948); "Further Reminiscences of Walt Whitman" (*MLN,* 1948); and "Trowbridge and O'Connor: Unpublished Correspondence, with Special Reference to Walt Whitman" (*AL,* 1951).

Emory Holloway's "More Light on Whitman" (*AM,* 1924) discusses Whitman's editorial experiences when he was with the Brooklyn *Evening Star* in 1845-46. (There is only a brief mention of this episode in Holloway's *Whitman,* 1926.) Portia Baker's "Walt Whitman and *The Atlantic Monthly*" (*AL,* 1934) examines Whitman's relationships with the members of the *Atlantic* circle and the reasons for the minimal attention which the magazine gave him, both in publishing his work and reviewing his books. There is a companion article by the same author in *AL* (1935): "Walt Whitman's Relations with Some New York Magazines." In his "Walt Whitman, the *Galaxy,* and *Democratic Vistas*" (*AL,* 1951), E. F. Grier brought to light new information about Whitman's connections with an important New York monthly. The article prints for the first time the correspondence between Whitman and the Church brothers, proprietors of the *Galaxy*, and follows the genesis and development of *Democratic Vistas* through articles which appeared in their magazine.

Among the articles which have helped to clarify particular episodes in Whitman's life, five deserve mention here. In 1856 or 1857 Whitman contracted a small debt to James Parton, the biographer, which the detractors of the poet, during his life and after his death, asserted he never paid. New information about this affair, which partially clears his name, is supplied by O. S. Coad's "Whitman *vs* Parton" (*Jour. of the Rutgers Univ. Library,* 1940). Using manuscripts in the Library of Congress, C. I. Glicksberg cleared up a hitherto obscure period in Whitman's life in his "Walt Whitman in 1862" (*AL,* 1934). In this same year Whitman received a letter from an "Ellen Eyre" which possibly implies that they had had sexual relations. Allen *(The Solitary Singer)* can make little of this episode but Emory Holloway in "Whitman Pursued" (*AL,* 1955) suggests that the name conceals the identity of Ada Clare, an actress, or of Mrs. Juliette H. Beach, of Albion, New York, one of Whitman's many female pursuers. Between 1865 and 1873 Whitman held several Federal clerkships; information about these was assembled in an important article by Dixon Wecter, "Walt Whitman as Civil Servant" (*PMLA,* 1943). In the summer of 1876 Whitman began to stay for long periods at the Stafford farm on

Timber Creek, near Kirkwood, New Jersey. Bathing in the stream and in the mud and basking in the sun relieved his paralytic condition and refreshed him generally. These visits are described in Sculley Bradley's "Walt Whitman on Timber Creek" (*AL,* 1933).

Four articles of a more general biographical interest remain to be mentioned. That untiring literary detective Emory Holloway gathered together some of the evidence of the poet's anonymous self-puffery in "Whitman as his own Press-Agent" (*AM,* 1929). Edward Hungerford's "Walt Whitman and his Chart of Bumps" (*AL,* 1931) demonstrates the extraordinary consequences in Whitman's life and art which derived from that important day in July 1849 when he had his bumps read by Lorenzo Fowler and received from him the flattering "Phrenological Notes on W. Whitman." Whitman was so proud of his large, but not too large "organs" that he had the "Notes" bound into copies of the 1855 *Leaves of Grass.* (For a refutation of some of the ingenious conclusions worked out by Hungerford, see Frances Winwar, "Walt Whitman's 'Dark Lady'," *University Review,* 1943.) Whitman's fondness for the theater as a young man, his preferences among actors, and his obiter dicta about actors and their styles have been studied by Floyd Stovall, "Walt Whitman and the Dramatic Stage in New York" (*SP,* 1953). Gustav Bychowski's "Walt Whitman—A Study in Sublimation" (*Psychoanalysis and the Social Sciences,* 1951) is a reputable examination of Whitman's sex life. Like most psychoanalytical interpretations of the life of a writer, however, it uses the poet's verses as if they were being spoken from the analyst's couch.

In concluding this section, attention should be called to Harvey O'Higgins' "Alias Walt Whitman" (*Harper's,* 1929; reprinted in book form by the Carteret Book Club, 1930). This attack on Whitman as a mediocre journalist, a borrower of the styles of other authors, a writer of anonymous blurbs of his own work, a narcissist who posed as a "fine brute" of a man is important only because it is typical of the way in which many who have disliked Walt Whitman the man have written about his life. An effective answer to O'Higgins and all the detractors was made by F. I. Carpenter in his "Walt Whitman's 'Eidolon' " (*CE,* 1942) which demonstrates why Whitman's "pose" (it would be more accurate to call it a "mask" or "persona") was necessary to him as a person and as a poet.

VI. Criticism

The mass of writing about Whitman which may be termed critical (some of it only very loosely) is enormous. The reasons why this great cairn has been piled up are not in the least obscure. Whitman has always attracted antagonists eager to show that he is a shallow thinker and a second-rate poet. But his defenders and explicators have been more numerous than his detractors. Year by year they have added stones to the cairn of criticism and commentary—Whitman as Hegelian, Whitman as Transcendentalist, Whitman as the Prophet of Personalism or Democracy or World Government, Whitman as the Most Genuinely American of Our Poets, Whitman as the Christ of Our Age. Because Whitman lived to be seventy-three, wrote much editorial prose in his youth, much poetry in his middle years, and talked unceasingly to his disciples in his Camden days, the scholiast (with *Leaves of Grass* and *With Walt Whitman in Camden* before him) could turn out an almost endless series of papers cut to this general pattern: "Walt Whitman and ——." Fill the blank with "Prostitution" or "Brigham Young" or "Eugenics" or "John Dryden," and another article is conceived. Much of this sort of commentary is picayune, but much of it, also, has helped to give us a clearer idea of Whitman's mind and the relation of his thought to his poetry. The reader must therefore be warned that this section will be long in spite of the fact that a stout effort has been made to eliminate items which are trivial or by now out of date.

1. *General Studies: Books and Articles*

Several of the biographies described above are, of course, concerned with understanding and evaluating Whitman's poetry and prose. Chief among these are the studies by Perry (1906), G. R. Carpenter (1909), Catel (1929), Schyberg (1933, 1951), Arvin (1938), Fausset (1942), and Canby (1943). Deserving special mention here is Roger Asselineau's *L'Evolution de Walt Whitman* (1954). The long second part (La Création d'une Œuvre) of this monumental biography is divided into two sections: "L'Evolution des grands thèmes" and "Les progrès de son art." Nearly every conceivable aspect of Whitman's thought and style is covered systematically. Without doubt Asselineau's treatment of these subjects is the best we have.

The year 1955 saw the publication of three studies which are mainly evaluative in character. The symposium edited by Milton Hindus—*Leaves of Grass One Hundred Years After*—contains essays by W. C. Williams, Richard Chase, L. A. Fiedler, Kenneth Burke, David Daiches, and J. M. Murray. All these essays, with the exception of Chase's which is biographical, reassess Whitman's achievement from the vantage point of the centennial year of *Leaves of Grass*. Their general drift may be summed up in the words of one of the contributors: Whitman "is a poet whom we must begin now to rescue from parody as well as apotheosis." Three lectures delivered at the Library of Congress in the centennial year have been printed as *Walt Whitman, Man, Poet, Philosopher*. The lecturers who addressed themselves to these topics were, respectively, G. W. Allen, Mark Van Doren, and David Daiches. Richard Chase's *Walt Whitman Reconsidered* (1955) stresses Whitman's place among nineteenth-century writers, American and European. (Chase's theory of "Song of Myself" as "the profound and lovely comic drama of the self" is, to say the least, aberrant.)

Only a very few book-length critical studies stand out in the mass of earlier writing about Whitman. O. L. Triggs's *Browning and Whitman, A Study in Democracy* (1893) has the virtues of a period piece. It attempts to show how the contributions of science, philosophy, and ethical truth, informed by the spirit of romanticism, emerge in the poetry of both Browning and Whitman and make their work a part of "modern prophetical literature." John Burroughs' final words on his poet friend, *Whitman, A Study* (1896), is still of use because he read Whitman correctly as the emancipator of those who hoped for the triumph of democracy and science, the believers in realism and positivism, and those possessed of a "religious hunger that flees the churches." Basil De Selincourt's *Walt Whitman, A Critical Study* (1914) was the most ambitious work of its kind before the appearance of the recent appraisals mentioned above. (Incidentally, it is of interest that this is a volume in a series of "modern monographs" which included studies of Synge, Henry James, Ibsen, and Hardy.) Though many of De Selincourt's conclusions are vitiated by his romantic view of Whitman (he serenely accepts the New Orleans lady of "gentle birth" and the six illegitimate children), his comments on the constructive principles, unity, and style of the poetry were remarkable for their time.

Of the many general critical articles or chapters devoted to Whitman ten or so are significant. Important in its time because of its length and fairness, and the prestige of the writer was E. C. Stedman's section on Whitman in his *Poets of America* (1885). W. S. Kennedy's "Drift and Cumulus" (*Reminiscences of Walt Whitman* 1896) can be taken as an "official" pronouncement of the Camden disciples. George Santayana's "The Poetry of Barbarism" (in *Poetry and Religion,* 1900)—the "Barbarians" are Whitman and Browning—has probably evoked more defenses of Whitman than any essay by a detractor. Santayana's style drives his barbs deep: Whitman "has approached common life without bringing in his mind any higher standard by which to criticize it; he has seen it, not in contrast with an ideal, but as the expression of forces more indeterminate and elementary than itself; and the vulgar, in this cosmic setting, has appeared to him sublime." On the other hand, P. E. More's essay on Whitman (*Shelburne Essays,* 4th Ser., 1906) is more sympathetic than one might expect, especially so in its discussion of Whitman's experience of war and death. Surprisingly modern in its understanding of the complexities which a critic of Whitman faces is Stuart Sherman's essay in *Americans* (1922). (It contains, incidentally, an excellent refutation of Santayana.) Though the Whitman essay in D. H. Lawrence's *Studies in Classic American Literature* (1923) is not the equal of his essays on Cooper, Poe, and Melville, it contains some brilliant insights. As one would expect, Whitman was for V. L. Parrington "a great figure, the greatest assuredly in our literature" ("The Afterglow of the Enlightenment—Walt Whitman," in *The Beginnings of Critical Realism in America,* 1930). There is considerable pathos in this chapter since it was written when Parrington despaired of American democracy and could only hope that Whitman's message might still help to awaken his countrymen "in a time of huge infidelities, in the dun breakdown and disintegration of all faiths." Another sympathetic general study, written in his happiest impressionistic vein, is contained in four chapters of Van Wyck Brooks's *The Times of Melville and Whitman* (1947). H. S. Canby's Whitman chapter in *LHUS* is admirably concise and comprehensive. The best critical study of Whitman in English is the long fourth book of F. O. Matthiessen's *American Renaissance: Art and Expression in the Age of Emerson and Whitman* (1941). As the title of this section indicates—"Only a Language Experiment"—Matthiessen's primary aim is to get at the secret of Whitman's penetration and force as a poet, but the subsections entitled "Vision and Attitude" and "Whitman's Landscapes" explore other aspects of his art and thought.

2. *Fundamental Ideas: Religion, Philosophy, Science, Nature*

Attempts to define Whitman's religion have not been notably successful. He has been described variously as a mystic, a pantheist, a panpsychist, a possessor of "cosmic consciousness," a personalist (his own term). Whitman's friend Dr. R. M. Bucke, the Canadian psychiatrist, was so much impressed by the poet's particular kind of mystical insight—his capability of receiving "ineffable light—beyond all signs, descriptions, languages"—that he wrote a book about it, *Cosmic Consciousness, A Study in the Evolution of the Human Mind* (1901). Here Whitman appears in the company of Gautama the Buddha, Jesus, Paul, and less eminent possessors of this faculty. Charles Cestre examined the relations between Whitman's mysticism and his poetical powers in "Walt Whitman: Le mystique, le lyrique" (*RAA,* 1930). Whitman as monist and pantheist is discussed in Maynard Shipley's "Democracy as Religion" (*Open Court,* 1919). Whitman described his whole program, and, necessarily, the kind of faith required for its fulfillment, in an influential essay, "Personalism," which he wrote for the *Galaxy* in 1868. Bronson Alcott took up the concept of personalism and introduced it into American philosophy. (See G. W. Allen's *Walt Whitman Handbook* for an excellent brief discussion of this movement.) How Whitman's concept accords with the latter-day development of this subphilosophy is indicated by William Maxwell: "Some Personalist Elements in the Poetry of Whitman" (*The Personalist,* 1931). The relations between some of Whitman's beliefs and those of the Oriental mystics are discussed in W. N. Guthrie's *Walt Whitman (The Camden Sage) as Religious and Moral Teacher* (1897). O. F. Pucciani's "Walt Whitman and the Nineteenth Century" (*Art and Action,* Twice a Year Press, 1948) provides a good general review of the part Whitman played in the movement away from traditional Christianity caused by the new historical relativism.

The studies which have been made of various facets of Whitman's philosophy are more rewarding than those which deal with his religious nature. Maximilian Beck's "Walt Whitman's Intuition of Reality" (*Ethics,* 1942) asserts Whitman's fundamental belief to be "that the value of anything that exists does not lie in its specific quality, in what it is, but purely in its own being." In his attempt "to identify the value of pure reality with that of life," Whitman anticipated both Nietzsche and Bergson. Somewhat similar conclusions were reached by H. A. Myers in his excellent article "Whitman's Consistency" (*AL,* 1936). Using a comparative method which yielded surprisingly good results, R. D. O'Leary in his "Swift and Whitman as Exponents of

Human Nature" (*Ethics,* 1914) contrasts effectively Swift's dualism and Whitman's monism. The section on Whitman ("Whitman and the Civil War") in Ralph Gabriel's *The Course of American Democratic Thought* (1940) demonstrates how Whitman inferred from the doctrine of the fundamental law, not determinism (as did many of his contemporaries), but humanism. The specific problem of Whitman's Hegelianism has been discussed by two scholars: M. C. Boatright, "Whitman and Hegel" (Univ. of Texas *SE*, 1929) and Olive W. Parsons, "Whitman the Non-Hegelian" (*PMLA,* 1943). (The second article is in large part a refutation of Boatright's conclusions.) There are also two studies of the similarities but more particularly the differences between Whitman's Transcendentalism and that of the Concord group: Norman Foerster, "Whitman and the Cult of Confusion" (*NAR,* 1921) and Leon Howard, "For a Critique of Whitman's Transcendentalism" (*MLN,* 1932). The chapter on Whitman in F. W. Conner's *Cosmic Optimism, A Study of the Interpretation of Evolution by American Poets from Emerson to Robinson* (1949) is mainly concerned with the "high-water mark of 'cosmic optimism' " which was reached in Whitman's writing; but the chapter also contains an excellent review of Whitman's interest in other contemporary philosophies, chiefly those emanating from Germany.

As for Whitman's interest in natural phenomena and his knowledge and use of scientific ideas, it will be sufficient to mention Joseph Beaver's *Walt Whitman—Poet of Science* (1951). It takes cognizance of earlier studies by Cooke, Dugdale, and Arvin, but goes beyond them in the amount of evidence cited. Beaver defends Whitman vigorously against those critics who have found his firsthand knowledge of nature slight and confused and his reading in popular scientific literature only superficial. He is possibly too severe in his critique of Norman Foerster's chapter on Whitman in his *Nature in American Literature* (1932). But this chapter has been relied on uncritically by later biographers and Foerster was certainly in error in his belief that Whitman misnamed his birds and could scarcely tell one star from another. In Foerster's defense it must be said, however, that these strictures occupy only a few pages of his essay.

Society and Politics

Whitman is known the world over as the poet of democracy and has inspired many a writer to champion the democratic society. Yet it is an astonishing fact that few articles of importance have been written about his social thought or his political views. The older essays on these subjects are too rhetorical to be of much value. (For example, see Edward Dowden, "The Poetry of Democracy: Walt Whitman," in *Studies in Literature,* 1878, and F. B. Gummere, "Whitman and Taine," in *Democracy and Poetry,* 1911.) C. J. Furness' "Walt Whitman's Politics" (*AM,* 1929) has a promising title but the article does little more than show, by examining a sheaf of manuscript notes, that Whitman studied the Constitution in order to enlighten himself on the legal aspects of the slavery question. Although H. A. Myers' "Whitman's Conception of the Spiritual Democracy, 1855-1856" (*AL,* 1934) concentrates on a brief period in Whitman's life, it emphasizes a facet of his political thought which is important in his poetry after the volumes of 1855 and 1856. In "Walt Whitman and the American Tradition" (*VQR,* 1955) Floyd Stovall has studied to good effect the relation of Whitman's thought to the basic concept of the free individual, the moral law, and progress. Of interest chiefly because it reveals Whitman's influence on a group of English workingmen is J. W. Wallace's pamphlet, *Walt Whitman and the World Crisis* (Manchester, 1920). Alice L. Cooke's "Whitman's Background in the Industrial Movements of his Time" (Univ. of Texas *SE,* 1935), though slight, assembles some useful information. Not even the leftist critics have said much of value about Whitman's propaganda poetry. Samuel Sillen's anthology, *Walt Whitman, Poet of American Democracy* (1944, reissued 1955), arranges the poems conveniently to stress particular social themes, but the Introduction is loose and rambling. Of more interest, because of its Marxist approach and Russian origin, is the translation of D. S. Mirsky's "Walt Whitman: Poet of American Democracy" (*Dialectics,* Critics Group, 1937). Leadie M. Clark's *Walt Whitman's Concept of the American Common Man* (1955) may serve as a useful corrective to the view of Whitman as the undiscriminating admirer of all the races of mankind and of the men and women of all classes. The fact remains that the best analyses of Whitman's social thought are to be found in three books already mentioned: Arvin's *Whitman* (1938), Allen's *Walt Whitman Handbook* (1946), and Asselineau's *L'Evolution de Walt Whitman* (1954). There are two articles which contain interesting evaluations of Whitman's strictures on American society: Emory Holloway, "Whitman as Critic of America" *(SP,* 1923), and M. E. Curti, "Walt Whitman, Critic of America" (*SR,* 1928).

3. *Literary Technique*

Some of the most important recent Whitman studies have been concerned with his literary techniques and his growth as an artist. Earlier admirers of Whitman often felt they had to apologize for his lack of artistry, stressing instead the value of his message. Gradually it has become apparent that Whitman was a member of the company of nineteenth-century poets who were attempting to free poetry from the restrictions of the traditional metrical and stanzaic forms. Eventually it was discovered that he had, indeed, been one of the most powerful leaders in this movement. What is surprising is that critics and scholars required so much time to develop the concepts and vocabulary required for explaining Whitman's art.

Whitman's friend W. S. Kennedy made a beginning in two sections of his *The Fight of a Book for the World* (1926)—"The Growth of Leaves of Grass as a Work of Art" and "Elucidations and Analyses of Difficult Poems in Leaves of Grass." He also provided a useful tool in this volume, "Index of Dates Covering All the Poems of All the Editions of Leaves of Grass." Killis Campbell's "The Evolution of Whitman as Artist" (*AL,* 1934) carried further the work begun by Kennedy. The most important studies of Whitman's artistic growth have been based on comparisons of versions of the poems as they were revised from edition to edition of the *Leaves.* O. L. Triggs made the first (and quite superficial) investigation of this sort in 1902, "The Growth of 'Leaves of Grass' " (*Complete Writings,* x). This method of studying Whitman has been used with excellent results in three recent books: G. W. Allen, *Walt Whitman Handbook* (1946); Frederick Schyberg, *Walt Whitman* (1951); Roger Asselineau, *L'Evolution de Walt Whitman* (1954).

Several useful studies have been made of the organizing principles to be discerned in *Leaves of Grass.* Though the article is brief there are interesting ideas in I. C. Story's "The Structural Pattern of Leaves of Grass" (*Pacific Univ. Bull.,* 1942). Examining the "Main Drifts in Whitman's Poetry" (*AL,* 1932) Floyd Stovall discovered that Whitman employed three different organizing themes at different stages of his poetical career (love of freedom, love and death, spirituality). Though the article strains to make its point, there is novelty and some merit in Ferner Nuhn's "Leaves of Grass Viewed as an Epic" (*Arizona Quart.,* 1951). G. W. Allen discusses one of the recurrent organizing principles of Whitman's poetry in "Walt Whitman's 'Long Journey' Motif" (*JEGP,* 1939). Whitman's use of the Hegelian dialectic in shaping his poetry (particularly in "Chanting the Square Deific" and "Out of the Cradle") is explored by A. H. Marks in "Whitman's Triadic Imagery" (*AL,* 1951).

In 1896 W. S. Kennedy attempted to explain Whitman's technical effects, in "The Style of Leaves of Grass" *(Reminiscences of Walt Whitman),* but he did not command the critical vocabulary adequate to his task. In 1929-30 there appeared three excellent studies which led the way to further explorations of Whitman's techniques. Jean Catel's *Rythme et langage dans la 1re édition des "Leaves of Grass"* (Paris, 1930) examines first the transition in Whitman's writing from the rhetoric of his early prose, published and unpublished, to the rhetorical verse of the 1855 edition. The second half of this monograph deals with particular features of his early poetical style, from vocabulary to the rhythmical grouping of lines. Lois Ware's "Poetic Conventions in *Leaves of Grass*" (*SP,* 1929) shows that Whitman was not as wildly radical in technique as his early defamers declared. Also in 1929, Autrey N. Wiley studied the "Reiterative Devices in *Leaves of Grass" (AL).* (The devices are epanaphora or initial repetition and epanalepsis or repetition within the line.) The complexities of a much debated feature of Whitman's technique are discussed in Mattie Swayne's "Whitman's Catalogue Rhetoric" (Univ. of Texas *SE*, 1941). D. W. Schumann explores the same subject in a larger frame of reference in "Enumerative Style and its Significance in Whitman, Rilke, Werfel" (*MLQ,* 1942). A subject in need of further development is Whitman's vocabulary. The chapter on "La langue—innovations et traditions" in Asselineau's biography is not adequate. Beyond this there is only a handful of articles: Rebecca Coy's "A Study of Whitman's Diction" (Univ. of Texas *SE,* 1936), and four papers by Louise Pound—"Walt Whitman and the Classics" (*Southwest Rev.,* 1925), "Walt Whitman and Italian Music" (*AM,* 1925), "Walt Whitman's Neologisms" (ibid.), and "Walt Whitman and the French Language" (*American Speech,* 1926). The publication of E. H. Eby's *A Concordance of Walt Whitman's "Leaves of Grass" and Selected Prose Writings* (Seattle, 1949-54) will lighten the task of whoever undertakes a thorough study of Whitman's diction.

Two excellent studies of Whitman's prosody make use of earlier efforts to explain the rationale of his verse and add important new contributions. The chapter on Whitman in G. W. Allen's *American Prosody* (1935) is concerned more with the devices the poet used (parallelism, the "envelope," phonetic recurrence, initial, medial, and final reiteration, etc.) in order to give rhythmical shape to his poems than with his meters. The conclusions reached by Sculley Bradley in his "The Fundamental Metrical Principle in Whitman's Poetry" (*AL,* 1939) can be summed up in his own words. "His revolution centered on three things: a new emphasis, to the point of organic use, upon ancient repetitive devices . . .; the construction of stanzas and larger units on the basis of rhythmic balance and parallelism; his conscious rejection of syllabic meter in favor of that more ancient and native English meter based on the rhythmic 'period' between the stresses." Long before American scholars began their investigations of Whitman's prosody a remarkable treatise on this subject was published in Italy, Pasquale Jannaccone's *La Poesia de Walt Whitman e L'Evoluzione delle Forme Ritmiche* (Torino, 1898). Jannaccone's fine ear for rhythm and his extensive knowledge of metrics enabled him to analyze Whitman's verse accurately and perceptively. His little book should be better known than it is. For a modern poet's insight into Whitman's art one should read Randall Jarrell's shrewd and sympathetic "Some Lines from Whitman" (*Poetry and the Age,* 1953).

4. *Whitman as Critic*

Whitman's critical writing has not been much studied. Fortunately the two most extensive surveys of the subject supplement each other: the chapter on "Whitman" in Norman Foerster's *American Criticism* (1928) and M. O. Johnson's "Walt Whitman as a Critic of Literature" (*Studies in Lang., Lit. and Criticism,* Univ. of Nebraska, 1938).

5. *Explications*

A number of useful explications of particular Whitman poems should be mentioned. These articles will be listed here alphabetically according to the poems which they treat. G. L. Sixbey, " 'Chanting the Square Deific'—A Study in Whitman's Religion" (*AL,* 1937); S. K. Coffman, Jr., " 'Crossing Brooklyn Ferry,' A Note on the Catalogue Technique in Whitman's Poetry" (*MP,* 1954); W. L. Werner, "Whitman's 'The Mystic Trumpeter' as Autobiography" (*AL,* 1936); Leo Spitzer, " 'Explication de Texte' Applied to Walt Whitman's 'Out of the

Cradle Endlessly Rocking' " (*ELH,* 1949); C. F. Strauch, "The Structure of Walt Whitman's 'Song of Myself' " (*English Journal,* 1938); Clarence Gohdes, "A Comment on Section 5 of Walt Whitman's 'Song of Myself' " (*MLN,* 1954); Paul Morgan, "New Significance to Whitman's 'Song of the Exposition' " (*Univ. of Texas Library Chronicle,* 1952); G. F. Cronkhite, "Notes: Walt Whitman and the Locomotive" (*Amer. Quart.,* 1954). (This studies the background of the locomotive symbol in "To a Locomotive" and "Passage to India.") Analyses of Whitman poems appear frequently in the *Explicator.*

6. *Parodies*

Parody is a form of criticism. It is also flattery by indirection, and Whitman enjoyed the sound of his own name, whatever the context. The compilation made by H. S. Saunders, *Parodies of Walt Whitman* (1923), proves that he is one of the most parodied poets in English. It also proves that several excellent wits have had their fun with his catalogues and his apostrophes to lowly persons, places, and things. Among them are H. C. Bunner, Quiller-Couch, Julian Sturgis, Carolyn Wells, Ezra Pound, Christopher Morley, and G. K. Chesterton.

7. *Sources and Influences*

Though Whitman was a desultory reader during most of his life, he read widely and in many different fields. Since he often kept extensive notes or pasted up articles which struck his fancy, scholars have been able to identify many of the works which influenced him. In "Notes on Whitman's Reading" (*AL,* 1954), Floyd Stovall tracked down the sources of 112 items printed by Bucke in *Notes and Fragments* (1899), and reprinted in Volumes IX and X of the *Complete Writings* (1902). This article contributes appreciably to our knowledge of Whitman's reading before and immediately following the publication of the 1855 *Leaves of Grass.* A less systematic study is David Goodale's "Some of Walt Whitman's Borrowings" (*AL,* 1928). In "Possible Sources of Some of Whitman's Ideas and

Symbols in *Hermes Mercurius Trismegistus* and other Works" (*MLQ,* 1953) Esther Shephard presents the ingenious theory that Whitman drew on various esoteric writings, in particular the *Divine Pymander* of Trismegistus, for the symbols which decorate his books, but there is a good deal of conjecture in her article.

Studies of the influence of English writers on Whitman are chiefly concerned with Shakespeare and Carlyle. The first extensive investigation of Shakespeare's influence was R. C. Harrison's "Walt Whitman and Shakespeare" (*PMLA,* 1929). This was followed by C. J. Furness' "Walt Whitman's Estimate of Shakespeare" (*Harvard Studies and Notes in Philol. and Lit.,* 1932) and R. P. Falk's "Shakespeare's Place in Walt Whitman's America" (*Shakes. Assoc. Bull.,* 1942). The tenor of these three articles is that Whitman's early repudiation of Shakespeare's feudalism prevented for a time an appreciation of his poetry. Citing passages from Whitman's journalistic writing, Floyd Stovall, in his "Whitman, Shakespeare, and Democracy" (*JEGP,* 1952), corrects the views of Harrison, Furness, and Falk and concludes that Whitman was aware, before he wrote *Leaves of Grass,* of Shakespeare's unrivaled greatness as a poet though he was "critical of his work as it relates to American principles and practice of democracy." In another article published in 1952, "Whitman's Knowledge of Shakespeare" *(SP),* Stovall demonstrates that much of Whitman's early knowledge of Shakespeare was derived from performances of the plays he attended, and that Whitman's notes on Shakespeare's career (printed in Bucke's *Notes and Fragments*) derive from J. P. Collier's biography, first printed in 1844. Three articles deal with Whitman's reactions to Carlyle's ideas: Gregory Paine, "The Literary Relations of Whitman and Carlyle with Especial Reference to Their Contrasting Views on Democracy" (*SP,* 1939); F. M. Smith, "Whitman's Poet-Prophet and Carlyle's Hero" (*PMLA,* 1940); and also by Smith, "Whitman's Debt to Carlyle's *Sartor Resartus*" (MLQ, 1942). Paine contends that though Whitman made a vigorous reply to Carlyle's

"Shooting Niagara, and After?" in his "Democracy," in the end he believed that Carlyle's fears for democracy were to some extent justified. Smith holds to the view that Carlyle may have had as much influence on the "gestation" of *Leaves of Grass* as Emerson did.

Whitman's indebtedness to German thinkers and writers has been much debated. Richard Riethmueller surveyed the subject generally (and rather superficially) in the *German American Annals* (1906)—"Walt Whitman and the Germans." More substantial is R. P. Falk, "Walt Whitman and German Thought" (*JEGP,* 1941). W. B. Fulghum, Jr., produces good evidence, in "Whitman's Debt to Joseph Gostwick" (*AL,* 1941), that Whitman was indebted to Gostwick's popular handbook, *German Literature* (1854), for information about the German philosophers. Sister Mary Eleanor discusses another possible intermediary in her "Hedge's *Prose Writers of Germany* as a Source of Whitman's Knowledge of German Philosophy" (*MLN,* 1946).

Well-documented articles which assess other writers or works influential in Whitman's career are few and may be briefly mentioned: G. W. Allen, "Biblical Echoes in Whitman's Works" (*AL,* 1934); J. C. Mathews, "Walt Whitman's Reading of Dante" (Univ. of Texas *SE,* 1939); F. I. Carpenter, "The Vogue of Ossian in America" (*AL,* 1931; Carpenter believes Whitman's interest in Ossian marks the culmination of the vogue in America); G. W. Allen, "Walt Whitman and Jules Michelet" (*Etudes Anglaises,* 1937); A. B. Benson, "Walt Whitman's Interest in Swedish Writers" (*JEGP,* 1932).

Whitman remarked to J. T. Trowbridge in 1860: "But for the opera I could never have written *Leaves of Grass.*" Evidence of the truth of this statement can be seen in many Whitman poems: in the overture-like first sections, in the intimate outpouring of lines spoken, as it were, directly to the reader in the style of the recitative, in the more formal but exalted aria-like passages set off in the text as if to notify the reader-singer of the change of mood. Few of the earlier biographers of Whitman paid much attention to this important subject and periodical writing about it is also scanty. Louise Pound looked briefly at "Walt Whitman and Italian Music" (*AM,* 1925). Examining another aspect of Whitman's pleasure in music, A. L. Cooke ("Notes on Whitman's Musical Background," *NEQ,* 1946) disclosed his interest in the musical revival which took place in Boston just after the Civil War and its influence on "Proud Music of the Storm." In 1951 R. D. Faner published *Walt Whitman & Opera,* a work which gathers together the evidence on this important subject. Faner lists the operas Whitman attended, quotes from his journalistic articles about singers and performances, culls out his allusions to musical forms and instruments, and then attempts to assess in detail the influence of operatic style on Whitman's poetry. Informative though this study is, the author occasionally runs into difficulty by trying to prove too much. Whitman actually knew next to nothing about the technical aspects of music, though there is no doubting the pleasure he derived from it and his desire to achieve in his poems the overwhelming emotional effects of grand opera. But Faner's attempts to discover Whitman using the sonata form ("whether he was closely aware of the details of the form or not" [!]) do not succeed. Nor is his chapter on "Melody" pertinent. No critic, to be sure, has entirely succeeded in working out this particular analogy between music and poetry. Georgiana Pollak's "The Relationship of Music to 'Leaves of Grass' " (*CE,* 1954) defines more precisely than Faner the influence of the recitative on Whitman's rhythms.

The subject of Whitman and music should not be dismissed without reference to the extraordinary number of musical compositions his poetry has inspired. (A partial list of these is given in *Walt Whitman, A Catalog Based Upon the Collections of the Library of Congress;* see also *Whitman Music,* compiled by H. S. Saunders, Toronto, 1945; typewritten.) Even more revelatory is the fact that many of the best modern composers have used his poems as libretti or as the inspiration of orchestral works. Chief among them are Ernest Bloch, Frederick Delius,

Roy Harris, Paul Hindemith, Gustav Holst, Charles Ives, William Schuman, and Vaughan Williams.

VII. Fame and Influence

Even before his death Whitman was becoming famous as a figure in world literature. He had been translated, not always adequately, into German, French, Danish, Dutch and Italian, and Russia had heard his voice in a few poems translated by Dr. P. Popoff in *Zagranichy (The Foreign Messenger.)* His English admirers were proud that they had taken him up at a time when his countrymen were still trying to ignore him. Whitman was vain of his growing reputation abroad and did everything he could to enlarge it. He and his Camden disciples kept every review or notice of his work which came from Europe or other parts of the world. (In 1926 W. S. Kennedy drew on this storehouse of criticism for his triumphant *The Fight of a Book for the World.*) Other American writers have exercised great influence abroad—notably Poe and Cooper—but none has enjoyed such a continuous and ever-expanding reputation. Each new generation of writers has found something to admire. (A typical statement of this recurrent enthusiasm for Whitman's poetry is Klaus Mann's "The Present Greatness of Walt Whitman," *Decision,* 1941.) By turns he has appealed to symbolists and Unanimists, to democrats, to members of the "intermediate sex," to Vedantists, to revolutionaries of the word and the act, to nationalists and internationalists. Meanwhile translations into new languages appeared—Spanish, Polish, Finnish, Jugoslavian, Roumanian, Czech, Portuguese, Hebrew, Japanese, Chinese. The wings of Whitman's soul were indeed plumed for far flights and it has made its "passage to more than India."

Though the subject of Whitman's fame and influence is a vast one, fortunately it has been excellently surveyed in Allen's *Walt Whitman Handbook* and in Schyberg's long chapter on "Whitman in World Literature" (*Walt Whitman,* 1951). Since Allen's chapter contains a good bibliography, all that it will be necessary to do here is to note the chief books and articles which were in print at the time his *Handbook* appeared and then review the more recent literature on the subject. (Holloway's bibliography—including translations—in the *CHAL* is extensive but of course it carries the subject only as far as 1918.)

Harold Blodgett's *Walt Whitman in England* (1934) was published more than twenty years ago, but it is not badly out of date since the wave of enthusiasm for Whitman in England began to recede in the first years of this century. Four studies deal adequately with the story of Whitman's fame in Germany: O. E. Lessing, "Walt Whitman and his German Critics" (*JEGP,* 1910); Grace D. Clark, "Walt Whitman in Germany" (*Texas Rev.,* 1920-21); Anna Jacobson, "Walt Whitman in Germany Since 1914" (*Germanic Rev.,* 1926); and Harry Law-Robertson, "Walt Whitman in Deutschland" (*Giessener Beiträge zur deutschen Philologie,* 1935). (Law-Robertson's dissertation contains a full list of German translations of Whitman and of critical estimates of them.) Though P. M. Jones later developed several of the ideas expressed in his "Whitman in France" (*Modern Language Rev.,* 1915), the article is still useful. Fernand Baldensperger's "Walt Whitman and France" (*Columbia Univ. Quart.,* 1919) is particularly interesting for its brief account of *le whitmanisme* of the 1910's. S. A. Rhodes's "The Influence of Walt Whitman on André Gide" (*RR,* 1940) shows conclusively that Whitman transformed Gide's life and career. Unfortunately the article says little about the revolt Gide led against Bazalgette's idealized translation of *Leaves of Grass* and his *Le Poème—Evangile de Walt Whitman* (1921), which is the most extraordinary piece of hagiography in all the Whitman literature. P. M. Jones's "Whitman and Verhaeren" (*Aberystwyth Studies,* 1914) finds no influence of the American poet on the "visionary of Belgium" but seeks to explain why Whitman and Verhaeren, before World War I, were "considered by the younger generation of Continental poets as the twofold source of inspiration in contemporary poetry."

In contrast with the frequent "rediscoveries" of Whitman in

Germany and France is the slight attention accorded him in Italy and Spain. What there is to tell in the case of Italy is summarized in Rea McCain's "Walt Whitman in Italy," *Italice* (1943). J. D. Ferguson's statement in his *American Literature in Spain* (1916), that "Walt Whitman, the latest important American author to reach Spain, enjoys the somewhat dubious distinction of being apparently more talked about than read," is confirmed by the fact that no Castilian translation of his poems appeared until 1912. Writing in 1938 J. E. Englekirk ("Notes on Whitman in Spanish America," *Hispanic Review*), averred that since the turn of the century Whitman has been "one of the leading spiritual forces in young Spanish America." This statement seems extravagant in the light of the rather meager evidence Englekirk offers in support of it. A better documented article, with an excellent bibliographical appendix, is Fernando Alegría's "Walt Whitman en Hispanoamérica" (*Revista Iberoamericana,* 1944). For Whitman's reception in Czarist Russia one must rely on Albert Parry's very amusing but not well documented "Walt Whitman in Russia" (*AM,* 1934). In the early years of the Soviet regime, at least, Whitman was extravagantly admired and imitated by the revolutionary poets. The difficult task of estimating his later influence has yet to be undertaken. One article brings the subject down to the 1930's—Leonard Spier, "Walt Whitman" (*International Literature,* Moscow, 1935).

For a listing of studies of Whitman's reputation and influence since World War II the reader should consult the "Walt Whitman Bibliography, 1944-1954" prepared by Evie A. Allen and G. W. Allen for the *Walt Whitman Foundation Bulletin* (April 1955). Of importance is C. B. Willard's *Whitman's American Fame, the Growth of his Reputation in America after 1892* (1950). Willard reviews the work of most of the biographers, the journalistic and academic critics, and the creative writers. Of special interest is his discussion of the part played in promoting Whitman's reputation by the Walt Whitman Fellowship and Traubel's magazine, *The Conservator.* Herbert

Bergman's "Ezra Pound and Walt Whitman" (*AL,* 1955) does not make out much of a case for the influence of Whitman on Pound but it prints for the first time Pound's essay, "What I Feel About Walt Whitman." W. D. Tempelman's "Hopkins and Whitman: Evidence of Influence and Echoes" (*PQ,* 1954) revives a much-debated question but is not very convincing. Earlier studies of Whitman's influence in Germany and the affinities between him and a number of German poets have been supplemented by two excellent articles: D. W. Schumann, "Observations on Enumerative Style in Modern German Poetry" (*PMLA,* 1944), and H. Pongs, "Walt Whitman and Stefan George" (*CL,* 1952). P. M. Jones's earlier studies of Whitman's influence in France have culminated in two judicious chapters of his *The Background of Modern French Poetry* (1951)—"Whitman and the Symbolists" and "Whitman and the Origins of the *Vers Libre*." Joseph Remenyi's "Walt Whitman in Hungarian Literature" (*AL,* 1944), though disappointingly brief, is indicative of Whitman's ever-widening influence. In "The Walt Whitman Myth" (*Américas,* 1954) Fernando Alegría points out that the older Spanish and Spanish-American attitude towards Whitman, which was largely influenced by Bazalgette and other European Whitmanians, is changing as the influence of more realistic biographical and critical studies is felt. His *Walt Whitman en Hispanoamérica* was published in Mexico City in 1954. Two especially useful features of this study are the copious quotations from Spanish-American critics of Whitman and analyses of the translations by Vasseur, Torres-Rioseco, Felipe, and Zardoya. G. W. Allen continued his investigations of Whitman's influence abroad in two brief but useful surveys, "Walt Whitman's Reception in Scandinavia" (*PBSA,* 1946) and a review of nine recent translations and books and articles about Whitman in foreign languages (*CL,* 1949). Allen's *Walt Whitman Abroad* (Syracuse, 1955), a volume of translated criticisms of Whitman, appeared too late to be discussed in this essay.

7

MARK TWAIN

I. Bibliography

BASIC IS Merle Johnson's *A Bibliography of the Works of Mark Twain, Samuel Langhorne Clemens; A List of First Editions in Book Form and of First Printings in Periodicals and Occasional Publications of his Various Literary Activities* in the much revised 1935 edition. But this must now be supplemented by "Mark Twain's Juvenilia" (*AL,* 1930); Ivan Benson's *Mark Twain's Western Years* (1938), which includes "Periodical Bibliography: Bibliography of the Writings of Mark Twain in the Newspapers and Magazines of Nevada and California, 1861-1866"; and E. M. Branch's "A Chronological Bibliography of the Writings of Samuel Clemens to June 8, 1867" (*AL,* 1946). The latest and best list of articles *about* Mark Twain is in Lewis Leary's *Articles on American Literature, 1900-1950* (1954) (to be referred to hereafter for full data as to scholars' articles as "Leary"). *LHUS,* III, 442-450, includes books and leading articles to about 1946. See also the *Twainian* for Oct. 1939, Dec. 1940, and Feb. and June, 1943. For articles current see *PMLA* and *AL* quarterly bibliographies.

II. Editions and Texts

The most complete and definitive edition is *The Writings of Mark Twain,* edited by A. B. Paine, 37 vols. (1922-25). There are also the Author's National Edition of *The Writings of Mark Twain,* 22 vols. (1899-1900); the Underwood Edition of *The Writings of Mark Twain,* 25 vols. (1901-07); and *Mark Twain's Works,* 23 vols. (1933). Much of Mark Twain's writing is to be found outside these collections. *Mark Twain's Speeches* (1910) and a more inclusive edition of 1923, the important *Notebook* (1935), and the *Autobiography* (2 vols., 1924) were all edited by A. B. Paine, along with the *Letters, Arranged with Comment* (2 vols., 1917). *Mark Twain in Eruption* (ed. Bernard De Voto, 1940) may be regarded as a third volume of the *Autobiography,* to be used with caution in the light of DeLancey Ferguson's findings in "The Uncollected Portion of Mark Twain's Autobiography" (*AL,* 1936). Dixon Wecter edited *Mark Twain in Three Moods* (1948), *Mark Twain to Mrs. Fairbanks* (1949), and *The Love Letters of Mark Twain* (1949), three collections of basic material. S. C. Webster's *Mark Twain: Business Man* (1946) includes letters as well as biography. Ivan Benson's *Mark Twain's Western Years* (1938) includes "Selected Mark Twain Western Items," and E. M. Branch's *Literary Apprenticeship of Mark Twain* (1950) includes "Selections from Mark Twain's Apprenticeship Writings" from 1852 to 1867.

Also especially noteworthy is W. F. Frear's *Mark Twain and Hawaii* (1947), a complete assembly of all his writing on that subject, with elaborate commentary. See also the following not in the collected editions: *The Curious Republic of Gondour* (1919); *Sketches of the Sixties,* by Bret Harte and Mark Twain (1926); *Adventures of Thomas Jefferson Snodgrass* (ed. Charles Honce, 1926); *The Washoe Giant in San Francisco* (ed. Franklin Walker, 1938); *Letters from the Sandwich Islands* (ed. G. E. Dane, 1937, 1938); *Letters from Honolulu* (ed. Thomas Nickerson, 1939); *Mark Twain's Travels with Mr. Brown* (eds. Franklin Walker and G. E. Dane, 1940); *Republican Letters* (1941) and *Washington in 1868* (1943), both edited by Cyril Clemens (see *AL,* Jan. 1943 for corrections); *Mark Twain's Letters in the Muscatine Journal* (ed. E. M. Branch, 1942); *The Letters of Quintus Curtius Snodgrass* (ed. E. E. Leisy,

1946); Walter Blair's "Mark Twain, New York Correspondent" (*AL,* 1939); E. E. Leisy, "Mark Twain and Isaiah Sellers" (*AL,* 1942); *Mark Twain's Letters to Will Bowen* (ed. Theodore Hornberger, 1941); C. B. Taylor's *Mark Twain's Margins on Thackeray's "Swift"* (1935); *Report from Paradise,* edited by Dixon Wecter, 1952 (two opening chapters of *Captain Stormfield's Visit* and "Letter from the Recording Angel"); H. W. Fisher, *Abroad with Mark Twain and Eugene Field* (1922), to be used with caution as the text is based partly on Fisher's memory; "Fenimore Cooper's Further Literary Offences" (*NEQ,* ed. De Voto, 1946); G. H. Brownell: "Two Hitherto Unknown Twain Tales" (*Twainian,* 1946), "Seven New Twain Tales Discovered by Chance" (*Twainian,* 1943), "Where and When Were These Twain Tales First Printed?" (*Twainian,* 1944), the first, second, and third of "American Travel Letters Series Two," reprinted from the *Alta California* (*Twainian,* 1947, 1949), and "Mark Twain's Letters in the San Francisco *Call*" (*Twainian,* 1949, 1952). Many of F. W. Lorch's valuable studies listed by Leary include citations from newspapers of Mark Twain's original lectures, as do two doctoral dissertations: S. T. Donner's "The Speaking and Reading of Mark Twain" (Northwestern Univ., 1946), and Jean C. Ervin's "Mark Twain, Speechmaker" (Univ. of Missouri, 1950). H. N. Smith of the University of California is the present custodian of the most considerable body of unpublished manuscripts owned by the Mark Twain estate. See De Voto's "The Mark Twain Papers" (*SR,* XIX, 10 Dec. 1938). C. J. Armstrong ("Mark Twain's Early Writings Discovered," *MHR,* XXIV, 1930) describes the Hannibal Papers presented to the State Historical Society of Missouri at Columbia. *The Yale University Library Gazette,* XVII, 1943, describes the Frear Collection available at Yale. The University of California has the Moffett Collection described in the *New York Times,* 19 September 1954. The Berg Collection of the New York Public Library has an important collection of Mark Twain manuscripts, and the William Dean Howells Papers at Harvard include

Twain's letters to Howells. The Boston Public Library, the Huntington Library, and the Princeton Library also have valuable Mark Twain collections, as does the Library of Congress.

III. Biographies

The first fairly important biography was by Archibald Henderson (London, 1911). This presented Mark Twain as a fellow Southern gentleman. Twain's friend and literary executor, A. B. Paine, published *Mark Twain, A Biography: The Personal and Literary Life of Samuel Langhorne Clemens* (3 vols., 1912), citing letters sparingly; these were to be edited in two separate volumes. Emphasis is placed on what is colorful, vivid and entertaining, and on those aspects of Mark Twain which show his integrity and fineness. In this biography, designed for the general reader, later experts have found many minor errors or lapses. F. W. Lorch has been especially diligent in examining various facets of Twain's career. See for instance "Mark Twain in Iowa," *Iowa Jour. of History and Politics* (1929), which supplements and sometimes corrects Paine's biography, basic as it is.

V. W. Brooks's *The Ordeal of Mark Twain* (1920, rev., 1933), as he himself later admitted, was written to prove a thesis. Twain is presented as a potential artist and satirist who was "thwarted" by being obliged to conform to a commercial-industrial America and its prudish Victorian taboos as these operated through his mother and his wife, and through Howells, the Rev. J. H. Twichell, and money-getters such as H. H. Rogers and Andrew Carnegie. What especially enraged re-revisionists such as Bernard De Voto was Brooks's notion that Mark Twain's Western frontier was "a desert of human sand!—the barrenest spot in all Christendom, surely, for the seed of genius to fall in." Perhaps not enough credit has been given Brooks for his sympathetic analysis of the good effects on Mark Twain's art of two experiences associated with the frontier—the craftsmanship of piloting and the craftsmanship of oral storytelling gained from Negroes and Westerners. Moreover, in riding his thesis, Brooks assembled a mass of evidence about

Twain's despair and his tragic sense which helped to show that he was more than a funny man. Brooks makes a sharp distinction between humor and satire, and accuses him of lacking courage to satirize spokesmen of the order which had befriended him. Here again his thesis leads him to belittle the satire in *The Innocents Abroad* (regarded as merely philistine and hostile to all art), the social criticism in *The Gilded Age* (regarded as centering on Philip Stirling's financial success story alone) and in *The Connecticut Yankee* (regarded as an attack on all beauty). His view of Mrs. Clemens as censor has been corrected by DeLancey Ferguson in "The Case for Mark Twain's Wife" (*UTQ,* 1939) and others. Brooks tends to neglect literary influences and the influence of science. His attack on *Huckleberry Finn* as essentially negative will be discussed later.

Whatever Brooks's faults, his book has been a catalyst. De Voto subtitled his *Mark Twain's America* (1932) "An Essay in the Correction of Ideas" and aimed it directly at Brooks's theory that the frontier thwarted Mark Twain. His counter-thesis is that "Mark Twain was a frontier humorist. His literary intelligence was shaped by the life of the frontier and found expression in the themes and forms developed by the humor of the frontier." De Voto amasses evidence to prove that in Twain's frontier there was

> an intense pleasure in the variety of the world—an exuberant delight which sprang from the frontier's energy. There was also the frontier's sharp perception—its ability to understand behavior and the motives which produce it. These form the basis of frontier humor which worked out in obscure newspapers the first formidable realism . . . in our literature. What this humor required was some one native to its pleasures and perceptions who could express them on the level of genius. . . . [Mark Twain] was . . . the expression of this humor at its highest level. . . . It was the basis of his mind, as it was the framework of his books. He was always a frontier humorist, who devoted himself to the production of laughter.

De Voto analyzes in detail and with great gusto the writings and techniques of A. B. Longstreet, G. W. Harris, J. G. Baldwin, T. B. Thorpe, Dan DeQuille, and others with whose work Twain was familiar. (His view that "the minds of Mark Twain and Artemus Ward, their methods, and their effects are antipathetic" has been sensibly questioned by Walter Blair in his generally eulogistic review in *AL,* 1933.) It should be noted that De Voto emphasizes the ruthlessness as well as the good aspects of the frontier. His criticisms of frontier elements in Twain's work are usually shrewd and stimulating, but he tends to be unduly harsh toward non-frontier work such as the "chaotic" *Connecticut Yankee,* and *Joan of Arc,* which he regards as "mediocre or worse." Those desiring a balanced view would do well to supplement De Voto's excellent study of frontier influences with Kenneth Andrews' scholarly and yet warmly sympathetic *Nook Farm: Mark Twain's Hartford Circle* (1950), which deals with the influence of the East during his twenty years (1871-91) with friends such as the C. D. Warners, Harriet Beecher Stowe, the Hookers, and Twichell (spokesman of Horace Bushnell's meliorism).

Edward Wagenknecht's main thesis in *Mark Twain: The Man and His Work* (1935) is that the man and his work are one. When he does express conclusions, they are generally sensible, and he favors interpretations sympathetic toward Mark Twain, although he thinks his wife's influence was "negative rather than positive." He assembles most of the main relevant evidence regarding his political, literary, and religious attitudes, without trying to explain them. Robert Spiller, in his review of Wagenknecht's book (*AL,* 1936), finds it mediatory rather than judicial as regards controversial issues. He thinks that "of a critical analysis surely we have a right to something more comprehensive in understanding and judgment." Yet Spiller concludes that partly because of Wagenknecht's fairness in citing opposing evidence his book is "among the most useful that we have on the subject" for introductory purposes, since it shows what the main problems are if it does not try to solve them. Wagenknecht mainly accepts the frontier thesis of De Voto, and accepts Miss Brashear's primary findings about eighteenth-century literary influences.

The best full-length biography is DeLancey Ferguson's *Mark Twain: Man and Legend* (1943), which corrects errors in the Twain legend and emphasizes his "career as a writing man" and "the forces which made him a writer." Ferguson necessarily presents a less colorful and vivacious personality than does Paine because he passes "over lightly, or ignor[es], his [Twain's] multifarious nonliterary doings." Within his limits, Ferguson's biography is rich in sturdy common sense and salty judgments. He offers valuable material on revisions in *Innocents Abroad* and *Huckleberry Finn.* Walter Blair's discriminating review (*AL,* 1944) finds much to praise but deplores the neglect of revisions of other work such as *Roughing It* and the slighting of details regarding Mark Twain's earlier career. (On the latter, Ferguson can be profitably supplemented by Ivan Benson and Edgar Branch.) Ferguson provides much more criticism of individual stories than does Paine, but the analyses are necessarily brief.

Dixon Wecter's untimely death prevented the completion of his proposed multivolume biography of Twain, and only *Sam Clemens of Hannibal* (1952) has since been published by his executors. Chapters xiii ("Instruments of Culture") and ix ("The Precious Dream of Death") stress the Hannibal element in the development of Twain's mind and personality; the first notes the cultural advantages of life in Hannibal, while the latter dwells on the violence to be seen in the frontier town, such as the shooting of the town drunk and Sam's watching through a keyhole the post-mortem done on his father. Wecter sometimes assigned greater importance to Hannibal experiences than seems warranted, but the book (based on exhaustive coverage of Hannibal newspapers and local history) filled a real need.

Studies of Mark Twain's growing despair will be more fully considered later in relation to his ideas, but a few predominantly biographical explanations may be mentioned here. In "The Devil and Samuel Clemens" (*VQR,* 1947) C. O. Parsons makes a psychological examination of Mark Twain's mind through his writings in order to show that he suffered from a guilt complex because of various childhood experiences, such as jealousy of his brother Henry. This, Parsons thinks, led him to condemn the moral sense or conscience. Much is made of Mark Twain's occasional condemnation of God and his sympathetic portrayal of the devil.

Brooks attributed Mark Twain's despair mainly to the suppression of his natural individuality and satirical genius in the midst of an industrial and Victorian environment. Kenneth Andrews (*Nook Farm)* emphasizes Twain's maladjustment, his later yearning for the River simplicities of his youth, and especially his dismay at a civilization which succumbed to money-lust and the "California sudden riches disease." Andrews cites a "very important" unpublished set of notes entitled "Villagers of 1840-43" contrasting what was good in that earlier age with the rapaciousness of the 1890's. Andrews and others have noted that the later stress on evil in work such as *The Mysterious Stranger* was but the accentuation of the evil chronicled (but balanced against good) in the era of *Huck.* DeLancey Ferguson in *Mark Twain: Man and Legend* (1943) finds deeply pessimistic moods as early as 1876 (in a letter to Mrs. Fairbanks) and thinks one may be too hasty in attributing *What is Man?* and *The Mysterious Stranger* "to the disasters of Mark's later years . . . The black moods were part of his nature, part of the price he paid for his lightheartedness. Later in life, as troubles thickened the moods came oftener, but the troubles did not cause them, they merely intensified them and gave them point." On the other hand Wagenknecht thinks all critics agree that Mark Twain's pessimism was not basically temperamental but that after Susy's death he "reasoned himself into despair." And of course his long obsession with the determinism of environment and heredity in relation to the whole scientific trend of the age must be taken into account, as suggested in H. H. Waggoner's "Science in the Thought of Mark Twain" (*AL,* 1937). De Voto's trenchant essay on "The Symbols of Despair" (in *Mark Twain at Work,* 1942), based on a close study of all the manuscripts culminating in *The Mysterious Stranger,* argues that blaming himself for the increasing disasters led him to the verge of insanity and that he "saved himself in the end, and came back from the edge of insanity" by formulating a determinism which absolved him of personal blame. In "Mark Twain's Despair: An Explanation in Terms of His Humanity" (*SAQ,* 1935), R. D. Altick attributed Twain's later despair to arrested development. According to Altick, Twain had been prepared in his youth to think of success in terms of being rich "at the expense of the development of his idealistic-intellectual-artistic side." When old age came he was unprepared for it.

III. Criticism

1. *Influences and Sources*

Brooks's disparagement of the frontier occasioned much defense of its influence on Twain, and since 1930, when F. J. Meine brought out his racy *Tall Tales of the Southwest,* Twain has been variously approached through the writings of such figures as A. B. Longstreet, W. T. Thompson, Sol Smith, J. J. Hooper, J. G. Baldwin, J. M. Field, G. W. Harris, T. B. Thorpe, and H. C. Jones. De Voto's *Mark Twain's America* especially emphasized Twain's *general* kinship with the spirit of these men, but attacked the quest for specific parallels and sources. Walter Blair in *Native American Humor* (1937) not only interpreted Twain's humor as the culmination or "summary" of a long indigenous tradition, but provided full bibliographical guidance and pointed out several convincing parallels such as that between Shillaber's Mrs. Partington and Tom Sawyer's Aunt Polly. Blair discusses narrative method, techniques, the use of frames and settings, characterization, the shadings of the vernacular, and even "the picaresque method."

His various studies, along with his peculiarly penetrating reviews of most of the major books on Mark Twain, have made him one of the foremost authorities. Twain's debt to European literary tradition has also received needed attention. Useful guides to his considerable reading will be found in H. A. Pochmann's master's thesis of 1924, "The Mind of Mark Twain" (Texas), now available in microfilm, and in Harold Aspiz' "Mark Twain's Reading—a Critical Study" (1949), a thorough dissertation directed by Wecter. Friedrich Schönemann's *Mark Twain als literarische Persönlichkeit* (Jena, 1925) was the first monograph published on Twain's analogues and literary debts. Though occasionally his findings are farfetched, he did useful pioneer work in calling attention to Twain's reactions to writers such as Swift, Goldsmith, Scott, Carlyle *(The French Revolution),* and Lecky. Those who do not read German readily will find useful the generous summary in E. H. Hemminghaus' *Mark Twain in Germany* (1939). O. H. Moore's stimulating study "Mark Twain and *Don Quixote*" will be discussed in the section devoted to the criticism of *Huckleberry Finn.* Minnie M. Brashear's *Mark Twain: Son of Missouri* (1934) combined much sympathetically presented cultural data on Hannibal and very important matter on Twain's debt to eighteenth-century writers such as Swift, Smollett, Goldsmith, Voltaire, and especially Thomas Paine. Her work is noteworthy in counterbalancing others' emphasis on the frontier.

Correcting De Voto's statement that John Phoenix (G. H. Derby) "suggested nothing whatever to Mark Twain," Gladys C. Bellamy proves conclusively in "Mark Twain's Indebtedness to John Phoenix" (*AL,* 1941) his indebtedness for five items, including the Whittier birthday speech. D. M. McKeithan, "Mark Twain's Letters of Thomas Jefferson Snodgrass" (*PQ,* 1953), shows these letters "probably owe more to W. T. Thompson's *Major Jones's Sketches of Travel* (1847) than to any single item." R. H. Wilson's "Malory in the *Connecticut Yankee,*" has been well studied in the University of Texas *SE* (June, 1948).

G. A. Cardwell's admirable *Twins of Genius* (1953) prints the interchange of letters between Twain and Cable—eighteen by Twain and twenty by Cable—from 1881 to 1906, and centers attention on their four months' lecture tour in 1884-85. Cardwell shows that Cable, whose *Dr. Sevier* had just been published and whose article defending Negro rights appeared during the tour, often received more newspaper praise than Twain did, and that earlier when writing *Huckleberry Finn* Twain had a very high opinion of Cable's liberal Southern views. Hence Cardwell suggests that if *Huck* excels Twain's earlier work in its insight into the Southern code and traditional way of life, this enrichment may have come from the general spirit of Cable. For "Cable was the only prominent southern writer of the time who had effected a fusion at all similar, the only one of Twain's friends who could easily have helped Twain to precipitate and order his ideas about the South."

B. A. Booth, "Mark Twain's Comments on Holmes's *Autocrat*" (*AL* 1950), concludes that it is "by no means impossible that a growing admiration for the Autocrat's urbane high comedy and for his infinite subtlety had its effect on Mark Twain's development." Twain always spoke of Holmes with "mingled reverence and affection"; both were in revolt against Calvinism, and both wrote of Jonathan Edwards as "insane." Ferguson thinks that as early as 1861 in the Snodgrass letters Brown's "source" is "obviously the young fellow John in *The Autocrat*."

E. H. Hemminghaus' "Mark Twain's German Provenience" (*MLQ*, 1954) "is not intended . . . to trace the influence of German writers upon Mark Twain," but only to determine the "extent of his reading and acquaintanceship with German writers."

The problem of Mark Twain's indebtedness to folklore may be studied in Constance Rourke's *American Humor* (1931; in the light of Walter Blair's very critical review in *AL*, 1932), in B. J. Whiting's "Guyuscutus, Royal Nonesuch and other Hoaxes" (*Southern Folklore Quart.*, 1944), and in V. R. West's monograph *Folklore in the Works of Mark Twain* (1930). One of the points at issue is precisely where folk-creations or legends stop and Mark Twain's artistic individualizing begins, as well as what is meant by "mythical elements."

A host of studies of individual influences can be located by consulting Lewis Leary's *Articles on American Literature, 1900-1950,* under Bellamy (Phoenix), Mrs. Field (Harte), Hemminghaus, Howe (Harte), Hoben, Laverty (Jane Taylor's influence on *The Mysterious Stranger*), Leisy, Long (Sut Lovingood), Lorch (many very able studies), McKeithan (Jules Verne), Mason, Moore, Mott, Orians, Roades (Cervantes and the *Yankee*), Schönemann (Adolph Wilbrandt), Stewart (Harte), Waggoner (scientists), Weatherly, Wecter, West (folklore), Wilson (Malory), Woodbridge (*Gesta Romanorum*), and H. G. Baetzhold's "Mark Twain's Prince and the Pauper" (*N&Q,* 1954) which shows that *The Prince* was suggested *not* by Charlotte Yonge's *Prince and the Page* but by her *Little Duke* (this study is derived from an able dissertation on "Mark Twain's Attitudes toward England.") F. A. G. Cowper thinks *The Mysterious Stranger* was indebted to Voltaire's *Zadig* and that it has some parallels to Goethe's *Faust;* Cowper's study is included in a volume *In Honor of . . . C. F. Johnson* (1928).

2. *Religious-Ethical Ideas*

There seems to be in print no full-length book on Mark Twain's religious-ethical ideas which gives proportionate and comprehensive representation of all their ingredients. V. W. Brooks doubtless overemphasized the effects of the Calvinism of his mother and his native environment, but even in Twain's later determinism Wagenknecht sees a kind of "inverted" Calvinistic predestination. In other words, Calvinism may have channelized his thinking and suggested the kind of questions he wanted answered, such as those of the responsibility for evil of "Our Father," the degree of man's personal responsibility, etc. Miss Brashear rightly emphasizes his early reading of Thomas Paine, spokesman of scientific and belligerent deism and anti-feudal republicanism, along with his reading of other eighteenth-century writers such as Hume and Voltaire. A. E. Jones in "Mark Twain and Freemasonry" (*AL,* 1954) states that in Twain's works there are more than a hundred allusions to Freemasonry, and quotes passages from Twain and from Albert Pike's authoritative work on Freemasonry indicating that the two men agreed that creeds are of human origin, that their diversity is to be explained merely by environmental differences, and that the "great unvarying laws" of nature should make man humble. Kenneth Andrews *(Nook Farm)* thinks Twain's revolt against his native Calvinism was surely aided during the Hartford years by the pervasive teachings of Horace Bushnell, which emphasized a natural goodness that is reflected in Colonel Sellers, Huck, Jim, etc. But this meliorism may have eventually seemed to Twain not to square with the facts of life. Thomas Paine may have influenced his hostility toward a politically established church and his strong anti-mediaevalism.

One of the best over-all analyses is that by Gladys C. Bellamy in *Mark Twain As a Literary Artist* (1950), in which she distinguishes four "bases" of his mind—moralism, involving free-willed responsibility; determinism; pessimism; and what she calls "patheticism," or a peculiar sympathy with individuals. She emphasizes the logical inconsistency of moralism and determinism. Whether Twain's theory of determinism was temperamental or logical, in actual practice he increasingly excoriated public figures he thought had done wrong; yet he wrote Twichell in 1904, "I wish I could learn to remember that it is unjust and dishonorable to put blame upon the human race for any of its acts." Miss Bellamy also develops the view that far from being a complete realist, he had a large residue of romantic ideals and illusions by which he measured realities. The confusion, she thinks, was one main cause of his pessimism. Paul Carus provides a documented description of "Mark Twain's Philosophy" in terms of determinism (*Monist,* 1913), but concludes that determinism alone could logically lead to optimism as well as to pessimism. De Voto, as we have seen, argued that determinism was used to evade the blame he heaped upon himself for the disasters which befell his family.

To treat comprehensively Twain's religious-ethical ideas, one ought to piece together in a proportionate way such ingredients and influences as his mother's Calvinism, eighteenth-century deism (of Paine, Voltaire, etc.), Freemasonry, Bushnellian immanence and meliorism, nineteenth-century evolutionism, determinism, his unstable compound of reason and feeling, his studies of the politically established church of the Middle Ages, and his combination of romantic illusions and humanitarianism and an unblinking observation of sordid realities and human cruelties, especially as presented by the era's newspapers. "When I read in the papers all about the rascalities and outrages going on I realize what a creature the human animal is" (Paine, 1336).

Although by no means exhaustive, H. H. Waggoner's "Science in the Thought of Mark Twain" (*AL,* 1937) is useful as an introduction to this important subject. Twain's references to the nineteenth-century scientists Darwin, Huxley, Haeckel, N. S. Shaler, and their followers such as A. D. White, Lecky, etc., are related to his use of geology to reinforce his growing belief in man's insignificance; to his theory that man is completely determined by heredity and environment, which constitute a "nature" that is "profoundly vicious, treacherous, and malignant"; and to his belief that human beings do not differ markedly from animals. The emphasis is on pessimism, and the optimistic implications of science are slighted—in fact *A Connecticut Yankee* is not even mentioned.

R. T. Oliver's "Mark Twain and Religion" (*Christian Leader,* 17 Feb. 1940), briefly emphasizes Twain's belief in religious freedom and a diversity of sects; his view that wars and their deadliness have increased during Christian ages; his view that the missionary movement was in part financially motivated; his acceptance of the beneficial results of mental healing through Christian Science which he condemned only for "what he considered to be the church's greed for money, and its failure to support any charities"; and his conclusion in *A Connecticut Yankee* that "even the great majority" of Catholic priests who were "on the ground among the common people, . . . were sincere and right hearted, and devoted to the alleviation of human troubles and sufferings."

F. C. Flowers, "Mark Twain's Theories of Morality" (*Mark Twain Quart.,* 1948), draws on a Louisiana State University dissertation which develops the unconventional argument that *What is Man?* (in which Twain urged us to "train your ideals upward . . . to confer benefits on your neighbor and the community") is not essentially an exposition of pessimism but of morality. Flowers tries to correlate this interpretation with the outspoken reformism in Twain's later writings on the exploitation of minority groups such as the Congo natives, Filipinos, Jews, and Negroes. This is a stimulating and original view. But a full-length, carefully balanced book on Mark Twain's religious-ethical ideas, genetically considered, is much needed.

3. *Political and Social Attitudes*

On this topic there is no comprehensive study in print. The broad outlines may be found in Wagenknecht's *Mark Twain,* and most of the other recent books include relevant sections. Miss Bellamy, under reform and humanitarianism, has much that is of great value. Miss Brashear does well in emphasizing Twain's kinship with the French revolutionary democracy of Thomas Paine's *Rights of Man* and the anti-traditional Enlightenment. The studies mentioned have made it clear that from the early days Mark Twain was a good deal of a moralist and humanitarian who used some of his humor for the satiric correction of political corruption. His chapters of *The Gilded Age* in part grew out of his experience as secretary to a Western senator in Washington and his alert observations there of the actual workings of the democratic process. Brooks charged that he did not dare satirize actual individuals and abuses, but A. L. Vogelback in "Mark Twain and the Tammany Ring" (*PMLA,* 1955) discovered his "Revised Catechism" in the New York

Tribune for 27 September 1871, which named names and by its deadly satire in a Biblical frame helped to bring members of the ring to justice. W. F. Taylor's chapter on Mark Twain in *The Economic Novel in America* (1942) is judicious in treating *The Gilded Age* as exposing the "forms of business and political piracy." He shows how, even if Twain slighted problems raised by the machine and industrialism, *A Connecticut Yankee* united praise of the machine with a Paine-like passion for social justice. (Twain's unpublished essay, "Knights of Labor," defended labor's right to organize.) Taylor concludes:

> As a business man [see S. C. Webster's *Mark Twain, Business Man,* 1946, on his printing business], he joined his contemporaries in glorifying the machine, fascinated with the possibilities of exploiting it and of controlling nature through it. As a satirist, he joined his contemporaries in attacking, never the machine itself, but certain economic abuses, such as speculation, which the machine, with its enormous release of energy, had made more dangerous. And as a pioneer democrat, inheritor of American liberalism, he joined his contemporaries in insisting on a wide diffusion of material comforts, and on the protection of the average man from economic, no less than from political or religious, tyranny . . . Within him, satirist, capitalist, and democrat worked toward the same object—that of enjoying the uses of the machine, and lessening the abuses.

Yet of course the typesetting machine bankrupted him and contributed to his pessimistic conviction that the later epoch was unique in rotting character by its wholesale greed. More might be fruitfully done, perhaps, in the way of investigating the precise extent to which Twain's frontier did in his case actually inspire in theory *and* practice the democratic ideas F. J. Turner attributes to the frontier in general.

John Gerber ("Mark Twain's 'Private Campaign'," *Civil War Hist.,* March 1955) throws light on Mark Twain's apparent indifference toward the war, as does F. W. Lorch's "Mark Twain and the 'Campaign that Failed' " (*AL,* 1941). G. H. Orians'

"Walter Scott, Mark Twain, and the Civil War" (*SAQ,* 1941) also illuminates his attitude while showing that he characteristically exaggerated Scott's vogue and influence in bringing on the war. D. M. McKeithan provides "More about Mark Twain's War with the English Critics" (*MLN,* 1948).

V. L. Parrington's essay on Mark Twain in *Main Currents in American Thought* is brilliant and spirited but one-sided. To him Twain represents "everything European fallen away," yet Parrington emphasizes his passionate democracy as "a product of the [European or French revolutionary] Enlightenment as it passed into the psychology of western Americans," retaining "the militant idealism of Jeffersonian times" and the "nature philosophy." Parrington skillfully connects *The Prince and the Pauper,* the "picaresque" *Huck,* the *Connecticut Yankee,* and *Joan of Arc* in their common attack on evil as bred by throne and altar, irrationality, and a credulous conformity to "unrighteous customs and laws of caste." Mark Twain taught that "the one sacred duty laid on every rational being is the duty of rebellion against sham," especially as seen in the revival of mediaevalism and caste and superstition by writers such as Walter Scott. Parrington thus makes Mark Twain's main period flamingly positive and constructive and humanitarian. He proceeds genetically, dividing Twain's development into six "definite stages" from a frontier "swaggering gayety" to the final disillusion of an "idealist who realizes how greatly he has been cheated by his dreams" as he concludes that mankind is not altruistic but rapacious in the midst of "the mad plan of a bleak mechanical universe." Parrington recognizes that Twain "inherited" the "technique" of a whole succession of frontier humorists who aided him as he "recreated some of the earlier types, translating Colonel Simon Suggs into Colonel Sellers, and Ransy Sniffle into Huck Finn." Such an approach, appealing as it is, needs to be balanced by the considerable evidence of occasional pro-British leanings and revulsion against some of the excesses of democracy, especially as assembled by A. L. Scott and Howard Baetzhold.

Turning from America to his view of Europe (the two aspects

of political and social attitudes which must be kept in mind), the best brief published study is A. L. Scott's "Mark Twain Looks at Europe" (*SAQ,* 1953), based on his University of Michigan dissertation, "Mark Twain as a Critic of Europe." (Robert Gilkey's dissertation, "Mark Twain voyageur et son image de L'Europe," Paris, 1951, was not available for discussion at the time this was written.) After pointing out that *The Innocents Abroad* praises some things in Europe (such as architectural wonders) and is not entirely vulgar condemnation, Scott proceeds in terms of four decades. In the seventies, after his genteel marriage, his views, culminating in *A Tramp Abroad* (1880) become more Irving-like, mellow and tolerant except as regards the French. In the eighties "extreme nationalism" inspired *Life on the Mississippi* (cf. the attack on Walter Scott, Ch. xlvi) and *A Connecticut Yankee,* partly because of Twain's wrath at Arnold's condescending censure, to which he replied by attacks on monarchy, hereditary aristocracy, and a politically established church. In the nineties, when Twain again lived abroad, his republican principles "waned, and his liking for aristocracy rose," although he attacked Czarist Russia, French Paul Bourget, and the persecutors of Joan of Arc. In *The American Claimant* (1892) and *Tom Sawyer Abroad* (1894) he regards England as "the most important country in the world," and though he attacked Rhodes, *Following the Equator* shows admiration for England's far-flung imperialism. In the 1900's he ceased to defend British imperialism, attacked Russia and Belgian colonization, but forebore attacking England because of her importance in world politics. Scott thinks that Mark Twain's "ultimate conclusion was that to worship rank and distinction was the valued and rightful privilege of all the human race," and that "thus died his republican ideals."

Paul Carter, drawing on an unpublished University of Cincinnati dissertation on "Mark Twain's Political and Social Ideas," analyzes briefly "The Influence of W. D. Howells upon Mark Twain's Social Satire" (Univ. of Colorado *Studies,* 1953). He does well in showing that far from being the stultifying influence Brooks imagined, Howells as a political liberal ardently encouraged satire in *The Prince and the Pauper* and *A Connecticut Yankee,* and urged Twain on to more slashing attacks on imperialism. Gibson in "Mark Twain and Howells: Anti-Imperialists" (*NEQ,* 1947) draws on his dissertation in reviewing the years 1898-1902, from the Boer War to General Funston's capture of Aguinaldo. While Howells wrote against imperialism "more steadily," Twain did so with "more fire." Because the general public was mainly for imperialism, Twain courted popular displeasure and loss of sales by his position. See also Paul Carter's brief "Mark Twain and War" (*Twainian,* 1942). A. L. Scott's "Mark Twain: Critic of Conquest" (*Dalhousie Rev.,* Spring 1955) cites the constant reprintings of his work as a refutation of current Russian charges that the United States is trying to silence voices opposing imperialism. Scott tries to illustrate briefly his thesis that "In China and Cuba, in Hawaii and the Congo, everywhere Mark Twain demanded that the little man be given a square deal . . . Mark Twain has done more than any other writer towards making the concept of liberty a part of the American heritage." F. R. Leavis in "The Americanness of American Literature" (*Commentary,* 1952) protests against the idea of Mark Twain as divorced from the European tradition and as merely a "frontier story-teller"; conversely, Leavis argues that only a "mature, subtle, and sophisticated" intellect could produce *Huck* and *Pudd'nhead Wilson,* and he thinks that the central theme of *Huck* is "the complexity of ethical evaluation in any society that has a complex tradition." Mark Twain, while indebted to the frontier, has "kept a vigorous hold on [his] heritage of civilization."

Earl Hilton, "Mark Twain's Theory of History" (*Papers Michigan Acad. of Science, Arts, and Letters,* 1951, pub. 1952), has done well in opening up a very important subject which merits further study. He argues that Twain "did not hold the evolutionary view of history" but "inherited the historical theory of the reformers of the late eighteenth-century Enlightenment." Hence his censure of the medieval church and feudalism, as opposed to his idea of progress and rationalism. This study is original in arguing (though the evidence is tenuous) that after the pessimism of 1901 he showed "a gradual recovery of spirits, and with it an attempt to construct a relatively endurable world on new principles," turning from a malignant nature to "the cumulative human experience crystallized in institutions . . ." This is a stimulating study, influenced by Carl Becker and Lovejoy. But more evidence and counterevidence are needed.

A few other relevant studies will be cited under the heading of individual works such as *A Connecticut Yankee*. Kenneth Andrews' *Nook Farm* contains much that illuminates Twain's political and social views in relation to those of his Hartford friends and to his turn from the Republican Party in 1884 when he came out for Cleveland. Howells said that while Mark Twain eventually "justified the labor unions as the sole present help of the weak against the strong," it was impossible to convert him to socialism.

4. *Literary-Aesthetic Ideas*

Recent scholarship has made it emphatically clear that, despite his lack of formal education, Mark Twain was a reasonably well read and highly calculating self-conscious literary artist, devoted to craftsmanship. "To me," he said, "the most important feature of my life is its literary feature." As in the case of Whitman, Twain's proper recognition was retarded by the failure of many critics to understand what he aimed at in his craft and by inept attempts to measure him by standards from which he revolted. In addition to a multitude of passages in his several volumes of letters and *Autobiography* and episodes sandwiched into his fiction (such as the satire on the "sensation" novel in *Roughing It*), his literary commentary includes such essays as "How to Tell a Story," "Harriet Shelley," "Is Shakespeare Dead?" etc. It will be remembered that his piloting developed peculiar powers of precise observation and memory, making him impatient with the vagueness of Scott and

Cooper. And his pragmatic oral testing of his stories on actual live audiences night after night on his tours, watching the faces of his listeners and revising repeatedly, resulted in a "natural" style which modern writers such as Hemingway have admired.

Three useful articles have been devoted to Mark Twain's literary theory since Brander Matthews' "Mark Twain and the Art of Writing" (*Harper's,* Oct. 1920). S. B. Liljegren in "The Revolt against Romanticism in American Literature as Evidenced in the Work of S. L. Clemens" (*Studia Neophilologica,* 1945) surveyed Twain's attacks on Scott and Cooper, and his satires on the earlier terror novel and ballads such as "Peter Bell" and "The Wreck of the Hesperus." (On this matter of romanticism and realism, consult Miss Bellamy, and the index in *Transitions in American Literary History* ed. H. H. Clark, 1953.)

G. W. Feinstein draws on his University of Iowa dissertation for a brief but able discussion of "Mark Twain's Idea of Story Structure" (*AL,* 1946) emphasizing the spontaneous flow of narrative, organicism, departure from the three unities, the art of the paragraph and the sentence, the illuminating incident, and the idea of form as the externalization of the writer's own individualized thinking. E. H. Goold's "Mark Twain on the Writing of Fiction" (*AL,* 1954) surveys such topics as his dependence on experience and observation; factuality and probability; authentic characterization; realistic dialogue; his allegedly weak plot construction; his idea that situation and incident should develop organically from the over-all plot and contribute to the logical development; his idea that there can be no complete originality; his idea of propriety. "He practiced and advocated the decorous Mid-Victorian realism of a Howells or a Thackeray rather than the stronger, naturalistic variety of Thomas Hardy or George Moore."

Drawing on his University of California doctoral dissertation on "Mark Twain's Novels: Principles and Practice of Realism," R. A. Wiggins in "Mark Twain and the Drama" (*AL,* 1953) supersedes earlier studies of this topic by Brander Matthews and Rodman Gilder. Wiggins effectively indicates Twain's considerable indebtedness to the drama in his lavish use of dialogue (about 80 per cent in his best books), "his structural emphasis upon scene," settings which often read like stage directions, attention to costuming, dramatic scenes, and the use of the "visual-kinetic style" in rendering certain episodes. He claims that Twain seldom rendered a character "in the round," but emphasized one dramatic trait.

A brief summary of Mark Twain's literary and critical views will be found in H. H. Clark's "The Influence of Science on American Literary Criticism, 1860-1910, Including the Vogue of Taine," in *Trans. of the Wisconsin Acad.* (1955).

5. *Language and the Vernacular*

Most of the critics of Mark Twain have noted the distinctively oral quality of his style. He told Howells, "I amend dialect stuff by talking and talking and talking it till it sounds right" (Ferguson, p. 175). "You write as a man *talks*," he advised an amateur in 1884, "and very few can reach that height of excellence." See also Mark Twain's "Concerning the American Language" (1882).

The chief studies of Twain's language are the following: R. L. Ramsay and F. G. Emberson, "A Mark Twain Lexicon" (Univ. of Missouri *Studies,* 1938); F. G. Emberson, "Mark Twain's Vocabulary: A General Survey" (Univ. of Missouri *Studies,* 1935); Katherine Buxbaum, "Mark Twain and American Dialect" (*American Speech,* 1927); C. J. Lowell, "The Background of Mark Twain's Vocabulary" (ibid., 1947); J. N. Tidwell, "Mark Twain's Representation of Negro Speech" (ibid., 1942), which concludes: "Mark Twain was both sincere and competent in his representation of the dialect of Nigger Jim. He revealed the salient low colloquial, Southern, and negro features of Jim's speech, not by a thoroughly 'consistent' spelling of every word, but by what is better, an accurate one." H. L. Mencken (*American Language,* 1930) says Mark Twain "deliberately engrafted" the American West's "greater liberty and more fluent idiom upon the stem of English, and so lent the dignity of his high achievement to a dialect that was as unmistakably American as the point of view underlying it." Thus he added great range and variety to "Boston" or "Oxford" English, a fact which enabled him to give sharp individuality to his fictional characters.

6. *General Critiques*

E. M. Branch, *The Literary Apprenticeship of Mark Twain* (1950), makes the most detailed analysis we have, chronologically arranged, of Twain's writings up to 1867 *(Innocents Abroad).* In addition, his book includes an incisive analysis of the thematic structure of *Huckleberry Finn* intended to prove that Twain's thinking was essentially continuous from his Nevada and California journalism to his later moralism, reformism, and pessimism. "The difference between Mark Twain's social and philosophic thinking in 1866 and in 1900 is a difference not in values and sympathies but in experience and insight." Refuting De Voto's argument that Washoe matured Mark Twain, Branch concludes:

> a farce, caricature, and banter replaced his earlier fumbling attempts to portray authentic, humorous character. Verbal trickery was preferred to the free flowing, colloquial language he knew so well. It is truer to say that much of what he learned in Washoe went into his mature work—often to its detriment—and that its very presence was often a mark of literary immaturity. When he left Nevada, Mark Twain was a far more practiced writer than he had been before, but too much of his practice had been along harmful lines.

Thus Hans Gottschalk (*JEGP,* 1952) finds Branch's book "scholarly, sound, but critically vague in that it does not really show how the apprentice became the writer." Like Gottschalk, DeLancey Ferguson praises Branch's analysis of *Huckleberry Finn* (*AL,* Nov. 1950), although he finds Branch repeats several common errors in using "biographical source material." Branch is interesting in showing how parts of Chapters viii, xi, and xiii of *Roughing It* come out of Mark Twain's writings of 1863, while (as Blair notes) other parts are revisions of some Sandwich Island letters and newspaper rehearsals. His interpretation of *Huckleberry Finn* will be treated later in connection with that book. Branch's work is supported by thirty-one pages of refreshingly precise notes.

Gladys C. Bellamy's *Mark Twain as a Literary Artist* (1950) has been highly praised by most scholars, and G. F. Whicher (*New York Times,* 13 Aug. 1950) says she "has set the appropriate keystone on the arch of Mark Twain criticism." Her two major contributions (after balanced analysis of Brooks and De Voto) are, first, her demonstration that Mark Twain was a conscious literary craftsman and painstaking artist; and second, her analysis of the conflict in his mind between freewilled and responsible moralism and a paralyzing determinism. The first is supported with "convincing proof," according to Walter Blair in his review (*AL,* Jan. 1951), but he thinks that the second may overemphasize Twain's admittedly weak philosophical thought at the expense of more literary criteria. Some may "feel that she has been so preoccupied with the thought in the works that she has not satisfactorily considered their form" in terms of the individual books' structure as a whole. He also suggests the need for more attention to ideas of craftsmanship in the essay on Cooper, to comments on humor in unpublished notebooks, to his early literary backgrounds and audiences, and to the revisions of earlier work which went into *Innocents Abroad* and *Roughing It.* In her aesthetic appraisal (which Blair does not think wholly convincing) she finds that "the ultimate significance of the work depends upon the quality of the [author's] conception." When this is harmonious and he achieves "detachment" he does his best work. Detachment, she thinks, is achieved by at least one of four devices: sympathetic identification with his characters such as Huck; settings remote in time or place; diminishing humanity also by remoteness in time or place; and portraying life as a dream, as in *The Mysterious*

Stranger. Whatever one may think of the schematization and aesthetic appraisal, her two special contributions are masterful in closely reasoned interpretation of fully assembled evidence, and no brief comment can suggest the richness of detail and insight in this even-tempered yet freshly vigorous book. Some of Miss Bellamy's comments on particular problems will be cited later.

As the work of one of our most experienced modern critics, H. S. Canby's *Turn West, Turn East* (1951), comparing and contrasting Mark Twain and Henry James in such a way as to throw the distinctive work of each into sharp relief, is one of the most readable and thought-provoking of current critiques. Canby thinks that both authors centered on independence and freedom, and that both "will live in literature by best describing what each called American innocence." Emphasizing the creation of personality, Canby thinks that Twain was far superior to James in the portraiture of characters (such as Colonel Sellers and Huck) and that he wrote "better English than Henry James," partly because he had "one of the most sensitive ears among craftsmen in language" and "great art is essentially oral." Canby has much to say about the reasons for Mark Twain's later "shift from a confident optimism to bitter cynicism," especially his increasing sensitiveness to suffering and inhumanity. While Canby emphasizes the river and Twain's environment, he also says that Twain owed something to his reading. He points out that "Mark Twain's best books are all accounts of a picaro," that Twain "devoured" picaresque stories in his pilot days, and that Colonel Sellers has a connection with *Don Quixote.* Unlike De Voto, Canby finds *Joan of Arc* "magnificent," coming after the brash *Yankee* whose ideal he compares to the "mechanical ideology" and "gadget state" of the Soviet dictatorship. Canby includes a précis of late "letters from Satan" violently attacking suppression and hypocrisy which W. M. Gibson, in his review, calls "perhaps the most important unpublished Clemens manuscript" (*AL,* 1952). Unlike Trilling and T. S. Eliot, however, Canby thinks Twain "ought to have been shot" for the conclusion of *Huckleberry Finn,* great as he thinks the book is as a whole.

Three comprehensive essays on Mark Twain in histories of fiction deserve mention. (Van Doren's in *The American Novel* is now somewhat out of date.) Alexander Cowie in *The Rise of the American Novel* (1948) devotes more than fifty pages to Mark Twain, supporting his careful concern with all sides of given issues by more than two hundred precise notes. In addition to analyses of the major books, Cowie has excellent summaries of Twain's opinions concerning political-social, religious-ethical, and literary questions. Cowie's critical judgments are rich in insight and his writing is spirited and readable. He is good at such phrases as Huck's helping readers escape "the pangs of adulthood." Edward Wagenknecht's *Cavalcade of the American Novel* (1952) devotes seventeen pages to Mark Twain, with notes which also cite recent scholarship effectively. As in his biography of Mark Twain, he follows De Voto's thesis, asserting that Twain "was that [Midwestern] frontier in literature . . . The whole thing [frontier thesis] hangs together beautifully; the picture is one, not many." And he adds that "Mark Twain inherited and fulfilled a tradition; he did not establish one." Wagenknecht is fair, however, in citing studies such as those by Olin Moore, Miss Bellamy, and Edgar Branch dealing with literary influence. He writes with much insight, with pleasing assurance, and often with eloquent sympathy both for the "fiction out of Hannibal" and the later crusading books of "History and Legend." A. H. Quinn has a shorter chapter on "Mark Twain and the Romance of Youth" in his *American Fiction* (1936). While "Huck is a picaresque vagabond," he is dismissed in about half a page. But Quinn has some thoughtful things to say of romantic elements in *The Prince and the Pauper* and *Joan of Arc,* although he is quite unsympathetic toward *The Connecticut Yankee,* disparaging the humor and finding "no veracity . . . in the abuses the Yankee seeks to rectify." These three authoritative histories of our fiction have, of course the advantage of placing Mark Twain in relation to what is before and after him in this genre.

Among the histories of American literature, space permits characterization of only three, Parrington having been cited elsewhere. The essay in *CHAL* (1921) was by S. P. Sherman. Although he feared that critics have been persuaded to take Twain's books too seriously, Sherman did regard Mark Twain as "one of our great representative men." His conclusion is especially suggestive: "Mark Twain counts as an influence because he is an innovator. The great notes of his innovation from *Innocents Abroad* to *A Connecticut Yankee* are: first, the disillusioned treatment of history; second, the fearless exploitation of 'the natural man,' or the next thing to it, 'the free-born American'; and, lastly, a certain strain of naturalistic pessimism." It should be noted that this is quite a different essay from the one Sherman did in his book *On Contemporary Literature* (1917), which is more outspoken in deploring Twain's anti-traditionalism, especially in *Innocents Abroad.* As he sees it, Twain's humor is "burly, not fine; broad, not profound," lacking the "historical depth" and the "prophetic" quality respectively of Carlyle and Whitman. Sherman thinks that Mark Twain was the spokesman of the democracy of the "divine average."

Dixon Wecter's twenty-two page essay in *LHUS* (1948) draws on his knowledge of the Mark Twain papers, of which he was custodian. Wecter notes the cruelties and evils Twain saw in his boyhood and chronicled in *Huckleberry Finn,* but concludes that "on the whole happiness outweighed grief." Especially instructive for those who struggle to bring unity out of Mark Twain's work is Wecter's finding contradiction or "dualism which self-observation would have shown running like a paradox through his nature: gullible and skeptical by turns; realistic and sentimental, a satirist who gave hostages to the established order, a frontiersman who bowed his neck obediently to Victorian mores [and visited Europe about twenty-five times], and an idealist who loved the trappings of pomp and wealth. Incessantly he contradicted himself on a variety of subjects. His was not a single-track mind, but a whole switchyard." Unlike some recent interpreters of *Innocents Abroad,* Wecter sees it as helping "to belittle our romantic allegiance to Europe, feeding our emergent nationalism." His unrivaled investigations of Twain's early years convinced Wecter that "fear of sex . . . seems to lie at the root of Mark Twain's nature . . . leaving woman not an object of desire but of reverential chivalry." Wecter thinks that one can "overstress" the "analogues" with Cervantes, but (like Miss Brashear) he finds that Twain "read widely if desultorily, and perfected his early journalistic manner until it became one of the great styles of American letters—easy, incisive, sensitive to nuances of dialect, rich in the resources of comedy, satire, irony, and corrosive anger." He lists his use of some nine types (or literary devices) which frontiersmen favored. He emphasizes the "distinctly artificial romanticism" of *The Prince, A Connecticut Yankee,* and *Joan,* but agrees that they also show "the iconoclast's itch to shatter that world of sham and injustice." After surveying the later pessimist, he ends with the reflection that on the whole Mark Twain finally "seemed a kind of ghost from America's buried life, recalling the nostalgia of her youth." This essay is on the whole one of the very best informed and illuminating essays we have.

Clarence Gohdes' essay in *LAP* (1951) is entitled "Mirth for the Million" and reflects some condescension not often found in Gohdes' other distinguished work. Mark Twain was "almost wholly indifferent to form," and the modern "critical attention" given work such as *Huckleberry Finn* is partly the result of "certain adventitious factors." One of these is the "cynicism which followed the First World War" which "bore Mark Twain to a lofty position among the intellectuals" and which led interpreters such as V. W. Brooks to exploit him as an illustration of "frustration." (Gohdes himself says, "As a thinker, Mark Twain is too inconsistent and too shallow to be of much importance . . .") Another factor is described as "the boom in the efforts to interpret American culture as the peculiar product of the 'frontier' " as associated with F. J. Turner and his disciples (such as De Voto?). The sale of more than two million copies of *Tom Sawyer* is "proof of its long-enduring power to delight children and at times their parents also." Gohdes does recognize that Colonel Sellers is "hilariously amusing," and that *Life on the Mississippi* has "matchless description." Although *Huck* is "sloppy in construction" in general, "putting the whole tale in the mouth" of the boy did help to increase the humor and reality and "illusion of unity." And he acknowledges briefly Mark Twain's great vogue in England, Germany, and Russia. Gohdes' suggestions about the two factors or "ideological movements" which "have served to attach to Clemens a greater intellectual significance than his contemporaries ever imagined" are stimulating but require scholarly testing.

7. *Studies of Huckleberry Finn*

DeLancey Ferguson's "Huck Finn Aborning" (*Colophon,* 1938) and his biography find that out of over 900 changes in the manuscript now at the Buffalo Public Library—changes which show how self-conscious Mark Twain's craftsmanship was—only about thirty were made by his wife. De Voto in *Mark Twain at Work* (1942) thinks this is quite a number, and he points out that only three quarters of the manuscript is available and hence there may have been other changes. Howells also read the proof sheets, much to Mark Twain's satisfaction. Arthur Scott (*AL,* 1955) has shown that Gilder published four parts (about a fourth of the whole) in the *Century,* making considerable alterations with the author's hearty approval. The book was published in England prior to the American edition. Jacob Blanck, "In Re Huck Finn" (*New Colophon,* 1950), has provided other bibliographical details. In his valuable account of "The Publication and Reception of *Huckleberry Finn*" (*AL,* 1939), A. L. Vogelback finds that it was reviewed immediately only in the *Century* (May 1885, by T. S. Perry favorably), but there was a good deal of sporadic newspaper comment about the book's being "vulgar," "coarse," and "inelegant," comment reflecting the genteel tradition. The publicity given the book by its being banned by the Concord Library and by Twain's reading from it on his lecture tours helped to sell about 40,000 copies within a few months of publication. Howells praised it only privately, but Joel Chandler Harris defended it as "wholesome" in the *Critic* (Nov. 1885) and wrote Twain that he regarded it as "the most original contribution that has yet been made to American literature."

Like most multifaceted masterpieces, *Huckleberry Finn* can profitably be viewed from many different angles. Wecter and others have illustrated the way in which, in some of the more memorable scenes and characters, Mark Twain drew on his memories of Hannibal and his boyhood. Kenneth Andrews *(Nook Farm)* and others have argued that the book owed much to Twain's "equilibrium in the middle eighties"; he was happy in his family life and successful as the author of *The Prince and the Pauper* (1882), and his leisurely revisiting of familiar haunts to finish *Life on the Mississippi* (1883) had tempered his detachment with a mellow nostalgia associated with scenes of his boyhood.

Those interested in the maintenance of a unified point of view have followed Henry James's friend, T. S. Perry, in his praise of the "autobiographical form." Every scene is "given, not described . . . What is inimitable, however, is the reflection of the whole series of adventures in the mind of the . . . hero," the fourteen-year-old boy who provides the tone and limits of the story, as well as the language and the rich illusion of reality. W. V. O'Connor (*CE,* 1955), in a stimulating article summarizing all the weaknesses of *Huck,* points out some exceptions in Chapters xvii and xviii. Some of the points which Walter Blair makes about *Tom Sawyer* involving a satiric reversal of the currently conventional boys' books might be made with reference to *Huck*. T. S. Eliot, in his introduction of 1950, praises the point of view but goes on to insist that Huck is "passive," in "subjection" to the river, and that he merely "sees the real world; and he does not judge it . . ." (Does such a statement overlook such passages as Huck's expression of a freewilled responsibility "to decide, forever, betwixt two things," and his saying the King and Duke in trying to rob Mary Jane made him "ashamed" of the human race?)

Then there is the question of joyousness versus evil in *Huck*. Critics such as Canby and Cowie feel that "delight" and an appealing escape "from the pangs of adulthood" predominate, following T. S. Perry, who stressed a "total absence of morbidness." But V. W. Brooks thinks the "moral" of the book is "that all civilization is inevitably a hateful error, something that stands in the way of life and thwarts it as the civilization of the Gilded Age had thwarted Mark Twain." This is repeated in Brooks's *Indian Summer*. J. M. Cox's study of Huck's "Sad Initiation" will be taken up shortly in another connection, but it emphasizes "two images, rebirth and death." And Philip Young in his book on Hemingway, with whom he constantly associates Mark Twain, claims that with the exception of the beginning and the end "every major episode in the novel ends in violence, in physical brutality, and usually in death," mentioning thirteen corpses. To Young, Huck "is really about as far from the carefree, laughing urchin he is almost universally taken to be as it is possible to get." Huck, followed by Nick Adams, illustrates "the Fall of Man, the loss of Paradise"; Huck's is the universal "story of innocence leaving its home and coming up against things which are not innocent." V. S. Pritchett in the *New Statesman and Nation* for 2 August 1941 has also stressed the theme of "cruelty," citing some eight instances. On the whole, however, it would seem that this emphasis on evil and death does not take into account the perspective of the book as a whole and Huck's boyish ability to see both good and evil and accept them, as emphasized by Kenneth Andrews in *Nook Farm*. Huck "cried a little" when Buck was shot in the feud, but as Andrews says, he "takes rascality for granted" and continues on his journey essentially "unaffected by the violence he sees." De Voto (*Mark Twain at Work,* 1942) recognizes the evils

Huck encounters but protests against symbolic interpretation and reading into the story of "metaphysical abstractions," such as the Fall of Man.

In contrast to V. W. Brooks's view of the moral of the book's being the idea that all civilization is "a hateful error" is the view of Parrington, Edgar Branch, Miss Bellamy, and others who emphasize the freeing of Jim from slavery and the satiric attack on inhumane institutions. Parrington relates *Huck* to Mark Twain's reformer's crusade in his other books against "unrighteous customs and laws of caste" and (following A. B. Paine) he makes *Huck* center on a conflict of "ethics" climaxed in having "to decide, forever, betwixt two things" involving Jim's status. Edgar Branch, in the most intensive analysis of the book to date, thinks it centers on the quest for freedom and the conflict between "two providences" which offer standards of right conduct: "Miss Watson's to behave and conform in selfish safety for fear of 'the bad place'; the Widow's to give unselfish aid to others. The alternatives are self-centered, conventional morality and humanitarian idealism," the latter of which Huck (assuming free will) chooses. Contrast Brooks's thesis about the hatefulness of all civilization. Part of the story certainly supports the thesis involving brotherhood. Trilling's introduction of 1952, for example, emphasizes the earlier passage where Huck tries condescendingly to tease Jim (who had grieved over Huck as lost) by leading him to think the storm was a dream, followed by Huck's repentantly coming to "humble myself to a nigger." When Jim realized that the debris caused by the storm proved Huck was making fun of him, he says (symbolically), "Dat truck dah is *trash;* en trash is what people is dat puts dirt on de head er dey fren's en makes 'em ashamed." However, while all this is surely an important and appealing element in the novel, this interpretation would tend to imply that Jim is the central character on whose escape everything is focused. Are there not several episodes of importance to which Jim has no relation—such as the Boggs-Sherburn story, the Shepherdson-Grangerford feud, and the Wilks story? Does this centering on Jim take into account the totality of the book? But Trilling's introduction, which came before Eliot's but develops his idea about the River being a God, is highly suggestive and charming as a whole, if more fanciful than scholarly. Like Eliot, Trilling finds "a certain formal aptness" in the disputed last nine chapters of the book. He regards Huck as "the least carefree of boys."

Huck is also interpreted as social history. De Voto, whose long and thoughtful studies command respect, concludes *(Mark Twain's America):* "The completeness of the society must be insisted upon . . . The portraiture which begins among the dregs with old man Finn ends with the Grangerfords. Between these strata has come every level of the South." Ferguson and Andrews also take this view.

Other critics find the clue to the form of *Huckleberry Finn* in its relation to the picaresque tradition, especially as that is represented by Smollett's translation of *Don Quixote.* Howells, who repeatedly mentioned picaresque elements in Twain's work, insisted that Cervantes' "free and simple design where event follows event without the fettering control of intrigue, but where all grows naturally out of character and conditions, is the supreme form of fiction," and since Twain's essay on Howells and his ardent letters to him show immense respect for his literary ideals, Howells may have reinforced Twain's devotion to Cervantes. In 1907, while Twain was still alive, F. W. Chandler in *The Literature of Roguery* (II, 488) argued that

> Huck . . . is a rogue with limitations. Although ready in lies, deceits, and disguises, and a petty thief, he is sound at heart [as Twain himself insisted, *Autobiography,* II, 174]. He scruples at helping to steal a "nigger"; he cannot bring himself to join with professional rogues in a swindle of moment [safeguarding Mary Jane's money from the king and duke]; he protects the weak, and is loyal to his friends. To the Don Quixote of the imaginative Tom Sawyer, he plays a delightful Sancho.

This brief generalization was elaborately documented by O. H.

Moore's "Mark Twain and Don Quixote" (*PMLA,* 1922), which finds some parallels also in *The Innocents Abroad* and in *A Connecticut Yankee* as a satire on chivalric medievalism. As early as 1860 Mark Twain called Goldsmith's *Citizen of the World* and *Don Quixote* "my *beau ideals* of fine writing" (*Letters,* I, 45). In Chapter xlvi of *Life on the Mississippi* Twain contrasts Scott's "chivalry silliness" and "the good work done by Cervantes" who "swept the world's admiration for the medieval chivalry-silliness out of existence." Incidentally, Moore's case has been much strengthened by the 1940 analysis of *Mark Twain's Travels with Mr. Brown,* by Franklin Walker and G. E. Dane, in which they find the Cervantes technique used in 1866 and 1867:

> Mark Twain's journey to New York [prior to the trip described in *Innocents Abroad*] was enlivened by the antics and conversation of his irresponsible imaginary companion, Brown—vulgarian, realist, and philosopher . . . An earthy philosopher, he acted as Mark Twain's Sancho Panza, interrupting sublime thoughts with skeptical comments. Thus he continued the role created for him in the Sandwich Island letters in which he had frequently shown himself "a bitter enemy of sentiment." It was he who reminded Mark Twain of the dirt and fleas when the correspondent grew poetic about the Hawaiian landscape. He also accompanied Mark Twain on his trip to Europe, where he tried to ride a donkey into a mosque and mistook the signs on water-closets for the names of French railway stations. However, when the Quaker City letters were revised for the *Innocents Abroad,* he disappeared; whereas part of him became Blucher and part Jackson, the grosser self was expurgated entirely. [Does this interesting change partly account for the lack of unity in point of view in *Innocents Abroad* which has troubled some scholars such as Walter Blair?] But years later some of his skepticism cropped up again in the character of Huck Finn.

O. H. Moore concludes that

> especially in *Huckleberry Finn,* Mark Twain parallels closely the masterpiece of Cervantes. He alters the character of Tom Sawyer so that, like Don Quixote, he is an omnivorous reader of romance, and desires to act out the roles of his favorite heroes. He alters also the character of Huckleberry Finn, transforming him from a very imaginative character to a prosaic Sancho Panza, a foil to the brilliant Tom Sawyer. For the romances of chivalry which turned the brain of Don Quixote, Mark Twain substitutes more modern romances, such as the Life of Baron Trenck, and *Monte Cristo,* which inspire the wild fancies of Tom Sawyer. In attempting the roles of his favorite heroes, Tom Sawyer falls into frequent altercations with Huckleberry Finn which resemble closely the arguments between Don Quixote and Sancho Panza. One or two episodes from *Don Quixote* are imitated directly in *Huckleberry Finn,* with acknowledgment by the author.

More important than any parallelism of details is the possibility that Cervantes provided Twain with sanction for expressing the two conflicting sides of his nature, the romantic and the realistic. Note also that this picaresque interpretation illuminates Twain's irony, his satire aimed at caste rituals such as the feud, and his sympathetic humanitarianism. (Parrington, III, 94, called *Huck* "the one great picaresque tale of the frontier" involving "rebellion against sham.")

There is of course no question that his materials are richly indigenous and based on his own earthy observations; the point is that these were poured into the picaresque mold. The theory accords with Twain's belief that narrative should be free, with "no law," and it makes sense of his warning that we should not seek in his book a plot (of the Aristotelian cause-and-effect kind). And the theory helps to explain Twain's responsiveness to both beauty and ugliness as well as his apparent contradictions: his frontier realism and his Victorian sentiment. In short, provided one does not claim any slavish imitation but interprets the picaresque tradition broadly, the theory of Mark Twain's following it offers an approach to *Huckleberry Finn* which would transcend by including most of the essentials in the other interpretations. This is especially true as regards the much-disputed question of whether the conclusion is a major flaw or part of a reasonable design by a self-conscious artist.

Defence of the disputed ending of *Huck* has come from those who stress, as does J. M. Cox in "Remarks on the Sad Initiation of *Huckleberry Finn*" (*SR* 1954), the idea that *Huck* is really the story of a boy supposed dead who seeks identification. Cox concludes that regardless of stylistic flaws, the final chapters are structurally "vital and necessary." In acknowledging he is "born again" and in his great vitality, Huck (according to Cox) "transcends the empty rituals of Tom Sawyer's universe and achieves mythic significance," Jim being "the conscience of the novel, the spiritual yardstick by which all men are measured." Lauriat Lane's "Why *Huckleberry Finn* is a Great World Novel" (*CE,* 1955) not only deals with the "total dramatic and moral irony," the passage from youth into maturity, and the epic representation of "all levels of society from the lowest to the highest," but stresses the rebirth-identification theme which is clinched "only" in the final chapters "when [Huck] is finally forced to assume this real self in the eyes of the world." Lane does not find Huck's final desire to escape further "sivilizing" inconsistent (as do some others) with the thesis that Huck has gone through a "maturing experience." Both Cox and Lane are richly suggestive on a "mythic" level, as are Eliot and Trilling.

H. E. Gerber ("Mark Twain's *Huckleberry Finn,*" *Explicator,* 1954) divides the book into five sections in terms of the alternation of land and river scenes, finding the climax in Chapter xxxi. Frank Baldanza ("The Structure of *Huckleberry Finn,*" *AL,* 1955) dismisses Cox's kind of symbol as well as emphasis on Jim's liberation and on the picaresque, and centers on "rhythmic stitchings" or the "principle of repetition and variation," of which he specifies a dozen instances, such as Tom's talk of Jim's keeping a rattlesnake in the Phelpses' cabin and

Jim's being bitten by one on Jackson's Island. These are interesting, but their meaning or significance is not very clear. Contrary to most recent critics, Baldanza says that "if we hold to any aesthetic standards at all, we hardly have the right to make extravagant claims for a book which we must admit in the same breath is negligible as a work of art." He does, however, bring his study to a final focus on the passage dealing with Huck's rebirth or identification, although Tom is likened to "Doubting Thomas"—"an oblique recall of the previous references to Moses and Solomon and the biblical kings."

Leo Marx in "Mr. Eliot, Mr. Trilling, and *Huckleberry Finn*" (*AS,* 1953) makes the best attempt to refute defenses of the ending, which Marx thinks a "failure." His weightiest argument is that Jim, who has hitherto grown in dignity, is now made to demean himself and to play a passive role to Tom's shenanigans; thus "the flimsy devices of plot, the discordant farcical tone, and the disintegration of the major characters all betray the failure of the ending."

On the whole the "frame" structure and the ending remain fascinating topics for debate.

8. *Studies of Other Individual Works*

L. T. Dickinson's are model studies: "Marketing a Best-Seller: Mark Twain's *Innocents Abroad*" (*PBSA,* 1947) and "Mark Twain's Revisions in Writing *The Innocents Abroad*" (*AL,* 1947). The latter demonstrates skillfully how his fifty-odd letters to the *Alta California* were revised in the interest of clarity, variety, decorum, toning down of irreverence, turning the "merely ludicrous into something rather subtly and richly humorous."

C. E. Shain's "The Journal of the *Quaker City* Captain" (*NEQ,* 1955) presents fresh evidence that Mark Twain exceeded a humorist's license in exaggerating the sanctimoniousness of Captain Duncan (with whom he later quarreled publicly) and in criticizing the directors of the cruise and the gossipy passengers.

While we await H. N. Smith's study, perhaps the best introduction to *Roughing It* is R. W. Paul's (Rinehart Series, 1953), which stresses regional aspects.

" 'That Hideous Mistake of Poor Clemens's'," as Howells named Mark Twain's much discussed address at the Whittier Birthday dinner given by the *Atlantic* in 1877, has been exhaustively and brilliantly studied in its social contexture by H. N. Smith (*HLB,* 1955). Especially interesting is his view that the behavior of the three rogues "is an anticipation of the behavior of the King and Duke on the raft in *Huckleberry Finn.*" In suggesting that the supposed New England writers were "imposters" Mark Twain wrote from an unconscious "impulse deep within" which challenged "the long-established proprieties of the literary life in New England." Many of Mark Twain's other minor works deserve this kind of fully oriented study.

Tom Sawyer should be approached in De Voto's edition of 1939 with its valuable prologue on "The Boy's Manuscript" written in 1870 or 1871 and here printed for the first time. De Voto treats the relation between the book and Mark Twain's boyhood friend Will Bowen and others, after whom he probably patterned his characters. Walter Blair's "On the Structure of *Tom Sawyer*" (*MP,* 1939) concludes that "it represented a fictional working-out of the author's antipathy to the conventional plot structure of juvenile tales," of the goody-goody boys' books then popular and already derided by books by J. J. Hooper, Max Adeler, and T. B. Aldrich. Blair shows that there are four "lines of action" in the plot: "the story of Tom and Becky, the story of Tom and Muff Potter, the Jackson's Island episode, and the series of happenings (which might be called the Injun Joe story) leading to the discovery of the treasure." Of the thirty-five chapters Blair finds only four which are not concerned with these four lines of action.

Lewis Leary, "Tom, Huck: Innocence on Trial" (*VQR,* 1954), argues that adventure (symbolized by Tom) at least as much as common sense (Huck) leads to the wiping out of evil as far as the boys are concerned. This very stimulating article, rich in insight, includes analysis of the intricate time-scheme as well as structure of these two boys' books; contrary to the usual view, Leary argues briefly that Tom grows and develops more than does Huck. Since at the end Huck still wishes to escape from being "sivilized," it is argued that he doesn't essentially change at all. But "Tom's solution [in the conclusion of *Huck*] is in the direction of Henry James's solution, of James Branch Cabell's, even of Ernest Hemingway's. It is escape through avoidance of what one wishes to avoid by creation of values of one's own which transcend reality because they seem finally more real than reality . . . Recognize the illusion, but cherish it."

A. L. Scott in "Mark Twain Revises *Old Times on the Mississippi*" (*JEGP,* 1955) points out some forty-five changes but says "several dozen might have been made by a conscientious proof reader." As a result of long study of Mark Twain, Scott adds that except for the revisions for *Innocents Abroad,* already studied by Dickinson, "Mark Twain's approach towards editing his own printed works was casual, perfunctory, and bored."

L. T. Dickinson's "The Sources of *The Prince and the Pauper*" (*MLN,* 1949) has been corrected as regards the debt to Charlotte M. Yonge's *Prince and the Page* by Howard Baetzhold (see above), but Dickinson provides valuable matter on historical works which Mark Twain followed "quite closely."

J. B. Hoben's "Mark Twain's *A Connecticut Yankee:* A Genetic Study" (*AL,* 1946) is a model investigation based on use of unpublished manuscripts. Especially interesting is Hoben's demonstration that Matthew Arnold's slurs on American civilization, our humorists, and Grant's grammar "evoked the spirit which transformed an unpromising sentimental romance into a promising satire" designed (in Twain's words) "to pry the English nation to a little higher level of manhood." Howells was called on for aid in revision; the revolutionary slant delighted him, and he thought it a "glorious book," simply "titanic." Mark Twain also says in an unpublished letter that E. C. "Stedman went through the book [the manuscript] and marked for the grave all that *he* could [of passages which might 'repel instead of persuade'] and I sacrificed them, every one." The supposedly timid and "genteel" Stedman (*Life and Letters,* II, 370-372) heartily approved of the book as it now stands, and even feared the public would overlook the attacks on the abuses of 1889. Walter Blair demonstrates (*Horse Sense in American Humor,* 1942) how the *Yankee* attacks (1) current spoils system appointments (in the fable about military exams) which Cleveland opposed, (2) the River and Harbor Bill (in the fable of King Arthur's evil appropriation and pork-barrel laws), and (3) the high tariff which Cleveland had flayed in 1887 (in the discussion by the Boss and the blacksmith of free trade). Robert Wilson's study of Mark Twain's use of Malory has been cited under "Influences and Sources," and it will be recalled that Olin Moore finds some influence of *Don Quixote* in the *Yankee* also (cf. Twain's Chapter xii). See also Sister M. T. Roades, "Don Quixote and *A Connecticut Yankee*" (*Mark Twain Quart.,* 1938).

As opposed to De Voto and those who stress the indigenous and mythic, as good a critic as the very conservative Stuart Sherman (*CHAL,* III, 17-18) concluded that *A Connecticut Yankee* "represents Mark Twain more completely than any other single book . . . . It displays every variety of his style from the mock-heroic and shirt-sleeve journalese of the Yankee's familiar vein to the careful euphonies of his descriptions of English landscape and the Dantean mordancy of the chapter 'In the Queen's Dungeons.' It exhibits his humour in moods from the grimmest to the gayest . . . [He is here] the representative of democratic America, preaching the gospel of commonsense and practical improvement and liberty and equality and free thought inherited from Franklin, Paine, Jefferson, and Ingersoll . . . *A Connecticut Yankee* is his *Don Quixote*, a sincere book, full of lifelong convictions earnestly held, a book charged with a rude iconoclastic humour, intended like the work of Cervantes to hasten the end of an obsolescent civilization" whose evils he traced to "monarchy, aristocracy, and an established church."

If one has misgivings about Leslie Fiedler's suggestion of homosexuality in "Come Back to the Raft Ag'in, Huck Honey" (*PR,* 1948), Fiedler's study of *Pudd'nhead Wilson* ("As Free as any Cretur'," *New Republic,* 15 Aug. and 22 Aug. 1955) shows much insight in discerning that here Mark Twain turns from his hope that evil could be remedied by changing outward institutions of state and church as in *A Connecticut Yankee* to his later view that evil is somehow ingrained in man's very nature. "Perhaps the supreme achievement of this book," says Fiedler, "is to have rendered such indignities [as Roxy's saying 'it's the nigger in you'] not in terms of melodrama or as a parochial 'special problem' but as a local instance of some universal guilt and doom . . . The false Tom . . . embodies also its 'dark necessity'—and must lie, steal, kill and boast until in his *hubris* he reveals himself as the slave we all secretly are." Fiedler stresses the book's "tragic inevitability" and finds it "superior" to *Huck* because, "morally, it is one of the most honest books in our literature." R. E. Spiller (*Cycle of American Literature,* 1955) says *Pudd'nhead Wilson* shows the beginning of Mark Twain's later extreme pessimism: "Basically it is an acceptance of the new position suggested by the science of Darwin and his followers that had apparently deprived mankind once for all of his free will to act in a mechanically predetermined universe." Thus *Pudd'nhead Wilson* takes on important new significance as a kind of watershed in Mark Twain's development.

Since Mark Twain said he originally began *Joan* as "a companion to *The Prince and the Pauper,*" Parrington in accord with his political-social interest linked these books illuminatingly with the *Yankee* as hostile to a "mean property consciousness" and to "bishops and kings" as contrasted with the faith that "peasants are people." On the other hand, Mentor Williams (in "Mark Twain's Joan of Arc," *Michigan Alumnus Quart. Rev.,* 1948) subordinates the castigation of "church bigots" and the King to the psychological problem of why Twain regarded *Joan* as "the best" of all his books, took "seven times the pleasure" in writing it he did in the others, and devoted more than four years to its preparation. Williams' answer is that his glorification of Joan fulfilled a deep spiritual and emotional need at a time when a sense of futility and his business failure, which was a result of misplaced confidence in the Machine, robbed him of hope. In Joan he found "by far the most extraordinary person the human race has ever produced," a find which (as Canby and Wagenknecht agree) greatly helped to temper his pessimism. "Joan was the measure of man's potentialities," Williams concludes. W. P. Trent's "Mark Twain as an Historical Novelist" (*Bookman,* 1896) concludes that Joan is not a complete success strictly as a historical novel because its elements are not "fused"—a verdict with which Ferguson agrees. But Trent finds that some scenes are "of imperishable interest and importance," and some events are "told with an insight, a *verve,* a humor that professed historians might well envy." E. H. Long ("Sut Lovingood and Mark Twain's *Joan of Arc,*" *MLN,* 1949) finds that Mark Twain modeled the scene in which the bull stung by bees disrupts a funeral procession on a tall tale of G. W. Harris. See also Bronia Sielewicz, "Joan and Mark Twain" (in *Joan of Arc, An Anthology of History and Literature,* ed. E. Wagenknecht, 1948), and Mary A. Wyman, "A Note on Mark Twain" (*CE,* 1946). Most major critics agree that what distinguishes *Joan* from its historical sources is not only Twain's invention of humorous characters and episodes, especially in the early chapters, but the fact that (as in *Huck)* the whole story is unified in point of view, being presented through the eyes of a devoted "page and secretary," the Sieur Louis de Conte.

"The Man that Corrupted Hadleyburg" has been the center of controversy since Brooks called it the first instance of Twain's completely outspoken exposure of the kind of supposedly incorruptible people in deference to whom he had been publicly silent. Miss Bellamy has argued that it merely climaxes a long and growing conflict between his "Moralism and Determinism" which accounts for the fact that "There is no continuity of motivation, no steadiness of emotional effect, no philosophical unity to the story." On the other hand, Everett Carter (*Howells and the Age of Realism,* 1954) argues interestingly that "on the scale of increasing sympathy, we generally find that the same ordinary, common people he celebrated in *Huckleberry Finn,* like Jack Halliday who led the townspeople of Hadleyburg in their scoffing of the Incorruptibles, ranked high, while the pretentious, self-righteous 'pillars of society' were very low." G. A. Cardwell ("Mark Twain's Hadleyburg," *Ohio State Archeol. and Hist. Quart.,* 1951) shows that Twain probably had in mind no one town such as Oberlin.

In "The Structural Problem of *The Mysterious Stranger*" (*SP,* 1952) E. S. Fussell attempts to ascertain Mark Twain's "adjustment of technique" to the realization of a fairly coherent theme. Assuming that a "general theory of solipsism" in the last chapter is Twain's final philosophical position, Fussell argues that this position is prepared for progressively (with some minor exceptions) throughout the book. "By putting his figures through these various progressive phases [of Satan's explication of the nature of "reality"] from unreality (literal materiality) to reality (solipsistic ideality), Twain has forced a certain degree of unity on his episodic structure; by treating each phase provisionally as if it were the only reality, he has eaten his cake all along and still has it at the end." Reference has been made under "Influences and Sources" to relevant studies by Laverty and Cowper. In his interesting essay on "The Symbols of Despair" in *Mark Twain at Work* (1942) De Voto has dealt with successive manuscript versions of *The Mysterious Stranger* which he interprets biographically as attempts in the midst of grief and self-accusation to save himself from insanity by shifting responsibility.

9. *Influence of Mark Twain*

Gohdes points out that the enormous European sale of Twain's books was aided by his various visits around the globe which "occasioned newspaper publicity astonishing in quantity and fervor." Malcolm Cowley ("American Books Abroad,"

LHUS) finds that "In the Kaiser's Germany, Mark Twain had been by far the most popular American author; there were exactly 100 translations of his various works between 1890 and 1913." The Russians bought 3,100,100 copies of his books, the demand for Mark Twain being second only to that for Jack London. Hence Mark Twain provided Europe with its most widely circulated image of the American and of our ideals, and must have done a great deal to condition European attitudes toward the United States. (One "curiosity" is M. Mendelson's *Mark Twain,* Moscow, 1939, a typical Soviet interpretation of nearly 300 pages, twisting Mark Twain's later pessimism into proof of the unsatisfying character of American civilization. "Disappointed in bourgeois society, Twain transferred his disillusionment to the entire human race.") Those interested in charting his vogue and the critical reaction to him will find ample guidance in Roger Asselineau's *The Literary Reputation of Mark Twain from 1910 to 1950: A Critical Essay and a Bibliography* (Paris, 1954), the latter running to 1,333 items and including articles from Europe and Latin America.

Unlike Stuart Sherman and Parrington, H. N. Smith thinks Mark Twain's ideas (stemming from the Enlightenment) tended to be naïve and thin in his later period, but he emphasizes the great influence of his style and craftmanship:

> And yet American literature of the twentieth century owes a substantial debt to the author of *Huckleberry Finn.* Writers as different from one another as Sherwood Anderson and Ernest Hemingway have acknowledged the influence of this book on their prose, and in addition one has to take into account the development of the humorous mode by writers like E. B. White, James Thurber, S. J. Perelman, and A. J. Liebling. These evidences demonstrate an important continuity in literary technique and attitude. Where the followers of Whitman [as a non-Western writer] have too often moved toward the loose oratory of Thomas Wolfe or Carl Sandburg, the influence of Mark Twain has encouraged discipline and craftsman-

ship. Paradoxically enough, the rank rabble party of Jacksonism turns out to have set in motion an austere cult of style that has given to American literature an esthetic tradition as pure and rigorous as that of the Symbolists themselves. (Smith's "Origins of a Native American Literary Tradition" in the collaborative *The American Writer and the European Tradition,* ed. Margaret Denny and W. H. Gilman, 1950.)

It will be recalled that in the first chapter of *The Green Hills of Africa* (1935) the Nobel Prize-winning Hemingway said: "All modern American literature comes from one book by Mark Twain called Huckleberry Finn . . . it's the best book we've had. All American writing comes from that. There was nothing before. There has been nothing as good since." Philip Young's *Hemingway* develops his debt to Mark Twain fully, in fact almost too extravagantly. But Mark Twain's influence on present-day literature is surely as pervasive as that of any of our nineteenth-century writers.

8

HENRY JAMES

I. Bibliography, Text, Manuscripts

THE STUDENT of Henry James has the inestimable advantage of starting with a definitive bibliography. Although F. A. King compiled a partial and chronological list of his writing to that date in *The Novels of Henry James*, by Elizabeth L. Cary (1905), the much fuller and more accurate listing of LeRoy Phillips in 1906 quickly superseded it. The revised edition of Phillips' book, *A Bibliography of the Writings of Henry James* (1930), gives descriptions of title pages, together with collations and other bibliographical data, of English and American first editions, notices of all subsequent editions then known which were printed from new type or plates, descriptions of books to which James made contributions or to which he wrote prefaces or introductions, notes on printed but "unpublished" plays, and short-title entries of collected editions of his works and of his contributions to periodicals. An index supplies an alphabetical list of titles of all his writings, whether books or essays, with reference to all then recorded printings. Even though, after more than fifteen years of intensive scholarship, this (to quote James himself) "mercilessly complete resuscitation" of his writings is still indispensable, a new bibliography, with more detailed collations of first editions, is promised by Leon Edel and Dan H. Lawrence. Other more selective listings, with far less bibliographical data, are found in Rebecca West's *Henry James* (1916), Michael

Swan's *Henry James: A Select Bibliography* (1950), *CHAL* and *LHUS*, the bibliography by Harry Hartwick in *A History of American Letters*, by W. F. Taylor (1936), *Selected Fiction*, edited by Leon Edel (1953), and the *Notebooks*, edited by F. O. Matthiessen and K. B. Murdock (1947). Partial listings are found in various critical works discussed below.

The most satisfactory list of books and articles about James is that compiled by L. N. Richardson and published first in *Henry James: Representative Selections* (AWS, 1941). It was reprinted without revision in *The Question of Henry James* (1945), a collection of critical essays edited by F. W. Dupee. Richardson includes prefaces and essays from books as well as articles from American, British, and some French journals. Although selective, there is little of importance that he has not discovered and listed. His occasional editorial comments are apt and temperate, and he provides an excellent summary of criticism of James in his Introduction. Satisfactory as the Richardson bibliography is, Eunice C. Hamilton was able to add a few titles prior to 1941 as well as to carry the listing through the year 1948 in her "Biographical and Critical Studies of Henry James, 1941-1948" (*AL*, 1949). She also includes some unpublished doctoral dissertations (a few of them early) and lists reprints of individual titles of the Works, 1930-48. Her list adds forty-four items from books as well as eighty-eight from periodicals, a testimony to the upsurge of scholarly and critical interest in James during these years. In her "Addenda" (*AL*, 1950), Viola R. Dunbar adds fifteen items from books to the listings of Richardson and Hamilton and thirty-three from periodicals, as well as a much fuller list of reprints, 1930-48, mainly of short stories and essays. For the period 1949 to date, the most satisfactory listings are still the reviews of current scholarship in *PMLA*, *AL*, *MHRA*, etc., and the full listings in *CBI*, *International Index*, *Articles on American Literature, 1900-1950*, by Lewis Leary (1954), etc.

Among special bibliographical studies, I. R. Brussel's descriptions and collations of those books by James of which the

English edition was the first, in *Anglo-American First Editions: Part II, West to East* (1936), makes a contribution to the history of copyright in the two countries rather than to the study of James, and Edna Kenton's "Some Bibliographical Notes on Henry James" (*H & H,* 1934) contains miscellaneous bits of minor information, including the opinion that "there is much unsigned work by James in various periodicals, never traced, much less suspected, all through the 1880 decade." A very full listing of volumes of reminiscences and letters of persons who knew James and who left firsthand impressions of him is to be found in Simon Nowell-Smith's *The Legend of the Master* (1948), and B. R. McElderry, Jr., has made a survey of the published letters of James himself (*BB,* 1952). Among other bibliographical notes are E. T. Bowden (*AL,* 1953), A. R. Ferguson (*AL,* 1949) and C. J. Weber (*Colby Lib. Quart.,* 1948). An evaluative summary of recent biographical and critical work on James is provided by J. W. Beach in a special introduction to the reprint of *The Method of Henry James* (1954).

The basic text for the study of James is still that of the novels, short and longer stories, critical essays, travel essays, and some plays as published during his lifetime. This text has never been reprinted in a collected and definitive edition. The so-called New York Edition, published by Scribner's in twenty-four volumes, planned and edited by James, plus two supplementary volumes, 1907-17, was thoroughly revised by the author and therefore represents in many cases a basically different text both in style and in other details that affect interpretation of character and incident. This edition contains the Prefaces by James. Its text, including these Prefaces, was reprinted in London, 1921-23 in thirty-five volumes, edited by Percy Lubbock, with the addition of all other fiction published by James during his lifetime. Neither of these editions is complete as James also omitted all his essays and plays. Furthermore, James often revised his novels, particularly the earlier ones, between the serial and the first book publications. A complete and definitive edition of the Works, or at least a variorum edition of the texts of the more important novels and tales is needed.

A definitive edition of the plays and notes toward plays is provided in *The Complete Plays of Henry James,* edited by Leon Edel (1949), and of the dramatic criticism by Allan Wade in *The Scenic Art, Notes on Acting and the Drama, 1872-1901* (1948). *Eight Uncollected Tales of Henry James* were collected and edited by Edna Kenton (1950), and the narrative version of *The Other House* was republished, with an introduction by Leon Edel (1924), as were some other items. There is no complete text of the critical and travel essays other than their first editions. Some new items were added by *Notes and Reviews by Henry James,* edited by Pierre de Chaignon la Rose (1921). The many other collections, selections, and new editions of the writings of James contain little or no new material or extensive editorial or textual notation. The problems of the Notebooks and the Letters are discussed below.

Manuscripts and papers of Henry James are of course widely scattered, but all those that were retained by the family were deposited by them in the Harvard College Library, which is now the official repository. These papers were first described by R. B. Perry (*Harvard Univ. Lib. Notes,* 1942). They contain principally letters and manuscripts of Henry James, Sr., Henry James, Jr., and William James. Under a restriction imposed by the family, these papers may not be used by students working toward a degree. The materials of Henry James, Jr., comprise thirteen boxes of letters to and eight boxes from various correspondents, thirteen boxes of manuscripts (mainly dramatic), and the manuscript of the revised version of *The American.* From various sources have been added other manuscripts, the most important of which are *The Princess Casamassima, The Portrait of a Lady,* "The Jolly Corner," "Confidence," and "En Province"; the originals of over five hundred letters to various persons; and several hundred transcripts of letters, including six boxes of those assembled by Percy Lubbock. Probably second in importance to this collection is that in the Library of Congress, and other small collections have found their way to those depositories, public and private, where American literary manuscripts are collected. Those in the Sterling Library of Yale University and the Brotherton Library in Leeds, England, deserve special mention.

II. Biography

The biographical study of James has been long delayed because of his own reticence, the feeling of his biographers that there is little that can be said about a life so uneventful in terms of action, the magnitude of the task, and the delay in making manuscript materials available to the student.

Recent criticism has obviated much of the difficulty created by the first two of these factors, and the James family has pretty much eliminated the last. Of published materials, the most revealing for biography are the three volumes of reminiscences which James dictated in his last years and left incomplete at his death. They are the memoirs of an old man, intricate and subjective, depending upon almost no documents or notes other than a few letters from his father and his cousin Mary Temple, but they have a special quality of self-revelation which a more formal record could not achieve. Written ostensibly to provide material for the biography of his brother William, they tell far more of his own place in the family circle than they do of William's, and a careful reading can reconstruct from these notes the peculiar quality of James's boyish personality. His own remark that his work is "vitiated perhaps by the effort to comprehend more than it contains" suggests the kind of revelation they achieve. Cornelia P. Kelley in *The Early Development of Henry James* (1930) demonstrates how useful these reminiscences are even while she is objecting that James not only found it difficult to get back to the mood of his early years but did not really wish to do so because he thought of the literary productions of those years as "hideous." The first of these three volumes, *A Small Boy and Others* (1913), covers the period of boyhood, the second, *Notes of a Son and Brother* (1914), concludes with the death of Mary Temple, commemorated as "the end of our youth," and the final volume, *The Middle Years* (1917), is but a beginning of the actual "middle years," and was edited by Percy Lubbock and published a year after James's death.

As supplement to these volumes, James prepared for the New York Edition of his works a series of prefaces in which he told the story of how he developed each of his themes into full narrative dress. Eighteen of these prefaces were collected by R. P. Blackmur under the title *The Art of the Novel* (1934), but neither Blackmur nor the editor of the letters, Percy Lubbock, seems to have known that the voluminous notebooks from which he worked had survived. Nine of these notebooks, covering the period from November 1878 to May 1911 (with some overlapping), turned up in the Harvard collection. Planned as early as 1873 as a depository for his ideas and materials of fiction, they are principally valuable as a source for studying the creative process of the novelist with reference to particular works and for the light they throw on general problems of James's life and his development as an artist. They were edited by F. O. Matthiessen and K. B. Murdock, with an introductory essay, as *The Notebooks of Henry James* (1947), with all the authority of meticulous scholarship, and perhaps more than the needed critical commentary. S. E. Lind raises an interesting and perhaps important point by calling attention to a distinction which he says James made between "Note-books" and "Journals" (*TLS,* 27 Nov., 1948). The editors of the *Notebooks,* in failing to recognize this distinction, were unable to explain why some of the entries deal with trivia, while others are more formal.

The story told by his boyhood reminiscences is taken up by the two volumes of *The Letters of Henry James,* selected and edited by Percy Lubbock (1920), with the assistance of James's niece, Mrs. Bruce Porter. *The Middle Years* opens with February 1869 and the first letter, addressed from London to his sister Alice, is dated 10 March of that year. Of the several thousand letters that passed through Lubbock's hands, he printed some four hundred, selected from a wide range of family and friends. Henry James was an excellent letter writer. He revealed himself freely if somewhat formally to those he trusted. It is therefore possible to reconstruct from his letters what he did and what he thought and felt about his experience. Only James himself could write his own life story, and this he never did in any systematic or complete fashion. The Lubbock selection, however, as S. P. Sherman points out in "The Special Case of Henry James" (*The Emotional Discovery of America,* 1932) and Virginia Woolf in *The Death of the Moth and Other Essays* (1942), tends to emphasize the British parts of James's life at something of a sacrifice of his American ties, and it also stresses the later rather than the formative stages of his career. Leon Edel is at work on a new and much fuller edition of the letters.

In addition to the letters in the Lubbock volumes, B. R. McElderry, Jr., reports (*BB,* 1952) that he found over seven hundred additional letters dispersed in more than 100 sources. He then describes the contents of almost 100 volumes or articles containing letters from James. Among these letters are those to W. D. Howells (*Life in Letters,* 1928), Mrs. Humphrey Ward (Janet P. Trevelyan, *Life,* 1923), Joseph Conrad (*Three Letters,* 1926), A. C. Benson (*Letters to A. C. B. and Auguste Monod,* 1930), Elizabeth Robins (*Theatre and Friendship,* 1932), Shane Leslie (*Horizon,* 1943), John La Farge (*NEQ,* 1949), and O. W. Holmes (*YR,* 1949). Those to T. S. Perry (Virginia Harlow, *A Biography,* 1950) are the earliest letters extant. To this list may be added several issues of the *Colby Coll. Library Quart.* (1943, 1953), the *Letters to Walter Berry* (1928), and the episode of Violet Paget's portrait of Henry James in her novel, *Lady Tal,* as revealed in letters included in articles by C. J. Weber and Burdett Gardner (*PMLA,* 1953, 1954).

Even though his life was, in most ordinary respects, uneventful, there was something about James that led his friends and acquaintances to tell stories about him and to quote and comment on the peculiarities of his personality and expression. Simon Nowell-Smith has gathered over one hundred sources of this kind and has thus revealed how a legend is born and nurtured (*The Legend of the Master,* 1948). An opening section questions the dependability of such evidence, with many examples of self-contradiction and distortion, but the following short excerpts succeed in painting a believable portrait, the worst sin of which would appear to be exaggeration. Among the most quoted sources are Edmund Gosse, Edith Wharton, Alice James, F. M. Hueffer, Violet Hunt, A. C. Benson, J. E. Blanche, and L. P. Smith. Janet A. Smith (1948) and G. S. Hellman (*Century,* 1926) have told the story of the friendship of Henry James and R. L. Stevenson, and E. K. Brown that with Joseph Conrad (*YR,* 1946). Conrad writes an appreciation of James in *Notes on Life and Letters* (1921), as does Hueffer in *Henry James, A Critical Study* (1916), and again in *Return to Yesterday* (1932) and *Portraits from Life* (1937). Edith Wharton pays tribute in *A Backward Glance* (1934). A serious misunderstanding brought a late end to a lifelong friendship with H. G. Wells. James's essay on "The New Novel" (1914) provoked the satiric fantasy *Boon* by Wells (1915), in which James was resolved, as he himself phrased it, into "an unmitigated mistake." Echoes of the controversy were heard for many years. H. M. Walbrook was among those who provided partial answers to Wells (*Fortnightly Rev.,* 1930) and L. P. Smith became involved by a reference to Wells in an article mainly on Santayana (*New Statesman and Nation,* 1943). Wells replied with a letter in the next issue, and Smith offered further brief reminiscences in the *Atlantic* for August. Most biographers deal with this controversy, but good critical summaries are E. K. Brown's "Two Formulas for Fiction" (*CE,* 1946) and Michael Swan (*Cornhill,* 1953).

More casual and not always reverent records of meetings with James are those of Robert Herrick (*YR,* 1923), Hamlin

Garland (*Bookman,* 1930), B. R. McElderry, Jr. (*AL,* 1952), Witter Bynner (*Critic,* 1905, and *SRL,* 1943), Sydney Brooks (*Harper's Weekly,* 1904), Muriel Draper (*Harper's,* 1929), Paul Bourget (*Camb. Jour.,* 1950), and Compton Mackenzie (*Life and Letters Today,* 1943), while Louise Boit tells of her knowing James as landlord at Lamb House (*Atlantic,* 1946), and Alice Broughton of taking his photograph (*H & H,* 1934). Marie P. Harris (*AL,* 1951) elaborates on the record of James as lecturer as earlier noted by Olivia H. Dunbar (*Critic,* 1905) and W. C. France (*Bookman,* 1905). The most revealing of all personal reminiscences of James, however, are the accounts of the young woman who served as his secretary during the latter years and who took his dictation for the late novels and the Prefaces. Theodora Bosanquet published in *Fortnightly, Living Age, Bookman* (1917), and *YR* (1920) the story, which was also told in *Henry James at Work* (1924), of how the master dictated directly to the Remington; and, by revealing his method, she stirred up a hornet's nest of controversy as to whether or not the involutions of his later style were a result of this descent to mechanization. Other aspects of his life are revealed in many incidental sources such as Mervyn Jones-Evans, in "Henry James's Year in France" (*Horizon,* 1946). The London *Spectator* (1915) prints J. W. White's interpretation of James's attitudes toward Germany, England, and the United States in the war years, while John Russell takes a more favorable point of view in "Henry James and the Leaning Tower" (*New Statesman and Nation,* 1943). Other minor biographical sources are the anonymous "Henry James and the English Association" (*Scrutiny,* 1946) and "Henry James at the Reform Club," by E. S. Roscoe (*Bookman,* 1925).

In spite of this wealth of sources, the biography of Henry James has not yet been written in full. Most biographical study has been offered casually as a frame of reference for critical reviews of the novels and tales or in conjunction with studies of the James family, especially Henry James the elder, his two sons, William the psychologist and Henry James the novelist, and their sister Alice.

Genealogical study begins with "William James of Albany, New York, and his Descendants," by Mrs. K. G. Hastings (*N. Y. Gen. & Biog. Record,* 1924) and with a chart of the family issued by Colby College Library in 1943, but the serious study of these interesting individuals and the effects of heredity and of close family ties upon them is earlier. Perhaps the first attempt to follow family traits through several generations was C. H. Grattan's *The Three Jameses: A Family of Minds* (1932). Although brief and none too thorough, this is the first study of the Irish immigrant grandfather William James and his Swedenborgian philosopher-son Henry James, Senior. The accounts of the more famous William and Henry of the third generation are full enough to allow dominant family traits and ideas to form a pattern of similarities and mutations that has psychological implication of great importance. *The Elder Henry James,* by Austin Warren (1934), develops the complex problem of the father more fully, and the definitive *The Thought and Character of William James,* by R. B. Perry (1935), fills out the portrait presented by the *Letters* (ed. by his son Henry James, 1920) of the brother to whom there was so subtle and profound a psychological tie. With the publication of the journals of the invalid sister, *Alice James: Her Brothers, Her Journal* (1934), by Anna R. Burr, further information about the mother and the lesser known brothers, Garth Wilkinson and Robertson, was also added. Later F. O. Matthiessen offered *The James Family: Including Selections from the Writings of Henry James, Senior, William, Henry, and Alice James* (1947). This is a careful study of the influence of the liberated religious faith and the skepticism of the elder James upon the two sons who disappointed the father's hopes for a new age of religion by applying his discovered freedoms to purely secular problems. More a source book than a finished biographical study, it is the authority, even though undigested, on the family as a whole. Matthiessen's theory is that William and Henry are arrayed on opposite sides of their father's antithesis between doing and being and so afford a study in contrast within a frame of identity. The Freudian implications of the crises in the lives of all three, of imaginary and real injury, and of a family unity that provided an escape from worldly responsibilities are not as fully developed as they are in the studies of Grattan, Edel, Quentin Anderson, and others. Comment on the two brothers had been offered earlier by Régis Michaud (*Revue de France,* 1922) and on the immigrant William and his son by H. A. Larrabee (*AS,* 1932).

The death of Henry James in 1916 took place at a moment in American literary history when critics were in the mood to emphasize sociological and psychological factors in the literary life. A whole group of critics, led by Van Wyck Brooks and V. L. Parrington, began to stress the connections between American literature and American life, which meant the place of the individual in the political and social development of the nation. Under this dispensation, the novelist of the international theme became the man without a country, the expatriate who never found a new loyalty. Rebecca West's short and brilliant study in 1916 is more a critique of the novels and tales than a biography, but it follows a strictly biographical pattern. Relating James's work closely to his early experiences and to the reaction of an American consciousness to European culture, she develops the paradox that, because he was both an American and a product of culture, "He could never feel at home until he was in exile." A summary of the essential biographical facts is followed by a discussion of the principal stories in a mood of appreciation for a nearly perfect art, tinged with scorn for the lack of passion in this novelist of the manners of a mannerless American-international set. To this biographer, James does not quite "come off," even though his masterworks decidedly do. The theory of frustration due to environment was soon given its fullest treatment by Van Wyck Brooks in *The Pilgrimage of Henry James* (1925). Here is a portrait of the American artist, alienated from his own society on the one hand because of its lack of culture and from the society of a more cultured European world because of his alien birth. Brooks's study is an important book in the history of Jamesean biographical criticism because it so overstated the paradox of the artist without a country that it revealed the fallacy as well as the core of truth in this simple formula. Others to develop the same formula in briefer form were Gamaliel Bradford in *American Portraits, 1875-1900* (1922), Thomas Beer in *SRL* (1925), Ernest Boyd in *Literary Blasphemies* (1927), Régis Michaud in *The American Novel Today* (1928), Matthew Josephson in *Portrait of the Artist as American* (1930), and Ludwig Lewisohn in *Expression in America* (1932). In later biographical critics who maintained essentially the same theory of expatriation, the emphasis becomes less doctrinaire and more subtle, beginning with Ferner Nuhn's *The Wind Blew from the East* (1942) and continuing with *Three American Travelers in England*, by R. C. LeClair (1945), Jean Simon's *Le roman Américan aux XXe siècle* (1949), and *Turn East, Turn West* by H. S. Canby (1951). This last book, a suggestive but somewhat baffling Plutarchian alternation between Mark Twain and James as representatives of the opposing American tendencies to turn West or turn East, builds upon the same critic's several essays in the *Saturday Review of Literature* and his essay on James in *Definitions, First Series* (1922), but reflects the changing critical currents of succeeding eras as it leaves doctrine behind while preserving an essentially social frame of reference for personality. The same change is to be noted in the later treatment of James's "exile" by Brooks in *New England: Indian Summer, 1865-1915* (1940), and in Constance Rourke's *American Humor* (1931).

Pelham Edgar attempted a direct answer to Brooks and his theory (*QQ*, 1932), and one of the purposes of his *Henry James, Man and Author* (1927) was to support his counter-theory by showing that James, the artist, soon exhausted his American material and that the move to Europe was good for both him and his art. Once this general approach to his problem is established in biographical terms, Edgar shifts to a topical organization of his comments on all of James's principal writings, grouping the stories according to their American setting, their general themes and the particular themes of the artist and of the supernatural, and concluding with chapters on the dramas, the letters, and the criticism. His discussion of each work is not exceptional, but shows a basically sound appreciation of James's intentions and methods. A feature of the book which gives it some of the distinction of being a "first" is its emphasis on the "major" or later novels which Edgar believes to be the best. He was perhaps the first critic to point to *The Golden Bowl* as the finest of James's stories, representative of his thinking and of his technique at their fullest development.

Since Edgar's book, the biographical study of James has progressed slowly but along the affirmative lines that he indicated. The much more rapid and emphatic changes in general critical attitude, which will be discussed below, have made it possible for the biographer to accept the role of the artist, as James describes it and embodies it, as legitimately American. The opening of the James family papers has dispelled some of the air of mystery about the facts of his life, and progress in psychological knowledge has helped to explain some of the problems and paradoxes in his personality. No single work could more effectively illustrate the change in modern aesthetic perspective than the unpretentious *Henry James,* by F. W. Dupee (1952) in the American Men of Letters Series. Dupee is able to take for granted the inner chronicle which James himself defines as the highest form of experience. With the paradox of alienation removed, the biographer can present a straight record of the known facts, of which he has many more than any of his predecessors, and to by-pass the need for explaining or justifying the life which his subject elected to live. Relatively weak in critical insight, especially into the later novels, this sketch is sound and well-balanced biography—standard until a fuller and more nearly definitive work appears.

That work is now in progress in the proposed three-volume biography by Leon Edel, of which *Henry James: The Untried Years: 1843-1870* (1953) is the first. This is the first biography to be based on a thorough study of the unpublished letters, journals, and other sources, as well as upon materials published but not previously used by a major biographer. This volume carries the story to 1870 and covers only "the fledgling years, the untried years." Its emphasis is upon those events like the fire in which James strained his back and the summer friendship with his cousin Mary Temple, and upon associations like those with his father and his brother William, which set the psychological patterns for his life and thought. The resulting portrait is that of a highly sensitive young man who was shaped into an original and unique personality by unusual circumstances of heredity and environment. In a reversal of the method of James himself and of many of his later critics, Edel thus prepares for an understanding of art by an analysis of the artist and of the materials available to him. R. C. LeClair has also completed a biography of the early years.

Edel's study of James goes back to about 1931 when he was working with the Prefaces and the plays, but his two *UTQ* articles (1933 and 1941) show a growing interest in the biographical problem. Like all students of James, he has been influenced by the trend toward psychoanalysis which is most dramatically evident in Edmund Wilson's essay on *The Turn of the Screw* and in the carefully reasoned but wholly doctrinaire article by Saul Rosenzweig, "The Ghost of Henry James" (*PR*, 1944). Starting with an "Oedipus situation" which he finds already highly developed in James, Rosenzweig posits a psychological castration theory which emphasized his frustration and caused a traumatic escape into fantasy leading to outright ghost stories, a neurosis that remained unresolved until he could identify himself with social action at the end. This theory was more or less accepted and literally interpreted by many critics and biographers in place of the Brooks theory of alienation or the generalized "homesickness" theory of Katherine Anne Porter (*KR*, 1943), notably, with some reservations, by R. P. Blackmur (*LHUS*, 1948), but Edel does a convincing job of discrediting it on the same kind of psychological evidence that Rosenzweig used in supporting it. He, with R. C. LeClair ("Henry James and Minny Temple," *AL*, 1949), and others accept the theory of a mental rather than a physical wound and proceed to a convincing analysis of his relationships with his immediate family and with Mary Temple as the basis of his creative personality.

III. Criticism

Although Henry James has been the subject of perhaps more critical essays than any other American novelist, basic research on him and his writings has lagged as much in other forms as in the biographical. Except for a few stories where the sources are obvious, there has been little documentation of the amount and kind of debt that he owed to English and European fiction, drama, and criticism, or of his influence, if any, on Joyce, Proust, Stein, and the whole company of the moderns. In spite of a seemingly endless series of articles on the obscurities and vagaries of his later style, there has been no systematic analysis of his language, grammar, and rhetoric, early or later. There is still much to be done in pinning down his actual scientific knowledge, especially in psychology, about which there has been much speculation but little real information as to kinds or sources. Other source materials should be made available, and at least his most important fiction should be edited and annotated.

On the other side of the ledger, it can be noted that at no time since the publication of his first critical essays in the *Atlantic*, the *NAR,* the *Nation,* and the *Galaxy* in the 1860's and of his first collection of short stories, *A Passionate Pilgrim, and Other Tales* (1875), has he failed for any long period to command well-considered critical attention both in England and America. Much of this commentary has been unfavorable and some of it stupid, but it has rarely been perfunctory or merely shallow. Because he announced, practiced, developed, and defended a consistent theory of literature himself and was always stubbornly resistant to the praise and blame of both his critics and his public, he provides an excellent measure of the changes in critical fashions of his day and since. For this reason, a more or less chronological review is the most satisfactory way of classifying and evaluating the research and criticism on him and his writings.

Three periods in Jamesean criticism may be distinguished with reasonable precision: the period of his lifetime to 1916; the period from his death, with its impressive array of commemorative and critical articles, to about 1934, when the Henry James issue of *H & H* brought forward a new group of commentators with a fresh approach to most of the now well-debated issues; and the period from 1934 to the present. Commemoration in 1943 of the centenary of his birth does not seem to have made any changes in the kinds of criticism then current although the amount of attention devoted to him has steadily increased, especially since 1950 when there seems to have been an upsurge of interest leading to somewhat more fundamental research than had previously been done.

1. *Contemporary Comment (1865-1916)*

These three periods coincide roughly with periods or trends in American literary history and criticism. Between 1865 and 1916 the major critical battle in the United States was that between "idealism" and "realism." The impetus of the romantic movement had thinned out to the lofty but somewhat stereotyped moral and aesthetic theories of the so-called "genteel" writers from Lowell to Stedman, whose standards were becoming fixed in a belles-lettristic pattern, whose methods were largely impressionistic, and whose range was limited. In his inherent gentility and in his stress on the problems of art, Henry James shared in this reactionary movement, but in other ways he defied it. Howells who, like James, accepted many of the genteel ideas and limitations, came out openly and strongly for that movement which most vigorously opposed idealism, i.e., realism, and James seemed to abet the revolt. The support of Howells, with its stamp of "realist," is the major factor in determining the issues and sides of the critical battle over James during his lifetime.

The detailed rises and falls in his reputation have been discussed many times and are now fairly well documented by two dissertations, the one on contemporary reviews of his work in the United States, the other in England. R. N. Foley's *Criticism in American Periodicals of the Work of Henry James from 1866 to 1916* (1944) and D. M. Murray's *The Critical Reputation of Henry James in English Periodicals, 1879-1916* (completed in 1948 and published in part in *AL,* 1952) together examine a large number of contemporary reviews and critiques, and provide, mainly in their footnotes, bibliographical references to most of the important and many of the trivial essays of this period.

In the United States, as Foley discovered, the most significant reviews are in the *Nation,* the *Critic,* the *Dial,* the *Atlantic, Harper's, Scribner's,* the *NAR,* and a few others, and the most influential general critical summaries were provided by a few of the recognized critics of the period, especially Howells, H. E. Scudder, and W. C. Brownell.

The review by Howells of *The Passionate Pilgrim* in the *Atlantic* (1875) deserves a special place in literary history for its courage and for its effectiveness in influencing the career of a fellow craftsman. The enthusiastic praise by the new editor of the major literary magazine of the time must have had great influence on this practically unknown writer and his potential public. Howells asserts that "his aim is high; he respects his material, he is full of his theme." He praises James's style and diction, his gift for the concrete, his humor and his psychological insight. While suggesting that his power lies in realistic writing, he nevertheless regrets that there are not more stories in the vein of "The Romance of Certain Old Clothes," a tale which James later repudiated. Other reviews followed, and in 1882 Howells attempted what was perhaps the first general summary of James's aims, methods, and accomplishments, this time in *Century*. In an apparently deliberate attempt to enlarge James's audience, Howells now explains that his friend is "an annalist and an analyst," an exponent of the "new realism," a man to be watched. He was still watching and praising in 1903, when he reviewed "Mr. Henry James's Later Work" in the *NAR* as an imaginary debate with James's unsympathetic feminine readers. His argument is that an artist who can so successfully depict life in general and feminine characters in particular can indulge with impunity in subtleties that some of his readers may not understand. This is a kind of realism that can be counted upon.

Others of James's critical contemporaries had mixed feelings about his work but agreed with Howells in classing him as a realist. T. W. Higginson, in *Short Studies of American Authors* (1880), recognizes James's powers, but objects to his lack of artistic control, by which he apparently means conventional plot structure. H. E. Scudder is more perceptive when, in an *Atlantic* review in 1882, he discovers in *The Portrait of a Lady* an inner "intellectual order" in that a part of James's method is a concentration on the elements within the story itself, a consistency which does not need to conform strictly to that of the world of reality. In *The Bostonians* (*Atlantic,* 1886) Scudder found the same fine workmanship but thought it spent on unworthy material, while in *The Tragic Muse* (*Atlantic,* 1890) he discovered a psychological realism which allowed the author to concentrate on the essentials of his tale and be true to the self-consistency of his art. This was Scudder's highest praise so far, and it anticipated the views of much later critics. Finally, in a note on *The Real Thing and Other Tales* (*Atlantic,* 1893) he declares James to be "the consummate artist in miniature story telling of this generation."

Among the many other favorably inclined reviewers of the day were Annie Macdonell who noted, in the *Bookman* (1896, and again in 1916 as a commemorative reprint), that James is a critic in his fiction and writes criticism as though it were fiction; and W. L. Cross who was one of the first to label James an "impressionist" in *The Development of the English Novel* (1899). Unfavorable reviews took several clearly defined lines. There were those who objected to him because they objected to realism in general; those who, like M. Logan in the *Nation* (1893), found in him only "form without substance"; those who attacked his style and found him obscure, like F. M. Colby in "The Queerness of Henry James" (*Bookman,* 1902) and "In Darkest James" (*Imaginary Obligations,* 1904); and those who like Claude Bragden (*Critic,* 1904 and 1905) really objected to James's moral point of view and did him more harm than good by attempted defences of his method of dealing with sublimated and distorted passion. James is attacked on grounds of lack of patriotism by J. C. Underwood (*Literature and Insurgency,* 1914) and his plays were depreciated by most dramatic critics including Harriet W. Preston in the *Atlantic* (1891) and Clayton Hamilton in the *Forum* (1909).

The critical summing up toward the end of James's career was done best by W. C. Brownell and Elizabeth Cary. Brownell was reviewing James as early as 1882 in the *Nation* where he acknowledged that *The Portrait of a Lady* was James's best work to that date and yet, like Howells and others, he regretted that in his increasing complexity James had sacrificed his ability to write in the manner of his early romances. A more comprehensive analysis appeared in the *Atlantic* (1905) and again in *American Prose Masters* (1909). Brownell really knows his subject and speaks with authority although his statements are philosophical generalizations rather than, in the manner of the later critics, references to character, plot, and text. He appreciates James's seriousness, discusses his obscurity and elusiveness, gives him the mind of a scientific critic with emphasis on disinterestedness (which is a defect in a novelist in that it sacrifices passion) and ends by regretting the style of the later novels. In a book in which acceptance as a "prose master" means the award of almost as much blame as praise by this lofty and judicial critic, James fares rather less well than the others. As critics, Brownell and James were not too far apart: both owed debts to Matthew Arnold and Sainte-Beuve, both emphasized ethical as well as aesthetic criteria, both dealt with the personality of the author as reflected in his work; but the difference comes in their degree of relative emphasis on ethical and aesthetic criteria. Brownell cannot forgive James for leaning so far in the direction of art as a substitute for life. This a realist should not do; nor should he open moral questions which approved standards have closed.

The first book to offer a full-scale critique of James's work was *The Novels of Henry James* (1905), by Elizabeth Cary. An expansion of an article in *Scribner's* the previous year, this small volume exhibits more good sense than depth, but it seems to have established the form for subsequent studies. Accepting the sparse biographical facts as generally known, it proceeds at once to an analysis and appreciation of James as an international novelist of a special and disappearing privileged class. It recognizes his skill at portraying national character and revealing the qualities of the external world of things as well as those of the internal world of the heart. Recognizing that James's center of interest is in the moral issues of character development, this critic does an excellent preliminary evaluation of Isabel Archer, Milly Theale, and Maggie Verver, among others. Later critics like E. C. Marsh (*Bookman,* 1909) and W. B. Cairns (*Dial,* 1916) speak as though to a monument and either praise the greatness of the collected works or speculate on the decline of popularity of this master of his art.

By 1907, when the revised New York Edition of his works began to appear, Henry James had received the verdict of his peers and contemporaries and he did not have too much to be happy about. His was a lonely grandeur; but already a new generation of critics was suggesting further difficulties. Philip Littell recalled a fifteen-year-old review of *The Sacred Fount* that he had written (*New Republic,* 1915) and expressed himself as not so sure now as he was at the time. John Macy, in his generally forward-looking book *The Spirit of American Literature* (1913), began to hint at the theme of alienation and to reject especially the later novels as irrelevant to American literature; and Herbert Croly in the *Lamp* (1904) attempted to deal carefully with the question of exactly what price James paid for his expatriation. He expresses himself as feeling that James abandoned America because its society was too "innocent" and he needed the society of London in which to develop. The wide gulf, he feels, between this American author and the literature of his fellow countrymen is to be lamented, but the achievement of Henry James is so extraordinary that it "is absolutely its own justification." Without knowing exactly how this achievement was to be recognized in American literary history, Croly predicted that a way would be found.

Probably in part because of the tradition of anonymous reviewing, the British commentary on James was neither as extensive nor as discriminating as the American. Murray finds that, after an initially generous reaction, British reviewers steadily cooled toward James. M. Sturge Gretton in the *Contemporary Review* (1912) presented an informed study of the text of the Prefaces as they were appearing in the New York Edition and found that, although they do not contribute much to theory, they aid greatly in an understanding of the novels, especially the later ones, and they help to answer the question of "whether their centres are living enough to carry the complexity their author lays on them." This is the old hollow-core objection which Oliver Elton had already answered in a penetrating review of the ghost tales and *The Wings of the Dove* (*Modern Studies,* 1907), anticipating much of the appreciation by later critics of the more enigmatical of James's tales; and Morton Fullerton was one of the few British critics to appreciate this excellence of the late great novels (*Quart. Rev.,* 1910).

In his later years, James associated himself with the aesthetic movement in British letters and became friendly with the writers for the *Yellow Book,* to which he contributed, and others of similar leanings. Among them several recognized his worth. Conrad describes him as "the historian of fine consciences" (*Notes on Life and Letters,* 1912), Max Beerbohm contributed a good-natured burlesque of James's style in *A Christmas Garland* (1912), and F. M. Hueffer wrote a whole book of praise not unmixed with sensitive critical insights, *Henry James, A*

Critical Study (1916). Hueffer attributes the master's greatness to the fact that "he, more than anybody else, has observed human society as it now is, and more than anybody has faithfully rendered his observations for us." He is the greatest of the impressionists because of the fact that "the supreme function of Impressionism is selection, and that Mr. James has carried the power of selection so far that he can create an impression with nothing at all." It was time for Rebecca West's sensible, vigorous, and revealing article on "Reading Henry James in War Time" (*New Republic,* 1915), which led directly to the stimulating little volume *Henry James* (1916), and inaugurated a new era in James biography and criticism. Rebecca West quarrels violently with James's pallid view of Europe, blisters with scorn his treatment of women and of passion, sees his early work as diluted by Hawthorne and his last novels as showing the signs of age "like white streaks in a black beard," but still manages to convey to her reader a vivid sense of the quality of his genius, especially in the stories of the middle period. On occasion Henry James "poured into his crystal goblet the red wine that nourishes the soul." Although she fails to make clear the source of this true inspiration, she seems to succeed in turning all her blame for the master's weaknesses into a single revelation of his central strength.

2. *Alienation (1916-1934)*

James's dramatic renunciation of his citizenship just before his death was a final paradox in a career that seemed to follow no conventional laws, for it meant that he was turning from his native country just at the moment when it was preparing to recognize its literary geniuses, in order to identify himself with a tradition in which he must always appear as something of an alien. His success during his lifetime in reconciling the idealistic and the realistic tendencies in art was a victory too easily won; there were more fundamental issues ahead, in which he could take no personal part.

The factors which most influenced Jamesean criticism in the

period 1916-34 were the discoveries by the historians that the United States had had a literary history of its own and that there was a very active and indigenous American literary movement then in progress At the same time, historical and philological research in all the modern languages was becoming more thorough and exacting than the older forms of literary study had been. The work of Henry James began to be examined, explained, and evaluated in relationship to its sources in his inheritance, education, and environment, and some of the needed factual research was undertaken. But all paths seemed to lead deeper into the morass of paradox; the more one understood of the man and his work, the less reason there seemed to be for the aura of greatness that increasingly surrounded that formidable shelf of the now nearly completed New York Edition (1907-17). The internationalism which had seemed to the earlier critics to be merely a limitation of material now deepened into a theory of alienation, for James did not fit into the nationalistic currents of the then popular historical scholarship or into the naturalistic movement which then was giving shape to American literature.

All of this was to develop in the next two decades; in 1916 the mood of both British and American critics was that of appreciative commemoration. Hardly a major periodical on either side of the water but published during that spring and summer an article by the best critical talent it could command in summary of the achievement of this great novelist. The *NAR* reprinted Howells' earlier essay on James's last novel together with a commemorative essay by Edith F. Wyatt; the *Dial* printed a sensitive appraisal by E. E. Hale; and the *Atlantic* turned to Helen and Wilson Follett for an almost reverent summing-up. James's central theme, these critics felt, is Renunciation—not in the Christian sense, but so that the soul "may live up to itself." His "studied formal exquisiteness" makes his tales seem increasingly austere and simple as his style becomes more complex. E. P. Dargan contributed to the *New Republic* an allegorical appreciation of James's "two cities"—that of Ars Longa and that of Cosmopolis, the city of art and the city of internationalism—while Anna Leach offered a more personal note to the *Forum* and W. L. Phelps another to the *YR*. In England, Percy Lubbock, who was then at work collecting the letters, offered a full and simple review of the man and his work to the *Quarterly Review,* making clear the critical distinction between the thing enacted and the thing described, and providing one of the best introductions to James's work up to then available. Among other appreciative and critical essays in this same year were Walter de la Mare's in *Living Age* and W. L. Randell's in *Fortnightly Review,* while Bliss Perry prepared a brief tribute for the American Academy of Arts and Letters in 1921.

Critical issues behind most of these commemorative essays faced backward rather than forward: What sort of a realist was Henry James? Did he have anything important to say about life or was his material so narrowly limited to one social class and to the international set that he defeated his own aims? Was he an idealist and a moralist or was he completely immoral? Had his later novels degenerated into vagueness and obscurity? The same frame of reference continued to influence literary historians for some time to come. F. L. Pattee, pioneer in the teaching of American literature on the college level, wrote a *History of American Literature Since 1870* (1917) and *The Development of the American Short Story* (1923) in which he presented James's work in this light with sympathy and comprehension. Linking him with Howells as a scientific realist, a term which he identifies with "the Classical Reaction against Sturm und Drang Romanticism," he credits James with standing for specialization, "all objective, external phenomena observed and recorded," his purpose in this short-length fiction being "to preserve for the future its author's observations upon the life and characters and manners of his epoch." G. E. DeMille, in *Literary Criticism in America, A Preliminary Survey* (1931) and A. H. Quinn in *American Fiction* (1936) make the same links with Howells and realism but find James limited in his range of experience and too "international" to give an accurate reading of American life, as does M. W. Sampson in his introduction to *The Ambassadors* (1930). The voice of neo-humanism—but one degree more critical than that of the idealists—was heard once again in S. P. Sherman's essay on "The Aesthetic Idealism of Henry James" (*On Contemporary Literature,* 1917). The distinctive quality of James's work, thought Sherman, lies in its existence solely on one level, that of the aesthetic experience. His love of beauty is shaped and controlled by his love of perfection. He lives in an imaginary world where the governing principle is a sense of style.

To counter this now more or less established critical formula there soon appeared the literary radicals with their theories of alienation and frustration for the American artist in general and for Henry James in particular. During 1923, Van Wyck Brooks published three articles in the *Dial,* which were trial flights for *The Pilgrimage of Henry James* (1925) and which defined the new socio-psychological approach to literary problems. As the implications of this approach are largely biographical, this book and others related to it have already been discussed in an earlier section of this essay, but the issue itself was critical. Dorothy Bethurum reasserted James's moral consciousness against Sherman's charge of pure aestheticism in *SR* (1923) and Edna Kenton took Brooks to task in the *Bookman* (1925), as did Alyse Gregory (*American Criticism,* ed. W. A. Drake, 1926), and S. T. Liljegren in *American and European in the Works of Henry James* (1920). Brooks carried his point one step further in "Henry James as a Reviewer" (*Sketches in Criticism,* 1932), in which he praises the reviews written before James had reached the age of twenty-four and attributes the "decay of Henry James" to his expatriation. In a humorous attack on Ezra Pound, Philip Guedalla took a similar psychological approach with his since famous formula of the three Jameses: James the First, James the Second, and the Old Pretender (*New Statesman,* 1919). Guedalla expresses his own preference (which was the same as Rebecca West's) for James II and explains the Old Pretender's reign as "a long struggle to get back to something he had somehow, somewhere lost." Literary historians of the time fell in with the formula to a greater or less degree, mixing it freely with that of realism. V. L. Parrington pronounced what is probably the most scornful dismissal of James in any serious literary history, in his *Main Currents of American Thought* (1930), dubbing him "the last refinement of the genteel tradition," while Harry Hartwick in *The Foreground of American Fiction* (1934) declared that, as an anti-naturalist, James should have been a neohumanist, but his lack of self-control made for diffuse, narrow, obscure, and unreadable novels. Carl Van Doren, taking a middle ground as did H. S. Canby, Norman Collins (*The Facts of Fiction,* 1932), and others, included in his history of *The American Novel* (1921; rev., 1940) a sane review of the principal novels and shorter stories, appreciative of their insights and their artistry, but he felt that James falls short of being a truly great artist because he is limited by his sense of contrastic nationalism and because of his attempt "in a democratic age to write courtly romances."

This hint of a new political approach had already been heard in an essay by J. C. Powys (*Suspended Judgments,* 1916) in which James was defined as a novelist of the polite leisure class that has time to explore its soul. It became even more overt in the early thirties when James's stock reached what was perhaps its all-time low with the application of the Marxian formula to literary history. C. H. Grattan in the *Nation* (1932) pointed out that James had identified himself with the parasitic leisure class of a dying culture rather than with the rising proletariat; Granville Hicks in his survey of recent American literature as measured by the Marxian hypothesis, *The Great Tradition* (1933), carried the charge one step further by suggesting that James's profession of the religion of art not only separated him from America, it separated him from reality so that he could not even write about his own restricted leisure and international class; and Robert Cantwell, in the *New Republic* (1934, 1937) gave James a ray of comfort with his thought that, in refraining from involvement in Fabian socialism and by being loyal to his own class, he escaped the fate of many novelists and, in his character of Owen Wingrave, gave a warning of the coming conflict even though he himself could not fully understand the significance of social change.

At the same time, the more systematic study of James was beginning in the universities. Dissertations were undertaken on aspects of his work during the twenties and thirties at the universities of Pennsylvania, Cornell, Ohio State, Munich, and Marburg. At Strasbourg, Marie Reine Garnier completed a careful and enthusiastic study of *Henry James et la France* (1927) in the Department of Comparative Literature, and at Paris, an American, Leon Edel, did his pioneer studies of *Les anneés dramatiques* and *The Prefaces of Henry James* (1931). One of the best of these special studies is *The Early Development of Henry James,* prepared at the University of Illinois by Cornelia P. Kelley (1930), a thorough critical analysis of all identifiable reviews, essays, and tales by James from 1864, the date of the earliest known review, to 1881, the date of *The Portrait of a Lady*. An even more specialized study of James's reviews and critical essays is *Henry James's Literary Criticism,* a Harvard dissertation (1928) by Morris Roberts who maintains both a careful objectivity and a consistent theory about James as a critic as he follows him from the early reviews, through *Partial Portraits* to the Prefaces and *Notes on Novelists*. Roberts shows how the critical mind was reflected in the fiction and deals fairly with the limitations and paradoxes of James's personality and art. Another special study on James as a critic is the introduction by Pierre de Chaignon la Rose to *Notes and Reviews by Henry James* (1921), a collection of twenty-five early reviews which appeared during 1864-66. Notes on individual stories began to appear in the journals with R. D. Havens' "The Revision of Roderick Hudson" (*PMLA*, 1925) and E. J. Goodspeed's suggestion that a Julia Newberry might have been the original of Daisy Miller (*Atlantic,* 1934). And, in addition to Edel's monograph on the drama, there had been brief notes on this subject by Brander Matthews (*Playwrights on Playmaking,* 1923) and Edna Kenton (*Theatre Arts,* 1928).

The most useful single work of scholarship during this period was the collection and editing of the *Letters* by Percy Lubbock. In his introduction to the first volume, Lubbock discusses "The Mind of the Artist" against a background of biographical evidence not available to any previous critic, and he carries his analysis further in his *The Craft of Fiction* (1921), in which he uses James—particularly *The Ambassadors*—to illustrate "the art of dramatizing the picture of somebody's experience." James, he thinks, carries this technique to the furthest limits of its possibilities. Lubbock's studies were reviewed favorably by Robert Herrick (*YR,* 1922), J. G. Huneker (*Bookman,* 1920), A. B. Walkley (*Fortnightly,* 1920), and H. D. Davray (*Mercure de France,* 1921), and gave stimulation to both the biographical and technical re-examination of James and his writings.

These new trends were reflected in the definitive work of Pelham Edgar and J. W. Beach. Edgar had already begun to turn his attention to technical problems in an article in the *Proceedings and Transactions of the Royal Society of Canada* (1918-19), in which he had spoken of James as a model of a "severe standard of technical excellence," acknowledged his indebtedness to Flaubert and Balzac, stressed his discipline in method as illustrated in *The Ivory Tower* and *The Ambassadors,* and called attention to his lack of real knowledge of "the region of unawareness." In the *National Review* (1924), Edgar carried his study on to an analysis of the space-time difficulty in fiction and to James's method of control through economy of method in the handling of the unities, and in the *Dalhousie Review* (1925) he gave a foretaste of his major book with an introductory analysis of the three big novels. The book itself, *Henry James, Man and Author* (1927), has already been discussed as biography, but is even more important as a comprehensive critical study of the whole corpus of James's writing. Refusing to make a choice between the early and the late novelist, Edgar proves conclusively that the differences are but two aspects of the same great genius.

The study of technique became the special province of J. W.

Beach with *The Method of Henry James* (1918), a full-scale critical analysis which provided material for the same author's chapters on James in *CHAL* (1917-21) and in his own survey, *The Twentieth Century Novel, Studies in Technique* (1932), as well as in miscellaneous articles including one on "The Novel from James to Joyce," in the *Nation* (1931), in which he points out that James represents the tendency which can be called dramatic whereas the method of Joyce is that of the post-impressionists in painting. Published first in 1918, *The Method of Henry James* was reprinted in 1954 with a useful introductory essay, revealing even more clearly than had at first appeared how very much of a pathfinder Beach really was. Accepting James's own thesis that the writing of fiction is an art and may be a highly complex and precise art, he blocks out his career into six stages from "Obscure Beginnings" through "Early Prime," and "Achievement" to "Full Prime." "It is a chief distinction of James," asserts this critic, "that he was the first to write novels in English with a full and fine sense of the principles of composition," and it can be said of Beach that he was the first critic of James to recognize this fact and to distinguish the fine points and the structural relationships implied by the approach through technique. All subsequent criticism of James has been built on the findings of this book.

While scholarship on James was thus progressing toward firmer foundations, criticism was called to a more exact reckoning by Ezra Pound, T. S. Eliot, and Edmund Wilson. Wilson issued the challenge perhaps most succinctly when, in a review of Pelham Edgar, he said (*New Republic,* 1927): "What is perhaps most needed now, in connection with James, is a thorough exploration of his fiction to find out what is actually in it—that is, precisely what is supposed to happen in each of his novels and stories and precisely what inferences we are supposed to draw." Wilson later furthered the cause by republishing in *The Shock of Recognition* (1943), T. S. Eliot's two brief notes on Henry James which he had written at Pound's invitation for a special James number of the *Little Review* back in 1918 and which Eliot had not republished in the interval. Eliot's shocking overstatements, of which "He had a mind so fine that no idea could violate it" is perhaps the most quoted, served to swing James criticism abruptly from a romantic to a neoclassic orientation and to reverse almost everything general critics had said up to this time about the man and his work. The alienation theme was revised to read: "There are advantages, indeed, in coming from a large flat country which no one wants to visit." And the kinship with Hawthorne, which had been thought of as largely a sentimental beginning of James's career, is given deep roots in the security of a cultural tradition (that of New England at mid-century) in which the literary man had leisure and social place, and by a reminder that it is in James's final and unfinished novel, *The Sense of the Past,* that the Hawthorne influence is most strongly felt. Such insights and insults made it possible for criticism to turn a positive and sympathetic mind onto those problems of control, discipline, limitation, and standards which the earlier romantic critics had looked at with more than a hint of jaundice. Pound's own notes in the same issue of the *Little Review,* "In Explanation," "Brief Note," "A Shake Down," and "The Middle Years," had a slightly different emphasis in that they dealt more with the content of James's thought, but they supplemented Eliot's in their enthusiasm for what James really was and was trying to accomplish. Finding that his art was great because it dealt with the personal tyrannies of people and with their efforts toward international understanding, Pound called attention to James's concern with the major forces in conflict in the modern world and with discovering an art through which he could give those forces expression in the lives of individuals. Their incoherence is perhaps more striking than their insights when these papers are read today as reprinted in *Instigations* (1920), but the direction of their influence is, like the comparing of James to a general by Gertrude Stein, in *Four in America* (1947) toward an affirmative re-evaluation in the coming age.

Other feathers in the wind, moving cautiously in the same

direction, were the special Henry James number of the British magazine, *The Egoist* (1918); an article on "The Clearness of Henry James" (*SR,* 1919) by R. D. Cornelius, in which attention is called to what James himself says in his Prefaces on the subject of method; another by W. L. Randell, "Henry James as Humanist" (*Fortnightly,* 1921), which is an early effort to defend James's understanding of people outside of his own class (an anticipation of Trilling on *The Princess Casamassima*); a third, "Henry James to the Ruminant Reader" (*The Arts,* 1924) by Edna Kenton, in which the study of James's "point of view" gives some basis for Wilson's Freudian interpretation of *The Turn of the Screw;* and another by Hélène Harvitt (*PMLA,* 1924) on the revisions of *Roderick Hudson.* But perhaps the best indication of new thinking in Jamesean criticism in this period came from Herbert Read in an article collected in *The Sense of Glory* (1930). Here the influence of Pelham Edgar and J. W. Beach is shown to be dominant, that of Brooks recessive, for Read sees James as raising and pointing a solution to most of the current problems of literary criticism in fiction: the problem of the form of the novel, that of the responsibility of the novelist, and that of the role of the novel today. Disregarding the evidence of his Americanism of material and feeling, Read also finds him standing for a kind of British integrity between the barbarities of America and Russia, "a calm, dominant, reticent and fastidious intellect, ordering the gathered forces of time to a manifestation of their enduring glory."

3. *The James Revival (1934-1954)*

The criticism of Henry James moved into a third phase in the middle 1930's with a resulting upsurge of interest in all aspects of his writing and thought that made him seem more alive and contemporary than were many writers who lived and wrote in this period. Part of the reason for this change in his critical reception was the mere passage of time with its clarification of some of the obscurities and objections that had stood in the way of his earlier readers; part was a basic shift in emphasis in American literary criticism and history in general, which happened to be of a nature to make James central in a new movement. During his lifetime James had been out of sympathy with both the waning gentility of the idealists and the literal realism of their opponents; he had fared even worse as an American writer when the emphasis of criticism and research was on nationalism and naturalism; but when the fashionable direction of critical thought shifted to the analysis of the work of art as such and to the psychology of the aesthetic process, his pioneering work in the theory and practice of fiction threw him into the center as the leader of the modern movement in the novel and short story, not only in American but in English literature as well.

This is not the place to review in detail the rise of reactionary tendencies in American and British critical thought of the thirties and forties, which have been loosely but conveniently grouped under the phrase, the "New Criticism." In America the influence of the expatriated Ezra Pound, Gertrude Stein, and T. S. Eliot was felt to lead in this direction as early as 1920; and those Southern writers associated with the so-called "Fugitive" group began about that time to call attention to the need for better means of analyzing the meaning of a work of art without reference to the extrinsic circumstances of its creation or to the personality of its creator, and to demand firmer standards and surer methods in literary art, as well as in religion and politics. This group, and others more or less associated with it in common aims, found in T. S. Eliot their perfect example and leader for poetry and criticism, but there was no living American or British novelist who satisfied their needs in intrinsic greatness and in devotion to the cause of art. Henry James was a ready-made "modern," and his work was complete and obviously distinguished. The "New Critics" therefore turned the full force of their talents upon him—together with Proust, Joyce, Kafka, and other European "moderns"—and, as their influence grew in academic circles, they brought to the study of James not only a new angle of vision but a good deal of basic and factual research, particularly into semantic problems approached through psychology. As a result, James received for the first time a critical evaluation which was sympathetic as well as thorough, and many of the old paradoxes in the interpretation of his life and work disappeared in the enthusiasm and the bickerings of critics who worshipped together at the altar of the master, differing only in the fine points of ritualistic observance.

The existence of a Henry James "revival" had been finally and belatedly recognized by the time of the centenary of his birth, 1943, and the reasons for it sought. W. H. Auden struck the keynote of the movement in his commemorative poem, "At the Grave of Henry James" (*Partisan,* 1941), when he turned from the confusions of the modern world for comfort to this "master of romance and scruple," but perhaps the underlying reasons were best expressed by Malcolm Cowley (*New Republic,* 1945) when he attributed the revival to a growing literary nationalism which was eager to claim a self-conscious artist and to a reaction against purely social and political standards in literature. Similarly deterministic explanations were offered by Isidor Schneider (*New Masses,* 1945) and Paul Rosenfeld who argued in the *Commonweal* (1946) that the revival was the result of naturalism's having run its course and, with her coming of age, America's rediscovery of her great novelist of the mind. Q. D. Leavis gave a more sophisticated explanation in *Scrutiny* (1947) when she attributed the change in interpretation of James to the shift of emphasis in criticism to myth and symbolism that began with William Troy (*Bookman,* 1931) and which leads into Blackmur's extraction of a theory of the artist by a study of the texts. Clifton Fadiman gave the credit for the change chiefly to Matthiessen and Rahv by setting up five points of an imaginary indictment against James and then showing how these critics helped to answer each of them (N. Y. *Herald-Tribune Books,* 1945), while Leon Edel demonstrated (*Atlantic,* 1948) how James had himself obscured his personality as the gulf between him and his readers widened during the latter years, and how, after 1943, the clutter of subjective criticism that had accumulated about him began to be blown away like "dandelion fuzz" as, with the studies and reprints of Matthiessen, the real James began to assert himself.

Whatever the reasons, it was clear that the work of Henry James had begun to emerge from misunderstanding when the *H & H* published a commemorative issue devoted exclusively to him in the spring of 1934. The editor, Lincoln Kirstein, proposed that James could serve as "an admirable point of departure for an inquest into the present condition of our literature" and that his contributors formed "a younger generation who, as yet, have not expressed their gratitude to the great novelist." Conspicuous by their absence from this symposium were the elder and the academic scholars, but the roll-call of those present included many who were to become leaders in Jamesean study in the next decade. Among these latter were Edmund Wilson, Stephen Spender, R. P. Blackmur, Edna Kenton, and Francis Fergusson. The old issues of realism, internationalism, obscurity, and the like were scarcely mentioned in these articles, but where they were, the bias was new. Lawrence Leighton suggested that James's sensibility to tradition was not merely a problem of European versus American civilization, but rather the record of a man fundamentally out of sympathy with his own times because of his temperamental devotion to "tradition, duration, continuity"; Stephen Spender proposed squeamishness rather than snobbishness as the cause of James's preference for European society, and Newton Arvin offered the usual variations on Marxist interpretation, describing James from *The Princess Casamassima* onward as "the chronicler of a festering society," lacking in the historical sense or in awareness of the forces stirring in the world of the almighty dollar, a view which Robert Cantwell seconded with less point. Edna Kenton's offerings in two articles were in the interest of factual and bibliographical knowledge, and in a third she pointed out that Henry James himself thoroughly discusses the problem of the artist-expatriate in his biographies of Hawthorne and Story.

Marianne Moore's note on the doctrine of being wholly oneself as the key to James's treatment of character and Francis Fergusson's on "The Drama in *The Golden Bowl*" were hints of general trends, whereas R. P. Blackmur's first printing of what was to become later his Preface to *The Art of the Novel* and Edmund Wilson's proposal of a Freudian interpretation for *The Turn of the Screw* opened up new vistas of critical study which will be discussed later in this essay. The several other essays in the issue are relatively inconsequential but help to fill out the most influential periodical publication in the history of Jamesean criticism. Its only rival, the commemorative issue of *KR* in the centennial year of 1943, contained articles of greater depth, but the new directions of criticism had by then been determined.

Although most of the people at first concerned in the James revival were not professional scholars, one of the first results of their positive attitude was a quickening of research activity. This took the form of edited and annotated collections, selections, and individual editions of his writing; of closer study of the text of his novels and tales, especially of his own revisions; of sporadic studies of the sources of his plots and characters; and of definitive work on his careers as dramatist and critic. All of this work taken together provides little more than a beginning of what needs to be done, but it is at least a beginning.

Henry James, Representative Selections, with Introduction, Bibliography, and Notes (AWS) by L. N. Richardson (1941) is an example of how a book of selections can be made into a handbook for research and criticism. Sympathetically, but with scholarly objectivity, Richardson considered all the problems of biography, style, literary theory and practice, social and political ideas, characterization, and basic philosophy in a well-planned introduction; his biblography provided the first comprehensive review of Jamesean scholarship and commentary; his chronological table collected the biographical and bibliographical facts of the novelist's career into a compressed table for ready reference; and his selections, with their editorial notes, provided a fair portrait of the early as well as the late James, of the critic as well as the writer of fiction, but not of the dramatist. This book has as yet no rival as a starting point for the study of James, although Oscar Cargill is at work on a handbook similar to that on Whitman by G. W. Allen and others in the same series.

The selection of tales from Henry James for special or popular volumes began during his own lifetime, but such volumes were few and inconsequential until a sudden deluge after 1943. Of the many published in recent years, only three or four are of scholarly importance. Perhaps most widely read are *The Great Short Novels of Henry James* (1944), edited by Philip Rahv, and *The Short Stories of Henry James* (1945), edited by Clifton Fadiman. These and other similar volumes of selections helped to crystallize the new approach to the interpretation of James, but the introductions were mainly biographical and relatively superficial. A few such collections, by emphasizing a particular aspect of James's work, helped to focus critical opinion. The best of these are the two edited by F. O. Matthiessen, *Stories of Writers and Artists by Henry James* (1944) and *The American Novels and Stories of Henry James* (1947). In both cases the selection and arrangement of the tales document introductions which add to understanding. The same can be said of *The American Scene* (1946), edited by W. H. Auden, and *The Ghostly Tales of Henry James* (1948), edited by Leon Edel. The problem of the periodically published but "uncollected" tales is discussed by B. R. McElderry, Jr., in *AL* (1949) and S. E. Lind (*AL,* 1951); and a total of thirteen such tales were collected in volumes edited by Albert Mordell (1919) and Edna Kenton (1950).

In similar manner the many edited printings of individual novels that appeared after 1943 added little information of scholarly import and few new critical insights, even though, taken together, they mainly reflect the positive aspects of the revival. A few have introductions which so illumine the text as to enhance or redirect interpretation. Among these are the introduction by Michael Swan to *What Maisie Knew* (1947), Lionel Trilling's introductions to *The Princess Casamassima* (1948) and *The Bostonians* (1952), Herbert Read's to *The Wings of the Dove* (1948), Carl Van Doren's to *The Turn of the Screw* (1949), and R. P. Blackmur's to *The Golden Bowl* (1952).

Although earlier critics like Herrick and Garland had objected to James's habit of constant revision of his text, the problem was first discussed dispassionately as one for scholarly solution by Richardson in 1941. The *TLS* in 1949 raised it again in its correspondents' column, whereat Leavis, West, Garnett and some others expressed preference for the earlier texts, while Leon Edel held that good scholarship requires a comparison of the two or more that James printed. No one in this exchange of opinion sided with James himself in preferring the later text; and the problem is not yet satisfactorily settled although each of James's many editors has had to make a choice, and some, including Richardson, have preferred the revisions.

A comparison of the text of the New York Edition with the early versions is the crux but not the whole of the issue. Edel proposed in an article on "The Architecture of James's New York Edition" (*NEQ*, 1951), that James had in mind Balzac's *Comédie humaine* in twenty-three volumes and therefore planned an edition of twenty-three volumes (later expanded to twenty-six) as a *Comédie* of international humanity. This would explain the omission of titles that really, on their merit, should have been included and would also explain his efforts to make the text of the earlier novels and tales more nearly like that of the later. But James had persistently altered the texts of these earlier works, both in adapting them from their magazine to their book form and as between editions. A. J. A. Waldock discussed this problem of the earlier texts in *James Joyce and Others* (1937), as did Simon Nowell-Smith in editing *The Reverberator* (1949). B. R. McElderry, Jr., pointed out (*MLN*, 1952) that there was less editorial skill in the changes between the *Atlantic* and the first book versions of *Watch and Ward* than in revisions of the New York Edition. A. F. Gegenheimer used "The Passionate Pilgrim" to emphasize James's interest in the exact word and the visual image in his revisions, and R. A. Gettman, in studying the 1877 and 1907 editions of *The American,* showed by parallel columns that James's changes were mainly stylistic—the addition of modifiers, the substitution of concrete for general words, and a considerable increase in the use of figures. Sentences, he found, are longer, although they refine and expand rather than alter the meaning. R. E. Young thought that he had discovered evidence of the carelessness of James in reading his own stories ("An Error in *The Ambassadors*," *AL,* 1950). An error in the order of two chapters in the first American and in subsequent editions was apparently not detected by James himself in editing the New York Edition. Leon Edel hotly debated the issue with Young in subsequent numbers of *AL* (1952). Edel's point that James saw the correct English rather than the garbled American edition through the press seems to be supported by these findings. Although most studies so far have limited their consideration to matters of style, Matthiessen made a good case in his thorough analysis of the changes in *The Portrait of a Lady* (*Henry James, The Major Phase,* 1944) for relating the changes in each case, as Viola Dunbar did in her study of Daisy Miller (*MLN,* 1950), to James's own interpretation of the central character. It would seem that the larger problem of the significance of textual variations has scarcely been touched.

Comparatively little has been done in tracing sources for James's plots, themes, characters, etc. Daniel Lerner and Oscar Cargill (*PMLA,* 1951) have presented a case for his classical knowledge by showing relations of *The Bostonians* and *The Other House* to the *Antigone* of Sophocles and the *Medea* of Euripides, and R. W. Short has indicated a kinship between James and euphuistic prose by an analysis of specific stylistic devices. In spite of biographical facts and James's own accounts of his reading and friendships, little precise study has been made of his debts to European novelists and dramatists. Herbert Edwards has followed up Edel's hint of Ibsen's influence in ethical theme and scenic method in the later novels (*AL,* 1952), Daniel Lerner has traced specific borrowings from Turgenev's *Virgin Soil* for *The Princess Casamassima,* concluding that this novel is James's most derivative work, and Viola Dunbar finds the same influence on *Roderick Hudson* as well as some influence of Dumas *fils* (*MLN,* 1948, 1952). W. C. D. Pacey's note on the influence of French novelists (*AL,* 1941) is too general to be convincing, but F. R. Leavis in *Scrutiny* (1946, 1948) and again in *The Great Tradition* (1948) gives a carefully documented examination of the influence of George Eliot's *Daniel Deronda* on *The Portrait of a Lady.* The Hawthorne influence which is so frequently discussed is given specific documentation by J. F. Lucke (*NEQ,* 1953) and Edward Stone suggests a debt of "Daisy Miller" to Cherbuliez (*PQ,* 1950) as well as a general influence of the enchantment of Rome in "The Last of the Valerii" (*BPLQ,* 1951). Originals for some of James's characters have also been suggested: Dr. H. L. Rypins, in an article held from publication for twenty-five years, attempted to identify Sir Luke Strett (*AL,* 1953), and Miriam Allott suggested (*MLN,* 1953) that the original of the Bronzino portrait in *The Wings of the Dove* might be the painting of Lucrezia Panciatichi in the Uffizi Gallery. Edel suggested that the fictional portrait of Jane Clairmont in *The Aspern Papers* might have drawn life from James's memories of his Great Aunt Wyckoff (*MLN,* 1952). The influence of James on others is suggested by Elizabeth F. Hoxie who blames nineteenth-century comments on Daisy Miller for the American vogue of chaperonage (*NEQ,* 1946) and by J. J. Robinson who seeks a direct influence of *The Middle Years* on Schulberg's *The Disenchanted* (*MLN,* 1952). It takes little imagination to realize that the influence of Henry James on other novelists extends far beyond these few hints, even though thorough study of the problem has not yet been made.

Another aspect of the James revival was the increasing study of his own criticism of fiction, painting, and the drama. As modern criticism became more interested in the theory of literature and the semantic analysis of the individual work, and less in mere impressionistic comment on men and books, James came more and more to represent the ideal critic as well as the ideal writer of fiction. The study by Morris Roberts in 1928, the republication of the early essays in *Notes and Reviews* in 1921 and the incidental study by Cornelia Kelley of the criticism along with James's other early work in 1930 had little immediate response. Laurence Barrett lists in a footnote to his valuable article, "Young Henry James, Critic" (*AL,* 1949), a half dozen earlier essays on this subject. Barrett concludes that the young Henry James was not only a good critic, he was much more influential than we have hitherto supposed. The real impetus to appreciation of the criticism came with R. P. Blackmur's collection of James's own Prefaces in *The Art of the Novel* (1934, 1948). In his Introduction, Blackmur succeeds in producing as sound and well rounded an essay on James as we have by separating out the principal topics touched upon in James's essays and presenting a rationale of his fictional method. Morris Roberts returned to the subject with an introduction to a volume of selections, *The Art of Fiction and Other Essays* (1948), in which he reviewed James's debt to the French and restated his belief that criticism and fiction are inseparable in the work of the master. R. W. Stallman quoted generously from James in *The Critic's Notebook* (1950) and R. W. Short attempted (*PMLA,* 1950) to systematize James's criticism of fiction by adopting his own terms, "action and character, register and centre, and scene and picture." Two critics called attention to James's appreciation of the plastic arts, especially painting: Jerome Mellquist in "From Henry James to Paul Rosenfeld" (*SR,* 1946) called for a further study of James's three works of art criticism, but F. O. Matthiessen, in "James and the Plastic Arts" (*KR,* 1943), had already shown that James not only used painters as subjects of his stories, but that he learned from painting as well as from the theatre some of the most useful of his methods, particularly in his later novels.

Matthiessen finds in painting a source for the abundance of images and scenes that gave his art compositional permanence. As a dramatic critic also James came into late appreciation. Allan Wade suggested in an article in *Theatre Arts* (1943) that James might have developed into an important dramatic critic because he appreciated the role of the theatre in society; and then he collected James's scattered essays on this subject into a volume, *The Scenic Art* (1948).

James's own unhappy excursion into the drama was treated lightly or dismissed by early critics, but modern research and criticism has done a thorough job in this department. Attention was redirected to this aspect of his work when the critics began to realize that much of his art of fiction was essentially dramatic, especially in the later novels where it was apparent that his experiment with playwriting, although perhaps a failure in itself, had contributed much to the development of the technique of his novels. As an increasing number of his stories were dramatized by others, the critics began to call attention to the essentially dramatic quality of all of his work. Francis Fergusson in "James's Idea of Dramatic Form" (*KR,* 1943) summarized the problem. James's formal plays were failures, Fergusson believes, because, in attempting to conform to the "well-made play of the Scribe tradition," he was forced to choose subjects which did not interest him. When he gave up writing for the stage and wrote dramatically in the novel form, he succeeded in developing a drawing room drama in which the ideal spectator views an action "in the round" from many angles. Although modern drama has tended toward more romantic forms, this "classic" conception of form is still needed. Fergusson had earlier offered *The Golden Bowl* (*H & H,* 1934) as evidence of what James had learned from playwriting, and Leon Edel had discussed it in his pioneering Sorbonne dissertation (1931). Others took up the same theme: Jacques Barzun (*KR,* 1943) proposed that his dramatic art lay somewhere between comedy and tragedy in that his debt to the romantics had developed a kind of "aesthetic melodrama"; Donald Peacock (*The Poet in the Theatre,* 1946) thought that he had learned from drama his sense of moral crisis, his sense of architecture and direct presentation of action, and his analysis of human behavior. Morris Roberts (*Rev. of Eng. Studies,* 1946) felt the same "sense of present action without an elaborate scene" in *The Golden Bowl,* F. R. Leavis (*Scrutiny,* 1948) found *The Europeans* to be a comedy of manners enriched by its symbolic and poetic interests and organized as a dramatic poem, and P. N. Furbank (*Essays in Criticism,* 1951) agreed with Leavis that, in the understanding of the art of direct expression, James had a dramatic sense from the start.

All of this discussion of the effect of James's playwriting and his use of dramatic structures and techniques called for a restudy of the plays themselves and their stage history. This Leon Edel supplied in *The Complete Plays of Henry James* (1949). This single volume contains the fifteen complete and two unfinished plays. It is thoroughly documented by reference to contemporary sources and by a general introduction and explanatory notes for each play in which the full biographical and circumstantial facts are given. This, with Edel's edition of the narrative form of *The Other House* (1947), supplies all the data needed for the subsequent commentary on this subject by B. R. McElderry, Jr. (*Arizona Quart.,* 1952), S. E. Lind (*Amer. Quart.,* 1951), Herbert Read (*World Rev.,* 1950), F. W. Dupee (*Nation,* 1950), and Henry Popkin (*NEQ,* 1951). There was not much more to say.

One further practical result of the research and criticism on James during this period was the discovery of a more reasonable place for him as an American writer in general histories of American literature and of fiction. W. F. Taylor (*A History of American Letters,* 1936) recognized his position as an artist who found life itself to be an art, as did E. A. Baker (*The History of the English Novel,* 1938), Charles Cestre (*La littérature américaine,* 1945), Alexander Cowie (*The Rise of the American Novel,* 1948), Edward Wagenknecht (*Cavalcade of the American Novel,* 1952), Clarence Gohdes (*LAP,* ed. A. H.

Quinn, 1951), J. F. Cahen (*La littérature américaine,* 1950), C. Arnavon (*Historie littéraire des Etats Unis,* 1953), and Marcus Cunliffe (*The Literature of the United States,* 1954).

There was a tendency, however, among the French, Italian, German, and even some British critics to regard James either as a British writer or as an expatriate American not really representative of the national literature and therefore not as interesting as Poe, Thoreau, Whitman, and many others. H. Lüdeke and Jean Simon (*AL,* 1934) reported little on James in Germany or France, and the late European criticism is not as full nor as particularized as it is on other major American authors. Among the more perceptive of the critical essays of this period, written by Europeans in their own languages, are those by C. Cestre (*RAA,* 1932), Maria L. Asteldi (*Studi di letteratura inglese,* 1940), Giulio Castiglioni (*Maestri del Pensiera e dell' educazione; Profili,* 1944), B. Quvamme (*Edda,* 1944), Luigo Berti (*Inventario,* 1946-47), Pierre Brodin, "Présence de Henry James," in *Ecrivains américains du XXe siècle* (1946), Irène Simon (*Les formes du roman anglais de Dickens à Joyce,* 1949), and Jean Simon, *Le roman américaine au XXe siècle* (1949). Probably the best general summary of recent criticism of James by a European is Heidi Specker's "The Change in Emphasis in the Criticism of Henry James" (*English Studies,* Amsterdam, 1948). Based on Dupee's anthology, this review features the work of S. B. Liljegren but discusses most of the recent trends, and finds that a study of the criticism of James almost provides a history of American literary criticism. C. Arnavon similarly reviewed the French criticism of James in *Les lettres américaines devant la critique française* (1915), and information on the European reception of James was kindly supplied to this writer by Professors Maurice Le Breton and Hellmut Bock. Among published European dissertations on James, two concern his treatment of women, that by Lotte Borchers (Berlin, 1929) and that by F. Noel (Paris, 1942) but European scholars have been slow in undertaking research on James. Since 1945 Maurice Ie Breton and Hellmut Bock report a number of unpublished doctoral dissertations. These few references can not do more than to suggest the range and variety of European commentary on James, nor can this essay touch upon his reception in Japan and the Orient, where unquestionably he is known. A study of translations and commentary in languages other than English is much needed.

It would appear, however, that the point of view of the "New Criticism" was taking hold in other countries as it had been in England and the United States in the decade 1945-55. The summing up of all criticism to that date was made by F. W. Dupee in *The Question of Henry James: A Collection of Critical Essays* (1945). Almost half of the essays in this volume reflect the new attitudes and methods, even though not all of the leading critics are represented. These attitudes are remarkably consistent, the new questions to be asked and the new methods to be used in answering them appear time after time, and the same few critics are generally accepted.

Of these critics F. O. Matthiessen provides the best transition from the recognized aims and methods of the older scholarship to those of the new criticism. His thinking takes its start in his comparison of James with Hawthorne in *American Renaissance: Art and Expression in the Age of Emerson and Whitman* (1941). Picking up the problem of James from a discussion of Hawthorne's theory of fiction, he uses Hawthorne's term "Romance" as distinct from the novel and thus develops his case in the context in which James himself would have set it. At the start, he feels, James reflected Hawthorne's method of romance, but he renounced Hawthorne when he turned from romance to realism. In the later novels, he returned to Hawthorne's material, but improved on his method by understanding his limitations. In his symbolism, he perfected the allegory in which Hawthorne failed and he thus provided a link between Hawthorne and T. S. Eliot who best represents the modern philosophy of art. This is the idea which other critics had touched upon but had not grasped with the same breadth of understanding. Bernard Smith in *Forces in American Criticism*

(1939) had likewise started with the trend toward realism as something more than a method but had lost his way by imposing a doctrinal value-judgment on his findings, and Alfred Kazin in *On Native Grounds* (1942) had understood that James's problem was the problem of his generation, i.e., the effort to establish "a primary sense of realism in American letters," but he had not developed the point either in this volume or in his essay in the *New Republic* (1943) where he got so far as to suggest that both William and Henry James worked with a conviction that life has a meaning because it "always returned to the central self." Some other critics of the older schools also moved in this new direction by retaining the problem of "realism" as central, but avoiding its narrower definitions, among them Mary Colum (*From These Roots,* 1937), G. B. Munson (*UKCR,* 1950), and R. P. Falk in an excellent series of historical essays (*Essays . . . to Lily B. Campbell,* 1950; *NCF,* 1952; *Transitions in American Literary History,* 1953; and *The Development of American Literary Criticism,* 1955), in which he traces more accurately than anyone else has so far done the variations on the theory and methods of realism in the latter half of the nineteenth century. His final conclusion is that James did not accept realism because he was too much concerned with the personal in literature to be interested in a term which was so strongly social in its implications, but that, by delimiting the organic conception of the earlier idealists to its technical application to the work of art, he became the reconciler of the ideal and the real and so the central figure in a transitional era. This is a far more detailed development of the problem than was Matthiessen's but it is based on the same assumptions and similarly helps to tie the old with the new approaches to the criticism of James.

Matthiessen himself soon moved on from this base, through his researches in the James family papers, which produced his edition of the notebooks and his book on the family; but at the same time he brought to bear upon James his critical thinking learned from his study of Eliot and the modern movement in poetry. He was aided in making the application of this critical idiom to fiction by his collections of the tales dealing with the problem of the artist and of the American, but he brought his central ideas to a focus best in *Henry James, the Major Phase* (1944), a frontal attack upon the elder critics of both the genteel and the Brooks-Parrington schools. Using Edith Wharton's text, "For him every great novel must first of all be based on a profound sense of moral values and then constructed with a classical unity and economy of means," he concludes that the traditional misconceptions have arisen from the attempt to divorce content from form as well as from the mistaken notion that James's devotion to art was an alienation from life. This is the point from which the new criticism takes its start, and it was made emphatically clear by Matthiessen's analysis of the four later novels, *The Ambassadors, The Wings of the Dove, The Golden Bowl,* and *The Ivory Tower.* With his rich knowledge of the artist in James and just how he worked, Matthiessen does not succumb to the fallacy of himself divorcing the work of art from the artist, but he places his emphasis where James placed it, on the sense of life to be gained from a thorough analysis of a single character in the setting of life's problems which determined it. He thus can see these novels on the three levels of ethical import, of personality, and of structure and expression, as James himself saw them.

Matthiessen's emphasis on "the major phase" was accepted by Jamesean criticism pretty generally because it called attention to James's theories of life and art at the point at which their expression was most complex and therefore their study most rewarding. Reviews by Louise Bogan (*Nation,* 1944), Malcolm Cowley (*New Republic,* 1945), E. K. Brown (*YR,* 1945), and J. S. Wilson (*VQR,* 1945) were generally favorable, but F. R. Leavis produced a minority report in *Scrutiny* (1947), declaring a cleavage that influenced much subsequent criticism. Leavis became the spokesman in this essay for those who still preferred the early and middle James and who felt that these later novels were elaborations without substance; but most of the contemporary and the younger students and critics of James followed Matthiessen into a closer and closer (and often pedantic and repetitious) analysis of these later works, particularly of the characters of Lambert Strether, Milly Theale, and Maggie Verver. Among these were Randall Stewart (*UKCR,* 1943), Morris Roberts (*YR,* 1947), Michael Swan (*Henry James,* 1953), and G. H. Bantock (*Cambridge Jour.,* 1953). Other "neglected" novels were brought up for reconsideration as studies in good and evil also: the unfinished two, *The Ivory Tower* and *The Sense of the Past; The Awkward Age, What Maisie Knew, The Spoils of Poynton,* and *The Turn of the Screw,* more or less as a group dealing with Hawthorne's "sin of sins," the violation of the human spirit; *The Bostonians* and *The Princess Casamassima* as studies of society, and *The Sacred Fount* (*New Statesman and Nation,* 1947, and *ELH,* 1949) as a rejected study of evil; and Annette Kar (Baxter) (*Amer. Quart.,* 1953) and Lotus Snow (*UTQ,* 1953) wrote of the theme of innocence. With the emphasis of Leavis and some others on the early novels, there was little of James's fiction that did not come in for reconsideration in these years.

Although the best way to describe the change in attitude might be merely to say that twentieth-century moral philosophy was more congenial to James than was the moral philosophy of his own day, it is possible to point to three influences which helped to bring about the change. They were pragmatism with its generally relativistic view of all problems; Freudianism with its emphasis on the personality through unconscious motivation; and Marxism with its rigid view of social structure and social change. James himself, of course, experienced only the first of these, but by the time of the James revival, all three had been modified and absorbed by the critics into a relativistic moral base for the study of the individual in society.

The shift of moral emphasis was disturbing to those critics who did not accept the new morality themselves. Yvor Winters in *Maule's Curse* (1938) made a study of the discrepancy between an inherited moral sense and the moral relativity of the

American experience in a number of American writers, past and recent. This discrepancy he found illustrated in James's isolation of ethical choice from the natural frame of moral ideas and his treatment of it as an element of character and of plot only. Herein lay James's strength as a novelist of character and his weakness as a moral thinker. For slightly different reasons Graham Greene, in an essay in *The English Novelists,* edited by Derek Verschoyle (1936) and translated into French in *La Table Ronde* (1950), and F. X. Connolly in an essay in *Thought* (1950), found a discrepancy between the sense of evil, religious in its intensity, that drove James to write and the form that his interpretation took. Others found James's underlying morality frankly relativistic and welcomed the change. Philip Rahv (*New Republic,* 1943) showed how this view allowed James to confront the contradictions and ambiguities of life with a sense of history and a sense of humanity that supplied the irony for his art, while Joseph Firebaugh (*VQR,* 1951, and *Jour. of Aesthetics and Art Criticism,* 1953) attempted to get at James's relativism by accepting the views of some of his characters as the views of the novelist himself. J. H. Raleigh (*PMLA,* 1951) did a more systematic examination of James's empiricism and made the point that, by his analytical treatment of human relationships, James gives an example of the atomistic quality of American culture. He argues further that James's true meaning is his technique, a commentary not only on James but on the rationale of American life as well. These are nearly all the efforts so far to study James's moral philosophy in itself and apart from his art; the critics who have merely accepted it as a factor in his art have been generally more successful in understanding it.

The use of psychoanalysis as an instrument of literary criticism has also helped in the reinterpretation of James's basic ideas. Efforts to make this application to biographical interpretation led, as we have seen, to devaluation of James as a man and artist, but the assumption that, even though he could not know Freudianism as such, he was himself well advanced in this kind of thinking, has been more successful in a few general studies like J. W. Shroeder's "The Mothers of Henry James" (*AL,* 1951) and as a means of analyzing certain of his stories. Among these are such obvious ones as "The Beast in the Jungle," "Maud-Evelyn," "The Jolly Corner," and incidentally many of the longer stories and novels, but the controversy on the subject has centered on "The Turn of the Screw," starting with Edmund Wilson's article in *H & H* (1934), in which he develops the idea that the governess-narrator of the story is herself a case of neurotic sex-repression and that the ghosts are nothing but Freudian symbols. Edna Kenton had advanced a similar theory as early as 1924 in *The Arts,* and Edmund Wilson had other things to say about Henry James (*PR,* 1938, and *New Yorker,* 1944, 1946), but the association of Wilson with Freudianism in James was firmly fixed by the controversy that this article aroused. Attention was incidentally called to the Demuth illustrations by J. L. Sweeney (*KR,* 1943) and other sources for the story were proposed by R. L. Wolff (*AL,* 1941), but few critics defended the theory.

Replies to the Wilson theory were slow in starting but eventually were many. N. B. Fagin suggested in *MLN* (1941) that the story might well be considered merely as "an allegory which dramatizes the conflict between Good and Evil" with a debt to Spenser and Bunyan by way of Hawthorne, but R. B. Heilman attacked directly in two articles (*MLN,* 1947, and *UKCR,* 1948) and in his *Forms of Modern Fiction* (1948). Heilman argues that James, in his Preface, is speaking of technical problems only and that there are many points in the story which cannot be explained by the Freudian hypothesis; on the other hand, there are religious overtones in the iterative imagery which reflect the Christian dualism of the struggle of Evil to overcome Good and to possess the human soul. Other interpretations which develop variations on this theme were offered by A. J. A. Waldock (*MLN,* 1947), Robert Liddell (*A Treatise on the Novel,* 1947), Oliver Evans (*PR,* 1949), G. A. Reed (*AL,* 1949), and F. X. Rollinger (*AL,* 1949). Evans and Reed argue that the story loses all point unless the apparitions are accepted in the spirit of fantasy and Rollinger goes so far as to point out parallels between James's story and certain cases reported by the Society for Psychical Research. More temperate views were offered by Katherine Anne Porter (*New Invitation to Learning,* 1942) and Carl Van Doren in a preface to the 1949 edition of the tale.

Identification of the moral with the social consciousness may have crystallized in the thirties with an increasing influence of the Marxian hypothesis, but again a doctrinaire approach which failed as an instrument of biography, when suitably mellowed, became an assist in criticism. Newton Arvin's view that, after *The Princess Casamassima,* James became the chronicler of a "festering society" was hardly recognizable in such a mild version as that of G. D. Snell (*The Shapers of American Fiction: 1798-1947,* 1947), where it is argued that James's characters, faced with the death of a society, have received no moral tradition to which to turn, but Snell's view that the inner life is the good life as opposed to the life of the "animal" people perhaps owes more to Darwin than to Freud or Marx. Adeline R. Tintner takes a more constructive view when she proposes (*PMLA,* 1946) that with *The Sacred Fount,* James undertook to "possess a civilization," specifically that of America, by understanding the given meaning in it, and Elizabeth Stevenson in *The Crooked Corridor: A Study of Henry James* (1949) uses a similar approach for a full length analysis and interpretation of all of James's fiction. Her thesis is that the crux of James's approach to life is the collision of the individual with society. This theory she elaborates in a "spiral of significance" which "begins with the national divergence of the American and the European, develops into the more essential contrast of innocence and experience, grows into the mature idea of the complementary nature of character and culture, and finally the halving of the world into energy and form." A similar but far less profound analysis is that of Andreas Osborn's *Henry James and the Expanding Horizon* (1948); but the best thinking on this subject centered around the interpretation of *The Princess Casamassima* and the few other novels and tales in which James touches upon the problems of a social class other than his own. Although this problem was discussed by Louise Bogan (*Nation,* 1938), C. F. Oliver (*Antioch Rev.,* 1947), George Woodcock (*SR,* 1952), and many others, the two principal critical positions are best expounded by Stephen Spender in *The Destructive Element* (1935) and in miscellaneous articles, and by Lionel Trilling in his prefaces to *The Princess Casamassima* (1948) and *The Bostonians* (1952). Spender sees James, in the early novels, as a modern writer in search of a moral subject, but one who is confronted by the fact that modern society is decadent. The only choice for the artist is therefore to make an art of life and a life of art. This James did, drawing upon his early experience but using this experience symbolically rather than literally in order to impose a clearer and more acceptable meaning upon life. In so doing, his unprecedented awareness of the present almost projects him into the future at the same time that it provides a violent flight into the past. In his commemorative evaluation of James (*N. Y. Times Book Review,* 1944) Spender explains James as a great moralist with two messages: the crime of the passion for things, and the irrelevance of social rules to morality or happiness. As he had earlier discovered James's best moral exposition in the late novels, specifically in *The Golden Bowl,* Spender again argues for James as a great writer because he loved what he wrote about and was therefore able to discover the life of the spirit in the most stupid of human characters. Thus ethics and social consciousness have become one.

Trilling's analysis of this problem is more subtle than Spender's. In his Introduction to *The Princess Casamassima* (1948) he attacks the problem of the "moral realism" of James's art at its source. This is the first thorough defense of a novel which was dismissed by previous critics because it attempted to deal with a sociological problem without a firsthand knowledge of the society and the social problems of the class concerned.

Trilling starts by accepting James's statement at its face value that "if you haven't, for fiction, the root of the matter in you, haven't the sense of life and the penetrating imagination, you are a fool in the very presence of the revealed and assured; but if you *are* so armed, you are not really helpless." James was so armed and could therefore overcome his ignorance of the anarchist movement and of the lower classes. Trilling presents a strong case for the power of the imagination to penetrate into areas of moral reality that are closed to mere factual knowledge. His own grounding in modern sociology and psychology enables him to help at least this one piece of James's "buried prose" to "kick off its tombstone." His tour de force reaches, in its effect, far beyond this particular novel because it reverses the direction of the earlier criticism of James as a social commentator and a moralist and makes his power as an artist into a power as a commentator on modern life. It is only a short step then to the conclusion that aesthetic criticism is always, at its best, an instrument of social and moral criticism. This is the implicit or explicit position of many of the best of the recent critics of James from T. S. Eliot to R. P. Blackmur.

The writers of *Scrutiny*, especially F. R. Leavis and Marius Bewley, were concerned ultimately with moral rather than social significance, but their immediate concern was with problems of expression and form. Both of these critics prefer the earlier to the later James, but they differ sharply in their reading. Leavis' studies in *The Great Tradition* and in the *Scrutiny* articles of 1946-48 have already been discussed as studies in sources. Bewley contributed two articles on James's debt to Hawthorne (1949) in which he contends that the influence was much deeper than merely that of one novelist on another; that both men belonged in a peculiarly American tradition in which moral sensibility is both sharpened and confused by the breakdown of a moral sense which could distinguish appearance from reality. An article specifically on "Appearance and Reality in Henry James" (1950) cut the issue even more clearly. Bewley here contends that the conflict between appearance and reality in James's work is a reflection of the American habit of maintaining a given set of ideals in spite of the facts. By thus creating ambiguities which dull the vision of evil, this tradition creates a kind of sensibility which is peculiarly American and which James shares with Hawthorne. Those novels in which appearance is "successfully and intelligibly correlated with reality," *The Portrait of a Lady* and *What Maisie Knew,* are masterpieces, but in the later novels and tales, *The Turn of the Screw* and *The Golden Bowl* for example, James's "destructive foray into the grounds for moral judgment" leaves unresolved issues which it is the duty of art to resolve. The result is moral and aesthetic chaos. Leavis attacked Bewley for taking some of James's stories too seriously, but did not disagree with his basic thesis, which Bewley repeated and elaborated by two more articles in the same journal. Although this issue does not seem to have been taken up and debated elsewhere, the idea that out of a systematic theory of art there can be developed, through moral sensibility, a satisfactory reading of life is the basis of many other thoughful and influential articles, among them "The Poetics of Henry James" by M. D. Zabel (*Poetry,* 1935), "Henry and William (Two Notes)" by Eliseo Vivas (*KR,* 1943), and "Sensibility and Technique (Preface to a Critique)" by David Daiches (*KR,* 1943). Daiches argues that James differs from other modern novelists like Proust in being moral at all, but he differs from older novelists in that they had specific moral meaning whereas in his novels "meaning is itself moral, and significance and moral illumination are coexistent."

The criticism of R. P. Blackmur follows much the same lines but is better informed and more sustained than that of any modern critic except perhaps Matthiessen. Blackmur's study of James began with his Introduction to the Prefaces in 1934, which put him in agreement with Matthiessen in emphasizing the later years as the "major phase" although he went beyond Matthiessen's analysis of the major novels themselves to a review, through James's eyes, of the entire fictional product of a lifetime. The theory that art is itself a higher form of conscience is next pursued into a group of ghost stories (*KR,* 1942) in a quest for a key to that supreme analysis of conscience, *The Sacred Fount.* Blackmur's central thesis reaches its most precise expression in an article in the commemorative issue of the *KR* (1943), "In the Country of the Blue." Here he sees James as placing the artist "between the earlier persons who master life by submitting to its conditions and the later persons who master what lies under the conditions by achieving a conviction of the self." The artist is thus an agent of transition for James into a deeper understanding of the ethical nature of art. In *Accent* (1945) he reviewed the current work on James and Melville with the observation that American writers are "deliberately self-pruned at the roots rather than at the branch and so do not realize the full tragic meaning of their society," and in *LHUS* he presented James's life and artistic development together, seeing the latter as a complex of dominant themes, derived in the first place from early experience but finally reaching full aesthetic unity of form and meaning in the four major novels of the last period. In "The Loose and Baggy Monsters of Henry James" (*Accent,* 1951) and in his preface to *The Golden Bowl* (1952), Blackmur develops further this idea of an "underlying classic form" as the vehicle in which "things are held together in a living way, with the sense of life going on." The classic is "the life that underlies the life we know." James's concern for this kind of form is obscured (and the critics have been fooled) by his emphasis on the individual consciousness. Echoing Eliot in another context, Blackmur concludes that James is a forerunner of the modern "disinherited sensibility," and that his apparent sterility is not in him but in the movement toward a mass society, which is stronger in America than in Europe, but is the main movement of modern times.

Incidentally, through all of this criticism runs the theory of expression which is based on the modern view of the symbol as the root of all language. Charles Feidelson, Jr., in *Symbolism and American Literature* (1953) discusses James in connection with earlier American authors; and among major analyses of specific novels or discussions of specific symbols are essays by W. M. Gibson (*NEQ,* 1951), Miriam Allott (*Essays in Criticism,* 1953), and Louise Daumier (*UKCR,* 1953). Quentin Anderson raised something of a critical storm by three articles, "Henry James and the New Jerusalem" (*KR,* 1946) and two others in *Scrutiny* (1947). The latter were commented on by F. R. Leavis in *Scrutiny* (1948). Anderson attacks the older view that James's consciousness or sensibility had no moral sanction other than taste, and then proposes that the theology and ethics which his father had derived from Swedenborg created in the son a realm of formal doctrine which he did not need to accept formally in order to make use of it aesthetically. Much evidence on the fundamental nature of the Swedenborgian system of symbols as the organizing agent in James's art is adduced, especially to provide the basis for his special feeling for the feminine sensibility as something above sex.

In general, Anderson's thesis has not been accepted and the structure of James's myth, symbol, and metaphor has been otherwise explained or not explained at all. Among the more suggestive treatments of this problem are those by Allen Tate (*SR,* 1950), William Troy (*New Republic,* 1943), and Austin Warren (*KR,* 1945). Warren developed his theory in an essay in *Rage for Order* (1948) in which he bases his argument on the distinction between the method of dialectic and that of myth-making, in that the one uses the reason to express ideas in literal words and the other uses intuition to create images and symbols. He finds two kinds of figuration in James: the "extended conceit" of metaphor, and the "emblematic perception" through which the whole truth of a character or a relation is revealed in a symbol. Perhaps that is a good point at which to leave the problem as to how and how not to study Henry James.

BIBLIOGRAPHICAL SUPPLEMENT

A Selective Check List, 1955-1962

This supplement, prepared especially for the present edition of *Eight American Authors,* lists selected materials published since the appearance of the original edition (*i.e.,* from 1955 to the early part of 1962). Items of 1955 mentioned in the original edition have not been listed again. When books are listed, articles contained therein are not listed. Abbreviations of periodical titles are the standard abbreviations used in *American Literature* or *PMLA*.

GENERAL AND MISCELLANEOUS

R. M. Ludwig, editor, *Bibliographical Supplement* [*1947–1957*], *L.H.U.S.* [Vol. IV], New York, 1959.

James Woodress, editor, *Dissertations in American Literature, 1891–1955, with Supplement, 1956–1961,* revised edition, Durham, N. C., 1962.

Marius Bewley, *The Eccentric Design,* New York, 1959 [devotes five chapters to Hawthorne, Melville, and James].

Richard Chase, *The American Novel and Its Tradition,* New York, 1957 [devotes four chapters to Hawthorne, Melville, James, and Mark Twain].

D. B. Davis, *Homicide in American Fiction, 1798–1860: A Study in Social Values,* Ithaca, New York, 1957 [touches upon Poe, Hawthorne, Melville, and Clemens].

Leon Edel, T. H. Johnson, Sherman Paul, and Claude Simpson, *Masters of American Literature,* 2 volumes, Boston, 1959 [has an Introduction to each of the eight authors].

L. A. Fiedler, *Love and Death in the American Novel,* New York, 1960 [treats of James, Poe, Hawthorne, Melville, and Mark Twain in seven of the chapters].

H. R. Floan, *The South in Northern Eyes 1831 to 1861,* Austin,

Texas, 1958 [considers Emerson, Thoreau, Hawthorne, Melville, and Whitman].

H. C. Gardiner, S. J., editor, *American Classics Reconsidered: A Christian Appraisal,* New York, 1958 [contains essays on Emerson, Hawthorne, Poe, Thoreau, Melville, and Whitman].

Clark Griffith, " 'Emersonianism' and 'Poeism': Some Versions of the Romantic Sensibility," *MLQ,* XXII, 125–134 (June, 1961) [comments upon Emerson, Poe, Hawthorne, and Melville].

D. G. Hoffman, *Form and Fable in American Fiction,* New York, 1961 [deals mainly with Hawthorne, Melville, and Mark Twain].

Edwin Honig, "In Defense of Allegory," *KR,* XX, 1–19 (Winter, 1958) [refers to Hawthorne, Melville, Poe, and James].

Leon Howard, *Literature and the American Tradition,* Garden City, N. Y., 1960 [devotes about ten pages to each of the eight authors].

Alfred Kazin, *Contemporaries,* Boston, 1962 [three essays, pp. 29–50, deal with Melville, Emerson, and Thoreau].

Harry Levin, *The Power of Blackness: Hawthorne, Poe, Melville,* New York, 1958.

R. W. B. Lewis, *The American Adam: Innocence, Tragedy, and Tradition in the Nineteenth Century,* Chicago, 1955 [deals with Thoreau, Whitman, Hawthorne, Melville, and James].

Agostino Lombardo, *La Ricerca Del Vero: Saggi Sulla Tradizione Letteraria Americana,* Roma, 1961 [contains essays on Emerson, Thoreau, Hawthorne, Melville, James, and Mark Twain].

Waldo McNeir and L. B. Levy, editors, *Studies in American Literature,* Baton Rouge, Louisiana, 1960 [contains four essays on Emerson, Poe, Melville, and James].

Leo Marx, "The Machine in the Garden," *NEQ,* XXIX, 27–42 (March, 1956) [for Hawthorne, Emerson, Thoreau, and Melville].

Perry Miller, *Errand into the Wilderness,* Cambridge, Mass., 1956 [notices Emerson, Thoreau, Whitman, Melville, and Poe].

———, *The Raven and the Whale: The War of Words and Wits in the Era of Poe and Melville,* New York, 1956.

Wright Morris, *The Territory Ahead,* New York, 1958 [contains five essays on Thoreau, Whitman, Melville, Mark Twain, and Henry James].

R. H. Pearce, *The Continuity of American Poetry,* Princeton, 1961 [discusses Poe, Emerson, and Whitman].

Georges Poulet, "Time and American Writers," Appendix to *Studies in Human Time,* translated by Elliott Coleman, Baltimore, 1956, pp. 323–345, 350–354 [treats of all the eight writers except Mark Twain].

L. D. Rubin, Jr., and J. R. Moore, editors, *The Idea of an American Novel,* New York, 1961 [deals with Hawthorne, Melville, James, and Mark Twain; and quotes views of all of the eight authors except Thoreau].

C. L. Sanford, "Classics of American Reform Literature," *AQ,* X, 295–311 (Fall, 1958) [for Hawthorne, Thoreau, and Mark Twain].

Charles Shapiro, editor, *Twelve Original Essays on Great American Novels,* Detroit, 1958 [includes essays by Malcolm Cowley, Granville Hicks, G. P. Elliott, and Richard Chase on *The Scarlet Letter, Moby Dick, Huckleberry Finn,* and *The Ambassadors*].

B. T. Spencer, *The Quest for Nationality: An American Literary Campaign,* Syracuse, New York, 1957 [for all eight authors].

Randall Stewart, *American Literature and Christian Doctrine,* Baton Rouge, Louisiana, 1958 [deals with Hawthorne, Emerson, Melville, Whitman, and James].

Richard Wilbur, Newton Arvin, K. S. Lynn, E. H. Davidson, Richard Chase, R. W. B. Lewis, H. N. Smith, and F. W. Dupee, Introductions to the eight authors in *Major Writers of America,* 2 volumes, New York, 1962.

Saburo Yamaya, "Poe, Hawthorne and Melville's 'Benito Cereno,'" *Stud in Eng Lit* (Hosei University), No. 4, pp. 21–32 (March, 1961).

POE

I. Books

Vincent Buranelli, *Edgar Allan Poe,* New York, 1961.

Joseph Chiari, *Symbolisme from Poe to Mallarmé: The Growth of a Myth,* London, 1956.

E. H. Davidson, *Poe: A Critical Study,* Cambridge, Mass., 1957.

Arnalds Grava, *L'aspect métaphysique du mal dans l'œuvre littéraire de Charles Baudelaire et d'Edgar Allan Poe, UNS,* N.S., XV, 1956.

J. C. Miller, *John Henry Ingram's Poe Collection at the University of Virginia,* Charlottesville, Va., 1960.

A. E. Murch, *The Development of the Detective Novel,* New York, 1958.

P. F. Quinn, *The French Face of Edgar Poe,* Carbondale, Ill., 1957.

S. M. Rein, *Edgar A. Poe: The Inner Pattern,* New York, 1960.

Kuno Schumann, *Die Erzählende Prosa Edgar Allan Poes: Ein Beitrag zu einer Gattungsgeschichte der "short story," FAGAAS,* Vol. V, 1958.

II. Articles

David Anderson, "A Comparison of the Poetic Theories of Emerson and Poe," *Person,* XLI, 471–483 (Autumn, 1960).

Roger Asselineau, "Introduction" to *Edgar Poe: Choix de Contes,* Paris, 1958, pp. 17–102.

S. S. Baskett, "A Damsel with a Dulcimer: An Interpretation of Poe's 'Eleonora,' " *MLN*, LXXIII, 332–338 (May, 1958).

Maurice Beebe, "The Fall of the House of Pyncheon," *NCF, XI*, 1–17 (June, 1956).

———, "The Universe of Roderick Usher," *Person*, XXXVII, 147–160 (Spring, 1956).

W. E. Bezanson, "The Troubled Sleep of Arthur Gordon Pym," *Essays in Literary History Presented to J. Milton French*, New Brunswick, N. J., 1960, pp. 149–175.

R. P. Blackmur, "Afterword" to *"The Fall of the House of Usher" and Other Tales*, New York, 1960, pp. 375–383.

Kenneth Burke, " 'The Principle of Composition,' " *Poetry*, XCIX, 46–53 (Oct., 1961).

Richard Cary, "Poe and the Great Debate," *TSLL*, III, 223–233 (Summer, 1961).

E. H. Davidson, "Introduction" to *Selected Writings of Edgar Allan Poe*, Boston, 1956, pp. vii–xxviii.

Willem Van Doorn, "Poe's Ulalume," *RLV*, XXIV, 395–404 (Sept.–Oct., 1958).

Hans Galinsky, "Beharrende Strukturzüge im Wandel eines Jahrhunderts amerikanischer Kurzgeschichte (dargelegt an E. A. Poes 'The Masque of the Red Death' und Ernest Hemingways 'The Killers')," *NS*, Beiheft III, 5–45 (1958).

J. W. Gargano, "Poe's 'Ligeia': Dream and Destruction," *CE*, XXIII, 337–342 (Feb., 1962).

———, " 'The Black Cat': Perverseness Reconsidered," *TSLL*, II, 172–178 (Summer, 1960).

Ada Giaccari, "La Fortuna di E. A. Poe in Italia," *SA*, V, 91–118 (1959).

———, "Poe nella critica italiana," *SA*, V, 51–89 (1959).

Richard Gimbel, " 'Quoth the Raven': A Catalogue of the Exhibition," *YULG*, XXXIII, 139–189 (April, 1959).

Laura Hofrichter, "From Poe to Kafka," *UTQ*, XXIX, 405–419 (July, 1960).

P. C. Holt, "Poe and H. N. Coleridge's *Greek Classic Poets:* 'Pinakidia,' 'Politian,' and 'Morella' Sources," *AL*, XXXIV, 8–30 (March, 1962).

J. B. Hubbell, "Poe and the Southern Literary Tradition," *TSLL*, II, 151–171 (Summer, 1960).

R. D. Jacobs, "Poe among the Virginians," *VMHB*, LXVII, 30–48 (Jan., 1959).

———, "Poe's Earthly Paradise," *AQ*, XII, 404–413 (Fall, 1960).

Joseph Jones, " 'The Raven' and 'The Raven': Another Source of Poe's Poem," *AL*, XXX, 185–193 (May, 1958).

George Kelly, "Poe's Theory of Beauty," *AL*, XXVII, 521–536 (Jan., 1956).

———, "Poe's Theory of Unity," *PQ,* XXXVII, 34–44 (Jan., 1958).
H. H. Kühnelt, "Die Aufnahme und Verbreitung von E. A. Poes Werken im Deutschen," in *Festschrift für Walther Fischer,* Heidelberg, 1959, pp. 195–224.
———, "E. A. Poe und Alfred Kubin: Zwei künstlerische Gestalter des Grauens," *Wiener Beitrage zur englischen Philologie,* LXV, 121–141 (1957).
Stuart Levine, "Poe's *Julius Rodman:* Judaism, Plagiarism, and the Wild West," *Midwest-Quart,* I, 245–259 (Spring, 1960).
F. H. Link, *"Discovery* und *destruction;* eine Interpretation von Edgar Allan Poes *MS. Found in a Bottle," NS,* X, 27–38 (Jan., 1961).
Dwight MacDonald, "Masscult and Midcult," *PR,* XXVII, 203–233 (Spring, 1960), 589–631 (Fall, 1960).
Carol H. Maddison, "Poe's *Eureka," TSLL,* II, 350–367 (Autumn, 1960).
A. H. Marks, "Two Rodericks and Two Worms: 'Egotism; Or, The Bosom Serpent,' " *PMLA,* LXXIV, 607–612 (Dec., 1959).
E. R. Marks, "Poe as Literary Theorist: A Reappraisal," *AL,* XXXIII, 296–306 (Nov., 1961).
J. E. Miller, Jr., " 'Ulalume' Resurrected," *PQ,* XXXIV, 197–205 (April, 1955).
S. L. Mooney, "The Comic in Poe's Fiction," *AL,* XXXIII, 433–441 (Jan., 1962).
S. P. Moss, "Poe and His Nemesis—Lewis Gaylord Clark," *AL,* XXVIII, 30–49 (March, 1956).
———, "Poe's Infamous Reputation: A Crux in the Biography," *ABC,* IX, 3–10 (Nov., 1958).
Charles O'Donnell, "From Earth to Ether: Poe's Flight into Space," *PMLA,* LXXVII, 85–91 (March, 1962).
John Ostrom, "Second Supplement to the Letters of Poe," *AL,* XXIX, 79–86 (March, 1957).
Mario Praz, "Poe, genio d'esportazione," *Approdo,* IV, iii, 3–15 (1958).
G. T. Pugh, "Poe: An Induction," *EJ,* XLV, 509–516, 552 (Dec., 1956).
P. F. Quinn, "Four Views of Edgar Poe," *JA,* V, 138–146 (1960).
D. A. Randall, "The J. K. Lilly Collection of Edgar Allan Poe," *IUB,* No. 4, pp. 46–58 (March, 1960).
J. A. Robbins, "Edgar Poe and His Friends: A Sampler of Letters Written to Sarah Helen Whitman," *IUB,* No. 4, pp. 5–45 (March, 1960).
E. A. Robinson, "Order and Sentience in 'The Fall of the House of Usher,' " *PMLA,* LXXVI, 68–81 (March, 1961).
Armando Rojas, "Edgar Allan Poe en la America hispana," *Revista Nacional de Cultura,* Nos. 142–143, pp. 152–161 (Sept.–Dec.,

1960).
Sergio Rossi, "E. A. Poe e la Scapigliatura lombarda," *SA,* V, 119–139 (1959).
Dorothy J. Samuel, "Poe and Baudelaire: Parallels in Form and Symbol," *CLAJ,* III, 88–105 (Dec., 1959).
S. G. Sandler, "Poe's Indebtedness to Locke's *An Essay Concerning Human Understanding,*" *BUSE,* V, 107–121 (Summer, 1961).
James Schroeter, "A Misreading of Poe's 'Ligeia,'" *PMLA,* LXXVI, 397–406 (Sept., 1961).
R. E. Spiller, "The American Literary Dilemma and Edgar Allan Poe," in *The Great Experiment in American Literature: Six Lectures,* edited by Carl Bode, New York, 1961, pp. 3–25.
Edward Stone, "Usher, Poquelin, and Miss Emily: The Progress of Southern Gothic," *GaR,* XIV, 433–443 (Winter, 1960).
William Wasserstrom, "The Spirit of Myrrha," *AI,* XIII, 455–472 (Winter, 1956).
Jean-Paul Weber, "Edgar Poe ou le thème de l'horloge," *NNRF,* VI, 301–311, 498–508 (Aug.–Sept., 1958).
T. N. Weissbuch, "Edgar Allan Poe: Hoaxer in the American Tradition," *NYHSQ,* XLV, 291–309 (July, 1961).
P. M. Wetherill, "Edgar Allan Poe and Madame Sabatier," *MLQ,* XX, 344–354 (Dec., 1959).
William Whipple, "Poe's Political Satire," *UTSE,* XXXV, 81–95 (1956).
Richard Wilbur, "Introduction" to *Poe: Complete Poems,* New York, 1959, pp. 7–39.
J. S. Wilson, "The Personality of Poe," *VMHB,* LXVII, 131–142 (April, 1959).

EMERSON

I. Writings of Emerson

Dante's Vita Nuova, translated by Ralph Waldo Emerson, edited and annotated by J. C. Mathews, Chapel Hill, N. C., 1960.
The Early Lectures of Ralph Waldo Emerson, Vol. I, 1833–1836, edited by S. E. Whicher and R. E. Spiller, Cambridge, Mass., 1959.
The Journals and Miscellaneous Notebooks of Ralph Waldo Emerson, Vol. I, 1819–1822, edited by W. H. Gilman, A. R. Ferguson, G. P. Clark, and M. R. Davis, Cambridge, Mass., 1960; Vol. II, 1822–1826, edited by W. H. Gilman, A. R. Ferguson, and M. R. Davis, Cambridge, 1961.

II. Biographical and Critical Studies

1. *Books*

E. G. Berry, *Emerson's Plutarch,* Cambridge, Mass., 1961.

K. W. Cameron, *An Emerson Index: Names, Exempla, Sententiae, Symbols, Words and Motifs in Selected Notebooks of Ralph Waldo Emerson,* Hartford, Conn., 1958.

———, *The Transcendentalists and Minerva,* 3 volumes, Hartford, 1958.

———, *Ralph Waldo Emerson's Reading: A Corrected Edition with Photographs of Literary Concord, Emerson, and His Family,* Hartford, 1962.

———, *A Commentary on Emerson's Early Lectures (1833–1836) with an Index-Concordance,* Hartford, 1962.

William Charvat, *Emerson's American Lecture Engagements: A Chronological List,* New York, 1961.

W. R. Hutchison, *The Transcendentalist Ministers: Church Reform in the New England Renaissance,* New Haven, 1959.

P. L. Nicoloff, *Emerson on Race and History: An Examination of "English Traits,"* New York, 1961.

2. *Articles*

David Anderson. See POE, above.

J. Q. Anderson, "Emerson and 'Manifest Destiny,'" *BPLQ,* VII, 23–33 (Jan., 1955).

Rolando Anzilotti, "Emerson in Italia," *RLMC,* XI, 70–80 (March, 1958).

Newton Arvin, "The House of Pain: Emerson and the Tragic Sense," *Hud R,* XII, 37–53 (Spring, 1959).

Eduard Baumgarten, "Mitteilungen und Bemerkungen über den Einfluss Emersons auf Nietzsche," *JA,* I, 93–152 (1956).

R. D. Birdsall, "Emerson and the Church of Rome," *AL,* XXXI, 273–281 (Nov., 1959).

Robert Bloom, "Irving Babbitt's Emerson," *NEQ,* XXX, 448–473 (Dec., 1957).

K. W. Cameron, "A Garland of Emerson Letters," *ESQ,* No. 10, pp. 32–41 (1st Quart., 1958).

———, "A New Source for Emerson's Lectures," *ESQ,* No. 20, pp. 10–25 (3rd Quart., 1960).

———, "Early Background for Emerson's 'The Problem,'" *ESQ,* No. 27, pp. 37–46 (2nd Quart., 1962).

———, "Emerson and Melville Lecture in New Haven (1856–1857)," *ESQ,* No. 19, pp. 85–96 (2nd Quart., 1960).

———, "Emerson and Swedenborgism: A Study Outline and Analysis," *ESQ,* No. 10, pp. 14–21 (1st Quart., 1958).

———, "Emerson, Thoreau and Concord in Early Newspapers," *ESQ,* No. 21, pp. 1–57 (4th Quart., 1960).
———, "Emerson, Thoreau, and the Town and Country Club," *ESQ,* No. 8, pp. 2–17 (3rd Quart., 1957).
———, "Emerson, Thoreau, Elegant Extracts, and Proverb Lore," *ESQ,* No. 6, pp. 26–39 (1st Quart., 1957).
———, "Emerson's Recommendation of Whitman in 1863: The Remainder of the Evidence," *ESQ,* No. 3, pp. 14–20 (2nd Quart., 1956).
———, "History and Biography in Emerson's Unpublished Sermons," *ESQ,* No. 12, pp. 2–9 (3rd Quart., 1958).
———, "More Notes on Orientalism in Emerson's Harvard," *ESQ,* No. 22, pp. 81–90 (1st Quart., 1961).
———, "Notes on the Early Lectures," *ESQ,* No. 20, pp. 25–123 (3rd Quart., 1960).
———, "Some Collections of Emerson Manuscripts," Parts I, II, III, *ESQ,* No. 3, pp. 1–3 (2nd Quart., 1956); No. 5, pp. 20–21 (4th Quart., 1956); No. 6, pp. 21–23 (1st Quart., 1957).
———, "Thoreau and Emerson in Channing's Letters to the Watsons," *ESQ,* No. 14, pp. 77–85 (1st Quart., 1959).
V. L. O. Chittick, "Emerson's 'Frolic Health,'" *NEQ,* XXX, 209–234 (June, 1957).
B. B. Cohen, "Emerson and Hawthorne on England," *BPLQ,* IX, 73–85 (April, 1957).
R. L. Cook, "Emerson and Frost: A Parallel of Seers," *NEQ,* XXXI, 200–217 (June, 1958).
A. M. Cory, "Humor in Emerson's Journals," *UTSE,* XXXIV, 114–124 (1955).
Frank Davidson, "Emerson and the Double Consciousness," *Earlham Rev,* III, 1–15 (April, 1960).
Hans Doderer, "Der Junge Emerson und Deutschland," *Germanisch-Romanische Monatsschrift,* XXXVI, 147–161 (April, 1955).
The Emerson Society Quarterly, 1955—, edited by K. W. Cameron, published at Hartford, Connecticut.
J. E. Englekirk, "Notes on Emerson in Latin America," *PMLA,* LXXVI, 227–232 (June, 1961).
Robert Frost, "On Emerson," *Daedalus,* LXXXVIII, 712–718 (Fall, 1959).
Richard Greenleaf, "Emerson and Wordsworth," *Sci and Soc,* XXII, 218–230 (Summer, 1958).
S. L. Gross, "Emerson and Poetry," *SAQ,* LIV, 82–94 (Jan., 1955).
George Hendrick, "Influence of Thoreau and Emerson on Gandhi's Satyagraha," *Gāndhi Mārg,* III, 165–178 (July, 1959).
Vivian C. Hopkins, "Emerson and Bacon," *AL,* XXIX, 408–430 (Jan., 1958).
W. A. Huggard, "Emerson's Glimpse of the Divine," *Person,*

XXXVI, 167–176 (Spring, 1955).
Yukio Irie, "Emerson as a Monist," *Am Lit Rev* (Tokyo), XXIV, 1–9 (March, 1958).
P. F. Jamieson, "Emerson in the Adirondacks," *NYH*, XXXIX, 215–237 (July, 1958).
Alfred Kazin and Daniel Aaron, "Introduction" to *Emerson: A Modern Anthology*, New York, 1958, pp. 7–13.
H. L. Kleinfield, "The Structure of Emerson's Death," *BNYPL*, LXV, 47–64 (Jan., 1961).
A. J. Kloeckner, "Intellect and Moral Sentiment in Emerson's Opinions of 'The Meaner Kinds' of Men," *AL*, XXX, 322–338 (Nov., 1958).
J. J. Kwiat, "Robert Henri and the Emerson-Whitman Tradition," *PMLA*, LXXI, 617–636 (Sept., 1956).
Paul Lauter, "Emerson's Revisions of *Essays* (First Series)," *AL*, XXXIII, 143–158 (May, 1961).
———, "Truth and Nature: Emerson's Use of Two Complex Words," *ELH*, XXVII, 66–85 (March, 1960).
R. F. Lee, "Emerson through Kierkegaard: Toward a Definition of Emerson's Theory of Communication," *ELH*, XXIV, 229–248 (Sept., 1957).
R. N. Linscott, "Introduction" to *The Journals of Ralph Waldo Emerson*, New York, 1960, pp. v–xii.
B. R. McElderry, Jr., "Emerson's Second Address on the American Scholar," *Person*, XXXIX, 361–372 (Autumn, 1958).
Haynes McMullen, "Ralph Waldo Emerson and Libraries," *LQ*, XXV, 152–162 (April, 1955).
G. R. Mason, "Ralph Waldo Emerson," in *Great American Liberals*, Boston, 1956, pp. 41–51.
D. M. Murray, "Emerson's 'Language as Fossil Poetry': An Analogy from Chinese," *NEQ*, XXIX, 204–215 (June, 1956).
S. K. Padover, "Ralph Waldo Emerson: The Moral Voice in Politics," *PSQ*, LXXIV, 334–350 (Sept., 1959).
R. H. Pearce, "Frost's Momentary Stay," *KR*, XXIII, 258–273 (Spring, 1961).
R. C. Pollock, "A Re-appraisal of Emerson," *Thought*, XXXII, 86–132 (Spring, 1957).
H. F. Pommer, "The Contents and Basis of Emerson's Belief in Compensation," *PMLA*, LXXVII, 248–253 (June, 1962).
Jacques Roos, "Ce que Maeterlinck doit à l'Amérique," *BFLS*, XXXVII, 197–208 (Dec., 1958).
Louis Ruchames, "Two Forgotten Addresses by Ralph Waldo Emerson," *AL*, XXVIII, 425–433 (Jan., 1957).
Andrew Schiller, "Gnomic Structure in Emerson's Poetry," *PMASAL*, XL, 313–320 (1955).
C. F. Strauch, "Emerson and the American Continuity," *ESQ*, No. 6,

pp. 1–5 (1st Quart., 1957).
———, "Emerson as Literary Middleman," *ESQ*, No. 19, pp. 2–9 (2nd Quart., 1960).
———, "Emerson's 'New England Capitalist,' " *HLB*, X, 245–253 (Spring, 1956).
———, "Emerson's Sacred Science," *PMLA*, LXXIII, 237–250 (June, 1958).
———, "The Importance of Emerson's Skeptical Mood," *HLB*, XI, 117–139 (Winter, 1957).
———, "The Sources of Emerson's 'Song of Nature,' " *HLB*, IX, 300–334 (Autumn, 1955).
———, "The Year of Emerson's Poetic Maturity: 1834," *PQ*, XXXIV, 353–377 (Oct., 1955).
H. B. Van Wesep, "Ralph Waldo Emerson: Gentle Iconoclast," in *Seven Sages: The Story of American Philosophy*, New York, 1960, pp. 59–119.
René Wellek, "Emerson's Literary Theory and Criticism," in *Worte und Werte*, edited by G. Erdmann and A. Eichstaedt, Berlin, 1961, pp. 444–456.
S. E. Whicher, "Introduction" to *Selections from Ralph Waldo Emerson*, Boston, 1957, pp. xiii–xxi.
T. R. Whitaker, "The Riddle of Emerson's 'Sphinx,' " *AL*, XXVII, 179–195 (May, 1955).
William White, "Thirty-Three Unpublished Letters of Ralph Waldo Emerson," *AL*, XXXIII, 159–178 (May, 1961).
S. T. Williams, "Emerson: An Affirmation," *TSL*, II, 41–50 (1957).
Lawrence Willson, "The Great Reversal," *DR*, XXXIX, 5–18 (Spring, 1959).
Conrad Wright, "Emerson, Barzillai Frost, and the Divinity School Address," *HTR*, XLIX, 19–43 (Jan., 1956).
Nathalia Wright, "Ralph Waldo Emerson and Horatio Greenough," *HLB*, XII, 91–116 (Winter, 1958).
Hiromichi Yahagi, "The Position of Ralph Waldo Emerson in the Formation of Americanism," *Taisho Daigaku Kenkyukiyo*, XLV, 85–146 (March, 1960) [in Japanese].

HAWTHORNE

I. Books

Millicent Bell, *Hawthorne's View of the Artist*, New York, 1962.
L. J. Fick, *The Light Beyond: A Study of Hawthorne's Theology*, Westminster, Md., 1955.
H. H. Hoeltje, *Inward Sky: The Mind and Heart of Nathaniel Hawthorne*, Durham, N. C., 1962.

R. R. Male, *Hawthorne's Tragic Vision,* Austin, Tex., 1957.
A. S. Reid, *The Yellow Ruff and "The Scarlet Letter,"* Gainesville, Fla., 1955.
———, *"Sir Thomas Overbury's Vision" (1616) by Richard Nicolls and Other English Sources of Nathaniel Hawthorne's "The Scarlet Letter,"* Gainesville, Fla., 1957.
Arlin Turner, *Nathaniel Hawthorne: An Introduction and Interpretation,* New York, 1961.
Rudolph Von Abele, *The Death of the Artist: A Study of Hawthorne's Disintegration,* The Hague, 1955.
Edward Wagenknecht, *Nathaniel Hawthorne: Man and Writer,* New York, 1961.

II. Articles

Darrel Abel, "Hawthorne's Dimmesdale: Fugitive from Wrath," *NCF,* XI, 81–105 (Sept., 1956).
R. P. Adams, "Hawthorne: The Old Manse Period," *TSE,* VIII, 115–151 (1958).
———, "Hawthorne's *Provincial Tales,*" *NEQ,* XXX, 39–57 (March, 1957).
Quentin Anderson, "Introduction" to *Twice-Told Tales and Other Short Stories,* New York, 1960, pp. v–xii.
Eugene Arden, "Hawthorne's 'Case of Arthur D.,' " *AI,* XVIII, 45–55 (Spring, 1961).
S. S. Baskett, *"The* (Complete) *Scarlet Letter," CE,* XXII, 321–328 (Feb., 1961).
Lillian Beatty, "Typee and Blithedale: Rejected Ideal Communities," *Person,* XXXVII, 367–378 (Autumn, 1956).
Maurice Beebe. See POE, above.
Jesse Bier, "Hawthorne on the Romance: His Prefaces Related and Examined," *MP,* LIII, 17–24 (Aug., 1955).
Virginia O. Birdsall, "Hawthorne's Fair-Haired Maidens: The Fading Light," *PMLA,* LXXV, 250–256 (June, 1960).
Charles Boewe, "Rappaccini's Garden," *AL,* XXX, 37–49 (March, 1958).
Sister M. Hilda Bonham, "Hawthorne's Symbols *Sotto Voce,*" *CE,* XX, 184–186 (Jan., 1959).
Paul Brodtkorb, Jr., "Art Allegory in *The Marble Faun,*" *PMLA,* LXXVII, 254–267 (June, 1962).
Brother Joseph, "Art and Event in 'Ethan Brand,' " *NCF,* XV, 249–257 (Dec., 1960).
Merle E. Brown, "The Structure of *The Marble Faun,*" *AL,* XXVIII, 302–313 (Nov., 1956).
R. B. Browne, "The Oft-Told *Twice-Told Tales:* Their Folklore Motifs," *SFQ,* XXII, 69–85 (June, 1958).

Peter Buitenhuis, "Henry James on Hawthorne," *NEQ,* XXXII, 207–225 (June, 1959).

C. S. Burhans, "Hawthorne's Mind and Art in 'The Hollow of the Three Hills,'" *JEGP,* LX, 286–295 (April, 1961).

K. W. Cameron, "Genesis of Hawthorne's 'The Ambitious Guest,'" *Historiographer of the Episcopal Diocese of Conn.,* No. 14, pp. 2–36 (Dec., 1955).

———, "New Light on Hawthorne's Removal from the Customs House," *ESQ,* No. 23, pp. 2–5 (2nd Quart., 1961).

Maurice Charney, "Hawthorne and the Gothic Style," *NEQ,* XXXIV, 36–49 (March, 1961).

M. J. Clark, "The Wages of Sin in Hawthorne," *Brigham Young Univ Stud,* I, 21–36 (Winter, 1959).

R. W. Cochran, "Hawthorne's Choice: The Veil or the Jaundiced Eye," *CE,* XXIII, 342–346 (Feb., 1962).

B. B. Cohen. See EMERSON, above.

———, "*Paradise Lost* and 'Young Goodman Brown,'" *EIHC,* XCIV, 282–296 (July, 1958).

T. E. Connolly, "Hawthorne's 'Young Goodman Brown': An Attack on Puritanic Calvinism," *AL,* XXVIII, 370–375 (Nov., 1956).

F. C. Crews, "A New Reading of *The Blithedale Romance,*" *AL,* XXIX, 147–170 (May, 1957).

E. H. Davidson, "Hawthorne and the Pathetic Fallacy," *JEGP,* LIV, 486–497 (Oct., 1955).

W. B. Dillingham, "Structure and Theme in *The House of the Seven Gables,*" *NCF,* XIV, 59–69 (June, 1959).

R. A. Durr, "Hawthorne's Ironic Mode," *NEQ,* XXX, 486–495 (Dec., 1957).

H. G. Fairbanks, "Citizen Hawthorne and the Perennial Problems of American Society," *RUO,* XXIX, 26–38 (Jan.–March, 1959).

———, "Hawthorne and the Atomic Age," *RUO,* XXXI, 436–451 (July–Sept., 1961).

———, "Hawthorne and the Catholic Church," *BUSE,* I, 148–165 (Autumn, 1955).

———, "Hawthorne and the Machine Age," *AL,* XXVIII, 155–163 (May, 1956).

———, "Hawthorne and the Vanishing Venus," *UTSE,* XXXVI, 52–70 (1957).

———, "Man's Separation from Nature: Hawthorne's Philosophy of Suffering and Death," *Chri Schol,* XLII, 51–63 (March, 1959).

———, "Sin, Free Will, and 'Pessimism' in Hawthorne," *PMLA,* LXXI, 975–989 (Dec., 1956).

Marvin Fisher, "The Pattern of Conservatism in Johnson's *Rasselas* and Hawthorne's *Tales,*" *JHI,* XIX, 173–196 (April, 1958).

Edwin Fussell, "Hawthorne, James and 'The Common Doom,'" *AQ,* X, 438–453 (Winter, 1958).

Barbara Garlitz, "Pearl: 1850–1955," *PMLA,* LXXII, 689–699 (Sept., 1957).

R. F. Gleckner, "James's *Madame de Mauves* and Hawthorne's *The Scarlet Letter,*" *MLN,* LXXIII, 580–586 (Dec., 1958).

J. D. Gordon, "Nathaniel Hawthorne, the Years of Fulfillment: 1804–1853," *BNYPL,* LIX, 154–165, 198–217, 259–269 (March, April, May, 1955).

S. L. Gross, "Hawthorne's 'My Kinsman, Major Molineux': History as Moral Adventure," *NCF,* XII, 97–109 (Sept., 1957).

———, "Hawthorne and the Shakers," *AL,* XXIX, 457–463 (Jan., 1958).

———, "Prologue" and "Bibliography" for *A "Scarlet Letter" Handbook,* San Francisco, 1960, pp. 2–14, 152–161.

———, " 'Solitude, and Love, and Anguish': The Tragic Design of *The Scarlet Letter,*" *CLAJ,* III, 154–165 (March, 1960).

Augusto Guidi, "Le Ambiguità di Hawthorne," *SA,* I, 125–142 (1955).

R. D. Hathaway, "Hawthorne and the Paradise of Children," *WHR,* XV, 161–172 (Spring, 1961).

R. F. Haugh, "The Second Secret in *The Scarlet Letter,*" *CE,* XVII, 269–271 (Feb., 1956).

W. L. Hedges, "Hawthorne's *Blithedale:* The Function of the Narrator," *NCF,* XIV, 303–316 (March, 1960).

Hubert Hoeltje, "Hawthorne as Senior at Bowdoin," *EIHC,* XCIV, 205–228 (July, 1958).

E. M. Holmes, "Hawthorne and Romanticism," *NEQ,* XXXIII, 476–488 (Dec., 1960).

Carlo Izzo, "Un Metafisico della narrazione: Nathaniel Hawthorne," *SA,* I, 97–124 (1955).

Robert Kimbrough, " 'The Actual and the Imaginary': Hawthorne's Concept of Art in Theory and Practice," *TWA,* L, 277–293 (1960).

Murray Krieger, "Afterword" to *The Marble Faun,* New York, 1961, pp. 335–346.

B. W. Larabee and B. B. Cohen, "Hawthorne at the Essex Institute," *EIHC,* XCIV, 297–308 (July, 1958).

Marvin Laser, " 'Head,' 'Heart,' and 'Will,' in Hawthorne's Psychology," *NCF,* X, 130–140 (Sept., 1955).

H. A. Leibowitz, "Hawthorne and Spenser: Two Sources," *AL,* XXX, 459–466 (Jan., 1959).

S. O. Lesser, "The Image of the Father: A Reading of 'My Kinsman, Major Molineux' and 'I Want to Know Why,' " *PR,* XXII, 370–390 (Summer, 1955).

David Levin, "Introduction" to *The Blithedale Romance,* New York, 1960, pp. 7–19; to *The House of the Seven Gables,* New York, 1960, pp. 7–20; to *The Marble Faun,* New York, 1960, pp. 7–19;

to *The Scarlet Letter,* New York, 1960, pp. 7–20; to *The Scarlet Letter,* Boston, 1960, pp. vii–xxi.

A. J. Levy, *"The House of the Seven Gables:* The Religion of Love," *NCF,* XVI, 189–203 (Dec., 1961).

Michael Lloyd, "Hawthorne, Ruskin, and the Hostile Tradition," *EM,* VI, 109–133 (1955).

James Lynch, "Structure and Allegory in 'The Great Stone Face,' " *NCF,* XV, 137–146 (Sept., 1960).

J. T. McCullen, "Young Goodman Brown: Presumption and Despair," *Discourse,* II, 145–157 (July, 1959).

Joseph McCullen and John Guilds, "The Unpardonable Sin in Hawthorne: a Re-Examination," *NCF,* XV, 221–237 (Dec., 1960).

B. R. McElderry, Jr., "The Transcendental Hawthorne," *MQ,* II, 307–323 (Summer, 1961).

H. N. MacLean, "Hawthorne's *Scarlet Letter:* 'The Dark Problem of This Life,' " *AL,* XXVII, 12–24 (March, 1955).

Anne M. McNamara, "The Character of Flame: The Function of Pearl in *The Scarlet Letter," AL,* XXVII, 537–553 (Jan., 1956).

Hugo McPherson, "Hawthorne's Mythology: A Mirror for Puritans," *UTQ,* XXVIII, 267–278 (April, 1959).

Frank MacShane, "The House of the Dead: Hawthorne's Custom House and *The Scarlet Letter," NEQ,* XXXV, 93–101 (March, 1962).

Franco Marenco, "Nathaniel Hawthorne e il *Blithedale Romance," SA,* VI, 135–182 (1960).

A. H. Marks, "Who Killed Judge Pyncheon? The Role of the Imagination in *The House of the Seven Gables," PMLA,* LXXI, 355–369 (June, 1956).

———. See POE, above.

B. A. Marks, "The Origin of Original Sin in Hawthorne's Fiction," *NCF,* XIV, 359–362 (March, 1960).

Leo Marx, "Foreword" to *The Scarlet Letter,* New York, 1959, pp. vii–xii.

J. W. Mathews, "Hawthorne and the Chain of Being," *MLQ,* XVIII, 283–294 (Dec., 1957).

Barbara Melchiori, "Scenografie di Hawthorne e il dilemma dell'artista," *SA,* No. 2, pp. 67–81 (1956).

J. E. Miller, Jr., "Hawthorne and Melville: The Unpardonable Sin," *PMLA,* LXX, 91–114 (March, 1955).

P. W. Miller, "Hawthorne's 'Young Goodman Brown': Cynicism or Meliorism," *NCF,* XIV, 255–264 (Dec., 1959).

Patricia Moyer, "Time and the Artist in Kafka and Hawthorne," *MFS,* IV, 295–306 (Winter, 1958–1959).

P. B. Murray, "Mythopoesis in *The Blithedale Romance," PMLA,* LXXV, 591–596 (Dec., 1960).

Truman Nelson, "The Matrix of Place," *EIHC,* XCV, 176–185

(April, 1959).
F. B. Newman, " 'My Kinsman, Major Molineux': An Interpretation," *UKCR,* XXI, 203–212 (March, 1955).
W. V. O'Connor, "Hawthorne and Faulkner: Some Common Ground," *VQR,* XXXIII, 105–123 (Winter, 1957).
C. R. O'Donnell, "Hawthorne and Dimmesdale: The Search for the Realm of Quiet," *NCF,* XIV, 317–332 (March, 1960).
Goshi Oomoto, "Solitude and Society in Hawthorne's *Twice-Told Tales,*" *Rikkyo Rev,* No. 22, pp. 37–54 (1961) [in Japanese].
B. J. Paris, "Optimism and Pessimism in *The Marble Faun,*" *BUSE, II,* 95–112 (Summer, 1956).
Louis Paul, "A Psychoanalytic Reading of Hawthorne's 'Major Molineux': The Father Manqué and the Protégé Manqué," *AI,* XVIII, 279–288 (Fall, 1961).
R. H. Pearce, "Introduction" to *The Scarlet Letter,* London, 1957, pp. v–x.
N. H. Pearson, "Elizabeth Peabody on Hawthorne," *EIHC,* XCIV, 256–276 (July, 1958).
———, "Hawthorne and the Mannings," *EIHC,* XCIV, 169–190 (July, 1958).
———, "Hawthorne's Duel," *EIHC,* XCIV, 229–242 (July, 1958).
Glenn Pedersen, "Blake's Urizen as Hawthorne's Ethan Brand," *NCF,* XII, 304–314 (March, 1958).
A. S. Reid, "A Note on the Date of *The Scarlet Letter,*" *FurmS,* IV, 30–39 (Winter, 1957).
———, "The Role of Transformation in Hawthorne's Tragic Vision," *FurmS,* VI, 9–20 (Fall, 1958).
E. H. Rosenberry, "Hawthorne's Allegory of Science: 'Rappaccini's Daughter,' " *AL,* XXXII, 39–46 (March, 1960).
E. H. Rovit, "Ambiguity in Hawthorne's *Scarlet Letter,*" *Archiv,* CXCVIII, 76–88 (1961).
J. D. Rust, "George Eliot on the *Blithedale Romance,*" *BPLQ,* VII, 207–215 (Oct., 1955).
Charles Ryskamp, "The New England Sources of *The Scarlet Letter,*" *AL,* XXXI, 257–272 (Nov., 1959).
E. C. Sampson, "Afterword" to *The House of the Seven Gables,* New York, 1961, pp. 279–286.
———, "Motivation in *The Scarlet Letter,*" *AL,* XXVIII, 511–513 (Jan., 1957).
J. W. Shroeder, "Hawthorne's 'Egotism; or, The Bosom Serpent' and Its Source," *AL,* XXXI, 150–162 (May, 1959).
Robert Stanton, "Hawthorne, Bunyan, and the American Romances," *PMLA,* LXXI, 155–165 (March, 1956).
———, "The Trial of Nature: An Analysis of *The Blithedale Romance,*" *PMLA,* LXXVI, 528–538 (Dec., 1961).
———, "Dramatic Irony in Hawthorne's Romances," *MLN,* LXXI,

420–426 (June, 1956).
C. N. Stavrou, "Hawthorne's Quarrel with Man," *Person*, XLII, 352–360 (July, 1961).
W. B. Stein, "'The Artist of the Beautiful': Narcissus and the Thimble," *AI*, XVIII, 36–44 (Spring, 1961).
———, "The Parable of the Antichrist in 'The Minister's Black Veil,'" *AL*, XXVII, 386–392 (Nov., 1955).
E. E. Stibitz, "Ironic Unity in Hawthorne's 'The Minister's Black Veil,'" *AL*, XXXIV, 182–190 (May, 1962).
Edward Stone, "The Antique Gentility of Hester Prynne," *PQ*, XXXVI, 90–96 (Jan., 1957).
C. F. Strauch, *et al.*, "Symposium on Nathaniel Hawthorne," *ESQ*, No. 25, pp. 2–36 (4th Quart., 1961).
W. R. Thompson, "The Biblical Sources of Hawthorne's 'Roger Malvin's Burial,'" *PMLA*, LXXVII, 92–96 (March, 1962).
Leo Von Hibler, "Hawthorne in England," *NS*, Heft 4 (1955), pp. 145–153.
William Wasserstrom, "The Spirit of Myrrha," *AI*, XIII, 455–472 (Winter, 1956).
Norris Yates, "Ritual and Reality: Mask and Dance Motifs in Hawthorne's Fiction," *PQ*, XXXIV, 56–70 (Jan., 1955).
Shiro Yokozawa, "Hawthorne's Use of Pearl in *The Scarlet Letter*," *Liberal Arts Rev.*, V, 16–26 (March, 1960).
Philip Young, "Introduction" to *The House of the Seven Gables*, New York, 1957, pp. v–xxiv.
Larzer Ziff, "The Ethical Dimension of 'The Custom House,'" *MLN*, LXXIII, 338–344 (May, 1958).
Camilla Zauli-Naldi, "La fortuna di Hawthorne in Italia: Nota bibliografica," *SA*, VI, 183–201 (1960).

THOREAU

I. Writings of Thoreau

Consciousness in Concord: The Text of Thoreau's Hitherto "Lost Journal" (1840–41) Together with Notes and a Commentary, edited by Perry Miller, Boston, 1958.
The Correspondence of Henry David Thoreau, edited by Walter Harding and Carl Bode, New York, 1958.
Thoreau's Translation of "The Seven Against Thebes" (1843), edited by L. M. Kaiser, Hartford, Conn., 1960.
Thoreau's Minnesota Journey: Two Documents, edited by Walter Harding, Thoreau Soc. Booklet No. 16 (1962).

II. Biographical and Critical Studies

1. *Books*

Walter Harding, *A Thoreau Handbook,* New York, 1959.
———, *Thoreau: Man of Concord,* New York, 1960.
———, *Thoreau's Library,* Charlottesville, Va., 1957.
H. B. Hough, *Thoreau of Walden: The Man and His Eventful Life,* New York, 1956.
Milton Meltzer and Walter Harding, *A Thoreau Profile,* New York, 1962.
C. R. Metzger, *Thoreau and Whitman: A Study of Their Aesthetics,* Seattle, 1961.
Sherman Paul, *The Shores of America: Thoreau's Inward Exploration,* Urbana, Ill., 1958.
———, *Thoreau: A Collection of Critical Essays,* Englewood Cliffs, N. J., 1962 [articles by William Drake, Edwin Fussell, Leo Stoller, *et al.*].
J. L. Shanley, *The Making of Walden, with the Text of the First Version,* Chicago, 1957.
J. S. Sherwin and R. C. Reynolds, *A Word Index to Walden: With Textual Notes,* Charlottesville, Va., 1960.
Leo Stoller, *After Walden: Thoreau's Changing Views on Economic Man,* Stanford, Calif., 1957.
J. G. Taylor, *Neighbor Thoreau's Critical Humor,* Logan, Utah (Utah State Univ. Monograph Series, VI), 1958.

2. *Articles*

R. C. Albrecht, "Thoreau and His Audience: 'A Plea for Captain John Brown,'" *AL,* XXXII, 393–402 (Jan., 1961).
J. G. Blair and Augustus Trowbridge, "Thoreau on Katahdin," *AQ,* XII, 508–517 (Winter, 1960).
Carl Bode, "Thoreau: The Double Negative," in *The Young Rebel in American Literature,* London, 1959, pp. 3–22.
J. C. Broderick, "American Reviews of Thoreau's Posthumous Books, 1863–1866: Check List and Analysis," *UTSE,* XXXIV, 125–139 (1955).
———, "The Movement of Thoreau's Prose," *AL,* XXXIII, 133–142 (May, 1961).
———, "Thoreau, Alcott, and the Poll Tax," *SP,* LIII, 612–626 (Oct., 1956).
Vincent Buranelli, "The Case Against Thoreau," *Ethics,* LXVII, 257–268 (July, 1957).
L. V. Cady, "Thoreau's Quotations from the Confucian Books in *Walden,*" *AL,* XXXIII, 20–32 (March, 1961).
K. W. Cameron, "Chronology of Thoreau's Harvard Years," *ESQ,* No. 15, pp. 2–108 (2nd Quart., 1959).

———, "Annotations on Thoreau's Correspondence," *ESQ,* No. 24, pp. 6–105 (3rd Quart., 1961).
———, "The Recent Sale of Thoreau Manuscripts," *ESQ,* No. 13, pp. 98–114 (4th Quart., 1958).
———, "The Solitary Thoreau of the Alumni Notes," *ESQ,* No. 7, pp. 2–37 (2nd Quart., 1957).
———, "Thoreau's Harvard Textbooks," *ESQ,* No. 23, pp. 19–111 (2nd Quart., 1961).
———, "Thoreau's New Poems," *ESQ,* No. 14, pp. 21–32 (1st Quart., 1959).
———, "Thoreau's Three Months Out of Harvard and His First Publication," *ESQ,* No. 5, pp. 2–12 (4th Quart., 1956).
———, "Young Henry Thoreau in the Annals of the Concord Academy (1829–1833)," *ESQ,* No. 9, pp. 1–42 (4th Quart., 1957).
———. See EMERSON, above.
R. C. Cosbey, "Thoreau at Work: The Writing of 'Ktaadn,'" *BNYPL,* LXV, 21–30 (Jan., 1961).
L. A. Cummings, "Thoreau Poems in Bixby Washington-University Manuscripts," *ESQ,* No. 26, 9–28 (1st Quart., 1962).
F. B. Dedmond, "Thoreau and the Ethical Concept of Government," *Person,* XXXVI, 36–46 (Winter, 1955).
Seymour Flaxman, "Thoreau and Van Eeden," in *Der Friede: Idee und Verwirklichung,* edited by E. Fromm, H. Herzfeld, and K. R. Grossman, Heidelberg, 1961, pp. 341–352.
Walter Harding and Carl Bode, "Henry David Thoreau, a Check List of His Correspondence," *BNYPL,* LIX, 227–252 (May, 1955).
Walter Harding, "The Influence of Thoreau's Lecturing on His Writing," *BNYPL,* LX, 74–80 (Jan., 1956).
———, "Thoreau's Fame Abroad," *BPLQ,* XI, 94–101 (April, 1959).
———, "Introduction" and Notes to *The Variorum Walden,* New York, 1962.
George Hendrick, "The Influence of Thoreau's 'Civil Disobedience' on Gandhi's *Satyagraha,*" *NEQ,* XXIX, 462–471 (Dec., 1956).
Clayton Hoagland, "The Diary of Thoreau's 'Gentle Boy,'" *NEQ,* XXVIII, 473–489 (Dec., 1955).
Joseph Hosmer, *et al.,* "Thoreau Annex," Thoreau Soc. Booklet No. 10 (Fall, 1955).
C. F. Hovde, "Nature into Art: Thoreau's Use of His Journals in *A Week,*" *AL,* XXX, 165–184 (May, 1958).
Joseph Jones, "Transcendental Grocery Bills: Thoreau's *Walden* and Some Aspects of American Vegetarianism," *UTSE,* XXXVI, 141–154 (1957).

Lauriat Lane, Jr., "On the Organic Structure of *Walden,*" *CE,* XXI, 195–202 (Jan., 1960).

Lewis Leary, "*Walden* Goes Wandering," *NEQ,* XXXII, 3–30 (March, 1959).

C. G. Loomis, "Henry David Thoreau as Folklorist," *WF,* XVI, 90–106 (April, 1957).

Christopher McKee, "Thoreau's First Visit to the White Mountains," *Appalachia,* XXXI, 199–209 (Dec., 1956).

Samuel Middlebrook, "Henry David Thoreau," in *Great American Liberals,* edited by G. R. Mason, Boston, 1956, pp. 69–79.

Perry Miller, "Afterword" to *Walden . . . and On the Duty of Civil Disobedience,* New York, 1960, pp. 249–255.

———, "Thoreau in the Context of International Romanticism," *NEQ,* XXXIV, 147–159 (June, 1961).

J. J. Moldenhauer, "Images of Circularity in Thoreau's Prose," *TSLL,* I, 245–263 (Summer, 1959).

Sherman Paul, "Introduction" to *"Walden" and "Civil Disobedience,"* Boston, 1957, pp. vii–xxxix.

K. A. Robinson, "Thoreau and the Wild Appetite," Thoreau Soc. Booklet No. 12 (1957).

Sreebrishna Sarma, "A Short Study of Oriental Influences upon H. D. Thoreau with Special Reference to His 'Walden,' " *JA,* I, 76–92 (1956).

Andrew Schiller, "Thoreau and Whitman: The Record of a Pilgrimage," *NEQ,* XXVIII, 186–197 (June, 1955).

J. L. Shanley, "The Pleasures of Walden," *Thoreau Soc. Booklet* No. 15, pp. 1–6 (1960).

Odell Shepard, "Unconsciousness in Cambridge: The Editing of Thoreau's 'Lost Journal,' " *ESQ,* No. 13, pp. 13–19 (4th Quart., 1958).

David Skwire, "A Check List of Wordplays in *Walden,*" *AL,* XXXI, 282–289 (Nov., 1959).

E. S. Smith, "A Thoreau for Today," *Mainstream,* XIII, 1–24 (April, 1960); 42–55 (May).

Laurence Stapleton, "Introduction" to *H. D. Thoreau: A Writer's Journal,* New York, 1960, pp. ix–xxix.

W. B. Stein, "*Walden:* The Wisdom of the Centaur," *ELH,* XXV, 194–215 (Sept., 1958).

Leo Stoller, "A Note on Thoreau's Place in the History of Phenology," *Isis,* XLVII, 172–181 (June, 1956).

C. F. Strauch, editor, "A Symposium on Teaching Thoreau," *ESQ,* No. 18, pp. 2–23 (1st Quart., 1960).

Denham Sutcliffe, "Foreword" to *A Week on the Concord and Merrimack Rivers,* New York, 1961, pp. vii–xiii.

Mabel L. Todd, "The Thoreau Family Two Generations Ago,"

Thoreau Soc. Booklet No. 13 (1958).
Johannes Urzidil, "Henry David Thoreau oder Natur und Freiheit," *CPe,* No. 30, pp. 13–31 (1956).
Lawrence Willson, "Another View of the Pilgrims," *NEQ,* XXXIV, 160–177 (June, 1961).
———, "The Transcendentalist View of the West," *WHR,* XIV, 183–191 (Spring, 1960).
———, "Thoreau and Roman Catholicism," *CathHR,* XLII, 157–172 (July, 1956).
———, "Thoreau and the French in Canada," *RUO,* XXIX, 281–297 (July–Sept., 1959).
———, "Thoreau and the Natural Diet," *SAQ,* LVII, 83–103 (Winter, 1958).
———, "Thoreau—Citizen of Concord," *ESQ,* No. 14, pp. 7–12 (1st Quart., 1959).
———, "Thoreau's Canadian Notebook," *HLQ,* XXII, 179–200 (May, 1959).
Kodo Yahagi, "On the Position of Henry David Thoreau in Relation to the Formation of Americanism," *Taisho Daigaku Kenkyukiyo,* XLIV, 1–40 (March, 1959) [in Japanese].

MELVILLE

I. Writings of Melville

Battle-Pieces and Aspects of the War, facsimile reproduction with an introduction by Sidney Kaplan, Gainesville, Fla., 1960.
Clarel: A Poem and Pilgrimage in the Holy Land, edited by W. E. Bezanson, New York, 1960.
The Letters of Herman Melville, edited by M. R. Davis and W. H. Gilman, New Haven, 1960.

II. Bibliographical, Biographical, and Critical Studies

1. *Books*

J. H. Birss, Gordon Roper, S. C. Sherman (Bibliography Committee of the Melville Society), compilers, *Melville Bibliography, 1952–1957,* Providence, R. I., 1959.
James Baird, *Ishmael,* Baltimore, 1956.
Merlin Bowen, *The Long Encounter: Self and Experience in the Writings of Herman Melville,* Chicago, 1960.
William Braswell, *Melville's Religious Thought: An Essay in Interpretation,* New York, 1959.
Dorothee Finkelstein, *Melville's Orienda,* New Haven, 1961.
R. H. Fogle, *Melville's Shorter Tales,* Norman, Okla., 1960.

Harrison Hayford, *The Somers Mutiny Affair,* Englewood Cliffs, N. J., 1959.
Hans Helmcke, *Die Funktion des Ich-Erzählers in Herman Melvilles Roman "Moby-Dick,"* Mainzer Amerikanistische Beiträge, Band I, München, 1957.
H. W. Hetherington, *Melville's Reviewers, British and American, 1846–1891,* Chapel Hill, N. C., 1961.
Leon Howard, *Herman Melville* (University of Minnesota Pamphlets on American Writers, No. 13), Minneapolis, 1961.
Klaus Lanzinger, *Primitivismus und Naturalismus im Prosaschaffen Herman Melvilles,* Innsbruck, 1959.
J. J. Mayoux, *Melville par lui-même,* Paris, 1958 (*Melville,* translated by John Ashbery, New York, 1960).
J. E. Miller, Jr., *A Reader's Guide to Herman Melville,* New York, 1962.
E. H. Rosenberry, *Melville and the Comic Spirit,* Cambridge, Mass., 1955.
M. M. Sealts, Jr., *Melville as Lecturer,* Cambridge, Mass., 1957.
Milton Stern, *The Fine Hammered Steel of Herman Melville,* Urbana, Ill., 1957.

2. *Articles*

Darrell Abel, "'Laurel Twined With Thorn': The Theme of Melville's *Timoleon," Person,* XLI, 330–340 (July, 1960).
D. D. Anderson, "Melville Criticism: Past and Present," *MQ,* II, 169–184 (Winter, 1961).
N. A. Ault, "The Sea Imagery in Herman Melville's *Clarel," RSSCW,* XXVII, 72–84 (June, 1959).
C. M. Babcock, "Some Expressions from Herman Melville," *PADS,* XXXI, 3–13 (April, 1959).
Laurence Barrett, "The Differences in Melville's Poetry," *PMLA,* LXX, 606–623 (Sept., 1955).
J. W. Beach, "Hart Crane and *Moby-Dick," WR,* XX, 183–196 (Spring, 1956).
Lillian Beatty. See HAWTHORNE, above.
Warner Berthoff, "'Certain Phenomenal Men': The Example of *Billy Budd," ELH,* XXVII, 334–351 (Dec., 1960).
W. W. Betts, Jr., *"Moby-Dick:* Melville's *Faust," LHB,* I, No. 1, 31–44 (1959).
Guido Botta, "L'ultimo romanzo di Melville," *SA,* III, 109–131 (1957).
H. C. Brashers, "Ishmael's Tattoos," *SR,* LXX, 137–154 (Winter, 1962).
William Braswell, "Melville's *Billy Budd,* as 'An Inside Narrative,'" *AL,* XXIX, 133–146 (May, 1957).
Glauco Cambon, "Ishmael and the Problem of Formal Discon-

tinuities in *Moby-Dick,*" *MLN,* LXXVI, 516–523 (June, 1961).

K. W. Cameron. See EMERSON, above.

G. A. Cardwell, "Melville's Gray Story: Symbols and Meanings in 'Benito Cereno,' " *BuR,* VIII, 154–167 (May, 1959).

J. G. Cawelti, "Some Notes on the Structure of *The Confidence Man,*" *AL,* XXIX, 278–288 (Nov., 1957).

William Charvat, "Melville and the Common Reader," *SB,* XII, 41–57 (1959).

M. D. Clubb, "The Second Personal Pronoun in *Moby-Dick,*" *AS,* XXXV, 252–260 (Dec., 1960).

C. H. Cook, Jr., "Ahab's 'Intolerable Allegory,' " *BUSE,* I, 45–52 (Spring–Summer, 1955).

G. R. Creeger, "The Symbolism of Whiteness in Melville's Prose Fiction," *JA,* V, 147–163 (1960).

Curtis Dahl, "Moby Dick's Cousin Behemoth," *AL,* XXXI, 21–29 (March, 1959).

T. R. Dale, "Melville and Aristotle: The Conclusion of *Moby-Dick* as a Classical Tragedy," *BUSE,* III, 45–50 (Spring, 1957).

A. G. Day, "Hawaiian Echoes in Melville's *Mardi,*" *MLQ,* XVIII, 3–8 (March, 1957).

Walter Dubler, "Theme and Structure in Melville's *The Confidence Man,*" *AL,* XXXIII, 307–319 (Nov., 1961).

Philip Durham, "Prelude to the Constable Edition of Melville," *HLQ,* XXI, 285–289 (May, 1958).

R. M. Farnsworth, "*Israel Potter:* Pathetic Comedy," *BNYPL,* LXV, 125–132 (Feb., 1961).

———, "Ishmael to the Royal Masthead," *UKCR,* XXVIII, 183–190 (March, 1962).

Marvin Felheim, "Meaning and Structure in 'Bartleby,' " *CE,* XXIII, 369–376 (Feb., 1962).

R. H. Fogle, "*Billy Budd*—Acceptance or Irony," *TSE,* VIII, 107–113 (1958).

———, "*Billy Budd:* The Order of the Fall," *NCF,* XV, 189–205 (Dec., 1960).

———, "Melville and the Civil War," *TSE,* IX, 61–89 (1959).

———, "Melville's *Clarel:* Doubt and Belief," *TSE,* X, 101–116 (1960).

C. H. Foster, "Something in Emblems: A Reinterpretation of *Moby-Dick,*" *NEQ,* XXXIV, 3–35 (March, 1961).

H. B. Franklin, " 'Apparent Symbol of Despotic Command': Melville's *Benito Cereno,*" *NEQ,* XXXIV, 462–477 (Dec., 1961).

Maxwell Geismar, "Introduction" to *"Billy Budd" and "Typee,"* New York, 1962, pp. xiii–xxvi.

W. M. Gibson, "Introduction" to *Moby Dick,* New York, 1959, pp. 9–14.

G. Giovannini and H. M. Campbell, "The Hanging Scene in Melville's *Billy Budd,*" *MLN,* LXX, 491–500 (Nov., 1955).

W. H. Gilman, Review of Horsford's edition of Melville's *Journal of a Visit to Europe and the Levant, AL,* XXVIII, 82–93 (March, 1956); a rejoinder by H. C. Horsford and a reply, *AL,* XXVIII, 520–524 (Jan., 1957).

Philip Graham, "The Riddle of Melville's *Mardi:* A Reinterpretation," *UTSE,* XXXVI, 93–99 (1957).

Dorothee Grdseloff, "A Note on the Origin of Fedallah in *Moby Dick,*" *AL,* XXVII, 396–403 (Nov., 1955).

J. J. Gross, "Melville's *The Confidence-Man:* The Problem of Source and Meaning," *NM,* LX, 299–310 (Sept., 1959).

Augusto Guidi, "Considerazioni su *Bartleby,*" *SA,* III, 99–108 (1957).

Allen Guttmann, "The Enduring Innocence of Captain Amasa Delano," *BUSE,* V, 35–45 (Spring, 1961).

Harrison Hayford, "Melville's Freudian Slip," *AL,* XXX, 366–368 (Nov., 1958).

———, "Melville's *Usable* or *Visible Truth,*" *MLN,* LXXIV, 702–705 (Dec., 1959).

———, "Poe in *The Confidence-Man,*" *NCF,* XIV, 207–218 (Dec., 1959).

C. H. Holman, "The Reconciliation of Ishmael: *Moby-Dick* and the Book of Job," *SAQ,* LVII, 477–490 (Autumn, 1958).

Leon Howard, "The Case of the Missing Whaler," *MSS,* XII, 3–9 (Fall, 1960).

C. B. Ives, "*Billy Budd* and the Articles of War," *AL,* XXXIV, 31–39 (March, 1962).

Margaret Jackson, "Melville's Use of a Real Slave Mutiny in 'Benito Cereno,' " *CLAJ,* IV, 79–93 (Dec., 1960).

David Jaffé, "The Captain Who Sat for the Portrait of Ahab," *BUSE,* IV, 1–22 (Spring, 1960).

———, "Some Origins of *Moby-Dick:* New Finds in an Old Source," *AL,* XXIX, 263–277 (May, 1957).

L. N. Jeffrey, "A Concordance to the Biblical Allusions in *Moby-Dick,*" *BB,* XXI, 223–229 (May–Aug., 1956).

B. C. Jones, "American Frontier Humor in Melville's *Typee,*" *NYFQ,* XV, 283–288 (Winter, 1959).

Koh Kasegawa, "*Moby-Dick* as a Symbolic Myth," *SEL,* XXXVI, 251–272 (1960).

James Kirsch, "The Enigma of Moby Dick," *Jour of Analytical Psych* (London), III, 131–148 (1958).

James Kissane, "Imagery, Myth, and Melville's *Pierre,*" *AL,* XXVI, 564–572 (Jan., 1955).

George Knox, "Lost Command: *Benito Cereno* Reconsidered," *Person,* XL, 280–291 (Summer, 1959).

H. H. Kühnelt, "The Bell-Tower: Herman Melvilles Beitrag sur

Roboterliteratur," *WBEP,* LXVI, 139–157 (1958).
———, "Der Humor in Melvilles *Moby Dick,*" *WBEP,* LXII, 111–121 (1955).
———, "The Reception of Herman Melville's Works in Germany and Austria," *Innsbrucker Beiträge zur Kulturwissenschaft,* IV, 111–121 (1956).
Patricia Lacy, "The Agatha Theme in Melville's Stories," *UTSE,* XXXV, 96–105 (1956).
H-J. Lang, "Melville's 'Billy Budd' und seine Quellen: Eine Nachlese," in *Festschrift für Walther Fischer,* Heidelberg, 1959, pp. 225–249.
Klaus Lanzinger, "Melvilles Beschreibung des Meeres in *Mardi* im Hinblick auf *Moby-Dick,*" *NS,* IX, 1–15 (Jan., 1960).
Lewis Leary, "Introduction" to *His Fifty Years of Exile* (*Israel Potter*), New York, 1957, pp. vii–xii.
R. F. Lucid, "The Influence of *Two Years Before the Mast* on Herman Melville," *AL,* XXXI, 243–256 (Nov., 1959).
Robin Magowan, "Masque and Symbol in Melville's 'Benito Cereno,' " *CE,* XXIII, 346–351 (Feb., 1962).
B. R. McElderry, Jr., "Three Earlier Treatments of the *Billy Budd* Theme," *AL,* XXVII, 251–257 (May, 1955).
Mordecai Marcus, "Melville's Bartleby as a Psychological Double," *CE,* XXIII, 365–368 (Feb., 1962).
J. C. Mathews, "Melville's Reading of Dante," *FurmS,* VI, 1–8 (Fall, 1958).
J. J. Mayoux, "La Langue et le Style de Melville," *EA,* XIII, 337–345 (July–Sept., 1960).
———, "Myth et symbole chez Herman Melville," *Inventario,* XV, 43–54 (1960).
J. E. Miller, Jr. See HAWTHORNE, above.
M. Millhauser, "The Form of *Moby-Dick,*" *JAAC,* XIII, 527–532 (June, 1955).
G. B. Montague, "Melville's *Battle-Pieces,*" *UTSE,* XXXV, 106–115 (1956).
Charles Moorman, "Melville's Pierre in the City," *AL,* XXVII, 571–577 (Jan., 1956).
J. B. Noone, Jr., "*Billy Budd:* Two Concepts of Nature," *AL,* XXIX, 249–262 (Nov., 1957).
W. V. O'Connor, "Melville on the Nature of Hope," *UKCR,* XXII, 123–130 (Winter, 1955).
T. B. O'Daniel, "Herman Melville as a Writer of Journals," *CLAJ,* IV, 94–105 (Dec., 1960).
R. V. Osbourn, "The White Whale and the Absolute," *EIC,* VI, 160–170 (April, 1956).
Marcello Pagnini, "Struttura ideologica e struttura stilistica in *Moby-Dick,*" *SA,* VI, 87–134 (1960).

J. Parke, "Seven *Moby-Dicks,*" *NEQ,* XXVIII, 319–338 (Sept., 1955).

L. R. Phelps, "*Moby-Dick* in Germany," *CL,* X, 349–355 (Fall, 1958).

———, "The Reaction to *Benito Cereno* and *Billy Budd* in Germany," *Sym,* XIII, 294–299 (Fall, 1959).

T. L. Philbrick, "Another Source for *White-Jacket,*" *AL,* XXIX, 431–439 (Jan., 1958).

———, "Melville's 'Best Authorities,' " *NCF,* XV, 171–179 (Sept., 1960).

William Plomer, "Introduction" to *White Jacket,* New York, 1956, pp. v–x.

Max Putzel, "The Source and the Symbols of Melville's 'Benito Cereno,' " *AL,* XXXIV, 191–206 (May, 1962).

Alfredo Rizzardi, "La Poesia di Herman Melville," *SA,* I, 159–203 (1955).

E. H. Rosenberry, "Melville's Ship of Fools," *PMLA,* LXXV, 604–608 (Dec., 1960).

Arthur Sale, "The Glass Ship: A Recurrent Image in Melville," *MLQ,* XVII, 118–127 (June, 1956).

H. H. Schless, "Flaxman, Dante, and Melville's *Pierre,*" *BNYPL,* LXIV, 65–82 (Feb., 1960).

———, "*Moby Dick* and Dante: A Critique and Time Scheme," *BNYPL,* LXV, 289–312 (May, 1961).

M. M. Sealts, Jr., "The Ghost of Major Melvill," *NEQ,* XXX, 291–306 (Sept., 1957).

———, "Melville's Burgundy Club Sketches," *HLB,* XII, 253–267 (Spring, 1958).

J. D. Seelye, "The Golden Navel: The Cabalism of Ahab's Doubloon," *NCF,* XIV, 350–355 (March, 1960).

Franz Stanzel, "Der Ich-Roman: *Moby-Dick,*" Chapter III of *Die Typischen Erzählsituationen im Roman, WBEP,* LXIII, 60–92 (1955).

C. N. Stavrou, "Ahab and Dick Again," *TSLL,* III, 309–320 (Autumn, 1961).

W. B. Stein, "Melville and the Creative Eros," *LHB,* I, No. 2, 13–26 (1960).

———, "Melville's Comedy of Faith," *ELH,* XXVII, 315–333 (Dec., 1960).

———, "The Moral Axis of 'Benito Cereno,' " *Accent,* XV, 221–233 (Summer, 1955).

———, "The Old Man and the Triple Goddess: Melville's 'The Haglets,' " *ELH,* XXV, 43–59 (March, 1958).

M. R. Stern, "Introduction" to *"Typee" and "Billy Budd,"* New York, 1958, pp. vi–xxv.

———, "Some Techniques of Melville's Perception," *PMLA,*

LXXIII, 251–259 (June, 1958).

G. T. Tanselle, "Herman Melville's Visit to Galena in 1840," *Jour of Ill State Hist Soc,* LIII, 376–388 (Winter, 1960).

W. R. Thompson, "Melville's 'The Fiddler': A Study in Dissolution," *TSLL,* II, 492–500 (Winter, 1961).

———, " 'The Paradise of Bachelors and the Tartarus of Maids': A Reinterpretation," *AQ,* IX, 34–45 (Spring, 1957).

Willard Thorp, "Afterword" to *"Billy Budd" and Other Tales,* New York, 1961, pp. 325–334.

Eleanor Tilton, "Melville's 'Rammon': A Text and Commentary," *HLB,* XIII, 50–91 (Winter, 1959).

Akira Tomita, "How to Read *Moby-Dick,*" *Rikkyo Rev.* (Tokyo), No. 16, pp. 1–16, 53–55 (1955).

W. Y. Tindall, "The Ceremony of Innocence (Herman Melville: *Billy Budd*)," in *Great Moral Dilemmas in Literature,* New York, 1956, pp. 73–81.

Dan Vogel, "The Dramatic Chapters in *Moby Dick,*" *NCF,* XIII, 239–247 (Dec., 1958).

Vern Wagner, "Billy Budd as Moby Dick: An Alternate Reading," in *Studies in Honor of John Wilcox,* Detroit, 1958, pp. 157–174.

Kurt Wais, "Die Errettung aus dem Schiffbruch: Melville, Mallarmé und einige deutsche Voraussetzungen," *DVLG,* XXXIV, 21–45 (1960).

J. A. Ward, "The Function of the Cetological Chapters in *Moby-Dick,*" *AL,* XXVIII, 164–183 (May, 1956).

W. T. Weathers, "*Moby Dick* and the Nineteenth-Century Scene," *TSLL,* I, 477–501 (Winter, 1960).

R. B. West, Jr., "Primitivism in Melville," *PrS,* XXX, 369–385 (Winter, 1956).

Otis Wheeler, "Humor in *Moby-Dick:* Two Problems," *AL,* XXIX, 203–206 (May, 1957).

Lawrence Willson, "Yet Another Note on *Moby-Dick,*" *DR,* XXXV, 5–15 (Spring, 1955).

Phil Withim, "*Billy Budd:* Testament of Acceptance," *MLQ,* XX, 115–127 (June, 1959).

S. C. Woodruff, "Melville and His Chimney," *PMLA,* LXXV, 283–292 (June, 1960).

Nathalia Wright, "*Pierre:* Herman Melville's *Inferno,*" *AL,* XXXII, 167–181 (May, 1960).

Saburo Yamaya, "The Inner Struggle in Melville's *Pierre,*" *Jour of Humanities* (Hosei University, Japan), No. 3, pp. 101–120 (1958).

———, "Melville's 'Inland Voyage to Fairyland,' " in *Essays in English and American Literature,* Tokyo, 1961, pp. 185–205.

———, "A New Interpretation of Melville's *Moby-Dick,*" *SEL,* English Number 1961, pp. 59–81.

———, "Poe, Hawthorne and Melville's 'Benito Cereno,'" *SEL,* No. 4, pp. 21–32 (March, 1961).
———, "The Stone Image of Melville's *Pierre,*" *SEL,* XXXIV, 31–57 (No. 1, 1957).
Elémire Zolla, "Melville e l'Abbandono dello Zodiaco," *Par,* XI, 3–41 (Aug., 1960).

WHITMAN

I. Writings of Whitman

The Collected Writings of Walt Whitman, G. W. Allen and Sculley Bradley, General Editors. Volume I, *The Correspondence, 1842–1867;* Volume II, *The Correspondence, 1868–1875,* edited by E. H. Miller, New York, 1961.
Walt Whitman, *An 1855–56 Notebook Toward the Second Edition of Leaves of Grass,* with an introduction by H. W. Blodgett, a foreword by C. E. Feinberg, and additional notes by William White, Carbondale, Ill., 1959.
Walt Whitman, "Criticism," *Lit R,* IV, 49–59 (Autumn, 1960).
"'Kentucky': Unpublished Poetic Fragments by Walt Whitman," edited by William White, *PrS,* XXXII, 170–178 (Fall, 1958).

II. Bibliographical Lists and Collections

Evie A. Allen, "A Check List of Whitman Publications, 1945–1960," in *Walt Whitman as Man, Poet, and Legend,* 1961, pp. 179–244.
Dorothy Bowen and Philip Durham, "Walt Whitman Materials in the Huntington Library," *HLQ,* XIX, 81–96 (Nov., 1955).
Rena Grant, "The Livezey-Whitman Manuscripts," *WWR,* VII, 3–14 (March, 1961).
William White, "Whitman: A Current Bibliography," in *WWN,* I–IV (Jan., 1955–Dec., 1958) and *WWR,* V–VIII (1959–1962).
———, "Walt Whitman's Short Stories: Some Comments and a Bibliography," *PBSA,* LII, 300–306 (4th Quart., 1958).
C. B. Willard, "The Saunders Collection of Whitmania in the Brown University Library," *BBr,* XVIII, 14–22 (May, 1956).

III. Biographical and Critical Studies

1. *Books*

G. W. Allen, *Walt Whitman as Man, Poet, and Legend,* Carbondale, Ill., 1961.
———, *Walt Whitman,* New York, 1961.
Roger Asselineau, *The Evolution of Walt Whitman: The Creation of a Personality,* Cambridge, Mass., 1960.

Richard Chase, *Walt Whitman* (University of Minnesota Pamphlets on American Writers, No. 9), Minneapolis, 1961.
Geoffrey Dutton, *Whitman,* New York, 1961.
Emory Holloway, *Free and Lonesome Heart: The Secret of Walt Whitman,* New York, 1960.
R. W. B. Lewis, editor, *The Presence of Walt Whitman: Selected Papers from the English Institute* [meetings of 1960 and 1961], New York, 1962 has essays by S. E. Whicher, Paul Fussell, Jr., Richard Chase, R. H. Pearce, Samuel Hynes, J. E. Miller, Jr., and James Wright.
E. H. and Roselind S. Miller, compilers, *Walt Whitman's Correspondence: A Checklist,* New York, 1957.
J. E. Miller, Jr., *A Critical Guide to "Leaves of Grass,"* Chicago, 1957.
J. E. Miller, Jr., Karl Shapiro, and Bernice Slote, *Start With the Sun: Studies in Cosmic Poetry,* Lincoln, Nebr., 1960.
———, *Walt Whitman,* New York, 1962.
R. H. Pearce, editor, *Whitman: A Collection of Critical Essays,* Englewood Cliffs, N. J., 1962 [has essays by John Kinnaird, R. H. Pearce, James E. Miller, Jr., Walter Sutton, Perry Miller, Richard Chase, and Josephine Miles, and other selections].
P. D. Westbrook, *The Greatness of Man; An Essay on Dostoyevsky and Whitman,* New York, 1961.

2. *Articles*

R. P. Adams, "Whitman: A Brief Revaluation," *TSE,* V, 111–149 (1955).
———, "Whitman's 'Lilacs' and the Tradition of Pastoral Elegy," *PMLA,* LXXII, 479–487 (June, 1957).
G. W. Allen, "Introduction" to *Leaves of Grass,* New York, 1955, pp. v–xx.
———, "The Problem of Metaphor in Translating Walt Whitman's 'Leaves of Grass,' " *Eng Stud Today* (Bern), ser. 2, 1961, pp. 269–280.
G. W. Allen *et al.,* "Special Symposium Issue—Whitman: 1960," *WWR,* VI, 3–16 (March, 1960).
Roger Asselineau, "État présent des études Whitmaniennes," *EA,* XI, 31–40 (Jan.–March, 1958).
———, "Introduction" to *Walt Whitman: Feuilles d'Herbe* (*Choix*), Paris, 1956, pp. vii–xxiv.
———, "Un Inédit de Walt Whitman: 'Taine's History of English Literature,' " *EA,* X, 128–138 (April–June, 1957).
———, "Whitman et Wordsworth—Étude d'une influence indirecte," *RLC,* XXIX, 505–512 (Oct.–Dec., 1955).
R. P. Basler, "Introduction" to *Walt Whitman's Memoranda During the War* [&] *Death of Abraham Lincoln,* Bloomington, Ind.,

1962, pp. 1–46.

H. W. Blodgett *et al.*, "Special Symposium Issue—Whitman: 1960 [Part II]," *WWR*, VI, 23–35 (June, 1960).

H. W. Blodgett *et al.*, "Walt Whitman Symposium," *ESQ*, No. 22, pp. 2–28 (1st Quart., 1961).

Fredson Bowers, "The Earliest Manuscript of Whitman's 'Passage to India' and Its Notebook," *BNYPL*, LXI, 319–352 (July, 1957).

———, "The Manuscripts of Whitman's 'Song of the Red-Wood-Tree,'" *PBSA*, L, 53–85 (1st Quart., 1956).

———, "The Walt Whitman Manuscripts of 'Leaves of Grass (1860),'" in *Textual & Literary Criticism*, Cambridge, Eng., 1959.

Sculley Bradley, "The Teaching of Whitman," *CE*, XXIII, 618–622 (May, 1962).

C. A. Brown, "Walt Whitman and the 'New Poetry,'" *AL*, XXXIII, 33–45 (March, 1961).

Glauco Cambon, "Ancora su Whitman," *Aut Aut*, No. 42, pp. 469–485 (Nov., 1957).

———, "La Parola come emanazione (Note Marginali sullo stile di Whitman)," *SA*, V, 141–160 (1959).

———, "Walt Whitman in Italia," *Aut Aut*, No. 39, pp. 244–263 (May, 1957).

———, "Whitman e il mito di Adamo," *Aut Aut*, No. 40, pp. 315–330 (July, 1957).

K. W. Cameron, "Emerson's Recommendation of Whitman in 1863: The Remainder of the Evidence," *ESQ*, No. 3, pp. 14–20 (2nd Quart., 1956).

Abe Capek, "Introduction" to *Walt Whitman: Poetry and Prose*, East Berlin, 1958, pp. 15–21.

———, "Walt Whitman: A Centennial Re-evaluation," *Philologica* (Prague), VII, 30–45 (No. 2–3, 1955).

V. K. Chari, "Whitman and Indian Thought," *WHR*, XIII, 291–302 (Summer, 1959).

Richard Chase, "Foreword" to *Specimen Days*, New York, 1961, pp. ix–xvi.

Henry Chupack, "Walt Whitman and the Camden Circle," *Proc. N. J. Hist. Soc.*, LXXIII, 274–299 (Oct., 1955).

S. K. Coffman, Jr., "Form and Meaning in Whitman's 'Passage to India,'" *PMLA*, LXX, 337–349 (June, 1955).

Alice L. Cooke, "Whitman as a Critic: *Democratic Vistas* with Special Reference to Carlyle," *WWN*, IV, 91–95 (June, 1958).

Malcolm Cowley, "Introduction" to *Leaves of Grass: The First (1855) Edition*, New York, 1959, pp. vii–xxxvii.

———, "Walt Whitman's Buried Masterpiece," *SatR*, XLII, 11–13, 32–34 (Oct. 31, 1959).

J. M. Cox, "Walt Whitman, Mark Twain, and the Civil War," *SR*,

LXIX, 185–204 (April–June, 1961).
David Daiches, "Imagery and Mood in Tennyson and Whitman," *Eng Stud Today* (Bern), ser. 2, 1961, pp. 217–232.
———, "Walt Whitman as Innovator," in *The Young Rebel in American Literature,* edited by Carl Bode, London, 1959, pp. 25–48.
C. T. Davis, "Walt Whitman and the Problem of an American Tradition," *CLAJ,* V, 1–16 (Sept., 1961).
Federico De Maria, "Walt Whitman, Poeta di Ieri e di Sempre," *CV,* XIII, 462–474 (1958).
E. H. Eby, "Walt Whitman and the Tree of Life," *WWR,* VII, 43–51 (Sept., 1961).
J. E. Englekirk, "Whitman en castellano," *Atlántico* (Madrid), No. 2, pp. 73–87 (1956).
C. E. Feinberg, "A Whitman Collector Destroys a Whitman Myth," *PBSA,* LII, 73–92 (2nd Quart., 1958).
L. A. Fiedler, "Introduction" to *Whitman,* New York, 1959, pp. 7–22.
Frederic Fleisher, "Walt Whitman's Swedish Reception," *WWN,* III, 19–22 (June, 1957); 44–47 (Sept.); 58–62 (Dec.).
Robert Forrey, "Whitman and the Freudians," *Mainstream,* XIV, 45–52 (Jan., 1961).
K. H. Francis, "Walt Whitman's French," *MLR,* LI, 493–506 (Oct., 1956).
Manuel García Blanco, "Walt Whitman y Unamuno," *Cultura Universitaria* (Venezuela), No. 52, pp. 76–102 (Nov.–Dec., 1955).
Clarence Gohdes, "Nationalism and Cosmopolitanism in Whitman's *Leaves of Grass,*" *WWR,* V, 3–7 (March, 1959).
R. J. Griffin, "Notes on Structural Devices in Whitman's Poetry," *TSL,* VI, 15–24 (1961).
Clark Griffith, "Sex and Death: The Significance of Whitman's *Calamus* Themes," *PQ,* XXXIX, 18–38 (Jan., 1960).
Phyl Hentges and Pierre Hentges, "Walt Whitman, poète d'un nouveau monde," *Nouvelle Critique,* VII, 84–104 (Sept.–Oct., 1955).
Maurice Herra, "Feuilles d'Herbe en Europe et en Amérique Latine," *Europe,* XXXIII, 137–145 (Nov.–Dec., 1955).
C. C. Hollis, "Names in *Leaves of Grass,*" *Names,* V, 129–156 (Sept., 1957).
———, "Whitman and the American Idiom," *QJS,* XLIII, 408–420 (Dec., 1957).
———, "Whitman and William Swinton: A Co-operative Friendship," *AL,* XXX, 425–449 (Jan., 1959).
Herbert Howarth, "Whitman and the Irish Writers," in *Comparative Literature: Proceedings of the Second Congress of the International Comparative Literature Association,* Chapel Hill, 1959, II, 479–488.

A. C. Howell, "Walt Whitman, Singer of the American Spirit," *ELL* (Korea), No. 4, pp. 265–278 (Oct., 1957).

S. J. Idzerda, "Walt Whitman, Politician," *NYH*, XXXVII, 171–184 (April, 1956).

A. N. Jeffares, "The Barbaric Yawp," in *The Great Experiment in American Literature: Six Lectures*, edited by Carl Bode, New York, 1961, pp. 29–49.

Joseph Jones, "Carlyle, Whitman, and the Democratic Dilemma," *ESA*, III, 179–197 (Sept., 1960).

Renaud de Jouvenal, "Walt Whitman," *Europe*, XXXIII, 91–107 (Nov.–Dec., 1955).

S. J. Kahn, "The American Backgrounds of Whitman's Sense of Evil," *Scripta Hierosolyminata*, II, 82–118 (1955).

———, "Whitman's 'Black Lucifer': Some Possible Sources," *PMLA*, LXXI, 932–944 (Dec., 1956).

S. J. Krause, "Whitman, Music, and *Proud Music of the Storm*," *PMLA*, LXXII, 705–721 (Sept., 1957).

J. J. Kwiat. See EMERSON, above.

Paul Lauter, "Walt Whitman: Lover and Comrade," *AI*, XVI, 407–435 (Winter, 1959).

Elias Lieberman, "Walt Whitman," in *Great American Liberals*, edited by G. R. Mason, Boston, 1956, pp. 83–95.

John Lovell, Jr., "Appreciating Whitman: 'Passage to India,' " *MLQ*, XXI, 131–141 (June, 1960).

A. L. McLeod, "Walt Whitman in Australia," *WWR*, VII, 23–35 (June, 1961).

Leo Marx, "The Vernacular Tradition in American Literature: Walt Whitman and Mark Twain," *NS*, Beiheft III, 46–57 (1958).

Iwao Matsuhara, "Walt Whitman in Japan: From the First Introduction to the Present," *Thought Currents in Eng. Lit.* (Tokyo), XXIX, 5–42 (Jan., 1957).

C. R. Metzger. See THOREAU, above.

F. D. Miller, "Before *The Good Gray Poet*," *TSL*, III, 89–98 (1958).

———, "Introduction" to *Walt Whitman's Drum-Taps (1865) and Sequel to Drum-Taps (1865–6)*, Gainesville, Fla., 1959, pp. vii–lix.

J. E. Miller, Jr., "Introduction" to *Walt Whitman: Complete Poetry and Selected Prose*, Boston, 1959, pp. xix–liii.

———, "Whitman and Eliot: The Poetry of Mysticism," *SWR*, XLIII, 113–123 (Spring, 1958).

———, "Whitman and the Province of Poetry," *ArQ*, XIV, 5–19 (Spring, 1958).

———, "Whitman in Italy," *WWR*, V, 28–30 (June, 1959).

L. S. Morris, "Walt Whitman, o Poeta da Identidade," *Kriterion*, XL–XLI, 438–452 (1958).

E. S. Oliver, " 'The Seas Are All Cross'd': Whitman on America and

World Freedom," *WHR,* IX, 303–312 (Autumn, 1955).
Saburo Ota, "Walt Whitman and Japanese Literature," *Asia and the Humanities,* Bloomington, Ind., 1959, pp. 62–69.
R. H. Pearce, "Toward an American Epic," *HudR,* XII, 362–377 (Autumn, 1959).
C. E. Pulos, "Whitman and Epictetus: The Stoical Element in *Leaves of Grass,*" *JEGP,* LV, 75–84 (Jan., 1956)
William Randel, "Walt Whitman and American Myths," *SAQ,* LIX, 103–113 (Winter, 1960).
Teut Riese, "Walt Whitman als politischer Dichter," *JA,* III, 136–150 (1958).
D. A. Ringe, "Bryant and Whitman: A Study in Artistic Affinities," *BUSE,* II, 85–94 (Summer, 1956).
Clara Rising, "Vistas of a Disillusioned Realist," *WWR,* VII, 63–71 (Dec., 1961).
Henri Roddier, "Pierre Leroux, George Sand et Walt Whitman ou l'éveil d'un poète," *RLC,* XXXI, 5–33 (Jan., 1957).
E. H. Rosenberry, "Walt Whitman's All-American Poet," *Del Notes,* XXXII, 1–12 (1959).
T. J. Roundtree, "Whitman's Indirect Expression and Its Application to 'Song of Myself,'" *PMLA,* LXXIII, 549–555 (Dec., 1958).
G. R. Roy, "Walt Whitman, George Sand and Certain French Socialists," *RLC,* XXIX, 550–561 (Oct.–Dec., 1955).
Andrew Schiller. See THOREAU, above.
Esther Shephard, "Walt Whitman's Whereabouts in the Winter of 1842–1843," *AL,* XXIX, 289–296 (Nov., 1957).
Gerhard Stebner, "Whitman—Liliencron—W. H. Auden: Betrachtung und Vergleich motivähnlicher Gedichte," *NS,* IX, 105–118 (March, 1960).
Floyd Stovall, "Leaves of Grass," *Univ. of N. C. Extension Bull.,* XXXV, 19–29 (Jan., 1956).
———, "Walt Whitman: The Man and the Myth," *SAQ,* LIV, 538–551 (Nov., 1955).
Fumi Takano, "Walt Whitman's Spiritual Pilgrimage," *SEL* (Tokyo), XXXIV, 59–75 (No. 1, 1957).
E. W. Todd, "Indian Pictures and Two Whitman Poems," *HLQ,* XIX, 1–11 (Nov., 1955).
H. R. Warfel, "'Out of the Cradle Endlessly Rocking,'" *TSL,* III, 83–87 (1958).
———, "Whitman's Structural Principles in 'Spontaneous Me,'" *CE,* XVIII, 190–195 (Jan., 1957).
S. E. Whicher, "Whitman's Awakening to Death: Toward a Biographical Reading of 'Out of the Cradle Endlessly Rocking,'" *SIR,* I, 9–28 (Autumn, 1961).
William White, "The Walt Whitman Fellowship: An Account of Its Organization and a Checklist of Its Papers," *PBSA,* LI, 67–84

(1st Quart., 1957), 167–169 (2nd Quart., 1957).
———, "Walt Whitman's Short Stories: Some Comments and a Bibliography," *PBSA*, LII, 300–306 (4th Quart., 1958).
C. B. Willard, "Ezra Pound's Debt to Walt Whitman," *SP*, LIV, 573–581 (Oct., 1957).
Lawrence Willson, "The 'Body Electric' Meets the Genteel Tradition," *NMQ*, XXVI, 369–386 (Winter, 1956–1957).

MARK TWAIN

I. Writings of Mark Twain

"Ah Sin," A Dramatic Work by Mark Twain and Bret Harte, edited by Frederick Anderson, San Francisco, 1961.
The Art, Humor, and Humanity of Mark Twain, edited, with commentary and notes, by Minnie M. Brashear and R. M. Rodney, with an introduction by Edward Wagenknecht, Norman, Okla., 1959.
The Autobiography of Mark Twain, edited by Charles Neider, New York, 1959.
The Complete Humorous Sketches and Tales of Mark Twain, edited with an introduction by Charles Neider, New York, 1961.
The Complete Short Stories of Mark Twain, edited with an introduction by Charles Neider, New York, 1957.
Concerning Cats. Two Tales by Mark Twain, with an introduction by Frederick Anderson, San Francisco, 1959.
Contributions to the "Galaxy" 1868–1871 by Mark Twain (Samuel Langhorne Clemens), edited with an introduction and notes by B. R. McElderry, Jr., Gainesville, Fla., 1961.
Mark Twain and the Government, selected and arranged by Svend Petersen, Caldwell, Ida., 1960.
Mark Twain-Howells Letters: The Correspondence of Samuel L. Clemens and William D. Howells 1872–1910, edited by H. N. Smith and W. M. Gibson, with the assistance of Frederick Anderson, 2 volumes, Cambridge, Mass., 1960.
Mark Twain: Life as I Find It: Essays, Sketches, Tales, and Other Material, the Majority of Which Is Now Published in Book Form for the First Time, edited with introduction and notes by Charles Neider, Garden City, N. Y., 1961.
Mark Twain of the "Enterprise": Newspaper Articles & Other Documents 1862–1864, edited by H. N. Smith, with the assistance of Frederick Anderson, Berkeley, Calif., 1957.
Mark Twain on the Art of Writing, edited with a foreword by M. B. Fried, Buffalo, 1961.
Mark Twain: San Francisco Correspondent. Selections From His

Letters to "The Territorial Enterprise": 1865–1866, edited by H. N. Smith and Frederick Anderson, San Francisco, 1957.

Mark Twain's Letters to Mary, edited with commentary by Lewis Leary, New York, 1961.

The Pattern for Mark Twain's "Roughing It": Letters from Nevada by Samuel and Orion Clemens 1861–1862, edited with an introduction by F. R. Rogers, Berkeley and Los Angeles, 1961.

Traveling with the Innocents Abroad: Mark Twain's Original Reports from Europe & the Holy Land, edited by D. M. McKeithan, Norman, Okla., 1958.

The Travels of Mark Twain, edited with an introduction and notes by Charles Neider, New York, 1961.

II. Biographical and Critical Studies

1. *Books*

Frank Baldanza, *Mark Twain: An Introduction and Interpretation,* New York, 1961.

Walter Blair, *Mark Twain & Huck Finn,* Berkeley and Los Angeles, 1960.

Pascal Covici, Jr., *Mark Twain's Humor: The Image of a World,* Dallas, 1962.

Paul Fatout, *Mark Twain on the Lecture Circuit,* Bloomington, Ind., 1960.

P. S. Foner, *Mark Twain: Social Critic,* New York, 1958.

Caroline T. Harnsberger, *Mark Twain: Family Man,* New York, 1960.

Lewis Leary, *Mark Twain,* University of Minnesota Pamphlets on American Writers, No. 5, Minneapolis, 1960.

E. H. Long, *Mark Twain Handbook,* New York, 1958.

K. S. Lynn, *Mark Twain and Southwestern Humor,* Boston, 1960.

D. M. McKeithan, *Court Trials in Mark Twain and Other Essays,* The Hague, 1958.

Milton Meltzer, *Mark Twain Himself: A Pictorial Biography,* New York, 1960.

Dorothy Quick, *Enchantment: A Little Girl's Friendship with Mark Twain,* Norman, Okla., 1961.

F. R. Rogers, *Mark Twain's Burlesque Patterns; As Seen in the Novels and Narratives 1855–1885,* Dallas, 1960.

R. B. Salomon, *Twain and the Image of History,* New Haven, 1961.

A. L. Scott, editor, *Mark Twain: Selected Criticism,* Dallas, 1955.

H. N. Smith, *Mark Twain: The Development of a Writer,* Cambridge, Mass., 1962.

A. E. Stone, Jr., *The Innocent Eye: Childhood in Mark Twain's Imagination,* New Haven, 1961.

Arlin Turner, *Mark Twain and George W. Cable: The Record of a*

Literary Friendship, East Lansing, Mich., 1960.
Edward Wagenknecht, *Mark Twain: The Man and His Work,* revised edition, Norman, Okla., 1961.

2. *Articles*

R. P. Adams, "The Unity and Coherence of Huckleberry Finn," *TSE,* VI, 87–103 (1956).
Jerry Allen, "Tom Sawyer's Town," *National Geographic,* CX, 120–140 (July, 1956).
Paul Baender, "Mark Twain and the Byron Scandal," *AL,* XXX, 467–485 (Jan., 1959).
H. G. Baetzhold, "Mark Twain: England's Advocate," *AL,* XXVIII, 328–346 (Nov., 1956).
———, "The Course of Composition of *A Connecticut Yankee:* A Reinterpretation," *AL,* XXXIII, 195–214 (May, 1961).
W. C. Barrett, "On the Naming of Tom Sawyer," *Psychoanalytic Quart.,* XXIV, 424–436 (Sept., 1955).
Warren Beck, "Huck Finn at Phelps Farm—An Essay in Defense of the Form of Mark Twain's Novel," *Archives des Lettres Modernes,* Nos. 13–15, 31 pp. (June–Sept., 1958).
R. E. Bell, "How Mark Twain Comments on Society through Use of Folklore," *MTJ,* X, 1–8, 24–25 (Summer, 1955).
Walter Blair, "The French Revolution and *Huckleberry Finn,*" *MP,* LV, 21–35 (Aug., 1957).
———, "When was *Huckleberry Finn* Written?" *AL,* XXX, 1–25 (March, 1958).
———, "Why Huck and Jim Went Downstream," *CE,* XVIII, 106–107 (Nov., 1956).
Edgar Branch, "Mark Twain and J. D. Salinger: A Study in Literary Continuity," *AQ,* IX, 144–158 (Summer, 1957).
R. B. Browne, "Mark Twain and Captain Wakeman," *AL,* XXXIII, 320–329 (Nov., 1961).
Frances V. Brownell, "The Role of Jim in *Huckleberry Finn,*" *BUSE,* I, 74–83 (Spring–Summer, 1955).
L. J. Budd, "Mark Twain Plays the Bachelor," *WHR,* XI, 157–167 (Spring, 1957).
———, "The Southward Currents Under Huck Finn's Raft," *MVHR,* LXVI, 222–237 (Sept., 1959).
———, "Twain, Howells, and the Boston Nihilists," *NEQ,* XXXII, 351–371 (Sept., 1959).
G. A. Cardwell, "Mark Twain's Failures in Comedy and *The Enemy Conquered,*" *GaR,* XIII, 424–436 (Winter, 1959).
P. J. Carter, Jr., "Mark Twain: 'Moralist in Disguise,' " *UCSLL,* No. 6, pp. 65–79 (Jan., 1957).
———, "Mark Twain and the American Labor Movement," *NEQ,* XXX, 382–388 (Sept., 1957).

———, "Olivia Clemens Edits *Following the Equator*," *AL*, XXX, 194–209 (May, 1958).

———, "The Influence of the Nevada Frontier on Mark Twain," *WHR*, XIII, 61–70 (Winter, 1959).

Carla Consiglio, "La prosa di Mark Twain e i suoi influssi," *SA*, IV, 175–197 (1958).

———, "Nota bibliografica su la fortuna di Mark Twain in Italia," *SA*, IV, 198–208 (1958).

Pascal Covici, Jr., editor, "*Dear Master Wattie:* The Mark Twain–David Watt Bowser Letters," *SWR*, XLV, 105–121 (Spring, 1960).

J. M. Cox, "*A Connecticut Yankee in King Arthur's Court:* The Machinery of Self-Preservation," *YR*, L, 88–102 (Autumn, 1960).

———, "*Pudd'nhead Wilson:* The End of Mark Twain's American Dream," *SAQ*, LVIII, 351–363 (Summer, 1959).

———. See WHITMAN, above.

L. P. Coyle, "Mark Twain and William Dean Howells," *GaR*, X, 302–311 (Fall, 1956).

Sherwood Cummings, "Mark Twain and the Sirens of Progress," *JCMVASA*, I, 17–23 (Fall, 1960).

———, "Mark Twain's Social Darwinism," *HLQ*, XX, 163–175 (Feb., 1957).

———, "Science and Mark Twain's Theory of Fiction," *PQ*, XXXVII, 26–33 (Jan., 1958).

———, "What's in *Huckleberry Finn?*" *EJ*, L, 1–8 (Jan., 1961).

Curtis Dahl, "Mark Twain and the Moving Panoramas," *AQ*, XIII, 20–32 (Spring, 1961).

Henry Darbee, editor, "Mark Twain in Hartford: The Happy Years," *AH*, X, 65–80 (Dec., 1959).

Chester Davis, "Mark Twain's Religious Beliefs As Indicated by the Notations in His Books," *Twainian*, XIV, 1–4 (May–June, 1955); 1–4 (July–Aug.); 1–4 (Sept.–Oct.); 3–4 (Nov.–Dec.).

A. A. Durocher, "Mark Twain and the Roman Catholic Church," *JCMVASA*, I, ii, 32–43 (Fall, 1960).

A. E. Dyson, "Huckleberry Finn and the Whole Truth," *CritQ*, III, 29–40 (Spring, 1961).

Paul Fatout, "Mark Twain, Litigant," *AL*, XXXI, 30–45 (March, 1959).

———, "Mark Twain's Nom de Plume," *AL*, XXXIV, 1–7 (March, 1962).

———, "The Twain-Cable Readings in Indiana," *IMH*, LIII, 19–28 (March, 1957).

Herbert Feinstein, "Two Pairs of Gloves: Mark Twain and Henry James," *AI*, XVII, 349–387 (Winter, 1960).

L. A. Fiedler, "Duplicitous Mark Twain," *Com*, XXIX, 239–248

(March, 1960).
R. W. Frantz, Jr., "The Role of Folklore in *Huckleberry Finn,*" *AL,* XXVIII, 314–327 (Nov., 1956).
M. B. Fried, "Mark Twain in Buffalo," *Niagara Frontier,* V, 89–110 (Winter, 1959).
Otto Friedrich, "Mark Twain and the Nature of Humor," *Discourse,* II, 67–86 (April, 1959).
Dewey Ganzel, "Twain, Travel Books, and *Life on the Mississippi,*" *AL,* XXXIV, 40–55 (March, 1962).
J. W. Gargano, "Disguises in *Huckleberry Finn,*" *UKCR,* XXVI, 175–178 (March, 1960).
J. C. Gerber, "Mark Twain's Use of the Comic Pose," *PMLA,* LXXVII, 297–304 (June, 1962).
———, "The Relation between Point of View and Style in the Works of Mark Twain," in *Style in Prose Fiction: EIE,* edited by H. C. Martin, New York, 1959, pp. 142–171.
Donna Gerstenberger, "Huckleberry Finn and the World's Illusions," *WHR,* XIV, 401–406 (Autumn, 1960).
Carson Gibb, "The Best Authorities," *CE,* XXII, 178–183 (Dec., 1960).
W. M. Gibson, "Introduction" to *A Connecticut Yankee in King Arthur's Court,* New York, 1960, pp. vii–xxiii.
E. J. Gordon, "What's Happened to Humor?" *EJ,* XLVII, 127–133 (March, 1958).
T. A. Gullason, "The 'Fatal' Ending of *Huckleberry Finn,*" *AL,* XXIX, 86–91 (March, 1957).
R. A. Hall, Jr., "Cultural Symbolism in Mark Twain's Connecticut Yankee," *AION-SG,* II, 127–140 (1959).
H. L. Hill, "Mark Twain's Book Sales, 1869–1879," *BNYPL,* LXV, 371–389 (June, 1961).
———, "Mark Twain's 'Brace of Brief Lectures on Science,'" *NEQ,* XXXIV, 228–239 (June, 1961).
———, "Mark Twain's Quarrels with Elisha Bliss," *AL,* XXXIII, 442–456 (Jan., 1962).
———, "The Composition and the Structure of *Tom Sawyer,*" *AL,* XXXII, 379–392 (Jan., 1961).
J. B. Hoben, "Mark Twain: On the Writer's Use of Language," *AS,* XXXI, 163–171 (Oct., 1956).
Ruth Hudson, "A Literary 'Area of Freedom' between Irving and Twain," *WHR,* XIII, 47–60 (Winter, 1959).
Robert Hunting, "Mark Twain's Arkansaw Yahoos," *MLN,* LXXIII, 264–268 (April, 1958).
A. E. Jones, "Mark Twain and Sexuality," *PMLA,* LXXI, 595–616 (Sept., 1956).
———, "Mark Twain and the Determinism of *What Is Man?*" *AL,* XXIX, 1–17 (March, 1957).

Charles Kaplan, "Holden and Huck: The Odysseys of Youth," *CE*, XVIII, 76–80 (Nov., 1956).

H. E. Klingelhofer, "Mark Twain, Edited and Bowdlerized," *MSS*, XI, 2–12 (Fall, 1959).

S. J. Krause, "Twain's Method and Theory of Composition," *MP*, LVI, 167–177 (Feb., 1959).

Nita Laing, "The Later Satire of Mark Twain," *MWQ*, II, 35–48 (Autumn, 1960).

R. D. Lakin, "Mark Twain and the Cold War," *MWQ*, II, 159–167 (Winter, 1961).

Lewis Leary, "Standing with Reluctant Feet," in *A Casebook on Mark Twain's Wound*, edited by L. Leary, New York, 1962, pp. 3–32.

Florence B. Leaver, "Mark Twain's *Pudd'nhead Wilson*," *MTJ*, X, 14–20 (Winter, 1956).

F. R. Leavis, "Mark Twain's Neglected Classic," *Com*, XXI, 128–136 (Feb., 1956).

F. W. Lorch, "Hawaiian Feudalism and Mark Twain's *A Connecticut Yankee in King Arthur's Court*," *AL*, XXX, 50–66 (March, 1958).

———, "Mark Twain's Lecture Tour of 1868–1869: 'The American Vandal Abroad,'" *AL*, XXVI, 515–527 (Jan., 1955).

R. D. Lundy, "Mark Twain and Italy," *SA*, IV, 135–150 (1958).

John Lydenberg, "American Novelists in Search for a Lost World," *RLV*, XXVII, 306–321 (No. 4, 1961).

Dwight MacDonald, "Mark Twain: An Unsentimental Journey," *NY*, XXXVI, 160, 162, 164–168, 171–178, 181–196 (April 9, 1960).

D. M. McKeithan, "The Morgan Manuscript of *Pudd'nhead Wilson*," *EIUES* (Uppsala), XII (1961), 64 pp.

D. H. Malone, "Analysis of Mark Twain's Novel *Life on the Mississippi*," in *The Frontier in American History and Literature*, edited by Hans Galinsky, Frankfurt a/M, 1960, pp. 80–93.

———, "Mark Twain and the Literature of the Frontier," *ibid.*, pp. 65–79.

Leo Marx, "The Pilot and the Passenger: Landscape Conventions and the Style of *Huckleberry Finn*," *AL*, XXVIII, 129–146 (May, 1956).

———. See WHITMAN, above.

W. R. Moses, "The Pattern of Evil in *Adventures of Huckleberry Finn*," *GaR*, XIII, 161–166 (Summer, 1959).

Robert Ornstein, "The Ending of *Huckleberry Finn*," *MLN*, LXXIV, 698–702 (Dec., 1959).

C. O. Parsons, "The Background of *The Mysterious Stranger*," *AL*, XXXII, 55–74 (March, 1960).

Alma Pellegrini, "Mark Twain alla scoperta dell'Europa: 'The Innocents Abroad,'" *SA,* IV, 109–134 (1958).

J. Q. Reed, "Mark Twain: West Coast Journalist," *Midwest Jour,* I, 141–161 (Winter, 1960).

E. A. Robinson, "The Two 'Voices' in *Huckleberry Finn,*" *MLN,* LXXV, 204–208 (March, 1960).

G. M. Rubenstein, "The Moral Structure of *Huckleberry Finn,*" *CE,* XVIII, 72–76 (Nov., 1956).

Pat Ryan, "Mark Twain: Frontier Theatre Critic," *ArQ,* XVI, 197–209 (Autumn, 1960).

Paul Schmidt, "River vs. Town: Mark Twain's *Old Times on the Mississippi,*" *NCF,* XV, 95–111 (Sept., 1960).

———, "The Deadpan on Simon Wheeler," *SWR,* XLI, 270–277 (Summer, 1956).

Friedrich Schönemann, "Mark Twains *Huckleberry Finn* (Zum 70. Geburtstag, 1885–1955)," *Archiv,* CXCII, 273–289 (Feb., 1956).

M. S. Shockley, "The Structure of *Huckleberry Finn,*" *South-Central Bul,* XX, 3–10 (Winter, 1960).

H. N. Smith, "Introduction" to *Adventures of Huckleberry Finn,* Boston, 1958, pp. v–xxix.

———, "Mark Twain as an Interpreter of the Far West: The Structure of *Roughing It,*" in *The Frontier in Perspective,* edited by W. D. Wyman and C. B. Kroeber, Madison, 1957, pp. 205–228.

———, "Mark Twain's Images of Hannibal: From St. Petersburg to Eseldorf," *UTSE,* XXXVII, 3–23 (1958).

———, "*Pudd'nhead Wilson and After,*" *Mass Rev,* III, 233–253 (Winter, 1962).

Eric Solomon, "*Huckleberry Finn* Once More," *CE,* XXII, 172–178 (Dec., 1960).

R. W. Stallman, "Huck Finn Again," *CE,* XVIII, 425–426 (May, 1957).

A. E. Stone, Jr., "Mark Twain and the Story of the *Hornet,*" *YULG,* XXXV, 141–157 (April, 1961).

Tony Tanner, "The Lost America—The Despair of Henry Adams and Mark Twain," *Mod Age,* V, 299–310 (Summer, 1961).

———, "Samuel Clemens and the Progress of a Stylistic Rebel," *Brit Assn for Am Stud Bul,* ns, No. 3, 31–42 (Dec., 1961).

———, "The Literary Children of James and Clemens," *NCF,* XVI, 205–218 (Dec., 1961).

Arlin Turner, "Mark Twain, Cable, and 'A Professional Newspaper Liar,'" *NEQ,* XXVIII, 18–33 (March, 1955).

Edward Wasiolek, "The Structure of Make-Believe: *Huckleberry Finn,*" *UKCR,* XXIV, 97–100 (Dec., 1957).

A. R. Wells, "Huck Finn and Holden Caulfield: The Situation of the Hero," *OUR,* II, 31–42 (1960).
Anne P. Wigger, "The Composition of Mark Twain's *Pudd'nhead Wilson and Those Extraordinary Twins:* Chronology and Development," *MP,* LV, 93–102 (Nov., 1957).
N. W. Yates, "The 'Counter-Conversion' of Huckleberry Finn," *AL,* XXXII, 1–10 (March, 1960).

HENRY JAMES

I. Writings of Henry James

The American Essays, edited with an introduction by Leon Edel, New York, 1956.
"Autobiography in Fiction: An Unpublished Review by Henry James," edited by Leon Edel, *HLB,* XI, 245–257 (Spring, 1957).
"Henry James: Fourteen Letters," edited by Henry Brewster, *Botteghe Oscure,* XIX, 182–194 (Spring, 1957).
The Future of the Novel: Essays on the Art of Fiction, edited with an introduction by Leon Edel, New York, 1956.
Henry James and H. G. Wells: A Record of Their Friendship, Their Debate on the Art of Fiction, and Their Quarrel, edited, with an introduction, by Leon Edel and G. N. Ray, Urbana, Ill., 1958.
"Henry James and the Bazar Letters," edited by Leon Edel and L. H. Powers, *BNYPL,* LXII, 75–103 (Feb., 1958).
The House of Fiction, edited by Leon Edel, London, 1957.
Literary Reviews and Essays by Henry James on American, English, and French Literature, edited by Albert Mordell, New York, 1957.
The Painter's Eye: Notes and Essays on the Pictorial Arts, edited with an introduction by J. L. Sweeney, Cambridge, Mass., 1956.
Parisian Sketches: Letters to the "New York Tribune" 1875–1876, edited with an introduction by Leon Edel and Ilse Lind, New York, 1957.
The Selected Letters of Henry James, edited with an introduction by Leon Edel, New York, 1955.
" 'A Tragedy of Error': James's First Story," edited by Leon Edel, *NEQ,* XXIX, 291–317 (Sept., 1956).

II. Bibliographical Items

Maurice Beebe and W. T. Stafford, "Criticism of Henry James: A Selected Checklist with an Index to Studies of Separate Works," *MFS,* III, 73–96 (Spring, 1957).
Leon Edel and D. H. Laurence, editors, *A Bibliography of Henry*

James, London, 1957, and Fair Lawn, N. J., 1958; *idem.,* 2nd edition revised, 1961.

J. R. Russell, "The Henry James Collection," *URLB,* XI, 50–52 (Spring, 1956).

III. Biographical and Critical Studies

1. *Books*

Quentin Anderson, *The American Henry James,* New Brunswick, N. J., 1957.

E. T. Bowden, *The Themes of Henry James: A System of Observation through the Visual Arts,* New Haven, 1956.

Oscar Cargill, *The Novels of Henry James,* New York, 1961.

F. C. Crews, *The Tragedy of Manners: Moral Drama in the Later Novels of Henry James,* New Haven, 1957.

Leon Edel, *Henry James* (University of Minnesota Pamphlets on American Writers, No. 4), Minneapolis, 1960.

C. G. Hoffman, *The Short Novels of Henry James,* New York, 1957.

Alexander Holder-Barell, *The Development of Imagery and Its Functional Significance in Henry James's Novels* (Cooper Monographs, Vol. 3), Bern, 1959.

Helen Horne, *Basic Ideas of James' Aesthetics as Expressed in the Short Stories Concerning Artists and Writers,* Marburg, 1960.

D. W. Jefferson, *Henry James,* Edinburgh, 1960, New York, 1961.

Dorothea Krook, *The Ordeal of Consciousness in Henry James,* Cambridge, Eng., 1962.

L. B. Levy, *Versions of Melodrama: A Study of the Fiction and Drama of Henry James, 1865–1897,* Berkeley and Los Angeles, 1957.

H. T. McCarthy, *Henry James: The Creative Process,* New York, 1958.

Robert Marks, *James's Later Novels: An Interpretation,* New York, 1960.

Albert Mordell, editor, *Discovery of a Genius: William Dean Howells and Henry James,* introduction by Sylvia Bowman, New York, 1961.

Richard Poirier, *The Comic Sense of Henry James: A Study of the Early Novels,* New York, 1960.

W. H. Tilley, *The Backgrounds of "The Princess Casamassima"* (Univ. of Fla. Monographs, Humanities, No. 5), Gainesville, 1961.

J. A. Ward, *The Imagination of Disaster: Evil in the Fiction of Henry James,* Lincoln, Nebr., 1961.

Christof Wegelin, *The Image of Europe in Henry James,* Dallas, 1958.

2. *Articles*

P. G. Adams, "Young H. James and the Lesson of His Master Balzac," *RLC,* XXXV, 458–467 (July–Sept., 1961).

Miriam Allcott, "Form versus Substance in Henry James," *Rev of Eng Lit* (Leeds), III, 53–66 (Jan., 1962).

A. Alvarez, "Intelligence on Tour," *KR,* XXI, 23–33 (Winter, 1959).

C. R. Anderson, "Henry James's Fable of the South," *SAQ,* LIV, 249–257 (April, 1955).

———, "James's Portrait of the Southerner," *AL,* XXVII, 309–331 (Nov., 1955).

Jacques Barzun, "The Blest Group of Us," *Griffin,* V, 4–13 (June, 1956).

Gerhard Baumgaertel, "The Reception of Henry James in Germany," *Sym,* XIII, 19–31 (Spring, 1959).

Millicent Bell, "Edith Wharton and Henry James: The Literary Relation," *PMLA,* LXXIV, 619–637 (Dec., 1959).

Joan Bennett, "The Art of Henry James: *The Ambassadors,*" *ChiR,* IX, 12–26 (Winter, 1956).

Leo Bersani, "The Narrator as Center in *The Wings of the Dove,*" *MFS,* VI, 131–144 (Summer, 1960).

R. P. Blackmur, "Introduction" to *The Wings of the Dove,* New York, 1958, pp. 5–17; *"The Aspern Papers" and "The Spoils of Poynton,"* 1959, pp. 5–18; *"Washington Square" and "The Europeans,"* 1959, pp. 5–12; *The American,* 1960, pp. 5–13; *The Portrait of a Lady,* 1961, pp. 5–12; *The Tragic Muse,* 1961, pp. 5–15.

V. F. Blehl, "Freedom and Commitment in James's *Portrait of a Lady,*" *Person,* XLII, 368–381 (July, 1961).

Paola Bompard, "Una Nota su *The Golden Bowl,*" *SA,* II, 143–162 (1956).

J. C. Broderick, "Nature, Art, and Imagination in *The Spoils of Poynton,*" *NCF,* XIII, 295–312 (March, 1959).

Peter Buitenhuis, "From Daisy Miller to Julia Bride: 'A Whole Passage of Intellectual History,'" *AQ,* XI, 136–146 (Summer, 1959).

———, "Henry James on Hawthorne," *NEQ,* XXXII, 207–225 (June, 1959).

Oscar Cargill, "Henry James as Freudian Pioneer," *ChiR,* X, 13–29 (Summer, 1956).

———, "Henry James's 'Moral Policeman': William Dean Howells," *AL,* XXIX, 371–398 (Jan., 1958).

———, "Mr. James's Aesthetic Mr. Nash," *NCF,* XII, 177–187 (Dec., 1957).

———, "Gabriel Nash—Somewhat Less than Angel?" *NCF,* XIV,

231–239 (Dec., 1959).
J. A. Clair, "*The American:* A Reinterpretation," *PMLA,* LXXIV, 613–618 (Dec., 1959).
D. P. Costello, "The Structure of *The Turn of the Screw,*" *MLN,* LXXV, 312–321 (April, 1960).
C. B. Cox, "Henry James and Stoicism," *E&S,* VIII, 76–88 (1955).
C. R. Crow, "The Style of Henry James: *The Wings of the Dove,*" in *Style in Prose Fiction: EIE,* edited by H. C. Martin, New York, 1959, pp. 172–189.
Nemi D'Agostino, "Sul Teatro di Henry James," *SA,* II, 163–177 (1956).
Howell Daniels, "Henry James and 'An International Episode,'" *Bul of the Brit Assn for Am Stud,* N. S., I, 3–35 (Sept., 1960).
A. B. Donovan, "My Dear Pinker: The Correspondence of Henry James with His Literary Agent," *YULG,* XXXVI, 78–88 (Oct., 1961).
J. R. Dove, "The Tragic Sense in Henry James," *TSLL,* II, 302–314 (Autumn, 1960).
F. W. Dupee, "Introduction" to Henry James's *Autobiography,* New York, 1956, pp. vii–xiv.
Sister Mary Durkin, "Henry James's Revisions of the Style of *The Reverberator,*" *AL,* XXXIII, 330–349 (Nov., 1961).
R. A. Durr, "The Night Journey in *The Ambassadors,*" *PQ,* XXXV, 24–38 (Jan., 1956).
Leon Edel, "The Literary Convictions of Henry James," *MFS,* III, 3–10 (Spring, 1957)
———, "Henry James: The Dramatic Years, Biographical Chapters," prefaced to Henry James, *Guy Domville,* Philadelphia, 1960, pp. 13–121.
———, "The Text of *The Ambassadors,*" *HLB,* XIV, 453–460 (Autumn, 1960).
———, "Time and *The Ambassadors,*" *MLN,* LXXIII, 177–179 (March, 1958).
———, "Introduction" to *The Portrait of a Lady,* Boston, 1956, pp. v–xx; to *The Ambassadors,* Boston, 1960, pp. v–xviii; to *The House of Fiction: Essays on the Novel,* London, 1957, pp. 9–19; to *Roderick Hudson,* New York, 1960, pp. vii–xvii; to *The Tragic Muse,* New York, 1960; to *Watch and Ward,* New York, 1960, pp. 5–18.
Donald Emerson, "Henry James and the American Language," *TWASAL,* XLIX, 237–247 (1960).
———, "Henry James and the Limitations of Realism," *CE,* XXII, 161–166 (Dec., 1960).
J. J. Enck, "Wholeness of Effect in *The Golden Bowl,*" *TWASAL,* XLVII, 227–240 (1958).
Alberta Fabris, "Note su *The American Scene,*" *SA,* VI, 255–273

(1960).
Herbert Feinstein. See TWAIN, above.
A. R. Ferguson, "The Triple Quest of Henry James: Fame, Art, and Fortune," *AL,* XXVII, 475–498 (Jan., 1956).
Francis Fergusson, "The Golden Bowl Revisited," *SR,* LXIII, 13–28 (Winter, 1955).
J. J. Firebaugh, "The Idealism of Merton Densher," *UTSE,* XXXVII, 141–154 (1958).
———, "A Schopenhauerian Novel: James's *The Princess Casamassima,*" *NCF,* XIII, 177–197 (Dec., 1958).
J. K. Folsom, "Archimago's Well: An Interpretation of *The Sacred Fount,*" *MFS,* VII, 136–144 (Summer, 1961).
Edwin Fussell. See HAWTHORNE, above.
R. L. Gale, "Art Imagery in Henry James's Fiction," *AL,* XXIX, 47–63 (March, 1957).
———, "Henry James and Italy," *SA,* III, 189–203 (1957).
———, "Religion [*sic*] Imagery in Henry James's Fiction," *MFS,* III, 64–72 (Spring, 1957).
———, "*Roderick Hudson* and Thomas Crawford," *AQ,* XIII, 495–504 (Winter, 1961).
J. W. Gargano, "*The Spoils of Poynton:* Action and Responsibility," *SR,* LXIX, 650–660 (Oct.–Dec., 1961).
———, "*What Maisie Knew:* The Evolution of a 'Moral Sense,'" *NCF,* XVI, 33–46 (June, 1961).
R. E. Garis, "The Two Lambert Strethers: A New Reading of *The Ambassadors,*" MFS, VII, 305–316 (Winter, 1961–1962).
H. K. Girling, "'Wonder' and 'Beauty' in *The Awkward Age,*" *EIC,* VIII, 370–380 (Oct., 1958).
R. F. Gleckner. See HAWTHORNE, above.
H. C. Goddard, "A Pre-Freudian Reading of *The Turn of the Screw,*" *NCF,* XII, 1–36 (June, 1957).
M. A. Goldberg, "'Things' and Values in Henry James's Universe," *WHR,* XI, 377–385 (Autumn, 1957).
A. L. Goldsmith, "Henry James's Reconciliation of Free Will and Fatalism," *NCF,* XIII, 109–126 (Sept., 1958).
Caroline Gordon, "Mr. Verver, Our National Hero," *SR,* LXIII, 29–47 (Winter, 1955).
M. E. Grenander, "Henry James's *Capricciosa:* Christina Light in *Roderick Hudson* and *The Princess Casamassima,*" *PMLA,* LXXV, 309–319 (June, 1960).
M. E. Grenander, B. J. Rahn, and Francine Valvo, "The Time-Scheme in *The Portrait of a Lady,*" *AL,* XXXII, 127–135 (May, 1960).
James Hafley, "Malice in Wonderland," *ArQ,* XV, 5–12 (Spring, 1959).
F. J. Hoffman, "Freedom and Conscious Form: Henry James and

the American Self," *VQR*, XXXVII, 269–285 (Spring, 1961).

L. B. Holland, *"The Wings of the Dove," ELH*, XXVI, 549–574 (Dec., 1959).

Viola Hopkins, "Visual Art Devices and Parallels in the Fiction of Henry James," *PMLA*, LXXVI, 561–574 (Dec., 1961).

A. E. Jones, "Point of View in *The Turn of the Screw*," *PMLA*, LXXIV, 112–122 (March, 1959).

Mark Kanzer, "The Figure in the Carpet," *AI*, XVII, 339–348 (Winter, 1960).

Jean Kimball, "The Abyss and the Wings of the Dove: The Image as a Revelation," *NCF*, X, 281–300 (March, 1956).

———, "Henry James's Last Portrait of a Lady: Charlotte Stant in *The Golden Bowl*," *AL*, XXVIII, 449–468 (Jan., 1957).

S. J. Krause, "James's Revisions of the Style of *The Portrait of a Lady*," *AL*, XXX, 67–88 (March, 1958).

Earl Labor, "James's 'The Real Thing': Three Levels of Meaning," *CE*, XXIII, 376–378 (Feb., 1962).

Gerald Levin, "Why Does Vanderbank Not Propose?" *UKCR*, XXVII, 314–318 (June, 1961).

L. B. Levy, "Henry James's *Confidence* and the Development of the Idea of the Unconscious," *AL*, XXVIII, 347–358 (Nov., 1956).

R. W. B. Lewis, "The Histrionic Vision of Henry James," *JA*, IV, 39–51 (1959).

Ellen D. Leyburn, "Virginia Woolf's Judgment of Henry James," *MFS*, V, 166–169 (Summer, 1959).

E. H. Long, "Introduction" to *Short Novels of Henry James*, New York, 1961.

John Lydenberg. See TWAIN, above.

———, "The Governess Turns the Screws," *NCF*, XII, 37–58 (June, 1957).

B. R. McElderry, Jr., "Henry James's 'The Art of Fiction,' " *RSSCW*, XXV, 91–100 (March, 1957).

Umberto Mariani, "L'esperienza italiana di Henry James," *SA*, VI, 221–253 (1960).

Terence Martin, "James's 'The Pupil': The Art of Seeing Through," *MFS*, IV, 335–345 (Winter, 1958–1959).

W. R. Martin, "The Use of the Fairy-Tale: A Note on the Structure of *The Bostonians*," *ESA*, II, 98–109 (March, 1959).

Barbara Melchiori, "The Taste of Henry James," *SA*, III, 171–187 (1957).

Giorgio Melchiori, "Un Personaggio di Henry James," *SA*, II, 179–194 (1956).

Michael Millgate, "The Novelist and the Businessman: Henry James, Edith Wharton, Frank Norris," *SA*, V, 161–189 (1959).

A. D. Moody, "James' Portrait of an Ideal," *MCR*, No. 4, pp. 77–92 (1961).

Wright Morris, "Henry James's *The American Scene,*" *TQ,* I, No. 3, 27–42 (Summer–Autumn, 1958).
Kenneth Murdock, "Introduction" to *"The Turn of the Screw" and "The Aspern Papers,"* London, 1957, pp. v–xi.
Simon Nowell-Smith, "Without Benefit of Bibliography: Some Notes on Henry James," *BC,* VII, 64–67 (Spring, 1958).
John Paterson, "The Language of 'Adventure' in Henry James," *AL,* XXXII, 291–301 (Nov., 1960).
Rebecca Patterson, "Two Portraits of a Lady," *MWQ,* I, 343–361 (Summer, 1960).
R. H. Pearce, "Introduction" to *The American,* Boston, 1962, pp. v–xxi.
R. A. Perlongo, *"The Sacred Fount:* Labyrinth or Parable?" *KR,* XXII, 635–647 (Autumn, 1960).
Norma Phillips, *"The Sacred Fount:* The Narrator and the Vampires," *PMLA,* LXXVI, 407–412 (Sept., 1961).
L. H. Powers, "Henry James and the Ethics of the Artist: 'The Real Thing' and 'The Liar'," *TSLL,* III, 360–368 (Autumn, 1961).
———, "Henry James and Zola's *Roman expérimental,*" *UTQ,* XXX, 16–30 (Oct., 1960).
———, "James's *The Tragic Muse*—Ave atque Vale," *PMLA,* LXXIII, 270–274 (June, 1958).
———, "Mr. James's Aesthetic Mr. Nash—Again," *NCF,* XIII, 341–349 (March, 1959).
———, *"The Portrait of a Lady:* 'The Eternal Mystery of Things,' " *NCF,* XIV, 143–155 (Sept., 1959).
———, "A Reperusal of James's 'The Figure in the Carpet,' " *AL,* XXXIII, 224–228 (May, 1961).
Ralph Ranald, *"The Sacred Fount:* James's Portrait of the Artist *Manqué,*" *NCF,* XV, 239–248 (Dec., 1960).
J. L. Roberts, "An Approach to Evil in Henry James," *ArQ,* XVII, 5–16 (Spring, 1961).
Robert Rogers, "The Beast in Henry James," *AI,* XIII, 427–454 (Winter, 1956).
A. H. Roper, "The Moral and Metaphorical Meaning of *The Spoils of Poynton,*" *AL,* XXXII, 182–196 (May, 1960).
S. P. Rosenbaum, "Letters to the Pell-Clarkes from Their 'Old Cousin and Friend' Henry James," *AL,* XXXI, 46–58 (March, 1959).
E. H. Rosenberry, "James's Use of Hawthorne in 'The Liar,' " *MLN,* LXXVI, 234–238 (March, 1961).
M. F. Schulz, "The Bellegardes' Feud with Christopher Newman," *AL,* XXVII, 42–55 (March, 1955).
John Silver, "A Note on the Freudian Reading of 'The Turn of the Screw,' " *AL,* XXIX, 207–211 (May, 1957).
R. M. Slabey, "Henry James and 'The Most Impressive Convention in All History,' " *AL,* XXX, 89–102 (March, 1958).

Lotus Snow, "The Disconcerting Poetry of Mary Temple: A Comparison of the Imagery of *The Portrait of a Lady* and *The Wings of the Dove,*" *NEQ,* XXXI, 312–339 (Sept., 1958).
———, "Some Stray Fragrance of an Ideal: Henry James's Imagery for Youth's Discovery of Evil," *HLB,* XIV, 107–125 (Winter, 1960).
J. L. Spencer, "Symbolism in James's *The Golden Bowl,*" *MFS,* III, 333–344 (Winter, 1957–1958).
W. T. Stafford, "James Examines Shakespeare: Notes on the Nature of Genius," *PMLA,* LXXIII, 123–128 (March, 1958).
R. W. Stallman, "The Houses That James Built—*The Portrait of a Lady,*" *TQ,* I, 176–196 (Winter, 1958).
———, " 'The Sacred Rage': The Time-Theme in *The Ambassadors,*" *MFS,* III, 41–56 (Spring, 1957).
———, "Time and Mrs. Newsome's 'Blue Message': A Reply to Leon Edel," *MLN,* LXXVI, 20–23 (Jan., 1961).
Franz Stanzel, "Der personale Roman: *The Ambassadors,*" Chapter IV of *Die Typischen Erzählsituationen im Roman, WBEP,* LXIII, Wien, 1955, pp. 93–121.
W. B. Stein, "*The Ambassadors:* The Crucifixion of Sensibility," *CE,* XVII, 289–292 (Feb., 1956).
———, "*The Portrait of a Lady: Vis Inertiae,*" *WHR,* XIII, 177–190 (Spring, 1959).
———, " 'The Pupil': The Education of a Prude," *ArQ,* XV, 13–22 (Spring, 1959).
A. E. Stone, Jr., "Henry James and Childhood: *The Turn of the Screw,*" *Stetson Univ. Bull.,* LXI, ii, 1–18 (April, 1961).
Floyd Stovall, "Henry James's 'The Jolly Corner,' " *NCF,* XII, 72–84 (June, 1957).
Michael Swan, "Henry James and the Heroic Young Master," *London Mag.,* II, 78–86 (May, 1955).
Tony Tanner. See MARK TWAIN, above.
Vincent Tartella, "James's 'Four Meetings': Two Texts Compared," *NCF,* XV, 17–28 (June, 1960).
H. L. Terrie, Jr., "Henry James and the 'Explosive Principle,' " *NCF,* XV, 283–299 (March, 1961).
Willard Thorp, "Foreword" to *"The Madonna of the Future" and Other Early Stories,* New York, 1962, pp. vii–xvi.
J. E. Tilford, Jr., "James the Old Intruder," *MFS,* IV, 157–164 (Summer, 1958).
I. Traschen, "Henry James and the Art of Revision," *PQ,* XXXV, 39–47 (Jan., 1956).
———, "James's Revisions of the Love Affair in *The American,*" *NEQ,* XXIX, 43–62 (March, 1956).
Parker Tyler, "The Child as 'The Figure in the Carpet,' " *ChiR,* XI, 31–42 (Winter, 1958).

Edmond Volpe, "James's Theory of Sex in Fiction," *NCF,* XIII, 36–47 (June, 1958).

Hisayoshi Watanabe, "Past Perfect Retrospection in the Style of Henry James," *AL,* XXXIV, 165–181 (May, 1962).

Ian Watt, "The First Paragraph of *The Ambassadors:* An Explication," *EIC,* X, 250–274 (July, 1960) [see also XI, 116–119].

Christof Wegelin, "The Rise of the International Novel," *PMLA,* LXXVII, 305–310 (June, 1962).

René Wellek, "Henry James's Literary Theory and Criticism," *AL,* XXX, 293–321 (Nov., 1958).

Nathalia Wright, "Henry James and the Greenough Data," *AQ,* X, 338–343 (Fall, 1958).

Walter Wright, "Maggie Verver: Neither Saint nor Witch," *NCF,* XII, 59–71 (June, 1957).

M. D. Zabel, "Introduction" to *Henry James: Fifteen Short Stories,* New York, 1961, pp. vii–xxx; to *In the Cage & Other Tales,* New York, 1958, pp. 1–28; to *The Art of Travel: Scenes and Journeys in America, England, France, and Italy from the Travel Writings of Henry James,* Garden City, N. Y., 1958, pp. 1–48.